PLANNED GIVING

Update Service

BECOME A SUBSCRIBER!

Did you purchase this product from a bookstore?

If you did, it's important for you to become a subscriber. John Wiley & Sons, Inc. may publish, on a periodic basis, supplements and new editions to reflect the latest changes in the subject matter that you **need to know** in order to stay competitive in this ever-changing industry. By contacting the Wiley office nearest you, you'll receive any current update at no additional charge. In addition, you'll receive future updates and revised or related volumes on a 30-day examination review.

If you purchased this product directly from John Wiley & Sons, Inc., we have already recorded your subscription for this update service.

To become a subscriber, please call **1-877-762-2974** or send your name, company name (if applicable), address, and the title of the product to:

mailing address: **Supplement Department**
                     John Wiley & Sons, Inc.
                     One Wiley Drive
                     Somerset, NJ 08875

e-mail: **subscriber@wiley.com**
fax: **1-732-302-2300**
online: **www.wiley.com**

For customers outside the United States, please contact the Wiley office nearest you:

Professional & Reference Division
John Wiley & Sons Canada, Ltd.
22 Worcester Road
Etobicoke, Ontario M9W 1L1
CANADA
Phone: 416-236-4433
Phone: 1-800-567-4797
Fax: 416-236-4447
Email: canada@wiley.com

John Wiley & Sons Australia, Ltd.
33 Park Road
P.O. Box 1226
Milton, Queensland 4064
AUSTRALIA
Phone: 61-7-3859-9755
Fax: 61-7-3859-9715
Email: brisbane@johnwiley.com.au

John Wiley & Sons, Ltd.
The Atrium
Southern Gate, Chichester
West Sussex, PO19 8SQ
ENGLAND
Phone: 44-1243 779777
Fax: 44-1243-775878
Email: customer@wiley.co.uk

John Wiley & Sons (Asia) Pte., Ltd.
2 Clementi Loop #02-01
SINGAPORE 129809
Phone: 65-64632400
Fax: 65-64634604/5/6
Customer Service: 65-64604280
Email: enquiry@wiley.com.sg

PLANNED GIVING

Management, Marketing, and Law
Third Edition

RONALD R. JORDAN
KATELYN L. QUYNN

John Wiley & Sons, Inc.

Published by John Wiley & Sons, Inc., Hoboken, New Jersey
Published simultaneously in Canada

For general information on our other products and services, or technical support, please contact our Customer Care Department within the United States at 800-762-2974, outside the United States at 317-572-3993 or fax 317-572-4002.

Wiley also publishes its books in a variety of electronic formats. Some content that appears in print may not be available in electronic books.

For more information about Wiley products, visit our web site at www.wiley.com.

Library of Congress Cataloging-in-Publication Data:

ISBN 0-471-44950-4

Printed in the United States of America.

10 9 8 7 6 5 4 3 2 1

About the Authors

Ronald R. Jordan is an assistant professor at New Mexico State University where he teaches courses on financial planning, consumer economics, and business and professional writing. He also consults with nonprofit organizations. He is a graduate of New England School of Law and was admitted to the practice of law in Massachusetts in 1975. Before he retired, he was the Assistant Vice President of University Advancement at New Mexico State University and former Director of Planned Giving at Boston University.

Katelyn L. Quynn is Executive Director of Development for Planned and Major Gifts at the Massachusetts General Hospital and Director of Planned Giving for Partners Healthcare System. She was named Planned Giving Professional of the Year in 1996, is a past President of The Planned Giving Group of New England (PGGNE), and former board member of the National Committee on Planned Giving. In 2003 she received the David M. Donaldson Award, from PGGNE. She graduated from Tufts University and Boston University School of Law.

Contents

CONTENTS

CONTENTS

CONTENTS

CONTENTS

CONTENTS

CONTENTS

CONTENTS

CONTENTS

CONTENTS

CONTENTS

CONTENTS

CONTENTS

CONTENTS

CONTENTS

IMPORTANT NOTE:

Because of the rapidly changing nature of information in this field, this product may be updated with annual supplements or with future editions. **Please call 1-877-762-2974 or email us at subscriber@wiley.com to receive any current update at no additional charge.** We will send on approval any future supplements or new editions when they become available. If you purchased this product directly from John Wiley & Sons, Inc., we have already recorded your subscription for this update service.

Preface

The Third Edition of *Planned Giving: Management, Marketing, and Law with CD-ROM* represents our efforts to present, in one volume, now in ten parts and 56 chapters, a state of the art text that provides assistance to everyone involved in the field of Planned Giving. This edition is completely rewritten, providing additional information on both the technical and practical sides of planned giving. In all cases, we have strived to make this text practical, not theoretical. Our goal is to present planned giving in context, so that planned giving is understandable to employees of nonprofit organizations and to professional advisors who practice in this field.

What we said in the first edition still applies today. "We began writing out of necessity—to fill a void, to document our ideas, and to share thoughts with our colleagues." We write this book to assist our colleagues, serve nonprofit organizations, and improve the level of knowledge so that donors receive information on concepts and strategies that help fulfill their philanthropic goals.

Please remember that all planned giving calculations included in this text must be updated to reflect current discount and annuity rates. Readers should update the calculations with their own planned giving software to recalculate payout rates, charitable income tax deductions, and other financial data. In addition, tax laws change regularly as do laws pertaining to planned giving and readers are advised to consult with competent legal or tax counsel.

The Third Edition contains a number of new chapters:

■ Chapter Four, "An Operational Plan for a Planned Giving Program." Beginning a planned giving program or expanding an existing one requires the development of a solid operational plan. An operational plan identifies the types of activities to be undertaken in the first 12–18 months of a new program or the next 24–36 months of an existing program. This chapter examines the drafting and implementation of an operational plan designed to match the nonprofit organization's style, pace, and politics.

■ Chapter Six, "Increased Management Responsibilities in the Development Office." In every development professional's career, promotions and new positions can mean additional management responsibilities. These responsibilities include supervising additional staff and overseeing or managing areas that are unfamiliar and outside of planned giving. This chapter explores the issues related to increasing management, including skill enhancement and managing staff, senior administrators, trustees, and volunteers.

■ Chapter Forty-eight, "Planned Giving at Educational Institutions." Educational institutions rely on private support, particularly planned gifts, to support the work of the institution. A planned giving program can be established in phases over time, first promoting gifts of securities, real estate, bequests and trusts, and endowed funds, then gradually adding life income gifts to the menu of gift opportunities. This chapter focuses on ways to expand or develop planned giving programs at educational institutions.

■ Chapter Fifty, "Health Insurance Portability and Accountability Act: Raising Funds in a Healthcare Setting." As of April 14, 2003, federal legislation entitled the Health Insurance Portability and Accountability Act (HIPAA) impacts the field of healthcare. Part of this act affects fundraising and regulates the extent that individually identifiable health information may or may not be used for fundraising purposes, unless a patient provides specific authorization for use of this information. This chapter explores the impact of this act on fundraising in healthcare settings.

CD-ROM

The CD-ROM contains over 250 documents that are divided into 7 categories.

1. Marketing Materials

2. Agreements

3. Correspondence

4. Administrative Documents

5. Exhibits

6. Presentations

7. IRS Forms and Tax-Related Documents

Before use, all forms should be reviewed and approved by the nonprofit organization's legal counsel. To maximize the use of the CD, we encourage each subscriber to print each document for placement in a three ring binder. To fully appreciate the documents, they are best seen in hard copy format for future study and modification. Like all forms, they represent one way to present information and they should be modified and customized to meet the needs of the particular nonprofit organization, the donor, and the situation involved.

We hope that the Third Edition of *Planned Giving: Management, Marketing, and Law* exceeds your expectations. As usual we are grateful to those who ask us to consider adding new material or chapters and we are grateful to donors who test the limits of our knowledge.

We welcome your ideas and suggestions that will in any way improve this text.

Acknowledgments

Writing a book takes teamwork, cooperation, and the participation of a number of individuals each of whom makes valuable contributions to the manuscript and text. The authors wish to thank the following individuals for their help in the production of this manuscript.

Ben Lipson, author of *J.K. Lasser's Choosing the Right Long-Term Care Insurance*, for his continued expertise and commitment to philanthropy.

Marjorie Houston, Director of Planned Giving at Wheaton College, Norton, Massachusetts for her useful article, "Mutual Fund Transfers for Charitable Gifts," and its updates.

Frank Minton and his staff at Planned Giving Services, Seattle, Washington, for providing information on the regulation of charitable gift annuities and updating it.

Trusts and Estates Magazine, 6515 Powers Ferry Road, NW, Atlanta, GA for permission to allow us to adapt from Marjorie Houston's article, "Mutual Fund Transfers for Charitable Gifts."

PG Calc, 129 Mount Auburn Street, Cambridge, Massachusetts, 617/497-4970, www.pgcalc.com. The authors wish to thank PG Calc and their fine staff for their generosity in allowing us to reprint PG Calc calculations and for creating such a wonderful product.

John Wiley & Sons, Inc. As usual it is always a pleasure to do business with the staff of John Wiley & Sons.

Michael Allard, Massachusetts General Hospital, for his expertise on HIPAA.

Ben Hinchey, Massachusetts General Hospital, for updating the PG Calcs used throughout the book.

Our families. The authors thank their families—Dianne C. Jordan and Derek Jordan and Barry, Henry, and Andrew Smith for giving us the time to develop and write this book.

Lastly, we thank our colleagues, donors, and employers who provide opportunities for us to learn our craft.

Ronald R. Jordan
Katelyn L. Quynn
July 2003

P A R T   O N E

Getting Started

CHAPTER ONE

What Is Planned Giving?

1.1   INTRODUCTION

Charitable giving has become big business in the United States, with gifts from individuals accounting for most of the philanthropic contributions. To encourage the continued private funding of charitable organizations, Congress has provided tax incentives for philanthropic individuals. No amount of tax benefits, however, will cause an individual who does not have donative intent to make a charitable gift. It is the donor's charitable intent that must be the motivating factor when making a gift. Planned gifts provide a way for philanthropic donors to make gifts to nonprofit organizations and simultaneously enjoy favorable and financial tax consequences.

Planned giving has two primary components: planning and giving. As charitable gift planners within our various organizations, we focus much of our energy on planning. We consider estate planning issues, financial ramifications, and tax benefits. Yet we must also remember that the second component, giving, is paramount for the transaction to be completed. When a donor makes a planned gift to a nonprofit entity, usually a religious, educational, health, arts, cultural, environmental, or social services organization, the donor irrevocably parts with the asset and cannot retrieve it if it is needed in the future. If the donor does not have a real desire to benefit a charity, then the planned gift in all likelihood will not or should not be made.

Planned gifts fall primarily into four categories: (1) outright gifts, whereby the nonprofit often has use of the asset immediately, such as gifts of securities, tangible personal property, and some real estate gifts; (2) bequests, whereby the donor uses or controls the asset during his lifetime and the charity receives the asset at the donor's death; (3) life income gifts, whereby a donor makes a gift today and receives a stream of income for life, and upon the donor's death the nonprofit has use of the remainder value of the gift; and (4) the creation of endowed funds.

The nonprofit should be in a position, at a minimum, to handle successfully those gifts made through securities, bequests, and charitable remainder trusts that are established by the donor and managed outside the nonprofit. The nonprofit also should be able to easily handle the creation of endowed funds. A complete program, however, will be a planned giving program that offers to donors life income gifts such as charitable gift annuities, deferred gift annuities, a pooled income fund, and the opportunity to make gifts of real estate. Such a program should be managed by at least one full-time professional and be supported by additional full-time staff members.

1.2 PLANNED GIVING FROM THE DONOR'S PERSPECTIVE

Planned giving is attractive to donors for many reasons. Through a planned gift donors often can make larger gifts than they thought possible, and for some donors this is the only way to make a substantial gift to charity. It often happens that when donors learn they can make a gift that (1) pays a stream of income for life, (2) increases the yield they may currently receive from other investments, (3) provides a charitable income tax deduction, and (4) reduces or eliminates capital gains taxes or estate taxes, they feel that they cannot afford *not* to make the gift. Planned giving also allows donors to be creative in making a gift. Real estate or tangible personal property that a donor is not using can be given to a nonprofit and thereby provide the donor with an income stream and various tax advantages. Conservative "blue-chip" stocks paying a 1 to 2 percent yield can constitute a life income gift and provide the donor with a substantially higher income stream, such as 6 to 9 percent. Planned giving options can encourage the charity-minded donor to act—to make the gift sooner than later.

1.3 PLANNED GIVING FROM THE ORGANIZATION'S PERSPECTIVE

A nonprofit organization attracts more donors and gifts by offering a complete range of giving options, including a variety of planned giving vehicles. Most life income arrangements, including charitable gift annuities, pooled income funds, and charitable remainder trusts, pay an income to a donor for life. This means that the organization must invest the gift to produce a yearly income stream to the donor; it does not have use of the principal of the gift until the donor dies. This unique obligation allows an organization to build its endowment and its future through its relationship with its donors. The charity pays out an income stream, based on actuarial tables, while continuing to invest the principal amount with the purpose of generating interest equal to or greater than the income paid to the donor. When older donors make a planned gift, the organization pays a high rate of return, assuming that the donor will live for fewer years. The nonprofit benefits by committing to an arrangement that brings a donor into the organization and strengthens a relationship that often results in additional gifts.

1.4 PLANNED GIVING FROM MANAGEMENT'S PERSPECTIVE

Planned giving staff can find themselves in conflict with the nonprofit's central administration, because the demand for current cash is frequently more valued than the promise of future support through planned gifts. This lack of common goal can create problems for the planned giving officer. Central administration may include the president of the organization, the vice president for business affairs, the treasurer, and general counsel, but also may include the vice president or director of development. The vice president for development may have hired a planned giving director, with the best intentions of creating or strengthening a planned giving program, but for any number of reasons may not fully support the planned giving effort or may emphasize raising outright gifts.

This section discusses issues that impact planned giving staff members in relation to their nonprofit. It examines the way planned giving should, ideally, be viewed within an organization, problems that may arise related to planned giving, and some specific actions that can be taken to make a planned giving program more successful.

1.5 A FOCUS ON THE FUTURE

Although most development staff members of a nonprofit focus on the need for current income and outright gifts, planned giving officers focus on the future. It is common to hear nonprofit presidents and vice presidents for development say, "We need cash today; we can't wait for tomorrow." A planned giving officer's response might be, "If the organization had established a planned giving program 10 to 15 years ago, we would not be so pressured to raise cash today." A development program must balance its efforts to bring in dollars today while building a foundation for the future.

There is no better way to provide for an organization's future than through planned gifts. A successful planned giving program stabilizes and balances a development program. During a recession, annual giving programs and major gifts may suffer, but planned giving programs generally prosper because planned gifts provide such substantial financial benefits to donors. Planned giving focuses on gifts that will materialize during a 50-year period, although most gifts are realized over a shorter, 3- to 5- to 10-year period. An appetite for current cash can short-circuit the ability to produce more substantial gifts that are nurtured and cultivated over time, and organizations may lose financial support if the process is rushed, thus producing disillusioned and, sometimes, alienated donors.

(a) Organizational Patience

A nonprofit organization that embarks on a planned giving program needs to adopt the notion of organizational patience, to recognize that it takes time for a planned giving program to work and for the planned giving officer to secure planned gifts. All too often, nonprofits expect instant success from the planned giving program. This rarely happens, and management can become impatient and disenchanted with the program. Instead, management must understand that a planned gift is often a large and complex gift that involves a number of financial and estate-planning decisions. Often the donor is elderly, and other players—attorneys, financial advisors, accountants, and family members—who frequently are involved may delay the process. Sometimes there are too many related considerations to rush a planned gift, but once the gift closes, a satisfied planned giving donor is often a repeat donor.

(b) The Decision Makers

In the quest for support, management sometimes substitutes its own judgment for that of the donor. Although planned giving officers can be influential in affecting the size, timing, and scope of a donor's gift, these decisions must be made at the donor's discretion. It is important for everyone involved to remember that the donor determines:

- The size of the gift
- The timing of the gift
- The form or structure of the gift

Planned giving officers must remind management that although they understand the organization's need for current cash gifts, decisions about any gift must be made by the donor.

1.6 EXPENSE VERSUS BENEFITS OF A PLANNED GIVING PROGRAM

Some organizations decide not to begin a planned giving program because the program is labor intensive and expensive to operate. Although it is true that there are significant challenges to a planned giving officer in learning and managing, and greater operational expenses for software, management, marketing, and education, a planned giving program usually provides an excellent return on the organization's investment. If an organization does not offer a planned giving program, it cannot compete for support among its peer organizations that do offer such programs.

It is important to note that many major gifts raised by planned giving officers do not come through planned giving. Frequently a planned giving officer asks for a planned gift from a prospect but instead receives an outright cash gift. Many donors are motivated to make a major gift to an organization after reading its planned giving marketing pieces; after discussions with a financial advisor, the donor decides to make a gift with cash rather than through a planned gift. Management should consider the benefits a planned giving program can bring to a development program apart from planned gifts.

1.7 PLANNED GIVING AND ANNUAL GIVING

Some development professionals believe that planned gifts divert support from an organization's annual giving program. The argument is that, in planned giving, very few new dollars are added to the program but are instead reallocated among other programs. Although annual giving donors often are converted into new planned giving donors, planned giving donors frequently become new annual fund donors. Most annual fund donors who become planned giving donors continue to support an organization's annual giving program, and the organization benefits greatly when the $50-per-year annual fund donor becomes a $20,000 planned giving donor. It is the planned giving officer's responsibility to encourage continued giving to the annual fund. Annual fund and planned giving programs should complement rather than compete with each other.

1.8 PERSPECTIVES FOR SUCCESS: LEADERSHIP, RESOURCES, AND STAFFING

Many professionals whose responsibilities lie in the area of planned giving also are involved in other development functions, which may cause a dilution of the planned giving effort and lead to management's becoming dissatisfied with planned giving efforts. To build a successful program, it is necessary for management to appoint one person to champion the planned giving effort. This individual must be able to devote at least half of his time to planned giving exclusively and must make the program a priority. Planned giving programs sometimes fail because no one is ultimately responsible for the program, given the charge to provide leadership, or given the time to make it work.

Furthermore, a planned giving program can fail if it has an inadequate budget and insufficient resources. Resources must be allocated and accessible for marketing, training, and other operating necessities. Programs also fail when staff turnover is so great that the constant flow of employees disrupts the program and confuses its donors. Management should focus energy on keeping its staff. At many nonprofits, staff members are not provided incentives to stay with the organization because of salary restraints and an absence of opportunities to advance. Because planned giving is generally a revenue-producing area, adequate financial incentive should be included in the program budget.

Competition for experienced planned giving professionals is great, and staff often change jobs because of better salaries offered by other organizations. Tenure in a development job is approximately two years, and management is just beginning to realize a return on its investment at about the time an employee is planning to move on. It is better management to reward a good staff member with financial incentives and opportunities for advancement with the organization.

1.9 PLANNED GIFTS NOW AND IN THE FUTURE

Planned giving has become one of the most attractive ways for individuals to make gifts to charity. Most of this country's wealth is now held by older Americans, those aged 60 and older, and younger entrepreneurs. As the population rapidly ages, baby boomers become middle aged, older Americans live longer, and concerns about healthcare increase. Many individuals want to control their assets while living, and a planned gift allows a donor to benefit financially from the gift while engaging in a relationship with the charity. The years ahead will likely bring the largest intergenerational transfer of wealth in U.S. history, as parents transfer assets to their children. This transfer creates the need for close examination of tax issues, beyond the traditional benefits of income tax savings. Passing wealth on to family members through planned giving options offers an attractive way to ensure current income for the individual and possibly additional family members while receiving tax advantages and providing for charity. Thus, nonprofits need to emphasize sophisticated planned giving techniques that provide needed benefits to donors while building their own future.

1.10 THE NEW PLANNED GIVING DONOR

Planned giving has changed over the years. No longer are the majority of donors elderly widows who, cultivated over tea, make the traditional donations to a husband's alma mater and the local hospital. Today's planned giving donor may just as easily be a young entrepreneur who establishes a charitable remainder trust with new stock holdings. Planned giving donors have become much more savvy and knowledgeable, and today's planned giving officer often has extensive contact with a donor's lawyer, financial advisor, trust officer, and/or accountant. Outside advisors usually are included in the process because of the range and complexity of gift vehicles available to donors of all ages, who have various personal and financial objectives. Planned giving officers need to monitor current trends in tax laws, estate planning, and financial planning and must learn to operate in the for-profit business world, bringing its energy and expertise to the nonprofit setting.

1.11 THE YOUNG PLANNED GIVING DONOR

Traditionally, planned giving donors were older, wealthier, and more well established. While generally this is still true, a younger planned giving donor has emerged at many nonprofit organizations. This donor has responded to the planned giving office's public education efforts to promote planned giving as part of the donor's overall financial and estate planning. Planned gifts like deferred gift annuities help donors prepare for retirement while they help the nonprofit. Contingent bequests name a nonprofit as beneficiary of a donor's estate in the event of the death of a donor who is unmarried without children or in the case of simultaneous deaths of a younger couple without children.

Many young donors, especially entrepreneurs and professionals, have the capacity and interest in making a mutually beneficial planned gift. Planned giving must be presented as an option that can complement, rather than compete with, the donor's financial objectives. Planned giving, properly presented, can do just that.

1.12 PLANNED GIVING IN A DEVELOPMENT OFFICE

Planned giving has evolved from a misunderstood and underused development function into a professional specialization. Traditionally, planned giving was not fully incorporated into many organizations' development programs. Planned giving officers spoke a foreign language and engaged in technicalities that other development officers did not understand and, perhaps, did not want to learn. Although the planned giving field employs special techniques, a successful planned giving program is built on solid development principles. The specifics of such a program can be learned, and a planned giving officer does not need to be a lawyer, banker, or accountant to be successful. The planned giving office, as an integral part of the overall development effort, should work closely with other areas in development to further office and organizational goals.

(a) Businesslike Approach

Although successful planned giving officers build on solid development skills, there are additional characteristics that they should cultivate to enhance the position and a professional image. For example, some development officers befriend prospects and become part of their lives by running errands and doing favors. Because of the technicalities of planned giving, in many ways it is more appropriate and easier for the planned giving officer to approach the donor at arm's length, treating the donor interaction as the business relationship it truly is. By addressing business issues at the outset of a meeting, the planned giving officer can resolve such matters and leave time for more relaxed, informal conversation. Both the planned giving officer and the donor know why the meeting was arranged, so it is best to tend to the business portion of the meeting as early as possible. Donors most often make their gifts to the fundraiser who is the most skilled and professional.

(b) Expertise and Training

A planned giving officer needs to present herself as a trained, experienced professional with knowledge in several areas, including law, banking, and finance. The greater the officer's knowledge, the better able she is to anticipate questions and solve gift-planning problems. Presenting herself as an expert in this field instills confidence in donors and co-workers alike. Taking courses in estate planning, financial planning, and federal income taxation, and becoming skilled as writers and effective speakers enhance such professionalism. Courses in communications and speech can improve presentations, and entrepreneurship, business, and marketing courses provide important perspectives to invigorate and successfully continue a planned giving program. Perhaps the most important skill a planned giving officer can have is the ability to work with all types of people. A planned giving officer needs to be a good listener and conversationalist. Cultivating personal interests such as travel, sports, and literature will allow points of commonality to arise in conversations with donors who share these interests. Such conversational ease helps in negotiating the terms of a planned gift.

(c) Personal Donor Visits

Never underestimate the value of a personal visit with a planned giving donor. A planned gift requires a donor to make choices related to family and finances, and a personal visit by the planned giving officer sometimes can make the difference between whether a gift is made or is not made. Donors appreciate the personal attention and are flattered that the gift is important enough to the nonprofit to warrant a special visit. Planned giving is a business that is best conducted face to face.

1.13 CONCLUSION

The business of planned giving has changed over the years, but it will always rely on interpersonal connections. Planned giving is also teamwork, building effective working relationships with donors, donors' advisors and families, and fundraising colleagues. It is a complex business that needs individuals skilled in using multidisciplinary approaches to solving problems.

Part of the job of a planned giving officer is to educate management about the differences between planned giving and development in general. The rewards of a planned giving program can be considerable; however, a successful program requires patience and time. Long-term planned giving programs provide a solid foundation for a nonprofit organization and an attractive option for many donors. Cooperation and a mutual understanding of the roles of development and planned giving can serve well any nonprofit organization.

CHAPTER TWO

Inside the Development Office

2.1 INTRODUCTION

Development offices are structured in a variety of ways, depending on the size and type of organization. A development office is often organized as a centralized department, where employees are managed by a main office and are physically located in a building housing the development office; sometimes the development office is a decentralized department, in which employees are physically located outside the office and report to a particular dean, physician, administrator, or department head. The development office also may be divided geographically according to regions of the country. In this case, development officers are responsible for raising money from donors within those areas and may be located within the particular regions or at organization headquarters. Many nonprofits use a combination of these organizational approaches.

A nonprofit organization's planned giving officers are part of the development team. Along with the development staff, a planned giving officer's goal is to raise money for the nonprofit and build relationships with donors. Most planned giving officers work from a centralized development office and work with all departments in the organization. The planned giving department identifies, cultivates, and solicits donors who choose to support the organization through a planned gift or an endowed fund. Planned giving officers specialize in handling gifts with tax and estate implications for donors. These include gifts of outright cash and securities; gifts that provide a lifetime income to donors, such as pooled income fund gifts, charitable gift annuities, and charitable remainder trusts; and bequests, real estate, and gifts of tangible personal property, such as art, jewelry, antiques, and collectibles.

This chapter describes the various fundraising activities in a development office, focusing primarily on larger organizations that contain separate development functions. In smaller organizations, it is not unlikely for several distinct functions to be included in one department, run by a single individual.

2.2 ANNUAL GIVING

The annual giving program is the foundation of any development effort; it is the development office's largest marketing arm and one that, over time, identifies a significant number of planned giving prospects. A development office uses annual giving to expand its base by soliciting donors for an annual, unrestricted gift through a personalized direct mail or telemarketing plan that segments the potential donor population. Within an educational setting, alumni of all schools and classes are solicited for the annual fund. Prospects to a hospital's annual fund are primarily patients, doctors, employees, and friends of the hospital, and for a museum the prospects include patrons, subscribers, friends, and volunteers. Depending on the size of the nonprofit and the maturity of the development program, the professional staff of the annual giving program may include a director, assistant directors, a reunion giving coordinator, and a coordinator for print and mail production.

The annual fund program has two main purposes: dollar acquisition and donor acquisition. A program's success is defined by its raising more dollars than in the preceding year, receiving a higher average size gift, showing a greater percentage of donor participation, and adding new donors to the annual fund base. Annual giving, one of the most expensive components of a development program, is labor intensive and financially expensive because of the costs of postage, printing and handling, and staffing. An organization may invest between $2.00 and $10.00 before the first annual fund dollar is produced from a new donor. There are several components to an organization's annual fundraising: direct mail, a telefund program, and special events. Each is explored in the following paragraphs.

(a) Direct Mail

Direct mail solicitation is the lifeblood of most annual fund programs and is the first and most used method of raising money. Through direct mail solicitation, nonprofits receive immediate cash, usually in small amounts, for operating expenses and program support. New prospects are solicited after graduation, a hospital stay, or a visit to the museum. Existing donors may be solicited based on the preceding year's gift or based on the donor's area of interest.

Most annual giving programs follow a process of segmentation, which divides the total target population into several components or subsections. This process permits a more individualized appeal and encourages development officers to learn about donors and their interests, based on the support provided to the organization and its departments. These annual fund donors are "raising their hands" to indicate that they want to be involved with and benefit the organization. Major gift and planned giving officers know that annual giving efforts generate prospects who usually, after a few years of supporting the annual fund, are upgraded to planned and major gift prospects.

(b) Planned Giving and Annual Giving

The direct mail solicitation and telefund card can include a brief statement promoting planned giving. For example, the following statement can be included:

> If you itemize your tax deductions, you can claim charitable gifts, like your gift to <ORGANIZATION'S> Annual Fund. You may also want to consider support for <ORGANIZATION> through a planned gift. A planned gift benefits <ORGANIZATION> and may provide an income and a charitable income tax deduction for the donor. Planned gifts include charitable gift annuities, pooled income funds, charitable trusts, and bequests. For more information on planned giving, please contact:
> <NAME>
> <TITLE
> <ADDRESS>
> <CITY, STATE ZIP>
> <TELEPHONE NUMBER>

(c) Telefund Program

Many organizations, in conjunction with their annual giving programs, operate a telefund or phonathon program. Telefund callers follow up on the direct mail effort by telephone, asking prospects and donors to make a gift to the organization's annual fund, turning a prospect's interest into a pledge of money to the organization. Telefund calls usually generate the financial support that has been solicited by mail. Telefund callers, whether volunteers, paid staff, or outside firms, operate in tandem with the direct mail program to solicit donors. Callers may work evenings, calling prospects throughout the country. Some organizations call on Sundays, and many call during the day to reach retirees who are at home. A number of organizations use automated computer telemarketing systems featuring monitors that show a donor's giving history and provide general information about the donor, as well as conversational scripts for the caller to follow when speaking with a donor. Callers may use headsets and autodialers to facilitate calling and to update addresses, confirm biographical information, and record pledges.

Personalized pledge cards are sent to donors to confirm their pledges. Pledge bills are then issued, usually three to four times a year, although some organizations bill monthly or even on consecutive weeks following the pledge. Most telefund callers receive several hours of training before making calls and are monitored and evaluated throughout their employment. Compensation is usually an hourly wage and may include incentives, based on a variety of performance categories. A professional telefund staff may include a program coordinator, nighttime supervisor, and staff assistants.

In addition to producing financial support, a telefund program gathers direct feedback from donors and prospects about the organization. Callers who speak with donors and prospects learn firsthand their perception of the organization, as well as their attitudes and feelings. This important information should be relayed to the development staff. Planned giving officers should educate telefund callers about planned giving so that callers can ask donors and prospects if they wish to receive information. This approach can disclose new planned giving prospects and confirm existing interest.

(d) Special Events

A third way to raise money for the annual fund is through special events. At educational organizations, class reunions provide a good opportunity for alumni to return approximately every five years to meet with old friends and faculty. In anticipation of homecoming, alumni relations directors and class agents plan events to encourage attendance and promote participation in a class gift, a gift that each class presents to the organization in honor of its reunion. Any gifts made by alumni of a particular class during their reunion year, including gifts to the annual fund, are usually counted toward the total class gift. The class gift solicitation is conducted by alumni volunteers recruited by the reunion giving coordinator and alumni representatives of each school and college. Solicitation is often by letter, composed and signed by a reunion gift chairperson, and a series of volunteer phonathons that reunite reunioners with their classmates. Planned gifts are a favored option for many reunioners, especially those in older classes, and planned giving officers should become involved with the tradition of the reunion program by having an opportunity to talk about planned gifts and their benefits. More reunioners are likely to participate in the class gift if planned giving options are presented.

Noneducational organizations use other types of special events to recognize annual fund donors. Many organizations offer lecture series to annual fund donors over the course of a year. Specialists from the organization may speak to annual fund members on a range of topics, and these presentations often are followed or preceded by a social reception. Some organizations also offer a once-a-year event to honor and recognize annual fund participants.

2.3 MAJOR GIFTS

Most development offices have several centrally based development officers who actively pursue prospects for major cash gifts. What constitutes a "major gift" varies among organizations. A major gift can range from $10,000 to $100,000 or more. Some organizations share major gift officers with several departments, and others have one or more full-time development officers concentrating solely on major gifts. The strategy for securing major gifts, which varies among development officers, includes identification, cultivation, and solicitation of prospects and donors. Because there is an overlap in donors and strategies, major gift and planned giving officers should work closely to coordinate solicitations and maximize gift potential. Many of an organization's largest gifts are made through a combination of cash, life income gifts, and bequests. For example, a planned giving officer may solicit a donor for a planned gift but may instead receive a major cash gift. So, too, a major gift officer may solicit a donor for a cash gift and learn that the donor is most interested in making a gift that provides him with a lifetime income. In light of their shared goal of raising money for the organization, planned giving officers should work with major gift officers to educate them about planned gifts, to help them become sufficiently comfortable with the concepts to offer planned giving options to their donors and prospects.

2.4 FOUNDATIONS AND CORPORATIONS

A foundations and corporations officer seeks support from foundations and corporations that make grants to nonprofits. Such grants may come from corporate earnings, charitable trusts, or monies invested through foundations for the sole purpose of distribution. Relationships can develop between the nonprofit and the charitable organization over time or grow out of an association of a trustee, administrator, or development officer with a particular foundation or corporation. Foundations and corporations tend to have specific criteria for giving, and their giving parameters can change annually. There is usually little overlap between the planned giving office and the foundation or corporation office unless a planned giving donor has a connection with a foundation or corporation that can result in a gift.

2.5 STEWARDSHIP

Some organizations have a separate stewardship office that oversees an organization's endowed restricted funds, those that are established for specific purposes, such as to award scholarship money to a student in a specific area of study. The primary responsibilities of the stewardship office are to cultivate the donors of these funds, serve as a liaison between the donor and the fund's beneficiary, prepare annual reports on the fund, and keep donors informed of additional donations to their funds. The stewardship office may also assist in establishing new funds by working with potential donors and departments on specific proposals, or oversee the creation of plaques for various naming opportunities or other forms of recognition. A good working relationship between the planned giving and stewardship offices can help strengthen donor relationships and increase gifts to an endowed fund. The stewardship office can cultivate donors by reporting to them and presenting stewardship events. See Chapter 54 for more information on planned giving and stewardship.

2.6 PROSPECT MANAGEMENT

Tracking prospects and following up on donor leads, an important process for a development officer, is particularly important for the planned giving officer, inasmuch as the duration for tracking a prospect from start to finish may be several years. Planned giving prospects require continued cultivation, and it is likely that a planned giving officer will become well acquainted with the donor over time. Thus, a system must be developed to facilitate the tracking process and to coordinate efforts among the organization's development officers. Many organizations have a separate prospect management system that oversees the tracking function. Prospective donors are more likely to give when they are approached by a single development officer presenting a clear and coherent organizational message. Efforts to elicit support can be undone or undermined by the accidental approach of several representatives of an organization to the same prospective donor. Before any individual, corporation, or foundation is approached for a gift, the development officer should check with prospect management for clearance.

Prospect management tracks solicitation activity throughout an organization, processing approvals for solicitations and providing development officers with progress reports on their prospects and activities. Prospect management can provide screening services and generate reports listing current top prospects by geographic area, program interest, school, year of graduation, age, or patient history—indicating their status or relationship to the organization. In many ways, the prospect management department provides monitoring and trafficking functions, coordinating efforts among development officers to avoid duplicate solicitations. Some organizations have a computerized prospect management system, which eliminates reliance on staff members.

Because planned giving prospects and donors are tracked for a potentially extended period of time, it may be important to establish a prospect management system specifically for planned giving. Such a tracking system can require more detail about prospects than afforded by the development office system. See Appendix, CD-ROM Documentation, Administrative Documents.

2.7 INFORMATION SYSTEMS AND COMPUTER OPERATIONS

A department of information systems or computer operations provides reports for a development office and supports computer users with training and consultation. The services of this department may include computer programming, systems analysis, and word processing. Like the department of prospect management, it is especially helpful in generating names of donors and prospect lists based on donors' giving history, relationship to the organization, and areas of interest.

2.8 GIFT REPORTING AND PROCESSING

The gift reporting and processing department keeps track of gifts and pledges made to the organization from the private sector, including individuals, foundations, and corporations. In general, government grants are not included in a development office's fundraising totals. The gift reporting department is responsible for maintaining donor records and processing gifts to the organization. Receipts are issued to donors from this office, as are acknowledgment letters.

2.9 RESEARCH

The research department provides research on prospects as requested by various offices and individuals in the development office. It is actively involved in the internal screening of prospects, through which it develops major prospects for the organization. This department also is called on to do background work on influential individuals who may be attending special events or who are being considered for trustee positions. The research department can be instrumental in identifying those prospects who are key executives at major corporations or who have significant financial holdings.

2.10 COMMUNICATIONS AND PUBLIC AFFAIRS

Many organizations, especially noneducational organizations, place the development office and the office of communications or public affairs under one vice-president. This relationship facilitates the inclusion of development promotional materials in all of the organization's publications. Depending on the size of the organization and the communications office, publishing, printing, and mailing may be done in-house. Communications department staff need to learn the language of development in order to write effective development pieces, and development staff need to understand the role of communications and appreciate its series of deadlines and production schedules.

2.11 ALUMNI RELATIONS

In most educational organizations, alumni relations is a part of the development department. In theory, both departments work as an integrated unit, but, in practice, they may not. For example, it is common for development and alumni relations departments to have territorial, philosophical, and functional differences. The office of alumni relations is sometimes a politically powerful department within an educational institution, because it works with many influential alumni leaders and volunteer groups. The alumni relations department hosts events and programs that are often considered "friend raising." Development officers, however, want to attend such functions specifically to meet development prospects and cultivate existing donors. The development office is charged with raising money, and the alumni staff, perhaps protective of alumni, may not want them to be solicited. Moreover, employees in alumni affairs may have access to alumni who wish to make a gift to the organization. Therein lies a problem for two offices that need to work together. A coordinated effort between the development and alumni offices can produce an integrated and cohesive message to their constituents.

Planned giving officers should make an effort to work with individuals in the alumni affairs department to promote planned giving. It is helpful to identify one or two individuals who are willing to learn about planned giving and will allow a planned giving presence at alumni events. Once trust grows and credibility is earned, planned giving efforts can increase.

2.12 CONCLUSION

The office of development is a complex structure within a nonprofit organization. The differences between the various departments of the office create a challenge in integrating the development effort. An understanding of the philosophies and goals of each department helps to determine where and how the planned giving department fits into the development office.

## CHAPTER THREE

Mobilizing the Nonprofit's Leadership

3.1 INTRODUCTION

Promoting a planned giving program to external constituents, such as donors, prospects, and financial advisors, is only one half of promoting a program. The other half is educating internal constituents. This chapter focuses on promoting a planned giving program to the people and departments within the nonprofit that can help the program to succeed. To ensure cooperation between the planned giving office and support departments, market the program to educate these other departments about planned gift options and about the expectations of the planned giving office concerning their part in the effort. Focus primarily on the vice-president for development, the organization's president, the board of trustees, volunteers (including deans, physicians, and administrators), the treasurer's office, general counsel, and the business office.

3.2 VICE-PRESIDENT FOR DEVELOPMENT

A planned giving officer working for a vice-president for development who understands and supports the planned giving program is in an enviable position. Most vice-presidents, although not specialists in this area, have a basic understanding of planned giving vehicles. They also know that to compete successfully with other nonprofits, the organization needs a planned giving program. The key to whether the vice-president for development supports the planned giving program is the value he places on planned giving efforts. The vice-president may instead encourage the planned giving officer to solicit donors primarily for outright major cash gifts and pledges, rather than for planned gifts. The vice-president for development who truly values the planned giving program will encourage the planned giving officer to take the time to set up a proper program and focus on planned gifts. The attitude of the vice-president directly affects the perception of the program by others in the organization, including development staff and employees in related offices.

There are a number of ways in which a vice-president for development can contribute to the success of a planned giving program:

- Provide direct access to the president and trustees when necessary and appropriate. Support at this level demonstrates that planned giving is important.

- Ensure a sufficient budget to run a planned giving program.

- Be patient in allowing marketing efforts and relationship building to translate into gifts.

- Offer an opportunity for continued professional training and education for the planned giving officer.

- Invite the planned giving officer to meetings that include the president and trustees, and provide the officer an opportunity to speak about planned giving.

- Give full credit for planned gifts within the nonprofit. Such recognition is important for donors and development staff, because it emphasizes the worthiness of planned gifts.

3.3 PRESIDENT OR CHIEF EXECUTIVE OFFICER OF THE ORGANIZATION

Support for a planned giving program begins at the top. The concern of the president or chief executive officer (CEO) of the organization for the planned giving program can add significantly to the program's success. An enthusiastic president can have a great impact on how the vice-president for development values planned giving efforts and how trustees and key volunteers view planned giving. The president is most likely to feel positive about planned giving once a valuable planned gift has been made to the organization. A president who has personally made a planned gift is uniquely qualified to speak about the value of planned gifts to other donors and to employees of the organization.

If possible, work with the president to round out his knowledge of the benefits of planned giving. Take the opportunity to talk about specific gift situations, and how a planned giving benefit helped to close the gift. By talking about specific financial benefits available to donors, such as stream of income, charitable income tax deductions, and elimination of capital gains taxes, the planned giving officer can educate the president about planned giving benefits and establish himself as the resident expert. The aim is to have the president of the organization endorse the planned giving program at every possible opportunity. A president who promotes planned giving influences others to take the program seriously and to support planned giving efforts. A president's backing can result in more help from trustees and, thus, increase giving to the program.

The president's role in development is not well understood. Some presidents or CEOs of nonprofit organizations may be uncomfortable with development and feel they are not good at it. However, most presidents are pleased when development efforts are successful and their organizations receive planned gifts. Involving the president of the organization in a successful solicitation is an excellent way to market the planned giving program to both the president and other staff members. Between the first and final moments of solicitation, there are a number of steps and strategies to be considered. The first question to ask is: Should the president be involved? If so, there are many opportunities for a president to interact with constituents. The encounter may be one on one at a large function or at a more intimate gathering in a private setting. It is important to select an appropriate forum that fits the president's style. Momentum, as well as gifts, can be lost by misreading the chemistry between the prospect and the president or by the lack of attention to the timing or details of the president's involvement.

Although it is sometimes difficult to judge the appropriateness of the president's role, consider the following guidelines:

- *Less involvement is usually better than more.* The president's time is valuable and should be protected. Involving the president less frequently but at more opportune times will enhance development effectiveness.

- *Lower expectations.* Have reasonable expectations about the president's willingness to be involved. Do not become disenchanted if the president does not seem interested in assisting with the development effort. In many cases, unwillingness is due to a lack of time, other priorities, or uneasiness in asking for money.

- *Consider the competition.* To impress prospects who are corporate executives, entrepreneurs, or very wealthy, it may be important to involve the president directly. It often happens that no one has a better presence than the president. Some donors are offended if they are solicited by anyone in an organization below the president's level. Keep in mind, too, that many donors are solicited by several organizations, and those other organizations may be involving their president in solicitations.

- *Remember that admirers want to be near the president.* Some prospects hold an organization's president in great esteem. With these prospects, the president can be exceptionally persuasive. Always consider involving the president with this type of prospect.

- *Prepare thoroughly.* Be sure to prepare the president before donor meetings or meetings in which development efforts will be discussed. Provide the president with donors' names, amounts of past gifts, and their current development interests. Remind the president if he has met the donor prospect on previous occasions.

- *Involve the president at events and programs.* A president may lose important opportunities to raise funds by failing to discuss the organization's need for financial support. Mentioning a development success or the organization's bottom line can provide an opening for such discussion. Help the president by coaching him to talk about the financial needs of the organization at every public event. Such opportunities can generate gifts to the organization.

- *Thank donors.* Even if the president is involved in no other way, make sure that he thanks donors after they give. If he is willing, have the president personally telephone new or large donors to thank them for their gifts. At a minimum, prepare a letter for the president's signature, thanking them for their gifts. Many organizations prepare letters for gifts of a certain amount, such as $10,000 or more, that are signed by the president. Donors respond favorably to a thank-you from a person at this level in the organization.

3.4 ROLE OF THE BOARD OF TRUSTEES

All too often, nonprofits fail to define expectations for board members and prospective board members. Organizations may place individuals on boards and ask for their help, but give them nothing to do. Often they fail to convey to board members what is needed from them and allow them to feel that they are fulfilling their responsibilities and expectations simply by lending their names to the organization. Nonprofit board members should be challenged to give or obtain financial support. One of the first jobs of any member of a board of trustees is fundraising. It takes money to drive a nonprofit, and the organization should be direct about this requirement; raising money is one of the major reasons for establishing a board in the first place. At the time of joining the board, members should be told of their financial obligation to make a gift, and gift giving or obtaining should be a condition of board membership. Board members should feel good about their financial support, knowing that their contributions can be influential in encouraging others to give.

It is important to educate trustees about the benefits of becoming involved in the program, whether in helping in decision making, in identifying and soliciting donors, or in becoming donors themselves.

(a) Importance of Trustee Giving[1]

Nothing validates a planned giving program as much as having a trustee make a planned gift to the organization. Such a gift serves to generate additional gifts from other trustees and donors. A trustee's planned gift creates a unique marketing opportunity, because the trustee can be profiled in planned giving newsletters and brochures. A trustee's making a personal planned gift demonstrates commitment to the organization, the program, and its objectives. Making a gift is a trustee's best opportunity to step beyond a policy-and-oversight role to become an active player, and a trustee who has made a planned gift is more comfortable in soliciting a prospect for a planned gift. For any planned giving program to succeed, prospective donors should know that board members are fully behind the planned giving effort. If not, a prospect may ask, "If the board members have not given, why should I be motivated to give?"

(b) Trustees as Fundraisers

Statistics show that the most successful fundraising campaigns have had significant trustee involvement. The ultimate responsibility for an organization rests with its board of trustees, and because the board is responsible for the spending of funds, it follows that board members should play an active role in the raising of funds. The trustees typically know the most about the organization's hopes for the future and how it plans to achieve its goals. Trustees are in the best position to tell the organization's story to others, to raise the level of awareness of donors, prospects, and community leaders. Outside their connection to the organization, trustees have developed other relationships that can be sources of financial support for the planned giving program. To increase program totals, trustees must be willing to help identify and solicit prospects who can make planned gifts. Fundraising at the trustee level is often between peers, and trustees should offer the opportunity to lend financial support to the organization to their friends, acquaintances, and business associates.

(c) Board of Trustees and Planned Giving

To begin a planned giving program, a planned giving officer may need to have extensive contact with the organization's board of trustees. If the organization does not have a pooled income fund or does not offer charitable gift annuities, board approval may be required to spend the necessary money to draft legal documents and pay for management of a planned giving program. Board members will need to see estimated costs outlined and fully described before approval and are likely to have questions about planned giving program revenue versus the money spent each year to keep the gifts invested and managed and to cover the costs of servicing donors.

It is essential to educate trustees on the importance of planned giving and what is required from outside legal counsel and an administrative manager in maintaining the planned giving vehicles. A board of trustees is likely to be made up of many distinguished, accomplished businesspeople, all of whom have different professional strengths and connections in the business world, yet may be unfamiliar with planned giving. Carefully outline to board members what is needed to run a successful planned giving program, a program that can handsomely support the organization for which they serve as trustees. Tell them about administrative and legal costs. Individual board members will likely have

---

[1] Adapted from J. W. Pocock, *Fund-Raising Leadership: A Guide for College and University Boards* (Washington, DC: The Association of Governing Boards of Universities and Colleges, 1988).

opinions about the program and suggestions as to the firms that should be used for legal counsel and investment services. Be clear about what the program needs, and do not select service providers based solely on an individual trustee's preferences. Although a particular law firm or bank may do a superior job in many areas, not many institutions specialize in charitable giving or planned gift management. If the wrong firm or institution is selected, the nonprofit may end up paying for hours of work that could have been done more quickly by an experienced lawyer or planned giving manager. Complex planned giving situations or scenarios should not be cases of first impression for the outside service providers.

3.5 DEVELOPMENT STAFF

The director of planned giving wants to bring more planned gifts into the program, and the general development staff can be a great help in bringing in more prospects and donors. The planned giving officer's job is to make the development staff feel comfortable enough with planned giving concepts to mention them to prospects, bringing the planned giving officer into the solicitation as it moves along. To help educate the development staff, schedule biannual planned giving training sessions and help attendees to understand the basic planned giving concepts. Include everyone in the office, especially those who have donor contact, including major gift officers, annual fund staff, those in acknowledgments, and the receptionist. Throughout the year, provide staff with new tax and planned giving information.

3.6 VOLUNTEERS

Some standard fundraising models contemplate that the leadership, direction, and implementation of a development effort are driven by its volunteers. The theory is that staff-driven programs are unable to access, cultivate, and solicit an organization's constituents. It is true that many major gifts come directly from volunteers themselves, and this is to be encouraged. But can an organization provide staff to support and sustain a volunteer-driven development program? Volunteer-driven programs may work best at older nonprofit organizations that have strong, long-standing traditions, such as Ivy League universities, small private schools, schools with a religious orientation, or those with strong athletic programs. Certain healthcare settings and arts programs also may foster strong volunteer programs.

Volunteers sometimes misunderstand the nature of development. They see involvement in an organization's volunteer activities as a way to accomplish their own social and political goals. A volunteer may attend volunteer meetings to gather with old friends and have lunch, rather than to focus on fundraising. To protect the budget for appropriate development events and programs, staff members must redirect volunteers' efforts by educating them about the importance of development and planned giving, and suggesting ways to help further development efforts. Volunteers often best serve planned giving programs by screening prospect lists for new donors, agreeing to solicit some key individuals for gifts, or making necessary introductions for staff members to solicit prospects. A volunteer who can work on his own, bringing into the program new donors who do not have a connection to the organization, is the most valuable type of volunteer.

3.7 VOLUNTEER FUNDRAISERS: DOCTORS AND DEANS

In certain organizations, there are opportunities for success in working with volunteers who can help identify and solicit planned giving prospects. Such volunteers include deans, physicians, and department heads.

(a) Working with Deans

Deans are usually grateful for any assistance from the development office. Yet a development officer who works for a school, college, or university and is based at one school or department within the organization may find a conflict between the various roles she is asked to play. The central development office may want the development officer to design fundraising strategies, identify prospects, interview faculty, and provide development leadership to the dean and to the school. The dean, however, may view the situation differently. Most deans have little knowledge of the role of a development officer. Development officers should be knowledgeable about their own jobs so that they can educate the dean about what is expected in regard to development. Hours lost on nondevelopment projects through performing other functions in the dean's office results in less financial support to the organization. Ultimately, the development effort at the school may be unsuccessful, perhaps causing both the central office and the dean to become disenchanted with development and the development officer.

Like presidents, many deans may not realize their own importance to the fundraising effort. A savvy development officer can educate the dean as to his role and provide the leadership needed to run a successful campaign. The goal is to maximize the dean's development activities. Keep the dean focused on the relationship between financial support and project enhancement and the need for additional scholarships and recruitment. Schedule a weekly appointment with the dean, or with an associate dean who reports to the dean, as a way to keep communication open, build a relationship, and learn about the school's priorities. Develop and follow an agenda for each meeting. This allows the development office to report successes to the dean on a regular basis, and to stay in touch with specific priorities and areas of interest.

(b) Working with Physicians

Doctors can be invaluable to the success of a development program within a healthcare setting. Patients often want to make their gifts to the doctor who treated them. If their doctor is willing to assist in raising money, this is ideal. First, a planned giving officer may need to convince the physician that the officer can help raise money for the physician's own programs. All programs need money, and doctors can be more helpful if they know that they can access the money raised. Try to maintain regular contact with the physician by telephone and written correspondence. Success in soliciting patients often follows from having a physician sign a letter, telephone a prospect, or agree to personally solicit a patient. Encourage as much physician participation as possible, because it can make a great difference in the fundraising effort. Working with physicians is covered more fully in Chapter 49.

(c) Annual Event for Internal Fundraisers

Consider hosting an annual event to thank those individuals in-house who have helped with development efforts. Ask one or two individuals to share with the group their experience working with the development office and a donor. This type of event is a public way to thank the volunteer and encourages others to help with development efforts.

(d) In-House Newsletter

Create an in-house newsletter to circulate to nonprofit staff, updating them on recent gifts made to the institution. This can help educate staff to the development office's efforts and encourage individuals to become involved in the process.

3.8 SUPPORTING OFFICES WITHIN THE ORGANIZATION

There are several key offices within an organization that can have a very significant impact on a planned giving program. The following paragraphs examine three such areas: the treasurer's office, the office of the general counsel, and the business office.

3.8 SUPPORTING OFFICES WITHIN THE ORGANIZATION

(a) Treasurer

It is often the case that the treasurer of an organization has been working at the organization for a long time. The treasurer may not be interested in making changes or may be unfamiliar with the value of a planned giving program. The treasurer and planned giving officer are likely to look at development-related functions differently. The planned giving officer's focus is to increase the number of planned gifts to the organization, yet the treasurer's office is also aware of the financial obligations connected with such gifts. Together, the treasurer and planned giving officer will deal primarily with investment and administrative issues of the program. Specifically, the treasurer is intimately involved with the administration and investment of the charitable gift annuities and charitable remainder trusts, and in making decisions about the use of an outside pooled income fund manager and its activities. If the treasurer of the organization is managing the charitable gift annuities and trusts in-house, first determine whether this arrangement is in the best interests of the planned giving program. Consider these four questions:

1. Are the donors and development staff best served and serviced by keeping the management of these gifts in-house?

2. Are the donors receiving the best possible rate of return while the remainder is protected for the organization?

3. Is the treasurer's office interested in continuing to manage the planned gifts in-house?

4. If management of planned gifts is moved outside the organization, who will pay the cost?

It is important to determine whether the arrangement is working for all players or, if the planned giving program is new, how the treasurer's office feels about administering the program. Whether to move the management of planned giving assets outside of the nonprofit is covered more fully in Chapter 56. Educate the treasurer and the treasurer's staff about the needs of the planned giving office and its impact on the organization's bottom line. Explain to them some details of planned giving; do not assume that they understand the intricacies of planned giving concepts. Explain, for example, that the payout rate to a donor who makes a charitable gift annuity is based on mortality tables, and that the goal of the nonprofit is to receive approximately 50 percent of the donor's gift, not to recover the entire amount of the gift. Let them know what they can do to help the program flourish. For example, the treasurer's office is often a starting point for inquiries from donors. Suggest that donor-related calls regarding planned gifts be directed to the planned giving office, and thank the treasurer's office staff regularly for the work they do on behalf of the development program.

(b) Office of the General Counsel

Work closely with the general counsel's office to help the planned giving program operate effectively. The general counsel's office may want to control much of the planned giving legal work, but many attorneys at nonprofit organizations are overworked and kept extremely busy with more pressing issues. It is unlikely that the general counsel has much experience in charitable giving, but she may feel strongly about trying to do the work in-house to maintain control over planned giving activities and to minimize outside legal costs. This function may prove to be a distraction to the general counsel. Once again, the planned giving officer should educate the general counsel about the legal complexities of planned giving work, stressing the technicalities of the different financial vehicles, gifts of real estate, and the various tax implications for donors. The general counsel probably will see that he or she cannot manage all or most of this work in-house.

Suggest a law firm or attorney as legal counsel for the program and discuss the firm's experience with planned giving. Stress that when a donor needs an answer quickly, the planned giving officer must have the independence to call an outside attorney without having to clear the request with the general counsel. Moreover, an outside attorney will not second-guess the planned giving officer's decisions, which affords a further measure of independence. The appropriate balance is to keep the general counsel informed of the planned giving effort and to maintain a level of professional independence. After all, it is the planned giving officer who is responsible for the program.

(c) Business or Real Estate Office

The business and planned giving offices work together primarily in handling gifts of real estate. A strong relationship is helpful when an organization goes through the complex process of accepting such a gift. Bring the business office into the process early by educating its staff members about what the planned giving office does and the benefits to the organization of receiving real estate gifts. Explain the gift process from beginning to end. Do not let the business office immediately reject a piece of real estate because of the complexity or time involved in closing the gift. Consider working with the business office to design a questionnaire for the development staff about accepting gifts of real estate. Such cooperation can put the planned giving office in a better position to navigate the potentially difficult waters of real estate gifts.

3.9 PLANNED GIVING TRAINING PROGRAM

A carefully designed training program should be used to educate internal constituents, including development staff members, about planned giving. It should define planned giving, alert staff members to the profile of a planned giving prospect, show how gifts can be funded, discuss various planned giving vehicles, illustrate how internal constituents can support the planned giving program. A sample planned giving training program is included in the Appendix, CD-ROM Documentation, Exhibits.

When organizing a training session, consider using overhead projections or handouts to demonstrate the financial benefits to donors who make planned gifts. Supply attendees with handout materials to read after the presentation is completed. Handouts can offer a summary of the session and should include planned giving calculations and, perhaps, a newspaper article of interest in this area.

Be careful about the length of the presentation; one hour is probably sufficient. Select a time of day when most people can attend, and give plenty of advance notice. Keep the presentation provocative and fun, and avoid getting too technical. Show attendees that planned giving is an interesting field, and that planned giving can help donors to make gifts they did not think possible—and help the organization to raise more money.

3.10 CONCLUSION

Educating an organization's internal constituents is critical to the success of a planned giving program. Keeping these constituents educated and involved is an important aspect of any planned giving program. Regular communication with all of these individuals helps the program to prosper.

CHAPTER FOUR

An Operational Plan for a Planned Giving Program

4.1   INTRODUCTION

Beginning a planned giving program or expanding an existing one requires developing a solid operational plan. An operational plan needs to be developed to identify the types of activities to be undertaken in the first 12 to 18 months of a new program or the next 24 to 36 months of an existing program. Before drafting the operational plan, the planned giving officer must fully understand the organization's style, pace, and politics. An operational plan needs to be realistic, well organized, and reflect a wide range of planned giving ideas depending on the maturity of the program. Periodically revise the plan to add new initiatives and ideas and eliminate those that do not produce a reasonable return. This chapter presents issues to consider in creating an operational plan.

4.2   PERSPECTIVE

When examining the planned giving program, adopt a fresh perspective. The nature of planned giving differs from almost every other area in a development office and is best exemplified by an entrepreneurial spirit and attitude.

Consider these six areas:

1. *Research.* Where does planned giving business come from?

2. *Product or service development.* What types of planned giving products or services should the nonprofit organization offer?

3. *Marketing.* How can the planned giving options be promoted through marketing?

4. *Outreach.* How can continued visibility be achieved with the community or nonprofit organization's constituents?

5. *Identification of new business.* Who are new planned giving prospects? Which existing donors or prospects need attention?

6. *Staff management.* Is the staff challenged and are assignments delegated appropriately?

4.3 PURPOSE OF THE PLANNED GIVING PROGRAM

Start the operational plan by stating the purpose of the planned giving program. "The purpose of the planned giving program is to raise funds through planned gifts such as life income gifts, gifts through estates and trusts, endowed funds, and to raise funds through assets other than cash." Include a statement indicating what is needed for the program to succeed. For example, "To succeed, a comprehensive educational, marketing, and outreach program must be established to inform donors, prospects, trustees, physicians/deans/administrators, staff, and friends about the benefits of making planned gifts."

4.4 GOALS OF THE PROGRAM

Outline the broadest goals of the planned giving program including:

- Identify new and solicit existing planned giving prospects and donors.
- Establish a strong marketing effort to promote planned gifts.
- Raise the visibility of the planned giving program internally and externally.
- Restructure existing support areas to provide services to the planned giving program.

Next take each program goal and further define the goal through specific activities. Include:

- Target fundraising goals.
- Target the number of planned gifts to be raised.
- Define marketing initiatives.
- Consider events, programs, and activities.
- Engage in Staff training.

4.5 DONOR CONTACT

Planned giving staff as well as other development staff needs to maintain regular contact with prospects and donors. Is the planned giving program connecting with its constituents? Is the program building a foundation to maintain a continued presence over a five-year period? How will contact be maintained? Staying in contact with prospects and donors usually takes place in three ways:

1. By letter

2. By telephone

3. By personal visit

While meeting in person is the most effective way to build a relationship, planned giving efforts should be geared toward one of these methods to promote contact with donors on a regular basis. Development, especially the business of planned giving, is a people-to-people business. Planned giving by definition requires regular contact over an extended period of time. Many planned gifts materialize only after a series of integrated efforts conducted over several years.

4.6 IDENTIFY NEW PROSPECTS AND SOLICIT EXISTING PLANNED GIVING PROSPECTS

Because planned gifts often take a period of years to materialize, it is necessary to build a large pool of prospects. To build this pool, consider these six steps:

1. Assist other development staff members with individual planned giving cases.

2. Identify and meet with existing donors to introduce them to planned giving concepts.

3. Upgrade bequest donors by asking them to consider a life income gift.

4. At an educational organization, identify members of a class who have made planned gifts and/or approach appropriate members of the classes celebrating their 25th, 50th, 55th, and 60th reunions. At other nonprofits, target other groups of donors (e.g., patients, patrons, attendees, or others, depending on the nonprofit) and organize those prospects around an event or activity.

5. Identify and work with one or two key volunteers who are willing to solicit others for a planned gift.

6. Establish bequest societies or planned giving committees.

4.7 ESTABLISH A STRONG MARKETING EFFORT TO PROMOTE PLANNED GIFTS

Establish a strong marketing effort to promote planned gifts through publications, mailings, and events. While planned giving budgets can be modest, resources are needed to reach new prospects and donors, especially when the number of staff members working on planned giving is limited. Remember to space marketing appeals so that appropriate follow-up can be accomplished. A comprehensive list of appeals follows. Select those actions that work best for the program.

(a) Publications

- Draft planned giving advertisements and articles for existing development newsletters or publications.

- Create a planned giving letter to send to planned giving prospects and donors.

- Run planned giving, financial planning, and estate planning columns in a development or planned giving newsletter.

- Revise annual fund reply devices to include a planned giving appeal.

- Create a general planned giving brochure to offer to donors and prospects.

- Identify and publicize organization-wide funding opportunities and needs through various existing publications.

- Draft an Inventory of Assets Booklet to help donors with estate planning matters and to identify assets that may be used to make a gift.

- Create an endowment book that lists existing endowed funds at the organization.

(b) Mailings

- Segment the database to develop a targeted population of donors who have made annual gifts of $25 or more for three or more years to send planned giving mailings.

- Segment the database to select donors or prospects who are 75 years old or older to send specific planned giving information, such as information on charitable gift annuities. If the donors' ages are not known, present a table showing payouts for donors at ages 65, 70, 75, and 80.

- Send donors 50 to 70 years old and donors who have made gifts of securities to the organization information about the organization's pooled income fund.

- Target donors 25 to 50 years old for a deferred gift annuity.

- Select all donors who have given $5,000 or more cumulatively to the organization to receive planned giving information.

- Target geographical areas for mailings by selecting donors living in zip code areas that indicate wealth.

- Prior to year-end, send existing planned giving donors and prospects a year-end tax letter that highlights the benefits of charitable giving and current tax tips.

- Mail a publication four times per year to all planned giving donors and prospects.

- Mail a "Ways to Give" brochure to retired faculty, staff, and administrators along with a letter showing the benefits of making a planned gift during retirement.

- Send a planned giving brochure with annual fund appeals.

(c) Events

- Host a series of seminars for donors, prospects, and friends of the organization to focus on preretirement planning, retirement planning, and financial planning to attract people who may be capable of making a planned gift.

- If appropriate, conduct seminars in regions of the country where many older donors live or vacation, including Florida, California, Arizona, and other locations.

4.8 RAISE THE VISIBILITY OF THE PLANNED GIVING PROGRAM

- Host a luncheon for all donors who have made a planned gift to the organization.

- Speak at a local retirement home about the benefits of planned giving, estate planning, and financial planning.

- Conduct planned giving seminars for area professional advisors.

4.8 RAISE THE VISIBILITY OF THE PLANNED GIVING PROGRAM INTERNALLY AND EXTERNALLY

Internal and external constituents should be educated about the ways to create planned gifts.

(a) Internal Constituents

- Educate development officers about trends in planned giving to make them feel comfortable about planned giving options, which they can present to donors and prospects.

- Interact with key internal staff, including the general counsel's office, representatives from the financial affairs and business offices, treasurer's office, and comptroller's office, to discuss the goals of the planned giving program and educate them about planned giving needs.

- Train and educate researchers, telefund callers, and annual fund staff to identify planned giving leads.

- Meet with department heads, administrators, physicians, deans, and program leaders to talk about planned giving and ways to identify planned giving prospects.

- Conduct screening meetings with volunteers, staff, and trustees for local and international planned giving prospects.

- Work individually with development officers to include planned giving in their operational plans.

- Assign staff members to serve as planned giving liaisons to particular departments. For example, assign a major gifts officer to focus on grateful patients connected to the Neurology Department to close a certain number of planned gifts each year.

- Clarify priorities for private support in each department, outline planned giving strategies to help accomplish priorities, and target specific prospects as potential planned giving donors.

(b) External Constituents

- Contact representatives from the banking, financial, and legal communities who can provide new business to the planned giving program, including attorneys, trust officers, bankers, financial advisors, and certified public accounts.

- Create a professional advisory committee to assist in marketing planned gifts. Invite these individuals to the planned giving office to attend workshops on charitable gift planning.

■ Conduct charitable gift planning, estate planning, and financial planning seminars in select geographical areas for donors and prospects.

■ Create and distribute a professional advisor's manual to lawyers, certified public accountants, trust officers, financial advisors, and others who may need information for clients or who can provide planned giving leads to the nonprofit. The booklet can provide information on estate planning, including wills, trusts and estates, and charitable gift planning. The booklet can be distributed with the organization's logo on the cover.

■ Host an annual luncheon/event for outside professionals to educate them about the organization and provide them with a social event outside of the office.

4.9   RESTRUCTURE SUPPORT AREAS TO PROVIDE SERVICES FOR THE PLANNED GIVING PROGRAM

Evaluate and restructure those areas that provide services to the planned giving program:

■ If the nonprofit has in-house planned giving services, determine if those services should be moved to a professional manager outside of the organization. If new programs need to be started, such as a pooled income fund or charitable gift annuities, determine what various outside providers offer and prices charged.

■ Create or update existing documents, such as a charitable gift annuity contract, pooled income fund trust agreement, and instruments of transfer.

■ Determine what area in the organization manages bequests. Decide whether the planned giving office should take over management of bequests.

The previous ideas may be incorporated into an operational plan or used as background information to support current goals.

4.10   INVENTORY EXISTING PLANNED GIVING TOTALS

Inventory existing planned giving files, if there are any, to establish a baseline starting point for the program. Determine the total number of planned gifts, including bequests, endowed funds, life income gifts, and gifts of assets other than cash and their amounts. Exhibit 4.1 is a Planned Giving Baseline that can be used to inventory planned gifts.

Exhibit 4.1   Planned Giving Baseline Totals

		Total $	Average Size $
#	Charitable Gift Annuities		
#	Deferred Gift Annuities		
#	Pooled Income Fund Gifts		
#	Charitable Remainder Annuity Trusts		
#	Life Insurance Gifts		

Exhibit 4.1 *(Continued)*

#	Real Estate Gifts
#	Bequest Intentions
	Total baseline of existing planned gifts (from inception of program)

Look at the overall quantity and quality of existing donors, and determine their financial capacity and interest in the organization. Using the model in Exhibit 4.2, list the total number of each type of gift, the total amount of those gifts, and the average size of that type of gift. Determine the years that each of these gifts were closed to develop a sense of what number and types of gifts close each year, so that priorities can be established.

4.11 PLANNED GIVING DATABASE

If a computer database retrieval system does not exist, consider purchasing a planned giving software package that retrieves information about each planned giving donor and prospect, including the donor's and prospect's address, telephone number, type of planned gift made or considered, age, and connection to the organization. Place all files on a minidatabase, and convert files to a system that enables the planned giving office to retrieve and sort data. The minidatabase enables the planned giving office to communicate more efficiently with donors and to help identify and target donors for seminars, cultivation, visits, mailings, and solicitations. To save money, create a database using a database software program.

4.12 PLANNED GIVING BUDGET

An operating plan should include a one-year planned giving budget. A sample budget is shown in Exhibit 4.2.

Exhibit 4.2 Planned Giving Budget

1000	Office Supplies/Materials			$
1001	Letterhead		$	
1002	Postage		$	
1003	Business Equipment		$	
1004	Files/Folders		$	
1005	Furniture		$ _____	
		Subtotal	$	
1010	Training/Education			$
1011	Conference		$	
1012	Subscriptions		$	
1013	Professional Memberships		$	
1014	Seminars		$ _____	
		Subtotal	$	

(Continued)

Exhibit 4.2 *(Continued)*

1020	Travel			$
1021	Air		$	
1022	Hotels		$	
1023	Restaurants		$	
1024	Rental Cars		$ _____	
		Subtotal	$	
1030	Computer Hardware/Software			$
1031	Planned Giving Software		$	
1032	Computer Laptops		$	
1033	Service Contracts		$	
1034	Telephone/Fax		$ _____	
		Subtotal	$	
1040	Professional Services			$
1041	Consultant		$	
1042	Legal Services		$	
1043	Financial Service Fees		$	
1044	Outside Administrators		$ _____	
		Subtotal	$	
1050	Marketing			$
1051	Design		$	
1052	Printing/Typsetting		$ _____	
		Subtotal	$	
1060	Salaries			$
1070	Programs and Events			$
1071	Workshops		$	
1072	Recognition Programs		$	
1073	Events		$	
1074	Outreach		$ _____	
		Subtotal	$	

Consider the following expenses to include as budget items in the operating plan:

(a) Travel

If the nonprofit has a national donor base, include local and national visits with donors and prospects as a travel expense. Remember to budget for airfare, hotel, meals, rental cars, taxicabs, telephone calls, and parking costs. Travel should be considered a high priority, because one-on-one meetings with prospects, followed by a solicitation, are more likely to produce gifts.

(b) Programs and Events

Budget for recognition events, outreach programs, and donor-related functions. Count on producing at least one donor event each year. When budgeting for an event, include the costs of food, rental space, parking, alcohol (if applicable), invitations, postage, flowers, token gifts, an honorarium for the speaker, and marketing the event.

(c) Marketing

Include the cost of printing and designing newsletters, ads, year-end letters, holiday cards, stationery, targeted mailings, business reply envelopes, and other marketing pieces and expenses.

(d) Postage

Include postage costs for targeted mailings, individual responses to donors, newsletters, and invitations.

(e) Legal Fees

Include funds in the budget to cover the cost of outside legal fees. The ability to call an attorney to answer questions is very important to a successful planned giving program—especially for a new program or when building a program. As the program matures, legal fees should increase. Estimate this amount based on the expected number of gifts to close this year, with a close look at which ones may require outside legal assistance. Overbudget rather than underbudget this expense. This cost should be separate from any legal advice obtained from the general counsel of the nonprofit organization.

(f) Outside Administration Fees

The budget should include the cost of planned giving services provided by an outside money manager. The administrative fees will likely include costs of maintaining the pooled income fund, gift annuity program, and charitable remainder trusts. Remember that as the program grows, so do the administrative costs. Budget additional amounts, if necessary, for outside consultants.

(g) Professional Development

Budget attendance for at least one professional seminar a year, individual one-day conferences, and the cost to attend local planned giving group meetings. If the organization offers charitable gift annuities, become a member of the American Council on Gift Annuities, which charges a modest annual membership fee.

Professional development is especially important when resources are limited. The planned giving officer needs to have as many resources available as possible.

(h) Computer Software

A planned giving program needs a software package with annual maintenance fees. If necessary, budget for an introductory training session to learn how to run the software.

(i) Books and Professional Newsletters, Subscriptions

Planned giving requires current reference materials, including books on planned giving; the Internal Revenue Code and Regulations; various tax, financial planning, and legal references; and list serves on the Internet. Keep money in the budget to pay for planned giving reference materials as needed. Subscribe to at least one monthly or bimonthly professional outside planned giving newsletter or service. This will help to supply information on current trends in planned giving and tax law changes. Also consider subscribing to the *Wall Street Journal*.

4.13 CONCLUSION

Everyone gets caught up in the day-to-day office routines. With some frequency, however, it is important to step back and assess the progress of the program. Although it is so easy to become distracted, constantly analyze productivity and focus on the bottom line, raising money. Develop an operational plan—one that is helpful and likely to be used and reused. Once developed, give it time to work and commit to it for at least one year. Read the plan quarterly and adjust accordingly, if appropriate. Make the plan the key working document, and distribute it to staff and selected nonprofit officials.

Managing a Planned Giving Program

CHAPTER FIVE

Hiring Staff

5.1   INTRODUCTION

Planned giving is a growth area in most nonprofits' development programs. Older, more established programs are hiring additional planned giving staff members, while younger, less mature programs are hiring their first planned giving officer or are looking to incorporate planned giving into their development programs. Whether the planned giving program is young or mature, hiring the right planned giving staff members can help determine the success of the program.

The rapid growth in planned giving is influencing decisions about whom to hire, and nonprofits are intensely evaluating the characteristics and qualifications of prospective development employees and the entire hiring process. This chapter is divided into four parts: the changing marketplace, attributes that often predict success for planned giving officers, the hiring process, and hiring a planned giving assistant.

5.2   THE CHANGING MARKETPLACE

Complicated and stringent tax laws, savvy and sophisticated donors, and increased competition for financial support have changed the world of planned giving. Those practicing it need to develop a diverse range of professional skills and innovative approaches. The success of a planned giving program is linked directly to the skills of the planned giving officer, who must understand tax law, banking, estate and financial planning, marketing, donor management, and people. Prospects, donors' financial and legal advisors, and the nonprofit's financial officers require this level of sophistication. Today's planned giving officer serves as a charitable gift-planning advisor working with and complementing the donor's professional advisors (financial planners, certified public accountants, and attorneys), who are regularly included in discussions about a donor's charitable gifts, especially large gifts.

Planned giving officers coming from business environments may be more likely to operate as entrepreneurs than those who have worked exclusively in a nonprofit setting, and can bring for-profit concepts about marketing, advertising, customer relations, case management, public relations, and budgeting to their nonprofit positions. The planned giving officer may equate launching a planned giving program to starting a business.

(a) Advanced Credentials

One reason that many nonprofit development offices are hiring planned giving officers from the fields of banking, law, finance, and accounting is the shortage of experienced staff within the development office and the growth of the planned giving field. Many nonprofits have discovered that the development office is not producing sufficient internal candidates with the requisite technical skills necessary for planned giving. Although a number of fine planned giving training programs offer information about planned giving concepts and principles, some development generalists may be reluctant to apply what they have learned about fundraising to the more technical and complex world of planned giving. For some individuals, understanding planned giving concepts can be intimidating, and communicating the concepts to a colleague, donor, donor's financial advisors, and the nonprofit's internal constituents can be even more so.

How do nonprofits cope with the changing workforce? Where do sophisticated planned giving officers come from? How does the planned giving office meet the demands and challenges of a changing marketplace? Increasingly, nonprofits are hiring employees with advanced degrees, such as doctor of jurisprudence (JD), master of business administration (MBA), and certified public accountant (CPA) certifications. In addition, practicing employees from other disciplines, such as law, accounting, and banking, are moving to nonprofit organizations. These candidates complement existing development staff members and can bring resources and a business perspective to the nonprofit.

(b) Credibility

The planned giving officer has an increasingly important role within the office of development as well as with external constituents, such as donors and professional advisors. A sophisticated planned giving officer provides credibility to a planned giving program at four levels:

1. The donor sees the planned giving officer as a skilled, technically proficient advisor.

2. A planned giving officer with an advanced degree or credential equalizes the interactions with a donor's financial advisors, all of whom speak the same financial language.

3. A skilled planned giving officer has heightened credibility when dealing internally with the organization's legal staff, business office, and treasurer.

4. Board members of the nonprofit, themselves perhaps attorneys or accountants, expect a high level of competence from the planned giving office.

A nonprofit's planned giving officer can also serve as a broker disseminating information about planned giving. A technically skilled planned giving officer frequently is called on by professional advisors to assist a donor or the advisor with a gift that may benefit a different nonprofit. He also may assist professionals at other nonprofits, not as a consultant but as a skilled colleague. Networking among planned giving officers and representatives from the nonprofit and financial communities enhances a planned giving officer's prospects for success and encourages the exchange of planned giving information and ideas. Ultimately, by educating others about planned giving, planned giving officers build their own programs while also contributing to the larger world of philanthropy.

(c) Transition Assistance

Education and transition workshops can help acclimate new planned giving officers to the demands of the job. Although professionals from other disciplines may be familiar with aspects of planned giving, law school, business school, or training to become a CPA do not provide a curriculum for charitable gift planning. Development staff members who move from other positions in the development office to planned giving also need instruction in the technical aspects of the job. To bridge the gap, new employees and internal candidates can take courses and join local planned giving groups. Colleagues at other nonprofits can assist in the transition.

A mentoring program with a senior member of the development staff can help educate the planned giving officer about the nonprofit environment and new job responsibilities. As with all development staff members, a thorough immersion in the nonprofit culture—its people, business practices, traditions, and history of successes and failures—can greatly assist the planned giving officer. An office retreat can promote professional relationships among coworkers, foster respect and trust, and assist in integrating new members with the existing development staff. Outside management or campaign consultants also may help orient new employees to the nonprofit environment and the fundamentals of development and planned giving.

5.3 ATTRIBUTES OF SUCCESSFUL PLANNED GIVING PROFESSIONALS

(a) The Desire to Learn

A willingness to learn is a personal investment by the employee in the mission of the nonprofit and the philanthropic community. Planned giving's technicalities demand training and retraining to stay current with tax issues and planned giving concepts. A candidate's resume shows much about the desire to learn. Has the candidate continued formal education through pursuit of a masters or other advanced degree? Has the candidate rounded out the depth of knowledge necessary in planned giving by taking courses in tax, estate planning, financial planning, or marketing? Has the applicant attended development and planned giving workshops and seminars sponsored by professional organizations? All of these activities show a desire to learn the business of planned giving.

(b) Productivity

Productivity is a measure of success based on volume and time spent on activities. In planned giving, it means that productive employees are able to generate gifts regularly and consistently both in quantity and in quality. A track record of productivity indicates a greater chance for success in the future. Planned giving officers should secure a designated number of gifts per month, quarter, or year; produce gifts in each of the planned giving options, utilizing a variety of assets; and build professional relationships with the nonprofit's constituents.

(c) Team Player versus Lone Ranger

It is generally thought that successful employees must be team players. Team players are valued within the nonprofit, but is planned giving always a team sport? The very qualities that make a person successful in planned giving can make that individual less of a team player and more of an independent professional. Successful planned giving officers must be cooperative and able to work with a variety of internal and external individuals, but they also must independently carry out the responsibilities of the job. They need to balance their attention between the nonprofit's external constituents—donors, prospects, professional advisors, and other members of the nonprofit community—and the internal staff involved in gift planning and administration—development directors, treasurers, executive directors, and board members.

(d) Communication and Interpersonal Skills

Effective verbal communication skills are essential in addressing groups of constituents and satisfying other public speaking aspects of a planned giving job. Presentations to donors, volunteers, and professional advisors illustrate the challenge of planned giving, combining solid interpersonal skills with technical proficiency. The planned giving officer should be as comfortable conversing with an individual donor as explaining the new tax act to a group of professional advisors. The officer also must be an effective writer to open up lines of communication to potential donors and develop printed marketing materials.

Conversation affords an opportunity for a donor to learn about the nonprofit and for the planned giving officer to learn about the donor's needs and charitable motivations. This requires effective speaking skills but, more important, demands sophisticated listening skills. Good listeners are sensitive to another person's attitudes, feelings, and perceptions, and can observe subtle nuances; a donor's nonverbal communication may be more revealing than anything that is verbalized.

(e) Integrity

In planned giving, integrity is a must. Planned giving officers represent nonprofit organizations and influence the perceptions of their internal and external constituents. Planned giving officers must maintain a high sense of integrity and ethical conduct, both professionally and personally. The nature of planned giving requires the professional to learn about the donor's personal and financial interests. A planned giving officer must respect the donor's privacy, provide assistance, and maintain an appropriate distance. Many donors see planned giving officers as quasi-financial advisors and often ask for advice on general financial matters apart from planned giving. Planned giving officers should provide information that is within the scope of their knowledge and act in the best interest of the nonprofit and donor. See Chapter 52 for a discussion on ethical issues affecting planned giving officers.

(f) Patience

To be successful in planned giving, patience is not a virtue, it is a necessity. Closing a planned gift can take months or years. The largest gifts often are produced because the planned giving officer was patient and acted in the best interests of both the donor and the nonprofit. Planned giving officers are not salespeople, driven by quotas. Sales-oriented planned giving officers can mistakenly believe that the goal is simply to raise money. Planned giving is a more thoughtful and complex process of developing a relationship that involves several questions:

- What is the donor's charitable motivation?
- Does the donor have overriding financial and tax considerations?
- What asset should the donor use to fund the gift?
- How does this gift complement the donor's overall financial and estate-planning goals?
- If other family members are involved, what is their role in the gift-planning process?

In the long run, simply moving from prospect to prospect does more damage than good to both the nonprofit and the donor. Nonprofits should retrain and refocus sales-oriented staff members on relationship building to encourage the planned giving officer to focus on the donor's philanthropic motivations.

(g) Volunteer Experience

Ideally, the resume of a planned giving officer should include previous volunteer experience with civic or charitable organizations. There is no better way to gain insight into the world of nonprofits than by serving as a volunteer. Many effective planned giving officers have a history of personal service and volunteerism through participation in a religious organization, college or preparatory school, political campaign, cultural organization, or community. During the interview process, probe into the quality and quantity of an applicant's previous volunteer experience.

5.4   THE PROCESS OF HIRING A PLANNED GIVING OFFICER

(a) The Job Description

The Appendix, CD-ROM Documentation, Administrative Documents includes a sample job description for a planned giving officer. Although descriptions vary from organization to organization, five common elements remain:

1. Title

2. Reporting relationship

3. Primary job functions

4. Educational qualifications

5. Benefits

An advertisement for a planned giving position should include, at a minimum, these five elements.

(b) The Advertisement

Most job descriptions are comprehensive and prohibit a complete printing in national publications such as the *Chronicle of Higher Education* or the *Chronicle of Philanthropy*. The Appendix includes an advertisement that is intended to generate interest from prospective planned giving candidates. See Appendix, CD-ROM Documentation, Administrative Documents. The advertisement should:

- State the name of the nonprofit and the location of the planned giving job.
- Describe general responsibilities of the position.
- Describe qualifications necessary for the job.
- Explain the application process.
- State the deadline for application.

Depending on the size of the organization and the scope of the job search, the advertisement can be placed nationally and locally in various nonprofit trade journals and development organization newsletters, and in regional or local chapter publications.

(c) The Search Committee

Practices vary among nonprofits regarding the use of search committees. If the organization does not use a search committee, it is helpful to have a number of individuals participate in the planned giving officer search process. Representatives may be appointed from the these groups:

- Central administration
- Development office
- Specific programs or departments
- External groups, such as a professional advisory committee or outside legal counsel
- Nonprofit volunteers or boards

(d) Resume Review and Sorting

A candidate's application package typically consists of a resume and a cover letter. Cover letters should speak specifically to the employer's position and should not be a generic response. Resumes should appear tailored to meet the specifics detailed in the job description and match the organization's qualifications. The search committee should test whether the candidate meets the expectations expressed in the job description:

- Does the applicant have the requisite years of experience?
- Does the applicant meet the formal educational requirements?
- Does the applicant possess adequate depth in experience?
- Is the experience relevant to the nonprofit's mission?

Some organizations routinely exclude candidates who make the following errors on their resumes and cover letters:

- Typographical errors
- Poor grammar
- Sentence or paragraph structure defects
- Unresponsive or generic replies

Many job postings elicit resumes and applications from 50 to 100 or more prospective candidates. Because handling candidates' applications is time consuming and tedious, it can be helpful to sort applications into three general categories, which may be graded as follows:

- "A" applicants meet the criteria enumerated in the job description and satisfy educational requirements.
- "B" candidates technically meet the qualifications, but lack specific job experience.
- "C" candidates fail to meet job qualifications.

This review is only preliminary; to be fair to all applicants, it is necessary to test the integrity of this initial categorization. Notes from the reviewer attached to each application eliminate the need to reread the same application and serve to refresh the reviewer's memory about a candidate's strengths and weaknesses.

(e) Telephone Interview

After the pool of prospective candidates has been narrowed down to between 7 and 10 serious candidates, telephone conversations can be conducted. Telephone interviews enable an employer to talk with a number of candidates efficiently and inexpensively and allow the interviewer to probe into a candidate's experience in planned giving. This step increases the opportunity to prequalify candidates for one or more of these criteria:

- Experience in planned giving and development
- General demeanor
- Telephone skills
- Interpersonal skills
- Salary expectations

Often the pool of candidates can be reduced after the telephone interview, leaving several viable semifinalists. From this step, the semifinalists can be invited to the nonprofit for on-site, personal interviews.

(f) Reference Checks

Prior to inviting prospective candidates for personal interviews, preliminary reference checks may be made, with the candidates' permission, to assess the candidates' work habits and personal traits, including:

- Overall strengths and weaknesses
- Verbal, written, and interpersonal skills
- Ability to work with a team
- Potential for success in planned giving
- Work habits

See Appendix, CD-ROM Documentation, Administrative Documents, for a list of insightful questions that may elicit meaningful responses from a candidate's references. These questions also can be posed to the candidate during the interview.

(g) The Interview

The purpose of the interview is for the candidate to learn about the nonprofit and for the nonprofit to learn as much as possible about the planned giving job applicant. If possible, applicants should be observed in a variety of different settings during the interview process:

- One on one
- Groups of three to five
- Large groups
- Business settings
- Social settings

In addition, the interview process should create opportunities for the candidate to meet the nonprofit's key members, especially those with whom the planned giving officer is likely to work on a regular basis. Outside general counsel, professional advisory committee representatives, and staff from the charity's business office can learn more about the candidate's technical skills, while board members and volunteers can examine the candidate's interpersonal skills.

(h) Following the Interview

Following the interview process and reference checks, the screening or search committee can meet to evaluate the strengths and weaknesses of each semifinalist. A comparison of each of the attributes included in Section 5.3 of this chapter can provide an objective analysis of each planned giving candidate's qualifications and potential for success in planned giving.

5.5 THE PLANNED GIVING ASSISTANT

The work of a planned giving officer is complemented by the efforts of a planned giving assistant who must be a versatile and adaptable employee. She must have strong interpersonal skills to work with donors and technical proficiency to produce planned giving projections and financial calculations. When the director is not available, the planned giving assistant must meet with prospects and donors and must support other nonprofit departments who depend on information from the planned giving office. As part of the development team, the assistant works with others from the business office, general counsel's office, and real estate office, as well as outside financial advisors who manage life income gifts on behalf of the nonprofit organization.

She must be aware of her skills and know her limitations. She must be cautious about exceeding her knowledge and circumspect in respecting a donor's privacy. The assistant should possess strong organizational skills to maintain accurate and complete files on every donor and prospect and assist with prospect management.

The planned giving assistant also is involved in developing training materials for development staff members, volunteers, and professional advisors. Planned giving agendas, worksheets, exhibits, and financial projections must be produced carefully to achieve the desired result. In addition, marketing materials such as ads, brochures, buckslips, and newsletters must be produced and personalized to meet the needs of a variety of the nonprofit's constituents.

Included in Appendix, CD-ROM Documentation, Administrative Documents, are a sample job description and an advertisement for the position of planned giving assistant. The documents can be modified to meet the specifications of the position and expectations of the nonprofit organization.

The assistant must possess many of the traits discussed earlier when hiring a planned giving officer and may have previously worked outside the nonprofit community. A transition and orientation program helps to focus the assistant on the goals, objectives, and organizational nuances of the nonprofit organization. Generally, the hiring of a planned giving assistant follows a process similar to the hiring of a planned giving officer: position announcements are prepared, search committees are mobilized, resumes are screened, interviews are scheduled, and references are checked. Although the search is conducted on a smaller scale, by no means is the hiring of the candidate of less importance to the office or to the nonprofit organization.

## CHAPTER SIX

Increased Management Responsibilities in the Development Office

6.1 INTRODUCTION

In every development professional's career, promotions and new positions can mean additional management responsibilities. Perhaps the job is a new position at another organization; or perhaps the planned giving officer has been promoted to planned giving director, a director of planned and major gifts, or director of development or chief development officer within the planned giving officer's organization. Regardless of the title, there likely will be new responsibilities, including supervising additional staff and overseeing or managing areas that are unfamiliar and outside of planned giving. This chapter explores the issues related to increasing management opportunities, including skill enhancement and managing staff, senior administrators, trustees, and volunteers.

6.2 NEW SKILLS, ABILITIES, AND THOUGHT PROCESSES

A new position will require learning additional skills that enhance the person's abilities and develop new ways of thinking. Just because the planned giving officer has mastered the technicalities of planned giving and successfully raised money from donors does not mean that she has honed the skills to successfully manage others or to oversee areas outside of planned giving, such as major gifts or research. New administrative skills will likely be needed, such as budgeting, working with human resources, facilities management, and drafting reports. A new, bigger position often involves becoming more broadly involved in the nonprofit, working with additional internal and external departments and constituencies. Often the new position requires becoming an ambassador from the department to the entire organization or its senior administrators. It may require public speaking. Additionally, managing staff, senior administration, trustees, and volunteers requires mastering skills such as team building, motivating others, and stewardship. The position may decrease contact with planned giving donors, resulting in less planned giving work and soliciting fewer donors for charitable contributions.

Consider the following as areas that may challenge existing skills. Evaluate strengths and weaknesses in these areas:

- Fiscal management
- Office management
- Human resources
- Facilities management
- Political skills
- Public speaking
- Writing
- Administrative skills

6.3   IS THE NEW POSITION A GOOD MATCH?

Consider whether this is a desirable job. Will the new position provide stimulating challenges, offer opportunities for growth and career advancement, and on a day-to-day basis provide enjoyable, substantive work? Soliciting planned giving donors, working outside of the office and working very independently, can be very different from working more closely with internal staff, managing and evaluating them, and working more with administration and becoming embroiled in political organizational issues.

When beginning the new position or after having done the work for six months or so, ask:

- Is this work interesting?
- Did expectations differ from reality?
- Is the job expanding capabilities and skills?
- Is this a stepping-stone to something else; if so, what?
- Are skills transferable from the previous position?
- Is this job enjoyable?
- What is missing?
- Can missing activities be included in the current job? How?

6.4   ADVANCE PREPARATION

If the planned giving officer has been raising funds from donors for many years, she is likely to be good with people. Having good people skills will help tremendously in the new position. To be a better manager, both with the development staff and the organization's senior administration, consider these next ideas to prepare in advance for the new job:

- Meet with every direct report on the staff and ask what they feel makes a good manager.
- Ask people how to communicate most effectively with them: e-mail, telephone, in person?
- Establish a regular system for meeting, whether one on one every week or as part of a larger group.
- Focus employees' individual skills. Ask people to take on specific projects at which they can succeed and in which they have an interest.
- Praise others often.

- Ask for feedback, both positive and negative. A manager cannot improve his skills if he does not know his faults. Evaluation can be made at the time of an employee's review or by anonymous feedback at an appointed time for all employees.

- Talk with other former planned giving officers and ask them how they like their new responsibilities, and what they would do differently.

- Attend management seminars, usually offered by someone outside of a development office.

- Read books on successful management. Buy them or check them out at the local library.

- Take a public speaking course to improve speaking skills and reduce fears.

6.5 TRANSFERABLE SKILLS: MOTIVATION, TEAM BUILDING, AND STEWARDSHIP

(a) Motivation

In a new position in the development office, new skills are tapped. Existing skills can be used but may be repositioned, perhaps for a new audience. For example, the new director may need to motivate senior administrators rather than staff. Determine which skills can be built on and where new resources should be brought in.

Motivating development staff is similar to motivating donors and prospects. Generate enthusiasm from staff to close major gifts or succeed in their areas of management in the same way a gift officer elicits gifts from prospects. Talk about the rewards associated with closing the gift: satisfaction of doing good, enjoying becoming a leader, training others. Complement individual staff members on what they do well, and motivate and encourage them through positive reinforcement.

Motivate senior administration, trustees, and volunteers to solicit major gifts by thanking them both casually and more formally in front of colleagues. Remind them that they set an example for others and further the work of the organization they love. When working with physicians, host the physicians at a formal program and have them tell their successful stories in front of other physicians. Let them receive recognition and praise. This both recognizes their efforts and motivates them to continue their work.

(b) Team Building

At a director's level, there is great opportunity to help build a team of development professionals to work together. The planned giving officer is already good at this, having worked with an organization's many areas internally and with donors' families and advisors to close a gift. Successfully managing a large team in a development office and closing gifts requires success in many different institutional departments. Bring different groups together and promote unity by doing things as a group; for example, host a regular meeting just open to major gift officers so that they can discuss solicitation strategies and learn from each other's expertise. Generate excitement and make noise when a big gift comes in; celebrate the gift. Hold meetings for managers in each area so that they feel a part of the whole program, vested in it to succeed. When appropriate, plan social events for members of the team outside the office.

When trying to build a team and a sense of teamwork consider:

- Hosting regular group meetings
- Celebrating gifts as they come in
- Investing in the group managers, giving them independence and autonomy
- Getting out of the office and socializing

(c) Stewardship of Nondonors, Administration, Trustees, and Volunteers

The work senior administrators, trustees, and volunteers do in development is likely to be outside their job description. The director needs to work with these individuals and thank them regularly, like donors, for their good work. Stay in touch with them over time, updating them on various donor situations and office issues that pertain to them. Consider hosting an annual dinner that will help to educate attendees about development and recognize their work. For those outside of the organization, such as volunteers, strive to make them feel like insiders, a part of the inner workings of the department and institution. Highlight them in organizational or development office publications. Recognize them at donor functions, commending their good work in front of the organization's president and other leaders. Steward all of these individuals like donors and prospects.

Remember to:

- Thank regularly.
- Provide periodic updates.
- Host a recognition event.
- Make volunteers feel like insiders.
- Provide publicity.

6.6 BUILDING STAFF

To help the director be successful in a new role, hire additional staff for specific skills the director is lacking. If the new job calls for great administrative skills and the development director is best at managing people, hire someone to fill that gap. From the new hire, the director can learn how to think administratively, how to gather and present data, and other organizational skills. No one is good at everything. Usually it is best to build on a person's already successful skills.

6.7 WORKING WITH A MANAGEMENT CONSULTANT

In the development office, role models may not exist in every area. Outside paid, professional expertise can be a great help for strategic planning and skill enhancement. When warranted, hire a management consultant for a specific amount of time, particularly when getting started. Consider selecting a consultant from the business world, one who may be focused on areas outside of fundraising. Ask colleagues and friends for a recommendation, especially colleagues at a senior level.

Determine exactly what is needed from the management consultant. What can the consultant provide? Help with budgeting, time management, staff interactions? Dealing with difficult personalities?

6.8 ESTABLISH MUTUAL EXPECTATIONS WITH THE CONSULTANT

Once a consultant is selected, try to determine what type of relationship will work best. Remember that the charitable organization is the client and that guidelines must be established that work for the development office and charity. Determine in advance:

- Length of time to work with the consultant (a year, six months, ongoing)
- Estimated cost
- Frequency of payment to the consultant
- Frequency of meetings (once a week, once every two weeks, once a month as needed)
- Availability for telephone consultations
- What needs to be produced, such as a long-range plan for the program or a staffing plan
- Necessity and frequency of written reports from the consultant
- Contracts
- Who will manage the consultant, and interaction with other development staff

## CHAPTER SEVEN

Measuring Performance for Planned and Major Gift Staff[1]

7.1 INTRODUCTION

Is the organization's overall development program successful? If so, it is likely that most members of the development staff are making sure that the program runs smoothly and is productive. In all likelihood, the majority of the success of the program, including meeting the department's financial and campaign goals, is because the major gift and planned giving programs are well managed and highly productive.

For development efforts to be successful, serious attention must be paid to the major gift and planned giving donors and prospects who are the heart of the development program as well as the staff who work with them. The major gift staff need to be fully engaged in the development process and regularly meet donors to cultivate, solicit, and steward them. Many managers for a planned and major gift program believe that some measurable standards and accountability for staff should be in place. Staff members who are nonperformers may become better performers with appropriate objective measures or they may choose to leave the organization, while good performers tend to become better performers. The challenge is to find the right standard for measurement, which will vary from organization to organization. There are few, if any, development-wide guidelines for accountability. How does a development office measure a major gift or planned giv-

[1] The authors wish to acknowledge David Dunlop, formerly at Cornell University, for teaching and inspiring development professionals to work with donors.

ing officer's success? First, the department must define a major gift and the job of the major gift and planned giving officer.

(a) What Is a Major Gift?

The definition of a major gift is as varied as the nonprofit organizations that raise such gifts. For some organizations, a major gift is $1,000 or $5,000. For many others, it is $25,000. As the number of fundraising campaigns increases, and goals soar into the billions, a major gift is likely to be a $100,000 gift or up to a $1 million gift. The definition is based primarily on the category of gifts that are the largest that the organization hopes and expects to receive, as well as its past experience in receiving gifts and its needs. At most organizations, a major gift may be either an outright cash gift or a life income or other planned gift. Refer to Chapter 14, "Planned Giving and Major Gifts," to learn more about how these areas differ.

(b) What Is the Major Gift or Planned Giving Officer's Job?

Once the charitable organization and staff members have agreed on the definition of a major gift, the development office, through its vice president or director of development, must define the major gift officer's job and performance expectations and then clearly communicate the expectations to the major gift or planned giving officer. The organization must be clear on what development and donor-related activities the major and planned giving officer should focus on as part of successful performance. Following are a number of possible parameters of what should be considered when defining a job, as well as how the officer's performance will be judged later.

(c) Criteria for Development Success

The way a major gift or planned giving staff member's success is measured varies depending on the type of organization, its size, needs, staff makeup, expectations, and culture of philanthropy. Most organizations, as part of overall success, evaluate major and planned giving staff on many of the following criteria:

- *Leadership*—Including the ability to manage donors and prospects; mentor new or younger staff members; take charge of donor meetings; and act appropriately assertive and self-confident. Whether a staff is large or small, a professional in a leadership role must act like a professional and set an example for others about how to conduct business. A major gift or planned giving officer should be actively on the road visiting donors and soliciting gifts, not in the office doing extensive paperwork. See Chapter 13, "Solicitation Strategies."

- *Teamwork*—The ability to work with staff members to close a gift or complete a specific activity. This is likely to include assisting in gift solicitations, sharing the spotlight and success with other staff members, and recognizing colleagues, from the researcher who identified a prospect, to the annual fund director who moved the prospect into the major gift arena. When the gift is completed, teamwork includes helping outside an area of responsibility and making concessions to support the collective good, such as relinquishing a prospect who could be solicited in another area that might result in a larger gift. For the planned giving officer, teamwork also means performing a variety of roles, including acting as an advisor and consultant to colleagues, and as an ambassador for the organization.

- *Professional knowledge*—Being up to date on the latest techniques and tax changes of life-income gifts and pursuing education and advancements for overall job-related knowledge. Focusing on new types of donors who can make philanthropic gifts, such as younger donors who have recently earned or acquired significant wealth.

- *Ethics*—Including working appropriately with colleagues and donors, especially elderly donors, and representing the nonprofit organization in the best way possible. Counting gifts in the most appropriate ethical manner. This is a very important criterion to focus on regardless of the size of the organization or how much it needs philanthropic support. The planned and major gift staff members are front-line representatives for the organization and must represent it with integrity.

- *Consumer relations/hospitality*—Contributing to the overall positive image of the organization; having the trust and respect of those within and outside the organization; and working well with donors and prospects. It means acting pleased with the donor's gift despite its size and doing everything possible for prospects whether they make a gift or a significant gift or not.

- *Accomplishing goals and objectives*—Raising money for the nonprofit in a timely manner. Staying focused on identifying donors, soliciting them for major support, and closing gifts. Specific ways of reaching a major planned or gift giving officer's goals and objectives are explored below in detail.

All of these measurements of leadership, teamwork, knowledge, ethics, consumer relations, and accomplishing goals and objectives should be examined when evaluating a planned and major gift officer's performance.

7.2   REACHING GOALS AND OBJECTIVES

Measuring a planned and major gift officer's ability to reach development goals and objectives is at the heart of successful fundraising. While the most basic measure is how much money has come in philanthropically to the organization at the end of the day, there are additional ways to measure development success.

(a) Financial Measurement

The most basic bottom-line measurement for a planned giving or major gift officer's reaching goals and objectives is the amount of money raised per month or year by the officer. This is likely to include gifts made through cash and securities, life income gifts, pledges, and perhaps bequest expectancies. Some charities expect that planned and major giving officers raise at least 10 times their annual salary. However, because financial markets can vary dramatically, and a donor's time line for finalizing a gift can be so unpredictable, solid major planned and gift giving officers can have a less successful year because a major prospect opts to defer his or her gift for a year, or a prospect dies suddenly or chooses to make a life income gift or bequest that might not be counted until the donor's death, or be deeply discounted. Planned giving and major gift officers also find that if a donor is rushed into making a decision about a gift, the gift is likely to be much smaller than what the donor could do, or the gift can be lost altogether. Generally, measuring performance strictly by money raised is an incomplete way to judge a planned or major gift officer's professional success.

(b) Other Performance Indicators: Activity

A better method to evaluate success is to measure activity more readily under the planned giving or major gift officer's control. For example, performance can be measured by:

- The number of personal visits per month or year the planned giving or major gift officer makes with individual prospects

- The number of solicitations made per month or year, including both direct personal solicitations and proposals sent by mail

- Time out of the office on the road meeting with donors and prospects, as a percentage of time, such as 30 or 40 percent

- Time spent with other staff working on donor solicitations

Activity can be further broken down by various moves, as seen below.

7.3 MOVES MANAGEMENT

Some organizations become very specific measuring performance on certain indicators. They ask planned giving or major gift officers to record and monitor their professional activities made with individual donors and prospects, using some variation of "moves management." A *move* is generally defined as a strategic step that moves an identified prospect toward closing a gift.

Under most moves management programs, a planned giving or major gift officer is assigned a number of prospects and donors for whom he is responsible. Depending on the charitable organization, the active caseload may be 125 to 150 prospects and donors, with an additional number of 100 or more prospects and donors carried by the planned giving or major gift officer although not currently active. A strategy is developed for each prospect by the major gift officer who is managing the prospect, and moves are planned for the next year. Activity is tracked, both by the major gift officer and by an individual in the development office assigned to prospect tracking or prospect control. If a move does not occur within six months, a prospect is reassigned to another major gift officer in the development office.

The definition of a move may vary from organization to organization, but a move is often broken down into categories of cultivation, stewardship, solicitation, and visit. The move is a way to measure performance, as well as seen as a step in the solicitation process. The moves categories include these specific definitions:

1. *Cultivational move*—A step performed by a planned giving or major gift officer that moves a prospect toward closing a gift, such as:

   - Introduction or cultivational letters

   - Telephone conversations

   - Greeting cards with a personal note

   - Invitation to or interaction at a special event

   - Personal thank-you letters

2. *Stewardship move*—Any activity that provides an update or report on a specific project, with the goal of keeping the organization in the donor's mind. Activity is usually initiated by the planned giving or major gift officer. Stewardship moves should occur on a regular basis, occur at least once a year, and may begin as soon as appropriate after the donor's gift is completed. Examples include:

   - Touring the charitable organization

   - Sharing a meal together

   - Sending an article to the prospect about the charitable organization or an update on some organizational activity

- ■ Visiting with a donor

- ■ Hosting a reception to honor the donor's gift

3. *Solicitation*—This move involves asking for something specific that includes a discussion of a gift of a specific dollar amount. Solicitations most often take place in person, but could be in the form of a written proposal, appropriately followed up. Senior staff and administration also may be involved in the solicitation.

4. *Visit*—A visit is face-to-face contact with a donor or prospect. This may include:

- ■ Personal meetings

- ■ A tour of the organization

- ■ Special event participation

- ■ A chance encounter if a significant gift-related conversation occurs

Moves related to cultivation, stewardship, solicitation, and visits allow a planned giving or major gift officer to measure his own performance, help others to measure their performance, and literally move donors and prospect situations to an outcome, whether positive or negative.

7.4 OTHER MOVES RELATED TO SECURING THE GIFT

Other types of activity may or may not fall into one of the preceding categories depending on how a moves program is established at the individual organization. The following activities may be considered cultivational or stewardship moves:

- ■ Strategy sessions with trustees, senior staff, or other members of the organization such as deans and physicians

- ■ Telephone calls that leave a message

- ■ Generic thank-you letters

- ■ Notes or telephone calls that confirm special-event attendance

- ■ Holiday cards

- ■ General invitations, newsletters, and promotional pieces from the planned giving or major gift officer that are not personalized

- ■ Assisting in a move that results in a closed gift

Most organizations require a planned giving or major gifts officer to make a specific number of moves to be considered successfully performing the job. For example, an organization may require that the officer visit 10 or more donors or prospects per month and additionally make 20 or more other moves with a donor or prospect per month.

7.5 ADDITIONAL WAYS TO REACH GOALS AND OBJECTIVES EXCLUSIVELY FOR PLANNED GIVING OFFICERS

Planned giving officers are in a unique position to reach goals and objectives in addition to the traditionally defined cultivational, stewardship, solicitation, and visit moves. Goals and objectives also may be measured by creating a strong marketing program for planned giving at the organization as well as raising the visibility of the planned giving program. Moves can be measured by performing some or all of the following:

(a) Marketing

- Drafting and placing a specific number of planned giving advertisements or articles in existing development newsletters

- Creating a planned giving newsletter

- Placing bequest cards around the organization

- Running an estate planning seminar

- Creating a new planned giving brochure

- Drafting and sending an inventory of assets booklet to donors

- Sending targeted planned giving letters

- Mailing a year-end tax letter to donors and prospects

(b) Raising Visibility

- Hosting a planned giving function

- Speaking about planned giving at a function/meeting older donors might attend

- Educating outside advisors about the organization and planned giving

- Managing a planned giving professional advisory committee

- Holding an event for outside advisors

- Speaking at a planned giving or development conference

(c) Administration of the Evaluation Process

Vice presidents and directors of development struggle with how best to administer the evaluation process. Typically, the donor base is large, and the pool of prospects and donors needs to be managed, assigning names to individual planned and major gift staff, and tracking progress over a specified amount of time, such as six months or a year. A good computer program can be helpful, as well as assigning one individual to the job of prospect management, working closely with the director of development or the director of major gifts in tracking donors and prospects. Additionally, planned giving and major gift staff members should, as in most professions, be evaluated on a regular basis.

(d) Annual Evaluation

It should be made clear upon hiring that the planned giving or major gift officer will be officially evaluated with a performance review once a year. Depending on the organization, a six-month review, especially for new staff members, may be helpful or warranted. When possible, share a blank copy of the review with the planned giving or major gift officer so that he knows the parameters of evaluation.

(e) Documenting Activity

Recording planned giving and major gift officers' activity is required at many charitable organizations. The frequency of submission varies. See Appendix, CD-ROM Documention for sample activity reports.

7.6   TEAM CONSIDERATION

To evaluate planned giving and major gift officers on successfully accomplishing goals and objectives, the development office may want to consider initiating team goals; for example, requiring that the development office as a team first meet an office-wide goal of raising a certain amount of money, such as that year's campaign goal, or asking staff to increase the number of members in their bequest society either by increasing individual members or increasing membership by an overall percentage of growth, such as 15 percent of existing membership. Then staff members may be divided into teams or small groups that are required to perform, as a group, a total number of moves. Doing this encourages staff members to work together, reducing competition and promoting teamwork.

7.7   FREQUENCY OF ACCOUNTABILITY AND TRACKING PROSPECTS

The director of development or director of major gifts will want to meet regularly with each planned giving and major gift officer to report on activity that has taken place with each donor and prospect under that officer's responsibility. Steps already taken should be documented, as well as next steps that need to be taken in every situation. As the director becomes better acquainted with each of the officer's prospects, there will be an opportunity to really focus on whether prospects are being appropriately moved along toward closing a gift. The tracking sheet provides categories that include the donor's name, connection to the organization, current status, proposed gift amount, and next step. Hopefully, planned and major gift officers do not spend more time tracking their work than meeting with donors.

On a periodic basis, it also may be helpful for trustees and senior administrators at the organization to be involved in the development process, further motivating planned giving and major gift staff to perform.

Over time, what is established will need to be reevaluated as the development staff grows, campaign goals are reached, and new priorities are established. As priorities change, the development staff may want to benchmark with other organizations to compare activities. New ideas will surface, as will new ways of working.

CHAPTER EIGHT

Managing Time
in Planned Giving

8.1   INTRODUCTION

Is there ever enough time in a day? Technology has made today's employee efficient but also has created increased demands and expectations. Employees are bombarded daily with e-mail, faxes, telephone calls (both traditional and cellular phones), and regular mail. Personal time has become more complex as many families have two working spouses and children attending school and participate in a multitude of personal and professional activities and lessons.

The planned giving world is faster paced than ever. Gone are the days of the charity's planned giving officer quietly working in the back room. Expectations are much higher today; many planned giving professionals are responsible for some or all of:

- Raising significant sums of money

- Identifying new planned giving prospects

- Meeting with donors and prospects

- Stewarding donors

- Working with outside advisors

- Drafting proposals and letters

- Attending donor events

- Managing staff

- Mentoring new hires

- Attending local planned giving council meetings

- Staying current on tax changes and planned giving updates

- Reading planned giving journals, loose-leaf services

- Drafting marketing materials

- Making planned giving presentations

How best to accomplish professional goals for the day or week? This chapter focuses on how to work most efficiently to accomplish work priorities.

8.2 GETTING ORGANIZED

For the big picture about creating a planned giving program, see Chapter 4. This chapter, by contrast, will help determine shorter goals and objectives for the next day, week, month, year, or five years. Regularly read the larger plan to stay on track, to ensure that each day, week, month, and year larger goals are nearer to being completed.

(a) Organize the Day and Week

At the beginning of the week or at the end of the previous week, make a plan for what should be accomplished in the following week. Write the plan on paper or on the computer or Palm Pilot—whatever works best. Next, determine and write down what is hoped to be accomplished each day of the week. If the director is organized, the week can be arranged efficiently. Be proactive and take charge of the workday.

(b) Block Off Hours

For organizing the week, make a list that includes "free" time—reserved as time to work on a specific project, or to leave some time to write. Much more can be accomplished during these blocks of time. For these hours of steady work to be successful, find a way to avoid interruptions and distractions. Consider closing the office door, disconnecting or forwarding the telephone, and turning the computer off to avoid reading e-mails if they act as a distraction. To cut down on colleagues' stopping by to chat, consider establishing "office hours," being available to staff during those hours. Also talk with colleagues, family members, and friends about how they can help with better time management, and ask them for their support.

(c) Managing the Calendar

Establish certain rules that control day-to-day office life. When setting the calendar for the day or week, consider:

- Holding no more than a certain number of meetings per day, such as three

- Beginning and ending all meetings at a certain time, so that work can be done at the beginning or end of the day

- Leaving free the day or afternoon before a trip to help prepare for the trip

- Leaving free the return day from a trip to catch up on e-mails and correspondence

- Having lunch brought in when meetings are scheduled at the lunch hour so that lunch is not missed

- Keeping mornings or afternoons free from meetings to concentrate on work

(d) Know Thyself

Everyone has certain weaknesses that cause them to lose work time. Determine how to work most efficiently by focusing on strengths and weaknesses. Is morning or evening the best time of day to work? Is there a three o'clock lull when a walk outdoors or around the office is needed? Are e-mails a distraction? Should personal telephone calls be reduced? Are conversations with colleagues distracting? Are hours before and after the workday good times to get things done? Is a day or two out of the office meeting with donors needed to change your perspective? Identify personal weaknesses and strengths to help schedule the day.

(e) Do the Most Difficult Tasks First

If a project or assignment is due at the end of the week or if a task is difficult to perform, do that work in the earliest part of the day or week. Doing other tasks first will waste energy dreading that other task, as its deadline continues to draw near. Try to finish that activity while energy is still available (such as in the morning if the employee is a morning person) and when there is still time to work on the task (such as at the beginning of the week before things become less predictable). For example, if a first draft of a planned giving presentation must be completed by the end of the week, begin the draft on Monday. By Friday, it should be comfortably completed or near completion. Or, if there is a donor who must be called this week, make the telephone call early in the week rather than putting off the call until Friday.

8.3 CONTROL THE OFFICE ENVIRONMENT

While juggling a series of assignments, such as talking with a donor, managing a direct report, and reading e-mail, find ways to set up the environment to be most productive and efficient. Consider the following practical suggestions to work smartly.

(a) Hire Great Staff

One of the most important keys to success when hiring staff members is to hire employees who can work together as a team. The planned giving staff can run calculations, handle donor calls, visit with donors, work on projects, and almost everything else that comes along. If competent and capable staff members are hired, they can grow in their jobs as more responsibilities are shared with them. Good staff members will even begin to close gifts on their own as they handle donor situations. When hiring, look for individuals who seem bright, flexible, conscientious, and adaptable, and who are quick learners and can multitask. Potential hires do not necessarily need planned giving or development experience; look for solid characteristics that can transfer to the planned giving environment.

(b) Delegate

Before immediately moving to handle a task, see if this is a job someone else on the staff can do. Ask:

- Who should be the representative at this meeting?

- Could an associate on the planned giving staff attend the meeting on investment policies?

- Where does this meeting rank on the priority list of meetings? If it is near or at the bottom of the list, can it be completely eliminated?

- Could someone else draft this letter or proposal to the donor?

- Could another staff member handle the donor interaction from start to finish? Perhaps there could be a policy that prospective gifts at a certain level are handled by other staff members.

- Does one staff member handle something better or most efficiently? Delegate!

(c) Hire a Great Associate Director

A great associate director can help the planned giving program and director tremendously. Let this person grow in the position to be able to handle almost everything. Also play to this individual's strengths and put her in charge of various functions, such as the bequest program, endowed funds, or presentations. Give the associate director lots of autonomy and let her do the job in her own style.

(d) Hire a Great Assistant

If the organization has the financial means to provide a good assistant, productivity will soar. Once a team learns how to work best together, the assistant can handle many responsibilities, such as:

- Making travel arrangements

- Managing the calendar

- Starting and perhaps finishing letters

- Signing names to letters

- Speaking with other representatives and employees at the charity

- Handling telephone calls

- Acting as a gatekeeper to protect time

- Summarizing highlights of planned giving journals

- Running planned giving calculations

- Responding to select voice mail messages

Be sure to provide good staff members with incentives to stay at the organization, working in the planned giving office. Give them as much responsibility as they are comfortable with and be sure to thank them publicly and privately often.

(e) Organize the Planned Giving Staff

Meet regularly with the planned giving staff as a team to get everyone moving along productively. On a semiregular or weekly basis, gather the team together to see who is working on what and which assignments can be delegated to other staff members both inside the planned giving team and in the development office. In this way, employees can equitably redistribute workloads, and tasks can be accomplished more efficiently. These regular meetings also give everyone an idea of the nature and scope of the work being done by individual members of the team.

8.4 MEETINGS

One of the greatest challenges in managing time is office and organization-wide meetings. While not wishing to eliminate all meetings, consider these tips for reducing the number of meetings attended:

- Make a list of all monthly meetings. Rank them in order of importance. Eliminate those meetings at the bottom of the priority list.

- Determine who really needs to be at the meeting and whether someone else from the staff can either be the representative at this meeting or should be asked to permanently handle the entire project.

- Suggest that the meeting take place by e-mail or conference call, cutting down on travel time to and from the meeting and perhaps reducing the amount of time spent in discussion.

- When meeting with others, meet at their office to be able to leave at the end of the meeting rather than continuing the discussion because the other person does not leave.

- Consider reducing hourly meetings to 50, 40, or 30 minutes.

- Suggest, where appropriate, that weekly meetings change to biweekly or monthly meetings.

- Combine some individual meetings to one group meeting where appropriate.

- Arrange meetings in which people stand (they will be shorter than seated meetings).

- Discuss with the vice-president or other supervisor the need to reduce some meetings, with the goal of spending more time with donors and being responsive to their needs.

- Draft an agenda for the meeting to keep people focused on the priorities.

8.5 TRAVEL TIME

Make the most of travel time. Many planned giving professionals travel regularly to other parts of the country for donor visits and planned giving conferences. Designate those hours in the air as time to work: complete proposals, read planned giving journals, work on staff evaluations, and the like. By working hard for three hours in the air or at the airport, a lot can be accomplished.

8.6 WORKING AT HOME

In today's telecommuting environment, more development professionals are having the opportunity to work at home at least part time. Working at home can provide significant benefits:

- It eliminates commute time.
- No colleagues will be dropping by the office to chat.

- E-mail and telephone use can be controlled.

- A block of uninterrupted time to work can be created.

- The environment is conducive to reading, writing, and working on projects that require more thought without office distractions.

(a) How to Begin

To make working at home viable, consider the following:

- Discuss the concept with the vice-president for development. Cite the number of people nationally working at home and/or those in the office who work at home. Explain the major advantage: being fully accessible to staff via telephone and e-mail while accomplishing more work at home. Try this in small blocks of time. If it works out well, time spent working at home can increase gradually.

- Start slowly. One or two days a month from home can be increased to one day a week from home.

- Make sure that children are at school, or have someone in the home to care for them. It is impossible to get work done at home if there are constant interruptions from children.

(b) What Is Needed

To work at home successfully, a number of items need to be assembled, including a computer and work supplies.

- A computer is the most important piece of technology to help with the work effort. Even if not working at home, a good home computer allows flexibility—which is of paramount importance when trying to balance home and work life. Consider saving long e-mails from work to read and respond to from home.

- Have a computer installed at home, complete with printer and fax machine, to draft planned giving letters, proposals, and other documents and respond to e-mail. Work with the charitable organization's information systems before the computer is installed to determine the best type of hookup so that the charity can be accessed most easily.

- Organize work supplies. At a minimum, find a clean, private place to keep supplies handy and a desk area to work from. Decide what supplies are needed and have them conveniently located and organized. Determine the office's policy on bringing supplies home. At a minimum, gather the following:

    - Desk supplies, including writing instruments, paper, and clips

    - Filing cabinet

To make the most of a day at home and to help the workweek run most efficiently, consider saving certain projects for the "work-at-home day" that require the most focused attention, for example, writing a planned giving proposal that has many technical components, digesting a new tax law, preparing a planned giving presentation, or drafting a colleague's performance evaluation. Also consider blocking off time to read and respond to lengthy e-mails from home.

(c) Telephone Calls

Depending on the amount of time working at home and the charitable organization and its financial position, consider installing a separate telephone line for business calls to avoid being interrupted by personal calls when working at home. When purchasing a new telephone, consider making it a portable telephone. Also consider using a caller identification system, available from the telephone company, to screen calls.

8.7 TECHNOLOGY

Make the most of technology that has been designed to help work run more efficiently. Take a closer look at these technological advances:

- *Hands-free headset.* Use this in the office while on the telephone so that hands are free to work on the computer, write, or clean off a desk. This is especially helpful when speaking with long-winded callers.

- *Handheld or personal digital assistant (PDA).* The technology in handheld computers is growing and changing rapidly. Many offices use PDAs to coordinate calendars office-wide. Excellent features include space to record engagements and to-do lists that keep running lists in one place, grouped by topic, rather than spread out on different slips of paper or Post-its. Consider including donors' names, addresses, and telephone numbers, as well as personal information to remember about them in the PDA.

- *Portable computer.* The new lightweight computers allow work to be done on documents while traveling out of the office and to correspond with the office via e-mail during business travel. It is much easier to read e-mails at the end of each day rather than return from a business trip to read many e-mails.

- *Business telephone credit cards.* This credit card for business telephone calls allows calls to be charged directly to, and paid by, the charitable organization. This is a great help because it allows the caller to eliminate putting in receipts for reimbursement checks. If policies permit, charge expenses directly to the charitable organization.

- *Cellular phones.* Cell phones save time when traveling to meet with a planned giving donor and running late; out of the office and needing to touch base quickly with a boss or assistant; boarding an airplane and wishing to check in with the office before flying; and driving and listening to voice mail messages or talking with someone in the office. Cell phones also can be used to check stock quotes, access websites, or provide other financial services.

8.8 GENERAL TIPS FOR SAVING TIME

- When scheduling for the day or week, remember that things generally take longer to accomplish than originally thought.

- Empower planned staff to answer questions and deal with problems. Communicate to others in the office which planned giving staff member handles what area so that colleagues know where to go with questions.

- Discourage colleagues and staff from dropping in the office to chat by establishing "open office" hours or encouraging correspondence by e-mail.

- Get enough sleep. Things always take longer when overly tired.

- Actively schedule some time each day to get out of the office. Breathing fresh air each workday will help employees wake up and be more alert.

- Drink a lot of water during the day to keep refreshed and hydrated. This is especially important if working in an airtight building. Keep a large bottle of water nearby.

- Bring healthful snacks to work to help perk up at midafternoon when blood sugar is low. Consider including portable foods like yogurt and fruit.

- Exercise.

- Balance workdays so that a variety of activities are accomplished each day. Spend some time in the office and outside of the office, seeing donors. Keep the day stimulating.

8.9 CONCLUSION

With all that is required of planned giving officers, it is important to try to make the most of all available work time. Explore how to organize the day, week, and year; control the office environment, manage meetings, travel time, working at home, and technology to help increase productivity. Work to incorporate many of the specific time-saving measures suggested in this chapter to focus time on where it is most needed, to make the planned giving program the best that it can be.

Evaluating a Planned
Giving Program

9.1 INTRODUCTION

At least once every three years it is important to take a fresh look, from start to finish, at the organization's planned giving program. Over the course of a few years the planned giving officer can easily depart from an intended focus. Planned giving staff must periodically recommit to specific goals and objectives. This is not to say that an evaluation and review should lead to abandonment of a current program. It may take only a modest adjustment to change course, especially when a planned giving officer and an organization are committed to building a high-quality planned giving program.

An evaluation of a planned giving program provides the opportunity for a planned giving professional to step back and assess the entire program, and look at the big picture to see where planned giving fits into the overall development effort and the charitable organization. The results of the evaluation allow the planned giving officer to build up areas that are working, increase staff efforts, and budget for those efforts that produce the greatest assets. Be sure to include representatives from the treasurer's office, business office, real estate office, and general counsel's office. Include any administrators from within the organization who may assist in the planned giving process. Work closely with other development staff members who can add significant input.

Professionals outside the organization also can help to evaluate the program. Enlist the aid of the outside asset manager and legal counsel and, where appropriate, outside financial advisors who have worked with the program or organization in the past. Some of these individuals may be able to offer for-profit techniques that may help the planned giving office work more efficiently and better serve its donors.

9.2 ANALYZE AND ASSESS

First, determine whether the staff is focused on the goals and objectives of the planned giving program. How long has it been since the program's priorities were redefined? Redefining and refocusing goals and efforts improves performance and enhances the opportunities for success. Examine each specific goal and, for each, deliberately decide whether the initiative falls within or outside the program's overall goals, objectives, and priorities. Review each year's operational plan to determine whether the program is doing what it is intended to do and whether the goals established for that year still make sense and are still priorities.

In reexamining the planned giving program, adopt a fresh perspective. The nature of planned giving differs from almost every other area of a development office and is best exemplified by an entrepreneurial spirit and attitude. Think of the things that need to be done to start a small business, and consider these seven topics:

1. *Research.* Where does planned giving business come from?

2. *Product or service development.* What types of planned giving products or services should the organization offer? Are there new ideas available that could be offered to donors and prospects?

3. *Marketing.* How can the planned giving business be promoted through marketing?

4. *Outreach.* How can continued visibility be achieved within the community or among the organization's constituents?

5. *Identification of new business.* How can new planned giving prospects be identified?

6. *Self-motivation.* Is the director of planned giving providing leadership?

7. *Staff management.* Is the staff challenged, and are assignments delegated appropriately?

9.3 TAKE INVENTORY

Begin by looking at the existing program in detail. Determine the number of total planned gifts under management, divided by type:

- Number of charitable gift annuities
- Number of charitable remainder trusts
- Number of charitable lead trusts
- Number of gifts to all pooled income funds
  - Growth
  - Balanced
  - High income

- Number of real estate gifts
- Amount of monies realized and expected from trusts and estates
- Number of trusts under outside management
- Number of tangible personal property gifts
  - Computer software
  - Artwork
  - Collections
  - Other
- Number of life insurance policies

Then determine

- The average gift size in each category
- The percentage of repeat donors
- Ages of current donors—average by gift type
- Gender (male/female) of current donors

Compiling this information will help to tell about the status of the current program and where the successes have come from in the past. It allows the planned giving officer to focus on those areas that have worked and are strong, and also to examine those areas that need building up. A planned giving action plan is included in Appendix, CD-ROM Documentation, Administrative Documents.

9.4 ESTABLISHING PROGRAMMATIC GOALS

Determine the future goals for the planned giving program, whether it is a new or existing program. If it is an existing program, look at previously stated goals and see how the program has succeeded in meeting those goals. What should be accomplished for the program over the next one to five years? Learn the program goals for the organization as a whole and for the organization's development office, and see how these goals can and should dovetail.

Many of the identified goals for the program may be financial. They may include:

- Increasing the total number of planned giving donors
- Increasing the average-size planned gift
- Managing more types of certain planned gifts; for example, building the program to include more charitable remainder trusts under management
- Finding a better investment return for donors, which may mean altering the current investment mix
- Raising the gift minimum on planned gifts, such as increasing the minimum on charitable gift annuities and pooled income fund gifts from $5,000 to $10,000
- Testing to determine whether gifts have been produced for each gift category

Some goals may not be financial but may include building donor contacts, increasing donor-related travel, and making more donor visits. Building new relationships could include working with individuals inside the charitable organization and strengthening ties with outside professional advisors.

9.5 IDENTIFYING PLANNED GIVING DONORS AND PROSPECTS

To increase the number of planned giving prospects and gifts, determine how the program has found its existing donors. List all of the planned giving donors and indicate how they became interested in planned gift options. Differentiate them in these ways:

■ *Donors who responded to marketing appeals.* This should include advertisements placed in organizational magazines or sent in annual appeals, and any other marketing efforts. In the future, when creating appeals, code each one so that the planned giving office can track and monitor all responses.

■ *Planned gift donors who were existing annual fund donors.* Calculate the number of annual fund gifts made over the number of years the donors participated and at what point, after how many years, they became planned giving donors. Note the average size of the donor's annual fund gift.

■ *Planned gift donors brought in by the planned giving program.* Look at those individuals who attended events who created a planned gift and were originally approached by a planned giving officer or a member of the development staff.

■ *Planned gift donors referred by outside development staff.* Provide the number of prospects who became planned giving donors because other development staff members talked with the prospect about planned giving and the planned giving office was later brought in to help close the gift.

■ *Planned gift donors referred by administrative staff or trustee.* Note the donors who were referred to the planned giving office by a member of the organization's administrative staff or by a trustee.

■ *Planned gift donors referred by other donors.* Determine if any prospects became planned giving donors because they were referred by other donors who discussed with them the benefits of making a planned gift.

■ *Planned gift donors referred by financial advisor, accountant, or attorney.* Count the number of donors who were brought to the planned giving program at the recommendation of their financial advisor, accountant, or attorney.

■ *Prospects approached by planned giving office "cold."* Determine the number of prospects who were approached by the planned giving office "cold," either by telephone call or letter.

Assembling this information can help to determine how to build the program's prospect base. For example, if the percentage of responses to marketing efforts is high, the program is likely to benefit from increased marketing efforts. If the number of donors identified from events is low, this information may suggest that more events are needed or that more staff members need to begin building relationships with donors at events. Or it could mean that the type of event taking place is not attracting enough donors or donors with strong giving potential and that the existing event strategy needs to be reworked.

9.6 ADMINISTRATION

Examine the way that the planned giving program currently is managed. Some of the following procedures may be taken for granted but could be done differently because the organization, development climate, or times have changed. Determine whether the planned giving program is best served with these existing functions:

■ Recording planned gifts: full face value, discounted amount, percentage of gift, or other formula

■ Accounting for gifts under Financial Accounting Standards Board (FASB) requirements

■ Managing in-house counsel versus outside counsel

■ Paying trust fees, either from a separate budget or from income generated by the gift

■ Managing gift assets outside of the organization or inside at the treasurer's office

9.7 EVALUATION OF STAFF FUNCTIONS

(a) Administrative Responsibilities

Nonprofits often operate with fewer staff than necessary, so employees must perform a wide variety of assignments and even a greater number of administrative duties. Over a period of time, administrative responsibilities may virtually paralyze a planned giving program. Although it may be difficult to avoid such assignments, planned giving officers need to stay focused on the job at hand. Any interruption in the program increases the length of time needed to close a gift, and this lag grows in proportion to the extent of the interruption. Today's efforts produce gifts for tomorrow, and as discussed earlier, the gestation period for planned gifts is frequently a minimum of six months and can be as long as five years or more. A periodic evaluation and restructuring of administrative responsibilities, in regard to staff assignments, scheduling, and efficiency, can allow the office to give sufficient time and attention to its primary objectives.

Remember that the president of the organization and the vice-president for development may not be concerned about the planned giving officer's outside planned giving council, the organization's new parking committee regulations, or the task force on ethics. They care about the bottom line, the money raised. It is important to maintain an appropriate balance between administrative assignments and those devoted to raising money.

(a) Involvement with Volunteers

A corollary to the rule of reducing participation in administrative or bureaucratic matters applies to working with development or planned giving volunteers. Such interaction can be seductive. Staff gradually can be drawn into a volunteer group's every effort and, instead of pursuing prospects, find themselves charged with drafting one agenda after another for what can become an endless series of volunteer meetings. Before committing to service a volunteer committee, recognize the great amounts of time, resources, and attention that are required. Time may be better spent by working one on one with a volunteer who is willing to assist with prospects and who has a proven track record of successful development.

(b) Working with Colleagues to Generate Gifts

Invite another staff member along on a prospect visit. A team approach can be educational and sometimes can help to remove various obstacles. Be willing, too, at a certain point to turn a case over to a colleague. A planned giving officer should not consider it a failure if a case is reassigned or if a colleague is able to close a gift that has been pursued for some time. No doubt the initial officer's efforts have helped to bring the donor to the point of making a gift. Sometimes the chemistry is better with one professional than another, and the first staff member then becomes available to pursue other prospects. This approach can greatly enhance the success of the development effort. Also consider inviting a colleague to help develop a new strategy for a gift that is not closing. Over time, in pursuing a prospect, the situation can become stale and the strategy unclear. An uninvolved colleague sometimes can provide an impartial opinion and a fresh perspective.

9.8 MARKETING

(a) Program Visibility

Planned giving, by its very nature, requires a high level of visibility. A planned giving officer can understand all the nuances of specific, technical planned gifts, but if she fails to reach and attract prospects and donors, very few gifts will be closed.

Examine existing marketing efforts. Is the program marketed correctly to achieve the heightened level of awareness necessary to increase the program's visibility? What methods are used to increase visibility? Are staff members segmenting proposals in order to produce personalized messages? If newsletters are bought from an outside source, are they too generic for the organization's constituents? Are new publications being produced at the organization that can include planned giving? Is the staff focused on and working with others who can help market the program to acquire new donors? Do not forget outreach efforts to professional advisors who can be a vital source of new donors. It is important to work with them to assist them and their clients in achieving their financial and philanthropic objectives.

Is there a clear case for support for the nonprofit organization? Have the organization's priorities been articulated both internally and publicly? Is there a marketing brochure or piece that clearly explains the organization's mission statement, needs, and priorities? Without a very clear picture of where the charitable organization is and where it hopes to be in the future, it will be very difficult to raise money. The planned giving officer must have a firm idea of what the organization hopes to achieve in the next several years, and must know its priorities and how gifts will be used, before money can be raised.

Marketing is a very valuable tool to use to attract donors to the planned giving program. Many facets of a marketing program must exist and work together to produce a strong effort. Examine the entire marketing effort, divided by marketing topic, to determine what areas need to be enhanced, changed, or eliminated.

(b) Marketing Planned Gifts—Print Copy

(i) Publications.   The various brochures and advertisements used to market planned gifts are enormously important. Begin by listing all publications that are available for a planned giving advertisement, donor profile, or article and see if a planned giving advertisement is included in the brochure. Are there brochures that do not have a planned giving marketing piece that could include one? Do nondevelopment-produced publications exist that would benefit from including a planned giving piece?

(ii) Advertisements.   The planned giving officer should determine whether

- The charitable organization is marketing all types of planned gifts that the organization wishes to encourage and accept.
- The advertisements are fresh, or whether new ones are needed.
- A new print design or logo is needed.
- Publications currently purchased from an outside vendor need to come from a new vendor.
- Market research needs to be done to ensure that the organization is sending the correct message to prospects and that the right message is being received correctly.
- The charitable organization is competing successfully with other nonprofit organizations.

(iii) Other Marketing Tools.   Explore other marketing venues to disseminate the word about planned giving. Determine whether the charitable organization is doing the best to market planned gifts through

- Letters
- Planned giving brochures
- Individual targeted mailings
- Inserts in annual fund mailings
- General educational letters

(c) Donor Contact

Periodically it is necessary to recommit to the pursuit of planned giving prospects. Gifts do not appear accidentally, but occur primarily because prospects are monitored within a formal program of follow-up. There is a direct correlation between donors pursued for gifts and gifts actually closed. The office may have lost touch with some prospects; contact them to remind them that the organization seeks their support. Send a letter or telephone prospects to reinforce the benefits of charitable giving and to remind them about the organization's needs.

Planned giving officers, as well as other development staff, should maintain regular contact with prospects and donors. Development, especially in the area of planned giving, is a people-to-people business. Planned giving by definition requires regular contact over extended periods of time. Many planned gifts materialize only after a series of integrated efforts conducted over several years.

Is the planned giving program building a foundation to maintain a continued presence over a five-year period? How will contact be maintained? Maintaining contact is a structured, and almost methodical, effort to stay in touch with prospects and donors over a period of time and is usually effected in three ways:

1. By letter

2. By telephone

3. By a personal visit or at an event

Although the last method is the most effective, planned giving efforts should use at least one of these types of contacts with donors on a regular basis.

Examine whether the planned giving officers are visiting enough donors. Look at the number of donor visits made each month to see if this number can or should be increased.

Determine whether planned giving seminars should be hosted to reach a larger planned giving donor and prospect audience. If they are already being done, what is the success rate in terms of closed, planned gifts? Have solid leads grown from the seminars? Should the seminars be held in a different part of the country where more planned giving prospects live? Is the planned giving office responding quickly enough to inquiries? Determine the office's typical response time and see if it can be improved.

(d) Working with Internal Constituents

Another important part of a marketing effort is working with individuals within the organization to educate them about planned giving. After identifying which individuals need to be educated or reeducated, follow up to regularly remind them that planned giving options exist and that they are a desirable option for many donors who wish to make a gift to the organization. These individuals may be able to generate planned giving leads. Remember that new people in the organization need to be educated too. Work with them individually or in groups.

(e) Development Staff

When was the last time the planned giving office hosted an in-house planned giving seminar for development staff members? Aim to instruct development colleagues at least two times per year on the benefits and mechanics of making a planned gift. The goal is to build individual development officers' confidence in talking with prospects about making a gift that could be a planned gift. Stress that development officers do not need to be experts in planned giving but should be comfortable discussing the basics.

Consider using case studies as an effective way to involve other staff members in the process and to publicly commend colleagues on their planned giving work. The planned giving officer conducting the seminar may learn as much from the session as the attendees.

Determine when the planned giving office last sent an article around the office that helped development staff to learn about planned giving or one aspect of it. Consider sending colleagues planned giving information that helps them with their own financial situations, such as information about changes in the tax law, saving for retirement, investment options, and legal issues in estate planning. Also determine whether telefund callers need to be trained about planned giving.

(f) Treasurer's Office, General Counsel's Office, Business Office, and Real Estate Office

Professionals in all of these departments at the charitable organization need to understand development and planned giving. Check to see the last time the planned giving office:

- Sent advisors an update about the planned giving program

- Shared recent planned giving successes

- Thanked advisors publicly for their help on a gift

- Included advisors on an invitation list for a development function

Over the years, it is easy to take these individuals for granted, but they need to be regularly reminded about planned giving and the opportunities planned gifts present. Consider hosting a reception or dinner that can recognize those individuals within the organization who have helped raise planned gifts.

(g) Trustees

If a planned giving seminar was presented years ago to trustees, it may be time to meet with them again. Individual trustees have likely changed, and now the planned giving program has a proven track record of success to report. It is important to keep the trustees involved in the planned giving process because they may have the ability to bring new donors to the program, make a planned gift themselves, or be an ally when a program decision needs to be made that requires trustee approval. If the planned giving officer or director does not have the opportunity to present something to the trustees personally, ask that a report be made by the vice-president for development or that a planned giving report be passed out at the trustee meeting.

Consider the following approaches with trustees:

- On an individual basis, target new trustees for a planned gift.

- If the planned giving program has a trustee "champion," regularly send him an update about the program.

- If there is a trustee who has made a planned gift, be sure to highlight that individual in a public way.

- Ask some trustees to write or speak to planned giving prospects about making a planned gift.

(h) Outside Advisors

Another important segment of the population to market to about planned giving is outside financial advisors. Over the years, the planned giving office probably has fallen into a set pattern of marketing planned gifts to these individuals. As the profession of planned giving grows, more advisors are becoming involved in planned giving both for expanding their businesses and to address their clients' needs. The planned giving office may need to educate advisors about planned giving and ensure that the charitable organization remains at the forefront of the advisors' thoughts as they begin to be cultivated by more nonprofit organizations.

Look at what has been done each year to work with these professionals, and evaluate the number of planned gifts received by working with outside advisors. Then see if more can be done to build an ongoing relationship. When working with outside advisors:

- Establish an outside professional advisory group if one has not been formed.

- Create an insider newsletter just for advisors.

- Host a lunch or breakfast at the organization for the professionals, giving them the chance to learn more about the organization and network with fellow professionals.

- Brainstorm new names to add to the outreach list. Look at the gifts that have come in over the last few years that included an advisor, and make sure that that individual's name is on the planned giving mailing list. Ask development colleagues to update the list, adding new names.

9.9   STAFFING

After many years of building a planned giving program, staffing needs change. One or two professionals running the program may no longer be enough, or some specific jobs may need to change. Every person has taken on additional jobs, and periodically each person's tasks must be examined to determine whether the program is being run as efficiently as possible. When exploring staffing needs:

- Establish mutually agreed-on goals.

- Determine each planned giving professional's responsibilities. Compare these responsibilities to those the individual assumed when first starting the job.

- Question whether everyone's job responsibilities are associated with raising money.

- Determine whether there are any jobs that should be assigned elsewhere in the department or organization.

- Determine whether there are jobs being done outside the development office that should be done by individuals in the planned giving office. For example, should someone from the planned giving office manage gifts from trusts and estates if they are handled in the legal or treasurer's office?

- Look to see if the planned giving office is running efficiently. Over time, people can fall into patterns of working that may not be the most efficient. Make sure that the office has standardized advertisements, documents, disclosure statements, letters, and appeals so that the new ones are not created every time they are needed.

When all is said and done, the bottom line is the amount of money that is raised. After one year, planned giving officers should be able to raise a minimum of three times their annual salary; successful planned giving officers who have been on the job for two years or more at the same organization should raise approximately 10 times their salaries. An alternative to measuring success by multiples of a person's salary is to gauge success by how well the person fulfills the goal of producing a minimum of 15 significant gifts per year, which converts to a little more than one gift per month. These quantifiable measures are helpful in refocusing job priorities to raise money.

It is easy to become caught up in day-to-day office routines. However, it is important to step back and, with some frequency, assess the progress of the planned giving program. Because staff can often be distracted by administrative tasks, it is important to constantly analyze productivity and focus on the bottom line: raising money.

Because there are a finite number of hours that can be worked each week, productivity is important. The key to evaluating productivity in the planned giving office is the answer to the question: Is the staff accomplishing its goals and objectives? If the answer is no, refocus energies and reevaluate the workload. Become proactive with donors and prospects, and discard projects that prevent or discourage productivity. To assess the workload, keep detailed records of weekly activities in a calendar.

Log the amount of time spent on the telephone speaking with colleagues, and honestly differentiate between work and social activities. Next, identify activities that are donor related and those that are not. This exercise helps to focus staff, increase productivity, and encourage development success. In addition, make a chart every few weeks that lists the names of donors and where they stand on the program's priority list. Focus activities on those donors who are closest to gifts or who need attention.

9.10 TECHNOLOGY

Some organizations use state-of-the-art equipment more readily than others. If the charitable organization does not have the following advances, consider requesting:

- Voice mail
- E-mail, as donors are increasingly communicating to charitable organizations through e-mail
- A Web page for the organization
- A toll-free telephone number for donors to reach the planned giving office
- Individual printers in each employee's office
- Portable computers to take on the road with donors
- Palm Pilots for senior-level employees

9.11 BUDGET/EDUCATION

Determine whether the current budget is adequate for existing and future planned giving needs. First, establish exactly what money is being spent on, and ascertain whether the planned giving office is getting the most for its dollars. Determine whether:

- There is satisfaction with planned giving conferences attended. Should others in the planned giving office also attend conferences?
- The local planned giving council is meeting educational and networking needs.
- The subscriptions to planned giving, development, and financial periodicals are meeting expectations.
- Expenditures related to marketing, software, donor-related travel, and events are being well spent.

9.12 POLICIES/PROCEDURES

After years of running a successful and growing planned giving program, the nonprofit organization may determine that the program does not have everything in place to keep up with its success. See whether the following need to be established or updated:

- Gift acceptance policy
- Substantiation requirements in donor acknowledgments
- FASB requirements
- Gift acceptance, review, or naming committees
- Endowed fund descriptions

9.13 STEWARDSHIP

(a) Donor Relations

Planned giving programs that are very successful at acquiring new gifts may not be as good at stewarding gifts. Do not let the planned giving program fall into this trap, because lack of stewardship eventually will take a toll on the program, preventing repeat gifts from donors. When was the last time that the program:

- Reported to donors on the use of their gifts? Let donors know the financial standing of their gifts, especially for those who created endowed funds? Ideally this should be done annually.

- Profiled a donor in an organization publication because he or she made a gift?

- Worked with surviving spouses and family members after a realized bequest?

- Worked to keep planned giving donors as annual fund donors?

(b) Bequest Society

For many organizations, the bequest society plays a primary role in stewarding donors and bringing in new gifts. In all likelihood, the bequest program has grown over the last few years, and it may be ready for a change. Ask these questions:

- What purpose does the bequest society currently serve or could it serve in the future?

- Is an annual bequest event needed? If the organization already holds an event, does the existing format need to be expanded or changed?

- Is the current recognition of donors at the bequest meeting still working? Does the organization need new membership tokens?

9.14 OUTSIDE SUPPORT

Outside support is critical to the success of a planned giving program. As the program grows, look at the following outside areas to determine whether the program is getting the most from these service providers or whether a change is needed.

(a) Asset Manager

(i) Investment Return to Donors

- Have the planned giving investments grown over the years in all gift categories?

- Are the organization and its donors satisfied with the investment performance?

- How well does the investment performance of the organization compare with that of other organizations?

- Is investment information shared on a timely basis? Are reports easy to read and understand? Can they be customized for donors if necessary?

- Does the pooled income fund's return attract donors? Does the charitable organization follow American Council on Gift Annuities rates? Under what circumstances would the organization decide to deviate from those rates? Does the organization need to establish maximum rates that it is willing to pay on charitable remainder trusts where the organization acts as trustee or cotrustee?

(ii) Service

■ Do all donors receive tax information and periodic checks on a timely basis?

■ Is the organization receiving the best service that is needed?

■ Are telephone calls returned quickly?

■ Is the organization receiving a can-do attitude from the asset manager to help close difficult or unusual gifts?

■ Are the fees reasonable?

(b) Legal

■ Does the organization have a strong in-house legal department or attorney? Is there a way to help educate the general counsel's office to better understand planned giving?

■ Does the organization have strong outside legal support? Can any work that is being done outside the organization be done inside?

■ Are there reasonable channels in place to reach outside counsel instead of using in-house counsel?

■ Is there an adequate budget for legal work?

(c) Planned Giving Software

■ Does the organization have the best planned giving software for its needs?

■ Are new programs needed?

■ Is updated training needed? Are there functions that the organization is ignorant of or does not understand that could help provide better information to donors?

(d) Consulting Help

Sometimes an audit of a program done by an outside consultant can help move a program to the next level. Determine whether a professional audit should be done, and identify the best person to conduct such an audit. See if the cost of a consultant will be worth the final product.

(e) Customer Surveys

Consider sending customer surveys to planned giving donors. Ask them what they consider to be the best and worst things about their relationship with the planned giving office and their gift process experience.

Look outside the program to see what can be learned from other organizations and colleagues both locally and nationally. What does the organization do well? What needs improvement?

CHAPTER TEN

Working with Nondevelopment Staff

10.1 INTRODUCTION

Over the past decade, most nonprofit organizations have sought to increase private support through expanded development programs. One method in support of this effort has been increased involvement by nondevelopment staff in development initiatives. Nondevelopment staff includes deans, department heads, faculty, departmental staff, institutional administrators, and nonprofit volunteer leaders and board members. This decentralized approach to development often results in additional private support from donors and prospects who are actively involved with nonprofit departments and nondevelopment staff. In addition, nondevelopment staff are well connected and work with volunteers and others connected to their department. The result of this initiative is that development has expanded to new levels of participation.

The process works as follows: Monies raised from development provide the financial resources to enable the nonprofit and its departments to fulfill its mission, achieve its goals, deliver its services, and offer programs to its constituents. In turn, nondevelopment staff members serve as advocates on behalf of the nonprofit organization, articulating needs, making the case for support, and representing the nonprofit to each of its constituents. Establishing partnerships between nondevelopment staff and development staff is essential in presenting clear and cohesive messages to donors and prospects.

This chapter discusses ways that planned giving officers and development staff members can build collaborative partnerships with nondevelopment staff to attract private support from department constituents.

10.2   PUTTING DEVELOPMENT INTO CONTEXT FOR NONDEVELOPMENT STAFF

For nondevelopment staff, the mainstream activities of the college, program, or department take precedence over development activities. To be successful however, development must also be a priority, one that requires a proactive stance by the nondevelopment department. They must understand that development does not just occur, but occurs only when it is undertaken intentionally. Although nondevelopment staff may not have time every day to engage in development, they must be aware of the importance of doing it and incorporating it into everyday activities. Planned giving staff can help nondevelopment staff to ease into the business of development. Because nondevelopment staff are experts about their department's business, with coaching, they have the potential to be great fundraisers.

Many nondevelopment staff members have misconceptions about development because few have actually worked with donors. The nondevelopment staff must understand that at its most basic level, development is about establishing relationships with interested individuals who could, if encouraged, provide financial resources through gifts to the nonprofit. Nondevelopment staff members involved in raising money need to learn to work with donors and prospects and understand the process and donors' attitudes. Key donor attitudes that nondevelopment staff should learn include:

- Donors feel good about their gifts and will often make them with the encouragement of staff members.

- Donors make gifts because it is important to them personally.

- Development is not taking resources from a donor; it is providing opportunities for donors to make gifts.

- A donor's gift indicates commitment and dedication and demonstrates belief in the organization.

To facilitate this understanding, planned giving officers can "coach" nondevelopment staff about the process of development and the expectations of donors. Planned giving officers can promote training programs to help nondevelopment staff members eliminate the fear of asking for a gift. Contrary to misperceptions held by some, donors enjoy relationships with nonprofit staff, including those whose duties involve fundraising. Fundraisers, whether departmental or development staff, are representatives of the nonprofit who provide valuable information to its constituents to build and sustain connections.

Nondevelopment staff must understand that development is a process that involves four stages—identification, cultivation, solicitation, and stewardship—and that each of these stages must occur at the right time involving appropriate staff members with particular donors and prospects. Each step of the process is geared to raise funds for the nonprofit organization or its departments, and all gifts include all the stages in the gift process. Nondevelopment staff must understand that development takes time to produce results, and it is not unusual to have a significant lag time between effort and result: Planned and major gifts can take one to three years or longer to occur. In addition, nondevelopment staff must be cautioned about unrealistic development expectations. After all, building a development program is hard work and requires commitment and perseverance.

Nondevelopment staff must come to realize that every person who is in some way involved with the department is a prospect. Most important, donors who are involved with a department may be more loyal to the individual department than to the nonprofit organization. In this case, nondevelopment staff may be more successful in fundraising than a central development staff member. No matter who raises the money, the nonprofit benefits.

10.3 COLLABORATIVE EFFORTS

Collaborative efforts among departments and the development office promote successful development programs. At some nonprofits, conflict among staff members and departments occurs in assigning and managing prospects and in determining how to divide the responsibilities for development. Some prospects receive extensive contact with development and nonprofit staff while others who may have the same capacity to give have never been cultivated.

Even nonprofits that historically have maintained tight control over prospects, reserving development activity only to development staff, have relaxed these controls. In most cases, this is based on a need to maintain a practical and organized system of allocating prospects to staff members. Prospects are likely to have relationships with departmental staff who share common interests. Development and nondevelopment staff working together, as a team, have a greater likelihood of success in raising funds and less opportunity for mixed messages being sent to prospects.

Development staff can help to identify prospects and donors on behalf of departments. Many of these donors support the department but have never met the department's staff. Others may be actively involved with the department but have never been approached for a gift. If the planned giving officer introduces prospects to departmental employees, development staff can provide linkage between the department and the donors, thus enhancing donor contact with departmental programs and activities that elicit additional support.

10.4 MARKETING

A development office provides a variety of development services to the nonprofit organization and its departments, yet some may not know that these services are available.

Marketing is one of the most important functions of a development office. Marketing means educating donors and prospects about the nonprofit's programs and also about ways donors can make planned gifts in support of these programs. Including a planned giving column in a departmental newsletter is a great way to generate new leads. Department heads are always happy to see responses to mailings. Development publications such as newsletters and charitable gift-planning guides can cultivate donors and train department staff. Development offices can provide much-needed training, skills development, and assistance in working with donors.

Depending on the nonprofit organization, a staff member can be assigned to a department or services may be shared with other departments. Development offices can be helpful in providing information on donors (gift records, degree information, and business status) and for designing development strategies that target particular constituents. At small nonprofits, development staff may serve in an advisory or consultant role that provides training to departmental staff or they also may accompany departmental staff in making calls on prospects. Planned giving officers, because of their centralized positions, typically work with many of the nonprofit's departments. Workshops on life income gift options, bequests, and estate planning offer opportunities to involve staff, volunteers, donors, and prospects.

10.5 EVALUATION AND ASSESSMENT

Prior to beginning a development program, departments should assess their services, delivery of those services, quality of programs, needs, and accessibility by constituents. Focus groups can provide valuable information on the worth of the department and the quality of its programs. A survey assessing strengths, weaknesses, and perceptions provides valuable feedback that can be used as the basis of a development campaign. Accreditation and self-assessment studies can focus a department on its ability to serve its constituents. Wish lists also can be helpful to identify potential areas of need.

10.5 EVALUATION AND ASSESSMENT

Once the results of the evaluation are available, planned giving and development staff can design a development plan to raise funds in support of development initiatives.

Included in Appendix, CD-ROM Documentation, Administration Documents, is a development plan for nondevelopment staff. This plan presents issues that must be addressed to prepare a development plan for departmental initiatives involving nondevelopment staff. The plan is a series of worksheets that should be completed by development and nondevelopment staff. Once completed, the worksheets become the development plan for the department. The plan is reproduced in Exhibit 10.1.

Exhibit 10.1   A Development Plan for Nondevelopment Staff

MAJOR CONSTITUENTS

A department's major constituents are known by key representatives within the department. A brainstorming session can help identify potential sources of support. Constituents can come from these groups:

1. Educational institutions: Alumni
2. Hospitals: Grateful patients
3. Arts/cultural organizations: Patrons/members
4. Friends
5. Past and present donors
6. Volunteers
7. Past and present faculty and staff
8. Vendors with whom the department does business or purchases products/services.
9. Parents or family members of key persons in the department.
10. Employers or industries who hire the department's employees.
11. Entities who depend on the department for research or technical support.
12. Past and present board members or advisory committees.
13. Those who attend or participate in the department's programs, services, or activities.

KEY ISSUES

To focus the development effort the following questions must be answered:

1. What are the department's needs?
2. Who are its constituents?
3. Which of the department's employees have valuable relationships with constituents?
4. Who, on behalf of the department, needs to be involved in working with the prospect?
5. Are there working committees and volunteers that can be mobilized?
6. Is there agreement on priorities and objectives?
7. Which types of gifts are appropriate to meet the needs?
8. Which type of solicitation is the most appropriate for the prospect?
9. Can the effort be sustained over time?
10. Is the entire department behind the effort?

DEVELOPMENT INITIATIVES

These development initiatives can be implemented to assist the department in its fundraising efforts:

1. Identify new prospects and cultivate existing donors.
2. Identify and work with volunteers who are willing to solicit others for a major gift.
3. Segment the database to develop a targeted population of donors who have made annual gifts of $100 or more for three or more years.

(Continued)

Exhibit 10.1 *(Continued)*

4. Segment the database to select donors or prospects who are 70 years or older to send specific development information, such as information on life income gifts and bequests.
5. Send a letter from the department head to all donors who have given $5,000 or more cumulatively.
6. Target geographic areas for focused regional efforts.
7. Create advertisements and articles for existing newsletters or publications.
8. Offer a planned giving, financial planning, or estate planning column in a newsletter.
9. Identify and publicize funding opportunities and needs through various publications.
10. At year end, send donors and prospects a year-end tax letter that highlights the benefits of charitable giving and current tax incentives.
11. Mail a "Ways to Give" brochure to retired faculty, staff, and administrators along with a letter showing the benefits of making gifts.
12. To outline the department's mission, host a series of events for donors, prospects, and friends of the organization who may be capable of making a major gift.
13. Host a luncheon for all donors who have made major gifts to the department.
14. Conduct screening meetings with volunteers, staff, and donors to identify new prospects.
15. Host a series of breakfast meetings for specific geographic regions.
16. Meet with staff to make them aware of fundraising needs. Meet with them in small groups or individually to discuss prospects. Distribute funding opportunities.
17. Have the next issue of the department newsletter devoted to the development program. Overprint to have the document serve as additional solicitation literature. State goals, objectives, needs, and fundraising opportunities.
18. Establish quarterly and yearly timetables, develop an action plan, establish goals, and assign responsibilities.
19. Guest lectures/symposiums: Recognize that those who attend events, programs, or activities are likely to be good prospects.
20. Focus on the process of identifying, cultivating, and soliciting prospects and donors.
21. Follow up with all attendees for every activity, event, or program.

IMPLEMENTATION

A department can implement a fundraising program by incorporating some or all of these steps:

1. Participate in the annual giving program.
2. Consult with the office of development for ways to include planned giving in the development program.
3. Organize staff in the field to meet with donors/prospects.
4. Draft model proposals and letters to individuals.
5. Establish a friends program.
6. Identify a top 100 list of prospects/donors.
7. Assign prospects/donors through prospect management to the appropriate college staff.
8. Place articles in magazines or newspapers.
9. Identify, cultivate, and solicit 20 to 25 prospects.
10. Follow up.

The next sections provide insights into prospect identification, cultivation, and solicitation. Strategies are offered on ways development staff can build partnerships with nondevelopment staff to facilitate the development process. Every individual who works with departmental constituents is part of the process, and each must share the responsibility with development staff to raise funds. Cooperative and collaborative efforts produce optimum results. The pace of the process must be regulated to meet the department's comfort level.

10.6 IDENTIFICATION OF DEVELOPMENT CONSTITUENTS

In most departments or programs, constituents are well known by key players within the department. In the university setting, alumni, friends, and corporations are often the most important constituents. In healthcare settings, the constituents include grateful patients, family members of grateful patients, physicians on staff, and retired employees. For museums and other arts and cultural organizations, prospects include patrons, sponsors, benefactors, staff, and volunteers. It is important for the department and nondevelopment staff to identify those individuals (e.g., faculty or administrators) with whom constituents have the closest contacts and who may therefore be most effective in the cultivation process. A nondevelopment staff member is the expert on the department's needs, objectives, goals, and constituents, while the development staff knows the development strategies that are likely to produce financial support.

Because nondevelopment staff members are often reluctant to engage in development, they struggle to find ways to capitalize on the goodwill that has been developed over the years. Converting the goodwill into financial support is the challenge of development. Occasionally nondevelopment staff may be overly protective of their constituents. They sometimes feel that fundraising efforts will alienate constituents.

Many nondevelopment staff involved in raising funds are surprised to learn that almost 90 percent of all funds raised come from individuals or their estates. One of the best ways for planned giving officers to demonstrate to nondevelopment staff the importance of individuals giving to the nonprofit organization is to present a pie chart showing sources of revenue. Sources of revenue include gifts by category such as by individuals, corporations, foundations, and other sources. When it comes to prioritizing the department's energy, it may be appropriate to focus a significant portion of time on individuals and to a lesser extent on foundations and corporations.

New department heads can help with the identification process by meeting with former department heads and present and past staff to learn the names of individuals who have been active with the department. Planned giving staff should monitor changes in department heads, as those taking over are candidates for a planned giving orientation. Work with new department heads by reviewing the existing files to identify the names of individuals who have requested gift information, attended programs or events, or in some way have been involved in the department's work. Past and current staff are themselves prospects, and many former staff members and retired faculty have made major gifts to benefit their departments. Provide bequest language to all present and retired departmental employees. Even modest bequests can provide significant resources to a department.

Almost every development office has a computer database that can be used to identify individuals who have made gifts in support of a specific program or department. Donors who have made a series of annual gifts are demonstrating an interest in the program, and these individuals need to be cultivated and nurtured by departmental staff. Many types of reports help to identify prospects. Each nonprofit attaches different names to such reports, but any report that demonstrates loyalty or provides information on cumulative giving, benchmarking data, and large gifts will yield insight and help to identify individuals that may become major gift prospects. A brainstorming session between the department staff and the development staff can identify appropriate constituents who are involved and interested in supporting the work of the department. A unit's constituents come from every level and association within the unit.

10.7 CULTIVATION OF CONSTITUENTS

The next step in the process is cultivation. Cultivation is a relationship-building process among the nonprofit department, its staff, and the prospect, and is the stage at which rapport is established between the solicitor and the prospect. Cultivation is all about contact—with the faculty, department heads, staff, administration, and other constituents. The contact is intentional and purposeful and is designed to further the development efforts. Ideally, cultivation occurs over a period of time during which the solicitor helps the prospect learn about the nonprofit department's mission, department focus, and needs, and helps the prospect to feel a part of the nonprofit. The prospect also learns how he may financially support the department's work. Once the prospects have been identified, it is vitally important for the unit to maintain open lines of communication to keep all constituents informed.

In the absence of cultivation and continued involvement between the nondevelopment staff and the constituent, no gift will ever occur. Planned giving staff members can help departmental staff find ways to cultivate constituents. One way to do this is to plan a planned giving workshop co-chaired by a department head and planned giving officers. See Appendix, CD-ROM Documentation, Exhibits, for a sample planned giving training program. Similar departments, especially those that "share" constituents, can host joint workshops and events. Events, meetings, and luncheons provide opportunities for the cultivation of prospects and donors. Educational institutions can host joint workshops for arts and cultural programs, such as the university's museum, library, and art gallery, that likely "share" volunteers. Medical nonprofits also can arrange events for related departments.

A number of activities can be initiated to create opportunities to accelerate the process. These focused activities bring interested prospects to the nonprofit to interact with nondevelopment and development staff.

(a) Events

Prospects enjoy relationships with individuals within the department and particularly enjoy attending seminars, symposiums, lectures, open houses, research presentations, programs, and social events, all of which serve as cultivation. Departments often believe that events are fundraisers. Events deplete departmental resources of labor and money. Often these events cost more in real resources to the department than they produce in terms of financial support. However, not everything needs to be measured in terms of current financial support. Events are a part of the cultivation of a prospect. Relationships are enhanced and information shared through cultivational events that in the future may produce financial support.

At events, departments should be encouraged to record the names of attendees through a guest book and distribute flyers or brochures to attendees that provide information about future programs or department activities. Flyers should include a response form so that the attendee can include name, address, and telephone number to request future mailings about departmental programs. These names are very valuable, and storing and retrieving such data are important to the department to identify interested prospects.

Departments need to understand that forms of cultivation must be done with consistency and perseverance as donors and prospects enjoy regular contact with a department. Regardless of the interval, donors and prospects should be able to count on the regularity of the activity. A program of systematic and regular contact is a major part of a unit's visibility to its constituents. Visibility is the cumulative and collective impression that donors and prospects have of the nonprofit's programs, mission, and service.

The process of cultivation involves building a long-term relationship, one that requires nurturing and continuity, and one that must be sustained continuously. Following the initial contact, it is important to sustain the interest of prospects, develop a productive relationship, and focus efforts on the value of development. Sustaining dozens of relationships is labor intensive and time consuming. However, newsletters and insider letters such as letters from the dean or department heads, including gift options and funding opportunities can help to sustain the interest over time while reducing the demand on personnel. To further promote the cultivation of the prospects, deans, department heads or faculty members can host breakfasts, luncheons, or meetings to provide a suitable forum to meet individuals and exchange information. Every event is an opportunity to focus on an initiative that could be enhanced through an infusion of financial resources. One or more attendees may respond favorably to the message. Planned giving officers who attend cultivational meetings can provide information on charitable giving to prospects. The mere presence of development and planned giving staff changes the focus of the meeting. Most important, in the early stages of development, nondevelopment staff members need the reassurance and support of development staff. Planned giving officers who understand the dynamics can provide valuable leadership to the effort.

Rather than developing a list of hundreds of prospects, it may be more efficient and productive to assign prospects to faculty and special staff members to deal with a smaller number, such as 10 to 25 prospects. Planned giving officers can help develop a workable list of key prospects. These individuals may be invited to a private luncheon, individually or as a group, depending on time and resources. Regional gatherings of alumni, friends, and those who have been involved with the department are an effective way to maintain contact. Discussions on departmental initiatives, activities, programs, and needs create awareness and promote further discussions about financial support. No effort should be initiated unless it can be sustained over time. Unsustained efforts cause damage by staff members who eagerly initiate a process but are unwilling or incapable of following up and sustaining the effort.

Not all parts of cultivation should be held at the nonprofit organization. Most prospects enjoy being visited at their homes or at neutral sites. Meetings held at the nonprofit tend to focus on the nonprofit, whereas those held off-site may be more balanced and may afford better opportunities for staff to get to know the prospect. Prospects also enjoy a chance to ask questions informally about the implications of a particular gift option.

(b) Advisory Committees

Advisory committees or advisory councils can assist departments in their cultivational efforts. Generally, the committee consists of distinguished individuals from a variety of backgrounds who are involved in the work of the department. These individuals may be industry representatives, corporate or business leaders, alumni, and faculty or staff. Representatives from each of the department's constituent groups help to balance the committee. The committee serves as a network providing feedback to the nonprofit from external constituents and helps to build relationships with committee members and the enterprises they serve. Term limits can be set to promote continuity and opportunity for others to participate. All have one thing in common: They are interested in the department and are willing to offer service or guidance. From a development standpoint, each member has the capacity to make a gift personally to the department, or, alternatively, they can secure financial support from others. Development staff or planned giving officers should be proactive and attend at least every other meeting to maintain a presence and focus on planned giving and development. Development and planned giving staff members should act as consultants to the department, sharing their expertise on gift-giving strategies and fundraising.

10.8 THE SOLICITATION

Individuals who have been cultivated usually are interested in providing financial support to benefit the object of their interest. Nondevelopment staff are often uncomfortable about this stage of development and may feel awkward asking someone for money; however, those being solicited usually are interested and committed to the work of the department, especially when relationships have been well established. A powerful bond is established when individuals and staff members share similar interests and what logically follows from that relationship is development-eliciting financial support for the program.

Nondevelopment staff must understand that donors and prospects may have single or multiple interests in a specific nonprofit organization. Donors with multiple interests are likely to provide financial support for a number of their special interests and yet maintain a "global" relationship with the nonprofit. Donors with singular interests, limited to a particular program or department, support that program and are prospects for that specific department. Global prospects should not be multiply solicited but should receive a coordinated and cohesive proposal inviting support that reflects the donor's varied interests. Conflicts occur in managing global prospects, because each department considers the prospect to be "owned" by that department. Centralized and coordinated messages and solicitations tend to produce larger gifts and minimize "donor fallouts" due to ill-conceived, perhaps inappropriate, contact methods. The prospect may have contact with many members of the staff, and it is from these multiple contacts that the prospect forms a collective impression of the nonprofit.

Explaining past and present achievements, goals and program objectives, and current and future needs along with a summary of their costs involves the prospect in the solicitation. A menu of needs and the financial support needed to accomplish the goals is an effective way to invite participation. If possible, appoint a representative from each of the constituent groups to develop a strategy and to participate in the solicitation of other members of the constituent group.

A number of strategies may be implemented to solicit a particular set of groups. Ideally, the preferred form of solicitation is a one-on-one personal contact. Personal contact may be made by a member of the unit's staff, a volunteer, a member of the development staff, or a planned giving officer. The solicitation also may be in tandem, with a member of the development staff and a member of the unit soliciting the prospect. When appropriate, planned giving officers can accompany departmental staff members to present life income gift options or bequest information. If there are a significant number of constituents and a shortage of staff, direct mail from the planned giving officer is an appropriate solicitation method. A well-drafted letter addressed to constituents, especially those located in geographically distant areas, can communicate the message and make the case for support. An accompanying response form providing details of the various needs, programs, and gift options can open the doors to prospects that may be interested in supporting one or more of the funding needs. Those who respond become prospects for one-on-one meetings or for telephone follow-up.

10.9 RAISING FUNDS FROM INDIVIDUALS

Individuals can make gifts in a variety of ways, including outright gifts, gifts from their estate, planned gifts, or a combination of these options. Finding the correct option that matches the financial capability of the donor increases the success of the development effort. Unfortunately, many nondevelopment staff members may not be aware of the option of making a gift through a donor's estate. The donors and nondevelopment staff must be educated not only about the department or program needs, but also about the ways donors can give. Booklets, brochures, and guides on charitable gift planning can help educate donors and staff members about the favorable tax consequences provided by charitable gifts. These materials also can help to create opportunities for donors to make gifts to the department. Nondevelopment staff must be educated about the choices of assets the donor has to make this gift and the assets. Planned giving officers should assess the needs of the department, the appropriateness of the type of gifts, and choice of asset that would be best for the department. The major assets are:

- Cash
- Securities, including stocks, bonds, and mutual funds
- Real estate: residential, commercial, vacant land
- Tangible personal property: art, antiques, collectibles, and collections
- Equipment: books, computers, software
- Retirement assets, including pension plans and individual retirement accounts

10.9   RAISING FUNDS FROM INDIVIDUALS

There are a number of ways constituents can make gifts to meet a unit's financial needs. Most often constituents will make annual gifts or a series of annual gifts in support of the program. Some businesses or corporations that are involved in the unit's work can make a leadership, major gift, or gift-in-kind. For other individuals, the gifts may be made through planned gifts, such as life income gifts or gifts through the donors' estates. A planned giving officer should counsel department staff on planned giving strategies and gift options. Individuals need to be nurtured, educated, and cultivated about the role and mission of the nonprofit and its departments, programs, and services. Many donors do not respond to annual fund solicitations but, in later years, make major gifts, planned gifts, or gifts through their estates in the form of a bequest. The annual appeals help to sustain interest, educate constituents, maintain contact, and stimulate financial support.

(a) Major Gifts and Gifts-in-Kind

Major gift prospects give because they are committed to the department and are willing to provide the financial support necessary to help the department do its job. Departmental major gift prospects can be accelerated to the gift-giving stage because of the bond that exists between the department and the prospect. These prospects often share a debt of gratitude to the department or its staff and are interested in making a gift to benefit the nonprofit. Planned giving officers offer options that are available to donors to make major gifts. The appropriateness of the choice of asset depends on the needs of the donor and the department. Planned giving is a method of funding the gift rather than an end in itself. The planned giving benefits are the incentives that can make a major gift materialize.

Donors often hold assets such as gifts-in-kind that can greatly enhance the resources of the department. Geologists may be able to contribute valuable geological collections that can contribute to the department's inventory. Museums may find that patrons or benefactors can contribute valuable artifacts to improve the museum's collections. At a hospital, a physician's collection of medical and scientific research can provide direct benefits to the nonprofit.

(b) Endowed and Current-Use Funds

All departments need cash today for current-use funds, but they also need funds to support the long-term needs of the department. Encouraging donors to make a gift for current use and a gift for an endowment raises money now and for the future. Current-use gifts provide immediate financial resources to the department for short-term goals, while endowed gifts provide support for long-term goals, providing stability. Unrestricted gifts of any amount usually can be placed in the endowment to benefit the entire nonprofit. Once the nonprofit's endowment has been established, the endowment should be professionally managed. Endowed funds are managed in perpetuity and make distributions that are based on a percentage of the principal value of the endowment. The distribution can be spent by the department or, with permission of the nonprofit, may be returned to the principal or reserved for future use. In most cases, endowments are restricted in that their income is designated to benefit a specific department or program at the nonprofit. Nonprofit departments and programs depend on endowment income to meet the operating budget and to continue programs from year to year. Endowed funds provide a foundation to a department and a receptacle in which to store funds. The distribution from these funds can be used for scholarships, operating support, program support, or any other purpose consistent with the intent of the donor and the needs of the department. Endowed funds can allocate the distribution by providing that, for example, 50 percent be used for scholarships and 50 percent be used for program support at the discretion of the department head.

(c) Raising Funds in Honor of a Department Leader

One of the most successful ways for departments to raise funds is in honor of a departmental leader. People make gifts to people, and people respond well to making gifts in honor of a distinguished individual. The individual should be well known, well connected, and ideally one with a long tenure who was revered. Almost every department has such an individual around whom such a minicampaign can be built. In most cases, the individual must agree to be part of the campaign, volunteering information on the names of individuals, businesses, friends, and family members who may wish to support the effort. A volunteer committee composed of representatives of the department along with others involved in affiliated businesses, corporations, or associations can help to identify prospects and organize the effort.

Funds can be raised for current use or preferably to establish a permanent endowment. A planned giving officer can draft an endowment agreement that facilitates the fundraising. A planned giving officer can help to raise major gifts, planned gifts, and bequests in support of the endowment. The department is likely to know prospects, and building a mailing list of interested prospects is critical because most of the prospects usually are contacted by direct mail. A brochure that summarizes the major contributions of the honoree can be very helpful. The brochure also should carefully explain the use of the funds and provide a response form for donors to make gifts. Planned giving officers should have input on the brochure to make sure that planned giving options are included in the response form. Multiyear pledges help to provide significant financial support, and committee members can actively raise funds one-on-one from friends of the department and other key constituents.

10.10 RAISING DONORS' SIGHTS

Both development staff and departmental staff must work together to raise donors' sights. Many donors make small gifts simply because, traditionally, that has been acceptable. Most minimums are based on historical patterns and do not reflect the higher costs of operating nonprofit organizations. Donors respond favorably to incremental choices about gift levels, and offering a wide range of options from $1,000, $5,000, $10,000, $25,000, or $50,000 and above often elicits gifts in each of these gift categories. Surprisingly, many donors will make larger gifts than their previous gift record would indicate and enjoy climbing up the cumulative gift ladder. Cumulative gift levels provide incentives to donors to reach the next highest gift category. Establishing recognition programs for annual gifts, cumulative gifts, and planned gifts encourages donors to make "stretch" gifts to reach the next level. Pledges that may be paid over a three- to five-year period also produce significant gifts. If offered as an option, many donors will commit to multiyear pledges that exceed their previous lifetime gifts.

10.11 AFTER THE GIFT—STEWARDSHIP

Once the gift has arrived, it is important for both the planned giving officer and the nondevelopment staff to acknowledge the donor's gift. The acknowledgment demonstrates to the donor that the nonprofit values the gift and intends to use it in accordance with the donor's wishes. Acknowledgments also lay the foundation for future gifts. It is important to recognize a donor's gift on a list of the department's donors, often referred to as a "roster" of donors. The roster may be printed in a newsletter or other communication by the department to its constituents. Most donors appreciate recognition; however, all donors should be asked for permission before including their names in any public roster of donors. Confirm with donors the way they would like their names listed for each gift, as many donors prefer to attribute the gifts to their business, spouse, or other source. Further, the department can recognize leadership as well as planned and major gifts at a public gathering or other appropriate forum.

10.12   DEALING WITH THE DOWNSIDE

With planning, cooperation, and communication, there is the opportunity for success, along with the potential for failure. Failure consists of frustration, distraction, and in development, a poor return on one's investment: failure to raise money. Development can be frustrating, and that frustration can be felt among staff and by staff when dealing with prospects. Prospects are not always the easiest to deal with, especially the wealthiest ones. It can be a challenge to meet with them, deal with them, and sustain their interest. Staff can be intimidated by donors, and donors often are likewise intimidated if they are not at least somewhat familiar with the options available to them and the way they operate. Donors and staff must be educated about the options, approaches, strategies, and opportunities available to the donor.

Nondevelopment staff members can become impatient with the development process. To prevent impatience, planned giving officers can assist in building a balanced portfolio of short-, medium-, and long-term prospects with varying gift potential. Using this approach, some prospects are likely to make gifts, sooner rather than later, helping the nondevelopment staff members to see some positive results to "buy time" waiting for the more complex and larger cases to develop.

10.13   CONCLUSION

A nonprofit's departments are fertile ground for development. Donors, prospects, and staff members are a rich, yet often untapped, source of individuals interested in planned giving. Accessing these prospects requires teamwork between the department's staff and the development office. Ideally, a partnership is formed with department staff members helping to educate prospects about the department's work, the development process, and charitable giving. When staff members work together, donors and prospects will see a unified approach, producing larger and more frequent gifts that will help the department do its work.

PART THREE

Managing Donors and Prospects

CHAPTER ELEVEN

The Planned Giving Prospect

11.1 INTRODUCTION

Why do donors make planned gifts to nonprofit organizations? To find the answer, perhaps we should start by asking why donors to nonprofits make gifts at all. Even in periods of economic uncertainty, philanthropy thrives as individual donors provide significant charitable support. As planned giving professionals, we need to look closely at why people make gifts and how we can work with donors to increase the number of planned gifts to our organizations. This chapter examines various topics related to planned giving donors: their motivations and characteristics, how to find planned giving prospects, and how to work with them in making a gift.

11.2 MOTIVATIONS

(a) Philanthropy

Pure philanthropic donors are truly the noblest—and scarcest—of all donors. They make gifts because they simply wish to better the world and view philanthropy as a personal duty. These donors often make their gifts anonymously and shun the spotlight. Attempts to recognize or honor them are politely rebuffed. Philanthropic donors usually seek out an organization to make a gift.

(b) Gratitude

Grateful donors are those who want to repay a debt to a nonprofit. They are often individuals who have received a service from the organization and feel indebted to it. They may be college graduates who feel that everything they have achieved in life is due to the education they received, patients who feel that medical care has saved their lives or greatly improved their quality of life, individuals who received social services in a difficult time, or those who want to support the religious organization they have believed in all their lives. Like purely philanthropic donors, grateful donors generally seek out an organization and set the gift-giving process in motion themselves. These donors are often eager to see their names included in contribution lists, because they want others to know that a debt is being repaid.

(c) Honoring Loved Ones

Many donors make gifts to honor loved ones. Such gifts sometimes are made to honor a person who is living, but more often are made as a memorial tribute to someone who has died. Donors of memorial gifts usually seek out the organization and have very specific ideas about how they want to honor the loved one. They often are motivated to create a named endowed fund that allows them to pay lasting tribute or erect a plaque that bears the loved one's name. Other family members may be involved in contributing to the gift. Planned giving is an excellent way to build a family gift, because the different financial, estate-planning, and tax needs of each contributor can be satisfied by various planned giving options. One donor may benefit most by making a gift of appreciated securities through a pooled income fund, whereas another family member may benefit more from establishing a charitable gift annuity or a deferred gift annuity. Donors also may make a gift through their estate to substantially augment an endowed fund. Individuals who are motivated to honor loved ones are excellent planned giving prospects.

(d) Nonprofit as Family Substitute

Many donors make gifts to nonprofits because they have no heirs to whom assets can be transferred, or because they do not wish family members to receive their money. In effect looking for substitute heirs, a donor may turn to a nonprofit organization as a replacement for a natural family. Many older donors are surviving spouses and do not have children. They may have been treated well by the nonprofit and enjoy the attention and recognition that philanthropy provides. In working with these donors, personal visits and correspondence are extremely important. They are often a nonprofit's wealthiest donors, and after a long relationship with the organization and the planned giving officer, and giving regularly to the annual fund, they may make major gifts through their estates. For these donors, it is especially important to show how a bequest can benefit the organization.

(e) Tax Benefits

One reason for making gifts is to realize financial or tax incentives. However, a donor must first have a philanthropic intent in making a gift. Tax benefits are attractive to the philanthropically minded donor. Avoidance of capital gains taxes, in addition to a reduction in federal estate taxes, is one of the strongest tax incentives. Such benefits from making a charitable gift are sometimes sufficient incentive to convert a prospect into a donor.

(f) Financial Benefits

Sophisticated donors, such as business professionals, have increasingly turned to nonprofit organizations as a way to maximize financial return while minimizing taxation. This relatively new breed of donors often uses an asset other than cash, such as securities or closely held stock, to fund gifts. They usually are looking for a stream of income or want to increase the yield they currently receive from low-paying investments. Most such donors are already working with financial advisors or are in the financial service business, which helps to facilitate the gift-giving process. Planned giving officers should identify these donors through marketing and educational efforts.

(g) Social Standing and Prestige

Some donors give to certain organizations because they wish to become their "insiders." They see their contributions as a form of membership dues. Others may give to well-established, long-standing traditional organizations so that they can be known as benefactors of those organizations. They perceive that their social standing will rise with each gift. Planned giving officers should pay special attention to events that allow donors at specific giving levels to socialize with each other. In addition to a perceived gain in social status, these events foster business and professional relationships among attendees.

(h) Insurance Policy

Some donors give to an organization because they want an "insurance policy" for the future. This practice is most prevalent at hospitals, but is also seen at other organizations. These donors want to make a gift so that they become known at the hospital. If anything were to happen to them, they believe they will be assured of getting first-class treatment because of their status as "big donors." A gift also may be made to ensure that a son or daughter is accepted into a school, college, or university. Donors may even express such motives when making gifts by asking, not so jokingly, "Does this mean that if something happens to me, I will get the best care?" or commenting, "I hope the university remembers this when my grandson applies for admittance."

Conversely, donors who have promised a gift also use their connections with the organization to avoid making the gift. They may say, for instance, that although the care they received was fine and the physician was excellent (they do not want to jeopardize their relationship with their physician), they had to wait a long time to be admitted, the nurses were inferior, or the food was bad. Or they say that they were planning to make a gift, but their nephew's application to the college was turned down.

It is important to refocus these donors on the reason that led them to want to make a gift in the first place. Remind them that the organization will benefit from their financial assistance or that a particular type of research needs to continue. Do not let the donor use one negative aspect to eclipse all the positive experiences.

(i) Recognition

In some donors, philanthropic intent becomes overshadowed by a desire for recognition. These donors seek to gain the most from their gifts and tend to favor high-profile opportunities, such as having their names engraved on a building. They also may complain loudly if their names are inadvertently omitted from a published donor list. Sometimes these donors may argue about the terms or size of the gift and try to work a deal to afford them the most recognition for the least amount of money. There are some who love the chase and the feeling of self-worth provided by the planned giving officer and the nonprofit organization. They are prone to name-dropping, mentioning other nonprofits that are courting them. To pursue donors of this type, tell them how important they are to the organization. Remind them of the publicity, social events, and recognition they will enjoy by making a gift. It may take several years in working with these donors to receive the gift, and it is important to reassure them that the planned giving officer will not abandon them once a gift is made. They love the attention and do not want to risk losing it by actually making the gift.

(j) No Donative Intent

It happens at least once in every planned giving officer's career. Repeated, strenuous efforts are made to close a gift from a prospect who has no donative intent. This prospect is often someone who is "just looking" for information, to see whether planned giving is a better (financial) option than a commercial alternative. The prospect may be someone looking for a "buyer" for an alleged "gift" of real estate, or someone who sees a planned gift purely as a solution to a problem, such as a way to avoid paying capital gains taxes. Unfortunately, some people turn to nonprofits when they want to get rid of an asset that they cannot sell, and if the prospect cannot sell the property, it is unlikely that the nonprofit can sell it.

Do not spend too much time on these prospects. If the donor does not have a connection to the organization or a strong desire to make a real gift, the gift will never be made, no matter how hardworking, clever, or persistent the actions of the planned giving officer. Cut losses early and move on to real prospects with donative intent.

11.3 PROFILE OF A PLANNED GIVING PROSPECT

Planned giving prospects are different from other development prospects, and their characteristics should be distinguished to better identify them. In general, planned giving prospects and donors share the following characteristics:

- *Age.* Although there are planned giving vehicles that benefit donors of all ages, most planned giving prospects are older. Their life experiences lead to valuing nonprofit organizations; they have lived long enough to accumulate wealth and are comfortable with giving some of it away. They may no longer need savings for a house or for children's education.

- *Wealth.* The majority of planned giving prospects have enough wealth to make a significant gift to a nonprofit organization. Because of their wealth, the favorable tax benefits offered by planned giving are an extra enticement.

- *Childless couples and single individuals.* Many planned giving prospects are childless and seek a place to leave their accumulated wealth. Many are single and have no immediate family members whom they wish to benefit at their death.

- *Surviving spouses.* Now alone, a planned giving prospect may want to honor the wishes of a deceased spouse who was connected to a nonprofit organization or to memorialize the loved one. The benefiting nonprofit is likely to have played a significant role in one or both of their lives.

- *Donative intent.* The planned giving prospect is connected to the organization, knows its needs, has supported it for many years at lower levels, and now wants to make a larger gift.

11.4 FINDING THE PLANNED GIVING PROSPECT

Planned giving donors come from a wide variety of backgrounds. Be open-minded about seeking planned giving donors and prospects, realizing that they can be found in all socioeconomic groups. The following paragraphs discuss a number of aspects that are important to building a planned giving donor base.

(a) Referrals from Development Staff

Ideally, other development officers will refer planned giving prospects to the planned giving office. For this system to work successfully, educate internal development staff members about planned giving so that they feel comfortable in referring prospects. Development colleagues must know that the planned giving officer will not "steal" their prospects or become too technical or cautious, thus scaring a donor away from making a gift. If a gift is made, be sure to share the credit for the gift. Seeking referrals from other development officers assumes that colleagues have donors or prospects to send to the planned giving office, which may not necessarily be the case. For a sample in-house training session agenda, see Appendix, CD-ROM Documentation, Exhibits.

(b) Marketing

It is important for a planned giving officer to build a personal donor base, because other development officers may not refer prospects. Greater autonomy is created if a planned giving officer can demonstrate success by bringing new donors into the organization. One way to do this is through marketing. Marketing identifies new planned giving donors, and a dialogue can begin with individuals who have identified themselves as interested in learning more about planned giving. Marketing is a long-term proposition, so begin as soon as possible. See Chapters 18 to 22 for a more complete discussion of marketing.

(c) Annual Fund Upgrades

A significant number of planned giving prospects exist in a nonprofit's annual fund base. To upgrade these prospects to planned giving donors, target annual fund donors who have made gifts at a particular dollar level over a number of years. For example, identify donors who have made gifts of $500 or more for each of the last three years. If the pool is large, reduce it by narrowing it to donors over a certain age (e.g., 65) who have made gifts of $100 or more for each of the last three years. Then begin a targeted marketing and direct mail program to provide information to this population throughout the year. Include letters about planned giving benefits, a planned giving brochure, gift calculations, invitations to events, news articles featuring the nonprofit, and newsletters. Follow up with these prospects over time, maintaining contact periodically to remind them of the benefits of planned giving.

(d) Rehabilitation of Old Cases

Review stale office files to uncover prospects who once asked for information about planned giving. Every development office has in its files some correspondence from prospects or donors who once inquired about making gifts through their wills or about planned giving. Review these files to find additional prospects. Send information about the planned giving program to each person, adding some personal calculations, news about the nonprofit, and the need to raise funds. It is likely that after a few attempts some viable planned giving prospects will surface.

(e) Events

When the organization or development office hosts events for donors and prospects, be sure to attend. Go through a list of attendees before the event and identify individuals who fit the planned giving profile. At the event, seek out prospects and mention the organization's funding needs. Talk about planned giving and how its benefits help donors to make gifts. If an individual has potential as a prospect, follow up with a letter and include information about planned giving. Keep in touch with such prospects, and over time new planned giving donors will be found.

(f) Suspect Meetings

"Suspects" are development prospects who are thought to have the capacity to make a gift to the organization but may have little connection to it. Suspect meetings, conducted with individuals associated with the nonprofit who may be able to screen and identify planned giving prospects, are another means of finding new planned giving donors. To prepare for a meeting that will focus on identifying suspects, create lists of people known to the individual attendees. For example, when working at a hospital and meeting with a physician, have a list of the physician's patients so that the physician can help identify individuals who may have the financial capacity and interest in supporting the hospital and the physician's work. It is particularly helpful if the physician or any member of a suspect meeting is willing to identify prospects and then become involved in the solicitation process.

(g) Board of Trustees

Another excellent source of planned giving prospects is an organization's board of trustees. Trustees are well acquainted with an organization's constituents, and they may be willing to assist in soliciting prospects. If the planned giving or development office is fortunate enough to have access to some trustees, invite a small group of them to meet at a convenient time. Because these people are volunteering their time, the meeting should last no more than an hour. Ask each trustee to identify potential planned giving prospects. Also ask whether the trustee will make an introduction to any particular prospects for the planned giving officer. Such introductions often lead to successful solicitations, because the prospect may be more inclined to make a larger gift.

11.5 WORKING WITH THE PLANNED GIVING PROSPECT

Now that the planned giving prospect has been identified and the prospect's motivation is understood, let us look at how to work with the prospect.

(a) Long-term Relationship

The relationship with the planned giving prospect is an ongoing one. The planned giving officer becomes well acquainted with this prospect, learning intimate details of financial and personal matters. Conversations are, ultimately, about making a gift to the organization, but much is learned about the prospect's feelings for the organization, family situation, relationships, finances, and hopes and fears.

(b) Basic Skills

As in any important relationship, basic interpersonal skills are needed in a relationship with a prospect. If the planned giving officer listens, rather than speaks, the prospect will tell what is needed to be known. Facilitate conversation by asking prospects questions about themselves. Find topics of common interest. Let prospects know that the organization cares about them. Honesty is essential. A prospect will quickly recognize its absence, and the planned giving officer will discover that it is hard to recover trust once it is lost.

(c) Background of Prospect

What should the planned giving officer know about a prospect at their initial meeting? First, understand the person's connection to the organization. Is the prospect a graduate? Grateful patient? Retired dean, physician, administrator, or staff member? Is the prospect a friend of the organization? This should be learned at the office before meeting personally.

Second, look at the record of the prospect's past giving to the organization if there have been any past gifts. How long has the donor been making gifts? At what level? Has giving been consistent every year? If not, what interrupted the giving? Has the donor made a planned gift? If so, what type? Determine whether there have been any dealings with the development office and, if so, whether they have gone smoothly. There may be an existing situation that is causing difficulties for the donor that the planned giving officer can solve. Files and data bases tell only a portion of the story; the real story comes directly from the donor during a face-to-face meeting.

Let the prospect tell what area or program he wishes to support. Do not rely on what the file indicates as the prospect's area of interest. Development officers can pursue, incorrectly, a prospect's alleged area of interest and then not understand why the prospect seems disinterested in making a gift. Over time, relationships and feelings can change, and what may have been of interest to a prospect earlier may no longer be of interest today.

Learn about the prospect's assets and whether she is trying to achieve a financial goal by making a planned gift. This will help in discussing the best way to structure the gift appropriately. The prospect may tell you her assets herself, but the planned giving officer also can pick up clues when observing a prospect's lifestyle and accomplishments.

Seek to uncover any outstanding personal matters that may be relevant. For example, does the prospect have a particular physical ailment, a sick spouse, or a disabled child? What personal factors may contribute to her making or not making the gift? These issues can play a significant role in negotiations with a planned giving prospect.

(d) Printed Materials

In most cases, a planned giving officer should arrive at a donor meeting with material to leave with the donor at the end of the meeting. Calculations for specific gifts are ideal to leave with the donor, but a Ways to Give brochure or any type of news release about the organization is also effective. The object is to keep the organization's name before the donor, emphasizing the need for funding.

(e) Making the Solicitation

A planned giving solicitation is different from any other type of development solicitation. A planned gift includes information on gift amounts, payouts, and tax benefits, and by discussing these necessities with a donor, the "ask" is being made. The planned giving officer certainly needs to discuss the organization's need for funding and the area of the organization that the donor is interested in supporting, but a planned giving solicitation often can initially focus on the financial benefits the donor receives through making the gift. If the donor has donative intent at this point, then whatever the financial obstacle to the gift, it is likely to be overcome. A planned giving solicitation can tend to focus more on how the gift will be made than on whether the gift will be made. Soliciting a planned giving donor is covered fully in Chapter 13.

11.6   CONCLUSION

Understanding the motivations of planned giving donors, identifying planned giving prospects, and learning to work successfully with these individuals is critical to a successful planned giving program. Planned giving donors are special; they cannot be grouped together with all individuals who make gifts to nonprofits. Recognition of their unique qualities can increase the number and amounts of planned gifts to nonprofit organizations.

CHAPTER TWELVE

Working with Donors

12.1 INTRODUCTION

Establishing a planned giving program is like starting a business. Products or services must be developed, donors' and prospects' needs must be known, and marketing must be done to "promote the business"—that is, to further the donor's charitable intent and the nonprofit's mission. Once developed, product lines and services must remain constant, and there must be continuity between staff and the nonprofit's constituents to promote confidence and build a loyal base. During the last decade, corporate America has shifted its focus toward providing service to its customers and clients. By surveying customers' attitudes, behaviors, preferences, and interests, corporate America has found ways to better meet customers' needs. Now major corporations offer solutions and individualized services to clients at the convenience of the customer. Law firms, certified public accountant (CPA) firms, and financial service industries also have learned to pay close attention to their clients' needs. The firms that have learned best have been the most successful.

In nonprofit organizations, donors are the nonprofit's customers; planned giving donors are the clients of a planned giving program. Understanding the needs of donors while building an environment to meet those needs promotes success for both the donor and the nonprofit.

12.2 A PLANNED GIVING OFFICE AS A SERVICE CENTER

A planned giving office is a philanthropic service center offering planned giving products and charitable gift-planning services. The office provides service to donors, prospects, nonprofit staff, and professional advisors regarding life income gifts, endowments, tax planning, estate planning, financial planning, and the use of assets other than cash for making gifts. The planned giving officer is a key component of the service center, providing professional expertise to donors and their advisors about each of the planned giving options. The service is client based, is built around long-term relationships that often involve extended family members, and is focused on personal goals, family needs, and business interests. A planned giving office, committed and dedicated to service, will generate planned gifts and financial support for the nonprofit from those to whom it provides its service. A planned giving office must make it easy for prospects to become donors by redefining the service it provides to its constituents.

12.3 MANAGEMENT

(a) Servicing Donors

The planned giving office staff members play an important part in building a successful planned giving environment. For donors who visit the office or telephone to request information, the first impression of the office starts with the receptionist. The receptionist should be trained and educated about the role of planned giving and the importance of customer service. He should be accessible, prompt, efficient, and responsive, greeting visitors, making them feel welcome, and reassuring them that they will have the opportunity to meet with a professional regarding their needs. Planned giving officers should be spontaneous and able to provide information quickly, demonstrating the willingness to deliver service that is so important in meeting donor needs.

Telephone inquiries also must be handled professionally and without delay. Inquiries demonstrate donor interest, and the way in which these inquiries are handled affects the end result. If it is not possible to take a call immediately, the call should be returned as expeditiously as possible. Some donors find it more convenient and efficient to use e-mail as a way to communicate. The telephone and e-mail provide a level of anonymity that allows donors to make inquiries and obtain information without feeling obligated or pressured to make a gift.

Financial calculations prepared on planned giving software and documents detailing the benefits of any specific gift option can be prepared. The planned giving officer can demonstrate several options at once, recalculating or fine-tuning as necessary. The ease with which information can be produced increases the donor's confidence level, allowing the software to be used to an advantage.

(b) Teamwork

The planned giving officer and staff members should cooperate and coordinate as necessary to produce the information for a donor easily and quickly. The staff should work as a team, knowing that each member plays an important part in serving the donor's needs. Responsibilities should be delegated, and there should be a division of labor that increases efficiency and productivity. For example, while the planned giving officer is meeting with the donor, an assistant can prepare the planned giving calculations. Sharing expectations with staff members clarifies the responsibilities and respective roles of each team member. Building an environment that promotes cooperation, communication, and collegiality among staff improves end results. Donors should be shielded from negatives such as office politics, software glitches, computer breakdowns, and other organizational problems, miscommunications, and mistakes. A mistake made by one is a mistake made by all. Donors have choices among nonprofits, and it is the collective impression of the nonprofit that counts. Planned giving involves many nonprofit departments, including the business office, accounting, gift recording, and the planned giving staff members. Success depends on the ability of these departments and individual employees to coordinate, manage, and meet the needs of the donor.

Once a bad impression has been created, it is hard to overcome; it may take months or even years to recover. When an error has been made, usually the best practice is to admit the mistake and apologize. Occasionally errors will occur, and it is important to develop a proactive stance in these situations. Work to regain the donor's confidence by correcting the mistake. If the donor has not yet discovered the mistake, consider calling her attention to it. For example, if payments to annuitants are late because of an accounting oversight, a quick telephone call to the annuitant will allay fear and restore confidence.

(c) Exceeding Donors' Expectations

For some donors, the planned giving officer is the primary contact with the nonprofit, so that officer must be capable of speaking on behalf of the nonprofit. The role of a planned giving officer is broad, and the donor appreciates a knowledgeable, informed planned giving officer who is an expert about the nonprofit, its mission, and charitable giving generally.

When donors deal with a nonprofit, they have expectations about the way in which their cases will be handled. Regardless of the level of a donor's expectations, it is the obligation of the planned giving office to exceed those expectations. A planned giving office that routinely exceeds expectations will build a loyal base of appreciative donors. Of course, if the level of service fails to exceed the donor's expectations, that too is noticed by the donor. Once a donor's expectations have been exceeded, it is important to continue the same level of service throughout the relationship between the donor and the planned giving office. There must be consistency in meeting deadlines and in producing the high-quality letters, printed materials, tax documents, and tax receipts that the donor has come to expect. Outside financial managers or trustees should be educated about the nonprofit's expectations of service to donors. Consistency is one of the hallmarks of good service.

(d) Delivery—Follow-Through

Following through on each request is a critical step in exceeding a donor's expectations and establishing a positive relationship. Each request, no matter how large or small, must be handled efficiently, with precision, accuracy, and attention to detail. Like any consumer, the donor appreciates fast and efficient service. A 24-hour turnaround time impresses donors and in most cases will exceed their expectations. Delivering quality and timely service to those who make requests establishes credibility and builds positive rapport. Donors learn that they can count on the office and often tell family members, colleagues, financial advisors, and other prospects about the experience.

12.4 EDUCATING DONORS

One of the most important elements of service is educating donors about the unique aspects of each of the planned giving options and the compatibility of an option with the donor's needs. Charitable gift annuities, deferred gift annuities, pooled income fund gifts, charitable remainder trusts, and lead trusts, along with bequests, are the primary "products" of a planned giving office. The donors must be educated not only about the nonprofit, its departments, programs, and mission, but also about the ways in which they can give. Knowledgeable donors can make larger and more frequent gifts. Booklets, brochures, and guides on charitable gift planning can help educate donors about the favorable tax consequences of charitable gifts. Planned gifts can take considerable time to conclude; following the initial contact, the challenge is in finding ways to sustain the interest of prospects to further the relationship. Sustaining dozens of relationships can be labor intensive and time consuming. However, newsletters and letters from key nonprofit department heads or staff members can help to sustain interest over time while reducing the demand on resources.

Donors also have choices about the types of asset (cash, securities, real estate, or tangible personal property) used to fund a gift. A planned giving officer must personalize the approach to match the donor's personality, needs, and assets. Some donors want tremendous detail, whereas others are more interested in the bottom line. Offering appropriate gift options, anticipating a donor's needs, and providing a proposal to match those needs increases the likelihood of success.

These questions may clarify the donor's goals and help in identifying the appropriate planned giving option:

- What is the donor trying to accomplish?
- What is the donor's motivation?

- Why has the donor chosen this time to give?

- What is the donor's past relationship with the planned giving office? With the nonprofit?

- Are external factors stimulating the gift, such as an interest in establishing an endowed fund in the name of another?

- Who else besides the donor is likely to be involved? The donor's family? The non-profit's staff?

- How will the gift be funded?

- Will others make gifts?

- Does the donor want to be formally recognized?

(a) Seeing the Transaction through the Eyes of the Donors

One of the best parts of a planned giving officer's job is working with the donors. Every donor is unique in the way he goes about achieving philanthropic objectives. A planned giving officer who views the gift through the eyes of a donor increases the probability of a gift. Planned giving staff often view the donor and the transaction from their side of the desk, neglecting to observe the unique set of circumstances that causes a gift to present itself. Donors may be motivated by a philanthropic desire to support the nonprofit, a need for income streams or tax deductions, or a desire to be publicly recognized—or it may be the first time in their lives when they have the financial resources or the interest to make a major gift. For some donors, a planned gift is the largest single financial transaction they have ever undertaken. Endorsing that check, deed, or stock power can be an unnerving experience. Donors can get "cold feet" when it comes time to make the gift. Individuals who purchase cars, homes, and other major consumer items sometimes back out at the last moment. A planned gift is a major financial transaction that requires careful consideration and thought. Some donors have limited philanthropic attention spans, so the planned giving officer must seize the moment to help make the gift occur.

(b) Simplify, but Do Not Oversimplify

Planned giving is complicated, and it is important to translate and interpret its complex concepts into an understandable language. Using planned giving jargon, tax terminology, and technical terms alienates and intimidates donors, raising barriers between the planned giving officer and donors. It is more effective for the planned giving officer to use language the donor understands. Although it is important to simplify language, one should not oversimplify planned giving concepts. These concepts are difficult to grasp, and it is important for the donor to fully comprehend the particular gift option. Face to face, the planned giving officer can read the donor's expressions, checking to see if the donor is comprehending the information. Examples and illustrations can help clarify the complexities of planned giving. Telephone conversations are more difficult to gauge, although gaps in conversation suggest a lack of comprehension or confusion. Once the donor demonstrates confusion or misconception, the planned giving officer must assist the donor in overcoming the confusion. Follow-up telephone calls can identify problem areas or questions for the donor.

(c) Know the Message

Donors can easily be discouraged by nonresponsive forms of communication. Body language and even subtle verbal expressions can frustrate donors who are intent on making gifts. Donors read demeanors, and the planned giving officer who is confident and supportive increases the probability of a gift. A planned giving officer who appears uncomfortable, uncertain, or tentative is likely to convey the wrong message to a donor who is enthusiastic and interested. No planned giving officer can know it all, but when faced with an unfamiliar inquiry, it is important not to discourage the donor. Many times a planned giving officer may not know enough about a particular department at the nonprofit, and it may be necessary to ask for help. Occasionally legal, tax, or charitable gift issues may present seemingly insurmountable problems, and it is important to have an attorney or consultant knowledgeable in planned giving to assist in these cases. Outside counsel can be very effective in dealing with a donor's financial advisor who needs technical assistance regarding the specific planned giving option. Knowing one's limitations is important so as to not overstate abilities or give inaccurate information. When help is needed, explain to the donor that it may be necessary to research the issue to provide the most accurate information possible. The information should be obtained and relayed to the donor in a timely fashion.

(d) Confirm Everything in Writing

The substance of every donor inquiry, conversation, communication, and meeting should be confirmed in writing. Confirmations accomplish several goals. They help to organize the issues regarding the gift, making it possible to present information in the most logical and sequential fashion. They also provide a second chance to explain the technical aspects of the gift option. Written documents provide the donor with an opportunity to review the information on a more personal basis in the privacy of his or her home. Letters clarify the issues, delineate the benefits, and reinforce the key points of earlier conversations. Confirmations also help avoid potential misunderstandings. Donors sometimes need to be reminded that the gift is irrevocable or that (in the case of a pooled income fund gift) the income stream may vary depending on the market performance of the fund's assets.

(e) The Personal Touch

Donors appreciate the personal touch, which includes following up with telephone calls, letters, or notes for informal donor requests and even hand-deliveries by the planned giving officer. A hand-delivered proposal is an effective way to show the donor her importance to the nonprofit. Hand-delivery also gives the planned giving officer one more opportunity to summarize the benefits of the gift option. A brief telephone call to the donor to confirm the donor's availability sets up the personal visit and eliminates wasted trips. Most donors are grateful for the "spontaneous" visit and appreciate the personal contact. In addition, the visit provides a chance to recap the benefits and answer questions. A follow-up telephone call following correspondence accomplishes a similar purpose. Questions can be answered, and the call confirms to the donor that he is important to the nonprofit and that the gift matters.

(f) Dealing with the Downside

With planning, cooperation, and communication, there is the opportunity for success—along with the potential for failure. Planned giving can be frustrating, and that frustration may sometimes be displayed to the nonprofit's constituents. Donors are not always easy to deal with. Staff can be intimidated by donors, and donors often are intimidated if they are not familiar with the available planned giving options and the way they operate. Nonprofit organizations also may be disappointed by the initial financial rewards of a planned giving program. Planned giving takes time, determination, continuity, and patience to succeed. It is important to be realistic and conservative about the time it takes to produce results. Over the years, a planned giving program can make major contributions to the nonprofit's bottom line. Building a balanced planned giving program—one that works to produce gifts of all sizes and types, using a variety of assets from each of the nonprofit's constituents—is critical.

(g) Evaluation

Corporations routinely evaluate their performance by sampling customer responses to recent experience with the corporation. In addition, staff members are asked to perform self-evaluations of their response and the service provided to the customer. A nonprofit's planned giving office can ask donors and staff members to evaluate performance. Included in Appendix, CD-ROM Documentation, Administrative Documents are copies of a donor survey and self-evaluation checklist. Periodic testing helps to identify problem areas and general issues that should be modified or corrected.

Following up with each inquiry also can help to stimulate prospects. Offering a series of planned giving training programs to nonprofit departments and staff members can generate further interest.

CHAPTER THIRTEEN

Solicitation Strategies

13.1 INTRODUCTION

Philanthropy is an investment in the present and the future. Donors, through their financial support, make investments in nonprofit organizations by providing resources for immediate and future needs. Philanthropy affords individuals the opportunity to preserve and promote ideals that they cherish and offers individuals a sense of belonging both to the nonprofit and to a larger group whose members have made a financial commitment to the charity.

Professionals who enter development and planned giving often ask for advice on ways to solicit prospects. They assume that a special script or dialogue will elicit a positive response and consequently a gift from a prospect. Of course, there is no magical array of words or one correct way to solicit a prospect for a gift. Successful solicitations are based on the donor's interest in the nonprofit and ability to make a gift, the planned giving officer's knowledge of the nonprofit and the donor, strong planning and preparation, a positive relationship between the officer and the prospect, and perseverance and patience.

This chapter is divided into 10 sections that explore the various stages of a solicitation. First, how to prepare for a solicitation, then, different types of solicitations are discussed and strategies for increasing the chances of success. Finally, the specifics of various gift options are discussed and a system for following up with donors is presented.

13.2 THE PLANNED GIVING OFFICER'S MIND-SET

(a) Belief in the Mission

Before commencing a solicitation, a planned giving officer should understand and be completely conversant with the nonprofit's mission and its charitable purpose. A rereading of the organization's mission or case statement can remind the planned giving officer of the charity's successes and its needs. Planned giving officers should meet with a variety of nonprofit representatives to obtain first-hand knowledge of the nonprofit's services and the people who make its work essential.

(b) Asking Is Not Taking

Individuals who are new to development sometimes view a solicitation as tantamount to taking the prospect's assets instead of facilitating a gift to support a nonprofit. A gift is a free act by the donor whereby the donor parts irrevocably with an asset. A successful solicitation matches the financial resources and interests of the prospect with the nonprofit's need to raise money to fulfill its mission. Planned giving officers serve as matchmakers, bringing a nonprofit's organizational needs together with the donor's interests and goals. The donor should participate fully in the process.

(c) Needs versus Needy

Nonprofits have needs but should never appear needy. Donors want to make gifts to successful nonprofits and know that their gifts have a positive impact on enhancing an already successful program. Occasionally staff members may translate needs into neediness, which evokes pity but does not usually result in financial support. It is more effective to show a donor blueprints of proposed new construction than to tour a deteriorating building. Nonprofits and their staff must evaluate their solicitations to make certain that they demonstrate the nonprofit's organizational needs.

13.3 PREPARATION

(a) Think Positively

To be successful in fundraising, a planned giving officer must develop a positive mind-set when working with donors. The following is a comparison of successful and unsuccessful approaches:

Successful Approaches	Unsuccessful Approaches
Be positive	Be apologetic
Be confident	Be imposing
Practice	Be fearful and nervous
Understand and explain the nonprofit's needs	Sound needy

(b) The Right Time Is Now

Some planned giving officers hesitate, waiting for the right time to ask. There is no one right time—the right time is *now*. A solicitation need not be perfect to be successful; if perfection is the goal, no solicitation will ever take place. A planned giving officer may delay a solicitation if the donor just made a gift, is ill, is grieving the recent death of a family member, or experienced a catastrophic business loss. However, waiting for the completion of a new brochure or the arrival of a research report should be avoided.

The more a planned giving officer is involved in soliciting prospects, the more comfortable he will become with the process. The planned giving officer should choose an appropriate timetable for soliciting a donor and move forward, rather than waiting for a more ideal time.

(c) Be Direct

Successful and experienced planned giving officers know that a one-on-one prospect solicitation is best conducted directly. Prospects can feel duped if a solicitation occurs at the conclusion of an hour-long social visit. Bring the solicitation and reason for the donor visit to the forefront. Treating the solicitation as a business meeting with an agenda focuses the planned giving officer on the business of raising money. Following the solicitation, there will be ample opportunity for social conversation.

(d) Know the Technical, Tax, and Legal Information

There is no substitute for knowledge when it comes to the tax consequences of charitable gifts or estate planning. Confusion on the part of the planned giving officer can deflate the donor's interest and directs attention away from gift giving. A reading of Chapters 22 to 34 may help the development officer in becoming conversant with some of the technical aspects of planned giving. If the planned giving officer does not know the answer to a donor's question, he should be honest and offer to find the answer for the donor. Anticipating likely technical questions is an effective way to prepare for a donor meeting.

(e) Know What Not to Say

Inexperienced development officers, because of nervousness or anxiety, have a tendency to speak too much and provide too much detail, especially by becoming overly technical about the tax and financial aspects of a planned gift. Often, less said is more effective and creates opportunities for the donor to fully participate in the conversation. Each approach must contemplate the prospect's personality, matching the needs of the nonprofit with the prospect's interests and the planned gift option with the prospect's financial needs.

(f) Practice

The phrase "practice makes perfect" applies to solicitations. Individuals who are new to planned giving should practice before a mirror or in front of family or friends who can provide direct feedback on approach, style, level of sincerity, and effectiveness. A video recording also provides an ideal opportunity to evaluate a solicitation. Role-playing is an effective way to prepare for a solicitation, especially if the role-playing is videotaped. The object of the practice session is not to memorize lines or make a speech, but to anticipate the flow of conversation, prepare for prospective questions, and develop appropriate responses.

(g) Research

Collecting basic background information is the first step in preparing for a donor meeting. Prior to a solicitation, the planned giving officer should develop a profile on the prospect that contains biographical, family, and occupational data, as well as philanthropic information, including the date of the donor's last gift, largest gift, cumulative gift total, gift designation, and gifts made to other charities. More sophisticated donor profiles may contain data on the prospect's interests, affiliations, civic and community involvement, and relationship with the nonprofit.

Internal records at the charity also can be an excellent source of information about prospects. A prospect's paper file can provide essential information on his relationship with the nonprofit. Former or long-term staff members and volunteers also may remember key information about prospects and donors. The nonprofit's computer system may supplement a donor's paper file with additional information on the prospect's giving history and the names of nonprofit personnel with whom the prospect has had contact. At many nonprofits, computer activity codes are used to indicate a donor's participation in select events and programs.

Although the importance of research should not be understated, planned giving officers should use listening and interpersonal skills to develop a donor profile in cases in which none exists. Planned giving officers should not be afraid to meet with a donor without having a full research profile of the person. The first meeting with a prospect can be used primarily for orientation, and second or future meetings can focus on a solicitation.

13.4   THE PLANNED GIVING PARTICIPANTS

(a) People Give to People

Philanthropy is a people business, and donors make gifts because they are asked to make a gift; the planned giving officer or volunteer can make a difference. Staff or volunteers, serving as ambassadors on behalf of the nonprofit, communicate the organization's needs and mission to donors. These representatives must establish long-term relationships with prospects and donors because major gifts secured through planned giving solicitations often take years to close. Planned giving officers therefore must be patient and invest time in building relationships that permanently bond prospects with the nonprofit. Planned giving is truly a people-to-people business.

(b) Volunteer Involvement

At many nonprofits, planned giving staff members work with volunteers and board members to make a solicitation. When volunteers are included, the staff member does not make the solicitation directly, but serves as an adjunct to the volunteer, making introductions, facilitating conversation, and providing technical support for the volunteer who is not a planned giving expert. Depending on the circumstances, the nature of the relationship, and the volunteer's motivation, the volunteer may play either an active or a passive role in the solicitation. Prior to the solicitation, the staff member should practice the solicitation with the volunteer to present a cohesive and coordinated message to the prospect. Properly trained volunteers can be exceptionally effective solicitors.

(c) The Planned Giving Officer's Personal Commitment

A volunteer is in a uniquely powerful position when soliciting a prospect. A volunteer who donates time and who has made a financial contribution to the nonprofit demonstrates commitment and dedication to the organization. A planned giving officer may achieve a similar commitment by making gifts to support particular programs of interest at the employing nonprofit. A volunteer can leverage her own role and personal investment of time and money; likewise when soliciting a prospect, a staff member who has made a gift will feel more comfortable soliciting prospects because of her own commitment. This investment can be persuasive during a solicitation because it shows a level of interest in the nonprofit's mission that demonstrates a deeper commitment than that of a traditional employee-employer relationship.

(d) Donors with Previous Giving Records

Donors with a gift history have already demonstrated loyalty and commitment to the nonprofit and are most likely to provide additional support. A planned giving officer soliciting previous donors should begin the conversation with an expression of appreciation for the donor's past support, which can even serve as the basis of the visit. A conversation about the donor's past support opens up lines of communication and sets the stage for discussions about additional support. Soliciting a prospect with a previous giving record is also a good way for new staff members to develop skills and confidence in soliciting and interacting with donors.

13.5 THE DONOR

(a) The Donor's Perspective

A planned giving officer should try to view the solicitation from the donor's perspective, as well as the nonprofit's, to better understand the donor's state of mind and potential reaction to the solicitation. Consider these issues from the donor's perspective:

- Financial resources
- Family circumstances
- Relationship to the nonprofit
- Motivation for making the gift
- Available assets

During conversations with the donor, be alert to these factors, because they can provide clues about how the gift will be made, the type of gift, and its size.

(b) Donor Alienation

Many nonprofit representatives falsely assume that asking for a gift could alienate the donor from the nonprofit. Prospects do not become angry when they are asked to make a gift; in fact, most prospects are honored and flattered to be asked to make a significant gift. Some staff members believe that if a donor is a prospect for a future gift of tangible personal property or a life income gift, a request for a current gift of cash will alienate the donor. Rather, current gifts of cash can cement the relationship between a donor and the nonprofit, making it more likely that the donor will follow through with a future planned gift.

(c) Educating the Prospect

Development professionals should assume that a prospect is unfamiliar with the details of the nonprofit's mission. Although most prospects have a general understanding of the public service provided by the nonprofit, the delivery or the nature of those services changes from time to time. Hospitals develop new centers of care or service different constituents; museums offer a new perspective or exhibits; educational institutions introduce new programs, centers, institutes, or projects; religious organizations may offer elder care programs or children's services. Educating the prospect on innovations or changes at the nonprofit is an essential preliminary step in a successful solicitation.

In addition to educating the prospect about the nonprofit's mission, the planned giving officer must educate the prospect about the available planned giving options. Carefully prepared letters and software calculations focus a prospect on the most appropriate gift options. A planned giving officer should go through the advantages and disadvantages of each viable gift option with the donor, allotting much time for questions. The planned giving officer also should encourage an interested donor to follow the visit with a discussion with the donor's financial advisor.

(d) Donor Commitment and Involvement

Prospects who see the work of the nonprofit and meet its beneficiaries are more likely to respond to a request for financial support. Many nonprofits offer tours or open houses to educate prospects about the nonprofit's mission and charitable purposes. Prospects who serve on a committee, volunteer group, or board are also more likely to understand the nature of the services offered by the nonprofit. Current and former board members, long-time loyal employees, and volunteers should always be included in a pool of potential prospects.

13.6   TYPES OF SOLICITATIONS

(a) Traditional Solicitations

A traditional fundraising solicitation is initiated from within the development office by a staff member, who may be assisted by a volunteer. At many nonprofits, prospects are screened, rated, and assigned to a member of the development staff based on the prospect's giving history, area of interest, and relationship to the nonprofit. Most traditional solicitations provide an extended time for cultivation during which the staff member educates the prospect about the nonprofit and involves the prospect in the charity's activities. The prospect is then solicited for a gift in support of a particular program of interest.

A planned giving solicitation may work somewhat differently. In a planned giving solicitation, the planned giving officer should bring to the meeting a portable computer or printouts of calculations for each of the planned giving options being considered. Calculations help to illustrate the financial benefits that the donor will receive by making a certain type of gift. Printouts should be prepared for a specific dollar amount that may be a target for the solicitation and also for the amounts of $10,000 and $100,000 because they can be multiplied or divided easily. If the donor rejects a request for a specific dollar amount, the solicitor must evaluate whether the donor is rejecting only the size of the gift or the idea of making a gift altogether.

(b) Peer Group Solicitations

Most prospects are part of a larger peer group. For example, an alumnus is a member of a class and a former hospital patient is associated with a particular physician or department. When viewing a prospect as part of a peer group, it may be helpful to solicit all members of the peer group for a gift, because individuals enjoy being part of a larger group and feeling that they share a common bond with their peers. No one likes to feel that she is the only one being asked to make a gift. Invite members of a peer group to attend a planned giving presentation illustrating gift options appropriate to the group. A member of the group who has already made a planned gift can persuade other members to do the same. Letters can be used to communicate with peer groups whose members are geographically dispersed.

(c) The "Cold Call"

The "cold call" is a solicitation without cultivation. In a cold call, the planned giving officer acts more like a salesperson than an advisor and simply asks for a gift. Most successful solicitations are predicated on patience, cultivation, and timing, but sometimes cold calls are necessary and unavoidable. They should be limited to situations in which there are few other options.

Cold calls may be by telephone or can involve a personal visit with a prospect without the customary relationship building that is part of the traditional solicitation. In most cases, a letter of introduction is sent to the prospect asking for an appointment. Geographically isolated prospects often appreciate the opportunity to meet with a representative of the nonprofit.

Although cold calls generally do not have a high success rate, they may be successful in these circumstances:

- When the prospect lives far away from the nonprofit. For example, a patient who received medical care at a hospital in another city may be solicited through a cold call by a member of the staff who is visiting the patient's geographic area.

- Upon conclusion of one-time regional nonprofit events, such as alumni events or charity receptions

- As part of a campaign for all members of a constituent group, such as the choir or members of the class of 1930

(d) Self-Identification

Many nonprofits recently have changed the traditional solicitation process. In addition to actively seeking prospects, they are asking individuals to identify themselves as prospects. These prospects respond to brochures, guides, and newsletters by completing reply devices that open up a line of communication between the nonprofit and the prospect. This sophisticated marketing strategy enables the nonprofit to communicate with each of its prospects and supplements the efforts of nonprofit staff members who cannot cover geographic regions outside of their local area.

Through self-identification, cultivation is minimal and the solicitation is mutual. These forums provide opportunities for planned giving self-identification:

- Printed materials, such as guides and newsletters that educate prospects about planned giving options

- Planned giving, estate planning, and financial planning seminars

- Check-off boxes for planned giving information on annual campaign return envelopes

By promoting a donor-friendly system that offers clear and concise information designed to educate the constituent, the nonprofit transforms the question from "Do you want to make a gift?" to "What size or type of gift do you want to make?" Through this approach, new and modest donors can be solicited successfully.

Small planned giving programs can be augmented by using informative, educational publications that allow development staff to reach donors who would otherwise be inaccessible. The publications carry the charity's mission to the nonprofit's constituents and promote opportunities to fulfill donors' philanthropic goals. Every publication should contain a response form that enables the prospect to communicate easily with the development office. In many cases, the prospect has already made the decision to make a gift. The more informed a donor is, the more likely he is to give.

The planned giving officer advises, provides information, and suggests gift options to the donor. Through self-identification, the fundamental nature of the relationship between the prospect and the planned giving officer is changed. The planned giving officer offers guidance as to the form of the gift that best matches the needs of the nonprofit, taking into consideration the resources of the donor and the asset that may be used to fund the gift. It is already known that the donor would like to make a gift; the question becomes how best to make the gift.

Donors communicate directly to the planned giving officer through response mechanisms included in publications. Answers to donors' inquiries or requests for information should ideally be processed within one to two business days. If there is no response from the prospect, the planned giving officer should follow up in one-month, three-month, and twelve-month intervals. See Appendix, CD-ROM Documentation, Correspondence, for sample follow-up letters.

Self-identification is an efficient, effective development strategy because:

- Serious prospects are more likely to contact the planned giving office because they are motivated to make a gift.

- The planned giving officer is seen as an advisor to the prospect.

- The process accelerates the usual time required to identify, cultivate, and solicit a donor.

- The prospect often makes repeat gifts.

- The size of the gift is often larger.

Successful self-identification requires the planned giving officer to:

- Develop a comprehensive marketing program.

- Provide correct information quickly.

- Educate constituents.

- Follow up with prospects.

Although this approach departs from traditional cultivation techniques, it may be used with existing groups of constituents, such as annual giving donors who have made repeat gifts. This is different from many development approaches, in that much of the contact may be conducted by mail or telephone rather than in person, as the printed materials solicit the prospect and then convert the prospect into a donor.

Nonprofits that can use this approach are those that have:

- A small staff

- National and international populations

- A new planned giving program

- Constituents in geographically isolated regions

Self-identification should be used as a supplement to, not in lieu of, traditional cultivation methods. Self-identification is a very practical solution to a complex problem: maintaining contact and opening up lines of communication with a nonprofit's constituents.

13.7 THE SOLICITATION PROCESS

(a) Cultivation

The next step in soliciting a prospect is cultivation. Cultivation builds relations between the nonprofit and the prospect. Ideally, cultivation occurs over a period of time during which the prospect learns about the nonprofit's mission and needs, is made to feel a part of the charity, and learns how she can financially support the nonprofit's work. Cultivation should not continue for so long that the planned giving officer cannot solicit the donor for a gift.

(b) Contacting the Prospect

Solicitations may be conducted by mail, by telephone, or in person and usually involve a combination of all three. Unless the prospect contacts the nonprofit, the nonprofit must initiate contact with the donor. To begin a solicitation, the planned giving officer may call or send a letter to the prospect to set up an appointment to meet. Before the meeting, the planned giving officer should familiarize himself with the nonprofit's mission and planned giving options.

(c) Telephone Conversation

A telephone conversation with a prospect alerts the planned giving officer to a number of factors:

- *Donor's motivation.* During the conversation, the planned giving officer can learn about the donor's motivation to make a gift, the seriousness of the donor's interest in pursuing the gift, and its anticipated timing.

- *Gift option.* The planned giving officer also can learn about the various gift options that interest the donor, the numbers of beneficiaries for a life income gift, and their ages. This valuable information enables the planned giving officer to prepare in advance planned giving calculations to discuss during a meeting and which can be sent with an accompanying letter prior to the meeting.

- *Assets.* The planned giving officer also may probe for information about the donor's assets, which may be used to fund the gift. Cash poses few problems, but it is helpful to know in advance the cost basis of noncash assets, such as securities, and, in the case of real estate, whether there is a mortgage on the property.

- *Designation.* Comments from the donor regarding the anticipated designation of the gift can provide the planned giving officer with an opportunity to prepare an agreement or fund description for a named endowed fund.

(d) Letters

A letter may be sent to a donor prior to or following the telephone call and is always used to follow up after a personal visit. A letter also can be used to provide information on the technical aspects of a planned gift option, including calculations and tax benefits specific to the donor. Most important, letters are used to confirm the date, time, place, and next step in the gift process. Consider these three elements of a follow-up letter:

1. *Tone.* The letter sets the tone for the next stage of the solicitation and can be used effectively to show appreciation to the prospect. It also provides an opportunity to reinforce the nonprofit's mission and its charitable services.

2. *Complex information.* A letter provides the planned giving officer with an opportunity to present information about planned giving options. Failing eyesight is common in later years and large-print letters can help donors to see the planned giving data.

3. *Supporting materials.* A letter also enables the planned giving officer to enclose additional materials about the nonprofit, its culture, and its traditions.

Exhibit 13.1 is a model letter.

Exhibit 13.1   General Inquiry Letter

<DATE>

Richard A. Johnson
126 Main St.
Boston, MA 02116

Dear Mr Johnson:

Thank you for requesting information about charitable gift planning at Academy for Learning. We appreciate your interest and are pleased to provide information which we hope will help you achieve your goals. Our staff works with individual donors and their professional advisors, including lawyers, CPAs, and trust officers to help donors accomplish the following:

- Establish an endowed scholarship fund.
- Produce a stream of income for life through one of <ORGANIZATION'S> life income gift programs.
- Reduce federal estate taxes.
- Obtain a charitable income tax deduction.
- Avoid or reduce capital gains taxes on transfers of appreciated property.
- Obtain membership in a <ORGANIZATION> leadership club.

You may choose to fund your gift through a variety of assets, including cash, securities (such as stocks, bonds, mutual funds, or closely held securities), real estate (such as a personal residence, commercial property, or vacant land), and tangible personal property (such as art, antiques, jewelry, or collectibles). In addition, the gift may be made in the form of a current gift, a planned gift, or a gift through your estate.

Enclosed is the latest issue of our <PLANNED GIVING NEWSLETTER>. If we can assist you, please feel free to contact the Office of Planned Giving at 555-1234.

Sincerely,

Joe Smith
Planned Giving Officer
Enclosure: PLANNED GIVING Newsletter

(e) The Personal Visit

A telephone call is usually the first step in setting up a donor meeting. In some cases, the planned giving officer must speak to an intermediary (secretary or spouse) prior to speaking with the prospect. Most intermediaries protect the prospect and are adept at deflecting requests. If possible, say little to the intermediary about the nature of the telephone call.

A personal visit is the preferred choice for a solicitation because it enables the planned giving officer to observe nuances in the prospect's demeanor and reaction to the conversation. Prior to the personal visit, the planned giving officer or member of the development staff should call to confirm the appointment. During the meeting, the planned giving officer should reference materials previously sent by letter and should bring an extra set in case the donor does not have the materials available.

(f) Planned Giving Calculations

The solicitation of a planned giving prospect focuses on educating the donor about different types of planned gifts. Prior to meeting with a prospect, the planned giving officer should be completely familiar with each element of a gift option, to anticipate questions about the tax consequences and financial advantages of the gift options. The planned giving officer should be familiar with all the data illustrated in the planned giving calculations.

The presentation to the donor should not be overly technical or complex, because too much detail can confuse a prospect. It may be effective to outline a general description of the mechanics of the gift and its financial benefits. To provide complete disclosure to the prospect, potential detriments, such as tax disadvantages, also should be explained. At the end of the meeting, the planned giving officer should summarize the key elements of the gift option and confirm everything in a follow-up letter. Although the financial benefits are significant, the most important part of a planned gift is the satisfaction of providing financial support to a worthwhile cause. Confirming the donor's philanthropic intent should be restated at the conclusion of the letter.

(g) Follow-up

One of the most important aspects of the solicitation is the follow-up, which is business-oriented and focuses on completing the gift. Any unresolved issues should be concluded, leaving no confusion in the prospect's mind about the gift. The follow-up may take the form of a letter, a telephone call, or a meeting, with or without the prospect's spouse or professional advisor.

- *Telephone call.* A follow-up by telephone is effective in resolving issues and helps to build relationships. The call reinforces the people-to-people aspect of the solicitation.

- *Letter.* A letter reconfirms technical information and provides an additional opportunity to present supplementary material about the nonprofit and its mission. A letter also may contain specific information about one of the nonprofit's departments or programs of particular interest to the prospect.

- *Meeting.* A subsequent meeting is the best form of follow-up. It may enable the prospect's spouse or professional advisor to participate in the process. Sometimes professional advisors and spouses can discourage a gift, and an opportunity to meet can provide a forum to discuss issues and resolve confusion.

(h) Closing the Gift

Bringing the solicitation to closure is one of the most important parts of the solicitation—one that tests the planned giving officer's skills. At this point, the planned giving officer needs to link the prospect's financial support to the nonprofit's mission. The ability to organize and synthesize information in a logical and coherent message is critical. Bringing the gift to resolution is perhaps the greatest and most rewarding challenge of the job.

To conclude a solicitation, it is helpful to use mutually agreed-on deadlines to encourage the donor to make a decision within a specified time frame. Deadlines, whether artificial or real, promote action and encourage prospects to become donors. The deadline may coincide with one or more of the following:

- Year-end closing—December 31
- Campaign stages
- Class reunions
- Homecoming
- Nonprofit's fiscal year-end

13.8 THE SIZE OF THE GIFT

Raising a prospect's expectations to reach a goal is critical to producing major gifts. Planned giving, through various tax and financial benefits, can enable donors to make larger gifts than many thought possible. Prospects' expectations can be raised by using one or more of these techniques:

- Discuss the size of other leadership gifts that have been made to support the development effort. Start high and emphasize the importance of leadership gifts; then, if necessary, scale back the size of the requested gift. If you start too low, it is difficult, if not impossible, to reverse the process and ask for a larger gift.

- Identify influential donors (if those donors have permitted use of their names) who have made major gifts.

- Use a gift range table to demonstrate the number of gifts needed at higher levels to reach a specific goal. See Appendix, CD-ROM Documentation, Presentation, for a sample gift range table.

- Offer two gift alternatives (either different amounts or different ways to make the gift at appropriate financial levels).

Donors with extensive gift histories can be solicited for a gift that represents a multiple of 10 to 500 or more times their largest gift; some donors make ultimate gifts at multiples of 1,000 times their previously largest gift. For example, if a donor consistently makes a gift of $25 to the annual fund, it is not unusual for his or her first planned gift to be $10,000, which represents 400 times the annual gift. It is more difficult to determine a target amount for the solicitation of prospects without giving histories. Two strategies can be used to influence the size of the donor's first planned gift:

1. *Endowed fund minimums.* A nonprofit can raise a donor's sights by setting appropriate minimums for endowed funds such as operating funds, fellowship funds, and scholarship funds. The minimum should be set at an amount that is within reach for many donors, yet represents a stretch to achieve and is an amount needed by the nonprofit to sustain the fund's objectives. A comprehensive list of endowed fund options and gift opportunities at all ranges helps to bring gifts in at all levels, including those at the highest levels. See Appendix, CD-ROM Documentation, Marketing.

2. *Planned gift minimums.* Most nonprofits have planned gift minimums of $5,000 to $10,000 for charitable gift annuities, deferred gift annuities, and gifts to the pooled income fund, and minimums of $100,000 for charitable remainder trusts. These minimums help to raise the level of a significant gift for most donors.

Some members of development staffs believe that solicitations should be made at extraordinary, sometimes unrealistic, levels. The problem with this approach is that the only gifts remembered are those that were successful. Under this theory, planned giving officers ask donors for sums of money that may be inappropriate to the donor's giving history, relationship to the nonprofit, capacity, and propensity to give. Many donors and prospects are offended by being asked for disproportionately large gifts, and irreparable harm can be done between the prospect and the nonprofit, perhaps even tarnishing the image of nonprofits.

An alternative strategy is to provide an opportunity for the prospect to raise the issue of gift size with the planned giving officer. Many times donors, on their own, stretch to make a gift that is much larger than the planned giving officer would have thought possible. Providing an opportunity to fully involve the prospect in discussing the gift's size often produces surprisingly large gifts in the planned giving officer's mind, but exactly the right size gift for the donor.

13.9 NEGOTIATIONS

A solicitation can be like a negotiation. Recognize that all parties have a role and stake in the outcome and that common ground must be established. Areas of common ground include the prospect's interest in one or more of the nonprofit's programs and the nonprofit's need to secure financial support. Negotiating with donors requires flexibility and maneuvering by both the donor and the charity. No donor should feel locked into a specific gift amount. The donor must be in control of the gift process and must determine the nature, timing, and scope of the gift.

(a) Never Get to No

Most initial personal visits do not immediately result in a planned gift; donors need time to reach a conclusion about making a planned gift. It is unrealistic to expect that the planned giving officer will return to the nonprofit with a gift; if he does, the gift is usually substantially smaller than it could have been. Allow adequate time for the donor to become involved in the process and comfortable with the concept of making a substantial gift. Short-circuiting the process by rushing the donor produces smaller gifts.

Inexperienced planned giving officers may phrase a solicitation as a question that results in a yes-or-no answer. In planned giving, the questions involved are more complex, and the answers are unlikely to be simply yes or no. Reinforcing the nonprofit's mission, its services, and the prospect's commitment to the charity, while presenting the prospect with fundable alternatives and appropriate gift options, will increase chances for success.

Gifts can be lost when inexperienced staff members see a solicitation as an all-or-nothing proposition. A gift at any level is always welcome, and a display of disappointment by the planned giving officer is always inappropriate. When soliciting a donor for a planned gift, a fundraiser can help the donor make a gift by spreading the gift over two to three years. Major gifts can be lost because a prospect is left with few alternatives. Offer a variety of gift options using different assets to help a prospect become a donor. The planned giving officer should remember that a first planned gift may be followed in later years by a larger gift.

(b) Overcoming Obstacles

A planned giving officer must be prepared for a donor's response. Many major donors have more experience at being the object of the solicitation than the planned giving officer has in making the request. Major prospects often are pursued by a number of nonprofit organizations and are quite adept at deflecting requests for financial support. Consider the following responses, which may be true or may be used as an excuse not to make a gift:

- "I would like to think about it."
  Delay. Donors must take time to consider the appropriate response to a request that affects their financial resources. Prospects for a planned gift can become overwhelmed by the complexity of the gift options. Some prospects delay making the gift because they are more motivated to obtain favorable financial and tax benefits and are less motivated by philanthropy. Uncovering the reason for the delay can help to reveal the donor's motivation. Prospects who lack donative intent are unlikely to move forward in the gift process. Setting a reasonable deadline can move the case forward.

- "I need to speak with my spouse."
  Spousal approval. Frequently a prospect pursues philanthropic interests on behalf of herself and her spouse. The prospect may be closer to the nonprofit and take the lead in their combined philanthropic pursuits, while the other spouse remains more passive. Dealing with a spouse who is absent from the cultivation and solicitation is a challenge for a planned giving officer. The active spouse often consults with the passive spouse, who surprisingly is often a key participant in the decision. The planned giving officer can help the gift process by making an effort to include both spouses, including addressing letters to both spouses, especially when both spouses are alumni, serve on the nonprofit's board, or have individually made previous gifts.

When prospects have not made previous gifts, the planned giving officer must determine whether the need for spousal approval is genuine or an attempt to deflect the request for financial support. This situation may be resolved by having either a meeting with both spouses to test the motivation of the active spouse or a mutually agreed-on deadline to complete the gift.

■ "Not as long as [Dr. Johnson] is president."
Displaced anger. Prospects may know the personalities and philosophies of the nonprofit's key members. Some prospects are favorably inclined to give but are put off by the actions, personalities, or philosophies of the nonprofit's president or by a board policy. Nonprofits can be unintentionally adept at providing prospects with excuses not to give. The planned giving officer needs to refocus the prospect on the nonprofit's mission and on the work it performs on behalf of its constituents. One way to do this is by reminding the prospect that individuals, whether presidents or board members, come and go, but that the nonprofit has provided valuable service for decades. The nonprofit outlasts any single individual, and the donor's financial support provides the nonprofit with resources to do its work.

13.10 FOLLOW-UP

Follow-up is a key ingredient for closing gifts. Often, donors are truly interested in making a gift but do not place it as their highest priority. It is the planned giving officer's responsibility to continue to stay in touch with the donor, over time, to complete the gift. This can take months or years. Without consistent follow-up, few gifts would be made.

To take advantage of follow-up opportunities, the prospect management report should be systematically reviewed. A systematic review focuses attention on prospects who need follow-up; the planned giving officer should create opportunities and excuses to stay in touch with prospects, keeping them interested in making a gift. A planned giving officer using a systematic review system can easily manage 50 to 75 prospects, tracking them by geographic region, anticipated date of solicitation, size of request, and gift history.

## CHAPTER FOURTEEN

Planned Giving and Major Gifts

14.1 INTRODUCTION

Traditionally, major gifts and planned gifts have been treated as separate and distinct classifications of gifts. This distinction applies not only to the gifts themselves but also to the staff members responsible for raising those gifts. There are a number of reasons for this distinction and the resulting division of labor. Major gifts have been around for as long as there have been nonprofit organizations, whereas planned giving is largely a vehicle of the twentieth century, which is a historical justification for this division. Of the two, major gifts have been valued more highly by nonprofit organizations because they provide immediate sources of revenue. Gradually, over time, the sharp distinction between major gifts and planned gifts has eroded, and the two types of gifts have evolved into an integrated and cohesive package of options for the donor.

Most nonprofit organizations now appreciate the role of planned giving as a vehicle to encourage donors to make larger gifts even if there is a delay in the use of the gift. Increasingly, nonprofit organizations are hiring directors or vice-presidents of major and planned gifts, and the major gift officers and development staff members working under them are expected to raise both major and planned gifts. Although planned giving will always have its unique technical and financial components, the distinction between planned gifts and major gifts is becoming more artificial than substantive. Even in the more traditional nonprofit organizations, the distinction has softened, and development staff members generally are responsible for raising both major and planned gifts regardless of the title they hold.

Planned gifts and major gifts should complement rather than compete with each other. The choice of the gift is a function of the needs of the donor and the donor's situation rather than a preconceived notion that one should raise either major gifts or planned gifts exclusively. Development staff members, regardless of their titles or duties, can share the responsibility to raise both major and planned gifts. Because donors do not understand the apparent and sometimes transparent division of labor that exists in development offices, development office staff members should present a seamless and integrated message designed to promote the most attractive gift options to the donor, maximizing the benefit to the nonprofit. Whether the gift is a planned or a major gift matters little. What matters is that the development staff has succeeded in helping the donor to fulfill his charitable interest for the benefit of the nonprofit organization.

Almost every individual of means in the United States is aligned with one or more nonprofit organizations and can be considered a possible major gift prospect. Many of these individuals support nonprofits through regular gifts of time and annual gifts but also look for ways to make a major gift, while still protecting family interests and securing their own financial well-being. Although major gifts are essential to nonprofit organizations, they never occur as frequently as needed. Few individuals have the financial resources to make the gift, and even fewer have been presented with a selection of appropriate options. Many donors with the most significant cumulative giving records make their first major gift through a planned giving vehicle. Planned giving opens the door to philanthropy, allowing interested, committed individuals to become philanthropists. Planned giving offers a blend of benefits that cushion the financial and psychological impact of an outright gift, enabling many individuals to make generous major gifts to nonprofit organizations. Income streams and favorable tax consequences provide incentives to many individuals, furthering the donor's interest in helping the nonprofit organization achieve its charitable purposes. Fine-tuning the payout and discount rates, carefully selecting the most appropriate asset to fund the gift, and comparing the benefits and detriments of each option are part of the attraction of planned giving. Many donors use assets other than cash to fund their first planned gift because the "cost" seems less; these assets often were acquired at a lower cost basis and are now worth substantially more. Assets that may be used to make a major gift include surplus assets, such as vacant land, a vacation home, or seldom-used lakefront property. Although the donor may consider such assets surplus property, they are extremely valuable gifts to a nonprofit organization.

Some donors who make planned gifts become outright major gift prospects eventually. First-time donors making large gifts may find it easier to make a planned gift. For many donors, an initial planned gift is like a dress rehearsal in preparation for future outright major gifts as well as additional planned gifts. If securing major gifts is a problem, planned giving can be part of the solution. Major gift and planned giving officers who work together, understand each other's jobs, and collaborate on major gift prospects will be more successful at the business of development.

14.2 DEFINITION

At most nonprofit organizations, a gift is classified as a major gift depending essentially on the size of the gift, the form of the gift, and the size of the nonprofit organization. Traditionally, a major gift is an outright gift in the amount of $10,000 to $50,000 to $100,000 or more depending on a donor's giving patterns to the nonprofit organization and the nonprofit's history and can be 10, 25, or even 100 times larger than the donor's previously largest gift. For some donors, a major gift can be the donor's first gift. No matter what the size, for both the donor and the nonprofit, a gift is a significant expression of commitment.

The majority of planned gifts are major gifts. The donor has chosen to fund the major gift using a planned giving vehicle or using assets customarily reserved for planned giving. While an outright major gift is more valuable to a nonprofit organization, for many donors an outright gift is not feasible. For example, an outright gift of $100,000 in cash can be used immediately by the nonprofit organization to support operations, programs, or capital projects. A planned gift of the same amount cannot be utilized until the death of the beneficiary, which might not occur for 10, 20, or 30 or more years. Another way to compare the relative value of a planned gift to a major gift is to compare the charitable income tax deduction of a major gift to that of a planned gift. An outright gift of $100,000 in cash produces a charitable income tax deduction of $100,000. Because it is an outright gift, the nonprofit can use the gift immediately. In the case of a planned gift, such as a charitable gift annuity with two beneficiaries, the donor receives a charitable income tax deduction of $24,000, or 24 percent of the value of the outright cash gift. In this case, the planned gift could be considered on its face to be approximately one-quarter as financially valuable to the nonprofit compared to the outright gift. Consequently, as a guide, when preparing proposals for prospects, the planned giving solicitation might be based on an amount four or more times greater than the outright major gift amount.

Planned giving is a method of funding the gift rather than an end in itself. The planned giving benefits are the incentives that can help to make a major gift materialize. Many more of these would occur if nonprofit organizations encouraged development staff members to collaborate on cases.

Planned giving includes several major gift alternatives, each of which can be used to produce major gifts from donors who are interested in supporting a nonprofit organization:

- *Life income gifts.* This major gift classification includes charitable remainder trusts, charitable gift annuities, deferred gift annuities, and pooled income fund gifts. Each of these options provides not only a stream of income to the donor and to the donor's spouse, if applicable, or to another beneficiary but also a charitable income tax deduction. Planned gifts are major commitments by donors to the nonprofit that express more than the gifts represent. A life income gift is truly a living gift, one that will support the donor during life and benefit the nonprofit in the future.

- *Gifts from the donor's estate.* Included within this important group are major gifts such as gifts through bequests or by will, or distributions through a trust. Bequests, a planned giving staple, are used by donors who wish to make a major gift upon their death. These gifts provide either a specific dollar amount, such as "$100,000 to XYZ organization," or all or a stated percentage of the donor's estate, such as "50 percent of the residue of my estate to XYZ organization." For donors who are unable to make an outright major gift, a bequest is most appropriate. Donors who have made planned gifts during their lifetimes sometimes make an additional gift through this method. Planned giving donors are excellent prospects for a major gift through the use of dispositive provisions in the donor's estate planning documents. These donors need to be cultivated. Often a bequest can finish funding a project dear to the donor. For donors who make major gifts through their estate, there is no greater way to show commitment than to share with the nonprofit the result of one's life's work so that the nonprofit may continue to perform services for its constituents.

- *Endowed funds.* Outright major gifts or planned gifts are used to support endowed funds in the name of the donor or to memorialize or honor a loved one. The principal of the endowed fund is managed in perpetuity, and a portion of the earnings from the principal is distributed to support the donor's wishes. Endowed funds are part of the nonprofit's endowment that provide financial stability and strength to the nonprofit.

- *Assets other than cash.* Many major gifts are made with assets other than cash, such as real estate, stocks, bonds, mutual funds, and tangible personal property like art, collectibles, and collections. Planned giving staff specialize in gifts of these assets, which can be used to make a major gift. Many times gifts are lost because the only asset considered was cash. Donors often hold assets that are far more valuable and appropriate for a gift than is cash, and many donors are more generous with gifts of noncash property than with cash. Planned giving officers should offer asset counseling workshops to nonprofit staff, donors, and professional advisors. Asset counseling involves reviewing the wide variety of asset options available to donors for making gifts. The appropriateness of the choice of asset depends on the needs of the donor and the nonprofit.

- *Structured gifts.* This option is attractive to donors who wish to make major gifts to nonprofit organizations. Through a structured gift, the donor and planned giving officer or major gift officer work together to reach an appropriate solution using a variety of giving methods. A structured gift is responsive to the wishes of a donor and is personalized to meet the donor's financial needs and charitable objectives.

The structured gift can include several components:

- An outright gift

- A pledge or commitment to a series of annual gifts over time

- A planned gift usually involving a life income gift

- A gift through the donor's estate

Structured gifts can be used to fund capital projects, chairs, endowments, and other significant projects that can be achieved only with major gift funding. The planned giving officer is actively involved in making the gift affordable, achievable, and feasible. Often used in capital campaigns (see Chapter 53), structured gifts also are used in a variety of major gift solicitations.

14.3   PLANNED GIVING AND MAJOR GIFT PROFILES

The reasons donors make gifts are as different as the donors themselves. There are, however, some general characteristics that emerge to form a profile of four types of donors likely to incorporate planned giving into their major gift strategies. Included in the appendix is a checklist that includes a list of donor characteristics that can help to form the profile of a planned giving prospect. See Appendix, CD-ROM Documentation, Administrative Documents, for a checklist to identify major and planned giving prospects. Like planned gifts, major gifts come both from donors who are well known by the nonprofit organization and from those who have had no previous relationship with the organization. Furthermore, individuals without any previous giving record may make major gifts.

Planned giving can be a vehicle to make a major gift happen. Many donors who want to support the nonprofit feel frustrated because the gift they can make would not satisfy the nonprofit's expectations. Donors who receive even a modest life income stream can sometimes reach the necessary gift level to make a major gift through planned giving. Major gift officers should be prepared to use planned giving options or seek the assistance of planned giving staff about donors for whom an outright gift is impractical. Likewise, planned giving officers should be prepared to raise major gifts without the aid of planned giving. Donors who have the capacity and inclination to make outright major gifts should be encouraged to do so. The following profiles may be helpful to identify major gift prospects for whom planned giving may be an option.

(a) Donors with a Giving Record

Planned gifts, major gifts, and annual giving are related. The annual giving program is the point of entry for the vast majority of donors. Donors with a record of continuous support to the annual giving program are excellent major and planned gift prospects and are ripe for a major gift. Donors with consistent giving records demonstrate commitment and interest in the nonprofit. Through continued cultivation, these donors must be upgraded from consistent annual-giving donors to major gift prospects.

Most planned giving donors are repeat contributors and make a number of planned gifts and major gifts over time. Some planned giving donors make a gift of all or a portion of the income they receive from their planned gift that, in turn, produces a new charitable income tax deduction, effectively eliminating the income. This gift can be used as an annual gift in direct support of the nonprofit organization or for one of its programs or to fund an endowed fund or current use award. See Exhibit 14.1 for a checklist to identify donors with a giving record.

Exhibit 14.1   Checklist to Identify Donors with a Giving Record

- A donor with a consistent annual giving record
- A loyal donor who has made gifts in three of the preceding five years
- Donors who have included the nonprofit organization in their wills or trusts
- Donors who have established memorial funds or endowed funds
- Donors who have made outright gifts of $1,000, $5,000, or $10,000
- Donors who have made planned gifts

(b) Individuals Who Have Established Relationships with the Nonprofit Organization

One of the most supportive groups are those donors who have an established relationship with the nonprofit organization, either with or without previous financial support. Depending on the nonprofit, they may be patrons, patients, alumni, friends, faculty, or staff. Often overlooked, long-term employees are valuable prospects for major gifts. Constituents, friends, or those who have a professional relationship with the nonprofit, such as colleagues with whom the nonprofit staff members share or conduct business, professional, or scientific research, are appropriate major gift prospects. At schools, "dual degree holders" are prime candidates because of their extensive relationship with the nonprofit. Individuals who received a bachelor's and an advanced or other professional degree owe much of their professional accomplishments to the nonprofit organization that granted these degrees. Many of these constituents may be eager to make a planned or major gift. See Exhibit 14.2 for a checklist to identify such individuals.

Exhibit 14.2   Checklist to Identify Individuals Who Have an Established Relationship with the Nonprofit Organization

- A nondonor who appreciates his or her relationship with the nonprofit
- A volunteer or board member
- A family with several generations of connections with the nonprofit
- Faculty or staff who provide financial support to their departments through payroll deduction
- Staff who have been employed by the nonprofit for 10 years or more
- Retirees or faculty emeriti
- Individuals who hold more than one degree from the nonprofit
- Donors who have attended more than three functions at the nonprofit within one year
- Donors who have received extended care
- Donors who have professional relationships with the nonprofit's staff members

---

(c) Planned Gifts, Major Gifts, and Family Dynamics

Often donors have to deal with a variety of family considerations when it comes to making a major gift. Sometimes there is conflict between the donor's interest in supporting a nonprofit organization and the donor's interest in preserving future resources for his family. Outright gifts can diminish reserves or leave donors who experience changed financial circumstances in conflict. A series of planned gifts allow donors to annually re-evaluate their financial status before making additional major gifts. Planned giving promotes philanthropy to those donors and their families because of the attractive life income streams, income and estate tax deductions, and possible capital gains tax avoidance. Planned giving complements tax, estate planning, and financial planning objectives and the need or desire to support one's family. Many donors use planned giving as an alternative to an outright major gift as a concession to a spouse who wishes to preserve family assets. Life income streams are seen as sufficient benefits for spouses who would be in conflict over an outright major gift.

In addition, families of donors who make life income gifts develop a permanent link to the nonprofit through the donor's relationship with the planned giving office and the income stream from the gift. A donor's financial well-being can be enhanced through the life income stream the donor receives. Families, too, come to understand the bond that forms between the donor and the nonprofit. After several monthly or quarterly payments, previously disinterested spouses can appreciate the value of life income gifts. A letter from the planned giving officer accompanying the payment reinforces the relationship between the donor and the nonprofit.

Surviving spouses, interested in establishing family endowments, in tribute or in honor of loved ones, use planned giving to fulfill their interests. These donors recognize the mutual benefits that planned giving affords to donors. These donors are able to become philanthropists supporting a nonprofit's mission through the creation of an endowed fund to honor a loved one, while obtaining benefits such as an income stream for life. Many of these donors make a series of gifts to the endowed fund, providing substantial benefits to the nonprofit. See Exhibit 14.3 for a checklist to identify these potential donors.

Exhibit 14.3   Checklist to Identify Donors with Special Family Considerations

- A surviving spouse
- A couple without children
- A donor for whom an endowed fund is appropriate to memorialize or honor a loved one
- Donors who have established an endowed family fund
- Donors from families who have generations of involvement with the nonprofit

---

(d) Financially Sophisticated Donors

Included within the broad category of financially sophisticated donors are professional advisors, such as attorneys and certified public accountants, as well as those in the financial services business. Employees of mutual fund companies, banks and trusts, and brokerage houses are astute in managing other people's money and their own. Businessmen and women, especially those with titles such as chief executive officer, chief operating officer, president, or vice-president, or individuals who work for corporate employers, are also important potential prospects. Entrepreneurs, especially those in small business or start-up companies, understand cash flow and the financial benefits that planned gifts can provide. These individuals are prime prospects for a major gift because they have the financial resources and savvy necessary to appreciate all of the benefits of a planned gift.

Many prospects, both financial professionals and regular investors, with extensive holdings in the stock market are exceptional candidates for a planned gift that can be used to complete a major gift. These prospects value the financial benefits that can be achieved through charitable remainder trusts or other forms of planned gifts that, like stocks, pay dividends and can appreciate in value over time. Planned gifts also reward donors with tax benefits that are helpful in offsetting income to reduce tax rates. Although planned gifts are not substitutes or alternatives to investment vehicles, they are charitable vehicles that complement a donor's financial investments, offering similar and familiar financial benefits.

Some donors see planned giving as a way to supplement retirement income. Deferred gift annuities offer streams of income that can be timed to begin at or during retirement. Retirees, especially those who were employed by the nonprofit, can enhance their income through planned giving and make a gift back to the nonprofit. Planned giving staff may wish to collaborate with their employee benefits office to share information with retirees about the benefits of charitable giving and the ways that planned giving can supplement retirement benefits. Many benefits offices allow planned giving staff to distribute information or make presentations at retirement planning workshops sponsored by the benefits office. Some will provide a list of retiring employees who may be contacted individually by planned giving staff members about the benefits of planned giving. These benefits are enough to push the donor forward to make a major gift.

Nonprofits also have as constituents individuals from lower-paying professions. The constituents include caregivers, nurses, social workers, teachers, artists, allied health professionals, secretaries, assistants, or curators. These individuals may have received their degrees from the nonprofit or may be employed by the nonprofit. The individuals are particularly appropriate prospects for a planned gift to supplement retirement earnings and Social Security. Though these individuals may not be well compensated, they may through marriage have access to wealth, may have inherited wealth, or during their lifetime may have proved to be exemplary savers. These prospects are often initially overlooked; yet they can be viable and loyal prospects if pursued for a major gift.

To a donor, the cumulative financial benefits of a planned gift, including an income stream and the charitable income tax deduction, can represent in excess of 50 percent of the gift. In addition, the donor receives intangible benefits, such as the good feeling that comes from making a major gift. Many donors recognize the true cost of a planned gift is actually much less than the face value of the gift. Describing in detail the benefits and costs of a planned gift to this group of prospects can produce results. Exhibit 14.4 gives a checklist for identifying financially savvy donors.

Exhibit 14.4 Checklist to Identify Financially Savvy Donors

- A professional advisor
- A donor with JD, PhD, MD, or DDS in his title
- A person who is familiar with investments and financial statements
- Graduates of professional schools
- Employees of financial institutions
- An entrepreneur or chief executive officer
- Donors with large holdings of investment assets, such as real estate, stocks, bonds, or mutual funds
- A donor interested in supplementing retirement earnings
- Attendees of a nonprofit organization's retirement planning workshop
- Donors seeking to stabilize income during retirement
- Individuals holding traditionally lower-paying professional positions who are long-term employees
- Donors seeking to provide benefits for spouses

14.4 IDENTIFYING MAJOR GIFT AND PLANNED GIVING PROSPECTS

Major gift and planned giving prospects can be found among individuals with traditional, yet often conflicting, demographic traits. These prospects come from every walk of life and can be middle age or very old, be of average wealth or very wealthy, be childless couples or those with extended families, have rural or metropolitan addresses, be new donors or donors from families with long traditions of philanthropy. For each prospect, the connection to the nonprofit must be explored and developed. The speed in which the case proceeds depends on the donor's knowledge of the nonprofit and the major gift and planned giving officer's skill in case management.

14.4 IDENTIFYING MAJOR GIFT AND PLANNED GIVING PROSPECTS

(a) Using the Nonprofit's Computer System

The nonprofit organization's computer center can provide reports on individuals who may be major gift prospects. The center may be able to retrieve the names of interested individuals, alumni, friends, or patrons who have not made gifts. Although the title of the reports and the data the reports contain vary from organization to organization, the following reports are generally available with accompanying data to rate and screen prospects.

- *Loyalty report.* A report that lists donors who have made gifts in three of the last five years or five out of seven years, without regard to amount. A computer printout showing names, addresses, and giving records for donors who have made gifts in the three last years provides a significant major gift prospect pool.

- *Cumulative giving report.* A report that lists donors' cumulative giving history.

- *Benchmark report.* A report that lists donors who are about to reach a cumulative gift level, such as $5,000, $10,000, or $100,000. This report can be helpful in upgrading prospects.

- *Largest single gift.* A report that lists donors who have made a one-time gift of, for example, $5,000, $10,000, or $100,000.

- *VIP report.* A report that includes alumni or friends who meet one or more of the following criteria: (1) cumulative gifts in excess of $5,000; (2) donors who have made gifts in three of the last five years; (3) individuals with a prefix or suffix such as CEO, CFO, president, vice-president, CPA, JD, MD, PhD, Honorable/Hon.; (4) individuals who have received recognition or who are past or present board members.

- *Zip code report.* A report that identifies and groups donors based on where they live.

The criteria contained in these reports is designed to identify prospects with potential for a variety of giving levels. These reports can be evaluated by staff members, board members, and others to rate or screen prospects.

(b) Using the Mail

Many major gift prospects are cultivated passively through the nonprofit's annual giving program. These annual giving appeals or phonathon requests, even if they go unheeded, bring news to the prospect about the nonprofit and are a form of communication and contact. It is always difficult to measure the impact of this one-way communication, but one thing is certain: Over time, the continuous, consistent, and sustained effort helps make some gifts materialize. Clearly, in the absence of the nonprofit's annual message, the job would be more difficult.

Each annual giving mailing should include a variety of information to help market planned and major giving options. Planned giving buckslips (see Chapter 19) can be included with each annual giving mailer, giving donors more choices and more information about charitable giving. The planned giving office can include information about planned giving in the envelope that contains a donor's annual giving receipt. Planned giving guides, newsletters, and brochures also spread the message to both donor and nondonor prospects, and many donors respond favorably to this information.

Regardless of the method of funding, major gifts set the pace, inspire others, and provide leadership to the nonprofit organization by challenging other donors to make major gifts. Although it may seem to make more sense to contact only those with a giving record, those without a giving record should also be considered potential donors. Although these individuals have heard the nonprofit's message but not responded to past efforts, they will have the planned giving and major gift options in their thoughts due to past mailings. A planned gift such as a life income gift is an opportunity to maintain contact with these potential donors and sustain interest. Lapsed donors may also be viable candidates for a planned giving mailing, helping to stimulate the interests of the former donors.

14.5 MOBILIZING THE NONPROFIT ORGANIZATION TO PRODUCE PLANNED AND MAJOR GIFTS

The nonprofit itself has a large number of individuals who themselves are prospects for major gifts or who can provide access to donors and prospects likely to make major gifts. This group includes central administration, deans, business and financial staff department heads, faculty, and development staff. Each is a prospect for a major gift, and each by virtue of her position has professional or business contacts involved with the nonprofit. Many major gifts come from this group of key, well-connected individuals.

(a) Working with Development Staff Members

The nonprofit's development and major gift officers should be an important source of planned giving referrals. At most nonprofit organizations, development officers are assigned major gift responsibilities for a large pool of prospects. Many times planned giving is not presented as a major gift option because the solicitor is uncomfortable with or lacks sufficient knowledge about the planned giving concepts and their applications and instead focuses on outright major gifts. Major gift cases are often complex and require careful orchestration, cooperation, and teamwork. On difficult cases, planned giving and major gift officers should be prepared to offer a variety of options. Sometimes the planned giving officer can act as an intermediary and other times as a consultant, brought in to deal with a technical aspect of a planned giving option. Too many gifts are lost because a major outright gift of cash is presented as the only option.

As an advisor or consultant to the major gift officer, the planned giving officer can accompany the major gift officer on a visit to the prospect. The major gift officer should explain to the donor the planned giving officer's role in the process. Planned giving officers are also used to dealing with a variety of the donor's financial and legal advisors. Major gift officers may be less comfortable in dealing with those individuals and in viewing charitable giving in the context of the donor's overall estate, tax, and financial planning objectives.

Much of the development process is similar for major gift and planned giving officers. The need to identify and cultivate donors and prospects and the methodology of doing so is similar. The difference occurs in the solicitation, where the form of the gift and the asset used to make the gift diverge. Solicitations of major gifts do not begin as planned giving solicitations but rather result in a planned gift. Major gifts become planned gifts because planned giving strategies are used to conclude the gift or because the gift was funded with assets such as securities, real estate, or tangible personal property. The donor's needs, interests, and available assets determine the classification of the gift. Therefore, it is necessary for major gift officers to identify planned giving concepts and strategies or at least consult with a planned giving officer to identify appropriate courses of action. Collaboration, information sharing, and strategizing are cooperative efforts that can produce results.

Building a solid working relationship with development staff is essential to foster successful collaborative efforts in major gift cases. Some development officers and major gift officers are hesitant to turn over the name of a potential prospect to a planned giving officer. This attitude is quite understandable, as the development officer may feel that to refer the prospect is to admit defeat; or, in the case of a successful solicitation, the development officer may feel that he has done all the work but that the planned giving officer may receive all the credit. Designing a development system that recognizes the need to share credit for successful solicitations among staff promotes collaboration and fosters teamwork. If major gift officers and planned giving officers collaborate in solicitations, each group should receive credit for their respective participation in the process. Failure to share credit discourages teamwork, as there is little incentive to work together. The development officer must know in advance that it is a policy of the planned giving office to share credit among all participants. This policy will encourage collaboration and the sharing of information about major gift cases, especially for problem cases for which a planned gift could be a solution.

(b) Working with Nondevelopment Staff Members

Nondevelopment staff include the nonprofit's department heads, faculty, staff, deans, and others for whom development is not a full-time responsibility. As nonprofit organizations expand their search for funds, more nondevelopment staff enter into the business of seeking major gifts. See Appendix: CD-ROM Documentation, Administrative Documents for a nondevelopment staff worksheet to identify major gift prospects.

When working with nondevelopment staff and major gift prospects who are unfamiliar with life income gifts, it is important to illustrate the benefits of the gift. These benefits include not only a charitable income tax deduction and an income stream but also the value of the remainder to the nonprofit. After all, donors are making a gift, and apart from the benefits that flow to the donor, substantial benefits also flow to the nonprofit organization. Although planned giving can be complicated, some nondevelopment staff who would be uncomfortable asking for an outright major gift feel quite comfortable asking for a planned gift. The planned gift not only seems easier but also feels less confrontational, since planned giving provides tangible benefits to the donor.

The words *planned giving* are "buzzwords" among donors, nonprofit staff members, volunteers, and professional advisors. Newspaper articles in the financial press and major market dailies have helped increase the awareness of the benefits of planned giving. Planned giving has increased in value at most nonprofit organizations, and a heightened awareness has reached the level of the nondevelopment staff. In some cases, the job of a planned giving officer includes tempering optimism among overzealous but well-meaning nondevelopment staff who may be involved in major gifts. Now more than ever, the planned giving officer must offer educational programs and printed marketing materials that explain the benefits and use of planned giving, demonstrating the ways it can be used to produce major gifts. The planned giving officer must control the dissemination of information so that it is accurate and must ensure that well-meaning nondevelopment staff do not inadvertently describe or misrepresent the gift options.

(c) Trustees and Boards of Directors

Trustees, members of the board of directors, or other nonprofit administrative bodies solicit major gifts on behalf of the nonprofit organization. These individuals can help to open the door to key persons likely to be interested in a proposal outlining several options at different gift levels. Volunteers, board members, and central administration charged with raising major gifts also may be less familiar with planned giving. This is true even for volunteers with backgrounds in law or accounting and professional advisors who work in the financial community. Professional advisors associated with the nonprofit organization are exceptional candidates for a planned gift and can be influential in raising the issue of philanthropy with their clients.

These individuals are a particular challenge since by virtue of their work they may find it difficult to ask for help or to admit their lack of specific knowledge about planned giving vehicles and concepts. They often speak broadly of planned giving concepts to donors and prospects but without the specificity necessary to make the major gift occur. These volunteers seldom participate in major gift workshops or planned giving training programs. The nonprofit can solve that problem at least partially by including planned giving training as part of a regularly scheduled board meeting.

For many members of the nonprofit organization's volunteer boards, planned giving is the most attractive major gift option. These boards often are challenged to make leadership gifts in support of campaign, capital, or operating funds. A planned gift helps board members with average resources make a major gift. Working alone or with a member of the development staff, the volunteer is assigned to manage a pool of prospects. Inexperienced volunteers can forget to include planned giving as a possible option. This can occur through oversight or because of a lack of familiarity with the planned giving options. Unfortunately, the words *planned giving* do not effectively or accurately convey the true meaning. Describing services, programs, functions, and vehicles helps to communicate the concepts of planned giving. This information is helpful to nonprofit staff members and to the nonprofit's external community, such as professional advisors, committees, and boards. Planned giving orientation sessions and workshops provide practical hands-on training.

(i) Major Gift Committees. Many nonprofit organizations have established major gift committees to assist in their development efforts. Representatives on these committees consist of key board members, volunteers, major gift prospects, and members who are likely to be connected or influential in the community. Members of the major gift committee are first asked to make their own leadership major gift to support the nonprofit organization. The first goal of every major gift committee is to have 100 percent participation in giving from among the members.

Many individuals considered for membership are recruited based on their ability to give or get major gifts. Some of these individuals may make their major gift through a planned gift. The 100 percent participation is an important goal to both internal and external committees. Other nonprofit boards are influenced by the activities of a major gift committee, and external constituents respond favorably to board members who have made their own major gifts first. Planned gifts enable many donors to make larger gifts than thought previously possible. These planned gifts greatly influence other current or potential donors as well as the size of the donors' gifts. The focus of the committee is to rate and screen prospects, design and implement development strategies to produce major gifts, and assign volunteers or staff members to solicit the prospects.

A member of the nonprofit's planned giving office should have a position on the committee for the purpose of training and educating the members about planned giving options. Committee members are likely to know background information about the prospects based on the committee members' relationship to the prospects. Members of the committee may know information about the appropriate size of the major gift and the assets that can be used to fund the gift. Nevertheless, many times planned giving as a major gift option is overlooked simply because the committee lacks the assistance of a planned giving officer.

(ii) Campaign Committees. Nonprofit campaign committee members, like major gift committee members, are both donors and volunteers who undertake key solicitation assignments. The members of the committee are recruited by key nonprofit staff members. This group shapes the campaign and implements the plan of action. Typically, the committee receives extensive training in the identification, cultivation, and solicitation of major gift prospects. A planned giving training program should be included as part of the nonprofit's training program as well. Each of the planned giving options should be illustrated, and planned giving guides and newsletters should be provided to each volunteer.

These members work with other donors and prospects at the highest levels. Campaign committees traditionally use a process of sequential fundraising, meaning that gifts first are solicited at the highest levels from those with the greatest capacity to make major gifts. These first early gifts determine the size of succeeding gifts, and this is where planned giving can be used to secure major gifts for the campaign. Gifts often are packaged as a structured gift to include some or all of the following: an outright gift, life income gift, pledge, and bequest. These structured gifts ensure the success of the campaign and set the example for other donors. All of the campaign's advance gifts form the nucleus fund, proving the axiom that 90 percent of the money comes from 10 percent of the donor base. If endowment building is part of the goal of the campaign, planned giving can be a particularly attractive option. Planned gifts frequently are used to establish endowed funds to support chairs, professorships, building funds, and other campaign-oriented goals.

(iii) Planned Giving Committees. Often nonprofit organizations create planned giving committees to assist in the identification, cultivation, and solicitation of donors and prospects. The

committee assists planned giving staff members by opening up doors to key prospects known by committee members. These committees include representatives such as planned giving donors, financial planners, bank/trust officers, and representatives from the legal and accounting communities. As its name implies and by tradition, these committees tend to focus exclusively on raising planned gifts. The committees work closely with planned giving staff members, but they also may serve as volunteer ambassadors to major gift staff who may need technical assistance or to a donor who could serve as a role model to a prospect. Committee members should understand that producing planned gifts is not the exclusive objective of the committee and that outright major gifts are of even greater value. Sensitizing volunteers to the use and misuse of planned giving options can improve results, enhance gift totals, and make service on the committee more rewarding for those members and the staff.

(iv) Regional Committees. Most nonprofit organizations have groups of constituents that are organized along regional or geographic territories. These groups host regional events, enlist volunteer support, and serve as extensions of the nonprofit. Group members serve as ambassadors to others in the region and may be involved in identifying prospects. They may even engage in solutions on behalf of the nonprofit. Donors from these regions often make their gifts as part of the region's commitment to the nonprofit. In turn, regions with great giving records command more attention, respect, and services from the nonprofit. Regional support encourages the nonprofit to offer exhibits, clinics, forums, or symposiums of interest to those in the region.

Regional groups enjoy having guest speakers from the nonprofit address the group. Planned giving staff members can find this opportunity exceptionally valuable, providing the chance to hold major gift workshops and training sessions for the members. These off-site meetings also enable staff to meet with existing donors and new prospects.

(d) Other Volunteers

A donor who has made a major gift through a planned gift can be an effective role model to other donors. Most nonprofit organizations have a well-connected and influential donor who can help carry the message to others. To begin, identify an individual who is well known, who takes pride in his professional and charitable accomplishments. Ask the donor for permission to do a story documenting the donor's motivation, relationship to the nonprofit, and views on philanthropy. Arrange for an informal interview. For example, if the individual is a graduate of the College of Engineering, collaborate with that college or department to coauthor a letter to send to all graduates from the college from 1955 on back. These profiles stimulate interest, comments, and feedback and, most important, generate leads that produce major gifts. Working with the planned giving officer, this donor can make calls on behalf of the nonprofit to other interested individuals. Many donors need to be shown an example and respond well to the challenge. A planned giving officer can suggest that the volunteer solicitor make the first call and set up a follow-up by the planned giving officer, perhaps with the volunteer. In that way, both the prospect and the volunteer can hear the presentation, one that will likely provide needed information to both parties.

## CHAPTER FIFTEEN

Negotiating the Gift of a Lifetime

15.1 INTRODUCTION

One of the greatest challenges facing charities is to secure exceptionally large gifts called *gifts of a lifetime*. Few charities have prospects who have both the capacity and propensity to make a gift of $10 million or more. For gifts between $1 million and $10 million, there is still a short supply of prospects. Except for the largest and most successful nonprofit organizations, the same generally can be said of charities for prospects capable of making gifts of $100,000 to $1 million.

There are, however, individuals with significant financial resources who have the capacity to make exceptionally large gifts. Traditional prospects such as surviving spouses, retirees, alumni, patients, and friends of the nonprofit organization have significant disposable wealth, as do high-tech entrepreneurs, corporate officers, and longtime employees. The much-discussed intergenerational transfer of wealth also should be creating greater opportunities for philanthropy at higher levels. Why are there so few gifts at these levels?

The reasons are many. Many wealthy donors are fearful of the process and are reluctant to discuss charitable gift planning. Some reasons have to do with the charity's failure to market to attract these donors and the readiness and ability to deal with large gifts. Inexperienced or unprepared staff may fail to recognize the signs and the capacity of the donor. Because there are so few gifts at these levels, most development staff members, planned giving officers, and nonprofit organizations are not ready to handle such a gift. Unfortunately, when a large gift does present itself, if it is mishandled, it may become a missed opportunity. What do charities have to do to market, manage, and land a gift of a lifetime? This chapter addresses the issues involved in securing a donor's gift of a lifetime.

15.2 DEFINITION

A gift of a lifetime is the largest gift that a donor could make at one time in her lifetime. For many donors, it is the largest single financial transaction that they have ever made or will ever make. As discussed, depending on an individual's capacity to give, the amount for a gift of a lifetime could be $100,000 to $10 million or more.

Before a donor will even make a gift of a lifetime, she will want to truly understand the mission of the nonprofit organization. No donor ever parts with a significant percentage of her net worth without first knowing and understanding the contribution that the particular nonprofit organization makes to humanity. Donors who make these gifts recognize the valuable role their resources play in helping a charity fulfill its mission.

15.3 MARKETING

A key component of the office of development and planned giving is to educate constituents about the services the charity offers through marketing. Educated prospects become donors, and some of them will make gifts of a lifetime. In the absence of education, donors feel little obligation to help, and fail to see reasons to make gifts of this magnitude. Ads and buckslips inviting donors to call with questions about charitable giving may elicit responses. Many mutual fund companies have successfully positioned themselves as financial service centers, and planned giving offices might imitate their approach by presenting their office as a charitable gift planning service center for donors.

15.4 PREPARATION

Gifts of a lifetime can occur as a result of careful planning and serendipity. Be prepared for both and be willing to work "outside the box." Many very wealthy donors are unconventional in the way they go about their charitable giving.

Often a gift of a lifetime combines donor passion with the nonprofit organization's priorities. Donors are motivated to provide funding for a project that is important to them. At the same time, these projects often fulfill key priorities of the nonprofit organization. The following is a checklist to help prepare nonprofits for gifts of a lifetime:

- Educate all constituents about the services the nonprofit provides to its constituents. Communicate the nonprofit's mission to everyone involved.

- Reach those who are well known to the nonprofit along with those who are not well known. Remember that the nonprofit's public impression is affected by many factors.

- Quiet institutions that fail to communicate will receive fewer gifts and fewer gifts of a lifetime.

- Create opportunities for donors to interact with the nonprofit.

- Sensitize development and planned giving staff to identify factors that might indicate wealth and propensity to give.

- Gifts of a lifetime occur when nonprofit organizations have the ability to act efficiently and expeditiously.

- Screen and evaluate prospect pools regularly.

- Invite different groups to evaluate prospects.

- Remember that many wealthy people go about their business quietly and may not be easily identifiable.

- Casual visits to a nonprofit or routine requests for information on charitable gift planning may mean more than they initially seem.

- Be prepared for serendipity. Wealthy donors do not always follow the herd.

- Stay in touch with all prospects. Follow up on every interaction.

- Be spontaneous and flexible.

15.5 CAPACITY

Donors must have the capacity to make a gift of a lifetime. *Capacity* refers to disposable wealth. How much can the donor contribute and still remain financially viable?

Wealth can be obvious, hidden, or disguised. However, there are a number of signs that indicate a donor may have the capacity to make the gift. The following signs indicate capacity:

- Large collections of valuable tangible personal property or artwork

- Donors who travel frequently overseas

- Donors who are childless

- Surviving spouses

- Those who seek the advice of development staff about charitable gift planning issues and planned giving

- Those who ask questions about estate and gift taxes, charitable income tax deductions, and capital gains taxes

- Individuals who are eccentric or unusual compared to other donors

- Those who are highly motivated to engage in charitable giving

- Those who are students of planned giving

- Alumni, patrons, or patients with consistent giving records

- Donors who periodically but regularly make large gifts

- Individuals who make gifts of appreciated stock or mutual fund shares

- Donors who own family-run or closely held businesses

- Individuals who are entrepreneurs

- Corporate employees or officers working in technology-based corporations

- Individuals who have inherited wealth

- Prospects who have second homes, vacation homes, or rental property

- Donors who live in a family homestead that several generations have occupied

- Individuals with forest land, farmland, or hobby farms

- Donors who live on or near the water

15.6 QUALIFYING PROSPECTS

In addition to identifying prospects with the potential to make a lifetime gift, it is important to "qualify" their capacity to give. Qualifying a prospect is a delicate and important process. Public prospects—those well known within the community—are relatively easy to qualify. Judgments about their capacity can be made based on:

- Occupation/title
- Personal residence
- Real estate holdings
- Education
- Board affiliations
- Memberships
- Corporate officer, director, or board of directors member
- Financials—salary, bonus, stock holdings, stock options
- Activities, interests, hobbies
- Family resources
- Awards
- Professional organizations

Once identified, the nonprofit organization's volunteer leadership and staff can confirm or refute assumptions made about a prospect's wealth. Many nonprofits use electronic screening services to evaluate or confirm a prospect's potential.

15.7 PROPENSITY

In addition to having capacity, donors also must have the propensity to make a gift of a lifetime. Propensity focuses on the donor's likelihood of making the gift. Identifying wealthy prospects without a propensity to support a particular nonprofit will not produce gifts. Cultivating, contacting, building relationships, and educating prospects about the nonprofit organization increases a donor's propensity to make a gift. Donor cultivation, involvement with the nonprofit organization, significant philanthropic motivation, donative intent, and belief in the nonprofit all promote the likelihood of a gift occurring.

15.8 TRIGGERS

A number of life-impacting events that can trigger the gift of a lifetime. These events greatly affect the donor in either positive or negative ways. Often charitable giving provides an appropriate way to channel energy and resources. The following is a summary of events that can trigger the gift of a lifetime:

- *Family events:* birth, illness, death, divorce, marriage, or remarriage
- *Significant dates or events:* retirement, birthday, wedding anniversary, anniversary of death of a loved one, 25th/50th reunion, other life crisis events like a medical condition or journey
- *Business or professional accomplishments:* business success, promotion, start-up, sale of business, launch of an initial public offering (IPO)
- *Internal and external influences:* inheritance, stock market peaks/lows, change of employment

Once the trigger occurs, the donor may initiate the action or the donor may respond to an action initiated by the charity (see Exhibit 15.1).

Exhibit 15.1   The Lifetime Gift Cycle

The diagram depicts the development lifetime gift cycle for a gift of a lifetime. The gift cycle depicts the clockwise evolution of the donor with the nonprofit and the intervention of a significant event that usually trigger the gift. The event may be significant to either the nonprofit (capital campaign) or the donor (retirement, death of a spouse). The nonprofit usually is viewed as a resolution for the event. *Note:* The significant conflict cause or event can occur at any time.

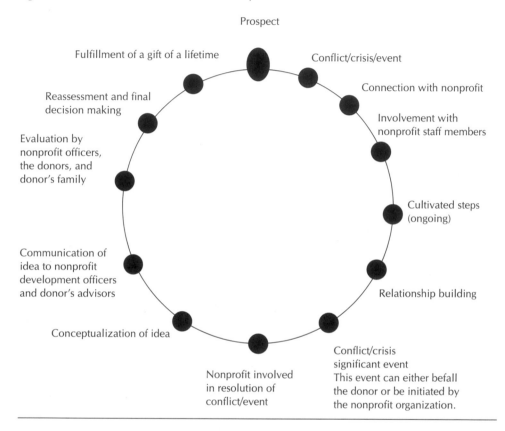

Prospect

Fulfillment of a gift of a lifetime

Conflict/crisis/event

Connection with nonprofit

Reassessment and final decision making

Involvement with nonprofit staff members

Evaluation by nonprofit officers, the donors, and donor's family

Cultivated steps (ongoing)

Communication of idea to nonprofit development officers and donor's advisors

Relationship building

Conceptualization of idea

Conflict/crisis significant event
This event can either befall the donor or be initiated by the nonprofit organization.

Nonprofit involved in resolution of conflict/event

15.9   WORKING THE GIFT THROUGH THE NONPROFIT ORGANIZATION

At some nonprofits, moving the gift through the organization is often more difficult than acquiring the gift from the donor. Nonprofit organizations are not used to dealing with the issues involved in a gift of such magnitude. Rather than greeting the donor and the gift with open arms, sometimes nonprofit organizations are paralyzed by the prospect of a gift of a lifetime. The complexity and size of these gifts can be overwhelming to some nonprofits and exhilarating to others.

To conclude a gift of a lifetime successfully, the planned giving officer or development officer must keep the nonprofit moving at the same pace the donor is moving. There is no benefit to moving the donor forward if the nonprofit is not at the same point. Gifts of a lifetime require synchronized management of both the donor and the nonprofit organization. Because of their size and complexity, several officials with the nonprofit organization are likely to have a voice in the cultivation and solicitation process.

15.10 DEALING WITH THE DONOR

(a) President

At a nonprofit, the most critical leadership position is the president, chief executive officer, or chancellor, depending on the organization. It is important for this individual to be involved in gifts in excess of $1 million at large nonprofits and for gifts of $100,000 or more at smaller ones. In addition, for any gift of which the donor is motivated to provide funding for a project of personal interest, it is essential to have the president endorse the project. For example, if a donor is championing a project that is outside the nonprofit's priority list, it is critical to have the president participate. Once a project is approved, the presidential seal of support will help the project move forward quickly within the organization.

Nonprofit organizations, especially large public ones, adhere to time-tested processes and are sometimes less responsive to donor-initiated projects. Public nonprofits include state-assisted universities, hospitals, and cultural and arts organizations. Private nonprofits are likely to be more responsive to donor-initiated projects because they depend so heavily on private support. Presidents cut through red tape and move gifts through the system.

(b) Vice-President of Development

At most nonprofits, the vice-president of development plays a pivotal role in gifts of a lifetime. In the event of a conflict within the institution, the vice-president of development can serve as an advocate on behalf of the donor to articulate the importance of the project to both the donor and the nonprofit. The vice-president negotiates and approves most agreements between donors and the nonprofit.

(c) Board of Trustees

The nonprofit's governing board is responsible for policymaking and for governance of the nonprofit. In addition, the board typically is responsible for approving all naming opportunities through which a donor's funds will be used to name a building or other capital project, or for approving major donor-initiated projects. Any large or complicated gift should have the approval of the chairman of the board and president.

15.10 DEALING WITH THE DONOR

Gifts of a lifetime can result from a calculated, structured "moves management" manner or they may emerge serendipitously. Of course, few gifts are truly serendipitous. Many gifts that appear to be serendipitous actually were a response to hard work sustained over a long time, marketing efforts, volunteer involvement, or the positive public image of the nonprofit. They may also develop from a combination of approaches.

As donors age, especially donors with sizable estates, they often spend considerable time studying estate planning issues. Wealthy donors are likely to consider these estate and tax planning issues:

- To whom should I transfer my estate?
- How much should each beneficiary receive?
- Which nonprofits have played an important role in my life?
- To whom shall I transfer my personal property? Artwork? Collections?
- How much can I afford to give?
- Over what time frame?
- What are the tax consequences of my gift?
- How can I fund the gift?
- When does groundbreaking on the project start?
- How does this affect my family or other projects?

After contemplating these issues, donors are often motivated to answer these questions, and if they are philanthropic, which many are, they may seek the advice of planned giving officers. A planned giving officer should consider the following:

- Listen carefully/engage in fact finding.
- Identify donor's goals.
- Identify family members, friends, and professional advisors who will assist donor.
- Evaluate all possible projects and their costs.
- Know the nonprofit organization's needs.
- Identify projects at high levels (and all levels) in need of funding.
- Develop subject matter funding needs.
- Consider nonprofit buildings that could house a donor's collection/papers.
- Become familiar with the nonprofit's physical plant and its naming opportunities.
- Be open-minded about a range of possible alternatives/seek new ways to do business.
- Use imagination.
- Ask others for advice.
- Collaborate with colleagues.

15.11 CHARITABLE GIVING AND FAMILY DYNAMICS

Family members also need to be included in discussion rather than left on the sidelines. Absentee spouses or other family members can impede progress. It is best to include members of the donor's family who are likely to influence the donor. Although charitable giving is an intensely personal issue, most donors' families greatly influence not only the size of the gift, but also the designation of that gift. Unmarried individuals or individuals who live with a partner also may need assistance from members of their family unit. For most large gifts, families operate in concert. Large gifts affect the availability of disposable income, and gifts to nonprofit organizations reduce resources that could be transferred to other family members such as children, nieces, nephews, and parents. Often, when family members learn more about charitable giving, they feel more comfortable with the concept of making a gift. They can share in the process to make it truly a family gift.

15.12 DEALING WITH A DONOR'S ADVISORS AND FAMILY

In most cases, the donor's decision to make a gift of a lifetime to a charitable organization will be influenced by the donor's friends, mentors, and professional advisors. This section starts by looking at those professionals who may have an opinion about the donor's gift. Then it moves to friends and mentors and the impact they may have on a donor's gift giving.

(a) Professional Advisors

Professional advisors are likely to have significant influence over the donor's decisions. These decisions include the way the gift will be funded, the assets used to fund the gift, and the timing of the gift. It is important to proactively bring advisors into the gift process. Leaving them on the sidelines increases the chances that they may become obstructionists.

Increasingly, professional advisors are becoming more involved in advising donors about their philanthropy. Planned giving and charitable gift planning seem complicated to practitioners who seldom become involved in charitable gift planning. Identifying qualified and competent advisors knowledgeable in charitable gift planning is critical. Beware of professional advisors who are unfamiliar with charitable gift planning techniques. Be cautious about advisors who divert the donor's attention to unacceptable alternatives or of those who discourage the donor from making a charitable gift. If they advise the donor against making the gift, make sure it is for the right reasons.

(b) Attorney

The donor's attorney can be helpful or hurtful when it comes to philanthropy. Most attorneys do not specialize in the field of charitable gift planning and may be unfamiliar with planned giving techniques. Even attorneys who are knowledgeable in estate planning and taxation may not understand the fine nuances associated with making a charitable gift. If they have a strong background in estate planning and taxation, they may be familiar with charitable giving, or those practicing in a large firm may be able to draw on the expertise of other lawyers in their firm who have a stronger charitable gift planning background.

The donor's attorney should be able to provide advice on how the gift fits into the donor's overall estate plan, the tax impact, and whether the gift should be made this year, next year, or spread over a number of years. The attorney may need to draft trust documents, such as a charitable remainder trust or a charitable lead trust. She should review gift or estate planning documents, endowed fund descriptions, gift annuity contracts, or pledge agreements. The charity's planned giving officer should work with the attorney to make the job easier.

(c) Stockbroker/Mutual Fund Companies

Stockbrokers, brokerage companies, and mutual fund companies are actively becoming involved in the charitable business. Many offer charitable gift accounts and information on the gift planning process. Because their income may be derived from the sale of products, they may not be eager to transfer assets out of the donor's account to a charity if that transfer will not trigger a commission. If their compensation is derived based on the value of all assets under management, their compensation may be reduced when assets are transferred to a charity.

(d) Certified Public Accountant

In most cases, the donor's certified public accountant (CPA) is familiar with the donor's tax situation. The CPA may be an excellent source of information about the donor's capacity to utilize charitable income and estate or gift tax deductions.

(e) Trust Officer

Trust officers may be in a position to help with a donor's charitable giving. This is especially true if most of the donor's income is in a trust, managed by this trust officer. Because many trust large trust companies or banks employ officers, they generally have resources to assist in estate planning and tax planning.

(f) Friends and Mentors

Friends and mentors, especially those who are philanthropic, can serve as a sounding board for individuals who are considering making a major gift or for those who are uncertain about which charity to support. These advisors may know individuals who serve on boards of charities and may understand the workings of a particular charity. Friends and mentors also may have colleagues and associates who have experience in philanthropy, and they may be helpful in providing information on charities that the donor is considering. For truly large gifts, most donors ask for the advice of at least one mentor or friend. Identify friends and mentors the donor relies on and, with the donor's permission, include them in at least one meeting.

15.13 FUNDING

If the donor's gift is a gift of a lifetime, the donor is likely to use a variety of charitable gift planning strategies and fund the gift using both an outright and a planned gift. In addition, the donor is most likely to use cash, appreciated stock, real estate, tangible personal property, or a combination of each. Many donors use a combination of several options and assets and make a structured gift. A structured gift consists of at least two of the following:

- Outright gift
- Life income gift (charitable gift annuity, deferred gift annuity, pooled income fund)
- Charitable remainder trust
- Charitable lead trust
- Bequest
- Pledge agreement

Structured gifts help make gifts of a lifetime affordable. They also allow the donor to make the gift over several years to maximize the benefits of charitable income tax deductions. The structured gift is described in Chapter 53.

15.14 TERMS OF THE GIFT

The terms of the gift should be documented in a written agreement or memorandum of understanding. These issues can be included:

- The amount of the gift
- Deadlines or timetable for donor to fulfill the gift requirements
- Finalizing the gift option, payout rate, planned gifts
- Donor's benefits, naming opportunities, plaques, lettering
- Purpose of gift
- Criteria for selection
- Documentation/agreements
- Restrictions and conditions
- Recognition/publicity

15.15 CONCLUSION

Gifts of a lifetime are rewarding to both the donor and the charity. These gifts promote permanent relationships between donors and charities. Properly planned, these gift provide mutual benefits for truly committed donors who wish to share their financial resources with worthy charities. Nonprofit organizations need to prepare for such an opportunity, anticipate donors' concerns, and identify ways to meet the challenges. Work within the charity to develop an organized approach to facilitate the gift. Realize that wealthy donors may conduct their business in nontraditional ways. Recognize the signs of wealth, and remember that wealth can be disguised. Gifts of a lifetime require organizational cooperation on behalf of the nonprofit. Nonprofits also must recognize the important role played by the donor's family members, friends, and advisors.

## CHAPTER SIXTEEN

Women as Planned Giving Donors

16.1 INTRODUCTION

Today women control approximately one-half of our nation's wealth. This is due to a combination of factors. Women outlive men by about seven years and on average become widows at just age 57. Some are inheriting money earlier; many are entering the workforce in record numbers. Women now head up Fortune 500 companies and own their own businesses. In addition to their own wealth, women are having more and more influence over corporate and foundation giving. And women are better educated now than ever before. Everyone has heard that trillions of dollars will be transferred from generation to generation over the next several years. Ask: Is the charitable organization, planned giving program, and staff doing enough to attract, maintain, and engage women in the philanthropic process?

16.2 GENDER-BASED DIFFERENCES IN GIVING

There are differences in ways that men and women benefit charitable organizations. Many female donors have different employment patterns from men, have often raised children and been removed from the workplace, and may have different financial challenges and therefore make their gifts differently. The planned giving program needs to take a look at this special donor group and examine why, how, and where female donors make charitable gifts.

16.3 WOMEN'S ACCESS TO WEALTH

A nonprofit organization should look closely at how a particular female prospect or donor has acquired her wealth. Like most donors—male or female—the donor is most likely to have obtained her money in one or a combination of ways: inheritance, marriage, and/or earned income. Consider asking these questions about the source of the prospect's or donor's wealth.

(a) Inheritance

- Has the donor/prospect inherited wealth?

- Does the donor's family have a history of philanthropy?

- Have the donor and her family given to this or another charitable organization over a sustained period of time?

- Is there a major naming opportunity (such as a building or program) at the organization named after the donor's family?

- Is there a way to increase or, if advantageous, redirect the donor's current giving?

- Will the donor's gifts continue when older family members die?

(b) Marriage

- What was the donor's financial situation before her marriage?

- Which spouse is making the decisions about philanthropy, or is it a joint decision?

- Do the spouses enjoy a good marriage?

- Will the giving to the charitable organization begin, end, or continue once the spouse dies?

- Is the charitable organization doing enough to engage the female spouse as a donor or volunteer in her own right?

(c) Earned Income

- Is the donor young?

- Is her wealth recently acquired?

- Is this donor still working? Should the donor be approached differently than a traditional solicitation of an older donor?

- Does this woman have specific expectations about how her money will be used?

- Is the donor in a job that will allow her earnings to continue at the same level?

16.4 FINANCIAL CHALLENGES FOR WOMEN

Women often have different financial concerns from men. They look at money differently and perhaps for good reason. Traditionally, women have been less involved in the household's financial decisions and feel less educated or certain about finances and investments. Many older women left financial decisions to their father, husband, or a trusted outside advisor. Life today has changed, and so has women's views of finances.

Because women live longer than men, they need to manage their money for potentially a long time, perhaps doing so without earning any income. Women who work still earn less than men who have the same job—about 25 cents less on every dollar earned. Most women's retirement plans trail their husband's; many women began to work later in life, after caring for children, and some worked just part time. Divorce rates also have contributed to women having less income. All of these realities affect how some women may view money and therefore charitable gifts and philanthropy.

16.5 TYPES OF DONORS

In addition to determining how a donor gained her money, examine other factors about the donor's life. This will help to determine her different motivations for giving, as well as help decide what approach to take with the donor, type of planned gift vehicle to suggest, and other parties, if any, to involve in the gift process.

(a) Surviving Spouse

- Is the donor a surviving spouse?
- Did the donor's spouse make gifts to the organization?
- Has the female donor continued to make gifts to the charitable organization?
- Does she support the same or different areas from her spouse?
- Is the organization stewarding the donor as a donor in her own right?

(b) Childless

- Does the donor have children?
- Is the donor looking to the organization as a substitute heir?
- Has the donor done sufficient estate planning that may include a bequest to the charitable organization?
- Is the charitable organization prepared and able to steward the donor for many years?

(c) Married with Children

- Is the donor's relationship with her children a strong one, or are they estranged?
- How old are the children?
- Do the children have independent financial means?
- Should any or all of the children be invited to participate in the gift process?
- Should the children be stewarded separately from the donor?
- Are the children prospects?

(d) Professional Women

- What is the woman's age?
- Is she married?

- Does she have children?

- How has she acquired her money?

- Is her earned wealth relatively new?

- Does she have time to be involved with the charitable organization?

- Is she familiar with planned giving concepts?

- How does she spend her free time? Does she have hobbies? Sit on any nonprofit boards?

- With whom does she socialize?

16.6 MOTIVATIONS FOR GIVING

Both women and men give for all types of reasons. Women may give to honor or memorialize the deceased. They may give because they feel that they owe a debt to the charitable organization. They may give for social standing or prestige. When examining a woman's charitable interest, try to determine her motivation. This will help determine how best to approach the prospect or donor and how best to cultivate and steward her. Following are some common motivations for most women's charitable gifts.

(a) Strong Relationship with Charity

Most women want to have a strong relationship with the charitable organization they support. Often they first work as volunteers or board members at the organization before giving any significant financial support. They learn about the organization from the inside and grow to know a lot about it. Many women see their gifts as a step forward in an ongoing relationship with the charity, helping to build a stronger relationship.

(b) Effecting Change

Many women see their philanthropic support as a way to make social changes, both at the organization and for the greater societal good. They want to see their gift make a difference in creating new attitudes, structures, and ways of doing business. They want to make a difference for people: in their education, healthcare, outlook, ability to learn, and quality of life.

(c) Seeing Results

Women may be more interested in accountability for their gifts than are their male counterparts. They want the charitable organization to be accountable for what is being done with the gift. Some women, especially younger women who have earned their wealth, may want to maintain some control over their gift once they have given it to the charity.

(d) Giving with Heart

Women tend to give with their heart. They are passionate about the cause they support. They like to invest personally in what they benefit. They usually do not make gifts and then walk away; women tend to invest their time and energy in the cause. They are also more likely to help during a crisis or disaster and to volunteer or serve on boards of charities that they support.

(e) Giving for Business Reasons

Women are earning more money, owning their own businesses, managing large corporations, and using their philanthropy to advance their careers. They are willing to "pay to play" when related to business. This type of female donor is more motivated to make a major gift.

16.7 GIFT PLANNING IMPLICATIONS

As seen above, women may relate to philanthropy and charitable giving differently than their male counterparts do. Consequently, the cultivation and solicitation process may be quite different. The following sections examine some specific ideas for nonprofit organizations to focus on when pursuing and dealing with female donors.

(a) Role of the Planned Giving Officer

It is wise for the planned giving officer, as well as the charitable organization, to pay attention to female donors and prospects. Female donors are perfect for planned giving arrangements. As planned giving donors or prospects, they are likely to be involved with the organization for a long time and enjoy the ongoing relationship. If the planned giving officer is a woman, she may connect as a woman with the female donor. However, some women prefer working with a male. Whether male or female, the planned giving officer should work on building the relationship with the female prospect or donor and plan to invest in the relationship over time.

(b) Building/Maintaining the Relationship

The charity's relationship with the female donor may take some time to develop and must be nurtured over an extended period of time. Continued contact over time is very important, as are regular personal visits. If the donor lives far from the charitable organization, a thoughtful memento from the organization is likely to be appreciated. Invest the time with the donor to bring her closer to the organization. If possible, get her involved in some way if she is not already involved with the charity. Consider her participation as a board member, committee member, or volunteer.

(c) Educating Female Donors and Prospects

Consider offering educational seminars about both the organization and charitable gift planning. These seminars can help women learn more about finances and investments, and make them feel part of a larger group that gives to the charitable organization, furthering their connection to the organization. Do not promote these as seminars "for women only," but as seminars for donors to the organization, alumni of the school, or patients of the hospital. Consider having a female speaker for the group.

(d) Stewardship

Because women tend to build and maintain a relationship to the organization, the nonprofit needs to be prepared to steward the donor or prospect over a long period of time. When staff members leave, a new connection in the development office should be made for the donor. The nonprofit should be careful to include those trusted by the donor, such as a spouse, advisor, child, or friend, in the gift process. Continue to cultivate the individual contacts the donor has with the organization, whether a favorite teacher, physician, or administrator. Be cautious about the way correspondence is addressed from the organization to the donor—some women may be particularly sensitive to not being included in correspondence to their husband, not being thanked, or being addressed in letters incorrectly as "Mr." or "Ms." if she prefers Mrs., and vice versa. Mistakes in stewardship can lead to a donor who no longer wishes to give—not because the donor no longer cares about the organization, but because she feels undervalued.

16.8 TYPES OF PLANNED GIFTS TO CONSIDER FOR THE FEMALE DONOR

Female donors' gifts to charity can take a variety of forms. These include bequests as well as life income gifts. In particular, consider the following gift options, which a nonprofit organization may find particularly appeal to female donors.

(a) Bequests

Bequests are generally one of the most popular gift options for female donors. Because some women may wish to preserve principal and are willing to take less risk than men, the bequest allows them to make a potentially large philanthropic gift, but hold on to their assets while living, in case they need the resources. This is a legitimate concern for women, knowing that they live longer and may suffer from more debilitating diseases as they grow older.

Encourage the female donor to begin with a charitable bequest to the organization. She will not be giving any money away now, but will be connected to the charitable organization over her lifetime. As her relationship to the nonprofit grows, consider soliciting her for a life income gift.

(b) Charitable Gift Annuities

When considering life income options, older female donors also tend to like the charitable gift annuity. Because this option provides the donor with a fixed, guaranteed rate of return, it responds to a cautious donor's wish to be able to count on having a set amount of income. Charitable gift annuities are also popular because the older donor receives a high rate of return, usually higher than many fixed-income investment vehicles, making them attractive to both women and men.

(c) Donor-Advised Funds, Supporting Organizations, and Private Foundations

As women are earning more money and becoming more involved in making their own decisions about philanthropy, organizations are likely to see an increase in the use of different giving vehicles by women. Giving options such as donor-advised funds, supporting organizations, and private foundations allow a donor more control over her giving, which many women—especially young women who have earned their wealth—seem to want. The nonprofit will be in a better position to accept these potentially large gifts if it understands the differences among the gift options and can offer them to certain donors.

16.9 WOMEN AND CHILDREN: THEIR PHILANTHROPY

If the charitable organization can offer something—like a philanthropy day for families at the charity or a course on family philanthropy—that helps female donors teach their children about philanthropy or involve them in charitable giving, the organization may have a distinct advantage. Many women learned about philanthropy at home and want to teach their children how to be responsible members of society who can benefit the world by giving of themselves and their money. Many women want to begin teaching their children with "hands-on" philanthropy: making food baskets for hungry families, collecting warm clothing for needy families, making baked goods for school fairs. Many mothers want to have their children see them as role models, helping others and leading by example.

Look for ways at the organization to bring families together in their giving. This also helps to educate the next generation about the organization. As a donor's children age and the family finances increase, the charitable organization may become a beneficiary of a family foundation or private foundation. When realistic, and when it will further the organization's interests, make giving a family affair. Be sure to recognize families for their support to the charity. Recognition dinners are great opportunities to honor families for their commitment.

16.10 WORKING WITH ADVISORS

There is likely to be someone else involved in any woman's philanthropy. As the planned giving officer, identify advisors, colleagues, and friends who may be involved, when appropriate. Include them in donor correspondences, meetings, solicitations, and visits to and from the charitable organization. The trusted advisor may be an outsider (e.g., a lawyer, certified financial planner, or certified public accountant), a family member (e.g., spouse, child, parent, or sibling), or even someone not in the room or not alive, such as the donor's husband or father urging the donor to give because this is what the husband or father would have wanted.

Because the planned giving officer often works with someone other than the donor when closing a gift, make sure that the real decision maker continues to remain in the process and is really making the philanthropic decisions. Sometimes a trusted advisor can go a bit too far, trying to work a deal, for example, and thwart the donor's interest in making a charitable gift. If this is happening, try to regroup and bring all of the players back together in the room to talk about the donor's wishes to benefit the organization.

16.11 CONCLUSION

Recognize that women and men approach and execute charitable giving differently. Women have various motivations for giving, make different kinds of gifts, and hope for certain results from their gift giving. Work with female donors to highlight these differences. Know the donor, her background, and her motivations for making charitable gifts. Engage family members and children when appropriate. Also, try to identify advisors who may be helping the donor make her gift.

## CHAPTER SEVENTEEN

Family Philanthropy:
Issues and Solutions

17.1   INTRODUCTION

Like many individuals, most donors operate as part of a family unit. Some families interact beautifully and have similar views about philanthropy. Other families have disparate views about philanthropy, and situations can occur where parents want to be philanthropic and their children are resentful about a prospective inheritance being given to charity. Other situations involve donors who have no children and wish to leave their money to a charity, and use advisors to help determine whether they should make a gift and the best way to give. Other family-related donor situations include families that agree about philanthropy and as a group support specific charitable endeavors. Planned giving officers must learn to work with all types of family units because they are likely to encounter all of these situations and more.

This chapter takes a broad look at philanthropy and families and how philanthropic objectives can be affected by intrafamily relations. It explores what planned giving officers should know before dealing with each type of donor situation outlined above, solutions to various obstacles, positive outcomes for involving families in philanthropy, and some gift options to use to engage families in giving.

17.2   ROLE OF THE PLANNED GIVING OFFICER

What is the role of the planned giving officer in various family dynamics? First, it is to close a gift for the organization if it is right for both the donor who wishes to make a gift and the charitable organization. The planned giving officer's role may also involve working with different family members, other than the donor, to ensure that the gift takes place and is a positive experience and has a positive outcome for all family members. If an advisor is involved, the planned giving officer's job may include helping the advisor to understand the gift process and be able to help complete the gift. Working with family members in philanthropic endeavors also may result in cultivating and stewarding family members who are not the actual donors, but are affected by the gift to the charitable organization.

17.3 BEFORE MEETING WITH THE DONOR

Gift scenarios evolve in a variety of ways. Some typical scenarios include: a prospect who calls and would like to talk about making a gift to the charitable organization; a prospect's responding to a charitable gift annuity advertisement; and the chief development officer asking for help with a donor situation. Among other things what, in the beginning, should the planned giving officer know?

After learning about the donor's age, connection to the charity, and program or project the donor wishes to benefit, determine what motivates the donor to make a gift. This should include the donor's general attitudes/motivations/feelings about philanthropy: Why does he wish to make a gift? Is she trying to give something back? Does he feel that he owes a debt? Is she looking for social recognition?

Recognize that family dynamics may affect whether the charitable gift is actually completed. The planned giving officer needs to determine who is making the gift. Is the prospect capable to make a gift? Does she own the property she wishes to give away? Then, who are the family members? Are there children/parents/siblings who will know about the gift? Will they be involved in the decision making around the gift? Are they for or against such a gift? Are there second marriages, stepchildren, and other relatives to explore? The planned giving officer needs to understand the donor's family philosophy, history, and feelings about gift giving. Is the donor making a gift to bring family members closer together, or could it force them apart? Is there a history of family philanthropy? Has any family member given to the charitable organization? These questions may not have answers initially, but the planned giving officer needs to try to determine these relationships and attitudes.

Checklist

- Determine who is making the gift.

- Identify immediate family members:
  - Mother
  - Father
  - Children
  - Siblings
  - Previous marriages

- Determine if there is past giving from any family members.

- Note any connection of family members to the organization.

17.4 FAMILIES IN SYNC/HARMONY

Family members who view philanthropy in the same way did not get that way by chance. Similar family values and a close family system draw individual family members together, resulting in shared values and a respect for each others' opinions. The family unit that together wishes to make a charitable gift is the most ideal and easiest for the planned giving officer to handle and learn from.

(a)   Working with the Philanthropically Compatible Family

The planned giving officer working with a harmonious family should work to bring all family members who are interested into the charitable gift process. Working with several family members may be more work for the planned giving officer to manage, but will be worth it in the end. Strive to steward all family members. The result should be a happy, satisfied family that is pleased with an initial gift and may wish to give again. The planned giving officer may see additional gifts from other family members (e.g., a son and his wife, grandparents), as well as future gifts at death.

It is relatively easy to involve all family members in the gift process. If the primary donor concurs, the planned giving officer can copy other family members on gift-related correspondence; recognize family members through a naming opportunity, such as a building, wing, or plaque; or include family names in an endowed fund. All family members should be invited to stewardship events, placed on mailing lists, and cultivated like prospects.

17.5   FAMILIES OUT OF SYNC/HARMONY

If all families were in perfect harmony, the planned giving officer would not need to read this next section. While ideal, rarely are donor situations easy, straightforward, or made up of family members who see things in the same way. It can be quite challenging for the planned giving officer to deal with and try to solve family issues related to philanthropy, which are rooted in family dynamics that have been in play long before the donor or prospect walked into the planned giving office.

What types of issues could the planned giving officer encounter? Potential challenging gift scenarios include:

- A donor who wishes to make a gift but jointly owns the property to be gifted with another family member who does not wish to make the gift

- A donor who is philanthropically oriented but his spouse is not

- A parent donor who wishes to make a gift but has children who are not philanthropic

- A donor who is philanthropic and whose family and/or advisor is not philanthropic and is suspicious of the charitable organization and its representatives

- A donor or prospect who becomes ill and a nonphilanthropic family member receives a power of attorney and does not intend to honor the donor's wishes

- A donor or donors whose children are alienated from their parents and later challenge a will that is leaving little or nothing to them because the bulk of the estate is going to a nonprofit organization

- A second marriage in which the second spouse is not supportive of the spouse's philanthropic interests

- A second marriage with a younger spouse (often the wife) who has children from a previous marriage or has children with the donor and prefers to see the donor's money remain in the family

Most experienced planned giving officers have seen these situations one or more times over the years. Some situations can be resolved while other times, no matter how hard the planned giving officer tries, the situation cannot be resolved. Consider the basic concepts below when working with families that are out of sync philanthropically.

17.5 FAMILIES OUT OF SYNC/HARMONY

(a) Concepts to Remember When Working with Families

- The decision to make a philanthropic gift belongs to the donor. It is not the spouse's, child's, planned giving officer's, or charitable organization's decision to make a gift.

- The ultimate decision to make a major gift may be seriously affected or threatened by the donor's other relationships, especially family and advisor relationships.

- Major and planned gifts take time; the planned giving officer who stays with the prospect over time may see positive results, but not necessarily quickly.

- Outside advisors can both tremendously help and hurt a potential gift. Advisors have a powerful impact on how they affect their clients. This can be unfortunate when a donor is philanthropically motivated and the advisor is not. Charitably minded advisors can be a great help in sorting out issues, distinguishing among personalities, and making difficult statements to family members.

(b) Strategies to Deal with Out-of-Sync Families

The planned giving officer should consider these five approaches in working with donors who have families that are not harmonious philanthropically:

1. *Evaluate the family.* Try to discover the way the family makes decisions and determine the family's hierarchy and leaders. Who is in charge and is likely to ultimately decide whether the gift will be made? Is the planned giving officer working with the real decision maker? A son working on behalf of his parents who wish to make a gift of real estate may not view things in the same way the parents do. The son may have his own agenda about the property that may not properly reflect the parents' thought process.

   An interesting donor situation that clearly illustrates this point involved a family that wished to make a charitable gift in memory of a daughter who had died in a terrible plane crash. While the immediate family grieved, the girl's uncle was placed in charge of the gift process. He seemed more motivated to work a deal to complete the gift than to actually make the gift. Once the planned giving officers were able to meet with the girl's mother—the ultimate decision maker—the gift was quickly completed.

   The planned giving officer also may want to examine individual family members to evaluate the potential impact that a major gift will have on a family member. For example, is there a child who would prefer to keep the philanthropic funds in the family? Would social recognition for this family member make it easier for her to make the gift? If so, consider how to recognize this family member in a public way.

2. *Include other family members.* The donor knows his family members best. If the donor suggests bringing various family members into the gift process, do so with the intent to embrace and steward the family members with the hope that they will feel favorable toward the charity. If the donor recommends leaving family members out of the philanthropic discussion, it is probably best to do so since it could actually hurt the process. The planned giving officer should take his or her cue from the donor.

3. *Engage the spouse.* It may be possible to engage a reluctant spouse in an organizational activity that will bring the spouse closer to the charitable organization. If she can become involved in an activity that she can call her own, it may create some enthusiasm and support for the organization. Begin by bringing the reluctant spouse into the organization through her spouse's philanthropic interests. As the planned giving officer begins to know the spouse better, determine the spouse's own interests and see what might be a strong philanthropic interest to cultivate. If the spouse is already connected to the organization, work to grow that connection.

4. *Legal safeguards.* If the donors are estranged from family members such as children who could challenge a will, protect the charity's gift in advance of a potential challenge. Work with the donor and his or her attorney to draft a will that addresses such issues. If necessary, have the donor's physician draft a note that can be placed in the donor's legal file stating that the donor was of sound mind when his or her will was made. Some donors use videotape recordings to preserve their state of mind at the time they draft a will if they expect challenges to their will.

5. *Involve an advisor.* If a family dynamic becomes too difficult to manage, an outside third-party advisor—often a lawyer, certified public accountant, or financial advisor who knows the family—may be helpful. The charitably minded advisor can be a great help in sorting out issues, distinguishing among personalities, and making statements to family members that the planned giving officer cannot say. Both the planned giving officer and the advisor must remember that it is the donor's decision to make a charitable gift; the decision does not belong to the advisor, who should ultimately try to help the donor satisfy his or her philanthropic wishes.

17.6 DONORS WITHOUT CHILDREN

A third type of family dynamic is the donor who does not have children. Not having children eliminates some hurdles for the planned giving officer, but can create others. When no children exist, they cannot prevent a gift from occurring. However, the planned giving officer can face some of these challenges from childless couples or individuals:

- An advisor with too much power. The advisor can step in and take on such a significant role that the planned giving officer may need to treat the advisor like a family member, because this is the way the donor regards the advisor.

- Many donors, whether childless or not, can be very needy. They demand the planned giving officer's time, attention, and praise. Donors who are older without children can rely on the planned giving officer as they do another friend or neighbor, which can blur the business relationship. Planned giving officers need to remember their primary role of representing the charity to secure a gift, not playing the role of a caretaker to a donor. Be aware of donor situations in which the planned giving officer is near the age of a donor's child or deceased/estranged child. This can foster an uncomfortable relationship if it veers from a professional to personal relationship.

- Donors without children often wish to make their legacy through a charitable gift and want recognition. The planned giving officer needs to offer a variety of recognition opportunities to capture the donors' interest. Named funds, plaques on buildings, and annual named lectureships can satisfy sought-after recognition.

- Where there are no children, other relatives may become quite important to the gift process. Eagerly include in stewardship opportunities loved ones who are fondly mentioned—a sister from Nebraska, an aunt from out of town. They can easily be invited to recognition events if the donor is interested in including them.

17.7 POSITIVE OUTCOMES FOR CHILDREN
FROM FAMILY PHILANTHROPY

If a family works together in its philanthropy, the members are likely to become a closer family unit, spending time and making decisions together. It is especially smart when parents can introduce their children to philanthropy at a young age. Benefits to the children include understanding and making decisions about philanthropic gifts to help others; learning about and connecting with the community; teaching them responsibility; understanding money; fostering leadership skills; building self-esteem; and helping them with their decision-making skills.

17.8 TOOLS FOR CONTINUING AND MAINTAINING FAMILY PHILANTHROPY

There are many different ways that families can engage in philanthropic decisions together, regardless of whether children are 5 or 50 years old. Bringing the family together to make philanthropic decisions gives family members more time together and enhances their communication. Whatever combination of philanthropic tools is used, parents should try to expose children to regular discussions about philanthropy; allow children to make some of the ultimate decisions about family philanthropy; be encouraged to participate in nonprofit site visits; and meet some of the recipients of the family's philanthropy. Families that are unable or unwilling to give financially can stay actively involved in philanthropy by volunteering at a nonprofit on a regular basis. A family can work together in a shelter, literacy program, or hospital. In addition, families can provide used clothing to people in need, donate blood on a regular basis, or bake brownies for the local firefighters for the holidays.

17.9 GIFT OPTIONS FOR FAMILY PHILANTHROPY

A number of gift options can help to foster philanthropy for family members. Private foundations, supporting organizations, and donor-advised funds are three to consider.

(a) Private Foundations

A private foundation is one mechanism for making family decisions about philanthropy. A private foundation may be an attractive option for families that have a substantial amount of resources, because the start-up costs and maintenance fees (legal fees, paperwork, filings) are expensive.

The private foundation offers donors a great amount of control over their giving. The family can form a board for the foundation that can be private and hand-picked by the family. Family members stay together over time to make philanthropic decisions and can choose which charities to benefit and do so with lots of freedom and spontaneity.

(b) Supporting Organizations

By establishing a supporting organization, a family chooses one or more charitable organizations to benefit. The supporting organization may support more than one nonprofit, but the nonprofits must be named at the time the supporting organization is established. The supporting organization will provide a family with less control than a private foundation, but there are fewer restrictions in making and maintaining a gift.

(c) Donor-Advised Funds

Through a donor-advised fund, a family can create a named fund with a charitable institution. Donors can make only nonbinding recommendations to the charitable organization for distributions from the fund. Most donor-advised funds can be established for a small amount of money, and the donors have flexibility in the timing of their gifts.

(d) Named Family Funds

A named family fund created at one or more individual charities is an excellent way to promote on-going family philanthropy for donors of modest means. Most nonprofits have a minimum of $25,000 or $50,000 to create a fund that can benefit one or more areas at the charity in the donors' name or in the name of a loved one who has passed away. Once the decision is made about where to establish a named fund, the family can make annual gifts in lieu of birthdays, anniversaries, and holidays. The family should visit the nonprofit and meet with its representatives at least once a year to receive updates on how the fund is progressing; meet its recipients; and tour any laboratories, libraries, classrooms, or projects that are benefiting from the family's philanthropy.

17.10 CONCLUSION

Family dynamics can play an important role in a donor's gift. Determine what type of family relationships exist and whether other family members may be involved in the gift process. Follow the strategies outlined in this chapter to help close the planned gift.

PART FOUR

Marketing

## CHAPTER EIGHTEEN

Drafting Planned Giving Documents

18.1 INTRODUCTION[1]

For planned giving officers and development staff members, developing documents is an important part of the job. Nonprofit employees must develop documents that take many forms, including the drafting of detailed proposals describing complicated gift options, marketing materials, correspondence to donors, professional advisors and staff members, exhibits, agreements, presentation materials, and IRS and tax-related documents. This chapter will help employees of development organizations draft, design, and develop a variety of documents that can accomplish their organization's goals.

Documents serve many purposes. They attract donors and prospects, help to deliver the nonprofit organization's message, and present charitable gift options in a professional manner. Documents also can enhance the image of the planned giving office and influence the public's perception of the nonprofit organization. Most important, thoughtful and well-written documents help to sustain and nurture relationships over time with those donors who share common goals with the nonprofit organization.

This chapter provides an organizational overview of the types of documents contained in the CD-ROM. In addition, this chapter discusses the issues that readers should consider while preparing documents, and it provides suggestions for developing good writing practices within an organization.

The CD-ROM contains over 250 documents to assist nonprofit development staff, mentors,

[1]This chapter is coauthored by Stephen A. Bernhardt, Ph.D., holder of the Andrew B. Kirkpatrick chair in Writing, University of Delaware, Department of English. He is coauthor with Edward L. Smith of *Writing at Work: Professional Skills for People on the Job*, NTC Publishing Group, Lincolnwood, Illinois, 1997.

and planned giving officers in their jobs. These documents serve as models, or templates, to be used in planned giving and development. The documents are divided into seven categories:

1. Marketing

2. Agreements

3. Administrative Documents

4. Correspondence

5. Exhibits

6. Presentations

7. Tax and IRS Documents

Each category is defined and exemplified in the next section.

18.2 TYPES OF DOCUMENTS

Planned giving officers prepare many types of documents for a variety of purposes. The documents and purposes are listed in Exhibit 18.1.

Exhibit 18.1   Documents and Purpose

Type of Document	Purpose
Marketing Documents	Communicate information to groups about charitable gifts to donors, prospects, and other constituents
Newsletters	Educate potential prospects about giving opportunities
Planned Giving Advertisements	Inform the public about the nonprofit organization and its services
Buckslips	Advertise a particular program with a focused informational piece of literature
Columns	Describe specific programs and gift opportunities through newsletters
Brochures	Educate the general public about detailed gift options, funding opportunities, and a broad array of named funds
Guides	Describe in a booklet the gift options, showing how planned gifts can provide financial benefits to the donor
Prospect Letters	Seek new relationships and cultivate existing ones
Agreements	Govern the use, scope, and purpose of a donor's gift
Endowed funds	Govern the use of funds transferred to establish a permanent endowed fund
Current Use Awards	Govern a donor's gift for immediate use
Specific Purpose Funds	Create chairs, professorships, or other specific funds
Other	Agreements that pertain to real estate gifts, tangible personal property, and other noncash assets
Administrative Documents	Administer the planned giving staff and manage the organization's contacts
Office Management	Assist in the administration of the office
Donor Management	Manage donors and prospects using special tools

Exhibit 18.1 *(Continued)*

Correspondence	Communicate, educate, and build relationships with individual donors
Donor Letters	Inform about planned gifts and the organization's accomplishments, cultivate relations
Prospect Letters	Renew relationships, cultivate existing ones
Professional Advisor Letters	Share information on charitable gift planning
Nonprofit Staff Member Letters, Memos, and Minutes	Educate about gift options and donor strategies internally
Exhibits	Teach and inform others through examples about the work of the organization
Estate Planning Documents	Attract donors, prospects, and staff
Materials for Workshops/Seminars	Educate faculty, staff, volunteers, and potential donors
Numerical and Data Based Documents	Demonstrate mathematical results and data trends
Agendas	Organize events, meetings, and workshops
Presentations	Educate others through speaking about planned giving programs
Planned Giving Presentation	Information about planned giving, life income gifts, gifts of assets other than cash, estate and tax planning
Presentation Thumbnail	Contains the same information as Planned Giving Presentation but in an outline format
Tax and IRS Documents	Meet tax requirements through a series of forms
Charitable Remainder Unitrusts	IRS-approved unitrust forms
Charitable Remainder Annuity Trusts	IRS-approved annuity trust forms
Pooled Income Funds	Pooled income fund documents

Each type of document performs some purpose for the organization. Notice that each purpose statement in Exhibit 18.1 begins with an *active verb*. In planned giving, donors *make* gifts, *transfer* stock, *support* nonprofits, and *write* checks. The verbs are italicized—they represent the action that shapes each document. Producing documents is all about doing something—accomplishing the work of the nonprofit organization.

In planned giving, the purpose of the document often is to explain the benefits of a specific gift option or to compare different gift options. Many of the documents are educational in nature. They are designed to educate donors, prospects, and professional advisors about the tax consequences and life income benefits of planned gifts. They also are designed to sustain and develop the relationship between the donor and the charity.

Whenever drafting a document, think first about purpose. The writer who is clear about the purpose has a much better chance of writing an effective document.

18.3 COMMUNICATE A MESSAGE FOR A PURPOSE

Documents must communicate information clearly and precisely to fulfill their purposes. The document's purpose drives all communication. Ask:

- What is the purpose of this planned giving document?

- What does the writer hope to accomplish? What is the intended outcome from this communication?

- What are the audiences' purposes? Why should donors want to work with the nonprofit and support the work of the organization?

18.4 KNOW THE AUDIENCE AND BE RESPONSIVE TO IT

Development documents are powerful tools that carry the nonprofit organization's message to all of the organization's constituents. Often the written message reaches donors and prospects in their homes and offices, places where the planned giving officer cannot yet enter. The message creates the opportunity for a dialogue between the nonprofit organization and its constituents. Introductory letters establish the beginning of a relationship that hopefully will continue over time, to the mutual benefit of both the donor and the nonprofit organization. Subsequent documents nurture relationships, helping those relationships grow and become more meaningful over time.

Instead of thinking about what the writer needs to tell the reader (self-centered thinking), think about the readers—who they are, what they want, what motivates them, what fulfills their goals (audience-centered thinking). Depending on the nonprofit organization, the reader could be an alumnus, a grateful patient, a patron, a volunteer, a vice-president, a faculty member, a professional advisor, or a board member. Each reader must be treated individually; the reader must be allowed to influence the tone and style of the document. When preparing to write, conjure up an image of the audience—think of specific people who come to mind. Imagine how they will respond to written communication. Talk to them, argue with them, and persuade them to consider a point of view.

Unsuccessful speakers, like unsuccessful writers, can fail to consider the audience. Consider these questions:

- Who is the audience?

- What are the goals that the nonprofit shares with potential donors? What does the reader want to achieve? (audience purpose)

- What is the audience's level of knowledge and experience?

- What does the audience need to know? What would they really like to know?

- What is the existing relationship between the nonprofit and the audience? What future relationship should be built?

Thinking through purpose and audience should help the writer formulate a strategy for written communication. The writer should be able to put in a very succinct statement the purpose and define the intended audience. The writer should be able to state clear facts about the audience that can be used to shape the document. Thinking clearly about the purpose of the writing and the intended audience forms the basis for effective communication and strong documents.

The worksheet in Exhibit 18.2 poses questions that may help to focus the writer.

Exhibit 18.2   Worksheet: Nutshell the Document

1. What is the purpose of the writing?

_____

2. Who is the audience?

_____

3. What does the audience need to know?

_____

4. How well does the writer know the audience?

_____

5. What is the nature of the document?

_____

Exhibit 18.2   *(Continued)*

6. What is the audience's goal?

_____

7. What is the writer's goal?

_____

_____

18.5   USE OUTLINING

Properly organized documents are usually first outlined. An outline allows the writer to plan the document much in the same way an architect draws a blueprint. Outlining allows the writer to divide the
document into smaller, more manageable units. Long, detailed letters with lots of information must be
outlined; otherwise the letter will likely confuse the reader. In addition, proposals, complicated gift documents, and marketing materials such as brochures, newsletters, and columns should all be outlined.
Outlining may seem to slow the pace, but in the long run, it improves efficiency and boosts productivity.

When preparing the outline, the writer should think about both what is to be covered and
about the order in which information should be presented. In most professional writing, the writer
should be prepared to state the purpose right from the start—to deliver the *bottom line up front*
(BLUF). The writer cannot fool readers or lull them into simply agreeing with the writer or acting in
a prescribed manner. Readers are suspicious of correspondence until they know who is writing, for
what purpose, with what intended result. The writer might as well state clearly the reason for the
writing, what the issues are, and why the writer is addressing that particular audience. When asking
for financial support, do not risk alienating the audience by playing coy.

When outlining the introductory paragraph, think about what should be accomplished. In
most cases, if the writer wants the audience to do something, it is best to come right out and say so.
The writer can be open about the purpose because the mission and project goals are shared with the
audience—the writer is presenting an opportunity to work together on something important. The
writer does not need to be blunt, but should be honest, direct, and open in the approach.

When organizing the body of the document, build on what audience members already know and
then extend their knowledge. This is a basic principle of moving from known or shared information to
new or unknown information. In the outline, be prepared to plan for some context or background information—stating what the writer and the reader already understand because of past dealings—before offering information on new developments, new initiatives, and/or new accomplishments.

Outline the major points and support each with examples, a brief story, some facts and figures, or a small surprise. At the top level of the outline, the writer should place the main points that
the reader needs to understand. If possible, these points should be tied to actions. At the lower levels
of the outline should be those nuggets that carry the day, that drive the point home. Each major
paragraph or section should be like a sandwich, with the more general statements or actions at the
beginning and end and the supporting material in the middle. One test of a good outline is to read
just the sentences at the top level of the document (the first sentence of each paragraph, or the first
and last sentence of each paragraph), and see if the sequence of topics or generalizations makes a
compelling and coherent argument on their own.

When completing the outline, think strategically about how to close the communication.
What specifically will the closing ask for? How will the point be driven home? What is the take-
home message for the audience? What does the writer want them to do as they finish reading? The
close of a business document is frequently "next steps," suggesting how to move forward from the
current position. Be clear about the proposed next steps.

When outlining, do not get hung up on format. Develop an outline strategy that is productive, not
one that follows an imaginary "correct way" to outline. The outline is a place to think and develop a
strategy. It should put into place prior thinking about purpose and audience. It should map a sequence of

■   157   ■

discussion and frame a coherent document. Time spent writing an outline will pay dividends when drafting the actual text, because the writer will be sure of the approach and will be working to a plan.

18.6 DEVELOP A FIRST DRAFT

Developing documents is a process that involves several steps rather than a single act. Many writers have unreasonable expectations, assuming that in one step they can move from draft to final on a document. For simple or standardized letters that may be possible, especially if the writer has written a similar document several times, but in most complex organizations, writers are confronted with new challenges, not well-rehearsed behaviors. Detailed, complex, or technical letters require a number of steps.

Some writers develop writer's block, an inability to face a blank page. These writers might begin again and again, trying to craft the first sentence. Or they may simply procrastinate, finding other work to do and putting off writing until they are faced with an imminent deadline.

If writers follow the process recommended thus far (thinking about purpose and audience, planning through outlining), they already have started writing and should be on their way to a strong draft. Writing is never easy, but planning makes it easier and more likely to be effective. Making progress in planning a document feels good, and the momentum keeps the writer progressing.

There are other ways to get a good start on a draft document. Consider these techniques:

- Talk through the document with a colleague.

- Make a list of everything the document should accomplish.

- Make a list of key words to be used in the document.

- Try drafting by writing as quickly as possible; then go back and make sense of what is on paper.

- Set aside time without interruption. Turn on the answering machine, ignore the e-mail, and close the door. Writing requires concentration.

- Work first on the most familiar or easiest parts. Begin writing at the middle, end, or beginning of the document, whatever is easiest and gets the words flowing.

- With long documents, work for a given amount of time, perhaps an hour, and then put it away until the next day, and then work again for an hour. Make steady progress.

- Use the word processor as a tool to help generate ideas, see connections, and keep track of thoughts. If the writer is working in one section and has a good idea for another section, he should stop and make a note. Use "stickies," index cards, notepaper, or leave placeholders to record information to be inserted later in sections or paragraphs.

- End a drafting section with a few notes about where to begin the next drafting section. Leave a place to begin on the next round.

Drafting is primarily about flow—getting flow, keeping flow going, managing flow. Many people notice that, once they get the flow going, writing becomes quite satisfying and they even resent interruptions. Attend to personal work patterns and recognize how to attain and maintain flow during drafting complex documents.

18.7 BRING OTHERS INTO THE PROCESS

Documents such as letters and proposals should be shared with a colleague for peer review. Getting a review improves the writing and helps to identify problems that may not be obvious to the writer.

Peer reviewers should offer constructive and objective criticism of the work. They can read in the role of the audience. Once a draft is in place, even if it is quite rough, be prepared to share it with others in the office.

Writers benefit when they let others look at their drafts, especially at an early stage. This involves a certain level of trust and openness, especially if the writer is asking a subordinate to look at an early draft. The reviewers should be asked to do more than say "Put a semicolon here" or "Why don't you say *donor* instead of *patron?*" The reviewers should play the role of the intended reader and tell the writer how they feel and react as they read the writing:

- Do they understand the writer's purpose?

- Do they understand the writer's goals?

- Do they feel respected and understood as they audience of the document?

- Do they feel persuaded that what the writer is asking for is reasonable, important, and good?

- Do they feel the document has the right information?

- Do they feel the document has the best strategy to accomplish its goals?

Many people are protective of their drafts, and they do not want other people to see work until it is finished. This is a mistake. The nonprofit organization needs to create a writing culture inside the organization, a culture that recognizes the value of teamwork and collaborative writing. A good way to do this is for the natural leaders in the organization to take the lead, share documents with others, and create an environment where people expect to help each other in significant ways.

18.8 MANAGE DOCUMENTS TO MEET DEADLINES

Planned giving documents must be planned, organized, developed, and managed to meet deadlines. Proper planning can make deadlines a helpful rather than a stressful experience.

(a) Timing

When planning a document, allow time for the various stages of planning, drafting, reviewing, revising, and preparing the final document to be published. Getting something on paper early in the process provides material to work with and helps create a sense of progress. Building early drafts and early reviews into the timetable ensures that documents have time to develop. Rushed work in desperate response to deadlines is not going to produce strong writing.

(b) Project Planning

There are many time management and project management tools on the market, and seminars are offered regularly on these topics. Adopt what is out there or invent an approach and tools. Most people benefit from a structured approach, supported by some kind of written plan, with activities, dates, staffing, and deliverables clearly marked. Treat writing as a work activity and map it out, working from the due date back through all the associated activities. This kind of backward planning, or planning with the end in mind, is essential for major initiatives, as when preparing marketing materials such as a "Guide to Charitable Giving." When finishing a big project, get the team together, look over the original plan, and figure out whether the project was well planned, where more time was needed, and how to manage things better on the next project.

(c) File Organization

Complicated documents take time and care to write. Developing a bank of planned giving letters and other documents can help writers meet deadlines. Taking time to properly label documents on computer or disk, with well-organized directories and files, can reduce the time spent searching for documents. Creating a document name—which includes the file name, date, and directory location or path for each document—is a great way to store and manage documents. Sometimes more time is spent looking for a document than writing it.

As the writer develops organized files, select some documents as models for new writers. While each writing situation is to some extent unique and must be responsive to particular details, many writers benefit from seeing good models. Also, the organization benefits from developing shared standards when they attempt to identify the best, most successful documents in their possession.

As nonprofit organizations mature, so do their document strategies. Many organizations develop a database of high-quality graphics and boilerplate text (text that can be reused in different documents). This is good practice, as long as the writer remembers to think about the current purpose and audience and strategically adapt the boilerplate. Fully mature organizations take advantage of technology by creating shared drives, where the organization's files are carefully stored and available to everyone in the group, so people do not waste time trying to find files on other people's machines or in file cabinets.

18.9 DESIGN AN EFFECTIVE DOCUMENT

Document production technologies have raised expectations for professional writing, and nonprofit staff must work hard to develop printed materials that are professional looking, usable, and effective. Marketing materials such as brochures, newsletters, and guides need careful design to organize the content of the document and to make it attractive to the reader. The selection of paper stock, font, color, graphics, number of columns, and width of columns affect the look and the impact of the document.

Try to write documents that are visually effective. Ask whether readers can immediately sense the purpose of the document. If a specific request is being made, is that request in a prominent position, so the donor knows the point of the document? Is there adequate white space between blocks of print, with short paragraphs and nice wide margins? Has the writer chosen print in at least 12 point, since many readers have fading eyesight? Since many traditional planned giving donors are growing older, consider using print in 13 or 14 point type.

For example, note the impact of different point type:

10 Point: Writing well is an important skill in Planned Giving.

12 Point: Writing well is an important skill in Planned Giving.

14 Point: Writing well is an important skill in Planned Giving.

16 Point: Writing well is an important skill in Planned Giving.

Most adults need print for body paragraphs in 12 point type.

Avoid overusing italics, especially for body paragraphs. It may suggest a more personal, handwritten approach, but in fact it is harder to read. Improve readability by adding a little extra space between lines of print and by not making the lines too long (30 to 40 characters/line is good). Space breaks between paragraphs and sections is also a good idea. If people must fill in forms, give them plenty of room to write and good directions.

Are documents legible, with good contrast of print on paper? Try to keep the documents looking clean; do not obscure the message with lots of clip art or by playing around with fonts and styles. Some organizations overdesign their materials, using too much color. Others print text over graphics or watermarks, making it difficult to read the materials. Select a look and design that matches the professional character of the organization.

Documents must be appealing and attractive, but not necessarily expensive. Select a design that is pleasing to the eye. Select paper that is an appropriate weight and color for the document. A very pleasing document can be created with a light-colored paper stock (buff or bone) together with a deep blue ink and perhaps one spot color to highlight the information and design.

Glitz increases the cost. Three-color (or more) pieces look great but cost a great deal to produce. Higher costs mean that fewer can be printed and mailed, thus reducing your ability to reach those who need to hear the nonprofit's message. Most donors are conscious of costs and value substance over form.

Consider developing a style guide for all publications. Form an identity with your readers, so they know and trust the organization. This can be accomplished, in part, by producing distinctive documents that audiences recognize as symbols of the organization.

18.10 TAKE ADVANTAGE OF DESKTOP PUBLISHING

Desktop publishing has brought the world of printed communications to a new level. Offices can now produce printed materials that are as good as, or better than, what can be bought. Instead of generically produced materials, the product can reflect the nonprofit organization's personality. To do the job well, quality computer hardware, software, and an experienced designer are needed. There are a number of appropriate hardware and software packages to choose from. Shop to find the best package to accommodate marketing needs and objectives. The largest expense will come in the first year; after that, a budget can be established to purchase updates and enhancements. A first-year budget of $4,000 to $5,000 should be adequate to establish the program, and $500 to 1,000 each year thereafter should sustain the effort.

(a) The Operator

Desktop publishing software packages are complex, and it is too much to assume that a skilled word processor can excel at desktop publishing. An operator should be sent to a training course, commonly offered at colleges and universities, in the specific software selected. The investment in time and money is well worth it. If possible, the operator should be a part of the planned giving team and be involved in the early stages. A positive relationship between the writer and the operator is helpful, because production of these documents requires teamwork, feedback, and collaboration.

If possible, bring in a graphic designer or document designer to help create brochures, posters, templates, letterhead, business cards, and perhaps a logo for the group. All these establish an identity for the organization. Talk to the people at a local college—those in technical and professional communication or graphic design. Sponsor a student project or internship and line up some talented students to help with design in the organization.

(b) Evaluation

Consider assembling a focus group to assess the publications and their usefulness. For example, assemble on a table the documents and publications used in the past year in the nonprofit organization. Get the team together. Bring in a couple of supportive donors or clients. Bring in the design person or someone from the university design or writing program. Look at the documents from a distance. Are they attractive? Does the reader want to read them? Do they look professional? Do they look like they come from the same organization, one with a confident and established identity? Self-evaluations and focus groups provide valuable feedback on the effectiveness of organizational publications.

18.11 USE LANGUAGE CORRECTLY AND EFFECTIVELY

A planned giving officer spends time learning the content of planned giving: the ins and outs of the law, the ways that organizations are structured, the various forms of giving and their benefits and limitations. It is also important that the officer be in absolute control of grammar and cultivate a strong professional style. This section offers principles for effective control of language to improve documents. Study these principles to sharpen the nonprofit's planned giving documents. Read and reread Strunk and White's wonderful text, *The Elements of Style*. A strong professional style is something to work toward.

Use informal and personal words: Some words bring a personal and conversational tone to correspondence. Referring to the nonprofit as *we* and to the prospective donor as *you* will create a sense of immediacy, something close to a conversation. The goal is to sound like a real person, a lively and interesting person, someone who is animated and optimistic about the organization's prospects. Do not go too far—do not offend by being too personal or pushy or straining too hard to be funny. Develop a light touch, a style that says the writer is not stuffy or pretentious, just an employee trying to do a good job and enjoying it.

Example: The decision has been made by the organization to solicit donations for an endowed fund with the goal of supporting students of color in their pursuit of higher education.

Suggestion: We've decided to raise an endowment to support our talented minority students.

Write using active verbs: Active verbs create active messages, particularly when the one doing the action is the subject and the action is captured by an active verb. Verbs provide the center of the sentence and can make writing sharp, clear, and lively. Sentences with passive or "to be" verbs (*is, are, was, were, be, being, been*) slow writing down and take away energy. Active verbs convey more than the action—they establish a sense of tone and the writer's attitude.

The next examples are passive and rewritten to active suggestions:

Example: It would be much appreciated if your reply were received by our office . . .
Suggestion: Please tell us what you think!
Example: It has been brought to the attention of the committee that gifts of real estate . . .
Suggestion: The committee understands that gifts of real estate . . .

Basic sentence structure calls for a subject followed by an active verb. Active verbs carry the action and are the most important words in the sentence. Compare these examples, where the writer finds the active verb and moves it closer to the subject:

Example: Through planned giving, the donor is provided with a sense of satisfaction.
Suggestion: Planned gifts satisfy the donor's wish to provide ongoing support.
Example: One option is provided by appreciated securities, which include such investment vehicles as stocks, bonds, and mutual funds . . .
Suggestion: Appreciated securities (stocks, bonds, and mutual funds) provide an option to. . . .

Do not be verbose: Large words are not necessarily better than small words. Most employees pick up the language of the workplace, and, unfortunately, much of what is said or written is verbose or grandiose. This style frustrates the reader and creates letters that do not communicate well. Large words fill space but seldom help the reader understand the point of the letter. Clean up these sentences, excise words that perform no function, say what is meant, and do not be driven by high-sounding phrases. Many adjectives and adverbs take up space and accomplish little.

Avoid jargon: Jargon is language that is used by individuals employed by a particular business or industry. The language of planned giving is full of legal and tax jargon: appreciated securities, charitable income tax deductions, discount rates, tangible personal property, generation skipping transfer tax, and charitable remainder trust. Although these words must and should be used in writing, they must not be used exclusively when dealing with individual donors and prospects. When they are used, explanatory language must translate the concept to something the reader understands. If a technical concept must be used, offer a scenario or a small example that allows the reader to understand the concept in terms of familiar situations and actions. Each reader has a different level of understanding, and it is important to personalize the message to meet the needs of a particular reader.

Do not overqualify: Qualifiers, routinely included in business and professional communications, detract from the message. Qualifiers include words or expressions such as *sort of, quite, very, perhaps,* or *almost.* These words affect the clarity of the message and effectiveness.

Example: The rate is quite high . . .
Suggestion: The rate is 8 percent . . .

Eliminate windy word clusters: Windy word clusters include phrases such as these: *in order to, in the event that, needless to say, in regard to, as a consequence of, as a matter of fact.* Like qualifiers, these phrases add nothing to the writing and only serve to cloud the message, which, for planned giving purposes, may already be confusing.

Example: In order to transfer the stock . . .
Suggestion: To transfer stock . . .

Be careful with "th" words: A number of words that begin with "th" can detract from the writing. Such words are routinely used to begin sentences but they might appear anywhere. *This, that, these,* and *those* create problems because they should refer to something that immediately preceded and that is in the reader's mind. Make sure the reference is clear. Or combine the sentences and avoid beginning new sentences with these words.

Example: Planned giving provides important financial benefits. This is attractive to many
                  donors.
Suggestion: Planned giving provides important and attractive financial benefits to donors.

Be economical and direct: Words become sentences, sentences become paragraphs, and paragraphs become documents. Every English composition professor teaches the importance of one topic–one paragraph, a concept that is often forgotten. Some writers write in circles or in choppy short sentences. Linear writers move the information forward in a logical and orderly sequence, never missing a step or an opportunity to develop the message. Look for ways to be economical with words so the writing moves smoothly and quickly to fulfill the goals.

Example: The charitable gift annuity pays a fixed rate and provides a tax deduction. The
                  deduction is $3,960.
Suggestion: The charitable gift annuity pays a fixed rate of 7 percent and provides a
                  charitable income tax deduction of $3,960, which can be used to offset income,
                  providing the donor itemizes his taxes.

Use parallel structure: Parallel structure means using similar grammatical constructions to express similar ideas. Parallel structures give writing balance and elegance.

Example: Many donors make gifts directly to the planned giving office, while the preference of others is to work through their bank and some like to use their broker.

Suggestion: While many donors make gifts directly to the planned giving office, others work through their bankers or brokers.

Notice how *bankers* and *brokers* become part of an economical, parallel, compound phrase.

    When used in series, words ending in "ing," "ed," "en" should have consistent endings.

Example: The art will be inventoried, and after cataloging, there will be a display . . .

Suggestion: The art will be inventoried, cataloged, and displayed . . .

18.12   RECIPE FOR A DOCUMENT

Documents include a variety of key elements. Ignoring or omitting one element can destroy the impact of a document. Four ingredients go into the recipe to produce quality documents:

Strategy: Strategy is the planning, preparation, and collaboration in document production.

Content: Content is the substance of the message.

Design: Design is the proper look, layout, and format of the document.

Language: Language includes the use of proper and effective sentence structure, strong word choice, and correct punctuation.

18.13   CONCLUSION

This chapter has offered productive ways to prepare documents to help writers become better communicators for planned giving. Developing documents will not suddenly become easy; it is likely to remain hard, although satisfying, work. Get others involved and make it a team effort. Always remember how much documents are related to success, since they are a primary means of communicating with those who are ready to help perform the good work of the nonprofit organization.

    Above all, remember that planned giving letters, marketing materials, and exhibits help to reinforce the image and sustain the relationship of the nonprofit organization with donors. These documents, properly structured with effective messages, attract planned giving donors and prospects. Documents are important tools in the business of planned giving. Use them wisely and the nonprofit will be rewarded.

## CHAPTER NINETEEN

Printed Materials
and Publications for
Donors and Prospects

19.1   INTRODUCTION

Professionals new to planned giving often attempt to compare planned giving to something they already know. Planned giving is not only development and interpersonal skills, public relations, and organizational and office procedures, but is similar to a business start-up with the planned giving officer in the role of entrepreneur. The most successful businesses are clear about the products they offer, understand the consumers they are trying to reach, and use marketing strategies to attract constituents. Often the most overlooked and crucial part of a planned giving program is marketing. Planned giving officers may focus on technical proficiency and the building of systems, such as prospect tracking and control, but can neglect the very area that brings prospects to a planned giving program. No amount of technical expertise will generate gifts to the organization unless individuals with donative intent learn about the program. Marketing is a comprehensive, integrated campaign designed to educate an organization's constituents about the organization and its needs for funding. Marketing creates a heightened level of visibility and awareness and projects a positive image of the nonprofit and its planned giving program. Marketing means not only educating prospects about planned giving vehicles, but also articulating the needs of the organization. This chapter describes the printed materials needed to market and promote a planned giving program to donors and prospects.

19.2 MARKETING FUNDAMENTALS

To be successful in attracting business to a planned giving program, it is necessary to understand basic marketing fundamentals. Continuity, repetition, and perseverance are key qualities. Planned giving materials must appear continually over a long period to educate donors and prospects. Each marketing piece, whether a newsletter, advertisement, or other publication, should be produced in a consistent style and placed in approximately the same location in a publication each time it appears. Remember that planned gifts do not usually close immediately, and it is the cumulative impact of marketing to a philanthropic donor over time, along with follow-up, that results in a donor's making a planned gift.

19.3 THE CASE STATEMENT

A case statement educates constituents about the needs of a program or project of the nonprofit organization. A case statement is a statement that makes a case for support; it can be an extensive document or booklet or as simple as a series of one-page integrated sheets. A case statement can focus exclusively on a particular department or program or on the major needs of the organization. Properly drafted case statements raise awareness about the organization's needs and, like a menu, offer a variety of funding options along with their corresponding costs. This often-neglected piece is one of the most important marketing tools a development program can offer. Some organizations believe that a case statement is needed only when the organization is involved in a development campaign, but a case statement is essential for every development program, every time money is needed. It communicates the organization's message to donors and prospects and helps to match interests with needs.

Many organizations spend too much time and money on the production of case statements. An organization may hire free-lance writers, graphic artists, design experts, and high-priced printers to create the statement. This product may be attractive, but all too often it fails to connect with its intended audience. The organization should consider, if possibly, drafting and producing the case statement in-house. One individual can be charged with the responsibility of drafting it, and others can participate in its creation.

(a) Steps to Create an Effective Case Statement

Five steps may be followed to draft an effective case statement:

1. Design a model that illustrates the components of a case statement. These should include a title for the project, its price, and a description outlining the needs of the organization, department, program, or project.

2. Meet with the necessary dean, physician, department head, program chair, or administrator to explain the purpose of the case statement and to gather information to identify the various components.

3. Determine how the development office will handle the information it receives from the various colleges, departments, or programs assisting in the preparation of the case statement.

4. Create realistic deadlines and timetables for production.

5. Use a desktop publishing program to create a standard format, layout, and design. Arrange for final approval by the appropriate person.

(b) How to Use a Case Statement

A case statement enables development professionals to show donors and prospects why the organization needs money and how specifically funds will be used, and helps donors to feel connected with the organization and its overall development effort. A case statement can help encourage a donor who has not completely committed to making a gift and can suggest particular areas that can benefit from the donor's planned gift.

19.4 GUIDE TO CHARITABLE GIFT PLANNING

A guide to charitable gift planning, or a "Ways to Give" brochure, outlines the many ways that a donor can make a gift to a nonprofit through a wide variety of assets. It is probably the most important brochure in planned giving, because it goes into detail about planned giving options. The brochure may be simple or deluxe, but to be effective, it must outline the different ways to give, show various giving levels and gift minimums, and provide information on taxes, financial planning, and estate planning. See Appendix, CD-ROM Documentation, Marketing. A typical table of contents includes seven items:

1. *Description of the organization.* Emphasize the prominent and unique features of the organization and the characteristics that separate this nonprofit from other nonprofits. Various design elements, such as bullets, can be used to highlight such features.

2. *About the development office.* Describe the services and programs the development office offers to prospects and donors. This section should be designed to open the door to inquiries and encourage communication between the organization and its constituents.

3. *Menu of assets.* Communicate to the donor the broadest range of asset options that can be used to make gifts. These options include cash, stock, retirement plans, real estate, and tangible personal property.

4. *Planned giving options.* Include a complete discussion of each of the planned giving vehicles offered by the nonprofit. This section should not be overtechnical or authoritative, but should pique a donor's interest. Include charitable gift annuities, deferred gift annuities, the pooled income fund, charitable remainder trusts, life insurance, and bequests. Use charts to illustrate financial benefits.

5. *Endowed funding levels.* Provide a summary of the organization's funding levels for establishing chairs, endowed funds, professorships, institutes, and scholarships. The inclusion of minimum giving levels helps to raise donors' sights for making a larger gift.

6. *Leadership and recognition societies.* Leadership and recognition societies help donors feel that they are part of a larger group, and some donors are motivated to increase their giving to reach certain levels in such societies. Include the name of a planned giving society and list its benefits to members, including special mailings, annual meetings or events, and other membership benefits.

7. *Staff.* Decide whether to include individual staff members' names, titles, and telephone numbers to facilitate contact between staff and donors. When individual employees leave, however, this information becomes out of date.

Once the brochure is printed, send it to donors who request information about making a gift to the organization and take a copy along on a personal visit. Make sure that other development officers are provided with a number of brochures to use when meeting with donors to talk about making gifts. Print many additional copies so that there will always be an available supply.

19.5 RESPONSE FORM

No planned giving communication or publication is complete without a reply device. A reply device, or response form, enables prospects to communicate with the planned giving office simply and easily. A perforated card, a card inserted into the spine of a booklet, or a tear-off device can be an appropriate response form. The card always should include the planned giving office's address and telephone number and spaces for the prospect's name, address, telephone number, and age. The card also should provide an opportunity to learn about a donor's capacity for giving by including a space for the donor to indicate the anticipated asset to be used to make the gift, and the approximate size of the gift. See Appendix, CD-ROM Documentation, Marketing.

19.6 NEWSLETTERS

A planned giving or development newsletter that includes planned giving information is a powerful tool in marketing a planned giving program. Consider including planned giving articles, ads, and testimonials in a development newsletter that is distributed organization-wide to donors and prospects. Create a newsletter specific to planned giving, and devote the entire issue to planned giving options or to a specific gift vehicle, such as real estate or charitable remainder trusts. Segment planned giving prospects into approximate age brackets and write a newsletter about deferred gift annuities. Then send it to donors or prospects in the age range of 30 to 50 years who would be most interested in learning about deferred gift annuities. Similarly, consider producing a newsletter that features pooled income fund gifts or charitable gift annuities, and send it to donors and prospects in appropriate age groups. Through such approaches, donors who would benefit most from a particular message are targeted.

Also consider segmenting prospects by geographic sections to match with asset options. For example, a newsletter that focuses on real estate may be sent to prospects in rural areas, where individuals may have more extensive real estate holdings. A newsletter that features gifts of stock can be directed to prospects in metropolitan areas. Remember to send the newsletter to outside advisors to enhance professional outreach. See Appendix, CD-ROM Documentation, Marketing, for a sample planned giving newsletter.

19.7 COLUMNS IN NONPROFIT PUBLICATIONS

A planned giving column placed in the nonprofit's newspaper, magazine, or newsletter affords another opportunity to communicate with planned giving donors and prospects. Emphasizing one or two planned giving vehicles or concepts per issue creates an opportunity to develop a library of informative, in-depth articles over time. These articles can be reprinted and sent as supplementary information to donors. They also can serve as the basis of a longer feature article in a newsletter, as well as training materials for staff. The planned giving officer should include a picture of himself as author and planned giving specialist so that donors become more familiar with the planned giving officer and feel more comfortable approaching him at donor functions. Include a response box with each column to facilitate requests for information. A sample planned giving column appears in Appendix, CD-ROM Documentation, Marketing.

19.8 PLANNED GIVING ADVERTISEMENTS

Use planned giving advertisements that can be placed in organization newsletters, newspapers, or magazines to attract new business to the planned giving program. Consider drafting straightforward, uncomplicated informational ads with bullets to highlight various gift benefits, as seen in Exhibit 19.1. Use one ad per gift vehicle or concept, and do not hesitate to repeat publication of the ad. Ads can be drafted and prepared by the planned giving office at little or no cost. See Appendix, CD-ROM Documentation, Marketing for a sample set of planned giving ads.

19.9 BUCKSLIPS

A buckslip is a valuable form of communication. An inexpensive document that is included with a mailing, it is usually smaller than a full page, often the size of a dollar bill, hence the name buckslip. Like a reply device, a buckslip enables a prospect to ask for more information. Buckslips should be enclosed with mailings such as an annual fund appeal or year-end tax letter. Use a buckslip as a way to encourage donors to request information about various life income gifts or establishing a named fund and tax, financial, and estate planning information (see Exhibit 19.2). A sample buckslip is included in Appendix, CD-ROM Documentation, Marketing.

A bank, trust company, or utility company may allow a nonprofit organization to include information about the nonprofit's activities in its mailing. This approach may work best when the nonprofit is the biggest or best-known organization in the area. It also works well with small nonprofits in rural areas. The use of buckslips may not be an option in major cities where there are dozens of nonprofits, but an inquiry is worth the effort. At one nonprofit, the planned giving officer spoke with banks in her city about including buckslips with bank statements to customers. The buckslips featured information about life income gifts and the ways in which these gifts can benefit donors as well as the nonprofit. On the reverse side of the card was a response form. Several banks included buckslips in their bank statements, and over a three-month period the nonprofit was able to place more than 65,000 buckslips in the hands of bank customers. Within a week several inquiries were received. This project has now run for several years and is a key component of the organization's marketing program.

Exhibit 19.1   Gifts through an Estate

Gifts through Your Estate Benefit
The Academy for Learning

Gifts through your estate provide important benefits to you and The Academy for Learning. Gifts may be made by will or trust, through which you may direct either a specific dollar amount ($25,000) or a percentage (25 percent). In addition, you may designate your gift to support a particular program or department of interest to you. Through your gift you can:

- Preserve current assets.
- Reduce or eliminate federal estate taxes.
- Make an enduring contribution to The Academy for Learning.
- Become a member of the <PLANNED GIVING SOCIETY>.

The Office of Planned Giving will be pleased to discuss ways to make a gift through your estate to benefit The Academy for Learning. Contact <NAME>, <TITLE>, <ADDRESS>, <CITY, STATE, ZIP>; <TELEPHONE>.

Exhibit 19.2   Buckslip: Life Income Gifts

The Academy for Learning
Life Income Gifts

Your life income gifts to The Academy for Learning pay dividends. There are several options to choose from depending on your age, your needs, and the way you fund your gift. A life income gift provides the following benefits:

- A stream of income for the lifetime of the donor and/or the donor's spouse
- A charitable income tax deduction
- An opportunity to establish an endowed fund in your name or in the name of a loved one
- Possible avoidance of capital gains taxes on gifts of appreciated property
- Membership in The Academy for Learning leadership club
- A reduction in federal estate taxes

The Office of Development will send you a personalized financial analysis that shows how a life income gift can benefit both you and The Academy for Learning. Please complete the form on the back of this card.

19.10   TESTIMONIAL ADVERTISEMENTS

A testimonial ad is a good way to illustrate the benefits of a planned gift. It features a donor or donors talking about the gift they made to the organization. These testimonials serve to educate other prospects about gift options, help prospects to feel part of a larger group of donors, and spark a prospect's feeling of similarity to the donor who has already made a gift. Testimonials are nontechnical and easy to read. They show "real-life" donors and tend to evoke an emotional response. Be sure to include a picture of the donor(s) in the ad. See Appendix, CD-ROM Documentation, Marketing.

19.11   LETTERS

(a) Anniversary Letter

Consider sending donors who have made life income gifts a letter on the anniversary of their last gift. Send calculations that show the benefit of making a new gift this year. A sample anniversary letter is included in Appendix, CD-ROM Documentation, Correspondence.

(b) Donors Who Have Made Security Gifts

Send donors who have made a gift of securities in the last year a letter telling them about the benefits of making a gift to the nonprofit's pooled income fund. The donor will likely be attracted to the avoidance of capital gains taxes enjoyed by making the gift. A sample letter is included in Appendix, CD-ROM Documentation, Correspondence.

(c) Retired Employees

If it is possible to obtain their names, send a letter targeted to retired staff of the nonprofit. Many worked at the nonprofit for many years and feel quite loyal. Those without children may see the charity as an heir substitute.

(d) Existing Planned Giving Donors

In November, send all planned giving donors a letter telling them about any tax changes in the upcoming new year or new benefits they may receive by making a planned gift.

- ■ *Planned giving information on annual fund appeal.* Be sure to include a check-off box for more information on the annual fund reply device. In this way, donors who are already interested in the nonprofit may take the opportunity to learn more about planned giving.

- ■ *Gift in honor or memory.* If the nonprofit is a hospital, place envelopes around the hospital that provides patients with the opportunity to make a gift in honor or memory of a loved one. A sample of in honor or memory language is included in Appendix, CD-ROM Documentation, Marketing.

- ■ *Planned giving information in annual or donor report.* Include planned giving information in the nonprofit's annual or donor report. A back page is an ideal location to include low-key language each year. Sample language is included in Appendix, CD-ROM Documentation, Marketing.

- ■ *Planned giving information in tax receipt.* The nonprofit might like to include planned giving information in tax receipts mailed to donors who have made a gift to the charity. This offers another opportunity to educate donors who already support the charity about planned giving opportunities.

- ■ *Institutional survey.* Nonprofits that send a survey to alumni, patients, subscribers, or members may wish to include language asking the individual to indicate whether she would like to receive information about making a planned gift. This language would be particularly appropriate for a survey from an alumni relations area or a hospital asking about patient services.

- ■ *Estate administration booklet.* Donors and prospects will appreciate an informative booklet that describes the duties of an executor or personal representative. Included in the booklet may be information about making a bequest to the nonprofit.

- ■ *Websites.* Most charities are creating Web pages that include information about making a gift to the nonprofit. Information can range from simple annual fund gifts to how to make a planned gift. Older donors are increasingly using computers for information and correspondence; many initially become attracted to this form of communication as a way to stay in touch with grandchildren. Websites need to be updated frequently or they become obsolete.

19.12 PIECES IN LOCAL NEWSPAPERS

If appropriate, test market, in a local community newspaper or trade paper, a planned giving column or ad about life income gift options or gifts of real estate. Use the newspaper to expand the donor population to include those not closely affiliated with the nonprofit but who might like to make a gift to the nonprofit. Target appeals to the constituency reading the ad; for example, place planned giving ads for charitable gift annuities in sections of the newspapers that are read by an older population. Remember to emphasize that these planned giving options are gift vehicles, not traditional investment options, and should be made by individuals with donative intent.

19.13 CONCLUSION

One of the most important components of any planned giving program is marketing. Planned giving is the department in a development office that is most likely to market. To stimulate business, the planned giving officer plays the role of entrepreneur on behalf of the program. Without a strong marketing effort, most prospects will not know about the giving opportunities offered by the organization. The use of marketing vehicles to help prospects identify themselves to the organization will, over time, result in a greater number of planned gifts for the organization.

CHAPTER TWENTY

Marketing the Noneconomic Benefits of Philanthropy

20.1   INTRODUCTION

Philanthropy has changed in the new millennium. A number of factors and events have greatly affected philanthropy generally and nonprofit organizations in particular. The Jobs and Growth Tax Relief Reconciliation Act of 2003 and the Economic Growth and Tax Relief Reconciliation Act of 2001 have diminished the tax benefits that charitable giving provides to donors who make charitable gifts. The stock market's volatility and poor performance has decreased donors' net worth and disposable assets. The weakened economy and recession has created economic uncertainty, and with that has come a challenge to consumer and business confidence, a loss of jobs, and a decline in business growth and expansion.

In a very positive way, the attacks of September 11 forced Americans to reconsider and reevaluate their personal value systems and the role that philanthropy plays in their lives. No doubt, philanthropy is emerging as one of the most important ways that individuals can contribute to society, and donors will continue to make charitable gifts to charities that reflect their personal goals, ideals, and value systems. Directly and indirectly, the nation's nonprofit organizations seek to attract donors to provide resources to enable these organizations to fulfill their missions. Noneconomic benefits include the many ways that donors and prospects enrich their lives because of their affiliation with a nonprofit organization. To articulate the noneconomic benefits of philanthropy, nonprofit organizations can use enrichment brochures to reach targeted audiences. This chapter examines these noneconomic benefits and makes suggestions on ways charities can develop strategies to ensure that this message reaches constituents through an enrichment brochure.

20.2   THE CHANGING FINANCIAL AND TAX CLIMATES

Charitable giving is changing. Previously, donors obtained greater economic benefits in exchange for their charitable gifts, including:

■ A larger charitable income tax deduction based on higher income tax rates provided greater benefits to donors. Now, with lower rates, donors pay for a greater percentage of their contributions.

■ Estate and gift tax charitable deductions that enable donors to avoid or diminish taxes by encouraging donors to make gifts to charity to reduce their taxable estates to amounts below the tax thresholds. Now, because donors are able to transfer to their heirs larger amounts of cash and property, donors will have fewer incentives to make charitable gifts.

■ Opportunities to fund gifts using highly appreciated assets such as stock. Now, although some donors still have considerable gains, the stock market is still well off its previous highs, leaving many donors with shrinking net worths and fewer highly appreciated securities that many donors prefer to use first when making charitable gifts.

■ Interest rates have likewise fallen, further reducing opportunities for many donors on fixed incomes to generate sufficient returns from certificates of deposit and bonds. Life income gift streams from planned gifts help donors supplement retirement income, wages, and investment earnings and may, in part, offset loss of income from fixed-income investments, making planned giving one of the more popular ways to make charitable gifts.

20.3 NONECONOMIC BENEFITS

Noneconomic benefits include everything that a nonprofit offers to its constituents, from participating in the organization's programs, attending a symposium, or participating in a seminar to discussing research with knowledgeable staff members. Noneconomic benefits also include the intangibles that come from philanthropy, including the good feeling that a donor experiences when a charitable gift is made. Through charitable giving, donors have opportunities to fulfill philanthropic objectives, giving greater meaning to their lives. These individuals also are invited to participate in the nonprofit's events, activities, and programs that develop social contacts and expand business and professional relationships. Further, donors have the chance to become more involved with the organization's professional staff and leadership.

What are the noneconomic benefits of philanthropy, and how should they best be communicated to the nonprofit's donors and prospects? The following illustrates some of the more important noneconomic benefits:

■ *Access to the nonprofit organization and its leadership.* Philanthropy provides opportunities for donors and prospects to access to individuals affiliated with the nonprofit. Depending on the nonprofit, these individuals include a wide array of nonprofit staff members, faculty members, deans, department heads, curators, medical staff, and executive leadership. Through philanthropy, donors with even modest gift records have a number of opportunities to meet the nonprofit's president and other executive officers. Some organizations create special groups, such as a President's Society, to recognize certain donors and give them regular access to certain senior administrators. Many donors consider these opportunities to be a very positive by-product of their philanthropy.

■ *Advocacy.* Nonprofit organizations are advocates on behalf of causes related to the nature of the charity. The causes are many and varied and can include the nonprofit's serving as an advocate on behalf of mainstream causes as well as for causes for whom there are relatively few supporters. The major causes include:

■ Environmental issues
■ Mental health issues
■ Poverty

- Literacy
- Disabilities
- Homelessness
- Programs for youths and young people
- Human rights
- Religious expression
- Educational opportunities
- Health care
- Community programs
- Arts and cultural programs
- Wildlife

Nonprofit organizations must remind their constituents of the important role that the charity plays in serving as advocates on behalf of others in need and for related causes.

- *Ambassadorship.* Nonprofit officers, staff members, and volunteers serve as ambassadors building goodwill, establishing networks, and organizing focused efforts on targeted issues. Nonprofit ambassadors can canvass regions and geographical areas and place individuals in strategically located positions building relationships that reflect the constituents' needs.

- *Association/affiliation.* Through involvement with nonprofit organizations, many donors identify themselves as being associated or affiliated with these nonprofit organizations. Donors and prospects enjoy the benefits of associating and affiliating with nonprofit representatives and other individuals who share common interests.

- *Research.* Constituents value the nonprofit's ability to gather and disseminate data, statistics, research, and other information pertaining to the shared interests of the nonprofit and the constituents.

- *Business contacts.* Through events, programs, and activities, philanthropy promotes opportunities for donors and prospects to develop business contacts and promote professional and business relationships. For example, the nonprofit's planned giving program can sponsor a planned giving committee. This committee brings together professional advisors and other individuals knowledgeable in the field of law, finance, investment planning, and related fields.

- *Sharing goals, values, and ideals.* Philanthropy creates opportunities for individuals to meet others who share similar goals, ideals, and values.

- *Social involvement.* Every nonprofit organization hosts activities that are largely social in nature. These activities include dinners, breakfasts, luncheons, and other events that create opportunities to meet others and develop social contacts.

- *Learning and education.* Seminars, workshops, and symposiums offer attendees the opportunity to increase their knowledge and sustain and broaden areas of interest.

- *Belonging.* For childless couples, surviving spouses, and individuals who are new to an area, nonprofit organizations offer a quasi-family with whom these individuals can share time and interests. At most nonprofit organizations, donors are recognized for their philanthropy that enhances the bond among donors and between donors and the nonprofit organization.

- *The nonprofit's power to organize, concentrate, and intensify impact.* Acting alone, individuals find it difficult to address and influence action. Nonprofit organizations make it possible to organize and mobilize action and people. Nonprofits also can concentrate, magnify, and intensify resources and attention on issues important to donors and prospects.

- *Professional management and financial services.* Through a nonprofit's foundation, treasurer, investment committee, and other financially related offices, donors receive a sense of assurance about the way their endowed fund is managed and invested. These offices relieve the burden that many donors experience. In addition, some nonprofits offer services to individual collectors providing advice, support, and curation assistance to develop displays and exhibits.

- *Legacy development.* Many individuals seek permanent ways to leave a meaningful legacy to society. Nonprofit organizations help donors fulfill lifelong dreams of establishing named endowed programs that carry on in perpetuity.

- *Volunteerism.* Nonprofit organizations provide opportunities for donors to engage in meaningful and rewarding work on behalf of the nonprofit. Through volunteerism, nonprofit boards, committees, and advisory groups rely on volunteers, most of whom are donors.

- *Charitable gift planning and counseling.* Planned giving offices perform valuable services counseling and advising donors and their professional advisors about charitable gift planning and planned giving techniques.

- *Positive feeling of well-being.* Through philanthropy, donors have opportunities to engage in truly important work and fulfill personal philanthropic goals and objectives.

20.4 ARTICULATING THE NONECONOMIC BENEFITS

As the economic benefits of philanthropy diminish, it is more important than ever to communicate the noneconomic benefits of philanthropy. Donors are more likely to support organizations that best articulate their services to society and define their place in the community. Nonprofits should clearly delineate the nature, scope, and focus of the services and programs they offer to their constituents. Donors select nonprofit organizations that they believe are worthy and deserving of their support.

20.5 ENRICHMENT BROCHURE

Unfortunately, some nonprofit organizations focus more on the economic benefits associated with philanthropy and fail to adequately inform donors, prospects, and the community about the intrinsic value of these noneconomic benefits. Now is the time for nonprofit organizations to reexamine the ways they educate their constituents about their mission, programs, services, need for financial support, and the noneconomic benefits of philanthropy. One way to do this is through an enrichment brochure.

At most nonprofit organizations, planned giving staff are actively involved in marketing and promoting both charitable giving and the organization. This is most commonly done through a variety of marketing documents, such as brochures, guides, and newsletters or through position papers or proposals developed for specific individuals. Most of these documents contain a description of the economic benefit of philanthropy—life income streams, charitable income tax deductions, and other related topics. The enrichment brochure is most typically produced as a publication, but it can be released online, allowing easy access to interested constituents and easy updating for maintenance of the publication. These brochures offer wonderful opportunities to promote the noneconomic benefits of philanthropy. Defining enrichment programs and preparing enrichment brochures is a great way for a planned giving program to develop goodwill both within and outside the organization with a wide variety of constituent groups. Including this information with planned giving documents enhances the usefulness of the document to the reader and improves its shelf life. Donors are much more likely to retain these documents.

This part of the chapter discusses the creation and use of enrichment programs and brochures that define and describe the noneconomic benefits of philanthropy available at nonprofit organizations.

20.6 ENRICHMENT PROGRAMS

One of the most effective marketing strategies to inform donors about the nonprofit's noneconomic benefits is through the drafting of an enrichment brochure. An enrichment brochure describes the noneconomic benefits that are available to the nonprofit's constituents. These brochures are particularly effective with the public and the community that the nonprofit serves. As described earlier, enrichment programs include programs, lectures, seminars, resources, and other activities such as museums, galleries, special collections, exhibits, or displays that are open to the public, the community, prospects, and donors. If necessary, individual brochures can be prepared for specific constituent groups.

Some charities use calendars and newsletters to provide information about current events, but an enrichment brochure is much more than that. Enrichment brochures provide information by areas of interest and give a broad view of the types of programs and resources that are available. To begin the brochure, each department in the nonprofit is invited to submit a description of programs sponsored by the department. Most departments are eager to promote their programs and most willingly participate in this process. Included are the department's name, address, telephone number, Web address, and the name of a contact person. This information is compiled for all interested departments and is included in the brochure along with a description of the types of enrichment programs offered by the department. The document can be supplemented with the nonprofit's mission statement, statement of purpose, by-laws, IRS letter of determination as a 501(c)(3) organization, and other related documents. Exhibit 20.1 is an example of a memorandum that can be sent to departments to invite their participation. This document is included in Appendix, CD-ROM Documentation, Correspondence.

Exhibit 20.1   Letter Describing Enrichment Brochure

MEMORANDUM

TO: <DEPARTMENT HEAD>

FROM: <PLANNED GIVING DIRECTOR>

DATE: <DATE>

I am pleased to enclose a sample page from <ORGANIZATION'S> enrichment brochure.

The purpose of this document is to educate donors, prospects, and the community about the ways that they may become involved with <ORGANIZATION.> We view this document as an important tool to be used in identifying and cultivating individuals who may be interested in becoming donors to <ORGANIZATION>. We also see this document as being helpful to members of the <VOLUNTEER LEADERSHIP GROUPS> that contact representatives throughout the community. No doubt, this document will also be very valuable to all departments and programs that are included in this document.

To the extent that your department offers programs or activities for the general public, please provide a narrative describing these activities. I would appreciate it if you would review this document and forward any suggestions or comments to me by <DATE.> However, if you need more time please let me know.

Information about events, programs and activities can be sorted by subject matter and cross-referenced. For example, a large university could offer several types of enrichment programs to its constituents. These opportunities and the enrichment brochure that follow are designed to promote enrichment programs at universities. Other nonprofit organizations can modify these enrichment programs to meet their needs. The following general categories offer a convenient way to organize the information for educational institutions:

- Alumni Programs
- Arts and Cultural Programs/Museums

- The Sciences/Astronomy
- Athletics
- Book Festivals and Fairs
- Business and Entrepreneurship Programs
- Computer Assistance and Resources
- Counseling and Referral Services
- Ethnic Programs
- Gift Shops and Bookstores
- Health Diagnostics and Referral Services
- Health and Fitness
- Hobbies and Leisure
- Home and Garden
- International Programs
- Centers and Institutes
- Languages and Linguistics
- Learning
- Libraries
- Literacy
- Publications and Subscriptions
- Recreation and Participatory Sports
- Special Events

The brochure can be nonprofits in-house, or outside designers can be retained to produce the document. Most nonprofits will find that the document can easily be produced in-house by current staff members or with the assistance of interested volunteers. If the nonprofit has a graphics or publication department, that department usually can offer technical assistance in producing the brochure. With a modest investment of time and effort, most organizations can produce a first-rate publication that will well serve the interests of the organization and its constituents.

Once the brochure has been produced in draft form, it is important to ask participating departments to approve the content pertaining to their representative sections. Exhibit 20.2 describes the approval process. This document is included in Appendix, CD-ROM Documentation, Correspondence.

As soon as the brochure is available, it should be distributed to all participating departments along with a document similar to Exhibit 20.3. This document is included in Appendix, CD-ROM Documentation, Correspondence.

Exhibit 20.2   Letter Describing Approval Process

MEMORANDUM

TO: <NAME>

FROM: <PLANNED GIVING DIRECTOR>

DATE: <DATE>

Thank you very much for participating in the development of our enrichment brochure that will be made available to the donors, prospects, and the community. Attached is a copy of your department's description, as it will appear in the brochure.

Please review and feel free to make any changes you feel are necessary. We encourage your input and comments. After you have made changes, please mark the "Changes made" selection, sign the approval form, and send the edited description to our office. If you are satisfied with the description as is, simply mark the "No changes necessary" selection, sign the approval form, and return.

❏   Approved. No changes necessary.

❏   Changes made and approved. See attached.

❏   Changes made. Second draft requested prior to approval.

APPROVED BY:

_____

Signature

_____

Printed Name

_____

Title

Exhibit 20.3   Letter Thanking Departments

MEMORANDUM

TO: «Dept»
                 «Contact name»
                 «Box»

FROM: <NAME>

DATE: <DATE>

SUBJECT: Enrichment Programs, Activities, and Resources for the Public

Thank you very much for participating in the development of our brochure describing enrichment programs, activities, and resources. We are excited with the final product and look forward to its potential impact on enhancing opportunities for donors and prospects to become more involved with
<ORGANIZATION>. We hope you are as pleased with this publication as we are. Enclosed are com-
plimentary copies. Thank you for your assistance in this project.

20.7   ENRICHMENT BROCHURE ILLUSTRATIONS

Exhibit 20.4 illustrates sample language that can be used to describe programs, activities, and enrichment opportunities at a nonprofit organization. The language can be modified to meet the needs
of a particular organization. This document is included in Appendix, CD-ROM Documentation,
Marketing.

20.8   DISSEMINATING ENRICHMENT BROCHURES

Once the enrichment brochure is printed, it should be distributed to a wide variety of individuals
and groups. The brochure should be sent to all donors, volunteers, prospects, and community leaders. The nonprofit's own publications should include information about the enrichment brochure
along with ordering information. In addition, the local press will often run stories on the programs
that are available at a particular organization. Exhibit 20.5 describes the enrichment brochure and
can be distributed along with a brochure to the press or to other organizations. This document is included in Appendix, CD-ROM Documentation, Correspondence.

20.8 DISSEMINATING ENRICHMENT BROCHURES

Exhibit 20.4 Enrichment Brochure

<ORGANIZATION>'s ENRICHMENT BROCHURE

<ORGANIZATION> <PROVIDE DESCRIPTION.> The <ORGANIZATION> offers programs for <DESCRIPTION>

The main facility houses <DESCRIBE> offering <DESCRIBE.>

With special emphasis on serving <DESCRIBE,> <ORGANIZATION> strives to offer programs to <TARGETED PURPOSES> in the following areas: <DESCRIBE>

Service is a vital part of the mission of <ORGANIZATION>. To this end, <ORGANIZATION> supports <DESCRIBE> with an emphasis on the needs of <DESCRIBE.>

<ORGANIZATION> means many things to many people. <ORGANIZATION> is committed to providing specialized assistance, information, and programs designed to address the <DESCRIBE PURPOSES> We hope this information is helpful to you and we invite you to participate in <ORGANIZATION>'s commitment to <DESCRIBE.>

ALUMNI PROGRAMS
ADDRESS, WEB ADDRESS
TELEPONE, CONTACT PERSON

The Alumni Association maintains and develops relationships between alumni and <ORGANIZATION>. The Alumni Association conducts a variety of programs such as chapter events, travel programs, career services, scholarships, publications, class reunions, and homecoming. The Alumni Association offers a wide selection of gifts bearing the <ORGANIZATION>'s logo including clothing, rings, watches, rocking chairs, and captain's chairs. Friend's memberships are available to the public.

ASTRONOMY
ADDRESS, WEB ADDRESS
TELEPHONE NUMBER, CONTACT PERSON

<ORGANIZATION> operates a planetarium and offers open houses the <DAY> of the month. Tours are available for classroom groups.

ATHLETICS
ADDRESS, WEB ADDRESS
TELEPHONE NUMBER, CONTACT PERSON

<ORGANIZATION> participates in the <CONFERENCE NAME> for intercollegiate athletics. As a member of <CONFERENCE>, <ORGANIZATION> sponsors <DESCRIBE OFFERINGS.> Sports facilities include <DESCRIBE.> Sports fans can support <ORGANIZATION>'s <ATHLETIC PROGRAM> by becoming members of <DESCRIBE> Priority seating is available for <DESCRIBE.> <ORGANIZATION> offers hospitality room privileges and game sponsorships.
<ACTIVITY and DESCRIPTION.> <DESCRIBE FEES>. Memberships available. Payment plans accepted. Call <TELEPHONE NUMBER>.

COMPUTERS
ADDRESS, WEB ADDRESS
TELEPHONE NUMBER, CONTACT PERSON

(Continued)

Exhibit 20.4 *(Continued)*

<ORGANIZATION>'s Computer Center is a community support lab which houses approximately <NUMBER> computers networked locally and available for <DESCRIBE USE> free of charge<OR DESCRIBE COSTS>. Although our computers are user friendly, if you're updating your resume, writing an important business letter, or creating a table or graph for a presentation <DESCRIBE SERVICES>, our employees are on hand to assist you with any questions or problems you may encounter. Computer Center hours are: <DESCRIBE HOURS OF OPERATION> Software/graphic scanners/printing services are also offered.

<NAME>DEPARTMENT
ADDRESS, WEB ADDRESS
TELEPHONE, CONTACT PERSON

The <Department> hosts workshops, readings, book festivals, and publishes literary magazines. Many of these programs and events are free and open to the public.

<DEPARTMENT> offers prose and poetry readings by nationally recognized authors and graduate students. Contact <NAME, ADDRESS, and TELEPHONE> for more information.

GALLERIES/MUSEUMS
ADDRESS, WEB ADDRESS
TELEPHONE, CONTACT PERSON

The <ORGANIZATION>'s gallery/museum is <DESCRIBE> The gallery presents <DESCRIBE> exhibitions annually, houses a permanent collection of over <DESCRIBE> collections, and sponsors extensive educational programs. The <ORGANIZATION'S GALLERY> features <DESCRIBE> exhibitions as well as <DESCRIBE> productions supplemented with lectures, workshops, performances, and field trips.

MUSIC
ADDRESS, WEB ADDRESS
TELEPHONE NUMBER, CONTACT PERSON

<ORGANIZATION>'s Department of Music hosts a wide variety of music programs, recitals, choirs, and orchestral ensembles. Brochures listing all upcoming musical events available at the <LOCATION> Join the <ASSOCIATION> that <DESCRIBE SERVICES.>

SPECIAL EVENTS
ADDRESS, WEB ADDRESS
TELEPHONE, CONTACT PERSON

If you're looking for big name entertainment, call the <NAME OF DEPARTMENT> at <ORGANIZATION>. Featured acts including <DESCRIBE> have appeared.

Exhibit 20.5   Letter to Press and Community Organizations

LETTER

<DATE>

<NAME>
<ADDRESS, CITY, STATE, ZIP>

Dear <NAME>:

It was nice to speak with you regarding our new publication about enrichment opportunities at <ORGANIZATION.> The purpose of this publication is to inform the donors, prospects, and the community about the many opportunities they have to participate in a wide variety of educational, social, cultural, and entertainment opportunities at <ORGANIZATION> along with <DESCRIBE OTHER PROGRAMS.> We thought that you might be interested in reviewing this booklet for the <NAME OF PUBLICATION.> If you think the publication would be helpful to your readership, we would be pleased to send complimentary copies to those who request a copy. Readers may request a copy by contacting the <NAME OF OFFICE, TELEHONE NUMBER, ADDRESS, and CONTACT PERSON.> A summary of the enrichment opportunities follows:

- Art/Art Programs (Pg. #)
- Astronomy (Pg. #)
- Child Care Resource and Referral (Pg. #)
- Computers (Pg. 12)
- Concerts/Special Events (Pg. #)
- Counseling Center/Career Center (Pg. #)
- Cultural Opportunities (Pg. #)
- Galleries/ Museums (Pg. #)
- Music: Symphony, choir, band, and opera (Pg. #)
- Placement and Career Services: Employment Opportunities, Job Fair (Pg. #)
- Sports Activities—Participatory and nonparticipatory sports including <DESCRIBE> (Pg. #)
- Theatre (Pg. 31)
- Volunteer Opportunities (Pg. #)

We hope you find this publication to be helpful and we look forward to hearing from you.

Sincerely,

20.9   CONCLUSION

Nonprofit organizations offer a variety of rich and rewarding opportunities for donors, prospects, and other constituent groups. Individuals affiliated with a nonprofit have opportunities to expand social and business contacts, learn about new topics, and engage the organization in a variety of interesting and meaningful ways. Noneconomic benefits provide incentives to individuals to become involved in philanthropy with one or more nonprofit organizations, enriching their lives.

These enrichment opportunities can be promoted through the use of an enrichment brochure that describes ways that constituents can participate through their affiliation with the nonprofit organization. Examine the types of noneconomic benefits offered by the nonprofit organization, and make a concerted effort to educate constituents about them through an enrichment brochure.

## CHAPTER TWENTY-ONE

Making Planned Giving Presentations

21.1 PRESENTATIONS

Planned giving presentations are an increasingly important component of a planned giving officer's job responsibilities. A presentation on planned giving provides an opportunity to introduce important technical and practical information about planned giving options and asset usage and communicates the nonprofit's message to its internal and external constituents. A presentation may be made to donors, prospects, friends, volunteers, board members, and professional advisors.

Presentations to an organization's donors and friends, and in the case of colleges and universities to alumni groups, serve as social gatherings for cultivation and reacquaintance with representatives from the nonprofit, which can strengthen the donor's bond with the nonprofit and in turn lead to increased financial support. Presentations to volunteers and board members are usually for training purposes, with the hope that the volunteer or board member will use the information for personal planning or to solicit planned gifts. Presentations to professional advisors are part of the nonprofit's public education and outreach program to educate the outside advisor about its needs and charitable gift planning options available to the advisor's clients.

A thoughtful and purposeful planned giving presentation can also serve as a solicitation of the attendees. By educating an organization's constituents through a planned giving presentation, the planned giving officer's actions amount to a solicitation of attendees. This important opportunity cannot be lost, so the presentation should be of the highest quality. Sophisticated audiences are accustomed to seeing savvy financial planners and investment brokers offer state-of-the-art presentations. These presentations use color, graphics, and audiovisual materials that maximize the opportunity to communicate potentially complicated information. Designing a high-quality presentation requires careful preparation and effective visual forms of communication such as slides, overheads, and transparencies.

This chapter explores the issues associated with planned giving presentations and offers a master set of exhibits that can be used or easily modified to meet the needs of the planned giving officer and the audience. See Appendix, CD-ROM Documentation, Presentations. The master set of exhibits is divided into six sections:

1. Introduction to Planned Giving

2. Life Income Gifts

3. Tax Consequences of Charitable Gifts

4. Estate Planning—Wills and Trusts

5. Asset Classification

6. Building Endowments

(a) Presentation Formats

Selecting an appropriate format is a critical first step in planning a successful presentation. The selected format should match the needs of the anticipated audience. Presentations to professional advisors are likely to include more detail and additional information on the technical aspects of planned giving, whereas presentations to volunteers and friends of the nonprofit are likely to be more informal and less technical.

There are a variety of formats to consider, each of which has its benefits and drawbacks:

- *Lecture.* A lecture format works well for nonprofit boards and committees and for large groups of alumni or friends of the nonprofit. However, it can be impersonal and may limit opportunities for interaction between the presenter and the audience.

- *Round table or U-shaped workshop.* This option works well for board members and nonprofit committees because it allows discussion and encourages interaction, as all attendees are visible to each other and the presenter. This format also provides ample workspace for participants.

- *Role playing.* Role playing can be an effective format for board members or volunteers. Role playing is participatory and enables all attendees to get to know each other while learning. It also provides an opportunity for participants to practice solicitations.

- *Case study.* The case study is particularly effective for professional advisors. As discussed later in the section on professional advisors, this format is familiar to attorneys, certified public accountants (CPAs), and investment advisors who may have received their training through the case study method.

(b) Anticipating the Audience

To deliver an effective and persuasive presentation that communicates and connects with the audience, it is necessary to consider the presentation from the intended audience's perspective. Consider these questions in adapting presentations to meet the needs of the audience:

- What is the relationship of the audience to the nonprofit?

- What is the audience's level of technical knowledge?

- What does this audience need to know about planned giving?

- Which assets is the audience likely to use to fund gifts?

- What is the audience's anticipated age group?

- Has this audience attended other planned giving presentations?

- Is the presentation structured to offer more than planned giving? For example, some audiences are interested in related topics such as estate and gift taxes, probate avoidance, and estate planning.

- How well do members of the audience know each other?

- How well does the audience know the presenter?

(i) Presentations to Nontechnical Audiences.   Nontechnical audiences may include the nonprofit's board members, volunteers, friends, donors, and prospects. These audiences appreciate general information about wills and bequests and income and estate taxation. Planned giving helps these individuals obtain income tax benefits, lifetime streams of income, and estate tax reduction; planned giving is seen as one way to meet financial needs while providing support to a worthy nonprofit.

(ii) Presentations to Technical Audiences.   Technical audiences include professional advisors such as attorneys, trust officers, accountants and investment advisors, and the nonprofit's financial officers. Professional advisors appreciate obtaining information that can assist them in working with their clients. They want information on reducing capital gains taxes, federal estate and gift taxes, trusts, bequests, and estate planning, along with information about making gifts of noncash assets such as real estate, securities, and tangible personal property, which may be given outright or used as a way to fund planned gifts. Because many are familiar with the case study approach typically presented in professional schools, this format offers a practical and familiar model. It serves as a point of reference for these advisors and is an approach that the speaker can modify to meet the experience level of the anticipated audience. A well-designed, influential presentation to professional advisors also offers the planned giving officer the opportunity to establish herself with the financial community. These advisors may contact the presenter about a variety of cases and situations, only some of which are likely to benefit the nonprofit organization sponsoring the presentation. However, over time, a number of important gifts may occur that will benefit the nonprofit.

The nonprofit's financial officers appreciate learning about the intricacies of planned gifts, especially as they relate to the nonprofit's investment obligation to produce the necessary income to meet payout rates for life income gifts. The information offered to these groups should be broader than just planned giving concepts, providing the presenter with an opportunity to place planned giving in context with other development programs and with tax, estate, and financial planning concepts.

(c) Audiovisual Materials

(i) Speaker's Outline.   Members of the audience should receive a copy of the speaker's outline and copies of any overheads. For many in the audience, distance from the speaker, poor vision, and poor hearing limit the opportunity to participate in the presentation. A personal set of materials enables each member of the audience to more actively participate in the presentation.

(ii) Supplementary Materials.   Flipcharts, greaseboards, whiteboards, and blackboards are effective devices for communicating with attendees. In most cases, the text should be preprinted for the presenter's convenience. These tools summarize information presented and can test the audience's understanding of the information presented.

(iii) Computers.   At many presentations, it is advantageous for the presenter to bring a laptop or notebook computer to illustrate planned giving concepts. The computer demonstrates the user-friendly nature of most planned giving software programs. Financial calculations can be produced immediately, and a well-designed presentation, coupled with calculations tailored to an individual's needs, can open opportunities to discuss potential gift options.

(iv) Overhead Transparencies.   Overhead transparencies provide an effective, inexpensive visual medium for the presenter to communicate information and ideas to the audience. To maximize the effectiveness of overheads, consider the following suggestions:

- ■ Use overheads that are either all portrait (vertical), $8^1/_2$ inches wide by 11 inches tall or landscape (horizontal), 11 inches wide by $8^1/_2$ inches tall, to orient the attendees to the visual form of communication.

■   **186**   ■

- Select a font that is visually clear and clean. Avoid the use of script fonts, which are often difficult to read.

- Use a blend of text, charts, and graphs to communicate.

- Limit text to emphasize key points and use only phrases, brief sentences, or bulleted points, not paragraphs. Use numbers or bullets to differentiate between ideas and concepts.

- Place a mark or a colored sticker in the right-hand top corner to help correctly place the overhead right side up.

- Always number each overhead and make sure that the number corresponds to the outline or copy of the overhead distributed to the audience. Attendees lose interest when they lose their place; this distracts the audience as well as the presenter.

- Print key concepts or words in advance or print on the overhead during the presentation to emphasize a special point.

Exhibit 21.1 is a model transparency from the master presentation plan, and included in Appendix, CD-ROM Documentation, Presentations. The presenter should be careful to position himself to provide the audience with an unobstructed view of the screen. The presenter should face the audience and use a pointer or colored pen, pointing on the overhead itself, not on the screen, so the presenter can maintain eye contact with the audience.

(d) Speaking Skills

(i) Duration. Presentations may be part of an all-day event at a nonprofit's open house or homecoming program, or a one-hour morning or evening session for volunteers, but ideally should not exceed 40 to 50 minutes in length. Include a question-and-answer session. If there are several sessions, breaks should be scheduled after each presentation, and the presenter should be sensitive to questions from attendees regarding gift options and discussions about specific assets such as stocks or real estate, which may indicate charitable motivation. Comments by attendees offer insight into the nature, size, and timing of a potential gift and its intended use. Additional staff members should be available to assist attendees and to provide the presenter with a break.

(ii) Vocal Delivery and Tone. The tone of the presenter's speech should vary from soft to loud, brisk to slow, high to low. The presenter should avoid a monotone or one-dimensional form of speech. If the presenter knows the audience, the tone may be informal. Attendees often are fearful that they will not grasp complex and technical information, so consider beginning the presentation with familiar, general information that helps attendees relax and learn. Enthusiastic, humorous, and self-effacing speech can disarm listeners.

Exhibit 21.1 Presentation: Why Do Donors Give?

Why Do Donors Give?

- Donative intent
- Philanthropic purposes
- Involvement with nonprofit
- Solicitation from staff members or volunteers
- Gifts in honor or in memory
- Repayment of a debt
- Nonprofit as a family substitute
- Tax/financial benefits

The presenter should speak at a comfortable and conversational pace. A pace that is too fast or slow can be distracting and frustrating to the attendees. Varying the pace can also serve to emphasize important points. The use of silence can signal the transition from one point to another. Repetition and reinforcement of key concepts and issues are critical to learning. Planned giving concepts are foreign to many attendees, and repetition of those concepts reinforces them.

(iii) Audience Participation. Each presentation should attempt to involve the audience. One way to do this in advance is to ask a likely attendee for permission to use him as a case study for the presentation. Using one or more attendees from different age brackets as case studies helps to involve all attendees in the presentation. In addition, most people learn and remember more when the planned giving concept is applied to a real-life example. If the presenter is not overly sensitive about her age, the presenter may use herself as a case study to introduce the benefits of life income gifts.

(iv) Practice. Prior to every presentation, practice with the information to be presented. Develop familiar and comfortable opening remarks to help make a connection between the presenter and the audience. Stage fright is caused by inexperience and a lack of confidence in the subject matter of the presentation. Inexperience may be overcome by practice and a lack of confidence can be overcome by knowledge. A brief anecdote by the speaker in the beginning is helpful in making a connection to the audience.

(e) Testimonials

An effective way to end a planned giving presentation is to conclude with a testimonial story about a planned giving donor who personifies the meaning of philanthropy. Most organizations have donors who, though not necessarily wealthy, have made a major sacrifice to reach deep into financial reserves to make a planned gift. These testimonials show attendees that they too can make significant gifts.

(f) Follow-up

After the presentation, the planned giving staff members should follow up, in writing, with all attendees to thank them for participating in the event. Attendees who indicated a specific interest in a planned gift option should be scheduled for a personal visit, and all attendees should receive future issues of planned giving publications.

(g) Summary

Consider the following when making presentations:

- Work to increase knowledge to become comfortable with the planned giving subject matter.
- Practice the speech.
- Never read or memorize a speech; always work from notes.
- Do not exceed the allotted time.
- Never say anything that could potentially offend any attendee.
- Maintain eye contact.
- Interact with the audience.
- Leave time for questions at the end.

21.1 PRESENTATIONS

Exhibit 21.2 is a Master Presentation Inventory Thumbnail presentation outline and is included in the CD-ROM.

Exhibit 21.2 Planned Giving Presentations

SECTION 1. INTRODUCTION TO PLANNED GIVING

PLANNED GIVING: BENEFITS OF CHARITABLE GIVING

What Is Planned Giving?
- Mutual benefits to donor and charity
- Gifts through wills and trusts
- Assists donors in making major gifts

Life Income Gifts
- Provides charitable income tax deductions, capital gains avoidance (20%), and estate tax reductions
- Endowments
- Other assets (real estate, stocks, bonds, mutual funds, tangible personal property)
- Financial stability to nonprofit

PLANNED GIVING: FUNDRAISING VERSUS DEVELOPMENT

What Is Fundraising?
- Outright gifts of cash
- Annual support
- Operating expenses
- Identifies prospects for major gifts

What Is Development?
- Long-term financial support
- Support at all levels
- Multitiered approach to raising money
- Integrated approach to raising money
- Development includes planned giving

WHY DO DONORS GIVE?
- Involvement with nonprofit
- Contact with staff members or volunteers
- Donative intent
- Philanthropy
- Gifts in honor or in memory
- Repayment of a debt
- Nonprofit as a family substitute
- Tax/financial benefits

GIFT RANGE TABLE

Gift	Number of Donors	Amount
$250,000	2	$500,000
$100,000	5	$500,000
$50,000	10	$500,000
$25,000	24	$600,000
$10,000	30	$300,000
$1,000	100	$100,000
	Total: 171	$2,500,000

TYPES OF PLANNED GIFTS
- Life income gifts
  - Charitable gift annuities
  - Deferred gift annuities

(Continued)

Exhibit 21.2 *(Continued)*

- Pooled income fund
- Charitable remainder trust
- Gifts from the estate
  - Will
  - Trust
- Funds
  - Endowed funds
  - Current-use awards
- Assets other than cash
  - Securities
  - Real estate
  - Nontraditional assets

SECTION 2. LIFE INCOME GIFTS

LIFE INCOME GIFTS

- Income for the lifetime of donor and/or second beneficiary
- A charitable income tax deduction
- Endowed fund
- Possible avoidance of capital gains taxes
- Leadership club
- A reduction in federal estate taxes

CHARITABLE GIFT ANNUITIES

- Income for life paid annually, semiannually, quarterly, or monthly
- A guaranteed return often greater than money market rates (for example, a donor at age <YEARS> earns <%>).
- Immediate charitable income tax deduction
- Reduction in capital gains taxes if the gift is made with appreciated securities
- A chance to support a program of interest
- Membership in a leadership club

Benefits of a $10,000 Charitable Gift Annuity

Ages(s)	Rate	Annual Income	Charitable Income Tax Deduction
65	%	$	$
70	%	$	$
75	%	$	$
70/68	%	$	$
75/73	%	$	$

DEFERRED GIFT ANNUITIES

- An immediate charitable income tax deduction
- Guaranteed income in the future, often at retirement
- An excellent yield (For example, a 40-year-old donor who makes a gift of $5,000 earns <%> at age 65.)
- A reduction in capital gains taxes if the gift is made with appreciated securities
- Membership in a leadership club

Benefits of a $10,000 Deferred Gift Annuity*

Ages(s)	Rate	Annual Income	Charitable Income Tax Deduction
40	%	$	$
45	%	$	$
50	%	$	$
55	%	$	$
40/45	%	$	$
50/55	%	$	$

*Deferred to Age 65

■   190   ■

Exhibit 21.2 *(Continued)*

POOLED INCOME FUND
- Increase yield
  - (Current rate is < % >.)
- Avoid capital gains tax on gifts of appreciated securities
- Receive an income for life
- Receive an immediate charitable income tax deduction
- Membership in a leadership club

Benefits of a $10,000 Pooled Income Fund

Ages(s)	Rate	Annual Income	Charitable Income Tax Deduction
60	%	$	$
65	%	$	$
70	%	$	$
75/68	%	$	$
75/73	%	$	$

CHARITABLE REMAINDER TRUST OPTIONS
- Income to beneficiary for life, remainder to nonprofit
- Charitable Remainder Annuity Trust: Fixed Payment, invade principal
- Charitable Remainder Unitrust 1: Straight fixed percentage trust, invade principal
- Charitable Remainder Unitrust 2: Net Income Unitrust
- Charitable Remainder Unitrust 3: Net Income Unitrust with a make-up provision

SECTION 3. TAX CONSEQUENCES

TAX CONSIDERATIONS
- The Jobs and Growth Tax Relief Reconciliation Act of 2003
- The Economic Growth and Tax Reconciliation Act of 2001
- Reduced Income Tax Rates
- Capital Gains: 15 percent for most investment assets
  - Example: Donor purchases stock for $50,000 and one year later the value is $150,000. The gain is $100,000 × 15% = $15,000
- The donor obtains a charitable income tax deduction for gifts of cash, up to 50 percent, and for gifts of property, up to 30 percent, of the donor's adjusted gross income. (Donor must be itemizer; excess may be carried over for up to five additional years.)
  - Example: Donor makes a gift by check for $75,000 and donor's adjusted gross income is $100,000. The donor may claim a charitable income tax deduction for $50,000 in year 1 and $25,000 in year 2.
- Long-term capital asset defined as an asset held for a year and a day
- Lifetime exemption and federal estate and gift taxes

Estate and Gift Tax Rates and Credit Exemption Amounts

Calendar Year	Estate and GST Tax* Credit Exemption	Gift Tax Credit Exemption	Highest Estate and Gift Tax Rates
2003	$1 million	$1 million	49%
2004	$1.5 million	$1 million	48%
2005	$1.5 million	$1 million	47%
2006	$2 million	$1 million	46%
2007	$2 million	$1 million	45%
2008	$2 million	$1 million	45%
2009	$3.5 million	$1 million	45%
2010	N/A (taxes repealed)	$1 million	Maximum gift tax rate equal to maximum income tax rate (35%)

*The GST exemption is indexed and is $1,120,000 in 2003.

(Continued)

Exhibit 21.2 *(Continued)*

- Marital deduction: Unlimited transfers between spouses
- Annual exclusion: $11,000 to each donee/year
  - Husband and wife: $22,000 to each donee/year

TAX DEDUCTIBILITY OF CHARITABLE GIFTS

- Donor must be an itemizer.
- For gifts of cash, donor obtains charitable income tax deduction limited to 50 percent of the donor's adjusted gross income and the excess may be carried over for up to 5 years.
  - Example: Donor makes a gift by check for $75,000 and donor's adjusted gross income is $100,000. The donor may claim a charitable income tax deduction for $50,000 in year 1 and $25,000 in year 2.
- For gifts of property (other than cash), a donor obtains a charitable income tax deduction equal to the appraised value, limited to 30 percent of donor's AGI.
- Gifts of real estate and nonmarketable securities must be appraised to ascertain value.
- Gifts of intangible personal property must be appraised (if over $5,000) and have a related use to the exempt purposes of the charity. If so, the donor obtains a charitable income tax deduction equal to the appraised value.

SECTION 4. ESTATE PLANNING—WILLS AND TRUSTS

ESTATE PLANNING AND CHARITABLE GIVING

- Financial planning
- Business assets
- Real estate
- Tax law
- Domestic relations
- Charitable gift planning

THE WILL: A ROAD MAP

- Transfer property from one to another
- Parties to a will: testator, witness, beneficiary, executor
- Formalities
- Codicils
- Updating a will/change in family circumstances—birth, death, divorce, remarriage, relocation
- Executor
- Guardianship
- Distribution of property—individuals and nonprofits

CHARITABLE PROVISIONS

- Specific bequest of cash ($25,000)
- Specific bequest of property
- Residue (all or a specific percentage of the remainder)

TARGETING DONORS FOR BEQUESTS

- Bequest programs
- Bequest forms
- Introductory bequest society letter
- Bequest ad
- A "thank-you" bequest ad
- Professional advisors

COORDINATING TITLE TO PROPERTY WITH THE ESTATE PLAN

- Sole ownership
- Joint ownershp with right of survivorship
- Tenancy in common
- Tenancy by the entirety

PROBATE

- The probate process
- Probate assets—assets owned solely in the name of the decedent

Exhibit 21.2 *(Continued)*

- Nonprobate assets
  - Assets that designate a beneficiary
  - Jointly held property
  - Property transferred to an inter vivos trust

DURABLE POWER OF ATTORNEY
- An important estate planning document that grants to another (holder) the power to act on behalf of the grantor.
- The power survives the grantor's incompetence.
- A traditional power of attorney lapses if the grantor becomes incompetent.
- According to the provisions of the durable power, the holder may do any act that the grantor could have conducted in his own right.

TRUSTS
- Parties—grantor, trustee, beneficiary
- Income versus remainder beneficiaries
- Transferring title to the trust corpus
- Powers governed by the document: buy, sell, mortgage, lease, rent, convey
- Distributions of principal and income
- Special provisions
  - Spray and sprinkle provisions
  - Provisions for minor children
- Charitable provisions

THE REVOCABLE INTER VIVOS TRUST (LIVING TRUST)
- Lifetime management plan
- Inter vivos transfers: Avoid probate
- Testamentary transfers: Do not avoid probate
- Revocable: Can be amended or revoked; no tax benefits
- Irrevocable: Completed transfer subject to gift tax (transferred during life) or estate tax (transferred at death).

CHARITABLE REMAINDER TRUSTS
- Income to beneficiary for life, remainder to nonprofit
- Donor obtains a charitable income tax deduction
- Donor avoids capital gains tax on gifts of appreciated property
- Income based on value of assets as revalued annually

BENEFITS OF $100,000 CHARITABLE REMAINDER TRUST FOR DONOR AGE 70

Payout Rate	Annual Income	Charitable Income Tax Deduction	
		Annuity Trust	*Unitrust*
5%	$5,000	$	$
6%	$6,000	$	$
7%	$7,000	$	$

OVERVIEW OF CHARITABLE REMAINDER TRUSTS
- Earn 5 to 7 percent income on gift.
- Receive an income for life for donor and a second beneficiary.
- Receive a charitable income tax deduction.
- Transfer appreciated securities to the trust and avoid capital gains taxes.
- Select own trustee.
- Select an annuity trust that pays a fixed, guaranteed dollar amount or a unitrust that pays a percentage of the trust as revalued annually.
- Support a program of interest and become a member of a leadership club.

TYPES OF CHARITABLE REMAINDER TRUSTS

Annuity Trust
- Fixed dollar amount based on value of initial assets
- Invade principal
- No additional gifts

(Continued)

Exhibit 21.2   *(Continued)*

Unitrust (Regular)
- Stated percentage
- Revalued annually
- Invade principal
- Additional gifts

Net Income Unitrust
- Stated percent or net income, whichever is less
- Revalued annually
- May not invade principal

Net Income Unitrust with Make-up
- Stated percent or net income, whichever is less with make-up
- Revalued annually
- May not invade principal

SECTION 5. ASSET CLASSIFICATION

ASSET CLASSIFICATION

Cash
Securities
- Stocks
- Bonds
- Mutual funds
- Closely held stock

Real Estate
- Personal residence
- Vacation property or second home
- Farm/ranch
- Commercial property
- Vacant land

Tangible Personal Property
- Art
- Antiques
- Books
- Collectibles/collections

A GIFT OF APPRECIATED SECURITIES
- Donor transfers appreciated securities.
- Donor obtains a charitable income tax deduction equal to the market value of the securities.
- Donor avoids capital gains taxes on the gain in the appreciated securities.
- Donor received gift credit for the market value of the securities.

GIFTS OF CLOSELY HELD STOCK
- Donor transfers closely held stock to nonprofit. Stock must not be restricted so as to prohibit transfer to a third party.
- Closely held stock is not publicly traded. To determine value, the stock must be appraised by one qualified to value business organizations.
- The nonprofit may redeem the stock to a closely held corporation or to the corporation's employees' stock option plan and the nonprofit receives a check for the redemption.
- The donor obtains a charitable income tax deduction equal to the appraised value of the stock.

TYPES OF REAL ESTATE
- Personal residence
- Farm or ranch
- Commercial property

21.1 PRESENTATIONS

Exhibit 21.2 *(Continued)*

- Vacation property
- Second home

GIFTS OF REAL ESTATE
- Guidelines
- Considerations in accepting gifts of real estate
- Types of real estate
- Tax considerations
- Gift options
- Outright gift or gift of a fractional interest
- Retained life estate
- Charitable remainder unitrust

GUIDELINES FOR REAL ESTATE GIFTS
- Nonprofits should not assume the role of a substitute buyer.
- Nonprofits need to establish safeguards and procedures (environmental audit).
- Nonprofits should not become an unwitting recipient of damaged goods.
- If the buyer cannot sell the property, how can the nonprofit?

CONSIDERATIONS IN ACCEPTING GIFTS OF REAL ESTATE
- Treating the gift as a sale
- Appraisal
- Gift review committee
- Gift brokering
- Gifts of mortgaged property

GIFT OPTIONS FOR REAL ESTATE
- Outright gifts and gifts of a fractional interest
- Retained life estate
- Charitable remainder unitrust

OUTRIGHT GIFT OF REAL ESTATE OR A GIFT OF FRACTIONAL INTEREST
- Appraised value
- Cost basis
- Donor obtains a charitable income tax deduction equal to the appraised value, limited to 30 percent of adjusted gross income

RETAINED LIFE ESTATE
- Donor age 75 owns a personal residence. Donor wishes to make a gift of the personal residence and retains the right to live in the home for life
  - Appraised value   <$>
- Benefits to donor
  - Charitable income tax deduction of   <$>
  - Right to occupy the property for life
- A gift of a personal residence or farm
- Donor obtains a charitable income tax deduction based on the appraised value of the property and the age of the donor
- Donor is responsible for maintenance, insurance, and taxes

CHARITABLE REMAINDER UNITRUST (Net Income Unitrust with Make-up Provision)
- Donor and spouse age 65 own vacant land or commercial property and wish to make a gift. Donors select the payout rate and receive a charitable income tax deduction and an income stream for their lifetimes, and avoid capital gains taxes on the appreciation of the assets. The property passes outside of the estate for federal estate tax purposes and avoids probate.

(Continued)

■ 195 ■

Exhibit 21.2 *(Continued)*

Appraised Value $500,000		Cost Basis $250,000
	Income Stream	*Tax Deduction*
5%	$25,000	$
6%	$30,000	$
7%	$35,000	$

GIFTS OF TANGIBLE PERSONAL PROPERTY

- Gifts of tangible personal property must have a use related to the exempt purposes of the non-profit organization.
- Charitable income tax deduction equal to fair market value (appraised value) if there is a related use.
- Charitable income tax deduction is limited to the cost basis if there is no related use.
- For property donated for resale, the charitable income tax deduction is limited to the cost basis.
- For property that an author or artist donates, which if sold would produce ordinary income, the charitable income tax deduction is limited to the donor's cost basis (cost of materials).

SECTION 6. BUILDING ENDOWMENTS

ESTABLISH A NAMED ENDOWED FUND

- Operate in perpetuity
- Award income annually
- May be established in the donor's name, family member as a memorial fund
- Benefit any designated department, program, or activity
- Support research, education, or scholarships

ESTABLISHING A SCHOLARSHIP

- Endowed
- Current use
- In memory or in honor
- Funded with a gift of cash, securities, or real estate through an outright gift, planned gift, or gift by will or trust

Marketing Planned Giving to Professional Advisors

22.1 INTRODUCTION

Marketing an organization's planned giving vehicles to prospective donors is a significant aspect of any marketing effort. However, a very influential segment of the planned giving market is made up of the professional advisors who represent these potential donors: attorneys, trust officers, financial advisors, certified public accountants (CPAs), stockbrokers, and insurance agents. These professionals often have extensive client bases and know their clients' net worth, tax situations, and real estate holdings. The advisor who works with these individuals is in a unique position to suggest the need for making a charitable gift and can recommend the nonprofit as an appropriate recipient. As the business of planned giving changes and grows, an increasing number of professional advisors are involved in donors' giving, and can greatly influence the donor's gift. This chapter discusses the importance of professional advisors and ways to market to generate business for the nonprofit or organization. In addition, the last portion of the chapter suggests a way to mobilize professional advisors through a professional advisory committee.

22.2 WAYS TO BEGIN

(a) Estate Settlement

In settling estates of which the organization is a beneficiary, a communicative relationship between the planned giving officer and the donor's attorney is an excellent means to ensure that the estate settlement process will develop smoothly and that the organization will obtain its maximum estate distribution as early as possible. A professional relationship allows the planned giving officer to call the attorney to check on the status of the case and the anticipated timing for the distribution of assets. It also sets the stage for the attorney to suggest the organization as a potential beneficiary of future charitable bequests from donors seeking to benefit a nonprofit.

(b) Outreach Mailing List

A planned giving officer who is starting a new program or expanding an existing one should consider compiling a list of professional advisors who have extensive estate, tax, or financial planning practices or have already had contact with the nonprofit. Include individuals who have settled estates for the nonprofit, act as donors' trust officers, stockbrokers who process gifts of securities to the organization, the outside planned giving manager who manages these funds for the nonprofit, and personal friends who are in these businesses. To educate these advisors about the organization and its planned giving program, include their names on a mailing list to receive selected publications about the organization. Send publications that carry planned giving advertisements and promotional material to inform these advisors about planned giving and how the planned giving office can act as a resource for them. Also send promotional pieces about the nonprofit. The eventual goal is to make the advisor sufficiently comfortable with planned giving concepts to suggest to appropriate clients the benefits of making planned gifts to the organization.

(c) Personal Visits

Next, select a number of advisors and meet with them personally to explain the concepts of life income vehicles. Do not be surprised if some of these professional advisors are not familiar with the intricacies of planned gifts. Although they have specialized knowledge in their own fields, planned giving is not usually covered in legal, accounting, or financial planning courses.

Offer to prepare calculations for these advisors. It is likely that the nonprofit has planned giving software that the outside advisor does not have. The planned giving officer may have to give extra attention to educating some professional advisors to dispel their fear that the nonprofit is competing with them for business. For example, as employees who are paid by commission, stockbrokers receive their compensation based on the pool of assets they manage or on the trades they make on behalf of their clients. Any transfer of stock to a nonprofit removes assets from their management, thereby reducing the brokers' opportunity for compensation or commissions. A gift of stock is neither a buy nor a sell, and, therefore, no commission is produced. One way to work with a broker is to have the donor transfer the stock to an account the broker creates in the name of the nonprofit. Once the stock is transferred to the nonprofit's account, the nonprofit orders a sale, and a commission is produced for the broker. Some trust officers also see nonprofits as competition inasmuch as a nonprofit may serve as a trustee for a trust and may have a pooled income fund located at a different trust company or bank.

To expand outreach, make an effort to identify other professional advisors who have extensive estate-planning and tax practices. These professionals can help to generate gifts that would otherwise not be available, by bringing to the nonprofit organization donors who have no past giving record or connection to the organization.

An illustration of this is shown in the following story. A $150,000 charitable gift annuity came into a nonprofit from a donor who had never been seen or contacted by anyone at the organization. The donor had met with a local attorney who, after reviewing the donor's estate plan, recommended that the donor could benefit by making a gift through a charitable gift annuity. The donor possessed low-yielding certificates of deposit, paying 2.5 percent. The advisor suggested that a charitable gift annuity could pay the donor 8 percent every year for life while he also gained a charitable income tax deduction. The attorney had a connection with the organization and was comfortable about requesting information from the planned giving office. After sending the appropriate information and calculations, meeting with the attorney, and then with the donor, the office completed the $150,000 charitable gift annuity. The organization would not have had this opportunity had it not been for the attorney who brought the donor to it. This example illustrates the value of establishing good working relationships with professional advisors outside the organization.

22.3 PLANNED GIVING PRESENTATIONS FOR OUTSIDE AUDIENCES

Another way to market to outside professionals is to take the organization's message outside the organization. This can be accomplished by speaking regularly to outside groups about the planned giving program, the services offered, and the gift options available. The following may present possible speaking opportunities: civic clubs, including Lions and Rotary clubs; CPAs' associations; estate-planning councils; bankers' associations; cultural groups, such as theater, museum, and library associations; and athletic booster clubs. It helps to bring a laptop computer to planned giving workshops to show an advisor or prospect personalized calculations on the spot.

22.4 MAILINGS TO PROFESSIONAL ADVISORS

When new brochures, publications, or newsletters are produced in the office, send copies to as many professional advisors as possible. Through receiving the latest newsletters and planned giving information, these advisors become educated about planned giving options, and the needs of the organization are reinforced. Take an altruistic approach to the outreach program; sometimes working with a professional advisor in a particular situation will result in benefiting another nonprofit. The planned giving officer should take heart, however, because next time the professional advisor may be a key player in making sure that a gift is made to the officer's own organization.

22.5 PUBLICATION IN A TRADE PAPER

Write a planned giving article for a local trade magazine. Publications that cater to lawyers, CPAs, trust officers, and bankers often are looking for new topics that will benefit their readership. An article that focuses on the benefits of charitable gift planning is likely to elicit inquiries and form new connections.

22.6 TECHNICAL OUTREACH PROGRAM

Host seminars on estate planning or financial planning for outside advisors. If possible, offer continuing education credits for their attendance. Planned giving concepts can be introduced. This type of outreach program may work best if the nonprofit is the biggest player in the area.

22.7 NONTECHNICAL OUTREACH PROGRAM

To bring outside advisors closer to the organization, host an outreach program consisting of a breakfast or luncheon followed by a program on a topic of interest to them. For example, at an educational organization, consider having guest faculty members speak about their area of academic expertise or inviting someone from the administration to speak about trends in education or policies of academic institutions. At a hospital, a physician might talk abut new medical discoveries, research, or treatments, or an administrator might talk about healthcare reform. An arts organization offers a special opportunity: Participants may attend a new exhibit, dramatic performance, or musical event.

Whatever topic, speaker, or program is chosen, make sure that the program is one that the professional advisors will want to attend. The purpose is to promote the organization and inform attendees that it is seeking funds and is interested in identifying potential donors. Strive to make the outreach program a positive, memorable event that professional advisors will want to attend each year. Careful cultivation of professional advisors can result in some unexpected and valuable gifts.

22.8 AMBASSADOR PROGRAM

If working at an educational organization, target alumni who are lawyers, accountants, or financial planners who can assist their alma mater and clients by recommending a planned gift to their clients. Focus on those advisors who live away from the area, in places that the planned giving officer may never reach. Send the ambassador information about the school and a form that he or she can send back to the school to receive planned giving software calculations or other information for clients. Ultimately, this idea can result in more planned giving prospects and bring the alumnae closer to the alma mater.

22.9 PLANNED GIVING MANUAL

Create a manual that provides information about making gifts to the nonprofit, and ask the advisor recipient to encourage gifts from friends and clients. The manual should include information about the charity as well as tax, technical, estate-planning, and planned giving information. Keep the following in mind when creating a planned giving manual:

- Consider the audience.

- Weigh the advantages of putting information in a three-ring binder.

- Determine the best way to distribute.

- Possible information to include:

    - Types of gift assets

    - Information about Internal Revenue Service (IRS) Forms 8283, 8282

    - Life income gift illustrations

    - Description of honorary society for donors

    - Gift uses and restrictions

    - Transferring securities to the institution

    - Disclosure statements for life income gifts

    - Organization's history, programs

    - Listing of planned giving office professional staff

22.10 THE PROFESSIONAL ADVISORY COMMITTEE

Nonprofits have many constituencies, including alumni, patients, patrons, friends, parents, staff, corporations, and foundations. One important constituency that is often overlooked is professional advisors. Professional advisors include attorneys, CPAs, brokers, investment advisors, financial planners, trust officers, and insurance professionals. These advisors assist clients in tax planning, estate planning, and financial planning. In addition, they are regularly asked for advice about charitable gift planning and may be consulted about the names of nonprofit organizations that would be appropriate beneficiaries for charitable gifts. Apart from their relationship with clients, they have a wealth of experience and expertise and can provide a valuable resource to nonprofits who wish to involve this well-connected group of professionals.

22.11   ESTABLISHING A PROFESSIONAL ADVISORY COMMITTEE

One way to serve this important group is to establish a professional advisory committee made up of key professional advisors in the region where the nonprofit operates. The advisors are invited to attend quarterly or semiannual meetings to learn about charitable gift planning, planned giving options, endowed funds, and the use of noncash assets such as real estate, tangible personal property, and securities. A committee of 25 to 35 advisors is a manageable group. To help manage the committee, a chair or co-chairs can be appointed from among the members to help provide leadership and direction. Staggered term limits can be established at one- to three-year intervals to provide continuity and opportunity for new members to serve.

To get started, interview practitioners who are known to have experience in the fields of estate planning and tax planning, along with professional advisors who have served as volunteers or board members for the nonprofit. These advisors will know of others who want to learn about charitable gift planning. To identify professional advisors, contact estate-planning councils. [To contact a local estate-planning council, contact the National Association of Estate Planners and Councils at www.naepc.org.] To help define the role of the committee and its relationship to the nonprofit, prepare a mission statement that provides the committee with a sense of direction and purpose, sets membership terms, and outlines responsibilities.

(a) Professional Advisory Committee Meetings

The first meeting of the professional advisory committee provides an opportunity for the planned giving officer to establish rapport, build professional working relationships, and most important, educate the professional advisors about planned giving and charitable gift-planning options. Committee meetings also fulfill an opportunity for social interaction among the committee members, which enhances their business and professional relationships. At the first meeting, provide each committee member with a package of information including reference materials on planned gifts, the use of noncash assets, and tax- and estate-planning options. Advisors are particularly interested in planned giving software printouts illustrating the benefits of these gift options. Because many professional advisors do not have access to these software packages, a planned giving officer who is willing to share this information can provide a valuable service to committee members. To illustrate the ease with which planned giving software can be used, bring a laptop computer and demonstrate the various gift options. One of the best ways to present information on planned giving is to preselect members of the committee to act as case studies to illustrate the various gift options and benefits they offer. To avoid surprise, a brief call in advance to committee members who represent different age brackets will not only involve the members in the presentation but also serve as a way to demonstrate the benefits. Real-life case studies crystallize the concepts and clearly illustrate the benefits of the gift options.

Once the first meeting is concluded, the planned giving officer can sustain interest by mailing a newsletter that focuses on particular gift options. Advisors who show interest in planned giving concepts can be invited to the office for a one-on-one session. The planned giving officer should not be surprised if she is invited to speak at a local meeting of attorneys, accountants, or bankers. Quite often, starting a professional advisory committee opens doors to other opportunities to become more involved with these key players. Over time, a network can be built that provides a free exchange of information among the nonprofit, the committee, and its members, all of which serve to open doors with prospects.

Speakers can include distinguished members of the bar or accountants from major accounting firms. To avoid perceptions of favoritism, establish a program committee to select the topic and identify speakers. In addition, the Internal Revenue Service (IRS) will provide speakers from its regional offices to speak on income taxation, gift taxation, estate taxation, or almost any other topic covered by the Internal Revenue Code. These speakers provide insight on the way the IRS views tax and charitable gift-planning issues and proposed regulations. Call the IRS's regional office for a list of speakers and their areas of expertise.

In many states, attorneys and CPAs need continuing professional education credit. Professional advisory committee meetings can qualify for continuing education credit if the nonprofit seeks approval, in advance, from the appropriate board of certification. Check with the state's bar and board of accountancy for requirements for continuing education credit.

22.12 PURPOSE OF THE COMMITTEE

Once the committee is established, representatives can be invited to participate in a variety of activities. Committee members can draft newsletters and articles, proof technical communications, and edit brochures. Members of the committee can participate in workshops, seminars, and homecoming or reunion events and can offer financial, estate, and tax-planning seminars at nonprofit events. A planned giving officer can serve as a moderator and supplement information provided by professional advisors by presenting charitable gift-planning alternatives that can help achieve a donor's tax and estate planning objectives.

One of the most important roles that a professional advisor can play is that of an ambassador, carrying the nonprofit's message to those who need to know. Professional advisors can be helpful in enhancing relationships with clients who are associated with the nonprofit. Many wealthy prospects acquired their fortunes without the aid of a degree in the economic boom following World War II, and often these prospects are not affiliated with an educational institution. These friends often enjoy their relationship with a program or department, although identifying these prospects is, at best, an inexact science. Often these friends tell their advisors of their philanthropic interests, and a professional advisory committee member who knows about your program can open the door.

(a) Information Sharing

The professional advisory committee should be viewed as a constituency of the nonprofit and one that needs to be cultivated, nurtured, and educated about the nonprofit and its gift-planning options. The committee should not be seen as a function of the nonprofit but rather as an independent resource, where there is a mutual sharing of information and resources between the staff of the nonprofit and the advisory committee. Consider establishing task forces within the committee that focus on life income gifts, life insurance, gifts of real estate, and public relations. These task forces can write articles, develop promotional materials, and draft gift acceptance policies and procedures. Seek professional advisors who have expertise in strategic business planning and marketing to help provide direction and a business focus for the office.

Because professional advisors need more detailed technical information than do donors, a resource library of books, articles, journal reprints, and software manuals can be of great assistance.

Professional advisors are also more than willing to share their expertise about their particular field of knowledge and provide a valuable resource for quick answers to questions while serving as a sounding board for ideas. One of the most important by-products of the professional advisory committee is the opportunity to brainstorm ideas and concepts with other professionals. Brainstorming sessions promote camaraderie and help to develop solutions to problems. However, the committee is not a substitute for the nonprofit's legal counsel or accounting firm. Occasional questions directed to the committee members are appropriate, but anything that requires more than a quick response should be directed to the nonprofit's counsel.

Form a subcommittee of the professional advisory committee to present a financial planning workshop. Invite the organization's constituency, as well as staff members, to attend. To advertise the workshop, prepare a one-page brochure and send it to the development staff, donors, prospects, and advisory committee members. If possible, include the brochure as an advertisement in a local newspaper. Structure the workshop to accomplish two purposes: (1) to educate prospects and donors about planned giving and (2) to showcase the professional advisory committee at an organizational gathering, which could result in additional business for the advisors. Invite members of the committee to plan next year's workshop. Offer additional regional workshops involving local professional advisors who are professional advisory committee members.

A sample agenda for a financial planning workshop is included in Appendix, CD-ROM Documentation, Exhibits.

(b) Advisors as Prospects

Apart from the professional relationship that advisors share with the nonprofit, professional advisors who are active and interested are themselves prospects. Serving as a member of the committee cements the relationship between the nonprofit and the professional advisors as the advisors learn more about the mission and charitable services of the nonprofit. The better informed a professional advisor is about the nonprofit's work, the more helpful he can be in cultivating clients and in choosing to provide personal financial support. Be sure to provide information about:

- Case statements

- Campaign documents

- Funding opportunities

- Mission statement

- View book

- Fact book

A tour of the nonprofit that provides an opportunity to meet with presidents, vice-presidents, deans, directors, and department heads is one of the best steps that can be taken in cultivating interest and in educating the advisors about the role of the nonprofit. Furthermore, professional advisors provide input and feedback on the way in which the nonprofit is viewed within the community.

22.13   WHAT TO EXPECT

After the program is up and running, what should the planned giving officer expect? It is quite likely that the organization will receive several inquiries each year from the committee. Follow up with each advisor on every inquiry to answer questions and to establish a professional rapport. These inquiries are much more likely to result in a gift, since the advisor and client have been preeducated and in many ways, the decision to make the gift has already been made, subject to the planned giving officer's confirmation of the details of the gift. Once advisors gain confidence in the staff and in the mechanics of the planned giving options, other gifts will follow.

Professional advisory committee members become involved with planned giving staff in developing solutions to tax and estate-planning issues through charitable gift planning.

22.14 CONCLUSION

Marketing a planned giving program to outside professional advisors is a way to educate professionals who may be in a position to bring gifts, through their clients, to the organization. Tell these professionals that the organization needs financial support and show them how their clients can be helped by making planned gifts. Consider the following strategies to reach outside professionals:

- Create a mailing list to keep professional advisors regularly informed about the organization and the planned giving services offered.

- Meet personally with outside professionals to talk about planned giving vehicles and help them to become comfortable with the concepts. Strive to alleviate their concern that the organization is competing with them for business.

- Form relationships with attorneys who are settling estates of donors to the organization. This helps to build a planned giving network and to monitor the estate settlement process.

- Form a professional advisory committee to bring outside advisors closer to the organization and perhaps to host a financial planning workshop for donors. During a workshop, use personalized planned giving calculations as examples.

- Speak regularly to outside organizations about planned giving to further expand an outside network and educate others about the benefits of planned giving.

- Showcase the organization to outside professionals by offering a program conducted by a speaker from the nonprofit who will address a topic related to the organization rather than one related specifically to planned giving.

- Maintain ongoing outreach efforts with the knowledge that, over time, they will generate new gifts to the organization.

Professional advisory committees are generally easy to maintain and do not require much attention between meetings. Although planned giving is a full-time job for the planned giving officer, keep in mind that committee members have their own professional commitments and that their time is limited. However, members are usually pleased to provide free advice on technical aspects of their particular professions. By alternating among committee members, the planned giving staff is able to obtain answers to questions while building solid professional working relationships with well-connected business players in the community. Also consider the merits of establishing a regional panel or a professional advisory committee to serve as a referral service to answer donors' questions about charitable gift planning.

Professional advisory committees may be informal or formal, structured or unstructured, and, depending on the nonprofit, may vary greatly as to their scope, duties, and responsibilities. They all share in common a commitment to provide service to nonprofit organizations and their constituencies. As the development program evolves and becomes more complex and sophisticated, the professional advisory committee can grow and accept new responsibilities and duties. Their flexibility and versatility are their prime advantages, and they can be modeled to fit the needs of any nonprofit organization.

Planned Gifts

CHAPTER TWENTY-THREE

Charitable Gift Annuities
and Deferred Gift Annuities

23.1 INTRODUCTION

Charitable gift annuities are the heart of a planned giving program. Along with bequests, they represent the first stage in the development of a solid life income gift component of the planned giving program. These gifts provide donors with an opportunity to benefit a nonprofit organization while receiving both an income for the rest of their lives and significant tax advantages. Gift annuities help donors to "leverage" their gifts, thus enabling them to make larger gifts. This chapter explores two important life income vehicles: charitable gift annuities and deferred gift annuities.

23.2 CHARITABLE GIFT ANNUITIES

Charitable gift annuities are among the most common and popular of the planned giving, life–income-producing vehicles. Through a charitable gift annuity, a donor makes a gift to a nonprofit organization and receives an income for life and, if desired, for another beneficiary's lifetime, and upon the death of the last beneficiary, the nonprofit receives the remainder. A portion of the income is tax free, and the donor claims a charitable income tax deduction. Charitable gift annuities are age sensitive and provide the greatest financial benefit to older donors, who receive the highest income rates.

CHARITABLE GIFT ANNUITIES AND DEFERRED GIFT ANNUITIES

The charitable gift annuity is a contract between the donor and the nonprofit. The donor makes a gift to the nonprofit, which is legally obligated to pay the donor a fixed amount of income for his lifetime. The transaction is, in reality, a bargain sale—part sale and part gift—because the donor is giving an amount to the nonprofit that exceeds the annuity promised by the charity. The annuity is backed by the general assets of the nonprofit, but is an unsecured obligation of the charity making the donor a general creditor of the nonprofit if for some reason it was unable to make payments to the donor. A charitable organization should be left with about 50 percent of the amount paid by the donor for the charitable gift annuity when the contract terminates.

(a) Gift Annuity Rates and the American Council on Gift Annuities

Planned giving software can be used to calculate a donor's annuity rate, which is affected by the number of beneficiaries to receive an income and their ages. Many nonprofits follow the recommendations of the American Council on Gift Annuities, a national organization that suggests rates for nonprofit organizations to offer to annuitants.[1] The recommended rates are the same for both sexes and ages. Although many nonprofits follow the American Council's suggestions, an organization may choose to deviate from the recommended rates. This most commonly occurs when a donor is intent on earning a specific rate of return or when a donor is "shopping" for rates among organizations. For instance, a donor indicates an interest in making a gift to a nonprofit but suggests that another organization is paying a higher rate of return. Based on the donor's age, health, and relationship with the organization, the planned giving officer, perhaps in consultation with the treasurer's office, can determine whether the organization wants to offer a higher payout rate to the donor. If a donor is asking for an unreasonable rate and the nonprofit is uncomfortable with it or thinks that the requested rate is not a good investment for the organization, it is wise not to proceed. If there is no donative intent by the donor, it is probable that the "gift" will not materialize. The American Council on Gift Annuities revises gift annuity rates periodically.

Although planned giving officers talk about rates of return, taxes, and investment strategies, it must be kept in mind that their organizations are nonprofits and are in the business of philanthropy. Nonprofits cannot and should not try to compete with banks, brokers, investment houses, and other commercial investments. Sometimes donors must be reminded that they are making charitable gifts. Exhibit 23.1 compares the benefits of a charitable gift annuity for donors of different ages.

Exhibit 23.1   Benefits from a $5,000 Charitable Gift Annuity.* Please see Appendix 23.1 (a) and (b).

Age	Payout Rate	Annual Income	Tax Deduction
65	6%	$300	$1,495
70	6.5%	$325	$1,549
75	7.1%	$355	$2,040
80	8%	$400	$2,320

* Actual deductions and rates are affected by the prevailing discount rate and payout rates suggested by the American Council on Gift Annuities.

(b) Tax Consequences of Charitable Gift Annuities

Various tax consequences occur when making a charitable gift annuity. The following paragraphs examine the donor's charitable income tax deduction, gift taxes, capital gains and income taxation, and estate tax consequences.

[1] The American Council on Gift Annuities, 233 McCrea Street, Suite 400, Indianapolis, IN, 46225-1030; (317) 269-6271.

23.2 CHARITABLE GIFT ANNUITIES

(i) Valuation of the Charitable Income Tax Deduction. Depending on age, a donor making a charitable gift annuity generally receives a charitable income tax deduction of approximately 40 to 50 percent of the gift. The exact value of the deduction is determined by subtracting the value of the annuity (life income interest) from the present value of the gift to determine the remainder interest to the nonprofit, which is equal to the donor's charitable income tax deduction. The value of the annuity is determined by applying the Internal Revenue Service (IRS) discount rate to the stream of payments over the life expectancy of the donor or other beneficiary. The IRS-determined interest rate is 120 percent of the federal midterm rate, which changes monthly based on the Treasury Bill rates (Internal Revenue Code [IRC] Section 7520). The federal midterm rate is defined as the average market yield on all options of the U.S. market that have a maturity over three years and less than nine years [IRC Section 1274(d)(1)]. The donor can use the discount rate for the month in which the gift is made or the rate for either of the two preceding months. The highest discount rate is usually selected to ensure the highest charitable income tax deduction. The donor obtains the charitable income tax deduction in the year the gift is made, and if the donor cannot use the deduction completely in the first year, it is carried forward for up to five additional years.

(ii) Gift Taxes. If a donor establishes a charitable gift annuity for the benefit of anyone other than himself or his spouse, and if the donor does not reserve the power to revoke the income payment from the charitable gift annuity through his will, he makes a taxable gift and may pay a gift tax on the present value of the charitable gift annuity. The taxable gift is not based on the stream of income paid to the beneficiary each year but on the total value of the charitable gift annuity at the time the gift is made. If payments to the third party begin within the year of the gift, the donor can use the $11,000 annual gift tax exclusion to eliminate or defray the gift tax due on the charitable gift annuity.

(iii) Capital Gains Taxes and Income Taxation. The donor who funds a charitable gift annuity with appreciated property held for more than one year will have to pay capital gains taxes, currently assessed at a rate of 15 percent for most investment assets, on that portion of the property that is used to purchase the charitable gift annuity. If the donor is the sole beneficiary or the first beneficiary, the gain can be spread out by reporting it over the donor's life expectancy. Otherwise, all the gain on the portion of the property used to purchase the annuity will be taxed to the donor in the year of the gift. If the donor wants her spouse to be the sole beneficiary, she should make an outright gift of the appreciated property to her spouse, which can be accomplished without tax consequences by using the marital deduction. The spouse can then make the gift to fund the charitable gift annuity. A portion of the stream of income received by the beneficiary will generally be excluded from gross income, because it is considered a tax-free return of capital. The rest is taxed as ordinary income and as capital gain income, if appreciated property is used to fund the gift. Once the donor reaches her life expectancy (calculated at the date of the gift), the entire amount of the annuity at the date of the donor's death will be taxed in the donor's estate.

(iv) Estate Taxes. If the donor is the only annuitant and the income stream ceases on her death, the value of the annuity is not taxed in her estate. If the donor's spouse is the sole remaining annuitant, the spouse's interest may qualify for the estate tax marital deduction. If a third person is the sole remaining annuitant the value of the third party's annuity will be taxed in the donor's estate.

(c) Acceptable Assets to Fund a Charitable Gift Annuity

Cash is the most common asset used to fund a charitable gift annuity. Donors also fund charitable gift annuities with securities, including stocks, bonds, and municipal bonds, but if the securities have appreciated, the donor will still have to pay some capital gains taxes on the gain in the "sale" part of the transaction.

CHARITABLE GIFT ANNUITIES AND DEFERRED GIFT ANNUITIES

Real estate can be used successfully to fund a charitable gift annuity. The organization must decide how soon payments to the donor should begin, based on how quickly the real estate can be sold and converted into cash to fund the gift annuity. Attention also must be paid to the agreed-on payout rate of the annuity to the donor in case the property sells for less money than anticipated. The organization also must consider the other costs associated with real estate, such as brokers' commissions and attorneys' fees, which may reduce the amount of sale proceeds to below the appraised fair market value of the contributed property. A full discussion of charitable gift annuities and real estate is found in Chapter 31.

(d) Considerations in Starting a Charitable Gift Annuity Program for Donors

Gift annuity programs, coupled with a comprehensive marketing effort, will likely bring new donors to a planned giving program. Charitable gift annuities are preferred gift options at nonprofits that have a solid donor base with a long tradition of giving to the annual fund. Before offering a charitable gift annuity program, confirm the existing potential for donors to raise their giving levels to the minimum required for a charitable gift annuity, which is $5,000 or $10,000 at most organizations. However, do not be disappointed if research shows a relatively small gift potential. The financial benefits of gift annuities often motivate donors to meet the minimum amount required.

(i) Gift Annuity Contract. It is generally inexpensive to begin a charitable gift annuity program; costs are substantially less than those needed in starting a pooled income fund. Because charitable gift annuities are contractual agreements, the only document needed is a one-page gift annuity contract that includes the annuity rate, the amount of payment, and the payment schedule, which is most often quarterly but may be monthly or annually. Once an attorney has drafted the form for the nonprofit, no other documents are needed, and only the nonprofit is required to sign the contract. See Appendix, CD-ROM Documentation, Agreement for a sample gift annuity contract. Some charities invite donors to "apply" for a charitable gift annuity, providing donors with a charitable gift annuity application form. A sample charitable gift annuity application form is included in Appendix, CD-ROM Documentation, Agreements.

(ii) Administration of Gift Annuity Program—Internal Versus External Management. If the organization does not currently offer charitable gift annuities and such a program is desired, it must decide who should administer the annuities—the treasurer or an outside firm. The organization's treasurer's office, if willing and able, can manage the program in-house. For this arrangement to be successful, excellent communication with the treasurer's office is essential. Therefore, the planned giving office and the treasurer's office should first discuss donor relations and reporting issues. The treasurer's office should be responsible for investment decisions and for sending tax forms to donors at year end. An organization is fortunate if the individuals in the treasurer's office understand the planned giving business and can work with the planned giving officer as partners. It is much less expensive to manage the program in-house than to pay an outside manager. However, sometimes there is an understandable tension between the treasurer's office and the planned giving office owing to their different goals. The treasurer's office is interested in keeping costs down and may not be completely sensitive to the goals of the development office. A planned giving officer, who is most interested in closing gifts, may be less attuned to the nonprofit's administrative obligations and may fail to understand investment concerns.

Alternatively, a nonprofit's charitable gift annuity program may be administered outside the nonprofit, usually by a bank, trust company, or investment firm. Bank and trust companies charge a minimum fee to administer a gift annuity program, and expenses increase as the number of charitable gift annuities grows. The charitable organization will be charged fees for administrative costs that include investment management, accounting costs, and fees for state and federal tax compliance. This arrangement makes it inexpensive to start a program, because only a small start-up fee is required in the beginning. If the nonprofit has a pooled income fund, consider using the services of the trustee of this fund to administer the charitable gift annuities so that the planned giving officer can work with the same staff on both programs. Even if the program is administered outside the organization, the treasurer's office will have to be involved when approving rates and endorsing the gift annuity contracts.

(iii) Insurance. Donors often want to know what happens to their charitable gift annuity payments if the nonprofit ceases to exist, suffers financial setbacks, or becomes bankrupt. The charitable gift annuity is an unsecured obligation of the charity. Some nonprofits choose to insure their charitable gift annuities to be certain that payments are met, whereas many others do not want to incur this additional cost or feel that it is unnecessary. Some states that regulate the issuance of gift annuities require a nonprofit to insure charitable gift annuities. If the nonprofit does not provide insurance coverage for the gift annuity payments, the planned giving officer must assure donors that the organization has substantial assets, tangible and intangible, that may be relied on to protect their income stream. In the unlikely event that an organization becomes bankrupt, donors will need to "line up" with other creditors to receive their payments. The planned giving officer should speak to the treasurer's or business office to determine the organization's insurance coverage. If a donor requires that the nonprofit purchase a commercial annuity contract to insure that payments will be made, the donor's charitable income tax deduction may be affected by the premium paid to the commercial carrier.

(iv) Marketing Charitable Gift Annuities. A successful marketing program for charitable gift annuities can result in many gifts to the nonprofit. Target ads, mailings, and educational pieces to older donors, those over 75 years of age who will receive the highest annual rate of return (see Exhibit 23.2). In addition to the high payout rate, many donors are attracted to the fixed rate of return. Educating prospects about these benefits will result in the creation of new charitable gift annuities. (For a more comprehensive discussion of marketing, see Part Four of this book.)

Exhibit 23.2   Life Income Gift Letter

<DATE>

<NAME>
<ADDRESS>
<CITY, STATE, ZIP>

Dear <NAME>:

Thank you for your interest in the <ORGANIZATION>. We appreciate your considering making a life income gift to the <ORGANIZATION> that can benefit both you and <ORGANIZATION>.

<ORGANIZATION> offers a number of options that can pay attractive rates to our donors. Our gift options also enable a donor to obtain a charitable income tax deduction, which provides important tax savings. The donor can choose to set up a permanently endowed fund in honor of a loved one. The minimum to permanently endow a fund is < $ >.

For individuals who are considering making a gift and obtaining a stream of income, there are a variety of options to choose from. Two of the most common planned giving vehicles are the Charitable Gift Annuity and the Pooled Income Fund. These options allow a donor to make a gift to benefit any department or program at <ORGANIZATION>, receive an income for life, and perhaps for a spouse's lifetime, and obtain a charitable income tax deduction at the time the gift is made. The Pooled Income Fund has an additional advantage in that gifts of appreciated securities can be made to the fund and the donor will avoid capital gains taxes. These vehicles require a minimum of < $ >.

I would be pleased to provide a personal financial projection illustrating the benefits of these gifts, so please send us your age and/or ages and the amount you anticipate contributing.

If I can be of further assistance please feel free to call me at <ORGANIZATION>. Thank you for your interest in <ORGANIZATION>.

Sincerely,

<NAME>
<TITLE>

23.3 STATE REGULATION OF GIFT ANNUITIES[2]

Gift annuities are a popular planned giving option issued by nonprofits around the country. In recent years, more states have enacted laws governing issuance of gift annuities.

(a) Brief History of Regulation

Charitable gift annuities have been issued since at least the 1920s, perhaps earlier. The question of state regulation originated in the 1930s with the New York Insurance Department. The department was concerned that charities have sufficient financial reserves to pay the lifetime income stream to a donor, that gift annuity rates not compete with commercial insurance rates, and that reserves be segregated and invested prudently.

Currently, regulatory requirements vary from state to state, making compliance burdensome for charities that offer gift annuities in many different states. The National Association of Insurance Commissioners approved both a model exemption act and a model regulatory act for gift annuities in December 1998, which were then sent to all state insurance departments. Since that time, as least 10 states that previously had no laws specifically addressing gift annuities have adopted exemption statutes, patterned after the model act. Other silent states may follow suit in adopting exemption statutes, and some highly regulated states may modify certain requirements, as New York did with respect to investment of reserve assets. Therefore, it is advisable for a nonprofit issuing annuities in multiple states to determine a method for keeping current on state regulation issues.

(b) Requirements to Become Authorized to Issue Gift Annuities

Requirements to issue gift annuities vary from state to state, but nearly all *regulated* states require a charity that issues gift annuities to have:

- A permit
- A segregated reserve fund
- An annual report that shows required reserves and a segregated reserve fund balance

Most regulated states also require the charity to have been in existence for a certain number of years before it can apply for a permit.

Depending on the state, a nonprofit can be required to file a variety of documents when it applies for permission to issue gift annuities. Such documents include financial statements, by-laws of the organization, articles of incorporation, a certificate of tax-exempt status, and an organizational chart. California may require detailed affidavits from the nonprofit's board members that disclose financial and personal histories. Filing fees generally range from $0 to $100; California charges more than $3,000. The time required to obtain a permit varies dramatically and some states limit the types of investments that can be held in a segregated reserve fund.

---

[2]Adapted with permission from Frank Minton and Edie Matulka, Planned Giving Services, 3147 Fairview Avenue F, Suite 200, Seattle, WA 98102.

23.3 STATE REGULATION OF GIFT ANNUITIES

(c) Regulation of Gift Annuities by State[3]

The following summarizes the regulatory status of various states as of February 2003. This information is always changing, and there may be regulatory initiatives under way that could change a state's current status.

States that specifically exempt gift annuities from regulation (some require notification or have other conditions that must be met):

Alabama	Kentucky	North Carolina
Alaska	Louisiana	Oklahoma
Arizona	Maine	Pennsylvania
Colorado	Massachusetts	South Carolina
Connecticut	Michigan	South Dakota
Florida	Minnesota	Tennessee
Georgia	Mississippi	Texas
Idaho	Missouri	Utah
Illinois	Nebraska	Vermont
Indiana	Nevada	Virginia
Iowa	New Mexico	
Kansas		

States that regulate gift annuities:

Arkansas	North Dakota	Oregon
California	New Hampshire	Washington
Hawaii	New Jersey	Wisconsin
Maryland	New York	

States in which the law does not specifically address gift annuities:

Delaware	Montana	West Virginia
District of Columbia	Ohio	Wyoming
	Rhode Island	

(d) To Register or Not to Register

Differences of opinion still exist over whether a nonprofit that issues charitable gift annuities in another state should register in that other state. Some attorneys still recommend that a nonprofit that does not have employees or an office in a state need not register in that state. Increasingly, other attorneys are advising their clients to register. It is clear that the states believe a nonprofit issuing annuities to their residents must register, regardless of where the nonprofit is situated. The American Council on Gift Annuities takes the position that nonprofits should comply with the laws of any state in which they issue gift annuities. When operating in a state that requires registration, the nonprofit should meet registration requirements and obtain state approval before beginning to issue gift annuities.

---

[3]Adapted with permission from a presentation to the Planned Giving Group of New England, February 1995, by Frank Minton. Status of regulation of gift annuities by state compiled by Frank Minton (Planned Giving Services, 3147 Fairview Avenue F, Suite 200, Seattle, WA 98102) and James B. Potter (Planned Giving Resources, P.O. Box 6930, Falls Church, VA 22040).

(e) Additional Benefits of a Charitable Gift Annuity Program

Because a charitable gift annuity is a contract between the donor and the charitable organization, the gift annuity offers more flexibility than other gift options. Charitable organizations may choose to accept funding for a gift annuity an asset such as real estate or closely held stock that could not be used to fund another gift, such as the pooled income fund. Additionally, the existence of the gift annuity fund may offer a solution to various gift planning problems; for example, when a donor, the probate court, and a charitable organization decide to terminate a charitable trust but still must make payments to a noncharitable beneficiary, the gift annuity fund could be used to receive the charitable trust proceeds and make payments to the beneficiary.

23.4 CHARITABLE DEFERRED GIFT ANNUITIES

A variation of the charitable gift annuity, the deferred gift annuity, is similar to an individual retirement account (IRA) in that a donor makes a gift to the nonprofit and the nonprofit agrees to pay the donor, and perhaps another beneficiary, a stream of income for life, beginning at a point in the future at least one year after the gift is made. At the last beneficiary's death the nonprofit has use of the principal. Many donors choose age 65 or above to receive the income stream, because they will have retired and expect to be in a lower tax bracket. Unlike the charitable gift annuity, the deferred gift annuity pays a higher rate to the younger donors, when there is a long period of time between the date of the gift and the drawing of income. The organization receives the donor's money today and invests it for many years, looking ahead to the time when income payments must be made. Exhibit 23.3 compares the benefits of a deferred gift annuity that is deferred over different periods of time.

Exhibit 23.3   Benefits from a $5,000 Deferred Gift Annuity Deferred to Age 65.* Please see Appendix 23.1 (c) and (d).

Age	Payout Rate	Annual Income	Tax Deduction
30	32.7%	$1,635	$1,034
35	25.6%	$1,280	$1,194
40	20.1%	$1,005	$1,328
45	15.7%	$ 785	$1,465
50	12.3%	$ 615	$1,565

* Actual deductions and rates are affected by the prevailing discount rate and payout rates suggested by the American Council on Gift Annuities.

(a) Tax Consequences of Deferred Gift Annuities

(i) Charitable Income Tax Deduction.   The donor participating in a deferred gift annuity plan claims a charitable income tax deduction in the year the gift is made. The deduction taken is typically quite high, averaging about 50 percent of the size of the gift. For example, a 56-year-old donor who makes a $10,000 deferred gift annuity to a nonprofit and begins to receive payments at age 75 obtains approximately $5,241 as a charitable income tax deduction. This figure will vary based on the donor's age and that month's current discount rate. It is important to note that a donor's charitable income tax deduction is affected by the frequency and timing of payments. More frequent payments will reduce a donor's charitable income tax deduction, as will providing the donor with a payment at the beginning rather than at the end of the payment period.

(ii) Gift Taxes. It is currently unclear whether a donor is assessed a gift tax when creating a deferred gift annuity to benefit another. The annual exclusion, discussed in Chapter 37, allows a donor to give up to $11,000 to one individual each year free of gift tax. However, the annual exclusion does not protect gifts of a future interest, which may include the deferred gift annuity because payments to a beneficiary do not begin immediately. Advise the donor who makes a deferred gift annuity to benefit someone other than her spouse that the law is unclear and she may be required to pay a gift tax. In the case of a donor making a deferred gift annuity to benefit a spouse, no gift tax is due because of the unlimited marital deduction.

(iii) Income Taxes. As in a charitable gift annuity, a portion of the income from a deferred gift annuity is treated as both a return on one's investment and taxable income from an investment. Therefore, the donor generally receives some tax-free income because part of the income is considered a return of the initial principal, which was already taxed. The part considered investment income is taxed as ordinary income, and as capital gains income if appreciated property is used to fund the deferred gift annuity. For a discussion on the estate tax consequences of a charitable deferred gift annuity, see the section on estate taxes earlier in this chapter.

(b) The Flexible Deferred Gift Annuity

Private Letter Ruling 9746050, dated August 15, 1997, recognizes a new concept for deferred gift annuities.[4] This private letter ruling allows a donor to select one date from among a list of dates contained in the contract to receive payment. The dates correspond to the age of the donor at several points in the future. For a traditional deferred gift annuity, the donor selects a single predetermined date to begin receiving payments. The payout rate and the charitable income tax deduction are based on the number of years the payment is deferred. For a flexible deferred gift annuity, the donor has a right to choose from among the list of possible dates the payout could begin.

For example, a donor, age 35, making a $10,000 gift to establish a flexible deferred gift annuity, requests the right to begin receiving income from dates corresponding to the following ages:

Age to Receive Payment	Annuity Rate	Annual Annuity	Charitable Income Tax Deduction
60	19.1%	$1,910	$1,538
65	25.6%	$2,560	$1,538
70	35.6%	$3,560	$1,538
75	49.6%	$4,960	$1,538
80	71%	$7,100	$1,538

Actual deductions and rates are affected by the prevailing discount rate and payout rates suggested by the American Council on Gift Annuities.

The earliest date on which the donor may begin to receive payments determines the annuity rate and the deduction. The donor's choices are typically incorporated into the deferred gift annuity contract. In this case, the donor obtains a charitable income tax deduction of $1,538, the

---

[4]Note: Private letter rulings are issued by the Internal Revenue Service in response to a question posed by a taxpayer. The IRS response is limited in scope to the specific taxpayer's case. Although a private letter ruling cannot be regarded as law, it does provide insight into the way the IRS may decide similar future cases dealing with the same issue.

lowest charitable income tax deduction from among the list, and the payout the donor receives is based on the date the donor selects. The donor may decide at age 50 that he wants to postpone payment of the annuity until age 53 or age 55. He cannot vary the amount of the annuity but may postpone the date of receipt.

Donors who are uncertain about their expected age of retirement may find the flexible deferred gift annuity to be an appropriate option. Like the IRA that allows the donor to select payouts within a range of years, this option allows the donor to postpone the decision about receiving income until the last moment.

The donor must provide the nonprofit organization with a statement requesting that payments begin 90 days prior to the receipt of payments. The nonprofit's accounting office may want to flag the gift for the first eligible date to remind the donor of the need to select a date. The nonprofit organization should otherwise follow the regular procedures for accepting deferred gift annuities.

23.5   MARKETING THE DEFERRED GIFT ANNUITY

Deferred gift annuities seem to be established most often by donors who are middle aged, have the financial resources to make a gift, and take the deferred income 5 to 8 to 10 years in the future. This age group could be most interested in establishing a deferred gift annuity when shown that annuity payments may be used to offset children's tuition or to care for elderly or aging parents while supplementing retirement benefits. Marketing efforts should target this prospect pool. It is worth noting that the younger donor who can benefit most from making a deferred gift annuity is often the least likely to make a charitable gift, especially a planned gift. However, establishing a deferred gift annuity is an ideal way for a younger donor to become a part of the organization at an early age and to gain recognition in the community.

23.6   ADMINISTRATION

As in the administration of charitable gift annuities in-house, it is important for the planned giving office to work closely with the business or treasurer's office in the administration of deferred gift annuities. The department that manages deferred gift annuities must provide a system to begin payments to donors at the agreed-on time in the future. If successful at bringing in deferred gift annuities, the planned giving officer must be confident that the charity can service the annuitants. Some nonprofits are able to process payments for deferred gift annuities and charitable gift annuities as part of their payroll systems.

APPENDIX 23.1(a)   6.5 PERCENT CHARITABLE GIFT ANNUITY

Appendix 23.1(a)

Deduction Calculations
Summary of Benefits

6.5 PERCENT CHARITABLE GIFT ANNUITY*

ASSUMPTIONS:

Annuitant	70
Principal Donated	$5,000.00
Cost Basis	$5,000.00
Annuity Rate	6.5%
Payment Schedule	quarterly at end

BENEFITS:

Charitable Deduction	$1,749.05
Annuity	$325.00
Tax-free Portion	$204.42
Ordinary Income	$120.58

After 15.9 years, the entire annuity becomes ordinary income.

IRS Discount Rate is 4%

*These calculations are estimates of gift benefits; your actual benefits may vary.

APPENDIX 23.1(b)   8 PERCENT CHARITABLE GIFT ANNUITY

Appendix 23.1(b)

Deduction Calculations
Summary of Benefits

8 PERCENT CHARITABLE GIFT ANNUITY*

ASSUMPTIONS:

Annuitant	80
Principal Donated	$5,000.00
Cost Basis	$5,000.00
Annuity Rate	8%
Payment Schedule	quarterly at end

BENEFITS:

Charitable Deduction	$2,320.40
Annuity	$400.00
Tax-free Portion	$285.28
Ordinary Income	$114.80

After 9.4 years, the entire annuity becomes ordinary income.

IRS Discount Rate is 4%

*These calculations are estimates of gift benefits; your actual benefits may vary.

Appendix 23.1(c)

Deduction Calculations
Summary of Benefits

15.7 PERCENT DEFERRED GIFT ANNUITY*

ASSUMPTIONS:

Annuitant	45
Age at Date of First Payment	[7/2/2023] 65
Principal Donated	$5,000.00
Cost Basis	$5,000.00
Annuity Rate	15.7%
Payment Schedule	quarterly

BENEFITS:

Charitable Deduction	$1,465.35
Annuity	$785.00
Tax-free Portion	$177.41
Ordinary Income	$607.59

After 19.9 years from the year the payments begin, the entire annuity becomes ordinary income.

IRS Discount Rate is 4%

*These calculations are estimates of gift benefits; your actual benefits may vary.

Appendix 23.1(d)

Deduction Calculations
Summary of Benefits

12.3 PERCENT DEFERRED GIFT ANNUITY*

ASSUMPTIONS:

Annuitant	50
Age at Date of First Payment	[3/20/2018] 65
Principal Donated	$5,000.00
Cost Basis	$5,000.00
Annuity Rate	12.3%
Payment Schedule	quarterly

BENEFITS:

Charitable Deduction	$1,565.75
Annuity	$615.00
Tax-free Portion	$172.31
Ordinary Income	$442.19

After 19.9 years from the year the payments begin, the entire annuity becomes ordinary income.

IRS Discount Rate is 4 percent

*These calculations are estimates of gift benefits; your actual benefits may vary.

CHAPTER TWENTY-FOUR

Pooled Income Funds

24.1 POOLED INCOME FUNDS

Recognized in 1969, when they were included in the Internal Revenue Code, pooled income funds constitute another important gift option to offer to planned giving prospects. The concept is simple: A donor makes a gift to a pooled income fund, which works somewhat like a mutual fund. The donor receives a variable income for life, and perhaps for another beneficiary's lifetime. The rate is market sensitive and may increase or decrease, depending on the earnings of the fund. The income stream must continue for the lives of the beneficiaries; an income stream for a specified number of years is not allowed. Donors generally receive their income payments quarterly, but could receive them biannually or quarterly as stated in the pooled income fund trust document. The donor claims a charitable income tax deduction in the year the gift is made, and at the last beneficiary's death the nonprofit receives the remainder interest. The remainder interest cannot be split among unrelated charities; it can go only to the nonprofit that established and controls the fund.

The fund is considered "pooled" inasmuch as a donor's gift is pooled with those of other donors; the larger amount of smaller gifts in the fund produces the opportunity for a higher rate of return than a single donor could achieve independently. Most organizations require a $5,000 minimum for a first gift to a pooled income fund, and additional gifts can be made, often at $1,000 or more. A pooled income fund enables a donor to make a gift of appreciated securities and avoid paying capital gains taxes on the appreciation. With a capital gains tax rate currently at a maximum of 15 percent, this offers a significant incentive. As rates have fallen, pooled income funds have fallen out of favor, and are encouraged less by organizations and seem to be used less by donors.

Many organizations used to choose to establish more than one pooled income fund so they could offer a range of investment options to donors. Typically, an organization that offers more than one pooled income fund will offer three, each with different objectives.

   1. *High-income fund.* A high-income pooled fund offers participants the highest possible rate of return that the organization can safely produce. For organizations that have had a high-income fund for many years, the income rates currently may range from 4 to 6 percent. Newer funds start at lower rates, because current investment market returns rarely reach those rates of return; older funds are likely to hold long-term bonds earning

interest at a higher rate than is available today. Although a high-income fund tends to be the most popular of the pooled income funds because it offers the highest yearly income to a donor, the charitable income tax deduction is the lowest available from any pooled income fund. Donors who seek a higher charitable income tax deduction and want to conserve more of the principal of their gift for the organization may choose a balanced or growth fund. (See Exhibit 24.1.)

2. *Balanced fund.* A balanced pooled income fund offers donors a lower rate of return. A balanced fund is invested in a combination of stocks and bonds, offering the donor a solid income stream as well as a greater charitable income tax deduction than is available from a high-income fund. A balanced fund preserves more of the principal of the gift. A donor with a life expectancy of 20 years or more may receive more income in later years from a balanced fund that has increased in value over the years than from a high-income fund, which rarely increases in value.

3. *Growth fund.* A growth fund offers the lowest rate of return to a donor. The growth fund is designed for the donor who wants the highest possible charitable income tax deduction from a pooled income fund gift and seeks to conserve as much of the principal as possible. As with the balanced fund, a very young donor may, in fact, receive more income over time from a growth fund that has substantially increased in value than from a higher-yielding fund.

An organization does not have to offer three pooled income funds and may never want to offer even one. Depending on the size of the organization and the potential of pooled income fund prospects, it may prefer to establish only one fund, probably a high-income fund, and add other funds as the donor base and program mature and pooled income funds become more popular again.

Exhibit 24.1 Benefits from a $5,000 Gift to the High-Income Fund.* Please see Appendix 24.1.

Age	Payout Rate	Annual Income	Tax Deduction
55	5%	$250	$920
65	5%	$250	$1,496.50
70	5%	$250	$1,857.55

* Based on a discount rate of 4%. Actual deductions and rates are affected by the prevailing discount rate and market performance.

(a) Tax Consequences of Pooled Income Fund Gifts

(i) Capital Gains Taxes. Donors can make gifts to a pooled income fund and completely avoid capital gains taxes on their gift. This is a significant incentive to make such a gift, especially for donors who have highly appreciated securities, because the capital gains tax rate for most investment assets is 15 percent. For example, if a donor sells securities for $1,000 that she purchased years ago for $100, the donor would be taxed at a maximum rate of 15 percent on the gain of $900 for a total capital gains tax of $135. If instead the donor makes a gift of the appreciated securities to a pooled income fund, she preserves the principal by avoiding the capital gains tax and obtains a charitable income tax deduction and a stream of income.

(ii) Gift Taxes.   If a donor makes a gift to a pooled income fund and either the donor or her spouse is the beneficiary of the income stream, no taxable gift is made. If the income interest is given to the donor's spouse, it may qualify for the gift tax marital deduction if a Qualified Terminable Interest Property (QTIP) election is made. See Chapter 25 for a further discussion of QTIP trusts. The assets are included in the donee spouse's estate, but the donee spouse will receive a charitable estate tax deduction for the amount going to the charity.

If, however, the donor makes a gift to a pooled income fund for the benefit of a third party other than herself or her spouse, the donor makes a taxable gift. If the third party has the right to currently receive income from the pooled income fund, the gift may qualify for the $11,000 annual gift tax exclusion. See Chapter 37 for a full discussion of gift taxes.

(iii) Income Tax to Beneficiary.   The income stream is taxed to the beneficiary (whether the donor, spouse, or a third party) as ordinary income. The only way to avoid this is for the donor to name himself as the first beneficiary and to reserve his right to revoke the income stream of the second beneficiary. This causes the income to be taxable to the donor, while alive, and includes it in the donor's taxable estate. Alternatively, if the donor does not want to be taxed on the income, he can make a taxable gift of the income interest to the designated beneficiary during his lifetime without reserving the right to revoke that beneficiary's income interest.

(iv) Charitable Income Tax Deduction.   A donor who makes a gift to a pooled income fund obtains a charitable income tax deduction in the year the gift is made. Planned giving software calculates the charitable income tax deduction by determining the value of the income stream over the life expectancy of the income beneficiary based on Internal Revenue Service (IRS) actuarial tables. The donor and charity may allow as many beneficiaries on the gift as they wish, but more beneficiaries will decrease the amount of the charitable income tax deduction. At the end of each calendar year, the planned giving software must be updated to include the rate of return earned that year from the pooled income fund. This information, which can be acquired from the organization that manages the fund, is necessary to compute accurately the donor's charitable income tax deduction. The deduction is based on the highest rate of return earned by the fund in the three preceding years. Since the assumed rate is well in excess of actual interest and dividend rates, the deduction for a gift to a new fund is often less than to an older fund, where the actual rate determines the deduction. Once this information is included in the software at the beginning of each year, the donor's charitable income tax deduction can be computed accurately.

(v) Estate Taxes.   Once a donor makes a gift to a pooled income fund, the value of the gift passes outside the donor's estate for estate tax purposes, except for the value of the life interest passing to a beneficiary other than the donor's spouse at the donor's death. In addition, the asset is removed from probate.

(b) Acceptable Assets for a Pooled Income Fund

A pooled income fund is a unique vehicle, and not all types of assets can be used for a gift to such a fund. Because each beneficiary's income is affected by all of the other donors' gifts, a donor cannot make a gift to the fund that will not immediately generate an income. Otherwise, the total amount of income in the pool would stay the same while the number of beneficiaries would increase, thus reducing all beneficiaries' income streams. Most gifts to a pooled income fund are cash and readily marketable securities, which generate income immediately. Closely held securities are not usually accepted into a pooled income fund, because they can be difficult to value, the transaction is time consuming, and a buyer is not always readily available. The private foundation self-dealing rules that prohibit sales, loans, leases, and other transactions with disqualified persons, generally including donors, may also prohibit a sale back to the donor or his family. Self-dealing occurs when a donor or her family retains an ownership interest in a business whose stock has been gifted. Tax-exempt securities are not permitted as gifts to a pooled income fund. If a donor wants to give tax-exempt securities, which typically do not appreciate significantly, he may sell them and then contribute the cash proceeds. Although theoretically gifts of real estate can be transferred to a pooled income fund, they are not appropriate for such a fund and are discouraged or forbidden by most organizations and outside managers. Only if the property can be immediately converted to cash can real estate be used successfully to make a pooled income fund gift.

(c) Establishing a Pooled Income Fund

Before establishing a pooled income fund, an organization should weigh and balance a number of considerations. The availability of a pooled income fund alone will not generate new donors to a planned giving program. Such a fund works best when the organization has a large group of existing donors and potential donors who can be further encouraged to make a gift through a pooled income fund. If the organization does not already have a substantial number of solid prospects or donors for the program, an option of this type may be too expensive to inaugurate. However, offering this gift option keeps an organization competitive with other nonprofits that offer pooled income funds. Most organizations with planned giving programs have pooled income funds, preferring not to lose prospects who want to make gifts of appreciated securities to such a fund, who otherwise might turn to another organization.

(i) Pooled Income Fund Documents. A lawyer who specializes in charitable giving should draft the necessary pooled income fund documents. These include a pooled income fund trust document, a pooled income fund prospectus, and instruments of transfer for making gifts. A donor should review all of these documents before making the gift. Samples of pooled income fund documents are included in Appendix, CD-ROM Documentation, IRS Forms.

(ii) Selecting and Working with a Trustee. A trustee for the pooled income fund must be chosen with care. The nonprofit may want to select an organization, such as a bank, trust company, or other investment company, that is experienced in managing pooled income funds. The planned giving officer should speak at length with the individuals who will manage the account. Many of the gift situations that are new and perhaps confusing to a planned giving officer will be routine to an experienced trustee. Thus, working with an experienced professional is a real advantage as the planned giving program attracts new prospects and donors who have questions about the fund.

Communication with the Trustee. Good communication and rapport between the charity and the trustee is critical to the successful administration of a pooled income fund, inasmuch as the gift process must be regularly coordinated with donors and the trustee. The planned giving officer is responsible for ensuring that the donor has completed the necessary paperwork for the gift and that the trustee has responded quickly and accurately to the donor. The planned giving officer must work with the donor and the trustee to ensure the proper receipt and valuation of the donor's gift and the receipt of the donor's income check, and that any direct deposits of a donor's check have been made. When a problem arises, the donor usually calls the planned giving officer, not the trustee, and it is important to outline expectations in the beginning and keep lines of communication open.

24.1 POOLED INCOME FUNDS

Trustee's Reputation.   The reputation of the trustee of a pooled income fund can be helpful in marketing the fund both to an organization's trustees and to donors. A bank, trust company, or other investment company with a well-known, highly regarded reputation is of substantial benefit to a planned giving program. The trustees of the organization can be secure knowing that the trustee of the pooled income fund is protecting the remainder value of the gift for the nonprofit and should be confident about investment performance providing a stable and secure return.

(iii) Establishing a Pooled Income Fund through a Community Foundation.   There are opportunities to offer a pooled income fund to donors while limiting the nonprofit's cost. Many community-based foundations offer pooled income funds under the name of the foundation enabling area nonprofits to participate in its fund. Donors to the organization can make a gift to the community foundation and designate the remainder of their gift to support the nonprofit. In general, the community foundation will insist on holding the funds indefinitely for the benefit of the nonprofit, distributing income only, rather than distributing the principal to the nonprofit upon the death of the income beneficiary. Participating nonprofits pay a nominal fee to join and a small yearly maintenance fee. From a development point of view, probably the most difficult feature of this arrangement is that the organization first has to secure the gift and then explain the idea of a community foundation administering the gift, as well as any restrictions the foundation has in paying out the gift. This may, however, be an inexpensive way to offer a pooled income fund to donors while assessing a program's progress. The organization can always start its own pooled income fund later if demand warrants such a step.

(d) Marketing the Pooled Income Fund

A well-marketed pooled income fund should produce responses. A nonprofit's marketing efforts should target two main groups: donors 50 to 70 years old who are comfortable with a variable rate of return and donors of any age who want to make a gift of appreciated securities to avoid capital gains taxes. Owners of appreciated securities who would receive a higher rate of return from a charitable gift annuity often decide to make a gift to a pooled income fund to avoid capital gains taxes. Use ads and news articles stressing the benefits of making gifts to the pooled income fund in targeting these groups. For a broader discussion of marketing in a planned giving program, see Part Four, Marketing.

APPENDIX 24.1(a)   POOLED INCOME FUND

Appendix 24.1(a)

POOLED INCOME FUND*

Deduction Calculations
Summary of Benefits

ASSUMPTIONS:

Beneficiary Age	55
Principal Donated	$5,000.00
Cost Basis of Property	$5,000.00
Current Estimated Income Rate	5%
Rate of Return Used for IRS Valuation	9%

BENEFITS:

Charitable Deduction	$920.10
First Year's Estimated Income (Future income will vary with fund earnings)	$250.00

*These calculations are estimates of gift benefits; your actual benefits may vary.

APPENDIX 24.1(b)   POOLED INCOME FUND

Appendix 24.1(b)

POOLED INCOME FUND*

Deduction Calculations
Summary of Benefits

ASSUMPTIONS:

Beneficiary Age	65
Principal Donated	$5,000.00
Cost Basis of Property	$5,000.00
Current Estimated Income Rate	5%
Rate of Return Used for IRS Valuation	9%

BENEFITS:

Charitable Deduction	$1,496.50
First Year's Estimated Income (Future income will vary with fund earnings)	$250.00

*These calculations are estimates of gift benefits; your actual benefits may vary.

Appendix 24.1(c)

POOLED INCOME FUND*

Deduction Calculations
Summary of Benefits

ASSUMPTIONS:

Beneficiary Age	70
Principal Donated	$5,000.00
Cost Basis of Property	$5,000.00
Current Estimated Income Rate	5%
Rate of Return Used for IRS Valuation	9%

BENEFITS:

Charitable Deduction	$1,857.55
First Year's Estimated Income (Future income will vary with fund earnings)	$250.00

*These calculations are estimates of gift benefits; your actual benefits may vary.

CHAPTER TWENTY-FIVE

Trusts

25.1 INTRODUCTION

Trusts are comprehensive, personalized asset management plans designed to accomplish specific purposes for the maker of the trust and the trust's beneficiaries. This chapter begins with a general look at trusts—terms, types, funding, and distribution—and then focuses on charitable trusts and how they are used as vehicles in charitable gift planning. See Appendix, CD-ROM Documentation, IRS Forms and Administrative Documents.

25.2 PARTIES TO A TRUST

There are a number of parties to a trust: the maker of the trust, the trustee, and the beneficiaries. A trust is established by a written agreement between the maker and the trustee.

(a) The Maker, Grantor, and Settlor

The maker of a trust, often called the grantor, donor, or settlor, is the person who creates the trust. If the trust is created by more than one person or by spouses, they are usually considered joint grantors or co-trustees. The grantor transfers the assets of the trust to a trustee, who manages the trust.

(b) Trustee

The trustee may be the grantor, another individual, or an institution such as a bank, trust company, or investment firm. The trustee manages assets for the benefit of one or more beneficiaries. The trustee holds legal title to the assets, and the beneficiary holds equitable title. Equitable title occurs in a fiduciary relationship when the trustee acts on behalf of the beneficiary. The common law traditionally requires that the trustee be held to the standard of a "prudent person," which means that the trustee is required to perform and make investment, distribution, and other decisions in a prudent or reasonable manner. A beneficiary who holds equitable title to the assets can sue the trustee for breach of a fiduciary duty, which includes waste, failure to act, or any act that is not prudent.

(c) Income and Remainder Beneficiaries

There are several types of beneficiaries; this chapter focuses primarily on income beneficiaries and remainder beneficiaries. Income beneficiaries are entitled to receive income earned from the trust's assets and, under some limited circumstances, principal for the trust term. Remainder beneficiaries receive the remaining principal of the trust upon its termination.

25.3 TRANSFERRING TITLE TO THE TRUST CORPUS

Property that is transferred to create a trust is called the trust principal, or corpus. If a grantor, Mr. Smith, transfers assets to himself as trustee of a family trust, he takes title to the assets as Mr. Smith, trustee of the Smith Family Trust. Transferring assets from a grantor to the trustee is generally a simple procedure. In the case of an automobile, the title is simply transferred at the Registry of Motor Vehicles. Title to real estate is transferred by deed. Bank accounts will have new signature cards completed in the name of the trustee for the trust, and brokerage account signature cards are reissued in the name of the trustee of the trust.

25.4 TRUST POWERS

The grantor of a trust defines the obligations and duties of the trustee through the trust powers, which are enumerated in the trust document. Trust powers may be extensive, permitting the trustee a broad range of financial powers, such as enabling the trustee to buy, sell, mortgage, lease, rent, invest, borrow, loan, or perform any other act so stipulated. Alternatively, the trust powers may limit the trustee to certain types of investments, such as Treasury bills or conservative equities.

(a) Distributions of Principal and Income

The trustee, in accordance with the terms of the trust, makes distributions to named beneficiaries. There are basically only two types of distributions that a trustee can make, principal and income.

The terms *principal* and *income* are defined under state law but may be modified by the terms of the trust document.

If the trust document permits, the trustee can make distributions of the principal of the trust to the beneficiaries. Distributions of principal can be made at the discretion of the trustee, at the request of a beneficiary, or upon the occurrence of a specific condition, such as upon the 21st birthday of a beneficiary. A beneficiary also may have the opportunity to make a withdrawal of principal during a specified time frame or "window." Such windows are often found in Crummey trusts, addressed in Section 25.5.

A trustee often is limited to making distributions of trust income to income beneficiaries. Income consists of the earnings generated by the trust principal. If the trust is invested in bank accounts, the income earned is interest; if invested in stock, income is paid out as dividends earned; for bonds, the interest may be referred to as yield or rate paid; and with real estate, it is the rental income.

(b) Special Provisions

The trust document can be drafted to include a number of provisions to assist beneficiaries with special needs.

(i) Spray and Sprinkle Provisions. According to certain provisions in the trust, the trustee may have discretionary power to distribute amounts of income or principal. These are called spray and sprinkle provisions. The trustee is permitted to spray and sprinkle, as with a garden hose, income and principal to beneficiaries in cases of specific need or simply at the trustee's discretion.

(ii) Provisions for Minor Children. The section on wills in Chapter 38 discusses the need to have a guardian appointed for the benefit of minor children. Spray and sprinkle provisions are especially important in the case of minors for whom trustees can make additional distributions. A trustee also can make payments for the benefit of a minor child or payments to meet an "ascertainable standard," which is a measurable and defined standard to meet expenses such as medical or educational costs.

25.5 GIFTS TO A MINOR

(a) Uniform Transfer to Minors Act

There are ways in which individuals, such as parents and grandparents, can transfer assets to a minor. Many states have adopted the Uniform Transfer to Minors Act (UTMA) or Uniform Gifts to Minors Act (UGMA), which provides an easy and inexpensive way to make a gift without the use of complicated trusts or guardians. Under UTMA, gifts to a minor are transferred to a custodian who holds the property for the minor child. The custodian, an adult or institution, is charged with the responsibility of the asset and, in cases requiring investment decisions, must act prudently and impartially. This person may charge a reasonable fee for services and is entitled to reimbursement of expenses. The custodian is obligated to turn over all property transferred under UTMA when the minor child reaches the age of majority, 18 in most states. The gift to the minor is considered an irrevocable transfer and therefore qualifies for the annual gift tax exclusion of $11,000. All unearned income paid to a minor under the age of 14, including income acquired through the transferred assets, is taxed at the parent's marginal tax rate. This tax is referred to as the "Kiddie Tax."

(b) Minor's Trust

A minor's trust is very similar to that provided by UTMA. This trust is sanctioned by Section 2503(c) of the Internal Revenue Code (IRC). Through a minor's trust, a donor transfers assets to a trustee to be held for the benefit of the minor. Funds may either be distributed or accumulated at the discretion of the trustee. Funds transferred qualify for the $11,000 annual gift tax exclusion. When the minor reaches the age of 21, the trustee must make the funds available. From a tax standpoint, a minor's trust avoids the Kiddie Tax, because the trust itself is treated as a separate taxpayer. The trust can limit income and invest for growth, thereby limiting the opportunities for taxation.

(i) Discretionary Payments and Ascertainable Standards.   When a trustee is permitted to make distributions at his discretion, these payments usually cannot be reached by the beneficiary's creditors or be attached in the event of a judgment in a lawsuit against the beneficiary. Because the payments are made at the discretion of the trustee, the beneficiary has no right to receive, expect, or demand regular distributions and has no present right to the assets. If the trustee is making distributions limited to an ascertainable standard, such as for education and living expenses, the payments are once again exempt from attachment.

(ii) Crummey Trusts.   The annual exclusion permits a donor to transfer up to $11,000 free of gift taxes, or $22,000 if the donor's spouse consents to split the gift and the donor files a federal gift tax return, Form 709. For a gift to qualify for the annual gift tax exclusion, the gift must be of a present, rather than a future, interest. A transfer of funds to a trust for the benefit of income or remainder beneficiaries to be paid in the future will not qualify for the annual exclusion, because it is a gift of a future interest. Donors may convert a gift of a future interest to a gift of present interest and thereby avoid gift tax consequences by using a "Crummey power" or other power such as a so-called 5 + 5 power ($5,000 or 5 percent). Such a power enables a donor to qualify a gift to an irrevocable trust for the annual exclusion by creating a window of time during which the beneficiary has the right to withdraw the money transferred.

The beneficiaries must be notified in writing by the trustee that they have a period of time, a window (generally 30 days), during which the funds may be withdrawn. The right to withdraw the funds during a window of time allows the gift to qualify for the annual exclusion, because in essence it is a gift of a present interest, rather than a future interest, and therefore no gift tax is due. The funding of the trust by the donor and the right to withdraw by the beneficiary both occur on an annual basis. In most cases, it is the intent of the donor that the funds not be withdrawn by the beneficiaries. Under the Crummey provision, the funds remain with the trustee of the trust and are then invested as part of the corpus of the trust for the beneficiary. In this case, the transfer by the donor qualifies for the annual exclusion, no part of the unified credit is used, and no taxable gift is otherwise made.

Crummey or similar provisions may be used in conjunction with a life insurance trust. The transferred funds are used by the trustee to pay premiums on a life insurance policy owned by the trust on the life of the donor. The beneficiaries of the trust are generally the heirs of the donor. The objective is to cause the policy proceeds to pass outside the taxable estate of the donor, because the trust is the owner of the policy. If the irrevocable trust is named as beneficiary, then the death benefit is payable to the trustee of the trust and will be added to the corpus of the trust for ultimate distribution to the income or remainder beneficiaries. The donor also may use income from a charitable remainder unitrust to fund an irrevocable life insurance trust.

25.6   REVOCABLE INTER VIVOS TRUST (LIVING TRUST)

A properly drafted revocable inter vivos trust can be a very effective lifetime management tool. *Inter vivos* means during life; the trust is established during one's lifetime. It is revocable in that the grantor may revoke or amend all or part of the trust. Usually the trust is funded during the grantor's lifetime, which means that the grantor transfers assets to the trust during life. A real value of an inter vivos trust is that any asset that passes under the terms of the trust, rather than under the will, avoids probate. In addition, any asset such as real estate or tangible personal property located in a state other than the state where the grantor is domiciled and where the grantor will be subject to probate may be held in the trust, thereby avoiding the extra burden of a separate probate proceeding, known as ancillary administration, in the other state. A revocable inter vivos trust may continue past the lifetime of the grantor for the benefit of the grantor's children, grandchildren, or other beneficiaries. A successor trustee, such as a bank or trust company, is often appointed to serve as trustee after the grantor's death.

All noncharitable trusts, including revocable inter vivos trusts, must provide for a termination of the trust in order to avoid what is known as the common-law Rule Against Perpetuities (now incorporated into the law of most states), which prevents such trusts from operating in perpetuity. A trust may terminate on the occurrence of a specific event, such as when the youngest beneficiary of the trust reaches the age of 21.

It is not usually possible or practical to transfer all assets a grantor owns to a trust during the grantor's lifetime. Any assets not transferred during life may be transferred at death through a "pour-over" provision in the grantor's will. This provision transfers any remaining assets to the trustee of the trust, and these assets are then managed as part of the corpus of the trust. Any asset that is transferred through a pour-over provision must pass through probate.

(a) Grantor Trust Rules

In a grantor trust, the grantor retains control and is considered to be the owner of all assets in the trust and may amend or revoke the trust. The grantor trust rules provide that if the grantor of a trust has retained incidents of ownership or control (elements that comprise a person's ownership) or has retained an interest in the property transferred to the trust, the grantor is treated as the owner of the trust for income tax purposes. The grantor is taxed on any income produced by a grantor trust. In addition, the grantor trust rules apply if the income from the trust may be applied to discharge a legal obligation of the grantor. Thus, a grantor who transfers mortgaged property to a charitable remainder unitrust, for which the trust is obligated to use trust income to pay the mortgage, may violate the grantor trust rules. The resultant violation of the grantor trust rules voids a charitable income tax deduction and may create other unfavorable tax consequences.

(b) Tax Implications

Because the grantor has all the elements of ownership and control over a revocable inter vivos trust, including the right to revoke and amend the trust, the grantor is taxed on any income that the trust earns and on any capital gains that the trust produces. For gift tax purposes, the grantor has not made a completed gift but has retained incidents of ownership and control over the trust. There is no gift tax due on any asset transferred to a revocable inter vivos trust. For federal estate tax purposes, all assets in a revocable inter vivos trust are includible in the estate of the grantor.

25.7 IRREVOCABLE TRUSTS

An irrevocable trust is one through which a grantor transfers property irrevocably to a trustee. The assets are outside the grantor's dominion, ownership, and control. Unlike revocable inter vivos trusts, irrevocable trusts, as the name suggests, may not be amended or revoked. The trustee is usually an institution such as a bank or trust company. Under some circumstances, the grantor may serve as one of several trustees but may not have control.

(a) Tax Consequences of Irrevocable Trusts

There are significant tax considerations in the treatment of irrevocable trusts. For income tax purposes, because the grantor retains no incidents of ownership, any income earned or capital gains produced are taxed to the trust (or its beneficiaries) and not to the grantor. Irrevocable trusts have their own individual tax identification numbers and are treated as separate entities for tax purposes. A transfer by the grantor to the trust is a gift for gift tax purposes.

(b) Charitable Gifts by Irrevocable Trusts

Through an irrevocable trust, a grantor transfers property irrevocably to a trustee, placing the assets outside the grantor's control. Unlike a charitable remainder trust, which is a tax-exempt trust, an irrevocable trust is fully taxable on income produced by the trust. Income earned or capital gains produced are taxed to the trust (or its beneficiaries) and not to the grantor. Irrevocable trusts are treated as separate entities for tax purposes.

Internal Revenue Code Section 642(c) allows a charitable income tax deduction for charitable gifts of income from the irrevocable trust but not of the corpus of the trust. To be deductible, the income must be income earned during the taxable year and paid to the charities pursuant to the terms of the trust instrument, although the trustee may elect to treat the gift as paid during the taxable year if the gift was made on or before the last day of the year following the close of the taxable year. The normal 30/50 percent limitations imposed on an individual's adjusted gross income do not pertain to irrevocable trusts. The trust can make a gift of 100 percent income without being subject to the ceilings on deductibility, so long as it is paid out in accordance with the terms of the trust instrument.

(c) Types of Irrevocable Trusts

Irrevocable trusts can be either inter vivos or testamentary. An inter vivos irrevocable trust is established during the lifetime of the donor, and any assets transferred to the trust during the grantor's lifetime avoid probate. Any assets that pour over to this trust must pass through probate. A testamentary irrevocable trust is established upon the death of the grantor, and all assets used to fund this trust pass through probate.

(i) Irrevocable Inter Vivos Trusts. There is a gift tax imposed on property transferred to an irrevocable inter vivos trust for the benefit of one or more individuals other than the donor or the donor's spouse, although a donor may use the gift tax credit exemption of $1 million to offset any gift tax. Because property transferred to an irrevocable inter vivos trust is beyond the control of the grantor, a complete gift is made for gift tax purposes since the donor has relinquished title and control of the asset. During his lifetime, a grantor can transfer up to $11,000 per year free from gift taxes under the annual exclusion, and a married couple, as joint grantors, can transfer up to $22,000 so long as the donor has a current right to trust income. The exclusion is indexed annually.

(ii) Irrevocable Testamentary Trusts. Property that is transferred by a grantor at death to an irrevocable testamentary trust passes through probate and is also assessed a tax for federal estate tax purposes. This property is deemed to be includible in the grantor's estate for federal estate tax purposes because the transfer is made testamentarily, upon the death of the grantor. Individuals should transfer assets that are likely to appreciate in value to irrevocable inter vivos trusts. It is generally more advantageous to pay a gift tax during life on the value of the assets before their appreciation than to pay an estate tax at death on the appreciated value of the assets. If the grantor lives for three years following the transfer, any gift tax paid on the transfer is excluded from his estate; whereas assets used to pay estate tax at death are themselves subject to estate tax. However, under current tax laws, assets that pass through a donor's estate for federal estate tax purposes receive a step up in tax cost or basis to date of death value, reducing capital gains tax on sale of the asset, whereas assets transferred during lifetime continue to have the grantor's original tax cost. See Chapter 37 for an additional discussion of changes under EGTRRA to step up provisions. This fact should be considered in lifetime gift planning.

25.8 CHARITABLE REMAINDER TRUSTS

Charitable remainder trusts are important gift-planning vehicles. They produce substantial financial and tax benefits for the donor, as well as gifts to charitable organizations. These trusts may be established either during life, through an inter vivos trust, or at death, through a testamentary trust. Charitable remainder trusts provide income to donors and beneficiaries, and upon the death of the beneficiaries or the termination of the trust term, the remainder is transferred to benefit one or more nonprofits. Charitable remainder trusts are established for life or lives of designated individuals or a period not exceeding 20 years. The Internal Revenue Service (IRS) in IRC Section 664 defines a charitable remainder trust as "a trust which provides for a specified distribution, at least annually, to one or more beneficiaries, at least one of which is not a charity, for life or for a term of years with an irrevocable remainder interest to be held for the benefit of, or paid over to, charity." There are two types of charitable remainder trusts, the charitable remainder annuity trust and the charitable remainder unitrust, which are discussed in subsequent paragraphs of this section.

(a) Self-Dealing and Trusts

A charitable remainder trust is subject to some of the limitations applicable to private foundations, including prohibitions against self-dealing. Self-dealing rules prevent a donor who has transferred property to a trust from dealing with the trust. The rules also prevent the donor's family from dealing with the trust. Actions considered to be "self-dealing" include buying, selling, and renting from the trust and continuing to do business with the trust. If a donor who has greater than a 35 percent interest in a corporation transfers stock in the corporation to a charitable remainder trust, the charitable remainder trust is prevented from selling assets to the corporation except under a special redemption or reorganization exception. The donor, the trustee, members of their families, and entities such as corporations in which they have substantial interests are "disqualified persons" and are prohibited from dealing with a trust that has been a recipient of the donor's property.

(b) Historical Tier System and the Taxation of Trust Income

Income produced by a charitable remainder trust and paid to a beneficiary is taxed to the beneficiary. Regardless of whether all income produced by the trust is distributed, the trust pays no income taxes on its earnings as long as it has no unrelated business income, such as debt-financed income. Distributions from a charitable remainder trust are characterized for tax purposes according to the historical income of the trust. For income tax purposes, distributions from the trust are taxed in the following order:

1. Ordinary income

2. Capital gain income

3. Tax-free income

4. Return of principal (corpus)

For example, all ordinary income earned by the trust in prior years or during the current taxable year must be distributed to the beneficiaries before any capital gains income. Only after all ordinary income and capital gains income historically earned by the trust has been distributed is tax-free income or a return of the initial principal permitted.

(c) Common Features of Charitable Remainder Trusts

There are a number of features common to charitable remainder trusts:

- *Income stream.* The grantor of a charitable remainder trust selects a payout rate that will provide a stream of income to the beneficiaries for their lifetimes. By law the rate may not be less than 5 percent or more than 50 percent. If the charitable organization designated as a remainder beneficiary subsidizes the drafting or administration of the trust, the payout rate should not exceed 7 percent in most circumstances. As the payout rate increases, the charitable income tax deduction to the donor decreases, and vice versa. The amount of payment is established at the time of the creation of the trust and should be selected to provide the grantor with the greatest tax benefits while still protecting the remainder value for the nonprofit.

■ *Charitable income tax deduction.* Donors who transfer assets to a charitable remainder trust receive a charitable income tax deduction that can produce significant tax savings. The amount the donor obtains as a charitable income tax deduction is the present value of the remainder interest passing to charity and is greatly affected by the number of beneficiaries and their ages. This deduction is approximately 50 percent of the value of assets contributed to fund the trust. The longer the stream of income is to be paid to the beneficiaries and the greater the rate of payout, the smaller the charitable income tax deduction.

■ *Capital gains taxes.* Assets such as securities that have appreciated in value can be transferred to a charitable remainder trust, enabling the donor to avoid entirely the capital gains taxes due on the gain.

■ *Gift taxes.* Transfers to a charitable remainder trust that provides income to the grantor do not have gift tax consequences. If the donor's spouse receives a present stream of income from the charitable remainder trust, the donor has made a gift to his spouse, but the gift qualifies for the unlimited gift tax marital deduction for federal gift tax purposes, thereby creating no gift tax consequences. If a donor provides a present income stream from a charitable remainder trust to a person other than a spouse, the donor has made a taxable gift of the income interest with gift tax consequences. If the gift is a present interest, the $11,000 annual gift tax exclusion may offset some or all of the gift, and if the value of the gift exceeds the exclusion, then the donor's gift tax credit exemption ($1 million in 2003 and beyond) may be used to eliminate or reduce any gift tax due. The gift tax annual exclusion of $11,000 is indexed.

■ *Estate taxes.* Assets transferred to a charitable remainder trust at a grantor's death will have estate tax consequences, depending on whether the interest to the beneficiary flows for life or for a number of years and whether the beneficiary is the donor, a spouse, or other beneficiary. Assets transferred to a charitable remainder trust that provides income only to the grantor and/or the grantor's spouse avoid federal estate and gift taxes. If the trust provides income to anyone other than the grantor and/or the grantor's spouse, then there may be gift or estate tax consequences.

■ *Probate.* If a trust is funded during a donor's lifetime through an inter vivos charitable remainder trust, all assets transferred to the trust avoid probate. Assets transferred at death, not held in trust, however, generally must pass through probate. Some states, such as Florida and Virginia, have statutory limitations on out-of-state trustees of trusts that receive assets upon the death of a grantor.

(d) Drafting a Charitable Remainder Trust

The IRS has provided model forms to be followed when drafting charitable remainder trusts and has stated that a charitable remainder trust that substantially follows the forms will not be challenged. See sample forms in Appendix, CD-ROM Documentation, IRS Forms.

(i) Naming of Trustee. For many charitable remainder trusts, an institution such as a bank, trust company, or investment firm serves as the trustee, although the nonprofit remainderman (one who is to receive the remainder of the trust) may serve as trustee or co-trustee of a charitable remainder trust. See Chapter 52 for a discussion on the advisability of a nonprofit organization's serving as trustee. As co-trustee, the nonprofit is most often paired with an institutional trustee. The

donor and the nonprofit should be aware that a nonprofit serving as trustee presents a potential conflict of interest. The conflict occurs in the selection of the investment assets of the trust. The income beneficiary may want maximum income, while the nonprofit wants to preserve the remainder; however, the nonprofit also wants to maintain the goodwill of the donor and the donor's family and cannot afford to ignore the income beneficiary's wishes.

(ii) Naming of Charitable Remainderman.   To qualify as a charitable remainder trust, a trust must designate a nonprofit having IRC 501(c)(3) status to receive the remainder. A donor can reserve the right to change the charitable remainderman without jeopardizing the charitable nature of the trust; however, there can be no noncharitable remainder interest created by the trust. A donor also can name more than one charitable remainderman. If the donor wants to deduct the gift to the maximum extent, that is, up to 50 percent of adjusted gross income for gifts of cash and up to 30 percent for gifts of appreciated capital gains property, precise language must be used to limit the remainderman not only to an IRC 501(c)(3) charity, but also to one having public charity status.

(e) Administration of a Charitable Remainder Trust

A charitable remainder trust is a separately managed trust and should not be established unless a minimum gift level is reached. The minimum varies among organizations but is often $100,000 or more. The trustee(s) is expected to manage and invest the trust assets prudently, balancing the interests of the income beneficiaries and remainder for the nonprofit. Exhibit 25.1 is an administration form for a charitable remainder trust.

(f) Five Percent Exhaustion Test

The 5 percent exhaustion test provides that if there is more than a 5 percent chance that the trust assets will be depleted so that the nonprofit remainderman will receive nothing, the donor is not entitled to a charitable income tax deduction. This is an issue for annuity trusts that pay out a fixed dollar amount regardless of the fluctuation in value of trust assets. Most types of planned giving software are designed to warn the user if the calculations indicate that there is more than a 5 percent chance of asset depletion.

(g) Charitable Remainder Trust Payout Limitations

The Taxpayer Relief Act of 1997 provides that for transfers after June 18, 1997, a trust cannot qualify as a charitable remainder unitrust or annuity trust if the annual payout exceeds 50 percent of the fair market value of the trust's assets. The Act provides that the value of the charitable remainder to a qualified charitable remainder unitrust or annuity trust must be at least 10 percent of the net fair market value of the property transferred on the date of the contribution. The 5 percent exhaustion test is still applicable for charitable remainder annuity trusts.

(h) Types of Charitable Remainder Trusts

The two types of charitable remainder trusts most often used in planned giving are the charitable remainder annuity trust and the charitable remainder unitrust. Although these types of trusts share many characteristics outlined earlier, they also have some differences. The type of trust selected by the donor will most often be based on the donor's risk tolerance, desire to secure a larger income, and desire to make additional gifts.

(i) Charitable Remainder Annuity Trust.   A charitable remainder annuity trust pays the beneficiary or beneficiaries a fixed, guaranteed dollar amount that represents not less than 5

Exhibit 25.1   Charitable Remainder Trust Administration Form

Donor's Name _____

Address _____

City _____ State _____ Zip _____

Telephone (Home) _____ (Office) _____

Date of Birth _____ Social Security Number: _____

Second Beneficiary _____

Address _____

City _____ State _____ Zip _____

Telephone (Home) _____ (Office) _____

Date of Birth _____ Social Security Number: _____

Type of Trust:

     Annuity: ☐

     Unitrust: ☐ Regular (Straight)   ☐ Net Income   ☐ Net Income w/Make-up Provision

Annual percent _____

Date of Gift _____ Amount of Gift _____

How was charitable remainder trust funded?   ☐ Cash   ☐ Securities   ☐ Real Estate

Has trustee received checks/securities? _____

Has trustee received signed trust agreement? _____

Has trustee sent confirmation letter to donor? _____

Attorney who drafted trust document:

     Name _____

     Address _____

     City _____ State ____ Zip _____

     Telephone _____

Who paid for drafting of document? _____

_____

Has donor been acknowledged by planned giving officer?   ☐ Yes   ☐ No

Has donor been acknowleged by president?   ☐ Yes   ☐ No

Terms of trust agreement: _____

_____

_____

_____

Has gift been credited?   ☐ Yes   ☐ No   Amount $

percent of the trust's assets. The donor selects the payout rate, which is usually between 5 percent and 7 percent. The amount is paid at least once a year, regardless of the trust's investment performance, and the trustee is required to invade the principal of the trust if necessary to meet the obligation of the payment. The annuity trust is most appropriate for conservative investors who seek security in a fixed payment. This trust is more risky for nonprofits, because the corpus may be diminished or depleted in order to make the required payment to the beneficiaries, thereby resulting in a smaller remainder interest to the charity. Once the trust is established, no additional contributions can be made to it; however, more than one charitable remainder annuity trust may be established.

Example 25.1

Mr. and Mrs. Dorsey, aged 70 and 75, make a gift to a charitable organization by establishing a charitable remainder annuity trust. The trustee is obligated to pay the Dorseys a fixed dollar amount regardless of the trust's investment performance. If the Dorseys' charitable remainder annuity trust is funded with $600,000 and pays out a 5 percent annuity, it will provide a fixed annual income of $30,000 a year for the Dorseys' lifetimes. The charitable income tax deduction for a $600,000 charitable remainder annuity trust is $251,190, based on the life expectancies of the Dorseys.[a]

---

[a] Based on a discount rate of 4 percent.

Funding Tuition through a Charitable Remainder Annuity Trust. Parents of students at secondary schools, colleges, and universities often ask for information about how to provide for their children's education. The cost of tuition represents a major financial burden for many families, and some early financial planning can help. Parents and grandparents often are surprised to find that charitable giving, providing attractive financial benefits and tax savings, can greatly assist in offsetting the expense of tuition. Consider the following ways that tuition can be generated each year through charitable gift planning.

Charitable Tuition Trust. Parents may consider establishing a charitable remainder annuity trust for a term of years to help offset the cost of a child's tuition. Such a trust, when used to pay for tuition, is called a charitable tuition trust. It is ideal for parents who would like to make a gift to a nonprofit, provide income to their children for tuition, and realize substantial tax savings. Parents usually establish a charitable tuition trust for four to six years, during which time the income from the trust is paid to the student and taxed at the student's lower income tax rate. At the termination of the trust, the trust property passes to the nonprofit as an endowed fund in the donor's name, with the income being used to support an educational purpose. The parent can designate the purpose of the fund, such as scholarship support or to benefit a program related to the student's area of study. The remainder may also be used for unrestricted support of the nonprofit.

A $25,000 charitable tuition trust established for a four-year period paying 7 percent generates an income of $1,750 annually and produces a charitable income tax deduction of $18,553.[1]

In addition to the charitable income tax deduction, additional benefits and further tax savings are possible by funding the tuition trust with long-term appreciated securities, which enables the donor to avoid capital gains taxes. All gifts are irrevocable, and the donor should consult with a lawyer, accountant, or financial advisor to ensure that the charitable tuition trust is structured to meet the donor's particular tax needs. A charitable remainder annuity trust for a term of years may be more broadly used to provide an income stream for a longer duration, 20 years maximum, so as to provide income for an extended period to offset educational costs for graduate work or to cover the cost of tuition for more than one child.

---

[1] Based on a discount rate of 4 percent.

*(ii) **Charitable Remainder Unitrust.*** There are three types of charitable remainder unitrusts, each of which is used for different purposes and affects a beneficiary's payout differently. See Chapter 44 for additional information on investment strategies.

Charitable Remainder Unitrust 1: Straight Fixed Percentage Trust.. This charitable remainder unitrust pays to the beneficiary a fixed percentage of the value of the trust's assets, valued annually. The amount paid is not dependent on the income produced by the trust, but is determined by multiplying the percentage payout rate by the fair market value of the trust assets valued annually, usually the last business day of the year. If the assets appreciate in value, then the payout percentage is multiplied by a larger corpus, producing a greater payment to the beneficiary. If the trust assets decrease, then a smaller payment is produced. The trustee is obligated to pay the fixed percentage of the trust assets and must invade the corpus if necessary to make the payment to the beneficiary.

Because the fixed percentage unitrust requires the trustee to invade the principal of the trust to make payments to the beneficiary, this trust generally invests in assets producing a total return that is likely to equal or exceed the payout; otherwise, the principal will be depleted, producing a smaller remainder value for the nonprofit. Depletion of the trust assets also produces a smaller return to the donor, inasmuch as the payout is based on a percentage of the annual value of the corpus. Therefore, it is advantageous to both the beneficiary and the nonprofit for the trust to invest in appreciating assets to preserve the capital and produce a payout stream equal to the predetermined payment rate.

Example 25.2 _____

Mr. and Mrs. Lloyd, aged 70 and 75, choose to make a gift through a charitable remainder unitrust of $600,000. The charitable remainder unitrust will pay the donors a predetermined percentage of the fair market value of the trust's assets, but not less than 5 percent, as revalued annually. If the payout rate is established for the Lloyds at 5 percent, the donors receive an annual income of $30,000 in the first year and a 5 percent payout each succeeding year, based on the annual valuation of the trust. However, if the rate is set at 8 percent, the annual income in the first year will be $48,000. This type of trust provides a hedge against inflation, because as the assets of the trust increase in value, so does the income. Additional contributions can be made to a unitrust. The Lloyds also receive a charitable income tax deduction that, if they cannot use the full amount in the first year, may be carried over for five additional years. The charitable income tax deduction for a charitable remainder unitrust with the rate set at 5 percent is $273,270; at 8 percent, the charitable income tax deduction is $176,256.[a] See Appendix 25.1(a) and 25.1(b), respectively.

_____

[a] Based on a discount rate of 4 percent.

Charitable Remainder Unitrust 2: Net Income Unitrust. The charitable remainder net income unitrust pays to the beneficiaries the stated percentage or the net income earned on the trust, whichever is less. Unlike Unitrust 1, this trust does not allow the trustee to invade the principal to make a payment. If the net income is zero, then no income is paid to the beneficiaries.

Net income unitrusts can be funded with growth stocks, to maximize returns, or other appropriate assets, whether liquid or not. Growth stocks may produce little or no income but instead are designed to appreciate in value. After a period of time the trust could convert the growth stocks, which would have appreciated in value, to income-producing stocks. The beneficiaries would then receive the net income produced or the stated percentage, whichever is less. Net income means interest and dividends but not long- or short-term capital gain. In recent years, investment return has increasingly consisted of capital gain. Consequently, income beneficiaries of many net income interests have complained about the inadequate return of such trusts. One solution is to define net income in the trust instrument to include net realized capital gains for the year. The IRS has recognized such a definition as a reasonable way to structure a net income interest to increase the payout. Only postgift appreciation may be treated as net income. The trust must be carefully drafted to achieve the right result. Of course, the stated percentage amount always imposes a cap on the amount that may be paid out in any year. See Chapter 40 for a discussion of a net income unitrust used for retirement purposes.

Charitable Remainder Unitrust 3: Net Income Unitrust with a Makeup Provision. The charitable remainder unitrust with a makeup provision is similar to a net income unitrust, except that the donor is entitled to a makeup of any income not paid during the term of the trust. The donor receives the stated percentage of the trust or net income, whichever is less. However, if the beneficiary receives net income payments that are less than the stated percentage, the makeup provision allows her to make up income in future years when the trust has net income that exceeds the stated percentage. It is appropriate to fund this vehicle with growth stocks or real state. Again, net income may be expressly defined in the trust to include realized capital gain.

Flip Trusts. A flip trust works especially well for donors who fund a trust with nonmarketable assets such as real estate or closely held stock, which may not be sold immediately. It also works well for beneficiaries who are relatively young and likely to have a fairly long life expectancy. For these donors, capital appreciation is an important part of the plan, and investing for total return enables capital appreciation to occur.

Total return is measured by income (interest and dividends) and capital appreciation, such as gains on the value of the corpus of the trust. For example, if the income is earned at the rate of 3 percent of fair market value and the trust calls for a payout of 5 percent, then the additional 2 percent is obtained from principal. If trust assets have appreciated the payout is made from the capital appreciation of the assets.

(i) Flip Unitrust Approved

The use of a flip trust has now been approved by the IRS. The flip trust is a charitable remainder unitrust that typically pays to the beneficiaries the lesser of the net income or a stated percentage. The flip trust need not hold any unmarketable assets. The trust may flip upon the date designated in the trust instrument such as the donor reaching age 65 or upon the death of the donor's spouse or other date outside the donor's control. The donor's retirement date is within the donor's control theoretically and should not be used as the conversion date. The flip trust is also appropriate for gifts of nonmarketable or low-income assets, such as real estate or closely held stock, or for other assets when there is likely to be a delay in the sale of the property. Upon the conversion of the assets to income-producing property or upon a designated date, the trust flips to allow distributions to be measured by the stated percentage. To qualify as a flip unitrust, three conditions must be met:

1. The trust must use the income exception distribution (net income) method or the straight percentage amount method until the conversion date, which may be sale of the nonmarketable assets used to fund the trust or another designated date. After the conversion date, the trust must flip to the straight percentage payout method (or income exception method if the trust began as a straight percentage payout trust) on a permanent basis.

2. If, while the trust is a net income method trust, the unitrust provides for a makeup account to recoup underdistributions, that account must be forfeited once the trust flips. This prevents income earned in excess of the stated percentage from being distributed once the trust becomes a straight percentage unitrust.

3. Once the trust has flipped, it may not change its status again.

The flip trust was pioneered by the late David Donaldson, Esq., a partner in the Boston law firm of Ropes & Gray, and presents a practical solution when dealing with nonmarketable assets.

25.9 QUALIFIED TERMINABLE INTEREST PROPERTY TRUST WITH REMAINDER TO A NONPROFIT

Through the use of a qualified terminable interest property (QTIP) trust, a donor can provide for a spouse and also benefit a nonprofit. A QTIP trust enables a donor to take full advantage of the unlimited marital deduction (see Section 25.11) by transferring assets to a QTIP trust. The spouse has a right to income for life and, in addition, may invade the trust corpus to maintain a standard of living or to cover healthcare costs. Upon the death of the surviving spouse, the remainder of the trust is distributed to a nonprofit organization.

Unlike a charitable remainder trust, whereby the donor receives a charitable income tax deduction, a charitable QTIP trust provides no income tax deduction to the donor, because the surviving spouse can invade the trust corpus. The transfer to the surviving spouse of QTIP assets qualifies for the estate tax marital deduction, enabling the first spouse who dies to avoid having those assets taxed in his estate. The property is includible in the estate of the surviving spouse, but because the remainder is distributed to a qualified nonprofit, the surviving spouse's estate receives an estate tax charitable deduction. Any income distributed to a beneficiary is taxable to the beneficiary and the QTIP trust itself is taxable, although it may deduct income paid to the surviving spouse. The trust will be taxed on capital gains that are not distributed by the trust.

25.10 CHARITABLE LEAD TRUSTS

A lead trust frequently is described as the opposite of a charitable remainder trust. The "lead" income is paid first to the charity, and after a number of years based on a term or a lifetime, the remainder is returned either to the grantor (a grantor lead trust) or to someone other than the grantor, such as the grantor's heirs or other beneficiaries (a nongrantor lead trust). Unlike a charitable remainder trust, a charitable lead trust does not have to meet the minimum payout of 5 percent. In addition, a charitable lead trust is a fully taxable trust, meaning that the trust pays taxes on its income and capital gains, unlike the charitable remainder trust, which is a tax-exempt trust, although the lead trust may deduct amounts paid to the charitable beneficiary pursuant to the terms of the governing instrument. Lower discount rates coupled with higher estate and gift tax rates provide opportunities for using charitable lead trusts.

(a) Grantor Charitable Lead Trust

A grantor lead trust can provide income to a nonprofit for a term of years or for a term measured by individuals' lives. The trust must be in either a unitrust or annuity trust form. Unlike a charitable remainder trust, the payout does not have to equal or exceed 5 percent of the trust assets, and unlike a charitable remainder unitrust, no net income with or without makeup provisions are possible. The grantor lead trust provides a charitable income tax deduction to the grantor. The grantor is able to accelerate, in the first year, the present value of the income payments to the nonprofit in the form of a charitable income tax deduction, subject to the limitations on deductibility. The grantor is, however, taxed on the income paid to the nonprofit, so the charitable income tax deduction may produce little tax benefit unless the donor is in a significantly higher tax bracket in the year of the gift than in later years during the trust term. If, however, the trust is funded with tax-exempt municipal bonds, the donor obtains a charitable income tax deduction and, because of the tax-free returns, is not taxed on the income. Grantor lead trusts have limited usage at the present time.

(b) Grantor Charitable Lead Annuity Trust

A grantor charitable lead annuity trust enables a donor to retain ultimate possession of an asset while making a generous gift to a nonprofit. This type of trust allows the donor to transfer assets, usually cash or securities, to a trustee. During the term of the trust, the trustee invests the trust's assets, providing a fixed dollar amount each year to the charity. Although the trust's term may be for the lifetime of one or more persons, a trust for a term of years is most common.

(c) Grantor Charitable Lead Unitrust

In addition to the annuity form of a charitable lead trust, there is also a unitrust form. Through a grantor charitable lead unitrust a donor transfers assets, usually cash or securities, to a trustee. During the term of the lead unitrust, the trustee invests the trust's assets and pays a fixed percentage of the value of the unitrust, as valued annually, to a nonprofit. If the unitrust's value increases, the payout to the nonprofit increases proportionately. Likewise, if the unitrust's value decreases, the amount donated also decreases. Although the term may be for the lifetime of one or more persons, most often a term of years (10 to 20) is used. Additional contributions can be made to a charitable lead unitrust at any time.

(d) Nongrantor Charitable Lead Trusts

A nongrantor charitable lead trust provides income to the nonprofit for a period of years, and at the end of the term of years the remainder is transferred to someone other than the grantor, usually the grantor's heirs. The grantor does not receive a charitable income tax deduction but receives estate and gift tax benefits, and trust income is not taxed to the grantor. If the nongrantor charitable lead trust is an inter vivos trust (established during life), the donor obtains a gift tax charitable deduction for the present value of the stream of income passing to charity. However, if the nongrantor trust is a testamentary trust (established upon the death of the donor), the estate obtains an estate tax charitable deduction for that value. The grantor pays gift or estate tax on the present value of the remainder passing to heirs or other individual beneficiaries. Grantors are able to use the nongrantor lead trust to help transfer assets to their heirs at reduced federal estate or gift tax rates. With proper consideration of generation-skipping tax consequences, grantors may pass a considerable amount of property to their grandchildren while substantially reducing taxes and benefiting a nonprofit. See Section 25.11 for a discussion of the generation-skipping transfer tax.

(e) Nongrantor Charitable Lead Annuity Trust

Through a nongrantor charitable lead annuity trust, a donor irrevocably transfers assets, usually cash or securities, to a trustee. During the term of the charitable lead annuity trust, the trustee invests the trust's assets and provides a fixed dollar amount each year to the nonprofit. These payments continue until the trust term ends. The term may be a specific number of years, the lifetime of one or more persons, or a combination of the two. When the charitable lead annuity trust term ends, the trust distributes all of its accumulated assets to family members or heirs. Any asset appreciation that occurs within the trust will be distributed to the trust's beneficiaries, free of additional gift or estate taxes.

(f) Nongrantor Charitable Lead Unitrust

During the lead unitrust's term, the trustee invests the unitrust's assets and pays a fixed percentage of the unitrust's value, as valued annually, to the nonprofit. The lead unitrust's term may be for a specific number of years, one or more lifetimes, or a combination of the two. When the lead unitrust term ends, the unitrust distributes the accumulated assets to family members or other beneficiaries.

25.11 TAX CONSEQUENCES

(a) Federal Estate and Gift Taxes and the Lifetime Exemption

The federal government and most state governments impose taxes on the transfer of property. The tax depends on whether the transfer can occur through a testamentary provision at death or through an inter vivos gift during a person's lifetime.

Many states impose an estate or inheritance tax at death, although most do not impose a tax in excess of the federal estate tax credit for state death taxes. A few states, such as New York, have a gift tax comparable to the federal gift tax. Outright charitable transfers to qualified nonprofit organizations are exempt from federal estate and gift taxes and, generally, from state estate and gift taxes. See Chapter 37 for a discussion of the impact of federal estate and gift taxes.

(b) Unlimited Marital Deduction

The unlimited marital deduction allows spouses to transfer an unlimited amount of property to each other without using up any of their lifetime gift or estate tax exemption. The transfer may be made either as a lifetime transfer (inter vivos) or a transfer at death (testamentary). There are both an estate tax marital deduction and a gift tax marital deduction. To qualify as a transfer under the marital deduction, the spouses must be married and the transfers must take place during the marriage. If a surviving spouse disclaims a property interest, then the marital deduction will not be allowed for that property. Any property interest subject to a mortgage that passes to a surviving spouse will be reduced by the amount of that mortgage.

(c) Generation-Skipping Transfer Tax

The generation-skipping transfer tax (GSTT) is imposed when one of three taxable events occurs:

1. *Taxable termination.* A taxable termination is a termination by death, lapse of time, release of power or an interest in a trust, if, after the termination, all interests in the trust are held by generation-skipping beneficiaries. Generation-skipping beneficiaries are persons two or more generations below that of the transferor. If, at the termination of an interest in property held in trust, assets are distributed to a person at least $37^1/_2$ years younger, or to a family member more than one generation younger than the transferor or to a trust for the exclusive benefit of those persons, this is a taxable termination with respect to the assets so distributed. A person generally has an interest in property held in trust if that person has a present right to receive income or principal from the trust or holds a power of appointment with respect to the trust.

2. *Taxable distribution.* A taxable distribution is a distribution from a trust to a skip person. A skip person is (1) a person two or more generations subsequent to that of the transferor or (2) a trust, (a) if all interests in the trust are held by skip persons or (b) if no person holds an interest in the trust and future distributions or terminations may be made only to skip persons. The distribution is subject to tax regardless of whether it is made from trust income or principal.

3. *Direct skip.* A direct skip is an outright transfer to or a transfer in trust for the benefit of a skip person from trust assets. A direct skip is a transfer of an interest in property that is a taxable gift or is includible in the estate of the transferor.

   In the case of a taxable termination or distribution from a trust, the tax is paid by the trustee. In the case of a direct skip, the transferor pays the tax. When a charitable remainder trust or charitable lead trust benefits a grandchild of the donor or another individual two or more generations below the grantor, full consideration of the impact of the GSTT must occur, and proper allocation of the GSTT exemption is vital.

(i) Exemption. The GSTT does not apply to any outright transfer to an individual that would qualify for the annual exclusion of $11,000 or for payments for tuition or medical expenses. However, transfers in trust, such as a transfer to a grandchild through a charitable remainder or charitable lead trust, are not protected from the GSTT though the transfer may qualify for the annual exclusion. In addition, every individual is allowed a $1,120,000 GSTT exemption in 2003 gradually increasing until, in the year 2010, when the GSTT is expected to be repealed. Spouses are permitted to pool the exemption so that a transfer may be treated as if one half were made by each. The exemption may be allocated to a specific transfer; however, once allocated the exemption is irrevocable.

APPENDIX 25.1(a)   5 PERCENT CHARITABLE UNITRUST

Appendix 25.1(a)

5 PERCENT CHARITABLE UNITRUST*

ASSUMPTIONS:

Beneficiary Ages	70
	75
Principal Donated	$600,000.00
Cost Basis of Property	$600,000.00
Payout Rate	5%
Payment Schedule	quarterly
	3 months to 1st payment

BENEFITS:

Charitable Deduction	$273,270.00
First Year's Income	$30,000.00
(Future income will vary with trust value)	

IRS Discount Rate is 4 percent

*These calculations are estimates of gift benefits; your actual benefits may vary.

APPENDIX 25.1(b)   8 PERCENT CHARITABLE UNITRUST

Appendix 25.1(b)

---

8 PERCENT CHARITABLE UNITRUST*

ASSUMPTIONS:

Beneficiary Ages	70
	75
Principal Donated	$600,000.00
Cost Basis of Property	$600,000.00
Payout Rate	8%
Payment Schedule	quarterly
	3 months to 1st payment

BENEFITS:

Charitable Deduction	$176,256.00
First Year's Income	$48,000.00
(Future income will vary with trust value)	

IRS Discount Rate is 4 percent

*These calculations are estimates of gift benefits; your actual benefits may vary.

## CHAPTER TWENTY-SIX

Private Foundations, Supporting Organizations, and Donor-Advised Funds

26.1 INTRODUCTION

Increasingly, planned giving officers are finding themselves working with donors to create gift arrangements that are more complex than traditional planned gift arrangements such as pooled income fund gifts, charitable gift annuities, and charitable remainder trusts. Due to greater donor education, advisors such as certified public accountants (CPAs) and attorneys being involved with a donor's philanthropy, and individuals accumulating greater wealth than they ever expected, people are becoming more interested in creating larger gifts and seeking greater control over their gifts. Private foundations, supporting organizations, and donor-advised funds are complex gift options that allow donors to make substantial gifts to charity and maintain greater involvement over time with their gift, and with the investment of their gift.

Planned giving officers need to educate themselves about the basics of each of these three types of gift vehicles in order to better work with donors and their advisors to establish gifts that are right for each donor and the charitable organization. In establishing one of these types of gifts, the planned giving officer will almost always involve a financial advisor, often the donor's and the charity's advisors, due to the complexity of these arrangements. This chapter covers private foundations, supporting organizations, and donor-advised funds, with emphasis on what the planned giving officer needs to know to offer and close these gifts successfully.

26.2 PRIVATE FOUNDATIONS

(a) Definition

Public charities enjoy favorable tax treatment under the Internal Revenue Code (IRC). By contrast, private foundations are subject to a range of taxes, limitations, and restrictions. Section 509 of the IRC describes private foundations as all organizations exempt under IRC in Section 501(c)(3). Section 509 states that all organizations must be divided into two main classifications, public charities and private foundations. Public charities must demonstrate their qualification under Section 509 (a)(1), (2), or (3) classifications to avoid private foundation status. A private foundation often is supported by one individual or family and may be very large, such as the Ford Foundation, or as small as the John Smith Family Foundation.

(b) Basic Deduction Rules

(i) Cash. An individual's charitable income tax deduction for a gift of cash to a private foundation is limited to 30 percent of the taxpayer's contribution base, which is likely to be her adjusted gross income with certain adjustments, or the excess of 50 percent of the contribution base for the taxable year after cost contributions to public charities, if less.

(ii) Appreciated Property. For gifts of appreciated property, donors may deduct the full fair market value of publicly traded appreciated stock contributed to a private foundation of up to 20 percent of adjusted gross income. A donor may not give more than 10 percent of outstanding stock of a company under this rule. All other gifts of long-term capital gains assets may be deducted. As with all charitable gifts, a donor may carry over unutilized charitable income tax deduction for up to five additional years following the year of the gift.

(c) Minimum Distribution Requirements

Section 4942 mandates that a private foundation must make, at a minimum, qualifying distributions equal to 5 percent of the fair market value of its net investment assets each year, regardless of actual income earned. Grants must be made to public organizations for charitable purposes. Distributions cannot be made to charities controlled by the private foundation or to its disqualified persons.[1] Gifts made to other private foundations other than operating foundations are not treated as qualifying distributions.

(d) Excise Tax on Net Investment Income

An excise tax of 1 percent is imposed on a private foundation's net investment income for 2003. The excise tax returns to 2 percent in 2004. This is basically defined as the excess of gross investment income and net capital gains over ordinary and necessary expenses paid or incurred either for

---

[1] A disqualified person is defined fully in IRC §§ 507 and 4946 and includes one who is a substantial contributor to the private foundation, foundation managers, such as officers and trustees, an owner of more than 20 percent of a corporation or other entity that is a substantial contributor to the private foundation, a member of the family of one named above, or a company or other entity controlled to an extent of 35 percent by those above, and a government official.

the production or collection of such income or for the management, conservation, or maintenance of property held for the production of such income.

(e) Prohibited Transactions

Tax laws and regulations restrict various activities and investments of a private foundation. Such restrictions are intended to discourage potential abuses by a private foundation of its tax-exempt status. The following acts are subject to substantial penalty taxes and are prohibited by a private foundation and those involved with it:

- Failure to meet the 5 percent minimum distribution requirement
- Acts of self-dealing such as sales, leases, or loans
- Holdings in business enterprises that are in excess of prescribed maximum amounts
- Investments that are speculative and which jeopardize the private foundation's tax-exempt purpose
- Payments for lobbying, or to individuals or other non-charitable activities

These prohibitions are discussed more fully below.

(f) Self-Dealing

A donor may be subject to excise tax penalties for pursuing various activities with the private foundation. These self-dealing transactions are prohibited between the donor and private foundation:

- Selling, exchanging, or leasing property
- Lending money on an interest-bearing basis from the donor to the foundation
- Paying compensation or other reimbursement of expenses by the foundation to disqualified persons unless such amounts are reasonable and necessary to carry out the foundation's tax-exempt purposes
- Transferring any income or assets from the foundation to the donor for the donor's use or benefit
- Transferring mortgaged properties to the foundation

(g) Excess Business Holdings

A donor cannot use a private foundation to preserve the control, management, and operations of a closely held business during his lifetime or after death. Specifically, a private foundation cannot hold more than 20 percent of a corporation's voting stock reduced by the aggregate holdings of all disqualified persons. A foundation may hold nonvoting stock only if all disqualified persons together hold less than 20 percent of the voting stock. The foundation may always own 2 percent of the outstanding stock of a company.

(h) Investments

Investments that may jeopardize a private foundation's tax-exempt purpose are prohibited. Such investments may include puts, calls, straddles, derivatives, and registered stock.

(i) Expenditures for Lobbying

Expenditures from a private foundation for lobbying and other activities to influence elections or legislation, or to make grants to certain individuals or noncharitable organizations involved, is strictly prohibited.

(j) Termination

A private foundation can terminate its status by becoming a publicly supported organization or it may go out of existence by distributing its assets to a public charity. It also may, under appropriate circumstances, distribute its assets to another private foundation.

(k) Who Should Create a Private Foundation?

An individual who wishes to make a substantial charitable gift but retain some control over the charitable disposition after contributing the asset is a good candidate for creating a private foundation. The donor must have the financial means to pay the cost of creating, administering, and managing the private foundation, including preparation of annual federal and state filings. This option works best for donors who wish to maintain some control over their gift, to benefit many different charities, to be involved with the investment of the foundation, and to allow their families to be actively involved in their philanthropy.

(l) Advantages and Disadvantages of Private Foundations

Donors, advisors, and charities can find both advantages and disadvantages in creating private foundations. When working with a donor or her advisor in establishing a private foundation, consider these advantages and disadvantages:

Advantages

- *Personal.* Creating a private foundation is in essence creating one's own personal charity. A board created for the foundation can be private and hand-picked.

- *Family oriented.* A donor and her children commonly comprise the board of a private foundation. A private foundation can provide a structure for a family's charitable activities. Family members can be involved early in making grants and helping future generations understand the meaning of philanthropy.

- *Control.* The donor and board have absolute control and can hire their own staff. They can choose which charities to benefit, and a private foundation provides lots of freedom and spontaneity in gift giving.

Disadvantages

- *Expensive.* Legal counsel must be obtained to create a private foundation. The start-up and administrative costs for creating a private foundation are high.

- *Detailed administration.* The donor is responsible for record keeping and tax return preparation for the foundation. Detailed reporting and allocation of expenditures is required. This adds to the expense of creating a private foundation and also adds to its complicated nature.

26.3 SUPPORTING ORGANIZATIONS

Another option to consider is the supporting organization. The supporting organization offers both the operational advantages of a private foundation and the tax advantages of the public charities they support. A supporting organization is subject to fewer restrictions than the private foundation but offers the donor less control.

(a) Definition

A supporting organization is a unique type of charitable organization because of its special relationship to a public charity. It is also classified as a public charity rather than as a private foundation.

26.3 SUPPORTING ORGANIZATIONS

Essentially, a donor, by establishing a supporting organization, chooses one or several charitable organizations to be benefited by the supporting organization, which will manage the funds. The supporting organization may support more than one charity, but all charities must be named at the time the supporting organization is established.

As with gifts to any public charity, donors may deduct up to 50 percent of adjusted gross income for gifts of cash to a supporting organization and up to 30 percent of adjusted gross income for gifts of appreciated property.

(b) General Requirements

A supporting organization must be structured to meet the following requirements of Section 509(a)(3) of the IRC:

- Organizational test

- Relationship test

- Control by nondisqualified persons test

(i) Organizational and Operational Test. The supporting organization must be organized and operated exclusively for the benefit of, perform the functions of, or carry out the purposes of one or more specified public charities. Generally, this test is satisfied if the supporting organization's documents state its purposes as being to support one or more designated organizations, as broad as those of the charity. The supporting organization, to satisfy the operational test, must make grants to further the supported organization or its charitable purposes.

(ii) Control by Nondisqualified Persons Test. Disqualified persons cannot control the supporting organization, directly or indirectly. For this purpose disqualified persons are those described earlier under the discussion of private foundations. Individuals who are employed or controlled by a disqualified person are also treated as disqualified persons. Therefore, a donor and his family can have only minority representation on the governing body of the organization if it is to qualify as a supporting organization. Prohibited control results if any of the following exist:

- Fifty percent or more of the voting power of the governing body consists of disqualified persons.

- A disqualified person has a veto power over the actions of the organization.

- A contributor retains the right to designate who will receive the income or principal from a contribution.

(iii) Relationship Test. This test requires that the supporting organization must be operated, supervised, or controlled by or in connection with the charity. This requirement is sometimes satisfied by meeting the "controlled by" test, but some are established under the "operated in connection with" test. The relationship test is usually satisfied in one of three ways:

1. *Controlled by.* A majority of the governing body of the supporting organization (either the board of directors or the trustees) is appointed by the charity. For example, Harvard University may elect the board members of a supporting organization, and essentially controls it.

2. *Supervised or controlled in connection with.* This test seems to be met only if both the supporting organization and the charity are under common control. Therefore, a majority of board members of the supported organization are made up of officers or trustees or representatives of the charity.

3. *Operated in connection with.* This is the most complicated and interesting of the three tests. To meet this test, the supporting organization must meet two different tests: the responsiveness test and the integral part test.

■ *Responsiveness test.* A supporting organization meets this test if it is satisfactorily responsive to the needs or demands of the supported organization. At a minimum, the charity must have a voice in the practice of the charity, typically by having one representative on the governing body of the supporting organization.

■ *Integral part test.* This test is met if the supporting organization maintains a significant involvement in the operations of one or more publicly supported organizations and such publicly supported organizations in turn depend on the supporting organization for the type of support that it provides. This typically means that the supported organization provides an amount of support to the supporting organization that is significant to its total operation or the operation of one or more of its programs.

Under this second test, neither the charity nor the supporting organization has total control. The charity can provide a voice and input. Usually, a three- to seven-person board is established, with one or several swing votes provided by an individual such as the donor's lawyer or financial advisor. The donor may serve on the board, but cannot control it.

(iv) Creation. A supporting organization can be created as either a corporation or a trust. Selection should be based on the donor's preference. The supporting organization created as a trust may be easier to create and operate, and is less expensive to create.

(v) Termination. A supporting organization can be terminated and the funds placed in restricted funds at the supported organizations.

(c) Who Should Create a Supporting Organization?

A donor who wishes to make a substantial gift to charity should consider establishing a supporting organization. This gift option is most appropriate for a donor who is willing to maintain less control over his gift than he would by creating a private foundation, but can enjoy fewer restrictions in making and maintaining his gift. A donor who wishes to make his gift using something other than cash or securities, such as real estate or closely held stock, is a good candidate for a supporting organization.

(d) Advantages and Disadvantages of Supporting Organizations

There are many advantages to qualifying for public charity status as a supporting organization over being classified as a private foundation. Supporting organizations provide donors with great flexibility, including what type of asset is used to fund the supporting organization, and allows more control over the timing of a donor's gifts.

Advantages

■ *No minimum distribution requirements*

■ *No annual payments.* No minimum amount of money in the supporting organization must be paid out annually, as with the private foundation that mandates a payout of 5 percent of asset value for annual distribution though the supporting organizations must pay out substantially all its net income.

■ *Higher income tax deduction.* There is better income tax deduction treatment.

■ *No excise tax.* A supporting organization avoids the private foundation excise tax, which is currently at 1 percent in 2003 and 2 percent in 2004, on its net investment income. This means more money is available for charity.

- *No self-dealing limitations*

- *No limit on holdings in business corporations and enterprises*

- *Allows risky investments.* There are fewer restrictions on speculative investments: A supporting organization can accept gifts of real estate, restricted stock, and closely held stock.

- *Support more than one organization.* A supporting organization can focus on making gifts to several institutions. Most supporting organizations benefit three to five charitable organizations.

- *Involvement with charity.* The donor can be involved with board members at the charities who will advise him, allowing the donor to work closely with and get to know more about the charitable organization(s).

Disadvantages

- *Less control.* Supporting organizations offer less control to the donor than a private foundation.

- *Less spontaneity.* The supporting organization can support fewer individual charities, and they must be named at the time of the supporting organization's creation, allowing for less freedom and spontaneity about where to make gifts.

26.4 DONOR-ADVISED FUNDS

Donor-advised funds offer a third option to donors who wish to support a charity and exercise more control and input than by making an outright gift, but prefer an alternative to the private foundation or supporting organization. Donor-advised funds are regarded, like supporting organizations, as public charities. They tend to be more flexible than private foundations, and are enjoying a growth of popularity. Many donor-advised funds are created through community foundations, but increasingly individual charities are offering donor-advised funds to donors.

(a) Definition

Through a donor-advised fund, a donor creates a named fund with a charitable institution. The fund can be a permanently endowed fund from which only income is distributed or be a fund from which principal and/or income can be distributed. The agreement creating the fund must state that the donor can make only nonbinding recommendations to the institution for distributions it makes from the fund. The donor's suggestions to the charity are advisory only; the donor does not exercise complete control over the workings of the fund.

(b) Basic Deduction Rules

A donor can deduct up to 50 percent of total income each year for cash gifts and up to 30 percent of adjusted gross income for gifts of appreciated property to a donor-advised fund.

(i) Investments. A donor may be given the opportunity to select investment options for the donor-advised fund. The options should be developed and controlled by the charity. The selections are advisory, not final or binding on the charity administering the donor-advised fund.

(ii) Charity's Obligations. The charity should have charitable programs that are separate from those selected by the donor to the donor-advised funds. It is desirable for the institution managing the donor-advised fund to recommend different programs and options to the donor that she may choose to support.

(iii) Limits on Grants.   All gifts from donor-advised funds must be made to properly qualified charitable organizations. Gifts should not be made for the benefit of the donor advisor, such as to a private foundation or any organization controlled by the donor or his family member or agent. Gifts should not be made to purchase tickets to benefits or in any situation in which the donor will receive direct or indirect benefit.

(iv) Donor Advice.   The donor may retain the privilege of making nonbinding recommendations to the charity about the timing, amount, and recipients of distributions from the donor-advised fund. All communication from the institution managing the donor-advised fund, whether written or oral, should make this limitation clear. The donor retains no legal rights obligating the charity to follow her suggestions.

Suggested ways to help ensure that the donor does not retain too much control include:

- The donor's advice must be consistent with objectives of the charity. For example, gifts to create a donor-advised fund at the Boston Foundation should be made with the understanding that the donor will recommend Boston area charities to receive gifts.

- The charity's need for gifts from the donor-advised fund must be consistent with its charitable purposes.

- Written and oral solicitations and communications specifically state that the institution managing the donor-advised fund must not be bound by the donor's advice.

(c) Why Charities Establish Donor-Advised Funds

If a charity offers donor-advised funds to be managed by the charity, it represents another option to offer to donors and a way to keep donors' assets close to the charity. Some charities such as colleges and universities that create such funds require that donors commit a portion, usually 50 percent or more, to the charity that manages the donor-advised fund. Most donors give more.

The complexity of the donor-advised fund can vary depending on whether the charity creates a separate legal entity for the donor-advised fund or invests the fund as part of its endowment.

(d) Donor-Advised Funds at For-Profit Organizations and Community Foundations

Many organizations offer donor-advised funds that can provide some of the advantages of a private foundation but avoid the administrative and reporting responsibilities. Most funds can be established quickly and easily, usually with a small minimum gift amount. The donor takes a charitable income tax deduction in the year the gift is made, but retains the right to make recommendations as to which charities shall receive funds over his lifetime or perhaps over the lifetime of a designated survivor. A donor's gift is pooled with other donors' gifts for investment purposes, and the donor can make his gift on his own timetable.

(e) Who Should Create a Donor-Advised Fund?

A donor-advised fund works well for a donor who wants to support a few named charities at a substantial level and for the donor who wants to support many charities at lesser amounts. A donor-advised fund may be a part of a community foundation or other charity. The donor who wishes to have the investment decisions and administration handled by someone else should consider establishing a donor-advised fund. In general, the donor must be willing to make her gift with cash, marketable securities, or shares in mutual funds.

(f) Advantages and Disadvantages of Donor-Advised Funds

Donor-advised funds are versatile in many ways and offer donors more control over their gift than an outright or life income gift. The donor can continue to be involved with his management and distribution of the contributed funds. The following outlines some advantages to creating a donor-advised fund.

Advantages

- *Small minimum to open.* Donor-advised funds often can be established for a small amount of money, such as $25,000. The fund can be added to at any time. Some nonprofits establish a higher gift minimum, such as $250,000.

- *Flexibility in timing of gift.* The donor can make a gift to a donor-advised fund and take an immediate charitable income tax deduction. The donor can later advise which charities should receive distributions.

- *Tax benefits.* The tax benefits are better than those of private foundations.

- *Less complex.* The fund is not required to file separate tax returns or accountings. Donor-advised funds are not subject to the private foundation rules.

- *Increase philanthropy.* Donor-advised funds bring more charitable dollars into the philanthropic community.

Disadvantage

- *Perception.* Some for-profit institutions that offer donor-advised funds may care less about philanthropy than about management of assets, and use vast marketing efforts to attract donors.

26.5 CONCLUSION

Private foundations, supporting organizations, and donor-advised funds offer three different alternatives for donors who wish to make gifts that provide them with more control than making an outright gift to a single charity. Exhibit 26.1 compares and contrasts these gift vehicles.

Exhibit 26.1 Gift Vehicles

Type	Status	Deductibility	Min. Distr. Requirements	Excise Tax	Prohibited Transactions	Control	Costs to Create and Maintain	Term of Years to Run
Private Foundations	Private	Cash 30% adjusted gross income apprec. secs. 20% adjusted gross income	5% annually of fair market value of net investments	Tax on net investment income	■ Failure to distribute minimum amount of foundation's income ■ Self-dealing ■ Excess business holdings ■ Certain investments ■ Expenditures for lobbying	■ Greatest amount available in terms of whom to support and how	High: Standard private foundation may cost $5,000–$10,000; annual cost for administration and filing $2,000–5,000/yr	No limit
Supporting Organizations	Public charity	Cash 50% adjusted gross income; apprec. prop. 30%	85% of net income	None	■ No self-dealing limitations ■ No limit on holdings in business corporations and enterprises ■ No restrictions on risky investments: can accept any type of appreciated asset such as restricted stock and real estate ■ No prohibitions on certain noncharitable expenditures	■ Less than private foundation ■ Supported organizations are limited and named at time of creation ■ Can make gifts to many organizations	Moderate: some cost involved in creating the supporting organization and keeping it running (about $5,000–10,000 to create and $2,000–$5,000 for annual accountings and returns). Works particularly well if the donor is interested and involved. Less complicated tax forms than private foundations	No limit

(Continued)

Exhibit 26.1 *(Continued)*

Type	Status	Deductibility	Min. Distr. Require-ments	Excise Tax	Prohibited Transactions	Control	Costs to Create and Maintain	Term of Years to Run
Donor-advised funds	Public charity	Cash 50% adjusted gross income; apprec. secs. 30%	None	None	■ Gift must be made to a public charity, not a private foundation ■ More restrictive as to investment options it will accept	■ Donor can offer nonbinding recommendations to charity on how to use gift ■ Use of the charity's investment expertise	Low for the donor: usually a small minimum gift amount to create ■ Legal fees low: legal counsel usually only needed as advisory ■ Little or no reporting or administrative responsibilities by the donor	Negotiable—often runs for parents' and children's lives

CHAPTER TWENTY-SEVEN

Endowed Funds

27.1   INTRODUCTION

Planned gifts are an important means of funding endowed funds. Although endowed funds may be established by outright gifts that do not involve planned giving, planned giving vehicles are often associated with establishing or augmenting endowed funds. An endowed fund is a gift arrangement established in perpetuity, through which the principal of the fund remains intact and usually only the income is paid out, most often on an annual basis. The principal is the amount of cash or property that was contributed by the donor, and the income is the earnings produced from the principal. Endowed funds may be established for any purpose and are commonly named after the donor or the donor's loved one. An endowed fund may be created to establish an endowed scholarship, project, program, institute, professorship, or chair.

27.2   ENDOWED NAMING OPPORTUNITIES

Endowed naming opportunities, such as endowed chairs, scholarships, and funds—named for the donor or another person—typically include planned giving as a funding mechanism. A printed list of endowed naming opportunities and their corresponding costs can help to raise a donor's philanthropic sights. Some competitive donors see the higher-level endowed fund options as a challenge to be met. The price associated with an endowed fund and the fund's wide range of opportunities alerts donors to the organization's needs and the cost of funding these needs. For every endowed fund, an agreement is created between the donor and the nonprofit. The agreement defines the obligations and the duties of both the donor in funding the gift and the nonprofit in making an award, selecting a recipient, and managing the principal of the fund. Typically, a development or planned giving officer and the donor discuss how to create the fund. The minimum level at many organizations is $10,000 to establish a named endowed fund, although it can be as high as $50,000. A donor may fund the endowment outright with cash, partially or completely through a planned gift, or through a bequest in the donor's estate. If the fund is established while the donor is alive, the donor has the opportunity to be recognized for establishing it and will perhaps have the chance to meet a fund recipient.

A named fund can grow with the help of family and friends. Often relatives and friends make gifts to a family fund in lieu of birthday or holiday presents. See Appendix: CD-ROM Documentation, Exhibits, and Exhibit 27.1 for additional information on ways to increase family funds.

Exhibit 27.1   Augmenting Endowed Funds

Building Your Endowed Family Fund

Over the years, the Office of Development has helped families increase the size of their endowed family funds, and we are pleased to share with you some of our ideas. We welcome the opportunity to develop a plan to increase your family fund to provide additional benefits to the <PROGRAMS> at <ORGANIZATION>.
Please consider the following ideas that have been successfully used to augment family funds:

- Make an annual gift to the fund. Over time such annual gifts may double the size of your family fund.
- Honor family members' birthdays, anniversaries, and weddings by making gifts to the fund in their names.
- Some families, in lieu of exchanging birthday or holiday presents, make a gift to the family fund.
- Make a planned gift and designate your gift to benefit your family fund.
- Through your will, leave a percentage of your estate or a specific dollar amount to your fund.
- Let friends, colleagues, and relatives know of your fund and invite their support.
- For memorial services, suggest that in lieu of flowers or fruit, gifts be made to your family fund at <ORGANIZATION>, <ADDRESS, CITY, STATE, ZIP>.

We welcome your suggestions. ***For further information, please contact:***

<NAME>
<TITLE>
<ORGANIZATION>
<ADDRESS>
<CITY, STATE, ZIP>
<TELEPHONE>

27.3   CREATING AN ENDOWED FUND

By creating an endowed fund, a donor makes a lasting contribution to the future of a nonprofit organization. An endowed fund provides annual support to teaching, patient care, maintenance, and research each year in perpetuity. Endowed funds help support faculty projects, scholarships, professorships, exhibits, lecture series, athletic programs, facility operations, and much more. There may be no more appropriate way to honor the memory of a loved one than to establish a memorial endowed fund. A named memorial gift fund becomes a lasting symbol of the bond between the organization and those who are forever honored and their families.

A donor can specify in writing the purposes that the endowed fund is to serve and how the fund is to be administered within the framework of the nonprofit's investment policies. Endowed funds can be created at any type of organization.

27.4   UMBRELLA FUNDS

Donors with the greatest gift potential often have multiple interests at the nonprofit organization. For example, at museums a donor may be interested in impressionist collections and also contemporary art, each of which may have a different curator or department head. Likewise, at hospitals a donor or a donor's family member may have been a patient in one or more of the hospital's departments. At educational institutions, it is not unusual to find donors holding double majors or dual degrees who enjoy attending university concerts, plays, and athletic events as well as the university's libraries, museums, and galleries. Donors' giving records usually reflect their interests and involvement with the nonprofit organization. Instead of departments competing for the donor's resources, it is more effective to offer the donor the opportunity to establish a single endowed fund that supports each of the donor's interests. An umbrella fund accomplishes this purpose.

An umbrella fund is an endowed fund that allows the donor to allocate the income from the fund to benefit more than one department or program. The donor allocates, through percentages, the distribution or income from the fund. For example, the umbrella fund may state:

Income from the fund shall be designated to support the following programs in the percentages indicated:
1. ____ percent (Description/Name of Department/Program)
2. ____ percent (Description/Name of Department/Program)
3. ____ percent (Description/Name of Department/Program)
4. ____ percent (Description/Name of Department/Program
5. ____ percent (Description/Name of Department/Program)

Through the umbrella fund, the donor may not only support multiple nonprofit departments, but also different funding objectives within one department. For example, the fund may provide support for lecture series, research, equipment purchase, fellowships, and support for operations for a single department.

Umbrella funds reflect the personal interests of the donor and become permanent and very visible symbols of the donor's philanthropic commitment. Donors become attached to these funds and have a sense of ownership over them and direct much of their charitable giving in support of these funds. These funds may be supported annually, through major gifts, planned gifts, and gifts from the donor's estate through a bequest or trust provisions. The remainder of a planned gift can provide additional resources to the umbrella fund upon the death of the donor. Additional gifts may be made at any time, and memorial gifts may be made to the umbrella fund by family members and friends.

Umbrella funds provide a solution to a donor's problem when she wishes to support a variety of nonprofit initiatives. Instead of diluting a donor's gifts, the donor's giving is concentrated on the umbrella fund, which distributes income consistent with the donor's wishes. The umbrella fund can be a positive organizational response to a donor with multiple interests. The donor will appreciate the coordinated efforts and centralized approach to giving, making it easy for the donor to make additional gifts. Recognition programs can be centralized at the nonprofit level and decentralized at the departmental level.

Donors should be directed to make bequests in the name of the fund to the nonprofit organization. The donor need not state the provisions of the fund in the estate-planning document. In this way, the donor can make changes to the gift agreement by reallocating percentages or change designations without rewriting the will or trust. Likewise, the remainder of the planned gift can be designated to benefit the donor's umbrella fund at the nonprofit organization.

27.5 SCHOLARSHIP FUNDS

At schools, teaching hospitals, and other organizations that include a formal teaching component, endowed scholarship funds provide assistance to worthy and financially needy students. A donor who creates a scholarship fund must consider who is an appropriate recipient. The donor may choose to provide assistance to a student with a specific major in a certain department or studying a particular subject that interests the donor. A graduate or an undergraduate student may be selected, and the donor can decide whether the candidate must be financially needy and/or academically worthy to receive the award. See Appendix, CD-ROM Documentation, Agreements, for a selection of scholarship fund agreements designed to meet a variety of purposes.

27.6 FUNDING ENDOWED FUNDS

A donor also must decide how to meet the minimum funding level required at the organization that is establishing the fund. The donor may fund an endowed fund with cash, through a planned gift, or through a bequest from his estate. In the case of a life income gift used to create an endowed fund, the remainder of the gift after the death of the life income beneficiary is available to fund the endowment. This is an important point, inasmuch as eager department heads can mistakenly believe that a life income gift is available at the time the gift is made. However, as with most planned gifts, the remainder is available only upon the death of the donor or beneficiary, and, depending on the vehicle selected, the remainder value may be less than the initial gift. Therefore, some organizations prefer to use the value of the remainder interest, rather than the value of the gift at the time the gift is made, to determine whether a donor has contributed a sufficient sum to reach the necessary endowed level. Another approach is to value the gift fully at the time of funding as long as the income stream is payable only to the grantor and to the grantor's spouse, and not to a series of other income beneficiaries.

27.7 CURRENT-USE AWARDS

An alternative to an endowed fund is a current-use fund. Current-use funds are established to make an award in the year the gift is made. These funds do not grow each year but provide current financial assistance to a recipient and are terminated at the end of the year. A donor can create a named current-use fund for as little as $1,000 at many organizations. This money often is used for books, supplies, operational expenses, or small specific projects. Because the fund exists for only a year, it is good practice to draft a fund description to avoid confusion or conflict, although a fund description is not absolutely necessary (see Exhibit 27.2). For a sample current-use award fund description, see Appendix, CD-ROM Documentation, Administrative Documents, (c) Endowed Fund Descriptions.

Exhibit 27.2   Agreement: Current-Use Award

The [Donor] Current-Use Award

Mr. Valerie and The Academy of Learning hereby propose to establish the [Valerie] Current-Use Award at [The Academy of Learning] in accordance with the wishes of the donor. The award shall be supported by a gift of [$].

The Award is defined and administered as follows:

The title of the award shall be the [Valerie, Current-Use Award at the Academy of Learning]. The Current-Use Award shall be used to support [Biology Program, Science Department] at [The Academy of Learning].

The award shall be used at the discretion of the Department Head to support [DESCRIPTION OF CRITERIA]. The [Valerie] Current-Use Scholarship Award shall be awarded in future years contingent upon the donor making additional gifts to fund the award.

Date	[DONOR]

Date	[NAME]
	[TITLE]

27.8 THE FUND DESCRIPTION

One of the most effective marketing tools in planned giving is the fund description. A personalized fund description is an excellent means of encouraging a donor to consider giving at a higher level to a fund established in the donor's name or in the name of a loved one. In anticipation of meeting with a donor, it is smart to draft a fund description for the donor that benefits the donor's area of interest. From the beginning, the donor is involved in the process and feels closer to the organization. The planned giving officer should explain to the donor how the money will be used and review any restrictions as to who will benefit from the gift. Donors often enjoy seeing their names associated with a program at the organization. The gratification in establishing an endowed fund is similar to that resulting from having a wing of a building or a room named in one's honor, but is achieved on a smaller financial scale.

Included in Appendix, CD-ROM Documentation, Agreements, (c) Endowed Fund Descriptions, are several standard fund description forms used to create an endowed fund in a donor's name (see Exhibit 27.3). Each donor who inquires about establishing a fund should receive a description that includes a statement of the fund's purpose, a brief biographical sketch of the donor, and a distribution clause for paying income or principal to recipients. No other document has been found to be more persuasive or beneficial to a donor who is considering making a gift. A great many gifts have been closed through the use of a fund description.

When meeting with a prospective donor, based on the planned giving officer's general knowledge of the donor, take a draft of a fund description to the meeting. Without knowing all the details, fill in the donor's name and any information known about her. Create the fund in an area in which the donor has expressed an interest. When meeting with the donor, present the fund description to her while explaining that she may choose to establish a fund to help financially needy students or to support a specific program of interest that has continuing needs each year. Remind the donor that this is a draft that can easily be changed to incorporate specific ideas or needs. Stamp the word "Draft" on the document. A donor who has the capacity often establishes a fund in her name with cash, rather than through a planned gift or bequest. Personalized fund descriptions are excellent development vehicles to convert prospects into donors.

Donors sometimes want to be involved in the selection of recipients of endowed funds. A donor who claims a charitable income tax deduction for a gift to a nonprofit cannot be the sole decision maker in selection of the recipient. If the donor were to select the individual who receives the financial benefit, the donor's charitable income tax deduction would be in jeopardy because, in effect, the donor would be paying a benefit to one person of her choice, or tuition, and as every parent learns, there is no charitable income tax deduction for tuition payments. The donor may, however, serve as a member of the selection committee comprising the organization's representatives.

Nonprofits should avoid dealing with situations in which a donor wants to place restrictions that exclude members of a particular ethnic or racial group from benefiting from an endowed fund. Such restrictions are discriminatory and, as such, potentially violate a variety of federal and state laws. Donors and nonprofits also should avoid using language so restrictive that it may prevent a candidate from being selected. Limitations should instead be expressed in the form of preferences.

Exhibit 27.3 Establishing an Endowed Fund

Establishing an Endowed Fund at The Academy of Learning

Name _____

Address _____

City _____ State _____ Zip _____

Telephone _____

Exhibit 27.3   *(Continued)*

We are pleased to draft an endowed fund for your review. Please complete and return this form to <OR-GANIZATION>.

1. Name of the endowed fund _____

2. Name of College, Department, or Program to benefit: _____

3. The fund will support:

   ☐ Scholarships   ☐ Equipment   ☐ Faculty Support   ☐ Operations   ☐ Lecture Series

   ☐ Departmental/Program Support   ☐ Other _____

4. Please describe the purpose of the endowed fund:

   _____

   _____

   _____

5. Name of University Representative to award earnings from endowed fund:

   Name: _____   Title: _____

6. Additional criteria, if any: _____

   _____

   _____

   _____

27.9   THE MECHANICS OF A FUND DESCRIPTION

What should a fund description look like? It should be no more than one or two pages long. Include the donor's name in the title and have signature and date lines at the bottom. In addition, these 13 steps are recommended:

1. Title the fund description with the donor's name, such as "The Diana Smith Endowed Scholarship Fund at (name of organization)." A donor usually responds to recognition and enjoys seeing her name, family name, or the name of a loved one included in the title.

2. State the names of the parties creating the fund. Generally, this will include one or more donors and the name of the organization: "XYZ University and Miss Diana Smith hereby propose to establish The Diana Smith Endowed Scholarship Fund at XYZ University."

3. Describe how the fund will be financially established, such as through a bequest, current gift, or a combination of both. This sentence enables the planned giving officer to discuss with the donor how the scholarship will be funded. Include language that permits additional gifts to be made to the fund.

4. Include a short background sketch of the donor(s). State their relationship with the organization and, if appropriate, some of their outstanding achievements. Donors enjoy including this information because it helps a recipient to know something about the benefactor and serves as a permanent memorial to the donor at the donor's death.

5. Restate the title of the fund several times in the body of the fund description.

6. State the fund's purpose. For example, "The income of the fund shall be awarded to a graduate student at the School of Medicine who wishes to study gerontology." Most often, a fund's purpose reflects the donor's interests.

7. Describe how the fund will be administered financially. For example, will the income be awarded on an annual basis? Will some of the income be returned to principal? State whether the principal can be invaded to make an award. Include a phrase reflecting the organization's investment policy as to whether income generated may be accumulated for future use or be returned to principal if an award is not made in a particular year. Explain the organization's investment policy to the donor.

8. State any restrictions. For example, must the recipient be financially needy, academically worthy, or have attained a particular grade point average? Are there geographic requirements for recipients? Should the recipient be focusing on a particular area of study? Again, most restrictions reflect a donor's interests. Strive to keep the fund limitations from becoming so restrictive that the organization is unable to award the scholarship each year because of an inadequate pool of eligible candidates.

9. Briefly inform the donor as to how the recipient will be selected. Will there be a selection committee composed of various representatives? Refer to committee representatives by title, and do not use specific individuals' names in the fund description, in case at some point in the future a representative no longer wishes to serve or leaves the organization. Use language similar to "Selection of candidates will be made by the Office of Financial Aid in consultation with the dean of the College of Liberal Arts." Keep in mind that the donor is prohibited from exclusively selecting the recipient.

10. Include a standard default clause to protect the organization if in the future it is unable to fulfill the terms of the fund. The clause may read, "If it becomes impossible to accomplish the purposes of this gift, the income or principal, or both, shall be used for scholarships in such manner as determined by the Executive Committee of (name of organization)." This language can frustrate many donors. Assure them that the wording is used to protect their gifts in case the school, program, or department they wish to benefit ceases to exist. If, however, the donor will not sign the description if such language is included, strike the wording in question and accommodate the donor's wishes.

11. Depending on the organization, include a statement requiring that approval of the fund be made by a specific governing board. For example, "The establishment of this fund is subject to the approval of (name of organization)'s Gift Review Committee." This provides an opportunity for the committee to review the fund description and determine the legalities of any restrictions.

12. Encourage the donor to participate by becoming involved in the drafting process. Involving the donor now ultimately benefits the organization and the donor. Be creative in drafting the initial fund description. Based on the organization's giving minimums and the donor's potential, decide whether the fund is an endowed fund or a current-use fund.

13. When working with a new donor, start at the highest funding level to encourage a "stretch" gift. A stretch gift produces a gift that is 5 to 10 or more times larger than the donor's previously largest gift.

In summary, a fund description is used to attract donors to make a generous gift to an organization. The description should appeal to the donor's sense of self and incorporate the preceding 13 steps. A fund description is one of the most important tools in closing this type of gift.

Appendix, CD-ROM Documentation, Agreements provides sample descriptions of endowed funds that can be modified to meet specific purposes. Exhibit 27.4 is a sample current-use scholarship award.

27.9 THE MECHANICS OF A FUND DESCRIPTION

Exhibit 27.4   Current-Use Scholarship Award

<Donor> Current-Use Scholarship Award

<DONOR> and <ORGANIZATION> hereby propose to establish the <DONOR> Current-Use Award at <ORGANIZATION> in accordance with the wishes of the donor. The award shall be supported by cash gifts made by <DONOR>.

The award is defined and administered as follows:

The title of the award shall be the <DONOR> Current-Use Scholarship Award. The fund shall be used in one year to support students majoring in <Department> at <ORGANIZATION>.

The scholarship shall be used to make an award of <$> to one or more students majoring in <MAJOR> who have attained an academic grade point average of <#> or better and are eligible by Financial Aid. The Award shall be made in the year <YEAR>. The <DONOR> Current-Use Scholarship Award shall be awarded in future years contingent upon the donor making additional gifts to fund the award. This fund may become permanently endowed through a gift from the <DONOR>'s estate at her death.

_____   _____
Date   [DONOR]

_____   _____
Date   [ORGANIZATION]

CHAPTER TWENTY-EIGHT

Endowed Chairs

28.1 INTRODUCTION

Many donors to charitable organizations wish to create academic chairs. These special gift opportunities provide donors with the ability to recognize a faculty member in the highest way possible, at the highest cost; price tags to create a chair can be in the millions. This chapter outlines ways donors can create chairs.

28.2 THE HONOR OF A CHAIR

An endowed chair is the highest compliment that a donor can bestow on an organization or individual. Sometimes a donor wishes to name a chair in honor of a faculty member, and may wish for that specific faculty member to be the first holder of the chair. This can be a wonderful opportunity to bring together the donor and the faculty member as well as bring the donor closer to the organization. Faculty sometimes initiate this gift option with donors and development staff because they are motivated to receive extra salary as well as be recognized with the organization's most distinguished honor. For many faculty members, a chair is their legacy to the organization to which they have dedicated their professional careers.

28.3 BENEFITS TO THE HOLDER OF THE CHAIR AND THE CHARITABLE ORGANIZATION

The holder of a chair receives supplemental salary support that can allow him to pursue academic interests he would most like to pursue, such as research, teaching, or some type of entrepreneurship. The holder also may be relieved from various administrative obligations that may be seen as tedious and time consuming. Most important, the holder is guaranteed an income for as long as he holds the chair.

A charitable organization wishes to create as many fully funded chairs as possible. The existence of chairs helps the organization to attract the best and brightest staff by both honoring them and providing them with additional salary.

28.4 PROFILE OF A DONOR WHO CREATES A CHAIR

What type of donor is most likely to fully fund a chair? Consider the following types of donors who might create a chair.

- *Entrepreneurs*. These donors are motivated by a personal interest to give a respected faculty member the opportunity to try something new, such as cutting-edge medical research, which could be seen as "out of the box." Such support might not otherwise be available as the venture may be risky or more forward thinking than the charitable organization or a government grant could support.

- *Faculty emeriti*. Retired faculty can be motivated to create a chair to help further the department and academic pursuits in which they are most interested.

- *Donors seeking naming recognition*. A chair can carry the donor's name, and for some donors this may be the ultimate naming opportunity, as the chair will exist in perpetuity.

- *Multigenerational alumni*. Because of the high price of a chair, many generations of a family may come together to fund the chair. This is a wonderful opportunity for a family to create and carry on a family legacy. A grandfather, son, and granddaughter who all attended the same university may wish to benefit the school with a chair carrying the family name.

- *Corporations and foundations*. Corporations and foundations that have an interest in a certain type of research can name a chair to pursue research. This is good marketing for the corporation and shows a spirit of working together between industry and a charitable organization.

- *Donors seeking a legacy*. Donors who are childless or wish to leave a lasting legacy through a nonprofit might consider creating a chair. The chair exists beyond the donor's lifetime and can be an excellent way to be remembered.

28.5 COST TO THE DONOR

The price of an academic chair ranges from organization to organization. Because a chair is considered the highest honor, it also has a high financial cost. Most chairs cost from $1.5 million to $3 million to create. The cost of a chair can increase at any time, but rarely does the cost go down. To keep pace with inflation, a charitable organization may systematically raise the cost required to fund a chair.

28.6 HOW CHARITIES INVEST FUNDS FOR CHAIRS

Each year, most charitable organizations pay out a small amount of the income earned by the chair, such as 3 to 5 percent. Additional income earned is added to the chair's principal. This helps to protect the principal amount of the chair and helps to keep pace with inflation. As the chair's principal grows in value each year, the 3 to 5 percent payout will be worth more.

28.7 WORKING WITH FACULTY/STAFF TO CREATE A CHAIR

Faculty members are often eager to have chairs created in their name and/or to be the holder of the chair. There is often little need to motivate faculty about this type of gift; skill is required, though, to work with certain faculty members who are the link to the donors who may have the ability to fund such an expensive gift. Otherwise reluctant faculty members can be encouraged to work with the development office when motivated by having a chair created in their name or becoming the holder of a chair.

When working with faculty members to create a chair, where one donor has not come forward, it is important to have access to a list of prospective donors. Ideally, the planned giving officer hopes to find one donor who will fund the entire chair. Start with the names of those prospects who have the financial means and potential interest in creating a chair. Next, assess the comfort level of the faculty members to determine how involved they will be in the development process. If a faculty member is uncomfortable, the planned giving officer or another faculty member may need to work closely with a prospect to explain the importance of the chair and help to close the gift.

28.8 TYPES OF CHAIRS

Chairs are generally of two types: at academic organizations they tend to be for academic research or teaching; at hospitals they may be for research, teaching (if the organization is a teaching hospital), and clinical care. In addition to providing additional salary for the holder of the chair, the chair can cover the cost of staff assistance. The chair also should cover expenses related to the faculty member's work, such as books and publication costs.

28.9 INDIVIDUAL VERSUS MULTIPLE DONORS TO FUND A CHAIR

A key to successfully creating a chair is through finding one donor who wishes to fund the chair. Working with one donor on structuring the gift is far easier than trying to reach a $3 million gift level by seeking smaller gifts from many donors who wish to contribute gifts ranging from $100 to $25,000. While well intentioned, success is rarely insured. Often chairs funded by many individuals languish at a low funding level, never reaching the required amount for a chair; chairs that are begun but not finished usually need to be "downgraded" to a fund that requires a smaller financial commitment, such as an endowed fund or lectureship. Unfortunately, donors and the faculty member to be honored and her family feel a sense of failure when the goal is not met. It is far better to identify and work with one major donor to create a chair.

28.10 WAYS TO FUND A CHAIR

Donors can fund chairs in many different ways. Because it is an expensive gift for most donors to make, some donors choose to fund a chair by combining several gift options: cash, a life income gift, and a bequest. Some organizations require the donor to make an initial cash gift to activate a chair, representing at least half of the funding price. For example, to establish a $3 million chair the donor must make a $1.5 million lifetime, outright cash gift. The cash part of the gift often can be paid over a number of years. The donor may then fund the remainder with a life income gift, such as a charitable remainder trust or a charitable gift annuity, and then complete the chair with a bequest.

Using a bequest to fund a chair is sometimes discouraged because the charitable organization may be concerned that there may not be enough money in the future bequest to cover what is needed for the chair, as the price of the chair may have increased from the time the donor finalized his will. Furthermore, the donor most likely will not enjoy seeing the chair activated if a major part of the chair is funded through a bequest.

28.11 THE INTERNAL PROCESS

Creating a chair can be complicated internally. There is much at stake (money, prestige) and sometimes multiple internal players who either want to enjoy the benefits of the chair or need to be involved with its creation. The process of creating a chair needs to be securely in place, and a designated leader of the process must be identified.

Many areas or individuals need to be consulted, including the development office's chief development officer; a representative from the department receiving the chair, such as a dean, chief of the department, or a senior administrator; a representative from the legal or finance office; and at some point the organization's president should be involved. If the chair is created at a teaching hospital but can be bestowed only by an academic organization, the hospital and university will need to work closely together to make the process appear seamless to the donor and the donor's advisor. Ideally, the planned giving officers from both organizations can coordinate information so that the planned giving officer from the teaching hospital can accurately represent the needs and wishes of the academic organization.

28.12 DRAFTING THE TERMS OF THE CHAIR

Organizations that offer chairs often have rigid terms for their creation. Despite the amount of the donor's gift, donors usually have little flexibility in changing a chair's basic terms. Boilerplate language is offered by the organization and tailored only slightly to the donor's individual wishes. Sample terms for a chair follow this section, and generally include all or some of the following:

- *Gift*. Announcement of the gift, by the donor(s), to benefit the named organization and department, and specific area.

- *Intent or field of endeavor*. This section outlines in detail the area benefiting from the donor's gift. It often includes a backup designation in case the area intended to benefit is no longer viable. For example, "If this field of teaching is no longer viable at <INSTITUTION>, then the president and trustees may assign the funds to benefit another area of close interest to the donor."

- *Selection of chair holder*. This section outlines who selects the holder of the chair. This is usually done by a small committee made up of one or more individuals, including a department head and member of the organization's administration.

- *Use of funds*. This section outlines how the chair's funds will be used, such as for salary support, research, and related expenses.

- *Completion of funding and naming of incumbent*. This section states the amount required to fund a chair and discusses at what financial level the holder of the chair can be named.

(a) Other Possible Sections

Some chair fund descriptions include term limits. Language states that the chair will be held for a period of years or for life. If a chair is held for a period of one to three years, this gives others in the organization an opportunity to hold the chair, which promotes friendly competition and provides incentives for excellence and innovation. Some organizations have a long-standing tradition of allowing the holder to stay in the chair for as long as she is able to work at the institution.

(b)   Sample Document

Exhibit 28.1 (also found on the CD-ROM) follows a sample document used to create a chair. This example illustrates a chair created at a teaching hospital, in conjunction with its medical school. It is created with a cash gift and a charitable remainder unitrust.

28.13   RECOGNITION

A gift this size deserves significant recognition by the charitable organization. The organization receiving this generous gift can do a variety of things to recognize it and honor the donor. The organization can host an elegant reception or dinner to honor both the donor and the holder of the chair, once the holder has been selected; or the donor can be taken to dinner by a small group including the president of the charitable organization, the holder of the chair, and the department head. Donors who prefer less social interaction might receive a keepsake from the organization, such as a plaque, clock, or silver bowl. The most important thing is to determine how the donor would like to be recognized and make the donor feel wonderful about completing such a significant and lasting charitable gift.

Exhibit 28.1   Creating a Chair: Sample Document

<DONORS> Chair in <DEPARTMENT>
at
<INSTITUTION>

Gift

This fund is established with a gift from <DONORS> to create a Chair at <INSTITUTION>, to be named the <DONOR> Chair in <DEPARTMENT>. Through the establishment of this Chair, the donors wish to benefit the field of <DEPARTMENT> generally and, in particular, surgical <DEPARTMENT>.

Intent or Field of Endeavor

It is the intent of the donors to support the Department of <DEPARTMENT> at the <TEACHING HOSPITAL>. The initial holder of the <DONOR> Chair in <DEPARTMENT> shall be a <SPECIALTY> who has attained the rank of professor or associate professor with a specialty in <DEPARTMENT> appointed in the Department of <DEPARTMENT> at the <TEACHING HOSPITAL> as provided in the next section. Subsequent incumbents shall be appointed in this field of medicine so long as <DEPARTMENT> remains viable to the teaching and research programs at <MEDICAL SCHOOL> and <TEACHING HOSPITAL>. If this field of medicine is no longer viable to the teaching and research programs at <MEDICAL SCHOOL> and <TEACHING HOSPITAL>, then the President of <INSTITUTION> College, upon the recommendation of the Dean of the Faculty of Medicine at <INSTITUTION> and with the advice of the Trustees of <TEACHING HOSPITAL>, may assign the use of the fund to support <INSTITUTION> activities at <TEACHING HOSPITAL> most closely related to the interests of the donors.

Selection of Incumbent

Upon the recommendation of the Dean of the Faculty of Medicine with the advice of the Chief of the Department of <DEPARTMENT> and the Trustees of <TEACHING HOSPITAL> the initial incumbent of the <DONOR> Professorship and subsequent incumbents shall be appointed by the President of <MEDICAL SCHOOL> .

Hospital Affiliation

So long as the present or similar affiliation exists between <MEDICAL SCHOOL> and <TEACHING HOSPITAL>, all incumbents of the <DONOR> Chair will serve in the latter institution. If the affiliation between the two institutions should terminate or so substantially change that the intent of the donors cannot reasonably be fulfilled, then the President, on the recommendation of the Dean of the Faculty of Medicine, may assign the chair to the department or area of instruction within the Faculty of Medicine most closely related to the interests of the donors.

Use of Funds

Income from the endowment, when fully funded, shall be used for support or supplement support for the salary, research, and related expenses only of the incumbent of the Chair. If there is no incumbent, the income may be used by <MEDICAL SCHOOL>, with the advice of the Chief of the Department of <DEPARTMENT>, to support academic activities at <TEACHING HOSPITAL> consistent with the original intent of the donors, may be held for later use, or may be added to the principal of the endowment fund, upon the recommendation of the Dean of the Faculty of Medicine.

(Continued)

Exhibit 28.1   *(Continued)*

Completion of Funding and Naming of First Incumbent

The chair will become fully funded and an income stream activated from the endowment when it reaches the sum of $3 million. The first incumbent may be named to the chair when a) the chair reaches the sum of $1.5 million, and b) the holder's salary and related fringe benefits shall be guaranteed by a combination of sources identified by the Trustees of <TEACHING HOSPITAL>; and c) provision shall have been made by the donors on an irrevocable basis to fund a charitable remainder unitrust with $1.5 million to complete the funding of the chair.

<MEDICAL SCHOOL>   <TEACHING HOSPITAL>

By: _____   By: _____

Title: _____   Title: _____

Date: _____   Date: _____

DONORS

_____

Mr. <DONOR>

_____

Mrs. <DONOR>

_____

Date
_____

## CHAPTER TWENTY-NINE

Bequests and the Bequest Society

29.1 INTRODUCTION

Gifts made through bequests form the foundation of a nonprofit development organization; approximately 80 percent of all money raised through planned giving comes from bequests. Many people who want to make a gift but cannot part with current assets find bequests an attractive way to give. Donors who make bequests to nonprofit organizations are often childless couples or individuals who view the nonprofit as a substitute for heirs, and their gifts can be substantial. Most nonprofit organizations have received bequests for years, even those that have not had a formal bequest or planned giving program. A nonprofit can take the first step in beginning a planned giving program simply by marketing and promoting bequests. This chapter focuses on issues related to bequests and what is needed to attract more gifts of this type to a charitable organization.

29.2 THE WILL

A will enables a donor to make a charitable bequest to a nonprofit organization. One reason donors make gifts through estates rather than during their lifetimes is to preserve assets for their own use and to maintain current control over the assets in case they want to change a bequest. A revocable trust often is drafted at the same time as the will, and the charitable gift may be included in the revocable trust. The will and revocable trust together often are called the estate plan. For a full discussion of wills and revocable trusts, see Chapters 38 and 25. The formal requirements for drafting wills are simple. Most states require the testator, the person making the will, to be 18 years of age or older and of sound mind, and to sign or execute the will in the presence of two or more competent witnesses. Most donors meet these requirements easily. The law of the state where the person is domiciled (where a person has his true permanent residence) will govern. To make a charitable gift to a nonprofit, the donor must either include the bequest to the organization in the body of the will or have a codicil drafted to include the bequest. A codicil (an amendment to a will) is a written document, often of one or two pages, which should be physically attached to the donor's existing will. The codicil, which may confirm the validity of the existing will, also includes new provisions and/or excludes old provisions from the existing will. Many donors make bequests through a codicil because it is less expensive and less time consuming than drafting a new will.

Donors should be encouraged to update their wills at least every five years. If a donor has a will that is five years old or older, a planned giving officer is providing sound advice by encouraging the donor to have a new will drafted. Let donors know that changes in family situations or in the tax law can make their wills obsolete practically overnight. The following require a will to be updated:

- Changes in family circumstances, such as marriage, divorce, birth, or death. Marriage revokes a will in its entirety (in most states) unless it is expressly contemplated in the will. Divorce or annulment generally revokes the disposition of property to a former spouse.

- Changes in the nature and value of a donor's property.

- Changes in state and federal laws, and in the interpretation of those laws.

- A move from one state to another.

29.3 SUGGESTED LANGUAGE

Donors often request sample bequest language so that they can make a gift through a bequest to an organization. Many bring this sample language to their attorneys, who incorporate some or all of the language into the donor's will. In the sample bequest language, be sure to include the full, legal name of the nonprofit. A one- or two-page document containing sample bequest language can easily be reproduced and sent with a cover letter explaining that state laws vary and the language should be carefully reviewed for consistency with state law. Also include sample bequest language in the organization's planned giving brochure to promote gift opportunities through bequests. Sample bequest language is included in Exhibit 29.1 and in Appendix, CD-ROM Documentation, Exhibits.

Occasionally a donor will suggest that the nonprofit pay for the cost of drafting a new will, with the understanding that the nonprofit will receive a major gift at the time of the donor's death. Because of a potential conflict of interest, nonprofits should avoid drafting donors' legal documents or paying outside counsel to draft them. In certain situations, perhaps based on the donor's close relationship to the organization, the nonprofit may agree to pay for a new will or trust.

Do not be discouraged if the process of having a donor make a gift through his estate becomes slow and cumbersome. Many people find the prospect of death frightening and will postpone the decision because it is emotionally difficult. Be patient with donors, allowing time for them to become more comfortable with this troubling issue. As with many planned giving options, it may take several years to finalize the paperwork and even more years for the organization to receive the benefit.

Most donors make gifts through their wills to a nonprofit in one of two ways: by means of a specific bequest or as a percentage of their estate.

(a) Specific Bequest

A donor can make a specific bequest by naming a certain sum of cash, securities, or property to be given to the organization. For example, the following language is appropriate for a bequest of a specific dollar amount:

I bequeath the sum of $_____ to (organization), (city, state, zip), to be used or disposed of as its board of directors in its sole discretion deems appropriate.

(b) Percentage of Estate

Often a donor's bequest provides for a percentage of the donor's estate to benefit the nonprofit. Because most donors do not know what the exact size of the estate will be at death, using a percentage

29.3 SUGGESTED LANGUAGE

Exhibit 29.1 Giving Society Membership Application

<PLANNED GIVING SOCIETY> Membership Application

Name _____

Mailing Address _____

<COLLEGE/IF ALUMNUS OR ALUMNA> _____

Relationship to the <ORGANIZATION> (if non-alumnus or alumna) _____

Type of Provision

I have made a provision for <ORGANIZATION> in my estate plan as follows:	Estimated Amount

1. Outright bequest in will: $_____
   (a) Specific dollar amount $_____
   (b   Specific property (*please describe*) _____

   _____
   (c) Share of entire residue of estate (_____ percent) $_____
2. Conditional bequest or will (*please describe conditions*) $_____

   _____
3. Trust under will or to be funded by will (*please describe*)

   (a) Charitable Remainder Trust _____ $_____

   _____
   (b) Charitable Lead Trust _____ $_____
   (c) Other _____ $_____
   4. As beneficiary of a life insurance policy $_____
   5. Other (please describe) _____ $_____

If your gift to <ORGANIZATION> is for other than <ORGANIZATION>'s general purposes, please describe any restrictions on the back of this form. Attachments or letters that further describe the above provision(s) are encouraged. In particular, a copy of the section of your will, trust agreement, other document containing the provision(s) will be appreciated. In the event of unforeseen circumstances that require any further change in the above estate planning provision(s), I agree to notify <ORGANIZATION> of such change.

_____   _____
Date   Signature

Please return this form to: <NAME>, <TITLE>, <ADDRESS>, CITY, STATE, ZIP>; <TELEPHONE>.

is a more appropriate way to divide the estate. It also enables the donor to benefit organizations and individuals in relative proportion.

Example 29.1

A donor wants to leave money to two nonprofits but does not know the value of his estate. By leaving 10 percent of his estate to the Salvation Army and 5 percent to the American Red Cross, the donor is demonstrating a desire to leave twice as much to the Salvation Army as to the American Red Cross. This approach is more satisfactory than leaving $10,000 to the Salvation Army and $5,000 to the American Red Cross. If the donor dies and leaves a net estate of less than $15,000, legal questions will arise about the amounts to be paid to each charity. A donor generally prefers to have the gift divided proportionately, in order to provide for all individuals or charities.

The following is sample bequest language for a donor who wishes to leave a percentage of his estate to an organization:

Share of, or entire residue of estate:
I devise and bequeath (all) or (_____ percent) of the remainder of my property to (organization), (city, state, zip) to be used or disposed of as its board of directors in its sole discretion deems appropriate.

29.4 STANDARD BEQUEST FORMS

Many organizations want donors to sign some type of bequest form that states in writing the donor's intention to leave a gift by will to the nonprofit. Like bequest intentions themselves, these forms are not binding, so why use them? An organization may want to have a donor sign a bequest form if the organization has a policy for crediting bequests. Another reason is to impress the donor with the seriousness of the intention: The organization views the gift seriously and will be counting on the donor's future support. Perhaps equally important, a signed bequest form satisfies the nonprofit's accounting procedures to credit a gift upon the donor's death.

Will donors sign bequest forms? Not always; in fact, probably fewer than half are willing to sign them. The most common reason for not signing a standard bequest form is that the donor is unable to estimate the size of her estate at death and therefore has no way of estimating the size of the bequest. A donor also may say that her lawyer, financial advisor, or trust officer advised against signing anything for fear that the standard bequest form will be viewed as a binding contract. Donors should be reminded that bequest intentions are revocable. The planned giving officer should explain that the organization wants the form on file to help determine future cash flow and to stay informed of a donor's intention, so that once the bequest is received the funds will be used to benefit the appropriate program designated by the donor. Despite the benefits of having a bequest form completed by the donor, do not be aggressive in asking a donor to sign a form. The risk is that the donor will be alienated and the nonprofit will lose the gift altogether. Raise the issue once with the donor, but if she does not follow through with a signature, set the issue aside. A sample standard bequest form is included in Appendix, CD-ROM Documentation, Administrative Documents.

29.5 LEGALLY BINDING DOCUMENTS FOR BEQUESTS

Courts in several states have upheld pledge documents that place an obligation on a donor to carry through with an intention to make a gift through a bequest. If consideration is provided by the nonprofit, a legally binding obligation may be created. *Consideration* (a legal term) is provided by the nonprofit if it performs an act, such as erecting a building in exchange for and in reliance on the donor's promise to provide funding. If consideration is provided by the organization, a charitable pledge agreement becomes binding. Even without consideration, a charitable pledge agreement may state that it is binding, thus obligating the executor of a donor's estate to transfer a certain amount of money to the nonprofit organization. A contract to make a will places an obligation on a donor to execute a valid will that recognizes the donor's obligation to make a bequest to the organization. Once the binding legal pledge or contract to make a will is signed, the donor's will should be amended if it does not currently provide for the gift to the nonprofit. Thereafter, no changes should be made to the donor's will that would decrease the organization's gift. State laws vary regarding the validity of these documents.

Because such documents are intended to be legally binding, their use may frighten donors. Exercise caution when working with these types of documents, and be sensitive to a donor's apprehension. A sample agreement to make a gift by will is included in Appendix, CD-ROM Documentation, Agreements.

29.6 TARGETING DONORS FOR BEQUESTS

Like other gift vehicles, bequests should be aggressively marketed to an organization's constituents; most donors and prospects should be solicited for a bequest, especially those who have made a planned gift to the organization. Conversely, donors who have already made a bequest should be solicited for a life income gift. Donors who make annual gifts and have consistent giving records are also excellent prospects for making a bequest. A series of annual gifts shows loyalty to the nonprofit, and loyalty generates bequests.

29.7 MARKETING BEQUESTS

To attract bequests to a planned giving program, it is necessary to fully market their benefits. Use the following marketing techniques to promote the value of bequests.

(a) Introductory Bequest Society Letter

If the organization does not have a formal bequest society in place, begin the process. Select a name for the society, perhaps naming it after one of the organization's founders or one of the first donors who made a bequest to the organization. Next, send out a letter to planned giving donors, prospects, annual fund donors, and anyone else who may qualify for potential bequest society membership, including trustees, administrators, and longtime volunteers. Inform them that the nonprofit is establishing a recognition program for all donors who indicate an intention to make a bequest or a planned gift to the organization. Consider including a survey asking potential bequest donors to indicate a time preference for attending a recognition event and to name topics they would like to learn more about. Inform them of the benefits provided by bequest society membership, such as a newsletter, annual luncheon, and membership pin or plaque. Follow up with telephone calls to donors if you do not hear from them. The response should give an indication of how soon to hold a recognition event. If the numbers are not sufficient to warrant hosting an event in the near future, continue to market the bequest society regularly and repeat this entire approach a year later (see Exhibit 29.1). A sample introductory bequest society letter is included in Appendix, CD-ROM Documentation, Administrative Documents.

(b) Bequest Ad

Include an ad in all publications, outlining the benefits of making a bequest to the organization. These benefits might be included:

- Make a gift without depleting current income.

- Support a program, department, or project of choice.

- Honor or memorialize a loved one through a bequest.

- Reduce estate taxes.

(c) "Thank-You" Bequest Ad

Include an ad in an organizational publication that thanks donors who have already remembered the organization in their wills. Ask donors to identify themselves to the planned giving office so that the organization can recognize and acknowledge their gifts. Include in the ad a response form to mail back with their names and addresses. Because so many bequests are made by donors without children, planned giving officers should identify these donors to recognize, cultivate, and include them in the planned giving program. Surviving spouses who may not be as close to the organization also should be cultivated. In all cases, this ad opens an effective line of communication to those who have most generously supported the nonprofit through bequests. A sample "thank-you" bequest ad is located in Appendix, CD-ROM Documentation, Marketing.

(d) Financial Column

Use a planned giving newsletter or other nonprofit publication to present a column that discusses the importance of a will and the benefits of making a gift through one's estate. Alert readers to specific programs or projects at the organization that can benefit from their bequests.

(e) Donor Profile—A Testimonial Ad

Everyone enjoys reading a story about a donor who left her entire estate to a nonprofit organization. Profile a donor in an organizational publication who feels strongly about the organization and has made a financial commitment through a bequest. Donor profiles provide role models and can be persuasive in demonstrating to other donors that they too can make gifts. An individual's real estate, cash savings, stock, mutual fund holdings, and tangible personal property often amounts to significant wealth, which can translate into a major gift.

29.8 CREDITING BEQUESTS

No organization seems to have solved the problem of how best to credit bequests that have been promised in a living donor's will. They are inherently difficult to deal with, because wills can be changed or revoked at any time. However, most bequest intentions are honored by donors. Nonprofit organizations have to find a way to credit future bequests that encourages development officers to seek bequests and to provide donors with proper recognition. These five suggestions have been adopted by various nonprofits for crediting bequest intentions:

1. Recognize donors who make bequest intentions as members of a bequest society. Add to the campaign totals only the money received once the bequest materializes.

2. Provide full credit to the donor for promised bequests that are accompanied by a signed bequest form from the donor.

3. Credit unrealized bequest intentions if certain requirements are met, such as the following:

   a. The donor must be of a certain minimum age, often 65 or 70.

   b. The amount of the gift must be a certain amount or percentage, based on a conservative estimate of the future value of the donor's estate.

    c. The bequest intention must be in writing on the organization's approved bequest form and accompanied by a copy of the relevant portion of the donor's will.

    d. The donor must have a preexisting relationship with the organization, such as service as a past or current trustee, dean, staff physician, administrator, or employee.

4. Count the bequest at full value, minus a discount, to arrive at a "present value" of the gift. The discount should reflect delay in receipt of the bequest based on the donor's life expectancy, inflation, or other factors. For example, assume that a donor makes a bequest of $1 million and the bequest is discounted at an annual rate of 5 percent. If the donor's life expectancy is 5 years, the value of the bequest is $783,526; if 10 years, the value of the bequest is $613,913, and if 15 years, the value of the bequest is $481,017.

5. Give full credit for a bequest intention if the donor has already made a substantial current gift to the nonprofit. Decide what the minimum amount is for a "substantial" gift.

Once an organization adopts a policy, it should be adhered to consistently. Part of the role of planned giving officers is staying focused on actually raising the gifts, and for most donors proper crediting is not the main issue.

29.9 RECOGNITION EVENTS

A well-run recognition event can be one of the best sources of new and repeat business for a planned giving program. When the organization is ready to host an event to recognize those who have made a bequest to the organization, include all donors who have made any type of planned gift to the organization. The key is inclusion, not exclusion. To have a successful event, there should be sufficient attendance to provide credibility to the program. Ten to twelve people are not enough for a formal luncheon, but could be appropriate for an informal reception. Expand the number of invitees to make those who attend feel that they are part of an elite group that makes special gifts. Consider using this occasion also as a cultivation event and invite prospects who will, it is hoped, make a gift to the organization. Special gatherings facilitate communication, and donors are likely to discuss business and future gifts at such events.

There are a number of issues to consider when planning a recognition event:

- *Timing.* Consider having the function during the daytime. Most older donors do not want to drive at night and will turn down an evening invitation, no matter how compelling. Choose a time of year when donors are at home, not during the summer or winter seasons when they tend to be away.

- *Location.* When selecting the location for the event, remember that many donors are elderly and will not want to climb flights of stairs. Wheelchair accessibility is also important, so a first-floor location is ideal. Mark the location well, and have volunteers available to direct attendees. Make sure that parking is readily available and close by; otherwise, provide shuttle buses or other transportation from the parking location to the event.

- *Marketing the event.* Donors like to feel part of a successful organization. Market the event to donors in the same way that planned giving vehicles are marketed. Remember that each event builds on the preceding event, and every year as new donors are gained the attendance should increase. Start the marketing process by sending a letter to all planned giving donors and to anyone else who is considered a planned giving prospect, announcing the upcoming program. Approximately three and a half months before the event, potential attendees should be told of the date and location and given information about the content of this year's program. Inform donors and prospects that they will receive an invitation shortly, which should be mailed approximately six weeks before the event. Include in newsletters and other publications the date of the event, as well as time, location, and any other relevant information. Call invitees to confirm attendance.

■ *Speaker(s).* Select a speaker for the event who is a present or prospective donor and who has had a positive experience with the planned giving office. If the speaker has been directly involved with the planned giving program, he is in an excellent position to promote planned giving as well as offer an interesting presentation. Most donors attend an event because they enjoy and appreciate the recognition and the feeling that comes with being a part of a special group. Identify roles for staff in the program, providing an opportunity to emphasize to the donors the staff's experience, the benefits of the program, and the needs of the organization. Consider sharing with attendees information about the highlights of this year's planned giving program.

■ *Donor recognition.* Most recognition events include the actual honoring of participants. Presenting bequest pins is one possibility. Donors will be delighted to receive the attention, and it encourages goodwill and future support.

To ensure the success of a recognition event, use a checklist, such as the one found in Exhibit 29.2, which includes the following elements. (See Appendix, CD-ROM Documentation, Administrative Documents.)

■ *Food.* Serving food is an important draw for every event. Keep in mind that many people do not eat red meat; consider serving chicken, fish, or a vegetarian meal.

■ *Bar service.* Offer beer, wine, mixed drinks, fruit juice, and nonalcoholic beverages to donors, unless the organization prefers that liquor not be served.

■ *Promotional materials.* Have available the recognition society's latest newsletter, along with a basic planned giving brochure and any materials about the program or organization that donors should see.

■ *Staffing.* Be free to greet and meet prospects, to talk with a donor who wishes to discuss making a new gift. Plan for additional staff to assist attendees at the event. Place staff members at a reception table to answer questions, distribute name tags, and help with coats.

■ *Audiovisual needs.* Inquire whether the speaker has particular audiovisual needs. Arrange for a podium, microphone, lighting, overhead projector, or any other necessary equipment.

■ *Photographer.* A photographer should be available to take pictures of donors at the recognition event. Use these photographs in the next planned giving newsletter to highlight the successful event. Send photographs to special donors as a keepsake of the event.

■ *Miscellaneous.* Do not forget flowers for tables, parking arrangements, coat checks, and name tags.

When the event is over, send a letter thanking attendees for coming. Thank them again for their continued support of the organization. Follow up immediately with donors who discussed making additional gifts. Also remember to send a note to invited donors and prospects who did not attend the event. Let them know how successful the event was, what they missed, and that it is hoped that they will be able to attend next year's program.

Exhibit 29.2 Bequests and the Bequest Society

VOLUNTEERS	NEEDED	ORDERED	CONFIRMED
Enlist chairperson			
Appoint committee			
Thank committee			
EVENT PRELIMINARIES			
Enlist speaker			
Book and confirm function space			
Requisition for labels			
Invitation copy			
Food ☐ Beverage ☐ Hotel ☐			
Requisition for food service			
Menu ☐ Guarantee ☐ Entree ☐			
Bar ☐ Liquor ☐ Wine ☐ Beer ☐			
Nonalcoholic drinks			
Hotel space			
Rooms ☐ Suites ☐			
Singles ☐ Doubles ☐			
Reception rooms			
Parking permits ☐ Passes ☐			
PUBLIC RELATIONS			
Brochures copy			
Posters			
Handouts/press kits			
Press releases/calendar announcements			
Media announcements			
Live coverage			
Biographies for introductions			
Photographer (hours needed) from: to:			
STAFFING			
Bartenders			
Coat-check attendants			
Staff			
ROOM SET-UP			
Flag ☐ Banner ☐			
Flowers			
Rugs installed ☐ Floor installed ☐			
Head table			
Chairs ☐ Tables ☐			
Water pitcher and glasses			
Display tables			
Coat rack			
AUDIOVISUAL			
Microphones ☐ P/A system ☐			
Podium ☐ Projector ☐ Screen ☐			
Overhead ☐ Flipchart ☐			
Tape recorder			
SUPPLIES			
Name tags			
Registration materials ☐ Desk supplies ☐			
Brochures ☐ Newsletters ☐			

PART SIX

Assets

Gifts of Securities

30.1   INTRODUCTION

Following gifts of cash, securities are likely to be the most common gifts made to a nonprofit. Gifts of securities include not only publicly traded stocks but also mutual funds, Treasury bills, notes, and closely held stock. Many nonprofits fail to emphasize adequately the range of securities that can be used to make gifts. A planned giving program should include gifts of all types of securities in marketing efforts, and the planned giving officer should learn how to assist a donor in making gifts of such assets.

Most organizations do not retain small blocks of stock given by donors, but instead convert the stock to cash. Donors should know from the beginning that, in all likelihood, securities donated to the organization will be sold. Donors can be quick to say that the value of the stock went up right after it was sold, and that if the organization had held onto it, the gift would have been worth a lot more. Save the organization from potential discord by disclosing to the donor the nonprofit's policy on gifts of securities.

A donor who wants to make a gift of securities usually either holds the securities in an account with a stockbroker or in a bank, or has the stock certificate(s) in his possession. Transfer of securities to a nonprofit differs, depending on how the securities are held.

30.2   SECURITIES HELD BY THE DONOR'S STOCKBROKER OR BANKER

In the case of securities held by a donor's stockbroker or banker, the donor or his stockbroker should call to inform the nonprofit organization that a gift of securities is to be made. The broker will need to know the organization's tax identification number, which allows the securities or their proceeds to be transferred to the nonprofit. In most cases, the nonprofit employs an outside broker to handle securities gifts. The donor's broker may establish an account in the nonprofit's name and transfer the stock to the nonprofit's account. The stock can then be sold directly from this account, resulting in a check being mailed to the organization for the proceeds, minus a broker's commission. The donor's broker must be particularly careful not to sell the securities until they are in the nonprofit's account, or the donor will incur a capital gains tax on any appreciation. As a charitable organization, the nonprofit is not liable for any capital gains taxes on the sale of appreciated securities.

Establishing a new account in the nonprofit's name, however, is an unnecessary extra step. The time needed to establish a separate account may cause a particularly unwelcome delay for a donor trying to make a gift on a certain day. The only benefit appears to be the commission generated for the donor's broker. A depository trust company (DTC) transfer, described in the following paragraph, is a more efficient way for a donor to give securities to a nonprofit organization.

Most securities are transferred easily and efficiently through a DTC. This electronic transfer system allows easy movement from one account to another and involves no physical exchange of stock certificates. The transfer can be made to the organization's account at a brokerage firm or to an outside manager administering pooled income funds, charitable gift annuities, and charitable remainder trusts. Once advised by the donor or broker that the securities are being sent, the planned giving officer must alert the appropriate persons that securities will be deposited in the organization's account. Otherwise, when the securities arrive, the receiving broker or fund manager may not know that they benefit the organization, potentially causing them to be rejected and returned to the issuing broker. Instructions for donors to transfer securities along with other related documents are included in Appendix, CD-ROM Documentation, Administrative Documents.

30.3 SECURITIES HELD IN THE DONOR'S POSSESSION

In some cases, the donor is in physical possession of stock certificates bearing her name. If the donor wishes to make a gift of the certificates, she should sign a stock power for each stock certificate that will be transferred to the nonprofit. A stock power is a document that allows the donee organization to sell the securities. For example, if a donor has a certificate for IBM stock and a certificate for Intel stock, the donor must sign a stock power for each certificate. Stock powers can be obtained from a broker, bank, or business stationery store.

If the transaction is negotiated by mail, the stock powers should be sent to the nonprofit in a separate envelope, apart from the stock certificates. The reason is that if the stock certificates and powers are sent together and then lost or stolen, anyone could sell the securities. Because one is not negotiable without the other, the donor can ensure their safety by sending them separately. Once the planned giving officer has both the stock powers and the stock certificates, they should be taken immediately to the organization's treasurer or outside investment manager.

Alternatively, the donor can endorse the back of a stock certificate, making the certificate immediately negotiable. The donor should sign his name exactly as it appears on the stock certificate. This is an appropriate method of transferring securities only if the certificates can be hand carried immediately by the planned giving officer to the treasurer's office or to the outside financial manager.

If the company issuing the stock is a small corporation, it may be convenient for the donor to ask the company to transfer the stock to the organization by issuing a new certificate promptly in the name of the organization. In that circumstance, the gift is made on the date when the company issues the new certificate.

A donor may want to make a gift to a charity with a stock certificate that represents more shares than she wants to transfer. In such cases, it is easy to give only a portion of the shares owned. The donor must instruct the broker, usually in writing, that she wants to give a specific number of shares to the organization while retaining the remaining shares in her account. The donor must enclose a signed stock power, with instructions as to when and where to send the gift. The broker then requests that two new stock certificates be issued, one to the charity for a specific number of shares and one to the donor for the remaining shares. One stock certificate is forwarded to the charity; the other is returned to the donor.

30.4 THE VALUE OF THE GIFT

The value of the securities given to the organization is the average of the "high" and the "low" of the security (the mean value) on the date the gift is made. If the gift is made on a Saturday, Sunday, or holiday, or on a day in which the stock was not traded, an average of the mean values on the preceding and succeeding business days must be used. If no high and low information is available (which is sometimes the case with bonds), bid and asked prices must be averaged. To determine the value of a stock gift, the planned giving officer can look at the *Wall Street Journal* for the day after the gift is made. The *Journal* quotes prices at the close of business on the previous day. To locate the stock, it is necessary to know the symbol or abbreviation for the name of the stock, which can easily be found in a stock guide or obtained from a broker. Because securities are traded on many different exchanges, more than one exchange may have to be checked, starting with the largest, the New York Stock Exchange. If the stock is not listed there, it may be listed on the American Stock Exchange, The National Association of Securities Dealers Automated Quoting System (Nasdaq), or one of the other stock exchanges.

Once the stock is located, take the average of the high and the low, called the mean, to find the value of the stock on the day the gift is made. Then multiply the mean by the number of shares the organization has received. The result will equal the value of the gift to the organization. For example, if a donor transfers 100 shares of stock that traded between $10 and $11 per share, the mean is $10.50 and the value of the gift (100 × $10.50) is $1,050.

30.5 THE DATE OF THE GIFT

If a donor sends a gift of securities through the mail either to a nonprofit or to the nonprofit's outside financial manager, the date postmarked on the envelope is the date of the gift. Therefore, if a donor wishes to make a year-end gift of securities and the envelope is postmarked in one year but received in the following year, the donor is still considered to have made the gift in the year the envelope was postmarked. If the donor personally delivers the stock certificate(s) and power(s) to the organization or to the planned giving officer, the day of delivery is the date of the gift. If the donor makes a gift of securities by telling her broker to transfer shares of stock from her account to a nonprofit, the date the stocks are actually received into an account in the name of the organization is the date of the gift. If the donor sends securities by special courier such as FedEx, the date the organization receives the securities is the date of the gift. Think about the date of the gift as the date when the assets are out of the donor's control, the time when he cannot recall them.

It is important that gifts of stocks be handled quickly and efficiently, because any market volatility can affect the value of the gift and potentially create unfortunate donor-relations problems.

30.6 THE DONOR'S CHARITABLE INCOME TAX DEDUCTION

If a donor has held gifted securities for more than one year (long term), the donor claims the fair market value of the securities as the charitable income tax deduction in the year the gift is made. The donor may deduct up to 30 percent of his adjusted gross income (assuming he has not made cash gifts to public charities in excess of 20 percent of his adjusted gross income) and any excess may be carried over for up to five additional years. If the donor has held the securities for less than a year or short term, the donor's deduction is limited to the cost basis of the securities. (Cost basis is generally the price originally paid by the donor.) If a donor wants to make a gift of securities that have decreased in value, he should instead sell the shares of stock, deduct the capital loss against any capital gain in accordance with the capital loss rules, and then contribute the cash proceeds to the organization. Otherwise, the donor will lose the benefit of the capital loss.

GIFTS OF SECURITIES

(a) Gift of Stock and Repurchase

As discussed earlier, a donor can make a gift of long-term capital gain stock and claim a charitable income tax deduction equal to the fair market value of the stock. A donor who owns substantially appreciated securities may, in fact, prefer to donate those securities in order to obtain a charitable income tax deduction and avoid paying capital gains taxes. The donor can then immediately repurchase securities in the same company, which thus gives her the added advantage of having a new basis in the new shares reflecting current market conditions.

A gift of stock followed by a purchase of similar shares, unlike a sale of stock and subsequent purchase, does not trigger the so-called wash-sale rules. Under the wash-sale rules, a loss sustained on a sale or disposition of stock is disallowed if a taxpayer acquires substantially identical stock within a period of 30 days prior to, or after, the sale. Because a gift is not a sale or disposition, the wash-sale rules do not apply.

(b) Gifts from Dividend Reinvestment Plans

Occasionally a donor will make a gift to a nonprofit of securities that have been purchased through a dividend reinvestment program. In a dividend reinvestment program, the dividend or income earned on the securities is reinvested, usually without fees or commissions, rather than paid to the donor. The shareholder is taxed each year on the dividend income, but the income is not paid out and instead is reinvested in new shares. In this way, the number of shares owned increases.

If a donor wants to make a gift of securities from a dividend reinvestment program, first the reinvestments must be stopped. The donor may not be aware that this has to be done, and the planned giving officer may have to inform her. In a letter advising of her intentions, the donor should instruct the agent holding the shares of stock to stop the reinvestment immediately. The agent will require the donor's Social Security number, the account number, and the nonprofit's tax identification number. The donor also must send a signed stock power (discussed earlier in this chapter) with her signature guaranteed for the reinvested shares. This must be sent in addition to any stock power already sent to the agent for full shares.

The agent will have to issue a new stock certificate in the nonprofit's name for any full shares and then liquidate the fractional shares. This transaction can take a significant amount of time to finalize. A gift through a dividend reinvestment plan is challenging in that it is difficult to determine the donor's cost basis. Each month, or quarter, as the dividend is reinvested, the donor owns a greater overall number of securities, and the monthly price of the stock is likely to change. The company issuing the stock may provide cost basis information. If not, the nonprofit's treasurer's office or an outside financial advisor may be able to assist in determining the donor's cost basis.

Gifts of reinvested stock often turn into two separate gifts: one gift of the full shares, which is delivered to the nonprofit relatively promptly, and a second gift of one or more fractional shares, which is probably delivered several months later. Most donors want to treat these as one gift, generating a charitable income tax deduction that can be taken in one year. However, if this transaction is done at year end and the fractional shares are not issued by the company until the new year, the donor will obtain a deduction for the fractional shares in the later year.

Any shares bought through the dividend reinvestment plan within one year of making the gift are, of course, short-term shares, and no deduction will be available for any appreciation over the cost basis.

30.7 ZERO COUPON BONDS

Zero coupon bonds are bonds sold by corporations and governments at a steep discount. The bond reaches its full value when it matures. The holder of a zero coupon bond must pay taxes each year on the accrued interest even though he does not actually receive the interest. The holder may defer taxes on the accrued interest when the zero coupon bonds are in a tax-deferred retirement account or may avoid such taxes on the interest component on tax-free municipal zero coupon bonds. If the bonds are sold before reaching full value, the owner will not receive the maturity value and may pay a penalty for selling before maturity. When an owner sells a zero coupon bond, he receives the value of the bond on the date of the sale. A donor who wants to make a gift of a zero coupon bond to a charity will receive a charitable income tax deduction for the market value of the bond on the date of gift.

Zero coupon bonds may be an attractive investment option for donors who want to fund a charitable remainder unitrust, paying the lesser of the net income or the percentage amount. Zero coupon bonds can be used to fund the trust, and since charitable remainder trusts are exempt from taxation, the interest will not be taxed until actually distributed to the income beneficiary in accordance with the terms of the trust instrument and so long as state governing law permits. Charitable remainder trusts are discussed in Chapter 25.

30.8   GIFTS OF SHARES OF A MUTUAL FUND[1]

A mutual fund company sells shares in its family of funds. Each fund invests in particular securities, depending on the fund's financial objective. Investors, assigned units or shares reflecting their investments, receive a statement, usually quarterly, telling them the value of their investments.

Donors can make a gift of their shares in a mutual fund to a nonprofit organization. A representative of the mutual fund assists the planned giving officer in transferring the mutual fund shares. The fair market value of a mutual fund is its public redemption price (net asset value) on the valuation date, which is quoted daily in the business section of most newspapers, including the *Wall Street Journal.* As with a gift of securities, the nonprofit can sell mutual fund shares once the shares are transferred to an account in the name of the nonprofit.

Owning shares in mutual funds has become very popular. Along with the number of individuals owning shares in mutual funds, use of the funds as gifts to nonprofit organizations has increased. Mutual funds are heavily regulated and are subject to many federal and state laws and regulations.

Shareholders who own mutual funds receive dividends and interest earned as well as capital gain distributions if the security is sold at a profit. If the shares have increased in value, there will be unearned capital gain, and when sold they will be taxed at capital gain tax rates. Therefore, when making a gift, the cost basis of the donated shares must be determined.

(a) Transfer Instructions

Transferring mutual fund shares is a time-consuming process, which may take two weeks to two months, or possibly longer, to complete. Keep the following in mind when using mutual funds as a charitable gift:

- *Transfer in kind.* Do not sell or redeem the shares, but transfer in the nonprofit's name, to avoid the donor's being responsible for capital gains taxes.

- *Timing.* As with other securities gifts, the mutual fund shares are not considered a gift until the shares have been transferred into the nonprofit's name. How quickly the shares are

---

[1] Adapted from Marjorie A. Houston, Director of Gift Planning, Brown University, "Mutual Fund Transfers for Charitable Gifts," by *Trusts and Estates Magazine* (March 1998):14. Reprinted with permission of the author and *T&E Magazine.*

transferred will depend on how long the fund responds to the transfer request and how complete the transfer request is.

■ *Determine how and where a mutual fund is held.* Mutual funds can be held in several forms: physical in certificate form, with a broker, or with a fund. When assembling the paperwork to accomplish the transfer, this information will be necessary.

(b) Required Transfer Paperwork

Most funds require several documents from the donor and the nonprofit to effect the transfer. Because the process varies with each fund, call the fund first to determine exactly what is needed. Some or all of the following may be needed:

■ *Letter of instruction from the shareholder.* The letter should state what is being given, when it should happen, to whom it is being given, the mutual fund account number, and the name of a contact person at the nonprofit. The letter must be signed with a signature guaranteed.

■ *Letter of instruction from the nonprofit.* This letter should confirm the source of the expected gift, convey a new account application and corporate resolution, and provide the contact name at the nonprofit.

■ *New account application from the nonprofit.* The nonprofit may be required to complete its own account application with the mutual fund.

■ *Corporate resolution from the nonprofit.* The corporate resolution will contain the name of the individuals authorized to accept gifts on behalf of the nonprofit and is stamped with the nonprofit's corporate seal.

■ *Form W-9 from the nonprofit.* This will contain the nonprofit's taxpayer identification number, and may be required by some mutual funds.

Each fund is governed by its own set of compliance regulations and transfer requirements. While the above requirements are standard procedure, some funds allow for on-line transfer of shares from one account to another existing account. An individual authorizes a fixed number of shares to be transferred to an existing account that the nonprofit has already set up. The donor needs to provide the mutual fund with the account information to affect the transfer. This requires collaboration between the donor and the nonprofit. The nonprofit must complete the fund requirements for establishing an account before the transfer. Funds held more than 10 years have considerable growth and are ideal for charitable gifts. For a sample letter to prospects who wish to make a gift of shares from a mutual fund, see Appendix, CD-ROM Documentation, Correspondence.

30.9 CLOSELY HELD STOCK

One of the most significant assets of a small business owner is likely to be the value of the company's closely held stock. Closely held stock, unlike publicly traded stock, is not freely marketable nor is its value as apparent or as easily determined. Closely held stock is most often found in family-run businesses or in private businesses with relatively few stockholders. It is private because it is not publicly traded, and in most cases there are restrictions on the transfer of the stock to third parties. The owner of closely held stock can give the stock to a nonprofit organization and deduct its market value. Because there are a number of important issues to consider in handling this type of gift, donors of closely held stock should consult with their attorneys or tax advisors.

(a) Valuation of Closely Held Stock

Closely held stock is not traded on any market; therefore, it is not easy to determine its value. Its value must be ascertained by an appraiser who is knowledgeable about corporate valuation. To approximate the value of the closely held stock, the planned giving officer or donor should contact the treasurer of the closely held corporation or business to obtain relevant financial information. A donor may not deduct a gift of closely held stock having a value of $10,000 or more unless he obtains a qualified appraisal and attaches Form 8283, summarizing the appraisal, to his federal income tax return for the year of the gift. (See a discussion of Form 8283 in Chapter 33, Section 33.5.)

(b) Restrictions on Transfer

Most closely held stock is subject to restrictions on its transfer to a third party. Many closely held corporations are family businesses or were started by friends or close associates who intended to keep the stock controlled by the original shareholders. As such, shareholders often have repurchase agreements that forbid the sale of stock to third-party purchasers without its first being offered to the other shareholders or to the corporation. Restrictions on transfer are usually located on the face of the stock certificate; however, all of the corporate documents, including the articles of incorporation, bylaws, and stock transfer agreements, should be read carefully for any restrictions on transfer. These restrictions may prevent the transfer of the stock or reduce its value.

(c) Arm's-Length Requirement

Donors who make gifts of closely held stock and nonprofits that receive closely held stock must do so with no strings attached, even though the nonprofit recipient may be eager to sell the stock promptly. Donors may attempt to place conditions on the transfer of closely held stock by trying to control the timing of the resale or redemption, or directing the sale of the stock to a specific third-party purchaser. As long as the nonprofit is free to accept or reject any offer to purchase or redeem the stock, the donor will not be taxed on the gain on sale by the nonprofit. Donors also may try to negotiate an agreement to sell the stock to a third party in order to maintain control of the stock. Donors considering a gift of closely held stock must be careful not to enter into a prior written agreement with either the closely held corporation or a potential third-party purchaser. The transfer should be an arm's-length independent transaction; otherwise, the donor may be taxed on the gain realized on sale. ("Arm's-length" indicates the lack of a close or preexisting relationship between the parties to the transaction.)

Consider a typical case in which a donor makes a gift of closely held stock to a nonprofit organization. To determine the value, the donor has the stock appraised and obtains a charitable income tax deduction equal to the appraised value of the stock. The appraisal must be conducted by an appraiser who is experienced in establishing such value. The nonprofit then asks the issuing corporation to redeem the stock and receives a check for the redemption price. It is important that the appraised price bear some relation to the redemption price, although it need not be identical. If the stock is sold within two years of the gift, the nonprofit is required to notify the Internal Revenue Service on Form 8282 (see Chapter 33, Section 33.7).

(d) Closely Held Stock and Debt

Sometimes a donor attempts to make a gift of stock of a closely held company to a nonprofit in a situation in which the donor's stock is subject to debt. Relief from debt is a taxable event, and a nonprofit that unwittingly assumes an obligation for the debt of a donor or accepts property that is subject to a mortgage, even though the donor is not personally liable, has conferred a benefit on the donor. This gift creates a gain to the donor, who is taxed accordingly.

(e) Sale to Third-Party Purchaser or to Employee Stock Ownership Plan

Instead of seeking redemption by the closely held corporation, the nonprofit can transfer the stock to a third-party purchaser as long as there are no restrictions that prohibit the transfer of the stock. Alternately, a nonprofit organization may sell contributed closely held stock to the closely held corporation's Employee Stock Ownership Plan (ESOP).

(f) Transfer to a Charitable Remainder Unitrust

In theory, a holder of closely held stock also may make a gift of the stock to a net income charitable remainder unitrust, which pays the lesser of net income or the percentage amount to the beneficiary. The owner of the stock transfers the stock to the trustee of the charitable remainder trust, who may ask the corporation to redeem the stock, to sell it to an ESOP, or to sell it to a third-party purchaser.

A redemption of closely held stock by a charitable remainder trust invokes the private foundation self-dealing rules. Self-dealing rules prohibit the donor and the donor's family from buying from, selling to, or dealing with a trust that has been the recipient of the donor's property. If a donor transfers shares of closely held stock to a charitable remainder trust and she and her family have as much as a 35 percent interest in the corporation, a redemption of those shares by the corporation violates the self-dealing rules unless a special procedure is followed whereby an offer to redeem is made to all holders of the class of stock being redeemed. If it appears that the self-dealing rules may be violated through the use of a charitable remainder trust, the donor may wish to consider the use of a charitable gift annuity, which is not subject to these rules. In addition, the trustee of a trust as a fiduciary is expected to make prudent investments. It may not be considered a prudent investment for a trustee to hold, indefinitely, a single asset with limited marketability, such as closely held stock.

30.10 S CORPORATION STOCK

Before proceeding with any gift of closely held stock, it is important to determine whether the stock is issued by an S corporation or is issued by a regular or C corporation. Like other corporations, S corporations offer their shareholders protection from personal liability, except that for tax purposes, they are similar to partnerships. An S corporation's gains and losses are allocated proportionately to each shareholder and are includible in the individual shareholder's tax return, which avoids the double system of taxation that occurs when a C corporation (regular corporation) pays tax and subsequently issues a dividend to its shareholders after tax. An S corporation must have no more than 75 shareholders and only one class of stock.

Donors may now make gifts of S corporation stock to nonprofit organizations without the risk of losing the S corporation status. Prior to the effective date of a 1996 change in the law, S corporation status would be lost if any stock in the S corporation was transferred to a nonprofit organization. Such a gift is deductible by the individual shareholder subject to his regular 30 percent to 50 percent limitation, but only to the extent of his basis in the S corporation stock.

Although the law now permits nonprofit organizations to hold S corporation stock, all income or loss flows through to the nonprofit holder of the stock as unrelated business taxable income or loss. In addition, any capital gains on the sale of appreciated S corporation stock will also be treated as unrelated business taxable income.

Although the new law permits a transfer without the loss of status, nonprofit organizations should proceed cautiously in accepting gifts of S corporation stock. The new law permits gifts only to charitable organizations described by Section 501(c)(3) and does not extend to transfers to a charitable remainder trust. A transfer of S corporation stock to a charitable remainder trust will still result in a loss of S corporation status.

30.11   PREFERRED STOCK—INTERNAL REVENUE CODE SECTION 306

Section 306 of the Internal Revenue Code provides that proceeds from the sale of certain preferred stock received as a tax-free stock dividend will be treated as ordinary income. Normally, closely held stock would be treated as capital gain property and its sale taxed accordingly. Ordinary income property that is contributed to charitable organizations may be deducted only to the extent of the cost basis rather than the fair market value of the stock, thus diminishing the benefit of making a gift of closely held stock.

Gifts of Real Estate

31.1   INTRODUCTION

An inquiry from a donor about a gift of real estate represents tremendous potential for a nonprofit organization—and nothing can be more exciting, challenging, and, sometimes, frustrating. Real estate typically can represent the largest single asset in a donor's estate; it therefore becomes an appropriate and valuable commodity with which to fund a gift. Nonprofits and planned giving officers must develop expertise and a system of safeguards in accepting gifts of real estate. The natural tendency for a planned giving officer is to be enthusiastic about the possibilities of a gift of real estate, but one who has experienced a substantial number of such inquiries realizes that caution must be exercised. For instance, individuals who have property that is unmarketable or environmentally damaged may have learned that some nonprofits, in their eagerness to acquire gifts, may fail to adequately screen or prequalify such property. It is critical to understand from the prospect's perspective why the property is being given away. What is the prospect trying to accomplish? What are the financial needs and the family situation? It is also important to know the prospect's age and whether she is in good health.

When working with a potential donor, be direct and explain that the nonprofit is not a substitute purchaser nor is it willing to accept damaged goods. A prospect may, after having a property on the market for a long time, assume that a nonprofit will take the property because of its proximity to the organization's location or because of the prospect's status as an alumnus, trustee, friend, supporter, or patient of the nonprofit. Explain that the organization is in the gift-receiving business and interested in receiving only real estate that is valuable, marketable, and sound. Before becoming too involved, prequalify both the donor and the property.

Factors to Consider in Accepting Gifts of Real Estate

- Determine whether the property is residential, commercial, industrial, vacant land, farmland, or rental property.

- If the property is residential, is it a single-family house, a condominium, a cooperative, or a duplex?

- Is it owner occupied?

- If it is commercial, what is its use?

- Have hazardous materials been used in the production of the commercial products?

- Has it been depreciated for tax purposes?

See Appendix, CD-ROM Documentation, Agreement.

31.2 ELEMENTS AFFECTING GIFTS OF REAL ESTATE

(a) Title to Real Estate

For an organization to accept a gift of property, its ownership must be established. Sometimes real estate can be the focus of a family or business dispute, resulting in disagreement among the owners as to the distribution of the property. Sometimes the prospect is just one of several co-owners of a property and cannot convey the property alone. It is important to identify the owner of property before proceeding with acceptance of the potential gift. See Chapter 38 on estate planning for a discussion of title to property.

(b) Real Estate Taxes

A property tax bill issued by the county or municipality in which it is located will provide information about the property. Some tax bills reflect 100 percent of the fair market value of the property, whereas others are based on a percentage of the fair market value. Call the assessor's office in the city or county in which the property is located to learn the financial relationship between the tax bill and the fair market value of the property. Fair market value is defined for tax purposes as the price that a willing buyer would pay to a willing seller in exchange for the property. The tax bill usually allocates the value of the property between the buildings and the land and takes into consideration the depreciable (buildings) and nondepreciable (land) portions of the property. These percentages are important in making calculations for special gifts of real estate such as retained life estates. A call to a local real estate broker also can help the planned giving officer to ascertain the value and marketability of the property.

(c) Appraisal of Property

A gift of real estate must be appraised by an independent appraiser to determine the property's value. It is important to differentiate between an appraiser and a real estate broker. A certified appraiser is one who is qualified to ascertain the true value of property. A real estate broker is not, for tax purposes, able to fix value but can only estimate a value for sale purposes.

It is the obligation of the donor to have an appraisal done, the cost of which is borne by the donor. The appraisal should be conducted no more than 60 days before the date of the gift, but may be conducted at any time up to the date of filing of the donor's federal income tax return for the year in which the gift is deductible. The cost of an appraisal is considered a miscellaneous itemized deduction that can be claimed on the donor's tax return, to the extent that the total of the donor's miscellaneous deductions exceeds 2 percent of his adjusted gross income. Because the obligation rests on the donor as taxpayer, the nonprofit should not offer to pay for the appraisal. The nonprofit should, however, conduct a second, independent appraisal of the property. Many organizations have simply accepted a donor's appraisal for determining value, and, unfortunately, sometimes a donor's appraisal price does not reflect the fair market value of the property. To avoid subsequent donor-relations problems and to protect its own interests, the organization should conduct its own appraisal.

31.3 FACTORS AFFECTING VALUE AND MARKETABILITY OF REAL ESTATE

(a) Restrictions and Easements

Real estate is often subject to restrictions or easements that affect its value or marketability. The deed to a property may include references to the existence of these potential flaws, and a visual inspection of the property may reveal others. A title check of the property at the Registry of Deeds in the county in which the real estate is located will disclose any restrictions, such as covenants, that may affect marketability of the property. A purported gift of real estate in which the donor retains an easement is considered to be a gift of a partial interest, for which no charitable deduction is allowed. See Chapter 32, Section 32.3.

(b) Environmental Hazards

Environmental hazards can take many forms and may be difficult to detect. For this reason, great caution must be exercised in accepting a gift of property so that it does not turn into a liability. It may be relatively easy to obtain a list of chemicals used in recent production or manufacturing of products on the site of a commercial property, but what about former uses of the site? In the case of residential property, vacant land, or farmland, it may be difficult to ascertain the presence of submerged oil tanks, fertilizers, or pesticides. A member of the nonprofit's staff who is knowledgeable about real estate should start by conducting an on-site inspection of the property. Depressions in the land, discoloration, and odors are often telltale signs of environmental problems. It is most important to remember that although the property is being offered as a gift, the transaction should be treated as a sale. Do everything possible to protect the organization, just as if the organization were buying the property for its own use.

If the organization is seriously interested in the property, the next step is to hire an environmental engineering firm to conduct an environmental audit. There are several levels of audits that can be conducted, depending on the particular site. Important information about the property also can be obtained from a municipality's building inspector, board of assessors, local real estate broker, conservation commission, zoning board, and planning board. Often a property's history is recorded in the memories of individuals who serve on the municipal board. A few telephone conversations may shed some light on the subject property and its potential environmental hazards.

(c) The Local Real Estate Market

A call to a local real estate broker can help in ascertaining the value and marketability of a property. A broker's knowledge of the local market includes the number of units on the market, the average length of time it takes to sell a piece of property, and the average asking and selling prices—all of which influence the value of a property under consideration.

(d) The National or Regional Economy

Most organizations prefer to sell a gift of property as soon as possible. The health of the regional and national economies greatly influences sales of real estate. Plant closings, high unemployment rates, and lack of consumer confidence are foreboding signs of sluggish real estate sales. If the owner was unable to sell a property that was on the market for an extended period, consider how easily the nonprofit will be able to sell it and who will bear the costs of ownership before it is sold.

31.4 TAX CONSEQUENCES OF GIFTS OF REAL ESTATE

Gifts of real estate provide many favorable tax consequences for a donor. Tax consequences of charitable giving are discussed in detail in Chapter 32, but consider the following tax considerations for real estate gifts.

- *Donor's charitable income tax deduction.* For gifts of appreciated long-term capital gains property, property held for more than a year (year and a day) a donor is entitled to claim a charitable income tax deduction up to 30 percent of her adjusted gross income in the year of the gift and may carry forward the excess for up to five additional tax years. Donors sometimes mistakenly believe that they may voluntarily spread the charitable income tax deduction over five years, but instead a donor is required to use as much of the deduction as possible each year up to the ceiling of 30 percent of the donor's adjusted gross income.

  Alternative accelerated charitable income tax deduction formula. A donor may elect to accelerate his charitable income tax benefit by deducting the charitable gift up to 50 percent of his adjusted gross income if he reduces the value of the contribution by the amount of the appreciation. In other words, the donor can claim a charitable income tax deduction equal to the cost basis of the property for up to 50 percent of his adjusted gross income. This election is useful only if the cost basis is not much less than the fair market value (appraised value).

- *Capital gains tax avoidance.* Capital gains taxes on gifts to nonprofits are avoided on outright gifts of real estate, gifts of real estate to a charitable remainder unitrust, and gifts of real estate to a pooled income fund.

- *Sale of a principal residence.* On the sale of a principal residence, taxpayers can exclude up to $250,000 ($500,000 if married filing a joint return) of gain on the sale or exchange of a principal residence. The property must have been used as a principal residence for two or more years during the five years preceding the sale. Some taxpayers will be able to sell older, larger homes, freeing up additional resources to be used to fund charitable gifts, but some taxpayers who have more than $250,000 of gain after sale ($500,000 if married and filing jointly) will be forced to pay tax on gain even though all sale proceeds will be reinvested in a new residence. Donors who find themselves in this situation may consider a gift of a fractional interest in the old residence to avoid or minimize tax. Planned giving staff may want to check local papers for a listing of real estate transactions to identify the names of donors or prospects who have recently sold property. If a donor makes a bargain sale of his personal residence, either outright or in exchange for a charitable gift annuity, he may use this exclusion to protect gain that may be generated in the transaction.

■ *Depreciation.* Commercial property or property used in a business, trade, or profession may be depreciated property. An owner depreciates property over a term of years as determined by the Internal Revenue Service (IRS) regulations. Depreciation is a method that permits the owner of property to deduct a percentage of the value of the property each year, until the value of the property is completely depreciated. Donors of depreciated real estate must reduce the cost basis of the property by the amount of the depreciation deducted. For an outright gift of property, a donor usually receives a charitable income tax deduction equal to the appraised value of the property. A donor's tax treatment resulting from an outright gift or a gift to a charitable remainder trust or a pooled income fund is not affected by the fact that the property has been depreciated; however, a gift to a charitable gift annuity or deferred gift annuity that requires capital gains taxes to be paid on the portion of property that is, in effect, sold to the charity is affected by the depreciation of the property since the cost basis is reduced by the depreciation.

31.5 WORKING OUT THE ARRANGEMENTS

(a) The Role of the Planned Giving Officer

Typically, it is the planned giving officer who receives the telephone call from a donor who wants to explore the possibility of making a gift of real estate to the nonprofit. Such a caller is usually one of two types: first, a caller who wants to "give" the nonprofit some real estate that he cannot sell, hoping to receive some tax benefits; the second is a prospect who cares about the organization, has a connection to it, and would like to make a gift of some real estate either outright or is eager to receive a lifetime income. The second type of caller is also likely to be emotionally attached to the property.

The planned giving officer should explore every inquiry and often can tell a legitimate gift opportunity from an inquiry that is unlikely to result in a gift. The planned giving officer should ask the caller what he hopes to achieve from the gift, whether the property has ever been on the market, and whether there is a mortgage on the property. The answers to these questions are excellent indicators of whether the real estate will ever be given to the nonprofit. The planned giving officer must remember that the organization wants to produce gifts that bring a benefit to the nonprofit, not a burden.

(b) Real Estate and the Donor's Advisor

Handling a gift of real estate is a challenging and complicated endeavor. It is further complicated by the likelihood that the donor will be advised by an attorney, accountant, or other financial advisor. Donors always should consult a financial advisor or attorney when contemplating a gift of real estate. However, charitable gift planning is a specialty, and there are few advisors who are experienced in handling such gift options without counsel from the nonprofit. Moreover, advisors often discourage donors from pursuing real estate gift options, because they do not fully understand the options or are not knowledgeable about a specific gift vehicle. The planned giving officer can help both the donor and the advisor by educating them about the positive and negative implications of a gift of real estate. Ask the potential donor to schedule a meeting for the donor, her advisor, and the planned giving officer. If the donor does not object, send a copy of all correspondence to the advisor so that everyone has the same information and the advisor is included in all negotiations. Become familiar with the names of experienced tax and financial advisors in order to provide a reference if requested by either a donor or another advisor.

(c) Emotions Related to a Gift of Real Estate

In addition to sophistication about the technicalities of a real estate gift, a planned giving officer also must have an awareness of the psychological and emotional attachments of a donor to her property. The adage "A man's home is his castle" becomes especially relevant when one has to part with it. Processing a gift of real estate takes time, sometimes years, and it is important not to force the gift but to be patient enough to allow the process to take its own course. There are usually a number of significant obstacles to overcome, and patience is truly a virtue, if not a necessity, in handling a gift of real estate.

31.6   OUTRIGHT GIFT OF ENTIRE PROPERTY OR FRACTIONAL INTEREST

The most common way to make a gift of property is to transfer it outright to the nonprofit. The gift is "outright" in that the donor transfers full ownership interest in the property. An outright gift of property frees the donor from paying real estate taxes and fees for maintenance and insurance. Capital gains taxes on the appreciation of the property also are avoided. At most nonprofits, a donor can use real estate to make a major gift.

A gift also can be a fractional interest in a property. A partial interest is created when a donor retains control or an incidence of ownership in property transferred to a nonprofit. Generally, a charitable income tax deduction is not allowed for a gift of a partial interest. An important exception to this rule permits a donor to make a gift of an undivided fractional interest of a donor's entire interest. A fractional interest in a property may be expressed as one-half, two-thirds, three-quarters, and so forth. Alternatively, the undivided interest may be expressed as a percentage. A gift of a fractional interest must convey an interest in each incidence of ownership, and the nonprofit must have the right to occupy or rent the property for its appropriate portion of the year. Because most real estate is held for more than a year and a day, the property is treated for tax purposes as a long-term capital asset and the donor obtains a charitable income tax deduction equal to the appraised value of the property. For more information on partial interests, see Chapter 32.

31.7   DENIAL OF CHARITABLE INCOME TAX DEDUCTION FOR A GIFT OF A USE OF PROPERTY

Nonprofit organizations often seek donors to provide the rent-free use of property owned by the donor, such as a vacation home, office space, or rooms at a bed and breakfast. The rent-free use of property is valuable to a nonprofit. However, the donor is not allowed to claim a charitable income tax deduction for a gift of less than the donor's entire interest and a gift of a use of property is a partial interest. Under the partial interest rules, a donor may not obtain a charitable income tax deduction for a gift of less than the donor's entire interest in the property except in the following situations:

- A contribution of an undivided portion of a donor's entire interest in a personal residence or farm

- A contribution of a remainder interest in a personal residence or farm

- A qualified conservation contribution

- A gift in trust

The donor's inability to claim a charitable income tax deduction for a gift of the use of real estate is the same regardless of whether the taxpayer is an individual offering space at a home or inn or a corporation offering hotel rooms for free or at a discount.

However, if the donor holds only a leasehold interest in the property—that is, the donor is a tenant who leases space—and makes a gift of the use of that entire interest, the donor is entitled to a charitable income tax deduction for the fair market value of that leasehold interest, if any. In this case, the donor has made a gift of his entire interest.

31.8 GIFTS OF REAL ESTATE WITH A RETAINED LIFE ESTATE

Another option in making a gift of a partial interest in real estate to a nonprofit is a gift of a retained life estate, whereby a donor makes a gift of a personal residence or farm and retains the right to occupy the property for life. The personal residence or farm does not have to be the donor's primary residence, but must be a personal residence other than rental property. As the life tenant of the property, the donor is still obligated to pay real estate taxes and fees for maintenance and insurance. The donor obtains a charitable income tax deduction for the value of the remainder interest (up to 30 percent of the donor's adjusted gross income), based on the donor's and life expectancy and the value of the property. See Appendix 31.1(a).

A retained life estate is an attractive option for a donor who would otherwise transfer a personal residence to the nonprofit at death. This type of gift is most appropriate for donors who are healthy and who wish to reside in the property for the immediate future. By accelerating the transfer and retaining a life estate, the donor retains the beneficial use of the property while obtaining a current charitable income tax deduction. The property also passes free of federal estate tax, as long as the life estate was created for the donor and/or the donor's spouse and the remainder is left to a qualified nonprofit organization. The value of the real estate after the retained life estate may be designated to fund a particular program or project at a nonprofit or may be used to establish an endowed fund.

(a) Charitable Income Tax Deduction

Calculating the charitable income tax deduction for a retained life estate is quite simple once the terminology and concepts are understood. The property is divided into two parts for the calculation: the nondepreciable portion (the land) and the depreciable portion (the building on the land). A local tax bill, for example, usually apportions the tax, based on the value of the land and the value of the buildings. Until an appraisal is conducted, a tax bill can serve to estimate the respective percentages of the depreciable and nondepreciable portions in calculating the charitable income tax deduction. It is important to realize that depreciation is a tax concept, rather than an actuality. In the long term, much real estate tends to "appreciate" rather than "depreciate," but for tax purposes it is always assumed to depreciate. The depreciable portion also is said to have a "useful life" determined by the age and type of the property measured in years. The appraiser determines the actual useful life, but for most properties, 45 years is an appropriate assumption. For purposes of the calculation, the property also has a salvage value—again, determined by the appraiser—which generally can be estimated at 25 percent of the depreciable portion.

Example 31.1 _____

A donor aged 75 wants to make a gift of a personal residence and retain a life estate. Assume the following information:

Appraised value of property	$600,000
Depreciable portion	$400,000
Nondepreciable portion	$200,000
Useful life	45 years
Salvage value	$100,000

In this case, a retained life estate in property having an appraised value of $600,000 produces a charitable income tax deduction of $360,987 (which, if not used in the first year, may be carried over for five additional years).[a] The donor also retains the right to occupy the property for life and is still responsible for the real estate taxes, maintenance costs, and insurance.

---

[a]Based on a discount rate of 4 percent.

31.8 GIFTS OF REAL ESTATE WITH A RETAINED LIFE ESTATE

(b) Release of Retained Life Estate

If a donor ever wants to vacate property subject to a retained life estate, the property can be rented to provide the donor with an income. Alternatively, the donor may choose to relinquish the remainder of the life estate, giving the nonprofit the right to occupy the property for the remaining years (see Exhibit 31.1). This action generates a new charitable income tax deduction based on the value of the donor's life estate at the time it is relinquished. (The donor has already deducted the remainder value.) As another alternative, the nonprofit could agree to purchase the donor's remaining life estate for cash or an annuity.

Example 31.2 _____

Assume that the donor in the preceding example chooses to release the life estate at age 80. The calculation for the charitable income tax deduction for a donor who releases a retained life estate is as follows:

1.	Assume appraised value of property (Five years later, donor now aged 80)	$650,000
2.	Value of depreciable portion	$425,000
3.	Value of nondepreciable portion	$225,000
4.	Salvage value (25 percent of depreciable portion)	$106,250
5.	Useful life	45 years
6.	Subtract from the fair market value the remainder value to determine the new charitable income tax deduction for the release of the life estate.[a] ($650,000 – $440,475 = $209,525)	

---

[a] Based on a discount rate of 4 percent.

If the donor no longer wants to occupy the property, the donor and the nonprofit can agree to sell the property and distribute the proceeds proportionately. The proportionate share for the nonprofit is based on the value of the remainder in relation to the value of the property. The donor's proportionate share is equal to the difference between the remainder and the value of the property.

Example 31.3 _____

If a donor aged 80 wants to vacate the property and the donor and the nonprofit choose to sell the property and divide the proceeds, the following calculation is used. Assume the following information:

Value of property	$650,000
Value of depreciable portion	$425,000
Value of nondepreciable portion	$225,000
Salvage value (1/4 of depreciable portion)	$106,250
Useful life	45 years

The nonprofit receives the value of the remainder, which is $440,474, and the donor receives the difference between the remainder and the fair market value, which is $209,525.25.[a]

---

[a]Based on a discount rate of 4 percent.

GIFTS OF REAL ESTATE

It is not necessary for purposes of the calculation of a gift or estate tax deduction to utilize a depreciation factor, and it is to the nonprofit's advantage to ignore the depreciation factor under the circumstances.

Exhibit 31.1   Form for Deed with Retained Life Estate

Quitclaim Deed with Retained Life Estate

I, Richard A. Johnson, 26 Main St., Boston, MA (the "Grantor"), for One Dollar ($1.00) consideration paid, grant to Academy for Learning, a Massachusetts charitable corporation with an address of 1 Stone St., Boston, with QUITCLAIM COVENANTS, a certain parcel of land with the buildings thereon, situated at 26 Main St., Boston, more particularly bounded and described as follows:

<DESCRIPTION OF PROPERTY FROM DEED TO GRANTOR>

There is expressly excluded from this conveyance, and the Grantor does hereby reserve for HIMSELF, the full use, control, income, and possession of all the premises for the remainder of HIS life. The Grantor shall not have the power to sell, mortgage, exchange, or dispose of the premises. The interest reserved in this paragraph is hereinafter referred to as the "Life Estate." The Life Estate may be terminated only by the death of the Grantor or by an instrument of release, executed by the Grantor or Grantor's legal representative in a form suitable for recording and delivered to Academy for Learning.

The Grantor hereby agrees that during the Life Estate, HE will do the following at HIS own cost and expense:

1. Keep the buildings on the premises insured against loss or damaged by fire (with extended coverage) in an amount sufficient to avoid being deemed a coinsurer and naming Academy of Learning as additional insured;
2. Pay all real estate taxes assessed on the premises, and if the expiration of the Life Estate is on a date other than at the commencement or expiration of any fiscal year, the taxes in such year all be apportioned between the Grantor and Academy of Learning;
3. Keep premises in substantially such repair, order, and condition as the same are in on the date hereof, reasonable use and wear excepted.

Consideration for this deed being nominal, no Massachusetts Deed Excise Stamps are affixed hereto, none being required by law.

WITNESS my hand and seal this _____ day of _____, 20__.

_____
<DONOR>

Commonwealth of Massachusetts

On this _____ day of _____ 20__, personally appeared before me, _____, and satisfactorily proved to me to be the signer of the above instrument by the oath of Martha Cooley, a competent and credible witness for that purpose, by me duly sworn, and HE, the said Richard A. Johnson acknowledged that HE executed the same.

_____
Notary Public

My Commission Expires: <DATE>

31.9 GIFTS OF REAL ESTATE TO CHARITABLE REMAINDER TRUSTS

(a) Charitable Remainder Trust (Straight Percentage Payout)

A charitable remainder trust provides the donor with an income along with a charitable income tax deduction for the value of the remainder to the nonprofit. In addition, using a charitable remainder trust avoids capital gains taxes on the transfer of appreciated real estate. A charitable remainder unitrust pays a beneficiary a predetermined percentage, but not less than 5 percent, of the fair market value of the trust's assets, as revalued annually. As the rate increases, the donor's charitable income tax deduction decreases. Donors who consider making a gift of real estate through a charitable remainder trust should remember two important rules. First, donors cannot obtain a charitable income tax deduction unless the trust is irrevocable. Second, donors cannot live in a personal residence that has been donated to a charitable remainder trust.

At present, the Internal Revenue Service has taken the position that a donor cannot transfer mortgaged property to a charitable remainder trust even with a hold harmless agreement in which the donor absolves the trustee from any financial obligation to discharge the mortgage. The donor may be able to transfer the debt to other real estate that he owns.

(b) Net Income Unitrust

A net income unitrust is ideal for a gift of real estate in instances when the donor wants to receive a life income and there is likely to be a delay in the sale of the property. Most pieces of real estate are non–income-producing assets, meaning that there is no stream of income available to pay the donor. The trustee cannot borrow to pay a stream of income without jeopardizing the tax-exempt nature of the trust. A net income unitrust is the solution to protect the nonprofit from the obligation to provide the beneficiary a stream of income. Through this option the donor receives either the stated percentage of the trust's value or the net income, whichever is less. However, upon the eventual sale of the property, the proceeds received by the trust are invested, producing a stream of income for the lifetime of the donor. In this way, a nonprofit can accept a gift of real estate without having to pay the donor income before the property is sold. The trust must receive from the donor sufficient cash or marketable securities to enable it to meet expenses such as real estate taxes, insurance, and maintenance costs until the property is sold.

(c) Net Income Unitrust with a Makeup Provision

Donors who want to make up lost income when making a gift of real estate through a charitable remainder unitrust should consider a net income unitrust with a makeup provision. Like a net income unitrust, a net income unitrust with a makeup provision permits a donor to receive the lesser of the stated percentage or the net income, but provides for a makeup of income lost during a delay in the selling of the property. Income lost during the delay may be recouped later if income in later years exceeds the stated percentage.

Example 31.4 _____

Assume that real estate worth $600,000 is transferred to a net income unitrust with a makeup provision. Assume that the donors are 75 and 77 years old and that they select a payment rate of 6 percent. Assume further that the property sells for $600,000 in year 1 and earns 8 percent in year 2. Because a net income unitrust with a makeup provision allows the donors to receive the stated percentage of the trust's value or the net income, whichever is less, in year 1 if no income is produced, the donors receive nothing. However, in year 2 the property produces 8 percent. The donors receive the 6 percent that they were entitled to receive in year 2 and a makeup of 2 percent toward the deficit or shortfall from year 1. This can continue each year until the deficit is completely recouped.

A donor also will receive a charitable income tax deduction in the year the trust is established, limited to 30 percent of adjusted gross income. In Example 16.4, the charitable income tax deduction for a gift of $600,000 to the charitable remainder unitrust described is $271,710 (based on a discount rate of 4 percent). If the entire tax deduction is not used in the first year, it can be carried over to offset income for up to five years. See Appendix 31.1(b).

Since a net income unitrust, with or without a makeup provision, may not pay out trust principal even after the real estate or other contributed assets are sold by the trust, it may be useful under some circumstances and with a sophisticated donor to create a "flip" unitrust, which may become a straight percentage payout unitrust in the year after the contributed property is sold. Thereafter, the trust can be invested on a total return basis and can pay out the straight percentage. See discussion of flip unitrusts in Chapter 25.

31.10 GIFTS OF REAL ESTATE TO FUND CHARITABLE GIFT ANNUITIES

(a) Charitable Gift Annuity

Real estate also can be used to fund a charitable gift annuity. (See Chapter 23 for further discussion on charitable gift annuities.) Unlike a net income unitrust with a makeup provision, a charitable gift annuity requires an immediate payment to the donor. Because there is almost always a delay in the sale of real estate, the nonprofit that accepts real estate to fund a charitable gift annuity has an immediate obligation to make a payment to the donor.

Why, then, use real estate to fund a charitable gift annuity? In most cases, it is not advisable unless the nonprofit expects to sell the property immediately. The nonprofit may also choose to accept property to fund a charitable gift annuity if it is interested in keeping the property for its own use. In a recent situation, a property was offered as a beachfront home for university retreats and events. The donors proposed that they receive a charitable gift annuity, which was not attractive to the university, because it would have to make immediate guaranteed payments to the donors. Another organization that wanted to use the property for events and retreats found the arrangement acceptable, and the gift annuity was completed.

Example 31.5

Assume that Mr. and Mrs. Jackson, aged 83 and 79, want to give their home and surrounding property valued at $600,000 to a charitable organization. In return, they want to receive a guaranteed fixed income for their lifetimes through a charitable gift annuity. The charitable gift annuity rate is often based on the rates suggested by the American Council on Gift Annuities,[a] according to the ages of the donors at the time their gift is made. For donors aged 83 and 79 making a $600,000 gift, the annuity rate is currently 7.3 percent, which produces an annual payment of $43,800. In addition, the donors receive a charitable income tax deduction of approximately $223,710.[b] When real estate is transferred to fund a charitable gift annuity, an irrevocable gift is made, which precludes the donors from continuing to occupy the property (unless they rent it at a market rental rate). The organization must be highly motivated to commit to making these payments before agreeing to a charitable gift annuity funded with real estate. See Appendix 31.1(c).

[a]The American Council on Gift Annuities, 233 McCrea Street, Suite 400, Indianapolis, IN 46225-1030, (317) 269-6271.
[b]Based on a discount rate of 4 percent.

(b) Charitable Deferred Gift Annuity

Unlike a charitable gift annuity, which requires an immediate payment, a charitable deferred gift annuity permits payments to the donor to be delayed to an agreed-on date of at least one year after the gift is made. Payments often are deferred five or more years after the gift is made. (See the discussion on charitable deferred gift annuities in Chapter 23.) Thus, payment to the donor is postponed until a time when it is likely that the property can be sold and can generate an income. Like a charitable gift annuity, the deferred charitable gift annuity is a contract between the donor and the nonprofit that provides a stream of income to the donor for life, but beginning at a predetermined date in the future. If the real estate used to fund a deferred charitable gift annuity is likely to be sold within one year, then payment should be deferred for at least a one-year period. A gift made through a charitable deferred gift annuity is irrevocable, and the donor is prohibited from continuing to occupy the property once it has been transferred to fund the gift. This is an underutilized gift option but one that is uniquely appropriate for real estate inasmuch as it contemplates beginning payments at a point in the future, which can coincide with the sale of the property.

Example 31.6

Mr. and Mrs. Novak, aged 60 and 56, want to give their home and surrounding property valued at $600,000 to a nonprofit organization and in return want to receive a guaranteed fixed income for their lifetimes. The deferred gift annuity rate is based on the donors' ages at the time the gift is made. For donors aged 60 and 56 making a $600,000 gift and deferring payments until ages 65 and 61, the annuity rate is 7.4 percent, which produces an annual income payment of $44,400 to begin in five years. The Novaks also receive a charitable income tax deduction of $62,622 in the year the gift is made (which they can use up to 30 percent of their adjusted gross income).[a] See Appendix 31.1(d).

[a]Based on a discount rate of 4 percent.

31.11 GIFTS OF REAL ESTATE TO POOLED INCOME FUNDS

Although, technically, a gift of real estate can be made to a pooled income fund, it is almost never advisable. Upon transfer of property to a pooled income fund, the donor is entitled to a stream of income based on the pooled income fund rate and the value of the property contributed. Non-income-producing real estate contributed to a pooled income fund dilutes the income paid to all donors in the fund. Unless the property is to be sold immediately, real estate should not be put into a pooled income fund, and most pooled income funds strictly prohibit the transfer of real estate to their holdings. (See Chapter 24 for further discussion of pooled income funds.)

31.12 GIFTS OF MORTGAGED PROPERTY

A gift of mortgaged property triggers the bargain sale rules. Bargain sale rules require the basis of the property to be allocated, part to the gift portion and part to the sale portion, for the purposes of computing the reportable gain. The sale portion is defined as the amount of cash received by the donor from the nonprofit or, in the case of a gift of mortgaged real estate, the amount of the mortgage. A potential gift of real estate with a mortgage calls for extra caution. How large is the mortgage in relation to the fair market value of the property? If the mortgage is substantial or if the donor is financially unable to pay off the mortgage prior to donating the property to the organization, the gift may be in jeopardy.

Nonprofits have had donors offer to make gifts of real estate, only to learn that a donor's mortgage equals or exceeds the fair market value of the property. In essence, the donor is asking the organization to assume responsibility for the mortgage. Whether or not the donor is personally responsible for the mortgage, if the property is transferred to a nonprofit subject to that mortgage, a benefit is conferred on the donor, who will recognize gain calculated as the amount of the mortgage reduced by an allocated portion of the donor's tax basis. Many organizations choose to refuse to accept all gifts of mortgaged property unless they are ready to employ sophisticated tax counsel and invest a substantial amount of time, money, and energy in the transaction. In addition to the adverse consequences to the donor, the sale of property by a nonprofit that produces a gain on gifted real estate subject to a mortgage generates income to the nonprofit that is taxed as unrelated business income. This tax treatment is imposed unless the property was acquired and the mortgage placed on the property more than five years before the gift and the charity does not assume or agree to pay the indebtedness. It is best for the donor to work with the lending institution to obtain a discharge of the mortgage on the property to be given.

(a) Bargain Sale

The best way to understand a bargain sale is to understand its application. A bargain sale is part gift and part sale and is effective when used in the case of a donor who has mortgaged property. Assume that a donor has property appraised at $600,000 with a mortgage of $100,000. To facilitate the transfer of the property to a nonprofit, the property is considered to be sold to the nonprofit for the amount of the mortgage, and the difference of $500,000 is gifted to the nonprofit organization. For this gift portion, the donor receives a charitable income tax deduction. The portion of the property that is considered sold to the organization has a value of $100,000. Depending on the donor's tax basis in the property, there may be a taxable gain on the sale portion.

A bargain sale is also effective in situations in which a donor wants to make a gift of property and needs cash for a down payment on a retirement home. The bargain sale permits the donor to receive cash while giving the balance of the property. The nonprofit uses its own cash reserves to give to the donor since it must wait for the ultimate sale of the property to receive cash. The nonprofit may wish to establish guidelines placing a ceiling on the amount of cash that the nonprofit is willing to use in a bargain sale. Each nonprofit determines the amount of cash it is willing to spend, and the decision usually is based on how motivated the organization is to acquire the gift. A general rule is that a nonprofit should not pay more than 15 to 20 percent of the appraised value of the property in a bargain sale. In addition, to protect its interests, the nonprofit should have an appraisal done.

It is important to remember that in this instance the nonprofit becomes the owner of the property, assuming the obligation for insurance, real estate taxes, maintenance costs, broker's commissions, and other expenses incurred prior to and in the course of the sale of the property. Many organizations ask the donor to make a gift to assist in paying some or all of the costs incurred in liquidating such property.

(b) Hold Harmless Agreements

In the case of a gift of mortgaged real estate (which is treated as a bargain sale), the donor may sign a hold harmless agreement to remove any financial obligation of the nonprofit to discharge the mortgage or to assume the donor's responsibility for payment. If a hold harmless agreement is used, the donor should consult his own tax advisor about whether any bargain sale or other adverse consequences follow.

(c) Tax Consequences

The tax consequences of a gift of mortgaged property can be illustrated by the following situation.

Example 31.7 _____

Assume that a donor makes a gift of real estate having an appraised value of $500,000, a cost basis of $100,000, and a mortgage of $75,000. Use the following calculation to determine the reportable gain:

1. Divide the sale price received by the donor (cash or relief from debt) by the appraised value of the property, which will produce a ratio (decimal) of sale price to appraised value.

$75,000 (mortgage amount) ÷ $500,000 (appraised value) = .15

2. Multiply the ratio (decimal) times the cost basis to arrive at the cost basis allocated to the sale price.

.15 × $100,000 (cost basis) = $15,000

3. Subtract from the benefit the allocated cost basis to determine the taxable gain on the benefit.

$75,000 − $15,000 = $60,000

In this case, the donor has a taxable gain of $60,000 and a charitable income tax deduction of $500,000 − $75,000 = $425,000, producing a net charitable tax benefit of $425,000 − $60,000 = $365,000.

Of course, the gain is likely to be taxed at favorable capital gain rates, whereas the deduction may be used to offset ordinary income taxes.

31.13 CONCLUSION

A gift of real estate represents a significant gift opportunity to both the planned giving officer and the nonprofit. Such a gift is complicated, not only for the donor and outside advisors, but for the nonprofit's planned giving officer, general counsel, business officer, and treasurer. The planned giving officer should educate and assist in-house officers in dealing with the various gift options and should include them early in any negotiations to define parameters and establish guidelines when accepting gifts of real estate. These other in-house staff members can assist the planned giving officer in making decisions about whether to accept a property, how long the organization may be willing to hold the property, and the amount of income that can be paid to a donor.

Appendix 31.1(a)

RETAINED LIFE ESTATE*

Deduction Calculations
Summary of Benefits

Retained Life Estate

ASSUMPTIONS:

Life Tenant Age	75
Value of Property	$600,000.00
Cost Basis of Property	$0.00
Value of Depreciable Portion	$400,000.00
Estimated Useful Life of Property	45 years
Salvage Value of Property	$100,000.00

BENEFITS:

Charitable Deduction	$360,987.00
	IRS Discount Rate is 4%

* These calculations are estimates of gift benefits; your actual benefits may vary.

APPENDIX 31.1(b)   6 PERCENT CHARITABLE UNITRUST

Appendix 31.1(b)

6 PERCENT CHARITABLE UNITRUST*

Deduction Calculations
Summary of Benefits

ASSUMPTIONS:

Beneficiary Ages	77
	75
Principal Donated	$600,000.00
Cost Basis of Property	$300,000.00
Payout Rate	6 percent
Payment Schedule	quarterly
	3 months to 1st payment

BENEFITS:

Charitable Deduction	$271,710.00
First Year's Income (future income will vary with trust value)	$36,000.00
	IRS Discount Rate is 4%

* Actual deductions and rates are affected by the prevailing discount rate and payout rates suggested by the American Council in Gift Annuities.

Appendix 31.1(c)

7.3 PERCENT CHARITABLE GIFT ANNUITY*

Deduction Calculations
Summary of Benefits

ASSUMPTIONS:

Annuitants	83
	79
Principal Donated	$600,000.00
Cost Basis	$100,000.00
Annuity Rate	7.3%
Payment Schedule	quarterly
	at end

BENEFITS:

Charitable Deduction	$223,710.00
Annuity	$43,800.00
Capital Gain Income	$30,835.20
Ordinary Income	$12,964.80

Total reportable capital gain of $313,575.00 must be reported over 10.2 years, until all of the gain is reported. After 10.2 years, capital gain income becomes tax-free.

After 12.2 years, the entire annuity becomes ordinary income.

IRS Discount Rate is 4%

* These calculations are estimates of gift benefits; your actual benefits may vary.

APPENDIX 31.1(d)   8.1 PERCENT CHARITABLE GIFT ANNUITY

Appendix 31.1(d)

8.1 PERCENT DEFERRED GIFT ANNUITY*

Deduction Calculations
Summary of Benefits

ASSUMPTIONS:

Annuitants	60
	56
Ages at Date of First Payment	[3/18/2008] 65 61
Principal Donated	$600,000.00
Cost Basis	$100,000.00
Annuity Rate	7.4%
Payment Schedule	quarterly

BENEFITS:

Charitable Deduction	$62,622.00
Annuity	$44,400.00
Capital Gain Income	$19,891.20
Ordinary Income	$24,508.80

Total reportable capital gain of $447,815.00 must be reported over 22.5 years, until all of the gain is reported. After 22.5 years from the year the payments begin, capital gain income becomes tax-free.

After 27.0 years from the year the payments begin, the entire annuity becomes ordinary income.

IRS Discount Rate is 4%

* Actual deductions and rates are affected by the prevailing discount rate and payout rates suggested by the American Council in Gift Annuities.

CHAPTER THIRTY-TWO

Conservation Easements

32.1 INTRODUCTION

Conservation easements or conservation restrictions help nonprofits preserve and conserve open space and, at the same time, offer significant income and estate tax benefits to donors. Although conservation easements have been available for years, tax changes increased the viability of conservation easements as a charitable gift-planning tool. In addition, the provisions of the Economic Growth and Tax Relief Reconciliation Act (EGTRRA) have furthered the use of conservation easements. The Act now more broadly removes restrictions on the locaiton of the property.

Through a conservation easement, a donor grants to a qualified organization the building or development rights to property owned by the donor. A conservation easement restricts development of a landowner's property, preserving views and open space. The rights to develop the property must be transferred to a charity or governmental unit. In turn, the landowner receives favorable tax benefits and the good feeling that comes from preserving and conserving real estate. The easement prevents or limits development of the property except that which is specifically allowed by the easement. In return, the donor receives a charitable income tax deduction equal to the difference between the value of the project before the easement was imposed and the value after its imposition. Of equal importance, the value of those rights is also excluded from the donor's estate.

Conservation easements can be valuable tools for planned giving and major gift staff members and important gift options for donors who wish to protect and preserve open-space views and conserve land. Landowners who own property adjacent to wetlands, parks, historic buildings, and property owned by a governmental agency or charity may see a conservation easement as the most appropriate way to preserve the property from being developed.

Like all charitable gifts, a donor must first have donative intent to make a gift. The donor must want to permanently preserve the conservation purposes of the real estate. A conservation easement imposes permanent restrictions on the land subject to the easement. Relinquished rights are given up in perpetuity. A donor often would realize greater financial reward by selling the property to a developer. The rules and regulations governing conservation easements, technically referred to as *qualified conservation contributions*, are spelled out in Treasury Regulation Section 1 170A-14. The authors have drawn extensively from these regulations in this chapter.

This chapter focuses on the important roles that conservation easements play in philanthropy. Nonprofit organizations that deal primarily with conservation land use and preservation issues no doubt regularly use conservation easements. Many other nonprofits and governmental entities with environmentally sensitive land holdings that benefit the public may wish to promote conservation easements and the attractive benefits they afford to interested land holders.

32.2   BENEFITS TO DONORS

A conservation easement provides the following attractive benefits to donors who are interested in land conservation issues, especially donors who own property adjacent to the property that is subject to the easement:

- Preservation of open space

- Preservation of wildlife habitat

- Land preservation

- Protection of scenic views

- Income tax benefits

- Estate tax benefits

- Local real estate tax reductions

Apart from the intrinsic benefits of preserving open space and promoting land conservation, donors receive favorable tax benefits in the form of a charitable income tax deduction, estate tax savings, and property tax restrictions. This topic is addressed in detail later in this chapter.

32.3   PARTIAL INTEREST RULES

With some important exceptions, the Internal Revenue Code (IRC) denies a deduction for a charitable contribution of any interest in property that consists of less than the donor's entire interest. One of the most important exceptions to the partial interest rule is that it allows a donor to make a gift of less than his entire interest in the property if the gift is for conservation purposes. The interest must provide a public benefit to preserve open space, preserve habitat, improve the view, or conserve water usage.

For donors who hold valuable real estate abutting conservation districts or who live in environmentally sensitive areas, views and access to open space are valuable property rights. Real estate ownership often is described as entitling the owner of the property to "a bundle of rights" with respect to the property. Subject to zoning requirements and other land use controls, these rights include the right to build, subdivide, lease, rent, and remove topsoil, clear-cut forestland, and a variety of other rights to develop the property. One of the most valuable is, of course, the right to develop the property fully and to build single family residences, motels, hotels, condominiums, or apartment houses. Relinquishing the right to construct such edifices decreases the value of the property substantially. In exchange for this decrease in value, the donor receives a charitable income tax deduction equal to the value of the relinquished property rights and the joy of preserving open space.

32.4 QUALIFIED DONEE ORGANIZATIONS

The qualified conservation contribution must be made to a donee that is a qualified organization. Qualified organizations include:

- A governmental unit

- A charitable organization that normally receives significant support in the form of contributions from the public [IRC Section 170(b)(1)(A)(vi)]

- A charitable organization that normally receives significant support in the form of contributions or earned income from the public [IRC Section 509(a)(2)]

- A charitable organization that supports and is controlled by an organization described by 2 or 3 above [IRC Section 509(a)(3)]

The donee charitable organization or governmental unit also must have a commitment to protect the "conservation purposes" of the gift and have financial resources to defend the restrictions of the easement. A deduction is allowed for a charitable contribution only if, in the instrument of conveyance, the donor prohibits the donee charity from subsequently transferring the easement unless the donee, as a condition of the transfer, requires the conservation purposes to be carried out. In addition, the subsequent transfer must also be to an organization that qualifies as an eligible donee.

32.5 CONSERVATION PURPOSES

The qualified conservation contribution must primarily be for these conservation purposes:

- Preservation of land areas for outdoor recreation by or for the education of the general public. The use of land for outdoor recreation or for education of the general public meets the meaning of conservation purposes so long as the general public has access to the protected property for those purposes.

- Protection of a relatively natural habitat of fish, wildlife, or plants or a similar ecosystem. A deduction is allowed even if the habitat or environment has been altered by human intervention so long as the first wildlife or plants exist in a relatively natural state. Significant habitats and ecosystems include habitats for rare, endangered, or threatened species of animal, fish, or plants and natural areas such as relatively undeveloped islands or natural areas that contribute to a local state or national park, preserve, or refuge.

- Preservation of open space for the scenic benefit of the public.

To qualify as a gift of property to preserve open space including farmland and forestland, the preservation (1) must be pursuant to a defined governmental policy and yield a significant public benefit or (2) the scenic enjoyment must be for the benefit of the general public and will yield a significant public benefit. Scenic enjoyment includes the preservation of the scenic character of rural or urban landscape and preservation of panoramas and views. To satisfy the requirement of scenic enjoyment by the general public, visual rather than physical access to or across the property by the general public is sufficient.

As described above, the preservation must yield a significant public benefit. In meeting the test that a significant public benefit is provided, these factors are considered:

- The uniqueness of the property to the area

- The intensity of land development in the vicinity of the property

- The consistency of the proposed open space use with public programs for conservation in the region

- The consistency of the proposed open-space use with existing private conservation programs in the area

- The likelihood that development of the property would lead to or contribute to the degradation of the scenic natural or historic character of the area

- The opportunity for the general public to use the property or to appreciate the property for its scenic value

- The importance of the property in preserving a local or regional landscape or resources that attracts tourism or commerce

- The likelihood that the donee will acquire equally desirable and valuable substitute property

- The cost to the donee for enforcement of the conservation restriction

- The population density in the area

- The consistency of the proposed open-space use with a legislatively mandated program identifying particular parcels of land for future protection

32.6 QUALIFIED REAL PROPERTY INTERESTS

The interest conveyed must be a qualified real property interest. Examples of a qualified real property interest include:

- *The donor's entire interest other than a qualified mineral interest.* A qualified mineral interest is the donor's interest in oil, gas, or other minerals and the right to access those minerals. Treasury regulations provide that "a real property interest shall not be treated as an entire interest other than a qualified mineral interest if the property was divided prior to the contribution to enable the donor to retain control of more than a qualified mineral interest or to reduce the real property interest donated." A donor may make a gift of an undivided fractional interest.

- *The qualified real property interest may also be a remainder interest.* In addition, perpetual conservation restrictions on the use of the real property also are qualified. A perpetual conservation easement or restriction as discussed above is a restriction granted in perpetuity on the use that may be made of real property including another interest that under state law has attributes similar to an easement.

- *The contribution must be exclusively for conservation purposes.* The qualified conservation contribution must be exclusively for conservation purposes, although a deduction will not be denied when incidental benefit is provided to the donor as a result of conservation restrictions limited to the use of the property. In addition, a deduction will not be allowed if the contribution accomplishes one or more enumerated conservation purposes but would permit destruction of other significant conservation interests. A use that is destructive of a conservation interest will be permitted only if such use is necessary for the protection of the conservation interests that are the subject of the contribution. The interest in the property given to the charitable organization and its successors must be subject to legally enforceable restrictions, such as being recorded in the Registry of Deeds or other department of land records. In the case of a remainder interest, the contribution will not qualify if the like tenant can use the property in a manner that diminishes the conservation values that are intended to be protected by the contribution. No deduction will be permitted for an interest in property that is subject to a mortgage unless the lender subordinates its rights in the property to the right of the qualified organizations to enforce the conservation purposes.

32.7 TAX CONSEQUENCES

As previously discussed, the donor obtains favorable tax treatment for the contribution of a conservation easement. The following section outlines the tax treatment of a gift of a conservation easement.

(a) Charitable Income Tax Benefits

A donor receives a charitable income tax deduction for relinquishing the development rights to the land. The charitable income tax deduction is equal to the relinquished value. The value of the land is determined by its "highest and best use" and, in most cases, development rights are an important part of the land's highest and best use. A five-acre tract of land with ocean view has multiple values depending on the land use. To determine the highest and best use, an appraiser examines the possible purposes of the property, for example, whether the land will be used for:

- One single-family residence
- Five single-family homes
- A condominium complex
- A hotel
- A commercial mall
- A park

Like other gifts of long-term capital gain property, the donor's charitable income tax deduction is limited to 30 percent of the donor's adjusted gross income, and any excess may be carried forward for up to five additional years.

The cost of the appraisal is typically an expense paid by the donor, reported as a miscellaneous itemized deduction, who must have the appraisal for his own income tax purposes. However, under certain circumstances, the cost can be negotiated and allocated between the donor and the donee organization. (See Chapter 33 for more information on appraisals.)

(b) Estate Tax Benefits

For wealthy donors, federal estate taxes remain a formidable obstacle. For many donors the value of real property represents a significant portion of their estates. Through a conservation easement, a donor reduces the value of the estate by the amount equal to the value of the relinquished property rights. This technique allows a donor to substantially decrease the value of the estate while substantially enjoying the use of the property.

A 1997 tax law allows the executor of an estate to grant a conservation easement on property owned by a decedent. Further, Congress has eased restrictions to donors who make conservation easements. The EGTRRA now allows estates of donors who have made gifts of conservation easements to receive estate tax benefits for up to 40 percent of the value of the property up to $500,000 in 2002.

(c) Property Tax Consequences

Local real estate property taxes are assessed on the property's value. The taxes are assessed by a municipality, county, or other governmental unit. For tax purposes, the property is allocated into two parts: (1) the value of the buildings and improvements to the land and (2) the value of the land itself. Since the value of the land is substantially diminished by a conservation easement, the donor's property tax bill often is reduced.

Since the donee charity or governmental unit that received the development rights is a tax-exempt organization, and since holding the development right is a part of the donee's charitable purpose, the value of the development right escapes local property taxes.

32.8 VALUATION

Like other gifts of noncash assets, donors and nonprofit organizations must confront the usual issues involving valuation and substantiation. In the case of a gift of a conservation easement or restriction on interest of the donor's entire project, the value of the contribution is the fair market value of the surface right in the property contributed. In the case of a contribution of any interest in real property, the depletion of mineral or other deposits diminishes the value of the property. In the case of a contribution of interest for conservation purposes, the current fair market value of the property must take into account any preexisting or limiting uses to which the property may be put. The value of the contribution in the case of a charitable contribution of a perpetual conservation restriction is the difference between the fair market value of the project before and after perpetual conservation restrictions were imposed.

These gifts are unique, so it is a challenge to identify comparable properties. If there is a substantial record of sales of easements comparable to the donated easement, the fair market value of the donated easement may be based on the sale prices of such comparable easements. If no substantial record of marketplace sales is available as a meaningful or valid comparison, as a general rule, the fair market value of a perpetual conservation restriction is equal to the difference between the fair market value of the property it encumbers before the granting of the restriction and the fair market value of the encumbered property after the granting of the restriction. The amount of the deduction in the case of a charitable contribution of a perpetual conservation restriction covering a property that is contiguous to other property owned by a donor and/or the donor's family is the difference between the fair market value of the entire contiguous parcel of property before and after the granting of the restriction.

(a) Fair Market Value of Property before and after Restriction

If before-and-after valuation is used, the fair market value of the property before contribution of the conservation restriction must take into account not only the current use of the property but also an objective assessment of how immediate or remote the likelihood is that the property, absent the restriction, would in fact be developed, as well as any effect from zoning, conservation, or historic preservation laws that already restrict the property's potential highest and best use.

Further, there may be instances in which the grant of a conservation restriction may have no material effect on the value of the property or may in fact serve to enhance, rather than reduce, the value of property. In such instance, no deduction would be allowable. In the case of a conservation restriction that nevertheless allows development, the fair market value of the property after contribution of the restriction must take into account the possible impact of the development. In the case of a conservation easement such as an easement on a certified historic structure, the fair market value of the property after contribution of the restriction must take into account the amount of access permitted by the terms of the easement.

Additionally, if a before-and-after valuation is used, an appraisal of the property after contribution of the restriction must take into account the effect of restrictions that will result in a reduction of the potential fair market value represented by highest and best use, such as the construction of one or several additional residences, but will, nevertheless, permit uses of the property that will increase its fair market value above that represented by the property's current use. The value of a perpetual conservation restriction shall not be reduced by reason of the existence of restrictions on transfer designed solely to ensure that the conservation restriction will be dedicated to conservation purposes.

(b) Allocation of Basis

In the case of the donation of a qualified real property interest for conservation purposes, the basis of the property retained by the donor must be adjusted by the elimination of that part of the total basis of the property that is properly allocable to the qualified real property interest granted. The amount of the basis that is allocable to the qualified real property interest shall bear the same ratio to the basis of the property as the fair market value of the qualified real property interest bears to the fair market value of the property before the granting of a qualified real property interest. When a taxpayer donates to a qualifying conservation organization an easement on a structure with respect to which deductions are taken for depreciation, the reduction required in the basis of the property retained by the taxpayer must be allocated between the structure and the underlying land.

(c) Substantiation Requirement

If a taxpayer makes a qualified conservation contribution and claims a deduction, the taxpayer must obtain an appraisal, maintain the appraisal, and keep written records of the fair market value of the underlying property before and after the donation, and the conservation purpose furthered by the donation that information shall be disclosed on Form 8283 attached to the taxpayer's income tax return for the year of gift. See Regulation Section 1.170A-13(c) (addresses substantiation requirements for deductions in excess of $5,000 for charitable contributions made after 1984) and Section 6659 (addresses additions to tax in the case of valuation overstatements).

(d) Protecting the Donee

As in the case of any gift of real estate, it is important to protect the donee. A site inspection of the property and possibly an environmental audit should be conducted. (See Chapter 31 for a discussion of issues regarding gifts of real estate.) At a minimum, a planned giving officer or other member of the nonprofit organization staff responsible for real estate should conduct a site inspection of the property.

    Aside from environmental concerns, the property should be free of mortgage, liens, or other encumbrances. The title of the property should be clear, and the property itself should accomplish the purposes of the gift. Often the subject property has been included in studies conducted by local conservation boards or committees, and it is easy to corroborate the value of the property and its significance for conservation purposes. These studies document the nature and quality of the lands and may also reference zoning classification. Check with local municipal government zoning and conservation boards for a local history of the land and its status within the community. Local realtors also can be helpful in determining value and suitability for its intended conservation purposes.

32.9 CONCLUSION

Despite their attractive qualities, conservation easements are underutilized by donors and donee organizations. Much more effort must be made to publicly educate all constituents about the use and desirability of conservation easements. Marketing materials may help to elicit responses from donors' interests in land preservation. As for conservation easements, an ad can be placed in the nonprofit organization's newsletters and in local newspapers to allow interested prospects and donors to self-identify their interest in preservation. In addition, public colloquiums on land use may attract the land-holding public.

    Conservation easements provide important benefits to donors and to the donee organizations that are beneficiaries of these easements. These benefits provide incentives to donors to make major gifts to preserve open space. Like all charitable gifts, donors must first have the donative intent to make a gift to help the organization fulfill its mission. Many worthy nonprofit organizations are committed to preservation and conservation. Bringing interested donors together with worthy organizations is the job of a planned giving officer. The following checklist will assist the planned giving officer in working with the donor in establishing a conservation easement.

Conservation Easement Checklist

- Obtain copies of deed/appraisal
- Conduct site evaluation
- Confirm zoning classification with local offices
- Contact local, regional conservation commissions
- Contact state or federal agencies
- Meet with related nonprofit departments:
  - General counsel
  - Real estate office
  - Gift review committee
- Prepare deed
- Title insurance policy/title search
- Draft agreement for the transfer of the property, including restrictions on use
- Execute deed and file in Registry of Deeds
- Acknowledge gift

CHAPTER THIRTY-THREE

Gifts of Tangible Personal Property

33.1 INTRODUCTION

This chapter discusses a number of topics related to gifts of tangible personal property. The first is an overview of the issues associated with making a gift of this kind to a nonprofit; the second is the various gift vehicles that can be funded with tangible personal property; and the third is recognition of gifts of services and out-of-pocket expenses.

A fourth section outlines the substantiation requirements for noncash gifts as mandated by the Internal Revenue Service (IRS), followed by a discussion of appraisals of gifts of tangible personal property. The final section deals with a nonprofit's gift review committee, designed to protect the organization from a variety of potential problems created by special gifts such as tangible personal property, real estate, and other restricted gifts.

33.2 OVERVIEW

(a) Definition of Tangible Personal Property

Tangible personal property is property that can be held physically, as distinguished from intangible property such as cash, securities, or real estate. A variety of tangible personal property may be used to make a gift, including these items:

- Furniture

- Art

- Antiques

- Coin and stamp collections

- Livestock (cattle, thoroughbreds, breeding stock)

- Jewelry

- Equipment

- Collections, collectibles

- Boats, yachts, recreational vehicles

- Automobiles

- Aircraft

- Books

- Clothing

- Software

(b) Holding Period: Long- and Short-term Property

A gift of tangible personal property held by a donor for a year or less is considered short-term property. A donor can claim a charitable income tax deduction for property held short term equal to the property's cost basis. The cost basis is the amount of money the donor paid for the property (purchase price). If the property is held long term (i.e., for a year and a day) and is related to the exempt purposes (charitable function) of the nonprofit organization, the donor obtains a charitable income tax deduction equal to the fair market value of the property. It may be advantageous for a donor to hold appreciated property long term so that the donor receives the larger charitable income tax deduction based on the fair market value when making a gift to a nonprofit, rather than on the property's cost basis.

(c) Transfer of Personal Property

To transfer ownership or legal title of tangible personal property from a donor to a nonprofit, a donor physically transfers the property to the nonprofit and the nonprofit formally accepts the property. In many cases a simple deed of gift drafted by the organization or donor is appropriate. A deed of gift is a writing that identifies or inventories the property, to be transferred, along with a statement signed by the donor demonstrating an intent to transfer. See a sample deed of transfer in Appendix, CD-ROM Documentation, Agreements.

Certain types of tangible personal property have a formal title transfer mechanism. For example, automobiles and recreational vehicles must be transferred at a registry of motor vehicles, and yachts and boats are transferred at the appropriate state agency or registry.

(d) Related Use

A donor who makes a gift of tangible personal property obtains a charitable income tax deduction, limited to the cost basis of the property, and may use the deduction in an amount up to 50 percent of the donor's adjusted gross income, unless the property has a use related to the exempt purposes of the nonprofit organization. For property that has a use related to the exempt purposes of the nonprofit, like other gifts of appreciated property, the donor claims a charitable income tax deduction equal to the fair market value of the property limited to 30 percent of the donor's adjusted gross income, if the property has been held by the donor for at least a year and a day to qualify as a long-term capital asset. In order for the property to have a related use, it must be "reasonable to anticipate" that the charity will use the property in a way related to the mission of the nonprofit for its exempt purposes. The related use limits only the charitable income tax deduction and does not apply to the estate tax charitable deduction or the gift tax charitable deduction.

To satisfy the related-use test, there must be a connection between the property and the nonprofit organization. For example, a gift of art is almost always related to the exempt purpose of the nonprofit if it is placed on display. A painting given to a museum clearly satisfies the related-use rule. The IRS, in a Private Letter Ruling, allowed a gift of art to a retirement home that placed the artwork on display in the home to satisfy the related-use test because the object enhanced the residents' living environment.[1] It follows that a strong argument can be made that a gift of artwork to be displayed at a university or hospital should also pass the related-use test. Examples of other gifts that pass this test include books donated to a school library and medical equipment given to a hospital. Property that a nonprofit sells upon receipt will not pass the related-use test because it is not being used by the nonprofit. Donors who are considering making a gift of tangible personal property should inquire as to whether the property will be used or sold by the nonprofit and may want to obtain a written statement from the nonprofit indicating the anticipated use of the property or under some circumstances to impose restrictions in the deed of gift on the use of the property.

(e) Gift of a Future Interest in Tangible Personal Property

Occasionally donors attempt to make a gift of a future interest in tangible personal property to a nonprofit organization. A future interest is a future right to ownership of the property subject to an intervening interest in, or the right to the use or possession of the asset. A gift of a future interest occurs when a donor transfers ownership by deed of gift to a nonprofit organization and retains the right to the use or possession of the property. For example, a gift of a future interest occurs when a donor attempts to make a gift of a piece of artwork to a museum subject to the donor's right to keep the artwork in the donor's home for life. A similar situation can occur when a donor lends tangible personal property to the nonprofit organization for display, retaining ownership, and including provisions in the donor's estate to transfer the property by specific bequest. In each case, the donor may not claim a charitable income tax deduction for a gift of a future interest in tangible personal property until the donor and all related persons have given up all reserved rights to use or enjoy the property. If the property is transferred to a charitable remainder trust, the trust may sell the property and the deduction is available at that time for the present value of the remainder interest in the property, using the *lesser* of the donor's tax basis or fair market value to determine value.

A gift of a future interest in tangible personal property is analogous to a gift of a retained life estate in a personal residence; however, the tax consequences are different. A charitable income tax deduction is allowed for a gift of a retained life estate in real estate but not for a gift of a future interest in tangible personal property. Through a retained life estate, a donor by deed transfers a future interest in a personal residence to a nonprofit organization subject to a life estate. The donor receives an immediate charitable income tax deduction equal to the fair market value of the remainder interest.

Donors can make a gift of a future interest in tangible personal property, but they may not obtain a charitable income tax deduction until all intervening uses have expired and the donors have relinquished all incidents of ownership, possession, and control.

---

[1] Priv. Ltr. Rul. 81-43-029. (Private Letter Rulings cannot be relied on as precedent.)

(f) Unrelated Use

Property that has an unrelated use or property that is immediately sold by the nonprofit is property that is not related to the purpose or function of the nonprofit's exempt purpose. As mentioned earlier, if the donor makes a gift to a nonprofit of property that has an unrelated use or is sold by the nonprofit, the donor obtains a charitable income tax deduction equal to the cost basis of the property, limited to 50 percent of the donor's adjusted gross income. A donor who wants to make a gift of tangible personal property for which there is no related use may prefer to sell the property and make a gift of the proceeds to obtain a charitable income tax deduction for the fair market value of the property. When selling the property, the donor pays any capital gains taxes due on the appreciation of the property. The nonprofit then receives less than it would if the donor gave the property and the nonprofit sold the contributed property.

(g) Ordinary Income versus Capital Gains Tangible Personal Property

Tangible personal property may be either ordinary income property or capital gains property. Tax treatment differs, depending on the classification of such property. For example, donors who hold tangible personal property that, if sold, would produce ordinary income or short-term capital gain, are entitled only to a charitable income tax deduction equal to the cost basis of the property regardless of its use by the charity.

For a gift of tangible personal property held by the donor as a capital asset, the donor may claim a charitable income tax deduction equal to the fair market value of the property if the donor held the asset for at least a year and a day and the nonprofit can use the property for its exempt purposes. For example, a breeder of thoroughbreds may own horses both for breeding and for sale. The horses for breeding are considered capital gains property, and a gift of these horses to a college of agriculture entitles the donor to a charitable income tax deduction equal to the fair market value of the horses. However, if the donor makes a gift of horses, which if sold by her would produce ordinary income, then the donor obtains a charitable income tax deduction limited to the cost basis.

Artists, authors, and playwrights who donate their personal artistic works are limited to a charitable income tax deduction equal to the cost basis of their work. Even those costs such as paints and canvas used by the artist may not be deductible; they may have already been deducted as business expenses. If the artist were to sell the work, ordinary income would be produced, hence the charitable income tax deduction is equal to the cost basis. Donors of tangible personal property sometimes wish to use their property to establish a planned gift that will provide an income stream and a charitable income tax deduction. The following section explores gifts of tangible personal property made to various gift vehicles.

33.3 GIFTS OF TANGIBLE PERSONAL PROPERTY TO PLANNED GIVING VEHICLES

(a) Charitable Remainder Trust

A gift of tangible personal property to a charitable remainder trust is not deductible at all, if the donor or any family member has a right to income from the trust. Even if the income is payable to persons unrelated to the donor, the gift fails the related-use test because the trust itself, unlike a nonprofit, does not have an exempt purpose. Therefore, a donor who makes a gift of tangible personal property to a charitable remainder trust may never obtain a charitable income tax deduction in excess of the remainder interest in the cost basis of the property. (See Chapter 25 for a discussion of charitable remainder trusts.)

(b) Pooled Income Fund

As in the case of a gift to a charitable remainder trust, a donor making a gift of tangible personal property to a pooled income fund obtains no deduction if he or his family members are entitled to the income. Even if the income is payable to individuals unrelated to the donor, the gift fails the related-use test because the pooled income fund is not a charitable organization. The donor is therefore limited to a charitable income tax deduction of the remainder in the cost basis of the property. Most pooled income funds specifically exclude gifts of tangible personal property to the fund. Like a gift of real estate, a gift of tangible personal property to a pooled income fund dilutes the income interest of all beneficiaries in the event of a delay in the sale of the personal property. (Chapter 24 discusses pooled income funds.)

(c) Charitable Gift Annuity or Deferred Gift Annuity

A gift of tangible personal property to fund a charitable gift annuity or deferred gift annuity is considered an outright gift to a nonprofit and, provided the organization uses the property for its exempt purposes in such a way that the property would otherwise satisfy the related-use test, the fair market value of the property is used rather than the cost basis in calculating the charitable income tax deduction for a gift annuity. However, many charities are unwilling to hold contributed assets acquired to fund a gift annuity and prefer to sell them to generate liquid assets to be used in paying the annuity. (See Chapter 23 for a discussion of charitable gift annuities and deferred gift annuities.)

(d) Gifts Made to Sell at Auction

A gift made to a nonprofit to be sold at auction does not satisfy the related-use test, because the nonprofit will not use it for its exempt purposes. The donor's charitable income tax deduction is limited to the cost basis.

33.4 RECOGNITION FOR OUT-OF-POCKET EXPENSES AND GIFTS OF SERVICES

The concept of recognition by a nonprofit of donor services or expenses differs from the IRS concept of tax deductibility. A nonprofit can choose to bestow campaign credit, club membership, or recognition for services or expenses that would not meet IRS rules for deductibility. Credit for out-of-pocket expenses incurred by a donor, such as for parking or meals, can be given if the donor submits receipts or check copies clearly indicating the service or material purchased. A volunteer may deduct such expenses as a charitable gift incurred in providing needed services to a charitable organization so long as expenses are reasonable.

The most common example of gifts of services is a volunteer's donation of time or expertise to a nonprofit. For instance, a lawyer may donate legal counsel or an accountant may give financial advice. There is no charitable income tax deduction for a gift of services. Donor recognition for donations of out-of-pocket expenses should be awarded within the organization only upon approval of the vice-president for development or the nonprofit's gift review committee.

33.5 SUBSTANTIATION REQUIREMENTS

When a noncash gift is made to a nonprofit, the IRS requires strict reporting. Both the donor and the nonprofit can be penalized if the reporting requirements are not followed.

(a) Form 8283 (Appraisal Summary)

Internal Revenue Service Form 8283 (see Appendix, CD-ROM Documentation, IRS Forms) must be filed by donors, including individuals, partnerships, and S corporations, who make gifts of noncash charitable contributions in certain circumstances. The need to file Form 8283 depends on the status of the taxpayer and the size and type of gift. The following is a summary of Form 8283 requirements:

■ *Gifts valued at $500 or less.* If a gift from an individual donor is valued at $500 or less, the donor does not have to complete Form 8283. However, if the gift to the nonprofit is one of a number of similar gifts donated to one or more charitable organizations, the individual should total the value of the gifts and follow the guidelines for a gift of the total amount. For example, an individual may donate five paintings worth $300 each to five different charities, bringing the total gift to $1,500. This donor is required to complete Form 8283, Part A, for a gift of $1,500. The organization should value the gift(s) for internal accounting purposes.

■ *Gifts valued between $501 and $5,000.* If a gift from an individual is valued between $501 and $5,000, the donation must be reported on Part A of IRS Form 8283, which should be attached to the donor's income tax return. An appraisal is not required. However, the organization should have a copy of the completed Form 8283 for its records.

■ *Gifts valued over $5,000.* If the amount claimed as a charitable income tax deduction exceeds $5,000, the IRS requires that the donor complete Part B of Form 8283, along with the signature of a qualified appraiser and the donee's charity.

■ *Gifts of nonpublicly traded stock.* Nonpublicly traded stock is stock that is not listed on an exchange or not regularly traded. If a donor makes a gift of nonpublicly traded stock, Part B of Form 8283 must be completed, regardless of the value of the stock. A qualified appraisal is required if the value of the stock exceeds $10,000.

(b) Gifts from Corporations

Donors that are publicly traded corporations must file Form 8283 only if the amount claimed as a deduction is over $5,000, and then it needs only to be partially completed in accordance with its instructions. A special rule applies for deductions taken by certain C corporations under Internal Revenue Code Section 170(e)(3) or (4) for contributions of inventory or scientific equipment. When Form 8283 is not required, the nonprofit should ask that a written statement of the gift's fair market value be forwarded for the organization's record-keeping purposes. When gifts of computer hardware or software are involved, each gift should be itemized separately.

33.6 APPRAISALS

A donor must obtain a qualified appraisal when the amount of a noncash gift reported as a charitable income tax deduction exceeds $5,000 unless the donated property consists of:

■ Publicly traded securities

■ Nonpublicly traded stock worth $10,000 or less

■ Property donated by C corporations

A qualified appraiser is an individual who is in the business of making such appraisals. The donor must attach a completed appraisal summary to his tax return.

(a) Art Worth $20,000 or More

In addition to the previously stated requirements for a gift of property, if the total deduction for a gift of art is $20,000 or more, the donor must attach a copy of the completed, signed appraisal (not an appraisal summary) and should be prepared to provide an 8 × 20-inch color photograph or a 4 × 5-inch or larger color transparency of the item. In cases in which the value is less than $5,000 or the donor is not an individual, the donor is encouraged, but not required, to submit an appraisal.

(b) Tax Deductibility of Appraisal

The cost of an appraisal is borne by the donor and is a miscellaneous itemized deduction. Because of the current miscellaneous deduction rules, it is unlikely that most donors will receive any tax benefit from such deductions since only miscellaneous expenses in excess of 2 percent of a donor's adjusted gross income are deductible.

(c) Acknowledgment Letters

The burden of substantiating a noncash gift falls to the donor. The nonprofit should not indicate values for gifts of property, nor should values be included in acknowledgment letters that are sent by the nonprofit to thank donors for their gifts.

33.7 THE GIFT REVIEW COMMITTEE

Many nonprofit organizations establish a gift review committee to approve all gifts of tangible personal property, property other than cash or marketable securities—including gifts of real estate—as well as all restricted gifts, before they are accepted by the organization. A gift review committee also should be consulted on complex, unusual, or potentially controversial gifts. However, it may decide to delegate certain decisions to an appropriate officer at the organization. The committee should be empowered to accept only gifts that can be sold, are of real value to the organization, or can be used by the organization without burdensome management.

The existence of a gift review committee may be useful in a number of instances. For example, when a donor who is well connected with the nonprofit wishes to make a gift of art to the organization, a number of issues must be considered. Is the gift of real value to the nonprofit? If not, is the relationship with the donor sufficiently important for the organization to accept the gift? Does the donor insist that the artwork be displayed rather than sold? If so, do liability issues arise? Will the artwork be safe and properly cared for? Will it be costly to the nonprofit to protect the gift? Where will the artwork be displayed in the organization? Who will make this decision? Questions of this type should be explored and answered before the gift is accepted.

A gift review committee plays an important role in gifts of real estate. For example, a donor wanting to make a gift of real estate may require that the nonprofit use the property for a specific purpose. The gift review committee would be asked to explore the relationship of the donor with the organization; whether the organization actually could use the property as specified; whether maintenance, taxes, and insurance are prohibitively expensive to accepting the gift; and whether the nonprofit has the capacity to manage the property.

(a) Suggested Composition

A gift review committee should be composed of several key officers of the nonprofit organization. The following individuals, or representatives from their offices, should be considered for membership in the committee:

- Vice-president for development
- Director of development
- Director of planned giving
- Vice-president for business affairs
- Comptroller/treasurer
- General counsel

(b) Procedures

A gift-in-kind description form, completed by the development officer working on the gift, should be submitted to the committee along with supporting documentation to help the committee in evaluating the gift. The gift description form should summarize information about the donor who is making the gift; describe the gift being made to the organization, including its value and potential use; and name the program or department that may use the gift. A sample gift-in-kind description form appears in Appendix, CD-ROM Documentation, Administrative Documents, (a) Office Management.

Once the gift review committee gives written approval of a gift, it can be accepted. When a gift is received by a certain department or office, that office should provide proof to the vice-president of development. Proof can be established by a shipping invoice or a letter that the gift is available for pickup. After a gift is received, the vice-president for development or the director of planned giving should send an acknowledgment of the gift to the donor and ask the president of the organization or a representative from the appropriate department to acknowledge the gift, as well as the staff member involved. Any acknowledgment of a gift may include its description but should not, however, include its value.

(c) Restricted Gifts

A gift review committee also should review and approve all restricted gifts to an organization. A restricted gift is any gift on which a donor places special, out-of-the-ordinary restrictions as to its use. For example, real estate donated to a hospital by an individual who requires that the property be used to house physicians from other countries is a restricted gift. Donors sometimes want to be involved in the selection of scholarship recipients for endowed funds. (For further discussion, see Chapter 27.) A gift for which the donor establishes criteria for eligibility, such as in the case of an endowed fund or scholarship, should be reviewed by the gift review committee. Discriminatory restrictions could cause the nonprofit to lose its tax-exempt status or the donor to lose the charitable income tax deduction for the gift.

Businesses that make gifts also may confuse charitable giving with employee benefits. A corporate donor may offer to make a gift to establish a scholarship fund that limits the pool of potential recipients to employees of the corporation. Such restrictions again place the charitable income tax deduction in jeopardy.

(d) Gifts of Real Estate

Before a gift of real estate is accepted by an organization, the gift review committee should approve and recommend acceptance of the property. A gift-in-kind real estate review form in Appendix, CD-ROM Documentation, Administrative Documents, completed by the development officer responsible for the gift of real estate, should be submitted to the committee. A gift of real estate involves many factors that can affect the decision to recommend acceptance of the property. These factors, discussed more fully in Chapter 31, generally include concerns about existing mortgages, ownership, zoning, environmental hazards, and marketability.

CHAPTER THIRTY-FOUR

Gifts of Major Collections

34.1   INTRODUCTION

A gift of a substantial and valuable collection can be an exciting challenge and rewarding opportunity for both a donor and the nonprofit organization. Gifts of collections can be made to a wide variety of charities. Art galleries, museums, educational institutions, and healthcare organizations are typical recipients, but so are many fine, smaller, community-based nonprofit organizations. Collections of art; geological, archaeological, anthropological, or historical objects or artifacts; and other gifts of tangible personal property may complement existing collections or may be the start of a new collection. Collections provide nonprofit staff members with research opportunities and attract visitors and guests who come to the nonprofit organization to see these collections transformed into new and exciting exhibitions. Exhibitions of valuable or unique collections can generate considerable public interest for a charity.

34.2   IDENTIFYING PROSPECTS

There are a number of ways to identify prospects who own collections. Ask donors and prospects about their interests and about whether they have collections. Visits to donors' homes provide opportunities to learn more about hobbies, collections, art, and other personal property. Marketing materials that illustrate the benefits of gifts of collections may encourage individuals who hold valuable collections to contact the charity. Develop marketing materials such as ads, buckslips, and newsletters that promote the benefits of such gifts. Professional advisors also should be included in marketing plans to promote the benefits of these gifts for both the donor and the charity. Included in Exhibit 34.1 is an ad for a collection. The ad can be placed in a variety of the charity's publications. In addition, consider placing ads in magazines devoted to the type of collection to be acquired. For example, a university with a substantial collection of artwork of the 20th century

Exhibit 34.1   Ad for Collection

<ORGANIZATION>

Do You Own a Valuable Collection? You Can Make a Gift of Your Collection to <ORGANIZATION>

You can make a charitable gift of your collection of art, antiques, geological, historical, and archaeological and anthropological artifacts, collectibles, and scientific instruments to <ORGANIZATION>. Your collection can augment an existing collection or can start a new one at <ORGANIZATION>. Gifts of these assets can provide attractive benefits to donors while offering valuable assets for display, exhibits, and research at <ORGANIZATION>:

- <ORGANIZATION> has professional curators experienced in managing collections.
- <ORGANIZATION> has attractive exhibition space for displaying and storing your collection.
- <ORGANIZATION> understands donors and their needs.

If you want to learn more about making a gift of a collection to <ORGANIZATION>, call the Office of Planned Giving. Please contact <NAME>, <TITLE>, at <ADDRESS>, <CITY, STATE, ZIP>, <TELEPHONE>.

may, through an ad, invite interested individuals or serious collectors to view the collection or arrange for a private tour. Through this effort, some individuals may self-identify as potential donors or prospects.

34.3 DONOR CONCERNS

Donors who have large collections often are faced with a difficult decision: What do I do with my collection upon my death? To whom should I transfer it? Who are appropriate beneficiaries? Which charity has adequate storage and display space? Must I divide the collection to make it feasible to be managed? If I divide the collection, is the value of the collection diminished? Who are appropriate charitable recipients? After donors consider these issues, they often realize that one of the best ways to maintain their collections in their entirety is to make a gift of their collections to charity.

(a) Family Members

Most donors with valuable collections want to preserve the collection intact. For many donors, dividing the collection among family members or friends is not an acceptable alternative. Most individual beneficiaries do not have sufficient space to adequately display and store the collection. Donors often confess that the decision about the management and maintenance of their collections is one of the most troubling issues they face. A charity that steps in to accept and maintain the collection is providing a valuable service to the donor and his family.

(b) Outside Advisors

Wealthy donors with valuable collections often rely on professional advisors such as attorneys or certified public accountants for tax and estate planning information. In addition, donors with large collections routinely associate with other collectors who own similar or related collections. These collectors are potential prospects for the charity, and they may be of assistance in setting up displays or serving as a member of a committee to oversee the collection. Invite both the donor's professional advisors and colleagues to the charity to outline the charity's plans for the donor's collection. Not including advisors fosters distrust, and they may sabotage the gift if they are not included.

(c) Emotional Issues

For most donors, their collection is their life's work and memories. Donors are often in love with their collections, and it is often very difficult for them to make a gift even if they understand the very positive benefits that come from such a transfer. Some childless couples treat their collections as if they were their children. They dote, fuss, and care for each and every piece of their collection. Many donors continue to add to their collections right up until the time of their deaths. Give donors time to get used to the idea of making a gift of their collections. Help them realize that the charity is a worthy and capable repository for their collections. Donors who own collections are intrigued knowing that others will have the chance to see their collections. In addition, a gift of a collection is likely to stimulate other gifts of similar collections.

(d) Costs

Donors who make gifts of collections should be counseled by a planned giving officer about the costs involved to manage a collection and that the property itself is non–income producing. (In some cases, the charity may charge a separate admission fee to help finance a worthy collection.) Collections must be managed, displayed, rotated, marketed, and curated, which is expensive. Each donor should be asked to make a gift in support of a donated collection or, more appropriately, to establish endowed funds to support the collection in perpetuity. Once donors understand the costs involved, they are much more likely to provide support to establish an endowed fund providing income to support the collection. Work with the donor to develop an annual budget to properly manage the collection as well as to determine the cost of admission to view the collection.

34.4 NONPROFIT ISSUES

Although collections can make wonderful charitable gifts, they also can be a burden to a charity. Often several nonprofit officials, including a curator, must be involved, and there also may be extensive costs. The charity must have a gift acceptance policy in place to govern gifts of collections. The following are issues that the nonprofit organization should consider.

(a) Nonprofit Officials

For major collections, it is necessary to involve a variety of nonprofit administrators. Handling, accepting, and managing a gift of a substantial collection is often quite complicated, and a nonprofit organization and its staff need to be prepared for such a gift. Staff involved may include a planned giving officer, development staff, president or chief executive officer, the board of trustees, and the academic or departmental staff responsible for managing the collection. The charity's gift acceptance policy may include the names of administrators who should be involved.

(b) Curator

The nonprofit organization should appoint a curator to oversee the collection. The curator organizes the displays and exhibits, maintains inventory, and coordinates publicity about the collections. Funding for the curator is provided by the nonprofit organization if managing the collection is part of the curator's routine duties. If the job of curating the collection falls outside the curator's duties, funding must be provided separately by the nonprofit, the donor, or a third party.

(c) Costs

Collections are labor intensive and expensive to manage. As discussed above, some significant collections must be curated, displayed, stored, maintained, rotated, insured, inventoried, and cataloged. Some charities take digital photographs for use in Internet catalogs. This catalog serves as a living inventory promoting research and marketing opportunities. Determine how the charity will underwrite or absorb the expense of a properly managed collection. If there are inadequate resources to manage the collection, ultimately the donor will be disappointed and the donor or her colleagues will not view the charity as a worthy recipient, discouraging additional gifts.

(d) Policies and Procedures

Policies, procedures, and a gift acceptance policy should be in place, along with a defined process to accept a gift of a collection. Most charities have restrictions on accepting gifts of collections. The nonprofit organization should follow the procedures of its gift acceptance policy for gifts of tangible personal property. The document outlines the policy and procedures to be followed regarding such gifts.

In addition to a general gift acceptance policy, some charities have a committee, often referred to as an art acquisition committee, that oversees the acceptance of gifts of collections or tangible personal property, especially artwork. If the charity has one in place, reread it carefully. If there is no policy, adopt one prior to the need. The policy should require a background check to be conducted on the donor and his family. The background check is conducted to prove that the donor and his family acquired the collection through appropriate means.

(e) Agreements

To transfer property from a donor to a charity, the donor typically executes a deed of gift, a memorandum of understanding, and a curation agreement. These documents are included in Appendix, CD-ROM Documentation, Agreements. The memorandum of understanding outlines the terms of the gift, the intended use of the collections, and the expectations of the donor and the charity. The curation agreement governs the duties of the curator, the requirements of the display, management of the collection, and publicity for public exhibitions.

34.5 DEPARTMENTAL ASSISTANCE

Like all gifts, a gift of a collection can be designated to benefit the charity itself or, more typically, one of its departments. Unlike other gifts, a gift of a collection requires the donee department to have specific knowledge and skill to manage the collection. Depending on the nonprofit organization, the department could be an academic department, a gallery or museum, a library, the charity's "special collections" department, or other department designated specifically for collections.

In accepting a collection, the donor, the development office, and the planned giving staff must develop a good working relationship with representatives of the charity's donee department. This department is responsible for developing and implementing a plan to manage the collection.

34.6 DEACCESSIONING

The term *deaccessioning* describes the sale, removal, exchange, or disposal of tangible personal property or a collection held by a charity. For example, a museum may receive two original paintings of the same subject by an artist. Instead of holding both, the museum may prefer to sell one and use the proceeds of the sale to purchase a new piece for the museum. Standards should be established and a formal process developed to deaccession property. Standards may include issues such as changes in legislation; state, federal, and international law; incompatibility of the collection with the scope and direction of the charity; irreparable damage to the collection; costs to upgrade the collection; unforeseen expenses to maintain a collection; or obsolescence. At the time a collection is transferred, donors should be advised about the charity's policy, procedure, and methodology for deaccessioning the collection.

34.7 EVALUATING THE GIFT

Before a large collection is accepted by a charity, it is important to evaluate the gift. These issues should be explored:

- Is the collection consistent with the themes of the charity's mission, and is it compatible with the charity's other collections?

- What are the costs associated with the management of the collection?

- Which of the charity's departments will have administrative responsibility for the collection?

- Where will the collection be displayed? Stored? Maintained?

- Has the collection been appraised? Should a second appraisal be conducted?

- Are there likely to be any unforeseen burdens placed on the charity if the collection is accepted? Display costs? Storage? Lighting?

- Is the collection likely to generate permanent or temporary interest among patrons, guests, and attendees?

- If the collection is accepted, may it be relocated to a different place at the charity in the future?

- Under what conditions may the collection be sold?

- Must the collection be maintained in its entirety? If so, for how long?

- Have appropriate members of the charity's staff assessed the historical, archaeological, anthropological, scientific, and artistic importance of the collection?

- Has a background check been conducted on the donor?

- Is it likely that the collection or any part of it has been obtained in an unethical, inappropriate, or unlawful way?

- Would displaying the collection in any way bring disfavor to the charity?

- Does the collection or any part of it contain unacceptable material?

34.8 UNACCEPTABLE COLLECTIONS

A number of international and federal laws govern the import or export or culturally sensitive property. In addition, other laws govern the possession of religious or cultural artifacts, archaeological resources, endangered species, and migratory birds. Check with the charity's general counsel or attorney for regulations that pertain to the charity and its collections and prospective collections.

A nonprofit organization usually should not accept collections that contain items that are sacred or hold religious significance, nor should collections of human remains (skulls, skeletons, etc.) be accepted without careful deliberation. Collections containing objects that are poisonous, contain hazardous materials, or are radioactive should not be accepted without prior approval or without separate funding. Collections that require special handling, such as temperature, climate, or humidity controls; air filtration; or light filtration systems, should have prior approval. Collections that require special or costly containers, display stations, or cases should not be accepted without careful consideration.

34.9 THE CURATION AGREEMENT

The curation agreement outlines the duties and responsibilities of the charity in handling and managing the collection. In addition, this document defines the role of the curator. These issues should be addressed in a curation agreement:

- Will the collection be loaned, given outright, or transferred at death by the donor?
- Will the donors underwrite the cost of managing the collection?
    - Display cases?
    - Rotation of collection?
    - Storage?
    - Insurance?
    - Publicity?
- Which department will oversee the collection, and who will be the curator?
- Define the duties of the curator:
    - Label, catalog, and inventory the collection
    - Create displays at the nonprofit
    - Develop displays for traveling exhibitions
    - Promote the collection through marketing materials
    - Maintain inventory and submit copy of annual inventory to donor and nonprofit
    - Chair the collection committee
- Rotation of collection
- Sale, trade, or exchange of pieces within the collection
- Promotion and marketing
- Insurance
- Permission to photograph, reproduce images, or display on Internet Websites
- Digitally or electronically record
- Emergency plans
- Cost of display space or estimated storage space based on square footage price

See Exhibit 34.2 for an example of a curation agreement and Exhibit 34.3 for an example of a memorandum of understanding.

GIFTS OF MAJOR COLLECTIONS

Exhibit 34.2   Curation Agreement for the Collection

<DONORS> and <ORGANIZATION> hereby agree to enter into a curation agreement for the <DONORS> gift of <NAME OF> collection to <ORGANIZATION>. This curation agreement outlines responsibilities of <ORGANIZATION> in accepting the gift and defines the arrangements for the transfer, management, display, and storage of the collection.

Description of Collection
The collection consists of <PROVIDE GENERAL DESCRIPTION OF THE COLLECTION>. In particular, the collection contains <NUMBER, COLOR, TYPE OF PROPERTY CONTRIBUTED IN THE COLLEC-TION>. Each piece of the collection has been inventoried and assigned an inventory number that is located in a catalog. A copy of the catalog is attached to this agreement and is incorporated by reference.

Curator
<NAME, TITLE> shall be appointed curator of the collection on behalf of <ORGANIZATION>. The curator shall be responsible for <DESCRIBE DUTIES OF CURATOR> and for maintaining inventory control on each item in the collection and shall provide an annual report to the donors detailing the location of each piece of the collection.

Selection Committee
A selection committee will be organized and once organized will be responsible for selecting pieces for display and for developing a system to restore the collection so that each piece will be on display at least <NUMBER> year out of <NUMBER>. The committee will consist of <NUMBER> members and shall include two representatives of the donors and three representatives of <ORGANIZATION>.

Initial Funding for Expenses
The cost of cataloging, labeling, transferring, maintenance, display, and storage shall be underwritten by the donors who have provided <$> to cover these expenses. The donors shall receive an annual accounting on the status of the account. The donors agree to provide additional funding during their lifetimes if the original amount is depleted.

Permanent Funding for the Collection
The donors and <ORGANIZATION> have agreed to establish an endowed fund to provide permanent support for the collection with funding provided by the donor in the amount of <$>. A copy of the endowment agreement is attached and is incorporated by reference to this agreement.

Publicity/Brochures
The curator, in consultation with the selection committee, shall draft a press release and other forms of communication regarding the collection. In addition, the curator shall prepare a brochure so that visitors and guests of <ORGANIZATION> will learn about the collection.

Management of the Collection
The curator shall prepare and manage the collection. The collection shall be maintained in its entirety and during the lifetime of the donors, <ORGANIZATION> will not sell, trade, or loan any piece of the collection without the approval of the donors. Upon the death of the donors, the committee will not sell, trade, or loan any piece of the collection without the approval of the selection committee.

Location
It is the intent of the donors that the collection be located in the <LOCATION> of the <NAME> building for a period of <NUMBER> years. After this period, the collection will not be moved without the approval of the selection committee.

Exhibit 34.2   *(Continued)*

Relocation

Should <ORGANIZATION> determine that the collection be relocated, <ORGANIZATION> can do so only if all of the following conditions are met:

1. The new space is equal to the square footage of the previous space.
2. The new building housing the collection is more specifically related to the collection than the previous building.
3. The donors consent to the relocation during their lifetime or, if the proposed relocation occurs following their deaths, their designee approves the move.
4. Describe other conditions.

Deaccessioning

The collection will be maintained in perpetuity. The collection can be deaccessioned only if the following conditions are met:

<DESCRIBE CONDITIONS>

Date	<DONOR>

Date	<ORGANIZATION REPRESENTATIVE>

34.10   TAX CONSIDERATIONS

A gift of a collection is a gift of tangible personal property. Like all gifts of tangible personal property, the property must have a use related to the exempt purposes of the nonprofit organization. If the property has a related use and the property is a long-term capital asset (held for a year and a day), the donor receives a charitable income tax deduction equal to the property's fair market value. If the property is worth $5,000 or more, the donor should have the collection appraised. See Chapter 33 for more information about the tax considerations of gifts of collections.

34.11   LOANED COLLECTIONS

As an alternative to an outright gift, donors may loan collections to nonprofit organizations. Some donors prefer to loan the collection or part of it during their lifetime. Upon their death, by bequest the donor may transfer the collection permanently to the nonprofit organization. Before accepting a loan of a collection, conduct due diligence on the loaned collection as if it were a permanent gift. A gift of a loaned collection is not a completed gift, and therefore the donor does not receive a charitable income tax deduction. A bequest of the collection does result in an estate tax charitable deduction. A donor may give an undivided fractional interest in a collection, allowing the charity to display the collection for one-half of a year. The donor then receives a charitable income tax deduction for one-half of the collection's value.

GIFTS OF MAJOR COLLECTIONS

Exhibit 34.3   Memorandum of Understanding Regarding the <DONOR> Collection

<DONORS'> and the <ORGANIZATION> hereby agree to enter into a Memorandum of Understanding regarding a gift of the <DONORS'> collection of <DESCRIBE PROPERTY>.

It is the intent of the donors to <TRANSFER> their entire collection of <DESCRIBE PROPERTY> to the <ORGANIZATION>. The donors agree to transfer <$> to provide for the cost of transfer, display, and storage. The donors agree to provide additional funding if needed.

The name of <LOCATION> will house select portions of the <DONORS'> collection of <DE-SCRIBE PROPERTY> and the balance of the collection shall be placed in storage. The collection should be managed by <ORGANIZATION'S> Department of <NAME>. It is the expectation of the donors that approximately <AMOUNT/PERCENTAGE> of the collection shall be displayed at all times, and that by rotating the collection, each piece will be on display at least two years out of five with the exception of specific pieces that may be on display permanently in the <LOCATION>. <ORGANIZATION> shall establish a five-member committee for the purpose of selecting pieces from the collection for display. <DONOR> and his designee shall serve as members of this committee.

The parties agree that the collection is to be maintained in its entirety and no sale or trade shall be made of any piece of the collection without the approval of <DONORS>. It is the intent of the parties that the collection shall be maintained in perpetuity by the <ORGANIZATION>.

The parties further agree that a brochure will be produced and printed for display at the <LOCA-TION>. The brochure shall describe the collection and detail significant pieces of the collection. The brochure will state that the collection was provided through the generosity of <DONORS>.

The Department of <DEPARTMENT'S NAME> shall maintain an annual inventory and a copy will be distributed to all parties.

_____	_____
Date	<DONOR>
_____	_____
Date	<DONOR>
_____	_____
Date	Head, Department of <NAME>
_____	_____
Date	<NAME>
	<TITLE>
	<ORGANIZATION>

34.12 CONCLUSION

A gift of a collection can be measured not only by its financial worth but also by the relationship that develops between the donor and the charity. Accepting a collection is a great way to better develop a relationship with a donor and her family, colleagues, and friends. A collection allows the donor and the charity to mutually benefit. A donor who makes a gift of a collection shows trust and belief in the nonprofit organization. From this relationship flows goodwill, additional contributions of collections, and, in many cases, significant financial support. Encourage staff members to consider both the benefits and detriments of collections. Be realistic about the costs associated with managing a collection. Properly document the acceptance of the collection and the duties, rights, and responsibilities of all parties.

Gifts of Life Insurance

35.1 INTRODUCTION

Life insurance is a valuable gift option that can be incorporated into a planned giving program. It is one of a range of charitable gift plans, products, and services that can be offered to an organization's development prospects. Although it has a place in every development program, life insurance should never be viewed as the salvation of the program, but as one arrow in the development quiver. Life insurance may be the most misunderstood and misused of all the charitable gift planning options. It is best used when it is the appropriate option for an individual donor, rather than featured as the centerpiece of a development program. Life insurance must be balanced by a wide variety of other planned giving options and by the organization's needs for current income and future support. This chapter deals with life, variable life, and universal life insurance, not term insurance. See Appendix: CD-ROM Documentation, Correspondence, for a sample letter in response to a request for information about a gift of life insurance.

35.2 DEFINITIONS

Life insurance is a leveraged gift, meaning that for a relatively small sum of money (the premium) a donor can produce a large death benefit. It may take years or decades before the nonprofit receives the death benefit. Gifts made with life insurance sometimes allow a donor to make a substantially smaller gift than he is capable of making and to receive credit from the organization greater than the actual value of the gift. However, for some donors the only way to make a significant gift is through life insurance. State law should be checked regarding life insurance gifts, not only for the state in which the nonprofit organization is located, but also for the state in which the donor resides.

This list defines terms associated with life insurance:

- The *subscriber* or the *insured* is the individual who takes out a life insurance policy.

- The *insurer* is the company or carrier of the life insurance policy.

- The *beneficiary* is the one who receives the benefit upon the death of the insured. The nonprofit is the beneficiary for charitable gifts of life insurance.

- The *premium* is the cost of the policy paid to secure coverage. It may be paid monthly, quarterly, or annually, or in certain cases as a single premium paid up front.

- The *owner of the policy* is the one who has the right to select the beneficiary and the right to cash in the policy. The nonprofit is often the owner of a gifted life insurance policy.

- The *death benefit* or *face value* reflects the amount of money that is paid to the beneficiary upon the death of the insured.

- The *cash surrender value* is the amount the subscriber or insured would receive from the insurance company if the policy were cashed in. The cash surrender value reflects the value of premiums paid and any investment growth, minus administrative expenses.

35.3 LIFE INSURANCE AGENTS AND PLANNED GIVING

Planned giving programs in need of development success sometimes become targets for life insurance agents. Sensing an opportunity, agents may encourage the nonprofit to mass market life insurance brochures to all donors, prospects, and those listed in the program's entire data base. Even worse, a planned giving officer may promote life insurance to the exclusion of other forms of planned gifts.

35.4 WAYS TO USE LIFE INSURANCE TO PROMOTE MAJOR GIFTS

Life insurance can be used like a bequest in that a donor, often older, transfers an insurance policy to a nonprofit organization. As in a bequest, the nonprofit receives a lump-sum payment upon the death of the insured. The policy may be either a fully or partially paid-up policy. There are different tax consequences for gifts of fully and partially paid-up policies, which are explored in subsequent paragraphs.

When a donor makes an outright gift of a life insurance policy to a nonprofit, he should name the nonprofit as owner and beneficiary of the policy. By so doing, the donor completely gives up ownership of the policy, waiving the right to assign or borrow against the policy or to change the beneficiary.

Well-intentioned donors sometimes have financial setbacks and are unable to continue paying the annual premiums, or their association with the nonprofit ends and they do not wish to complete payments. The lapsed policy then creates a problem for the nonprofit. The nonprofit must decide whether to continue to make payments or to cancel the policy, based on the amount of premiums contributed to date, thus reducing the death benefit and the ultimate gift to the nonprofit. Donors may be required to have a medical examination to determine insurability.

(a) Charitable Income Tax Deduction for an Outright Gift of a Paid-up Policy

If a donor completely relinquishes control over the policy by naming the nonprofit as owner and beneficiary, she obtains a charitable income tax deduction for the paid-up life insurance policy's replacement value, the cost to purchase an identical policy. If the replacement value exceeds the donor's basis (cost), the deduction is limited to the basis. The donor can deduct up to 50 percent of her adjusted gross income in the year the gift is made and can carry the deduction forward for up to five additional years.

(b) Outright Gift of a Partially Paid-up Life Insurance Policy

A donor may want to name a nonprofit as owner and beneficiary of a life insurance policy that is only partially paid up. It is necessary to ascertain whether the donor intends to pay the remaining premiums or if the nonprofit is accepting the obligation of continuing payments; both arrangements have advantages and disadvantages. If the organization assumes responsibility for making the payments, it must structure a payment procedure to ensure that payments are made in a timely manner. The better practice is to have the donor make the payments to the nonprofit. If the donor makes the payments directly to the life insurance company and is late in making a payment or stops altogether, the nonprofit is less likely to be informed and the policy could lapse and its value be lost altogether or significantly reduced. It is also more difficult for the organization to acknowledge a donor who is making payments directly to the insurer, and the donor may feel less connected to the organization than if he makes the checks payable directly to the organization.

If the donor makes the payments to the nonprofit and the nonprofit then makes the payments to the insurer, a stronger relationship is likely to build between the organization and the donor. Moreover, the planned giving officer is better able to monitor the payments and ensure that the premiums are paid on time. A life insurance gift that requires a donor to make annual premium payments is an excellent annual giving tool.

(c) Donor's Charitable Income Tax Deduction for a Partially Paid-up Policy

A donor's charitable income tax deduction for a partially paid-up life insurance policy is based on the value of the "interpolated terminal reserve." This is an amount that reflects the daily current value of the policy when it is donated between policy anniversary dates and is slightly more than the cash surrender value—the amount the insured would receive if the policy were cashed in to the insurance company. This amounts to the value of premiums paid plus any investment growth minus any administrative expenses. The charitable income tax deduction is limited to 50 percent of a donor's adjusted gross income.

(d) Donor's Charitable Income Tax Deduction When Donor Makes Premium Payments

If the donor makes insurance premium payments in cash directly to the insurer, her charitable income tax deduction may be limited to 30 percent of her adjusted gross income. The reason for this limitation is that the gift is considered "for the benefit of" the nonprofit, rather than a gift to the nonprofit. If the donor makes the payments directly to the charity, the charitable income tax deduction is increased to 50 percent of the donor's adjusted gross income.

35.5 POLICY DIVIDENDS

Life insurance policies produce earnings, or dividends, that can be paid to the owner or may reduce the costs of the insurance policy premiums. Dividends are typically insignificant, except in the case of exceptionally large policies. Many organizations find that a gift of dividends to the nonprofit is small, whereas the paperwork associated with the gift is quite time consuming, and choose not to promote this type of gift option.

35.6   SHORT-TERM ENDOWMENT POLICIES

Some development offices may see short-term endowment policies (STEPs) as a quick fix for a development program. Through a STEP, a donor makes a series of five to eight annual gifts to cover the premium on the policy. In the insurance business, these policies are called five-pay or eight-pay policies. The nonprofit is the owner and beneficiary of the policy. The annual premiums will produce a death benefit of 10 to 15 times the sum of the annual premiums, depending on the age of the donor. Short-term endowment policies often generate a greater benefit for the agent and the life insurance company than for the nonprofit. Short-term endowment policies programs also create crediting problems, discussed in a later paragraph.

35.7   STUDENT LIFE INSURANCE PROGRAMS

Some nonprofit educational organizations have considered using life insurance to insure current students as a way to build future endowment. Such students are usually linked categorically as honor students or members of an athletic team, a band, or an art club. The student agrees to be insured, names the nonprofit as the owner and beneficiary of the life insurance policy, and may have to have a simple medical examination. The money for the premium usually comes from a donor, the operating budget, or the endowment of the nonprofit. A single-premium life insurance policy on a student 22 to 26 years old costs approximately $5,000 for a death benefit of $350,000.

Although student life insurance programs can constitute a creative way to build endowments, there are significant public relations problems associated with these programs. In the event of a student's premature death, the nonprofit organization is negatively perceived to be a fortuitous beneficiary. It is wise to consider seriously the pros and cons before embarking on this type of program.

35.8   INSURANCE USED IN ASSET REPLACEMENT TRUSTS

Donors often struggle between a desire to achieve philanthropic goals and the need to preserve assets for their families. Life insurance may be a solution that enables a donor to make a major gift while putting the estate back into the position it was in before the gift was made. Donors can make a major gift and simultaneously fund an asset replacement trust that is irrevocable. The arrangement usually works as follows: In anticipation of receiving tax benefits, and possibly a stream of income from their gift, donors (typically a husband and wife) fund an irrevocable trust with cash naming as current beneficiaries individuals such as the donor's children. The trustee of the trust uses the cash from the benefits of the gift to fund a "second-to-die" life insurance policy on the donors that is owned by the trust. A second-to-die policy reduces the overall cost of the life insurance, because the policy accumulates retained earnings and pays a death benefit only upon the death of the surviving spouse. The second-to-die life insurance policy may be purchased for approximately 3 to 8 percent of the death benefit or face value of the policy. The actual cost depends on the insurance carrier and the age and health of the donors. Because costs vary, donors should shop for a carrier that offers competitive premiums, and because the death benefit will not be paid for some time, the donors should be sure to select a life insurance company that is financially secure. Upon the death of the survivor, the beneficiaries (typically the donors' children) receive the death benefit of the insurance policy. Because the death benefits pass outside the estate to the children, federal estate taxes are avoided. The funding of the irrevocable life insurance policy will be treated as a gift for gift tax purposes. Through an asset replacement trust a donor can make a major gift to a nonprofit but still provide for family members.

35.9 FUNDING A CHARITABLE REMAINDER NET INCOME UNITRUST/FLIP TRUST WITH LIFE INSURANCE

As discussed in Chapter 25, a donor can fund a net income or an income-only charitable remainder unitrust. A net income unitrust pays to a beneficiary, for life, the lesser of the stated percentage or the net income earned. This type of unitrust can be funded with life insurance on the life of the grantor, which will provide income to the grantor's spouse as a life-income beneficiary. Such a trust should be structured as a so-called flip unitrust, which, upon the death of a grantor, flips over to become a straight percentage payout unitrust, providing the spouse with an annual payment based on the fair market value of the assets. The grantor, through the unitrust, is able to make a series of payments to cover the cost of the premiums. The payments will be treated as additional cash contributions to the unitrust and as such will produce a charitable income tax deduction for the remainder value. Remember that a key characteristic of a unitrust is that additional contributions can be made to it, whereas only one contribution can be made to an annuity trust, which makes the unitrust the preferred vehicle for life insurance.

35.10 GUIDELINES FOR THE PLANNED GIVING OFFICER

(a) Exclusivity for Life Insurance Companies

The planned giving officer who wants to embark on a planned giving effort that includes life insurance must recognize that many donors, prospects, and friends of the organization are life insurance agents who work for specific companies. Board members also may have relationships with particular insurance companies or salespersons. Keeping this in mind, do not offer exclusivity to any one agent or company; otherwise, key individuals may become alienated. Never release a list of donor names to an insurance company representative. Prospects are valuable to the organization and must be protected.

Occasionally an organization develops a relationship with an insurance agent or company, and the question may arise as to whether a member of the development staff can become an agent of the insurance company to facilitate the issuing of policies. This is not advisable because it creates a potential conflict of interest.

(b) Reporting Requirements

A life insurance gift is a noncash gift and must be reported on Form 8283 (discussed in Chapter 33) if a donor claims a charitable income tax deduction for $5,000 or more. The donor is also required to provide a qualified appraisal of the policy.

(c) Crediting

There is no one answer as to how to credit gifts of life insurance. Life insurance policies can be credited based on the donor's charitable income tax deduction; an organization may choose to credit the life insurance gift based on its cash surrender value; or, in the case of a non-paid-up policy, the organization may credit the gift based on the premiums paid. A donor should never receive credit for a gift of the face value of the policy.

(d) Administration

A hidden aspect of gifts of life insurance is the staffing necessary to administer the policies. If the donor makes payments to the nonprofit to cover premiums, the nonprofit must issue a check to the life insurance company. Each life insurance company is different, however, and staff members should become familiar with the payment procedures. To make a claim for a death benefit on a policy in which the organization is a beneficiary, it is necessary to know that the insured has died. Many thousands of dollars in premiums are lost, having been paid toward policies on which nonprofits will never collect, simply because donors' addresses are lost and the nonprofits are unable to make claims.

## CHAPTER THIRTY-SIX

Gifts of Nontraditional Assets[1]

36.1 INTRODUCTION

Nonprofit organizations seek gifts that include cash, securities, real estate, and tangible personal property. Individuals who support a nonprofit, including its donors, employees, researchers, and faculty, may hold a variety of valuable but nontraditional assets, but both the nonprofit and the prospective donor may be unaware of their worth and unique requirements for transfer. These assets include intellectual property, such as patents, copyrights, trademarks, inventions, and royalties, and other types of property, including installment sales contracts, series EE and HH bonds, and oil and gas interests. In addition, corporate donors can make gifts of inventory; qualified contributions of inventory for the ill, needy, or infants; or certain scientific property for research. Special tax rules affect the charitable income tax deductions for gifts of these assets.

    This chapter provides an overview of the unique requirements involved in transferring intellectual property, inventory, installment sales contracts, and government bonds, as well as the issues involved in transferring gifts of oil and gas interests to nonprofit organizations. The chapter then examines the tax treatment for donors who wish to obtain charitable income tax deductions for gifts of such property and suggests ways to cultivate donors who hold these nontraditional assets. In many cases legal advice is required to assure proper transfer of the asset. Appendix, CD-ROM Documentation, Administrative Documents, includes donor intake questionnaires and a deed of gift form to assist planned giving officers in handling gifts of these types of assets.

---

[1] Portions of this chapter were adapted from David M. Donaldson and Carolyn Osteen, *A Manual: Tax Aspects of Charitable Giving* (Boston: Ropes and Gray).

36.2   INTANGIBLE ASSETS

The nonprofit takes on few, if any, ongoing obligations or responsibilities when accepting a gift of an intangible asset such as a patent, copyright, or royalty. Most of these assets are passive ones that require low maintenance and little care, but can provide important sources of income to nonprofit organizations. In most cases, the income stream is linked to the success of the underlying asset (e.g., a right to royalty income from a book is linked to the book sales). Alternately, if there is a market for the asset, it may be sold to a third party and the proceeds used to support the mission of the nonprofit, consistent with the wishes of the donor. When intangible assets are given to the nonprofit organization, they must be appraised by a qualified appraiser who is knowledgeable about intangible assets. Because nontraditional assets are noncash assets, Internal Revenue Service (IRS) Form 8283 must be filed by the donor with his federal income tax return for the year of the gift if the appraised value of the asset exceeds $5,000. Form 8282 must be filed by the charitable recipient with the IRS if the property is sold within two years.

(a) Patents

The holder of a patent can make a gift of the patent to a nonprofit organization. A *patent* is defined as a document granting the right to produce, sell, or receive profit from an invention or process for a specific number of years. A patent is considered a capital asset in the hands of the inventor or a transferor. (Capital assets are discussed in Chapter 33.) As with gifts of tangible personal property, a patent or other intellectual property must be appraised to determine its value. As long as the donor transfers her entire interest in the patent, including all rights to royalties, the donor receives a charitable income tax deduction equal to the appraised value of the patent based on the anticipated stream of income to be produced by the patent. For example, if a donor transfers a patent that is expected to produce $10,000 annually for 10 years, the present value of the gift, discounted at 8 percent, is $67,100. Appropriate steps to record the change of ownership of the patent must be taken to effectuate the gift.

(b) Copyrights

A *copyright* is an exclusive right to a publication, production, or sale of the rights to a literary, dramatic, musical, or artistic work, or the use of a commercial print or label, granted by law for a specified period of time to an author, composer, artist, distributor, or publisher. A holder of a copyright receives income for the right of another to use the copyright. A work that is copyrighted, such as a manuscript or a piece of art, consists of two parts: the copyright and the underlying work that the copyright protects. A transfer of either alone is considered a transfer of a partial interest. Under the partial interest rules, a charitable income tax deduction is not allowed for transfers of property in which the donor retains an interest or transfers less than the whole, except for certain prescribed circumstances. To be eligible for a charitable income tax deduction, a donor must transfer the work along with a written agreement transferring the copyright. Appendix, CD-ROM Documentation, Agreements, is a sample statement to transfer a work of art and copyright.

For purposes of estate and gift taxes, the donor may give either the work of art or the copyright without violating the partial interest rule and may deduct the fair market value of the gift. For purposes of the income tax deduction, the donor must give both the work itself and the copyright. Moreover, if the donor is also the creator of the copyrighted work of art, this property is ordinary income property, and the charitable income tax deduction is limited to the cost basis. If the donor is not the creator, and the donor's tax cost or basis is not derived from the donor's, but the donor is the holder of both the copyright and the work of art, then the donor receives a charitable income tax deduction equal to the current appraised value, as long as the property was held for a year and a day or longer.

(c) Royalties

A *royalty* is a share of the proceeds or product paid to the owner of a right, such as a copyright or patent, for permission to use it or operate under it. For example, the author of a book is paid a royalty by the publisher; the holder of a patent is paid to authorize its use by a manufacturer. The donor must transfer or assign the copyright along with the royalty payments. Under the assignment of income rule, a donor may not avoid being taxed on the income received by assigning the income to another while retaining the property that generates the income. If the donor transfers both the royalty payments and the copyright that produces the royalty, then the donor receives a charitable income tax deduction equal to the appraised value of the copyright and the value of future streams of income. When royalty payments are received by a charitable organization, they are specifically exempt from the unrelated business income tax.

36.3 INVENTORY

(a) Overview

Inventory includes products, goods, or stock purchased or produced for sale to a third party, such as by a manufacturer who sells to retail customers. Donors who make a gift of inventory to a nonprofit organization receive a charitable income tax deduction that may not exceed the cost basis of those goods, because this property is ordinary income property and the manufacturer is the creator of the property. For example, if a piano manufacturer makes a gift of one of its pianos, the manufacturer receives a charitable income tax deduction equal to the raw materials used to construct the piano, unless the cost of materials has already been deducted as a cost of doing business. If the same piano was sold to a dealer for the wholesale price of $3,000, and the dealer made a gift of the piano from inventory to a nonprofit organization, the dealer would receive a charitable income tax deduction equal to its cost basis, or $3,000 (again unless the dealer has deducted the acquisition cost as a cost of doing business). If the piano was sold by the dealer to a third party who held it for at least one full year following the date of acquisition and until it became a very valuable antique, a gift of that piano by the third party to a nonprofit organization produces a charitable income tax deduction equal to the appraised value of the property. If the property was appraised at $50,000, the donor would receive a charitable income tax deduction equal to the appraised value, or $50,000, assuming that the piano is used for the organization's exempt purposes. However, for purposes of a gift of inventory, it does not affect the donor's income tax deduction whether the nonprofit retains the gift of inventory or sells it to a third party.

(b) Qualified Contributions of Inventory

The Internal Revenue Code (IRC) permits certain manufacturers to make gifts to a nonprofit organization and obtain a charitable income tax deduction equal to the cost basis of the property plus 50 percent of the appreciation. Under IRC Section 170(e)(3), the manufacturer must be a regular or C corporation and the property must be manufactured by the donor and given to be used for care of the ill, needy, or infants. Under IRC Section 170 (e)(4), such gifts may be made by a C corporation that is the manufacturer of scientific property to be used for certain kinds of research or experimentation in the physical or biological sciences within the United States. The specific requirements for gifts of qualified contributions of inventory follow.

(i) Qualified Contributions—Gifts for the Ill, Needy, or Infants. For a gift to be considered a qualified contribution as defined in IRC Section 170(e)(4), the property transferred must meet these criteria:

- The property must have a use related to the exempt purposes of the nonprofit.
- The property must be used by the donee nonprofit solely for the care of the ill, the needy, or infants.

- The property must not be transferred by the donee in exchange for money, other property, or services.

- If the property is subject to regulation under the Federal Food, Drug and Cosmetic Act, the property must satisfy the applicable requirements.

- The donor must be a C corporation, not an S corporation.

- The donee must be a so-called public charity eligible to receive the said gifts, not a private foundation.

- The donor must receive from the nonprofit organization a written statement indicating that the property will be used consistent with the terms stated previously. Appendix, CD-ROM Documentation, Agreements, includes a sample statement.

(ii) Qualified Contributions—Gifts of Scientific Property Used for Research. Manufacturers also may make gifts of scientific property used for research and receive favorable tax consequences. To qualify a gift of scientific research property as a charitable contribution under IRC Section 170(e)(4), the property must meet these criteria:

- The property must be tangible personal property.

- The property must normally be considered inventory in the hands of the corporation or property held primarily for sale to a customer.

- The contribution must be to an eligible educational institution or to an eligible scientific research organization, such as a hospital or medical research center.

- The property must have been constructed by the donor corporation.

- The property contributed must be transferred within two years of the date of construction.

- The original use of the property must be by the donee.

- The property must be scientific equipment or apparatus used by the donee for research or experimentation, or for research training in the United States in the physical or biological sciences.

- The property must not be transferred by the donee in exchange for money, other property, or services.

- There must be a written statement regarding the use and disposition of this property. Appendix, CD-ROM Documentation, Agreements, includes a sample statement.

36.4 INSTALLMENT SALES

A donor can make a gift of an installment sale obligation to a nonprofit organization. An *installment sale* is a method of reporting gains from the sale of property when at least one payment is received in a tax year following the year of sale. Under the installment method, gain is prorated and is recognized in the years in which the payments are received. The installment treatment allows the taxpayer to defer the gain realized until such time as the deferred cash payments are made. A portion of the gain is taxable as received; the taxable amount is determined by multiplying the payments received in that year by the gross profit ratio for the sale. The gross profit ratio is equal to the anticipated gross profit divided by total contract price. For example, if the gross profit is $100,000 and the contract price is $900,000, the ratio is $100,000 ÷ $900,000, or 1/9. A gift of a note from an installment sale to a nonprofit organization, if permitted by the terms of the note, is treated as a disposition of the installment sale obligation.

Upon the disposition of an installment sale obligation, the donor would recognize the deferred gain and would be taxed immediately. Gain must be recognized to the extent of the difference between the basis of the obligation and its fair market value. The recognition of gain is not itself necessarily a bar to a gift of an installment sales contract, but it makes the gift unattractive if the donor wishes to avoid tax by making the gift. For donors who have already recognized much of the gain and where there is a relatively small portion of deferred gain, a gift of an installment sales contract may be an attractive option. A gift of an installment sale obligation will require that the donor obtain an independent appraisal and file Form 8283 as described earlier. Exhibit 36.1 illustrates the computation of an installment sale obligation.

Exhibit 36.1 Gift of an Installment Sale Obligation

In 1982, Mrs. Gordon sold a parcel of real estate for $20,000 in cash plus a note calling for 10 annual installments of $8,000 with annual interest at 10 percent, for a total purchase price of $100,000. If Mrs. Gordon's basis is $20,000, the total gain is $80,000. Under the installment method, the first payment of $20,000 consists of two parts: part one represents a $16,000 capital gain and part two represents a $4,000 return of cost basis. To determine the percentage of the gain, divide the cost basis by the sale price ($20,000 ÷ $100,000) or 20 percent and multiply it times the gain of $80,000; the result is $16,000. The balance of $4,000 ($20,000 - $16,000 = $4,000) is allocated to the donor's original cost basis. The payment made at the end of the first year, and for each succeeding year, of $8,000 consists of $6,400 as capital gain and $1,600 as cost basis. As each payment of $8,000 is made, 8 percent of the gain or $6,400 is recognized and the balance of $1,600 is allocated as cost basis. If Mrs. Gordon were to give the note to a charity in 1990 when eight of the installments had been paid, and after she had recognized $67,200 of the gain, Mrs. Gordon would be entitled to a charitable income tax deduction based on the then fair market value of the note. However, the gift of the note would trigger immediate recognition of the balance of the gain, $12,800, which represents the gain element of the last two unpaid installments. The nonprofit receives the remaining installments, providing a source of income. The nonprofit organization can also sell the installment sale obligation to a third party or can borrow against the obligation. The gift can be reported as a pledge or booked based on the present value of the stream of income.

36.5 SERIES EE AND HH BONDS

Series EE savings bonds are discount bonds purchased for 50 percent of their face value. The difference between their value at maturity and their purchase price is interest. The interest is taxed at the donor's ordinary income tax rate. The interest can be reported annually or deferred until maturity. At maturity, series EE bonds also can be traded for HH bonds that postpone the payment of income tax.

Series HH bonds can be purchased at face value only through the exchange of series EE bonds. These bonds pay interest semiannually until they reach maturity in five years. Donors may not make a gift of a Series EE and HH bond directly to a nonprofit organization without first being taxed on any accumulated income. The income from the bond is considered ordinary income, and the IRS does not allow a donor to avoid the taxation of ordinary income. To transfer the bond, the donor must redeem the bond at a Federal Reserve Bank or an appropriate national bank. Income taxes must be paid on the accumulated interest earned on the bond. The donor may then transfer the proceeds of the bond to a nonprofit organization and receive a charitable income tax deduction equal to the value of the proceeds.

36.6 GIFTS OF OIL AND GAS INTERESTS

For some donors, the value of an oil or gas interest may represent a significant asset, one that can be donated to a nonprofit organization. These gifts can be extremely complicated because they involve special considerations; in most cases, a planned giving officer will work with outside legal counsel specializing in gifts of such property. To help donors who wish to make gifts of these interests, a general understanding about gifts of oil and gas interests is essential. In many ways, a gift of an oil and gas interest uses several of the concepts discussed throughout *Planned Giving: Management, Marketing, and Law* and may even help to clarify their use. These gifts involve partial interest rules, classification of property between ordinary income and capital gains property, unrelated business income, and the assignation of income rule, along with many related planned giving tax concepts.

Oil and gas interests also can represent substantial liabilities to nonprofit organizations. Acceptance of gifts of oil and gas interests should be carefully considered by the nonprofit's gift review committee. Nonprofits that are not aware can become unsuspecting owners of a potentially risky asset. Increased environmental concerns, personal injury awards, and other operational dangers that attach to a gas and oil interest all mandate caution in accepting such gifts. In most cases, a nonprofit may not wish to accept a gift of a working interest in an oil or gas property (working interests are discussed later). Most nonprofits are not equipped to operate an oil or gas property, and, unless the gift is of significant value, the risk may exceed the benefit.

Oil and gas interests are classified as minerals that include solid natural substances such as gold, silver, and natural deposits. The rights of a land owner include both surface and subsurface rights, such as mineral rights. These mineral interests and the rights to extract the minerals may be separated from the surface rights. The right to the mineral interest consists of two parts, (1) the royalty and (2) the working interest, often referred to as the *mineral claim* or *operating interest*. The owner of the mineral rights has the right to extract the mineral from the property but typically does not own the surface under which the mineral resides. The owner of the minerals may transfer a variety of lesser interests to others. Some interests are limited in duration, such as for a term of years. The terminology of oil and gas interests is unfamiliar to most planned giving officers, so a brief summary follows.

- *Fee interests.* Fee interests represent outright and complete legal ownership of real estate.

- *Working interests.* The working interest is the interest in the oil and gas property that complements the royalty interest. The owner of the working interest is responsible for development and operation of the property. The owner of the working interest created by a lease may carve out other interests, such as a production payment or overriding royalty payment to a third party. These interests are coextensive with the working interest, meaning that they do not extend beyond the life of the working interest.

- *Royalty interests.* A royalty is a mineral interest that entitles the owner to a specified fraction of the production, free of development expenses.

- *Leasehold interests.* The holder of the working interest may in turn grant to a lessee a leasehold interest. In most cases, the lease will expire if the lessee fails to develop the property.

- *Overriding royalty interests.* An overriding royalty interest is created from the operating interest, and its term is coextensive with that of the operating interest. The interest is represented by a fraction.

- *Net profit interests.* A net profit interest is an interest in minerals offered as a share of gross production. A net profit interest is created from a working interest and has the same term.

- *Production payments.* A production payment is a right to minerals that entitles the holder to a specified fraction of production until the expiration of a period of time, or until a specified sum of money or a number of units has been met.

- *Carved-out production payments.* The owner of the mineral property may carve out, by selling, transferring, or assigning a portion of future production, with payment secured by an interest in the minerals. A carved-out production payment is treated as a mortgage loan on the mineral property rather than an economic interest. The income is taxed to the seller (the owner of the working interest) and is subject to depletion.

- *Economic interests.* A holder of an economic interest who receives income has a right to a deduction for depletion.

(a) Donor's Entire Interest

Under the partial interest rules applicable to outright gifts, such as gifts of oil and gas interests, no deduction is allowed for a gift of a partial interest unless it is an undivided fraction of the donor's entire interest. Accordingly, no deduction is allowed if a donor makes a gift of less than the donor's entire interest. Internal Revenue Service (IRS) regulations state that a gift of land in which the landowner retains the rights to minerals is a gift of a partial interest for which no charitable income tax deduction is allowed. No deduction is allowed if a fee owner grants a charity a leasehold interest in the oil and gas, or if a holder of a leasehold interest grants a charity a working interest, because in each case the owner has not given the charity all of the owner's rights or an undivided fraction of all the owner's rights. If, however, the donor owns an overriding royalty interest and gives a charity a one-half interest in that royalty interest, the gift is deductible because it represents an undivided fractional interest of all the rights possessed by the donor.

(b) Capital Assets

In most cases, oil and gas interests are capital assets in the hands of the donor, even though they may represent a right to the future income from the property. As discussed in Chapter 33, a *capital asset* is property that does not produce ordinary income upon its sale and is not held as property for sale to customers. To be a long-term capital asset, the property must have been held for at least a year and a day.

If the donor is in the oil and gas business, the oil and gas interest may not be a capital asset but rather ordinary income property, producing a charitable income tax deduction limited to its cost basis. Even if the donor is in the oil and gas business, if the interest can be characterized as real property used in a trade or business so as to qualify as so-called Section 1231 property, a gift of Section 1231 interest may generate a deduction based on fair market value. Under some circumstances, business real estate and depreciable business property are not considered capital assets. However, some business property qualifies as Section 1231 property; if gains from sale or disposition of this property exceed basis and allocable costs or losses, then the gain is treated as if produced from the sale of a long-term capital asset. Internal Revenue Code Section 1231 allows the taxpayer to treat gains and losses on sales as long-term gains and losses.

(c) Reduction for Ordinary Income

If the donated interest is a capital asset in the hands of the donor and represents the donor's entire interest, in calculating the charitable income tax deduction the donor is required to reduce the appraised fair market value by the amount of any ordinary income that the donor would have realized had the interest been sold. In the case of oil and gas properties, the most likely source of ordinary income is intangible drilling costs. Thus, if on the sale of the interest the donor would have to treat $100,000 of intangible drilling costs as ordinary income, the donor will have to reduce the charitable contribution deduction by the amount of the so-called recapture amount ($100,000). In other cases the donor would have been forced to treat some part of the sale proceeds as recaptured depreciation, (i.e., as ordinary income). In that case the donor's deduction is also reduced by the recaptured amount.

(d) Bargain Sale

A gift of property subject to an indebtedness is taxable as a bargain sale, even if the donor is not personally liable for the indebtedness. Such indebtedness is often referred to as *nonrecourse debt*. The at-risk rules require a taxpayer to be personally liable to receive tax benefits for oil and gas interests that are financed, and thus it is unlikely that an oil and gas interest will be subject to indebtedness unless the debtor has personal liability. Carved-out production payments are treated as loans for tax purposes, and thus a gift of a working interest (or an overriding royalty interest) from which a production payment has been carved out may be treated as a bargain sale on the ground that the transfer relieves the donor of the liability for the carved-out production payments.

(e) Valuation

In calculating the amount of the donor's charitable income tax deduction, first the fair market value of the oil and gas interest must be determined through an appraisal by a qualified expert. A reserve analysis is conducted on the property to determine the value of the oil or gas remaining. Assuming that the interest relates to property on which oil or gas has been found and that the property is producing revenue, the operator should be able to furnish the donor with a cash flow projection indicating the expected cash flow from the property. The future cash flow is first discounted by an appropriate factor to determine its present value; then, depending on the nature of the property, a further discount may be applied to reflect the risk that the projected cash flow may not be realized. If the interest represents a minority interest in a partnership, a further discount may be required to reflect the minority status, unless the charity can readily dispose of the donated interest. Exhibit 36.2 is an illustration of the computation to calculate a donor's charitable income tax deduction for a gift of oil or gas.

Exhibit 36.2   Gift of Oil and Gas Interest

Mr. Johnson is the owner of underdeveloped property which has the potential to produce oil or gas. Mr. Johnson acquired the property for $100,000 in 1993. To develop the property, Mr. Johnson invested $100,000 in intangible drilling costs and purchased equipment for $50,000. A qualified appraiser has valued Mr. Johnson's interest at $500,000 including equipment. Mr. Johnson's basis of $100,000 has been depleted. The following is used to calculate the charitable income tax deduction for a gift of Mr. Johnson's interest to a nonprofit organization.

The charitable income tax deduction is equal to the appraised value reduced by recaptured depreciation, depletion, and intangible drilling costs:

$500,000	Appraisal value
($ 20,000)	Recapture of depreciation of equipment
($100,000)	Recapture of intangible drilling costs
($100,000)	Recapture of depletion (depletion is allowed up to basis)
$280,000	Charitable income tax deduction

(f) Partnership Indebtedness

Oil and gas interests frequently are held in the form of an interest in a limited partnership. A gift of a partnership interest in property that is subject to an indebtedness requires the partner to treat the gift as if she had sold the partnership interest for her allocable share of the indebtedness, whether or not the partner is personally liable for the partnership liabilities.

(g) Unrelated Business Income

Before the charity accepts a gift of an oil and gas interest, it will want to determine what income (as opposed to cash flow) is projected for the partnership interest and whether that income will be taxable to the charity. The definition of *unrelated business income* excludes "all royalties (including overriding royalties) whether measured by production or by gross or taxable income from the property."

(h) Form of the Gift: Use of Oil and Gas Investments in Charitable Lead Trusts

In a depressed market for oil and gas interests, the discounts used in valuing an oil and gas interest may result in an appraised fair market value below the economic value of the investment to an investor who has the patience and resources to hold the property for a number of years. As such, although the discounts may discourage outright or remainder gifts of oil and gas interests, the same factors may make oil and gas interests an interesting vehicle for a lead trust. If an oil and gas interest produces sufficient return to meet the lead payout to the charity and has potential for future growth, as with most gifts of property likely to appreciate, the discounts used in valuing the interest help to guarantee that the donor's gift to his heirs will grow in value.

As in the case of an outright gift, a transfer of an oil and gas interest to a lead trust will result in the realization of gain to the extent of any liabilities attributable to the interest. The trustee of the trust and the donor will need to confirm that the transfer of the interest subject to indebtness is not an act of self-dealing as defined in Section 4941 and to assess the extent to which it may cause the trust to lose all or part of its income tax deduction, causing the trust's income to become taxable. Intangible drilling costs, subject to recapture, will result in the realized gain being taxed as ordinary income. However, for a lead trust, the donor is normally concerned only with a gift or an estate tax deduction; thus, the fact that the property given represents ordinary income property (which would cause a reduction of the income tax deduction) is of little consequence.

(i) Taxation of the Trust. Although a lead trust is always subject to some of the private foundation rules, such as the self-dealing rule, if the value of the lead interest exceeds 60 percent of the fair market value of the assets transferred to the trust, the trust will be subject to the jeopardy investment rules and excess business holdings rules. Therefore, an investment in the oil and gas partnership should be scrutinized to determine whether the investment is speculative and would jeopardize the ability of the trust to carry out its charitable purposes. If the lead trust holds an interest in a corporation or equivalent interest in partnership, the trust may not hold more than a 20 percent interest in that entity. For purposes of the calculation, its interest must be aggregated with those of the donor and members of the donor's family. Although the regulations specifically refer to a working interest in a mineral property as an investment that may jeopardize the charitable purpose of a private foundation, the fact that the interests involved are working interests in oil wells does not necessarily require the conclusion that the investment would jeopardize the carrying out of the trust's charitable purpose.

In determining whether the investment would jeopardize the trust's ability to meet the charitable purpose, the trustee should be entitled to take into account facts such as that the partnership interest represents an unleveraged interest in a great number of wells in a stable and profitable oil field that is not expected to require any further investment to continue the projected income stream. As long as the trustee can demonstrate that this is the sort of investment that would be made by a prudent businessperson, it would appear that the investment can be defended as one that does not jeopardize the ability of the trust to carry out its charitable purposes.

By contributing a partnership interest to a lead trust, the donor makes the trustee of the lead trust a partner in the partnership. A general partnership interest exposes the lead trust to all the risks of the business and in general is not appropriate for a charitable gift. A limited partnership interest or a limited liability company (LLC) interest exposes the trust to more manageable risks. In either case, the trustee is deemed to be engaged in the business of the partnership. If the partnership or LLC is throwing off income that would be unrelated business income if it were received directly by the charity, the ability of the lead trust to deduct a portion of the unrelated business taxable income is limited. In effect, the IRS disallows an unlimited charitable deduction for unrelated business income that is earned by a nonexempt lead trust; as a result, a trust's ability to deduct a distribution is subject to the same limitations applicable to contributions made by individuals.

(ii) Depreciation and Depletion. The trust instrument should be drawn so that depletion and depreciation deductions are allocated to the trust; otherwise, all or a portion of such deductions will follow the income distributed to the charity and will, therefore, be wasted.

(i) Gifts of Oil and Gas Interests to Charitable Remainder Trusts

Although it is possible to fund a charitable remainder trust with an oil or gas interest, it is seldom done. The discount factors mentioned earlier, which depress the value of the interest, also will depress the deductible value of the remainder interest. Moreover, though unrelated business income may, with careful planning, be absorbed by a lead trust without undue difficulty, any unrelated business income received by a charitable remainder annuity trust or unitrust will cause all income to be taxable. Thus, if an oil and gas interest is to be given to a remainder trust, the interest should be carefully analyzed to ensure that it does not involve unrelated business income.

36.7 TAX CONSIDERATIONS

Most of the basic tax rules for gifts of property such as real estate and tangible personal property pertain to gifts of the special assets discussed in this chapter. Property is classified as either ordinary income property or capital gains property according to the nature of the relationship of the property to the donor. The charitable income tax deduction is in turn based on the classification of the property. A donor who makes a gift of ordinary income property obtains a charitable income tax deduction that may not exceed the property's cost basis. For example, the owner of a gardening center that sells shrubs, plants, and flowers to the public may, in the case of a gift of shrubs, deduct the cost of the shrubs rather than the retail price unless he has already deducted the cost of the inventory as a business expense, in which case he will not get any additional deduction. *Capital gains property* is property held for at least a year and a day that would not otherwise be considered ordinary income property. If the property is a capital asset, held for a year and a day to qualify as a long-term capital asset, the charitable income tax deduction is equal to the fair market value of the property. If the nontraditional asset represents tangible personal property, such as a work of art, its use also must be related to the charity's exempt purpose if the donor is to deduct the full fair market value.

Unlike gifts of marketable securities, where the value of the asset is determined by the trading price, to determine the value of these special gifts, an appraisal must be conducted. In the case of a gift of inventory by a corporation, the rule governing the charitable income tax deduction is similar to a gift of tangible personal property made by the creator; the charitable income tax deduction is equal to the cost basis. See Exhibit 36.3 for an example.

Exhibit 36.3   Illustration of Classification of Property

An owner of thoroughbred horses may raise horses for sale to others as part of the owner's inventory; the owner may also race thoroughbreds. A sale of the horses held for sale to others will produce ordinary income, because they are part of the inventory in the hands of the donor. A gift of these horses to a nonprofit organization will produce a charitable income tax deduction that may not exceed the donor's cost basis in the property. The owner may also hold thoroughbreds for breeding that are considered capital assets; a gift of these breeding thoroughbreds produces a charitable income tax deduction equal to the appraised value, assuming they are used by the donee charity for exempt purposes, not for lease or sale. The way in which the horses are characterized in the hands of the owner determines their classification and the value of the charitable income tax deduction to the donor.

36.8 CULTIVATING PROSPECTS

One of the real challenges is educating the holder of nontraditional assets on the value of the gift to a nonprofit organization. These gifts can provide valuable income streams from royalties, or they may be sold and the proceeds used to establish endowments, professorships, or funds for research, exhibitions, or the construction or renovation of the nonprofit's facilities.

It is essential to cultivate donors who hold nontraditional assets. Cultivation should be directed at those nonprofit departments likely to have staff members or volunteers who are in the fields of medicine, science, engineering, agriculture, business, or art. Members of the faculty and nonprofit researchers may conduct research, provide support, or be consulted for advice on technical applications. Discussions with nonprofit personnel can help to identify holders of nontraditional assets.

For nontraditional assets, cultivation is the process of education. Newsletters, brochures, pamphlets, and presentations to groups likely to be involved can generate leads. Ads and guest columns in departmental publications can elicit responses. Included in Appendix, CD-ROM Documentation, Marketing, is an ad that can help to alert a donor to the attractive benefits of these gifts. Newsletters targeted to donors, friends, or others located in those states also may produce leads. Professional advisors are likely to have clients who hold such assets. In the case of oil and gas interests, some regions of the country, particularly in the southeastern and southwestern parts of the United States, are more likely to have donors holding these interests. A marketing strategy designed to educate donors about the attractive benefits of gifts of these special assets will, over time, produce results.

# PART SEVEN

Planned Giving Related Disciplines

The Tax Consequences of Charitable Gifts

37.1 INTRODUCTION

Charitable giving has become big business in the United States with gifts from individuals accounting for most of the philanthropic contributions. In 2002 over $370 billion in current gifts and bequests were made to nonprofit organizations. To encourage continued private funding of charitable organizations, Congress has provided tax incentives for philanthropic individuals. A donor's charitable intent must be the motivating factor behind making a gift. No amount of tax benefits will cause an individual who does not have donative intent to make a charitable gift. Planned gifts provide a way for philanthropic donors to make gifts to nonprofit organizations and simultaneously enjoy financial and favorable tax consequences.

    Currently, much of this country's wealth is held by older Americans, those age 60 and older. As the population rapidly ages, baby boomers become middle aged, older Americans live longer, and concerns over healthcare and Medicaid increase. The years ahead will see the largest intergenerational transfer of wealth in U.S. history, as trillions of dollars are expected to be transferred from parents to their baby-boomer children. This transfer of assets creates the need for close examination of tax issues, beyond the traditional benefits of income tax savings. Passing wealth on to family members through planned giving options offers an attractive way to provide secure, current income while receiving tax advantages and providing for charity. Charities need to emphasize planned giving techniques that provide needed benefits to donors while building for the charity's future.

As discussed, donors make gifts not because of tax considerations but because of philanthropic motivations that match the donors' interests. However, almost all donors are still motivated to make their gift "taxwise" seeking income, capital gains, estate, and gift tax relief through charitable giving. Planned giving staff members, donors, and their professional advisors must have a comprehensive understanding of the tax consequences of charitable contributions and the underlying tax considerations that can impact charitable giving.

Potentially, four different types of taxes may be involved when a donor makes a single charitable gift: income, capital gains, estate taxes, and gift taxes. In addition to federal taxes imposed by the Internal Revenue Code and assessed by the Internal Revenue Service, a state or local government, sometimes also may assess related taxes. The following is an overview of the tax consequences of charitable giving.

37.2 THE JOBS AND GROWTH TAX RELIEF RECONCILIATION ACT OF 2003

The Jobs and Growth Tax Relief Reconciliation Act of 2003 (JGTRRA) which was passed into law in May of 2003 provides a number of benefits to taxpayers, but impacts, in a small way, charitable giving. Federal income tax rates, capital gains tax rates, and the taxation of dividends are reduced, saving taxpayers money, but offering few new incentives for taxpayers to make gifts of investment assets. Taxpayers may find that the act returns additional discretionary income to their checkbooks and may use some of that surplus to make gifts to charity. The act does not diminish future income tax rate reductions included in the Economic Growth and Tax Relief Reconciliation Act; rather this new act accelerates some provisions of EGTRRA. The major provisions of the act that affect individual taxpayers are as follows:

1. Accelerated 10 Percent Bracket Expansion
   The 10 percent bracket is expanded to apply to $14,000 of taxable income for married couples, rather than 12,000 under EGTRRA.

2. Reduction in Income Tax Rates
   Income tax rates under EGTRRA were 10 percent, 15 percent, 27 percent, 30 percent, 35 percent, and 38.6 percent. The income tax rates were scheduled to be reduced under EGTRRA in 2004–2006. The Act accelerates those lower tax rates retroactive to January 1, 2003. The 2003 tax rates are now 10 percent, 15 percent, 25 percent, 28 percent, 33 percent, and 35 percent.

3. Reduction of Marriage Penalty
   The Standard Deduction for married taxpayers is increased to twice the amount for single taxpayers.

4. Reductions in Tax Rates on Dividends and Capital Gains
   The maximum tax rate on dividends paid by corporations to individuals and individual taxpayers' capital gains is reduced to 15 percent. For taxpayers in the 10 percent and 15

percent ordinary income tax rate brackets, the tax rate on dividends and capital gains taxes is reduced to 5 percent in 2003–2007 and 0 percent in 2008. The new rates apply to capital gains realized on or after May 6, 2003 and dividends received in 2003.

5. Increased in Child Tax Credit
   The amount of the child tax credit is increased to $1000 in 2003 and 2004, accelerating a scheduled phase-in between 2005 and 2010.

Most taxpayers who have the capacity to make major charitable gifts are in the upper tax brackets. Besides paying federal income taxes, in most cases these taxpayers pay state income taxes, assessed on a similar basis, although at lower rates. Donors who are citizens and residents of foreign countries and who have no U.S. income are not subjected to federal income taxation nor do they obtain the tax benefits of charitable giving. Canadian citizens who give to certain U.S. colleges and universities, designated by Revenue Canada because they accept Canadian citizens as students, are permitted to deduct their gifts for Canadian income tax purposes.

(a) Adjusted Gross Income

A donor's adjusted gross income (AGI; contribution base) is an important benchmark in calculating a donor's allowable deductions. The adjusted gross income is the donor's total income derived from all sources, minus deductions for alimony, individual retirement account (IRA) contributions, and other specific expenses and items. The AGI is the starting point for computing the charitable income tax deduction, medical deductions, casualty losses, and miscellaneous deductions. Some deductions may be available only subject to certain limits; for example, only medical expenses (for the donor, spouse, or a dependent) in excess of 7.5 percent of one's adjusted gross income are deductible.

(b) Taxable Income

A donor is taxed on income earned as well as investment income produced by the donor's assets. Personal exemptions and itemized deductions are subtracted from the AGI, resulting in taxable income. One of the most advantageous deductions to income is the charitable income tax deduction. There are two types of taxpayers for federal income purposes: nonitemizers and itemizers. Charitable contributions benefit only those taxpayers who itemize their deductions.

(i) Nonitemizers.   Nonitemizers most likely rent or own a personal residence without a mortgage. Home ownership provides important tax deductions for mortgage interest, real estate taxes, and home equity loan interest. Under current law, taxpayers may not deduct their charitable contributions unless charitable contributions, along with all other permitted deductions such as mortgage interest, real estate taxes, and state income taxes, exceed the estimated standard deduction levels of $7,850 in 2002 for married individuals filing jointly or $4,700 for taxpayers filing singly. Once these levels are reached, these taxpayers can become itemizers. The standard deduction levels are adjusted annually and are indexed to inflation. A donor may choose to accumulate contributions that would otherwise have been made over several years and make them all in a single year instead. By "bunching" ordinary deductions and charitable contributions, a donor may exceed the standard deduction thresholds and qualify as an itemizer. At the time this book went to press, legislative proposals were being considered that would allow nonitemizers to obtain charitable income tax deductions for gifts of cash to charity.

(ii) Itemizers.   For gifts of cash, itemizers may deduct the value of their contributions to public charities up to 50 percent of their contribution based on their AGI. If the entire deduction

cannot be used in the first year, it may be carried over for five additional years. If it is carried over, a donor is required to use as much of the charitable income tax deduction as possible each year up to 50 percent of the contribution base. In other words, a donor may not voluntarily apportion the contribution over several years.

For certain gifts of investment property, such as real estate or securities, if the property has been held for at least one year and a day and would produce long-term capital gain upon sale (a "long-term capital asset"), a donor may deduct the fair market value of the property, up to 30 percent of the donor's contribution base.

Cash gifts must be deducted before gifts of property. To the extent that a donor had given cash gifts greater than 37 percent of her contribution base, gifts of property will be reduced by the excess over 37 percent. Because gifts of cash must be applied first, it follows that the deductibility of gifts of property is affected by cash gifts. The 30 percent limit is not above the 50 percent limit, but is a sublimit within it.

37.3 FAIR MARKET VALUE

Fair market value is the price at which property would change hands between a willing buyer and a willing seller, with neither one being under an obligation to act and both having reasonable knowledge of the relevant facts. If the property is held for a year or less (a "short-term capital asset"), then only the cost basis of the property can be deducted, which is an amount that equals the purchase price of the property.

37.4 THE COST BASIS

The cost basis and the fair market value for cash are the same amount. For gifts of securities, such as stocks or bonds, the cost basis is the purchase price of the securities in addition to any costs associated with the purchase, such as commissions and transfer fees. For real property, the cost basis is the purchase price plus legal fees, recording costs, and settlement or closing costs plus the cost of improvements. For lifetime transfers (property that is transferred by gift), the cost basis to the donees (or recipients of the gift) is the donor's cost basis plus the value of any gift tax paid by the donor.

For property transferred to a donee through one's estate until 2010, the basis is stepped up to the fair market value of the asset at the donor's date of death. For example, if a donor inherited property from his father, his basis is the fair market value of the property as of the date of his father's death. If a donor continues to hold the property and the property appreciates and is later sold, then a capital gains tax is due upon the sale of the asset on the difference between the value of the property at his father's death and the value of the property upon sale. Under the EGTRRA, beginning in 2010, neither heirs nor beneficiaries will receive a stepped-up basis on inherited property in excess of certain amounts. Recipients will acquire the lesser of the fair market value or the decedent's basis plus up to $1.3 million for assets transferred to other beneficiaries and $3 million for certain assets transferred to a surviving spouse.

37.5 DEDUCTIBILITY OF GIFTS OF TANGIBLE PERSONAL PROPERTY

As discussed in Chapter 33, for a donor to obtain a charitable income tax deduction for the full fair market value of gifts of tangible personal property such as artwork, antiques, stamps, and coin collections, there is an additional requirement that it is reasonable to anticipate that the donated tangible personal property will be used in a way that is related to "the business of the charity." The "related use" rule is met if a donor makes a gift of a painting to a museum or a book to a library. This rule applies only to the charitable income tax deduction, not to the estate or gift tax charitable deduction. The purpose of the related use rule is to diminish the charitable income tax deduction for gifts of tangible personal property where there is no related use to the charitable organization's exempt purpose or where the property, even though related, will be sold by the charity immediately at an auction or other event. For most large charities, especially universities, arguably almost any gift of property, such as artwork, can satisfy the related use test since it could be used by at least one of the many departments or for display. However, if the donor knows that the charity intends to sell the property, the gift will fail the related use test. If the property is a gift of long-term appreciated tangible personal property and the charity uses it in a related use, a donor can deduct the fair market value of the property up to 30 percent of the donor's contribution base. If the gift of tangible personal property is unrelated, then the donor's deduction is limited to the donor's cost basis up to 50 percent of the contribution base.

If the donated property is not related to the business of the charitable organization, a donor may prefer to sell the asset and give the proceeds to the charity. In this case, a donor obtains a charitable income tax deduction equal to the proceeds less any capital gains taxes. If a donor makes a gift of "ordinary income property" (property used in her trade), then she may deduct the cost basis of the property, up to 50 percent of her contribution base, assuming she has not already deducted the cost as a business expense, in which case no deduction is allowed. Donors do not receive a charitable income tax deduction for the value of the use of their property, such as a ski condominium or vacation property, contributed for a weekend to a charity or that is auctioned at a charity auction. Only the donor's out-of-pocket expenses, such as cleaning or heating costs, associated with such use may be deducted as a gift.

Volunteers do not receive a charitable income tax deduction for a gift of services, such as time volunteering at the charity. However, the volunteer may receive a charitable income tax deduction for unreimbursed out-of-pocket expenses incurred while serving as a volunteer on behalf of the organization, including transportation expenses.

37.6   ACCELERATION OF DEDUCTION

Taxpayers may utilize an alternative to permit an increase in the percentage of income that may be offset by the charitable income tax deduction. A donor may increase the limitation from 30 to 50 percent of his contribution base for gifts of property if he elects to deduct the cost basis rather than the fair market value. If the asset has not appreciated significantly, he may prefer to elect to accelerate the deduction by choosing to deduct the cost basis rather than the fair market value limited to 50 percent of his contribution base. Example: If a donor bought real estate for $100,000 and the property has a current value of $105,000, she may choose to deduct the cost basis of $100,000 up to 50 percent of her contribution base rather than the fair market value of $105,000 limited to 30 percent of her contribution base income.

37.7   DEDUCTION REDUCTION PROVISION

EGTRRA reduced the value of deductions for upper-income taxpayers. Beginning in 2006, the phase-out provisions for deductions gradually will be reduced, and by 2010, they will be repealed. Until that time, taxpayers will have the total value of their itemized income tax deductions reduced by the lesser of (1) 3 percent of that portion of the AGI that exceeds a base level or (2) 80 percent of their itemized deduction otherwise allowable for the taxable year. The threshold amounts are indexed and change annually.

Itemized deductions include home mortgage interest, real estate taxes, state taxes, medical expenses, excise taxes, charitable deductions, and other miscellaneous deductions. The deduction reduction formula reduces the value of these types of deductions for certain taxpayers. This provision has a negative impact on the value of all deductions (except for medical, investment interest, or casualty and theft losses) including the charitable income tax deduction. However, most wealthy donors have involuntary types of deductions, such as state income taxes and real estate taxes in amounts that exceed the 3 percent threshold; therefore, charitable contributions, which are voluntary, may be considered on top of the 3 percent limit.

(a) Additional Provisions of the EGTRRA of 2001

The EGTRRA made a number of other changes that will impact taxpayers in the years to come. The following summerizes those changes.

- *Itemized deductions and exemptions.* Beginning in 2006 and by 2010, taxpayers will receive full benefit for all income tax deductions and exemptions.

- *Limitations on retirement plan contributions.* The limits on contributions to IRA and Roth IRAs will increase gradually: $3,000 in 2002–2004, $4,000 in 2005–2007, and to $5,000 in 2008–2010. From 2009 and forward, the amount will be adjusted to inflation. Individuals aged 50 or older may use catch-up provisions. The act also increases amounts that can be contributed to 401(k) and 403(b) plans—$12,000 in 2003, $13,000 in 2004, $14,000 in 2005, and $15,000 in 2006—subject to a number of restrictions. From 2007 forward, the limit is indexed for inflation.

- *Coverdell IRAs.* Increases the limit on contributions from $500 to $2,000. The act allows tax-deferred growth and tax-free distributions to pay for qualified expenses.

- *Qualified tuition programs (529 plans).* These plans will be made available to students attending private schools; however, withdrawals cannot be made until 2004. Taxpayers can contribute to both 529 Plans and Coverdell IRAs.

37.8 PLEDGE AND PROMISSORY NOTE

A pledge generates a charitable income tax deduction only in the year the pledge actually is paid. Likewise, a promissory note from a donor to a charity does not generate a charitable income tax deduction until the note is paid in full.

37.9 BENEFITS TO DONORS/QUID PRO QUO CONTRIBUTIONS

Donors can jeopardize their charitable income tax deductions and charities jeopardize their nonprofit status by improperly crediting the value of a charitable gift. If a donor makes a contribution to a charity and receives a benefit such as a product or service, the value of the benefit must be deducted from the contribution to determine the actual charitable income tax deduction. For example, if a donor makes a gift of $100 to a charity to attend a fundraiser, the fair market value of the meal, entertainment, and other benefits enjoyed must be deducted from the gift of $100 to determine the real value of the gift. The IRS requires charities that receive a gift of $75 and above for which a donor obtains a benefit to disclose the following information:

1. The amount of the contribution deductible for federal income tax purposes, which is limited to the excess of the money or the value of any property other than money contributed by the donor over the value of the goods and services provided by the organization.

2. A good faith estimate of the value of such goods and services.

In addition, in order for a donor to deduct a contribution of $250 or more, the charity must issue a receipt for the gift and must state whether (and give an estimated value if) any portion of the gift was made in exchange for a benefit.

Volunteers may deduct out-of-pocket expenses incurred in the course of traveling or otherwise contributing their services to the charity such as attending a board meeting, as long as they receive an acknowledgment recognizing the date of the volunteered service and a statement that the service was a benefit to the charity.

37.10   THE ORDINARY INCOME REDUCTION RULE

The ordinary income reduction rule reduces the value of the charitable income tax deduction for contributions by donors of assets that are characterized as ordinary income property. The rule applies only to the charitable income tax deduction, not to the estate tax deduction. Ordinary income property is property that would result in ordinary income or a short-term capital gain if the property were sold on the date contributed. Ordinary income properties are assets that a taxpayer sells or uses to produce ordinary income, such as a retailer who sells inventory to customers or an artist who sells items that the artist produced or created. Property is characterized as ordinary income property based on the nature of the property in the hands of the donor.

For example, sales of the following property would produce ordinary income:

- Short-term capital assets

- Inventory in the hands of a retailer, dealer, or merchant

- Artwork in the hands of the artist; a manuscript in the hands of the author

- Section 306 stock of which any dividend produced would be treated as ordinary income

- Certain property that has been subject to depreciation recapture

- Annuity or life insurance contract

For gifts of ordinary income property, a donor is entitled to claim a charitable income tax deduction equal to the cost basis of the asset. The rule limits the value of contributions of ordinary income property by donors to charities because the value of the charitable income tax deduction is reduced.

Artists, authors, or playwrights who donate their own works of art or manuscripts are limited to a charitable income tax deduction equal to the cost basis, which for an artist usually amounts to the cost of materials used to make the artwork (e.g., paint, brushes, and canvas for a painting), assuming that the cost has not already been deducted as a business expense, in which case no deduction is available. However, inventors who make gifts of their own patents are entitled to a charitable income tax deduction equal to the fair market value of the patent since patents are characterized as capital gains property rather than ordinary income property.

37.11   INCOME IN RESPECT OF A DECEDENT

As discussed earlier, most assets transferred at death receive a stepped-up basis, which means that the donee obtains a new basis in transferred property equal to the fair market value of the property at the date of the donor's death. However, items that are classified as income in respect of a decedent (IRD) do not receive a stepped-up basis. Income in respect of a decedent is taxable income that the decedent was entitled to at death but which was not included in any previous income tax return. The term *income in respect of a decedent* includes these categories of income:

- Wages

- Accounts receivable (for a cash basis taxpayer)

- Untaxed interest income on savings or Treasury bonds

- Deferred compensation such as IRAs and qualified plans

- Series EE bond interest

- Installment contracts

These types of income are subject to an income tax and also are includible in the decedent's estate. Beneficiaries receiving IRD items pay an income tax and receive an income tax deduction for the estate tax that was assessed against the estate for the IRD items. This partial double taxation of IRD items can be avoided if these items are gifted to charities, which do not pay income taxes. Unlike the charitable income tax deduction, which is limited by a percentage of the taxpayer's contribution base, there is no limit on the amount that an individual may contribute to charities for purposes of the estate tax charitable deduction.

Items classified as income in respect of a decedent may be transferred in one of two ways, either outright or to a charitable remainder trust.

(a) Outright Transfers

Income in respect to a decedent items may be transferred by will to a charity. These items should be transferred as a specific legacy to a charity or may be transferred through the residuary clause in a will if the charity is the recipient of the residue. Series EE bonds, for example, could be transferred to a charity through a specific legacy by will, or retirement plans could name the charity directly as the beneficiary.

(b) Charitable Remainder Trust

Income in respect to a decedent items also may be transferred to a charitable remainder trust. A charitable remainder trust is exempt from income taxation, and IRD items transferred to it avoid income taxation until the trust makes a distribution to the beneficiaries. See Chapter 40, Retirement Planning and Planned Giving, for more on IRD transfers to a charitable remainder trust.

37.12   DEDUCTIBILITY OF CHARITABLE CONTRIBUTIONS FOR BUSINESS ORGANIZATIONS

Business organizations, like individuals, can make tax-deductible charitable contributions to a charity. Several types of business organizations, including regular business corporations, known as C corporations, S corporations, and partnerships, have a different tax treatment for charitable contributions.

(a) C Corporations

A C corporation may deduct charitable gifts of cash or property and obtain a charitable income tax deduction limited to 10 percent of the corporation's taxable income (with certain adjustments) for the year in which the deduction is made. Like individuals, the corporation is permitted to carry over any excess for up to five additional tax years.

(b) S Corporations

An S corporation is a special type of corporation. An S corporation is limited to no more than 75 shareholders (with certain limitations on who those shareholders can be) who, along with the corporate entity, elect to be treated as an S corporation. An S corporation does not pay income taxes but instead passes through to its shareholders income, expenses, and profit or loss, all of which are included in the shareholders' individual tax returns. An S corporation can make charitable gifts, and, unlike a C corporation, the gifts are not limited to a ceiling of 10 percent of taxable income. Instead, the value of any charitable gifts is passed through to the shareholders. The charitable income tax deduction available to the shareholder is limited to the extent of the shareholder's basis in the stock. The deduction is still limited to the taxpayer's (shareholder's) contribution base levels of 30 percent for gifts of property or 50 percent for gifts of cash. Under previous tax law, a nonprofit organization could not own shares or an ownership interest in an S corporation; otherwise the S corporation status was lost. Now charities (but not charitable remainder trusts) may own S corporation stocks, although the value of the stock to the charity is greatly diminished. All income or loss flows through to the charity as unrelated business taxable income or loss. In addition, any capital gain on the sale of S corporation stock is taxed as unrelated business taxable income. See Chapter 30, Gifts of Securities, for more information on making gifts of S corporation stock.

(c) Partnerships

Under current tax law, a partnership is not entitled to deduct charitable contributions directly. The partnership itself files a tax return but does not pay tax because gains and losses from the partnership are passed through to the partners. A partnership's charitable contributions also are passed on to the partners.

37.13 DEPRECIATION

Depreciation is a tax concept that enables a taxpayer "a reasonable allowance for the exhaustion, wear and tear of property used in a trade or business, or of property held for the production of income." The depreciation deduction is applied against ordinary income earned by the taxpayer and effectively reduces the taxpayer's income tax liability. To be depreciable, an asset must have a useful life of more than one year. Items that have a useful life of less than one year are expensed, and the cost is recovered as a deduction against revenue in the year the item is acquired. In the case of repairs, the cost of repairs is expensed unless the repairs amount to capital improvements, in which case they are depreciated. There are several ways to claim depreciation. For example, in straight-line depreciation, the asset is deducted on a prorated basis over the useful life of the capital asset. The IRS has established asset depreciation tables for tax purposes to measure the useful life of any asset.

The impact of depreciation on an asset that is gifted depends on whether the asset is considered ordinary income property or capital gains property. The difference as to whether an asset is ordinary income property rather than capital gains property is based on the nature and use of the asset in the hands of the donor. Ordinary income property is property that, if sold, would produce ordinary income, such as art in the hands of an artist or property that, if sold, would produce a short-term gain. Capital gains property is property held for investment; some property used in a trade or business is treated as capital gains property. The donor may obtain a charitable income tax deduction for the full fair market value of the asset as long as the asset was held at least a year and a day and qualifies as a long-term capital asset. Certain depreciation of assets must be recaptured or taxed on the sale of the property. Under the ordinary income reduction rule, the donor of ordinary income property must reduce the full market value of that property by the amount of depreciation that would have been recaptured had the property been sold. The basis of an asset is important for gifts made to fund a charitable gift annuity since the difference between the fair market value and the cost basis is capital gain and is taxed accordingly. Although, such tax, in most cases, may be deferred at the time of the annuity payout. Long-term capital gains are not taxed when capital gain property is transferred outright to a charity or to a charitable remainder trust or a pooled income fund.

37.14 CAPITAL GAINS TAXES

Long-term capital gains taxes are assessed on the sale of an appreciated capital asset that has been held by the taxpayer for more than a year. The appreciation is measured by the difference between the fair market value of the asset and the original price, or cost basis less depreciation of the asset. As discussed under JGTRRA, capital gains are taxed at a maximum rate of 15 percent for most investment assets. Donors may gift long-term appreciated assets to a charitable organization and avoid capital gains taxes while obtaining a charitable income tax deduction equal to the fair market value of the asset.

37.15 FEDERAL ESTATE AND GIFT TAXES

Federal estate and gift taxes sometimes are referred to as wealth transfer taxes. Donors can make a transfer of property during their lifetime and be subject to a gift tax, or make a transfer of property at death and be subject to an estate tax. Under previous law, the estate and gift tax rate was "uniform," meaning that the same rate of tax was assessed regardless of whether the asset was transferred during life or at death. The estate tax is assessed on the value of the asset transferred and the amount needed to pay the estate tax whereas the gift tax is assessed only on the amount transferred. Now under EGTRRA, the estate and gift taxes are treated separately. For gift tax purposes, the new act caps the lifetime exemption equivalent at $1 million for estate tax purposes; the exemption equivalent is $1 million in 2003 and increases to $3.5 million in 2009. The generation-skipping transfer tax exemption is $1,120,000 in 2003. The same tax rate is assessed on estate and gift transfers until 2009. In 2010, the estate tax is scheduled to be repealed and the gift tax will be assessed on transfers in excess of $1 million at a rate equal to the taxpayer's income tax rate. The following table illustrates the applicable tax rates and exemptions:

Estate and Gift Tax Rates and Credit Exemption Amounts

Calendar Year	Estate and GST Tax* Credit	Gift Tax Credit	Highest Estate and Gift tax Rates
2003	$1 million	$1 million	49 percent
2004	$1.5 million	$1 million	48 percent
2005	$1.5 million	$1 million	47 percent
2006	$2 million	$1 million	46 percent
2007	$2 million	$1 million	45 percent
2008	$2 million	$1 million	45 percent
2009	$3.5 million	$1 million	45 percent
2010	N/A (taxes repealed)	$1 million	Maximum gift tax rate equal to maximum income tax rate (35 percent)

*The generation-skipping tax exemption is $1,120,000 in 2003.

Wealthy taxpayers with significant assets may wish to make charitable gifts rather than pay hefty estate and gift taxes. Many donors are motivated to reduce their estate taxes through lifetime charitable gifts supplemented by additional gifts to reduce their estate. Charitable gifts made during their lifetime are deductible for gift tax purposes. To be deductible for gift tax purposes, the contribution also must be deductible for income tax purposes.

When making a taxable gift of assets that are likely to appreciate in value, it is more advantageous to make a lifetime gift of the assets prior to the anticipated appreciation, thereby avoiding higher taxes later. This option is better than transferring the assets at death and paying the higher estate taxes on the asset plus its appreciated value. Charitable gifts made through a decedent's estate are deducted from the decedent's gross estate, which lessens the estate tax burden. To take advantage of such a deduction, the gift must be irrevocable. It may be made through a will, an irrevocable charitable remainder trust, or a revocable trust that becomes irrevocable at the donor's death.

Philanthropically motivated donors will always make gifts through their estates even if there is no longer an estate tax charitable deduction. For example, because donors do not exactly know how much of their estate they will need for their use during their lifetimes, many donors prefer to make the largest of their charitable gifts through their estates. For other donors, this legislation would be a disincentive to make charitable gifts. Check with the charity's general counsel for more information about legislative changes that may affect the estate and gift tax.

37.16   GIFT TAX ANNUAL EXCLUSION

A donor is entitled to an annual exclusion that permits a donor to make a present gift of up to $11,000 each year to any number of donees without gift tax consequences and without using up any of the $1 million lifetime exemption equivalent. Spouses can pool annual exclusions, enabling a couple to give up to $22,000 each year to any number of donees. The annual exclusion is adjusted and will increase gradually over time. Parents and grandparents who wish to take advantage of the annual exclusion can make gifts to their children and grandchildren while substantially reducing their estate tax liability. The annual exclusion applies only to gifts of a present interest and not a future interest, such as a deferred gift annuity. Charitable gifts are unaffected by the $11,000 annual exclusion limit that exists for gifts to individuals. In addition, gifts to charity do not diminish an individual's lifetime exemption; gifts to charities, regardless of amount, will not incur any gift tax.

37.17   PAYMENTS FOR TUITION AND MEDICAL BILLS

A donor also may give any amount, including an amount over $11,000, without gift tax consequences if the gift takes the form of a direct payment of tuition or medical expenses. The payment must be made by the taxpayer directly to the provider (university, hospital, etc.) rather than to an individual. For example, an individual can pay to a university on behalf of another individual a payment for tuition without being subject to a gift tax.

37.18   GIFTS BY HUSBAND AND WIFE/THE UNLIMITED
MARITAL DEDUCTION

When spouses contemplate making gifts, they should consider whether the gift should be made by an individual or as a couple. For federal gift and estate tax purposes, each spouse is considered to have contributed one-half of the purchase price of an asset if the property is held jointly. By transferring assets jointly instead of from a single spouse, they can elect to split gifts of property. In this manner, each spouse obtains one-half of the charitable income tax deduction. Current federal tax law provides spouses who are U.S. citizens with an unlimited marital deduction, allowing one spouse to make an outright gift to the other of an unlimited amount of marital property without incurring any federal estate or gift tax and without using any of their lifetime gift or estate tax exemption. The transfer may be made either as a lifetime transfer (inter vivos) or a transfer at death (testamentary). There is both an estate tax marital deduction and a gift tax marital deduction. To qualify as a transfer under the gift tax marital deduction, the spouses must be married and the transfers must take place during the marriage. If a surviving spouse disclaims a property interest, then the marital deduction will not be allowed for that property. Any property interest subject to a mortgage that passes to a surviving spouse will be reduced by the amount of that mortgage. If one spouse is infirm, that spouse may wish to take advantage of the marital deduction by gifting his interest in the property to the other spouse and having the healthy spouse donate the property to charity. This technique allows the healthy spouse to receive the full charitable income tax deduction for the donation including any contribution carryover that would otherwise expire at the first spouse's death.

37.19 STREAMS OF INCOME AND GIFT TAX CONSEQUENCES

A future interest is created when a gift is made of an interest that begins at a point in the future, such as a charitable remainder trust that provides income to a second beneficiary upon the death of the first. A gift of a future interest to an individual does not qualify for the annual gift tax exclusion of $11,000. A gift of a future interest to a spouse (other than through a charitable remainder trust) also does not qualify for the marital deduction. In both cases, there is no present interest created. A donor can avoid creating a future interest, and making a taxable gift, by reserving the right to revoke the future interest. The reservation of the right to revoke is generally exercisable by will and must be included in appropriate language in the legal document. In the case of a charitable gift annuity with an income stream paid to someone other than the donor or the donor's spouse, the charitable gift annuity agreement should include the following language:

"The donor may, by the donor's will, revoke the annuity to be paid to Mr. Donee X."

(a) Taxation of a Stream of Income from a Life Income Gift

Depending on the life income gift option selected (charitable gift annuity, deferred gift annuity, pooled income fund, etc.) and the beneficiary (donor, spouse, relative, etc.), there are different tax consequences associated with the gift of a stream of income. Generally, the gift of a present stream of income qualifies for the annual exclusion, but any gift of a future stream of income to another person raises gift tax considerations.

(b) Taxation of a Present Interest

For life income gifts such as charitable remainder trusts, charitable gift annuities, and pooled income funds, all of which may create a present stream of income for the benefit of another, the stream of income is an interest that is eligible for the annual exclusion of $11,000. If the stream of income is payable to a spouse, then the stream is also eligible for the marital deduction.

(c) Taxation of a Future Interest

If the stream is not a present interest but a future interest payable upon a contingency such as the death of a first beneficiary, the annual exclusion does not apply; nor in the case of a spouse does the marital deduction apply. In this case a donor may reserve the right to revoke the income stream, exercisable by will or during lifetime, although a lifetime right to revoke may disqualify a charitable remainder trust. This reservation has the effect of suspending the stream of income and making the gift incomplete. If the right to revoke is not exercised, then the present value of the gift to a nonspouse will become part of the donor's taxable estate.

In the case of a deferred gift annuity, an income stream is created to be paid beginning at a point in the future. When the annuity is payable to a beneficiary other than the donor, it is unclear under current tax law if the present value of the beneficiary's intent would qualify for the gift tax annual exclusion. If the present value of an income stream exceeds the annual exclusion or if the donor creates a future interest but fails to retain the right to revoke, there is a gift tax. Donors who create streams that exceed the annual exclusion subject to a gift tax can use the lifetime gift/estate tax exemption.

37.20 SALE OF A PERSONAL RESIDENCE

Under prior law, a taxpayer was subject to a capital gains tax on any gain realized from the sale of a principal residence unless the taxpayer purchased a replacement principal residence of equal or greater value within a specified period of time. Under that law, if the taxpayer was 55 years of age or older and did not replace the residence, the gain on the sale of the principal residence could have been offset by the one-time, lifetime exclusion that permitted a taxpayer to sell a principal residence and exclude up to $125,000 of the gain. New tax law permits a taxpayer of any age to exclude up to $500,000, if married filing jointly, of capital gain ($250,000 if single) upon the sale of a personal residence if the taxpayer lived in the residence for at least two of the last five years. The exclusion can be claimed more than once so long as the taxpayer lived in the residence for at least two of the last five years.

37.21 GIFTS OF REAL ESTATE SUBJECT TO A MORTGAGE

Donors who make a gift of mortgaged real estate obtain a charitable income tax deduction equal to the fair market value of the property minus the value of the mortgage. See Chapter 31 for an in-depth look at gifts of real estate.

37.22 TAX IMPLICATIONS OF A BARGAIN SALE

If a donor makes a partial gift, partial sale, or transfers real estate to a charity in exchange for a payment, the donor is making a bargain sale and the donor is taxed on the gain. Assuming the property is capital gain property, the gain is treated as a capital gain. The same is true in a charitable gift annuity situation. When a donor transfers capital gain property in exchange for a gift annuity, the donor will receive part ordinary income and part capital gain.

A bargain sale is treated for tax purposes as two transactions: one part sale and one part gift. The basis of the property has to be allocated between the sale portion and the gift portion to determine gain. To calculate the gain, divide the sale price by the fair market value of the property. This will produce a ratio expressed as a percentage. To determine the cost basis to be allocated to the sale portion, multiply the percentage (which is a ratio of the sales price to market value) times the cost basis of the property. Last, subtract from the sale price the cost basis allocated to the sale to arrive at the reportable gain.

37.23 SUBSTANTIATION REQUIREMENTS

A taxpayer who makes a gift of $250 or more must obtain a receipt from the charity to claim a charitable income tax deduction. The receipt or acknowledgment must state the amount of cash or the nature of the property received and must state whether the donor received any goods or services in exchange for the gift; if any were so received, the value of the goods and services must be stated. If the donor makes a gift of property other than cash and marketable securities, the donor needs to prove that the gift was made and also needs to substantiate value. The Internal Revenue Service (IRS) has specific requirements for the substantiation of noncash gifts, including forms and appraisals.

(a) Form 8283

The IRS requires that donors who make gifts having a value of $5,000 or more of any property other than cash or marketable securities to charitable organizations have a formal appraisal and report these gifts on Form 8283 (gifts of closely held stock with a value of $10,000 or more require an appraisal). Noncash contributions include gifts-in-kind such as artwork, musical instruments, real estate, antiques, jewelry, computer hardware and software, and securities. In each of these cases the determination of the value of the contribution is complex. The purpose of the appraisal and the Form 8283 is to require taxpayers who make noncash gifts to be honest and accurate in substantiating the value of those assets for charitable income tax deduction purposes.

37.24 APPRAISALS

For situations where an appraisal is necessary, the appraisal must be conducted by an independent qualified appraiser. Form 8283 is a summary of the gift appraisal and must be attached to the donor's federal income tax return (a partially completed Form 8283 is also required for some gifts that donor requires an appraisal). The cost of the appraisal is borne by the donor and is treated as a miscellaneous deduction subject to the 2 percent limit. The charitable organization recipient is not required to attest to the value of the property, but is required to acknowledge receipt of the gift on Form 8283. The appraisal must be conducted no more than 60 days prior to the transfer of the property and no later than the date the federal income tax return is filed for the year of the donation. Failure to obtain an appraisal and to file Form 8283 will result in a disallowance of the charitable income tax deduction. A "good faith" failure to obtain an appraisal is not a defense to the disallowance of the deduction. The appraiser's signature is required.

(a) Form 8282

In the event that the charitable organization sells the contributed assets reported on Form 8283 within two years from the date of the gift, the organization must file Form 8282 with the IRS. If the charity sells the asset for an amount that does not closely approximate the appraised value, the donor's charitable income tax deduction may be challenged.

37.25 PARTIAL INTERESTS

A charitable income tax deduction is not allowed for charitable gifts, whether made outright or in trust, that represent less than the donor's entire interest in the gift. The loss of the deduction applies to the charitable income tax deduction, the charitable gift tax deduction, and the charitable estate tax deduction. Partial interests are created when a donor retains a right or ownership interest in property transferred to a charity.

A number of important exceptions to this rule enable a donor to obtain a charitable income tax deduction:

- *Gift of the donor's entire interest where the interest is less than full property rights.* The donor may obtain a charitable income tax deduction for a gift of a partial property interest as long as that interest represents the donor's entire interest in the property and the partial interest was not created for purposes of the gift.

- *Gifts-in-trust.* As discussed above, the donor is entitled to a charitable income tax deduction for a gift of a remainder interest in trust as long as the trust is a qualified charitable remainder unitrust, charitable remainder annuity trust, or qualified pooled income fund. In addition, the donor may obtain a charitable income tax deduction for the gift of a lead interest (income interest) in a grantor charitable lead trust as long as the donor is taxed on the income of the trust.

■ *Gifts of a remainder interest in a personal residence or farm.* This exception permits the donor to obtain a charitable income tax deduction less depreciation for a gift of a remainder interest in a personal residence or farm. For example, in a retained life estate, the donor retains a life estate or the right to occupy the property for life, with the remainder to a nonprofit organization. The donor receives a current charitable income tax deduction for the present value of the gift of the remainder. A personal residence is defined as any residence used by the taxpayer as a personal residence, although it does not need to be the donor's primary residence. A farm is defined as any land used by the taxpayer in the production of crops, fruits, agricultural products, or livestock.

■ *Gifts of an undivided interest in a donor's entire interest.* An undivided fractional interest of a donor's entire interest often is expressed as a percentage or a fraction. If the donor transfers 25 percent or a one-quarter interest in property, he is conveying a portion of his interest. It is undivided in that the nonprofit's interest does not represent a certain right to a specific area or acreage but rather has use of the entire property for a certain fraction of the year.

■ *Gift of a partial interest in real property for conservation purposes.* A donor can obtain a charitable income tax deduction for a gift of less than the donor's entire interest if the interest is an easement or conservation restriction imposed for conservation purposes. Conservation purposes include the preservation, protection, or creation of open space, natural habitat, recreation, or historic preservation if the use is for public purposes or education. See Chapter 31 for more information on the use of conservation easements.

37.26 CONCLUSION

Nonprofit staff members and planned giving staff members must understand the tax consequences of a donor's charitable gifts. Four types of tax savings may be available, including a charitable income tax deduction, capital gains tax avoidance, gift tax deductions, or estate tax deductions. In addition, taxes assessed by a state also may be avoided or reduced.

To fully engage in philanthropy, a donor must first want to make a gift to help support the charity's mission. The tax benefits are provided to donors who wish to make a gift to benefit a charity. Few donors make gifts for tax purposes. The planned giving officer can help donors see the benefits of philanthropy, then show them ways to maximize the tax benefits of their gifts.

CHAPTER THIRTY-EIGHT

Estate Planning
and Planned Giving

38.1   INTRODUCTION

Estate planning involves the coordinated integration of several documents including a will, trust, durable power of attorney, and living will or healthcare proxy. Estate planning also involves assessing several aspects of a donor's personal life. It is important for planned giving officers to understand the basics of estate planning so as to fully appreciate a donor's financial challenges, personal goals, and philanthropic interests. Charitable gift planning should be incorporated into a donor's overall estate plan objectives, rather than dominating the effort. This approach is critical, inasmuch as many donors' ultimate charitable gifts originate from solid estate planning. Planned giving officers must see the overall picture, not just the slice that is planned giving. Estate planning can help an individual achieve three major financial goals: distributing the estate, reducing taxes, and avoiding probate.

38.2 RELATED DISCIPLINES

Estate planning is an umbrella that encompasses several aspects of business and law. Consider the implications of each of the following areas in estate planning.

(a) Financial Planning

Financial planning focuses on types of assets and their appropriateness as investment vehicles. Investment assets and objectives must be matched to achieve a donor's financial goals. Investment objectives and strategies, which can change over time, must be reevaluated regularly. For a complete discussion of financial planning, see Chapter 39.

(b) Business Organizations

Estate planning also considers a donor's private relationships with business organizations such as sole proprietorships, partnerships, corporations, and business trusts. It is important to be familiar with the donor's relationship to these entities and their holdings in order to understand the donor's assets and liabilities when assisting him with charitable gift planning and estate planning.

(c) Real Estate

Real estate is often the largest single asset a donor owns. Real estate holdings may be residential, commercial, industrial, farm, or vacant land. It is essential to understand the manner in which the donor has taken title to the property and the donor's relationship to any other owners. Real estate is governed by the law of the state in which it is located. For a complete discussion of gifts of real estate, see Chapter 31.

(d) Tax Law

Taxation, both federal and state, is an important consideration and incentive for most charitable donors. The adage "You can give it to the Internal Revenue Service or to your favorite charity" is true. Taxation can serve as leverage when it comes to charitable gift planning and can motivate philanthropic-minded donors to benefit nonprofits. Donors sometimes view charitable gift planning as the last tax shelter through which income, estate, gift, and capital gains taxes can be diminished or avoided entirely. The U.S. system of taxation permits and encourages taxpayers to make gifts to nonprofits, because without private support to our nation's charities, many educational, health, social service, environmental, and cultural programs would go unfunded. The nation's nonprofits ease the burden of the federal government in providing these charitable services. See Chapter 37 for a complete discussion of the tax consequences of charitable giving.

(e) Charitable Gift Planning

Charitable gift planning is another important aspect of a donor's estate plan. Rather than viewing charitable gift planning in the abstract, consider it as a part of a larger plan through which a donor can achieve financial and philanthropic goals. Charitable gift planning involves a comprehensive analysis of a donor's financial situation combined with an understanding and appreciation of the donor's wish to benefit a variety of individuals and organizations, of which some may be philanthropic.

(f) Domestic Relations

Domestic relations include relations with spouses and family, such as a situation in which it is necessary to provide special care to a disabled child or an institutionalized relative. Domestic relations plays a role in estate planning because various laws affect the relationship between families and the distribution of property. For example, in most states, marriage voids a will unless the will was made in contemplation of marriage. Divorce or annulment generally voids a distribution of property made to the former spouse but otherwise leaves the will intact. If a revocable trust is used, the provisions may still be valid after a divorce and the divorced spouses must revise their trusts.

38.3 INTESTACY

Perhaps surprisingly, more than half of all Americans die without a will, and the causes are many and varied. The reason may be an absence of legal services, a lack of knowledge, or a failure to understand the need for a will. Yet sometimes it is more complex, involving emotional and psychological factors that keep individuals from drafting a will. Some people feel that drafting a will puts them closer to death. Whatever the reason, the result is the same—intestacy. When a person dies without a will, he is considered to have died intestate, and the state where he is domiciled will, in effect, make a will for him. The laws governing this circumstance vary considerably from state to state. Intestacy produces undesirable results. Instead of the decedent's providing for a distribution of assets, the state determines the individual's distribution of assets and adds extensive and cumbersome legal formalities and extra legal costs. Often there is no consideration of the needs or wishes of the individual or of his family. Anyone can avoid intestacy simply by making a valid will.

38.4 THE WILL: A ROAD MAP

A will is a road map that gives directions in transferring an asset from one person to another person or to a charity.

(a) Parties

There are several parties to a will:

- The *testator* (or testatrix) is defined as the one who makes a will, who in most states must be at least 18 years of age.

- The *executor* (or executrix)—personal representative, in some states—is named in a will to carry out the wishes of the testator. The executor files the will, gathers the assets of the estate, collects income, pays taxes, and distributes the proceeds with the permission of the probate court (in some states, the district court).

- The *probate court* (district court) is the state court in which the decedent's will is filed and which oversees the administration of the estate. A will usually is required to be filed within 30 days of the date of death of the testator, in the probate court located in the county where the testator was domiciled at the time of death. A domicile is the place where the decedent lived and intended to make a permanent home. The location of a person's second home or vacation home is not a place of domicile, because there is no intent to make a permanent residence.

- An *administrator* (personal representative) is a person appointed by the probate court to perform the duties of an executor when a decedent dies intestate. A clause appoints a guardian to act on behalf of minor children of the decedent or a designated executor who is willing to serve in that capacity.

- A *beneficiary* is one selected by the maker of a will to receive property. A beneficiary should not be a witness to the decedent's will; otherwise the bequest to that beneficiary may be void or questions may arise regarding the validity of the will because the beneficiary's presence at the time the will was executed suggests that the beneficiary may have exercised undue influence.

- A witness to a will participates in the proper execution of a will and observes that the testator is of sound mind and is not acting under duress, undue influence, or fraud.

(b) Formalities

A will must be executed in accordance with certain legal formalities. It is necessary for the testator to sign the will, most often in the presence of two, and perhaps three, witnesses, depending on state law. Witnesses typically sign their names in the presence of each other and the testator. Most states provide for an attestation clause, whereby a notary acknowledges that the will was appropriately signed by the testator and the witnesses. The attestation clause enables a will to be presented in court without the necessity of having witnesses appear to offer proof that the will meets the required formalities.

(c) Codicils

Amendments or modifications to a will can be made through the use of a codicil. A codicil is most appropriately used for relatively minor changes to a will and must be executed with the same formalities as a will.

(d) Importance of Updating a Will

An out-of-date will may be as undesirable as the lack of a will. Many circumstances can make a will obsolete, including changes in family circumstances such as marriage, divorce, birth, adoption, and death; changes in state and federal law; changes in the nature and value of a person's property; and a move from one state to another. A will should be updated or reviewed at least once every five years and upon any change in family circumstances.

(e) Revoking a Will

A will can be revoked or voided by tearing, burning, or otherwise obliterating the will. To revoke a will in writing, the testator must sign a statement executed with the same formalities as a will, stating that the testator wants to revoke the most recently drafted will. A subsequently executed will revokes a prior will, but a statement revoking the prior will should be included in the new will.

(f) Contesting a Will

To contest a will, the contesting party must be one who has an interest in the estate, such as a potential beneficiary or a testator's heir. The party contesting the will must allege one of several specific grounds as to why the will is not valid. Such grounds include fraud, duress, undue influence, misrepresentation, or lack of capacity such as senility or drunkenness, which indicate that the testator was not of sound mind when the will was made. Ambiguities in a will may cause a will contest or an action by the executor in the probate court to seek instructions from the court to resolve the ambiguity. To help prevent a future will contest, an individual can be examined by a physician the day the will is signed. The doctor can include in the patient report a statement that the individual is in good health and is mentally sound. To have sufficient mental capacity to make a will, the testator must understand the extent of property owned, know the identity of his heirs, and be aware of those persons to whom assets are being distributed. A videotape recording provides an excellent opportunity to demonstrate that a testator is of sound mind.

38.5 PARTS OF A WILL

A properly executed will transfers property from the testator to beneficiaries. There are a number of standard provisions or clauses in a will, which include:

- A clause revoking all previously drafted wills or codicils
- A clause that directs the payment of all debts, taxes, funeral expenses, and administrative costs
- A clause naming an executor or a personal representative of the estate
- A clause appointing a guardian to act on behalf of minor children of the decedent
- Distribution clauses, which permit personal and real property to be distributed to specific beneficiaries
- A residuary clause that directs the distribution of the remainder or residue of the estate

(a) Naming the Executor

The executor of an estate handles the details of transferring a testator's wealth. The executor files the will in court and preserves the assets of the decedent's estate. This person's responsibilities include collecting any income due to the estate and paying bills and federal and state taxes. The executor also helps to locate the beneficiaries of the estate and makes distributions. The work of the executor is overseen by the probate court.

(b) Guardianship Provision

A guardianship provision is of great importance to any parent of minor children. A minor, under the age of 18 in most states, cannot legally make decisions on medical or health care issues, and contracts that a minor has entered into may be considered voidable. A simple clause that appoints a guardian to act on behalf of a minor enables the guardian, with court approval, to take action for the benefit of the child. In the absence of a guardianship provision, the probate or family court must be petitioned to request that an individual be appointed to act as guardian. There is considerable delay and expense for this process, which is entirely unnecessary in that it can be avoided or accelerated through a guardianship provision in the will. Estate planning requires planning for contingencies; it is not enough to appoint a single individual as guardian, executor, trustee, or beneficiary. For each, there should be a successor chosen to act or benefit in the event of the death, disability, or disqualification of the first chosen.

(c) Powers of Appointment

A power of appointment is an important means of transferring property. The donor of the power grants to the holder of the appointment, the donee, the right to designate beneficiaries to receive a transfer of property. The power of appointment may be a general or a special power of appointment. For example, a testator may create a trust under will, giving a child of the testator the right to appoint trust property to himself, his own children, or charity. Under a general power of appointment, the holder of the power can appoint the property subject to the power as he chooses, including to the holder or the holder's creditors, heirs, or estate. Because the donee has such extensive control over the property, all of the property over which the donee possesses the power of appointment is deemed to be includible in the estate of the donee for federal estate tax purposes unless the donee exercises the power of appointment prior to death, effectively making a lifetime gift, in favor of individuals other than the donee of the power. Even if it is exercised but the donee retains control, the property is includible in the donee's estate.

A special power of appointment permits the donee to select beneficiaries for the distribution of property with one critical exception: Neither the donee nor her estate may be a beneficiary. For example, a testator may create a trust under will, giving a child the right to appoint trust property to her children or charity but *not* to herself or her estate. Property subject to a special power of appointment, therefore, is not includible in the estate of the donee, because the donee may not designate or appoint herself as a beneficiary. A power to use assets of a trust that is limited by an ascertainable standard relating to health, education (tuition), support, or maintenance, is not considered a power of appointment. A power to provide for one's own comfort, welfare, or happiness is not considered to be an ascertainable standard, since it is not measurable.

(d) Distribution of Property

In technical terms, *legacies* are gifts of money, *bequests* are gifts of personal property, and *devises* are gifts of real estate. However, most commonly, all transfers of property made at death are referred to as bequests. Donors can make bequests of a specific dollar amount, a particular piece of property, or a percentage of their estates. See Chapter 29 for more information on bequests. Donors also can make gifts through a residuary clause in a will. A residuary estate consists of everything that is not specifically given away. A bequest of a fraction or percentage of the residue permits the donor who may not be able to estimate precisely the size of the estate to divide the estate among individual beneficiaries and/or to a nonprofit organization. The residuary clause is sometimes called the *remainder* or *residue* of the estate.

38.6   COORDINATING TITLE TO PROPERTY WITH THE ESTATE PLAN

For a will to transfer property from the testator to a beneficiary, the ownership or title to the property must be coordinated with the testator's estate plan. For example, spouses commonly take title to property as joint tenants with a right of survivorship. In this case, upon the death of one spouse, the property passes automatically, by "operation of law," to the surviving spouse; therefore, the first spouse to die cannot transfer her interest in the property by will. Once the surviving spouse inherits the property and holds it in his own name and not as a joint tenant, it is possible to transfer the property by will to a beneficiary.

It is important to understand the various ways in which donors hold title to property. There are several forms of ownership, including:

- *Sole ownership.* When property is held in sole ownership, the owner owns the entire interest in the property and may transfer the property to another by will.

- *Tenancy in common.* In a tenancy in common, two or more owners share an undivided interest in the property. A tenancy in common is a customary form of ownership for friends or family members but not spouses who own property together. Upon the death of one cotenant, that cotenant's interest in the property can be transferred by will to the cotenant's heirs. Ownership does not automatically pass to the surviving tenant in common, as in the case of a joint tenancy.

- *Joint tenancy with a right of survivorship.* Upon the death of one joint tenant, the property is transferred automatically to the surviving joint tenant and cannot be transferred by will.

- *Tenancy by the entirety.* A tenancy by the entirety, which exists in a limited number of states, is a special form of joint tenancy held only by spouses. Upon the death of one spouse, the property passes automatically to the surviving spouse.

- *Community property.* A number of states, primarily in the West and Southwest, are community property states: Arizona, California, Idaho, Louisiana, Nevada, New Mexico,

Texas, Washington, and Wisconsin. In many community property states, all property acquired during a marriage, except property acquired by gift, inheritance, or with separate funds, is presumed to be community property, with each spouse owning one-half of the property. Property acquired prior to a marriage is separately owned by the spouse who acquired the property.

38.7 PLANNING CONSIDERATIONS: PER STIRPES VERSUS PER CAPITA

An important consideration in estate planning involves the question of whether children are permitted to "step into the shoes" of a predeceased parent and take that parent's share of inheritance. Opinions vary as to the appropriateness of this action, depending on family circumstances. The testator may choose between distributions made *per capita* and *per stirpes.*

A distribution made per capita is a distribution made equally to the existing number of individuals with each person receiving the same amount regardless of whether the recipient is a child or grandchild. A distribution made per stirpes distributes shares equally by representation; if the person to receive the share from an estate is no longer alive, the children of that decedent would divide the share that the parent would have received equally among themselves. It is vital that anyone making a will address the issue of how children and grandchildren will share.

Example 38.1 _____

Assume that a mother and father leave property to their three children, Mary, John, and Bill. Mary predeceases her mother and father, leaving two children. Should Mary's children be permitted to acquire the property that Mary would have acquired from her parents (per stirpes), or should the gift to Mary "lapse" so that the property is divided (per capita) between Mary's two surviving siblings, John and Bill? If mother and father leave $100,000 to Mary, John, and Bill to be divided per capita, and if Mary predeceases her parents, John and Bill each take $50,000 and Mary's children take nothing. Alternatively, Mary's children may take an equal or per capita share with John and Bill, each receiving $25,000. If mother and father leave $100,000 per stirpes to Mary, John, and Bill, and Mary predeceases her parents, John and Bill each receive $33,333 and Mary's two children split her share, each taking $16,677.

38.8 PROBATE

Probate is a state-sanctioned system that oversees the administration of a person's estate. The concept of probate is confusing, because many people mistakenly believe that probate is avoided if a person has a will. A decedent's will is filed in probate (district) court and is probated (established as genuine and valid). The main purposes of probate are to collect the decedent's probate assets, protect and preserve the property of the estate, pay debts, file federal and state estate tax returns and pay taxes, cut off claims of creditors, determine who is entitled to receive the assets of the decedent, and distribute the property to them. Probate can be an expensive process. Apart from the filing fees and notification requirements, there may be significant executor's and legal fees involved in settling an estate. Probate fees may be billed hourly or may range from 3 to 8 percent of the estate's probate assets. For an estate worth $500,000 in probate assets, which are determined by the nature of the assets, fees of 3 percent amount to $15,000. In addition to being expensive, the probate process is also very time consuming and may last up to a year or longer.

(a) The Probate Process

The probate process is governed by state laws, each having particular requirements and time lines. In general, however, the probate process begins by having the decedent's will filed in the probate court in the county where the decedent lived. The court then issues a citation, which is a notice asking for the decedent's will to be allowed and the executor appointed. If a charity is entitled to a portion of the donor's estate, it will receive notice of the allowance of the will. Any party who has a basis for objection may object to the allowance of the will and file an appearance in court. If no one objects, the court is likely to allow the will and appoint the executor.

Once the executor is appointed, he can collect estate assets and pay outstanding debts of the decedent. The executor will pay any federal or state taxes owed and wait for the expiration of the period during which creditors can make a claim against the estate. The executor is then able to pay an organization's charitable bequest. When the estate is completely distributed, the executor will file a final accounting of the estate, showing the total amount of assets collected and distributed. After the court allows the final account and all tax and other filings have been made and accepted, the executor no longer has responsibility for the estate.

(b) Probate Assets

What is probate property? Which assets need to be probated? The answer depends on the way in which title to the assets is held. Probate property includes:

■ Assets, real or personal, owned in the name of the decedent

■ Property in which the decedent had an ownership interest as a tenant in common

■ Life insurance policies that name the decedent's estate as beneficiary

(c) Nonprobate Assets

The following assets are not probate assets:

■ Assets transferred by virtue of a beneficiary designation to a beneficiary other than the estate of the decedent. For example, pension and retirement benefits in which the spouse or other beneficiary is a named beneficiary pass outside probate. In most cases, life insurance should not be payable to the estate of the decedent but pass to the designated beneficiary outside the estate. It is appropriate to name the estate of the decedent as a beneficiary of a life insurance policy only when the estate does not have other significant liquid assets to pay debts, taxes, or funeral expenses.

■ Assets that pass automatically, by operation of law, to a joint tenant. This form of ownership includes joint tenancies and tenancy by the entirety, discussed earlier. It also may include property, such as bank accounts, for which there is a designated joint owner.

■ Any property that the testator has transferred during her lifetime to a revocable or irrevocable inter vivos trust (see Chapter 25 for a discussion of such trusts).

(d) Property Held Out of State—Ancillary Administration

Many individuals own property outside the state in which they were domiciled—real estate such as retirement homes, recreational property such as mobile homes, and boats or yachts. Any real estate or tangible personal property that a decedent owns in another state that is considered a probate asset requires a separate probate filing in that state. This process, called *ancillary administration,* results in additional expenses and delay. To avoid ancillary administration, any assets located in another state should be transferred to an inter vivos trust.

38.9   POWER OF ATTORNEY AND DURABLE POWER OF ATTORNEY

A general power of attorney permits the holder of the power to act on behalf of another individual, the grantor of the power. The power is assigned in writing, and any third party to whom the power is presented can deal with the holder of the power as if the holder were the grantor. A power of attorney lapses upon the incompetence of the grantor and therefore ceases to be effective.

A durable power of attorney survives the incompetence of the grantor and permits the holder to act, and third parties to rely, on the durable power. This important document can be used when a grantor lapses from competence to incompetence for a period of time or indefinitely, for example, while undergoing surgery or suffering from Alzheimer's disease. A durable power of attorney is an important legal document that can save a grantor's family considerable time and expense. In the absence of a durable power of attorney, the family of an incompetent person must petition the probate or district court to request the appointment of a conservator or guardian. The petition process is expensive and takes time, during which the business affairs and financial well-being of the family may be jeopardized. This entire process can be avoided by having a competent grantor create a durable power of attorney.

Once the durable power is established, the power to act is transferred from the incompetent person to the holder of the power as *attorney-in-fact,* which allows the holder to transact business. The holder of the durable power of attorney is permitted to perform the functions delineated in the power, including the ability to buy, sell, mortgage, lease, gather assets, discharge debts, and generally perform any act or conduct any business for the benefit of the grantor that the grantor could have conducted.

With respect to property jointly held by spouses, the signatures of both are needed in order to convey property such as real estate. If a spouse becomes incompetent, it is necessary to have a guardian or conservator appointed. However, if a durable power of attorney had been executed, the property could have been transferred by the competent spouse and the attorney in fact without probate court approval, thus reducing expense and delay.

38.10   HEALTH PROXIES AND LIVING WILLS

Most states provide individuals with an opportunity to choose to refuse artificial life-sustaining measures. Individuals who want to take advantage of this may do so by creating a living will or a healthcare proxy. A living will permits an individual's wishes to be honored if the individual does not want to be kept alive when his medical condition offers no reasonable expectation of recovery. In such a situation, all heroic measures, artificial means, and medications would cease. This point is most often reached when a person is in an irreversible coma or terminally ill.

Many states recognize the healthcare proxy, which allows the maker of the proxy to name a trusted individual to make healthcare decisions if the maker is unable to communicate his healthcare decisions. The healthcare proxy is used only for medical purposes. Like a living will, a healthcare proxy states when life support equipment should be disconnected and heroic efforts should cease. The healthcare proxy should be treated as a formal document, executed with the formalities of a will. Once the form is signed, the maker should distribute it to appropriate people, such as family members, doctor, lawyer, and clergy, so that the family and professional advisors know the individual's wishes. A sample healthcare proxy is included in Appendix, CD-ROM Documentation, Exhibits.

38.11   TALKING WITH A PROSPECT ABOUT ESTATE PLANNING
AND WEALTH

Professionals in the planned giving profession recently have begun to focus on what should be included in a conversation with a prospect or donor who is working on estate planning. Family dynamics are being explored, with parents being asked about their values and attitudes about money.

This includes their views on what is an appropriate inheritance for their children; how they believe money affects one's life, both positively and negatively; and the role of family members in financial decisions. These values may be more closely scrutinized as the profession sees an increase in the creation of private family foundations, supporting organizations, and donor-advised funds.

The nonprofit organization needs to be sensitive to a prospect's family issues while trying to engage those family members beyond the prospect or donor who may be involved with making a significant gift. The nonprofit's planned giving office should:

- Provide as much technical information as possible about the different giving options including family foundations, supporting organizations, and donor-advised funds.

- Include a spouse, children, and extended family members when appropriate, in the gift planning process.

- Act as a liaison, connecting the individual family members with others who can help educate, such as financial planners, lawyers, and others.

- Use a questionnaire, which family members can complete, to understand individual views toward wealth and philanthropy. A sample family questionnaire is included in Appendix, CD-ROM Documentation, Administrative Documents.

Appendix 38.1

GLOSSARY OF ESTATE PLANNING TERMS

Abatement: The order of reduction or elimination. For example, if a person leaves "five hundred dollars to John and the rest to my heirs," John receives five hundred dollars and the heirs' share may abate to zero if there is only five hundred dollars.

Ademption: 1. Disposing of something left in a will before death, with the effect that the person it was left to does not get it. **2.** The gift, before death, of something left in a will to a person who was left it. For example, Ed leaves a chair to Joan in his will, but gives her the chair before he dies.

Adjusted gross income: A technical federal income tax term that means, in general, the person's income minus deductions such as certain travel, work, business, or moving expenses, etc. For most people, it is the same as "gross" or total income. The term is used for personal income taxes, not for business taxes.

Administer: Settle and distribute the estate of a deceased person.

Administration: Supervision of the estate for a deceased person. This usually includes collecting the property, paying debts and taxes, and giving out what remains to the heirs.

After-born child: A legal principle that if a child is born after a will is made, the child should still inherit whatever children inherit unless the will specifically excludes late-born children.

Age of majority: Age at which a child gains full right to enter into binding contracts, make a will, vote, etc. This age varies from state to state (although it is often age 18) and from purpose to purpose.

Ancillary administration: A proceeding in a state where a decedent had property, but which is not the state where that person was domiciled or where his main estate has been administered.

Annual exclusion: The amount of money a person can give away each year to any individual without paying a federal gift tax and without using up any of the unified credit to which each person is entitled. The current amount is $11,000.

Assets: All money, property, and money-related rights owned by a person or an organization.

Beneficial interest: The right to profits resulting from a contract, estate, or property, rather than the legal ownership of these things.

Beneficiary: 1. A person or organization for whose benefit a trust is created. **2.** A person to whom an insurance policy is payable. **3.** A person who inherits under a will. **4.** Anyone who benefits from something or who is treated as the real owner of something for tax purposes.

Bequeath: To give personal property or money by will; to give anything by will.

Bequest: A gift by will of personal property; any gift by will.

Breach of trust: The failure of a trustee to do something that is required; includes doing things illegally, negligently, or forgetfully.

Charitable: A gift or organization is charitable for tax purposes if it meets several tests: A gift must be made to a government-qualified nonprofit organization to benefit humankind in general, the community in general, or some specific large group of people. In addition, the organization's and the gift's purpose must be for the relief of poverty; protection of health or safety; prevention of cruelty; for advancement of education, religion, literature, science, etc. A qualified organization must use its money and staff to advance these purposes, rather than to benefit specific individuals. If the gift and the organization meet these standards, the donor may deduct the gift from income and the organization is exempt from paying taxes.

Charitable remainder trust: A trust that benefits designated individuals for life or a period of years and then distributes money or property for charitable purposes.

Charitable trust: A trust set up for a public purpose, such as for a school, church, charity, etc.

Codicil: A supplement or addition to a will that adds to or changes it.

Community property: Property owned in common (both persons owning it all) by a husband and wife. "Community property states" are those states that treat most property acquired during the marriage as the property of both partners no matter whose name it is in.

APPENDIX 38.1   GLOSSARY OF ESTATE PLANNING TERMS

Community trust: An organization set up to administer charitable or public trust funds received from many donors in a particular community.

Competent: Having the right natural or legal qualifications. For example, a person may be competent to make a will if she understands what making a will is, knows that she is making a will, and knows generally how making the will affects persons named in the will and affects relatives.

Consanguinity: Blood relationship; kinship.

Conservator: A guardian or preserver of property appointed generally by a court for a person who cannot legally manage it.

Cy pres: "As near as possible." When the provisions of a deceased person's will or trust can no longer legally or practically be carried out, a court may (but is not obligated to) order that the assets held under the terms of the will or trust are used in a way that most nearly accomplishes what the person would have wanted. If the court does not use its cy pres powers, the will or trust may be held void and no longer binding. The doctrine of cy pres is now usually applied only to charitable trusts.

Decedent: A person who has died.

Declaration of instrument of trust: A document created by a person owning property regarding the use of property for the benefit of himself or others.

Deduction: A reduction of income for tax purposes. Itemized deductions are those expenses that may be subtracted from adjusted gross income and include certain medical payments; taxes; home mortgage interest; charitable contributions; professional expenses; etc. There are detailed tax rules for deducting each. As an alternative to itemizing deductions, a individual may choose the standard deduction, which is a specific scaled amount based on income.

Deed of trust: A legal arrangement similar to a mortgage by which a person transfers the legal ownership of land to independent trustees to be held until a debt on the land is paid off.

Distributee: Heir; person who inherits.

Domiciliary: Relating to a person's permanent home. For example, a domiciliary administration is the handling of a decedent's estate in the state of the person's legal residence, the primary or permanent home.

Donative: As a gift. For example, a donative trust is a trust set up as a gift for another person.

Donee: A person or organization to whom a gift is made or a power is given.

Donor: A person making a gift to another or giving another person power to do something.

Earned income: 1. Money or other compensation received for work; does not include the profits gained from owning property. **2.** The earned income credit is a tax break given to certain low-income workers.

Estate tax: A tax paid on the property left by a decedent; paid on the property as a whole before the property is divided and distributed. This is different from an inheritance tax, which is based on the property each individual inherits and is paid from each heir's separate share.

Estate trust: A trust that holds property for a surviving spouse (which may qualify for the marital deduction) or for others.

Estimated tax: Persons with income from sources other than salaries must estimate and pay income tax four times a year.

Executor: A person named in a will to administer the estate and to distribute the property after the person making the will dies.

Generation-skipping trust: A trust that transfers payment down to grandchild or great-grandchild or unrelated person at least $37^1/_2$ years younger than the donor, for example, a trust created by a grandmother giving the trust income to her children and ultimately the trust assets to her grandchildren. Assets transferred through generation-skipping provisions may trigger tax consequences that may be diminished through the use of a special lifetime exemption.

Gift: 1. Any transfer of money or property without payment or compensation equivalent to the value of the thing transferred. **2.** Any willing transfer of money or property without payment.

Gift tax: A tax imposed on a gift that is paid by the giver or by the person receiving the gift.

APPENDIX 38.1 GLOSSARY OF ESTATE PLANNING TERMS

Gifts to Minors Act: A uniform act, adopted by most states, that simplifies the transfer of property to a minor child and allows property to be held for a child without the need for a legal guardian. An adult acts as the child's representative and controls the property, and the child gets the interest dividends, or gains, which may be used for the child's support.

Gross estate: The total value of a decedent's property from which deductions are subtracted to determine the taxable estate on which estate taxes will be paid.

Gross income: Under the federal tax laws, gross income is all earned and unearned income minus "exclusions." It is formally defined as "all income from whatever source derived" in the Internal Revenue Code.

Heir: A person who inherits property; a person who has a right to inherit property or a person who has a right to inherit property only if another person dies without leaving a valid, complete will.

Holograph: A will, deed, or other legal document that is entirely in the handwriting of the signer. Some states require a holographic will to be signed, witnessed, and in compliance with other formalities before it is valid. Other states require less.

Incapacity: Lack of legal ability or power to do something. For example, a minor child has a legal incapacity to vote or make contracts.

Income tax: A tax on profits from business, work, or investments including capital gains tax imposed on sale of appreciated investment assets.

Incomplete transfer: An attempted gift or other transfer of property made by a person who keeps some of the control or benefits. If the person then dies, the value of that property may be included in his estate for tax purposes.

Infancy: In general, the legal status of a very young child. In some states this means the same as minority.

Individual retirement account (IRA): A tax-deferred account or other investment arrangement.

Inheritance: Property received from a dead person, either by the effect of intestacy laws or under a will.

Insanity: In deciding whether a person has sufficient mental capacity to make a valid will, some of the signs of insanity are "inability to understand the property being given away, the purpose and manner of its distribution, and the persons who are to receive it."

Intent: The resolve or purpose to use a particular means to reach a particular result. Intent usually explains how a person wants to do something and what that person wants done.

Issue: Descendants such as children or grandchildren.

Joint: Together; as a group; united; undivided.

Joint bank account: A bank account held in the names of two or more persons, each of whom has full authority to deposit or withdraw money; on the death of one joint holder, the survivor or survivors generally inherit the account assets.

Keogh plan: A tax-deferred retirement account established by a person with self-employment income; similar to an individual retirement account.

Kin: 1. Blood relationship. **2.** Any relationship.

Legacy: 1. A gift of money by will. **2.** A gift of personal property (anything but real estate) by will. **3.** A gift of anything by will.

Legacy tax: A tax on the privilege of inheriting something. This may be an inheritance tax based on the value of the property, or it may be a flat fee.

Legal heirs: 1. Persons who will inherit if a person dies without a will. **2.** Any heirs.

Legatee: A person who inherits something in a will.

Lineal: In a line. For example, lineal relationships are those of father and son, grandson and grandmother, etc.

Living trust: A trust that takes effect while the person setting it up is still alive, as opposed to one set up under a will. It is also called an inter vivos trust.

Living will: A document in which a person expresses his wish about the extent of medical treatment to be administered if unconscious because of a terminal disease or injury and that may designate a person to make decisions about treatment on his behalf.

Majority: Full legal age to manage one's own affairs.

Marriage: Legal union as husband and wife.

Mutual: Done together; reciprocal. For example, mutual wills are separate wills that were made out as part of a deal, each one made because of the other one.

Natural heir: 1. Child. **2.** Close relative. **3.** Anyone who would inherit if there were no will.

Next of kin: 1. Persons most closely related to a decedent. **2.** All persons entitled to inherit from a person who has not left a will.

Of age: No longer a minor; a person who has reached the legal age to sue, vote, make a will, etc.

Patrimony: 1. All rights and property that have passed or will pass to a person from parents, grandparents, etc. **2.** All of a person's property, rights, and liabilities that can be given a dollar value.

Per capita: "By head"; by the number of individual persons, each to share equally.

Perpetuity: 1. Forever. **2.** Any attempt to control the disposition of property by transfer in trust for noncharitable purposes that is meant to last longer than the life of a person alive when the transfer is made (or at least conceived by then) plus 21 years. Most states have adopted statutes incorporating some version of the common-law as the Rule Against Perpetuities.

Per stirpes: A method of dividing a dead person's estate by giving out shares equally "by representation" or by family groups.

Pour-over: A will that transfers some money or property to an existing trust is called a pour-over will, and a trust that does this is a pour-over trust.

Power of attorney: A document authorizing a person to act as attorney for the person signing the document.

Pretermitted heir: A child (or sometimes any descendant) either unintentionally left out of a will or born after a will is made. Some states have pretermission statutes that allow a child left out by mistake to take a share of the parent's property.

Privity: A relationship between parties out of which arises some mutuality of interest.

Probate: 1. The process of proving that a will is genuine and distributing the property in a manner specified in the will. **2.** In some states the court that handles the distribution of decedents' estates handles other matters such as insanity commitments.

Real estate: Land, buildings, and things permanently attached to land and buildings. Also called realty and real property.

Residuary: The part left over. For example, a residuary clause in a will disposes of all items not specifically given away.

Reversion: Any future interest kept by a person who transfers property. For example, John transfers his land in trust, providing income to charity for 10 years. His ownership rights during those years, his right to take back the property after 10 years, and his heirs' right to take back the property, after 10 years if he dies, are reversionary interests.

Revocation: The voiding of a document. For example, revocation of a will takes place when, for example, a person tears it up intentionally or makes another will.

Simultaneous Death Act: A law, adopted in most states, requiring that if there is no evidence as to who died first in an accident, each decedent's property will pass as if that person survived the others. Some states have a presumption that the younger, healthier person lived longer.

Special use valuation: The option of a person handling a decedent's land to have it valued for tax purposes on the basis of its current use, not what it would be worth if used most profitably. For example, land used for agricultural purposes may under certain circumstances be so valued, rather than valued on the basis of its development potential.

Spendthrift: A person who spends money unwisely who may need a trustee to look after her property and/or principal. This protection of a person's property against himself, or creditors, is called a spendthrift trust.

Sprinkling trust: A trust that gives the trustee discretion to distribute income to many persons at different times.

APPENDIX 38.1   GLOSSARY OF ESTATE PLANNING TERMS

Statute of Wills: Various state laws, modeled after an old English law, that require a will to be in writing, signed, and properly witnessed in order to be valid.

Step up (or down) in (cost) basis: An increase (or decrease) in the tax basis of property to fair market value at the date of death of the person from whom the present owner inherited the property.

Stock: Shares of ownership in a corporation.

Stock dividend: Profits of stock ownership paid out by a corporation in more stock rather than in cash. This additional stock reflects the increased worth of the company.

Street name: Stock or other securities held in the customer's account, in the name of the brokerage or other firm acting for the customer.

Succession: The transfer of property at death. Intestate succession is the transfer of property by law to heirs where that person leaves no will.

Survivorship: The right to own property after the death of another person.

Take: Acquire when a person inherits property.

Tangible: Capable of being touched; real.

Tax avoidance: Planning finances carefully to take advantage of all legal tax breaks, such as deductions and exemptions.

Tax rate: The percentage of taxable income or taxable estate paid in taxes. The federal income and estate taxes have graduated rates.

Taxable estate (or gift): The property of a decedent, or a gift, that will be taxed after subtracting for allowable expenses, deductions, and exclusions.

Testamentary: Having to do with a will. For example, testamentary capacity is the mental ability needed to make a valid will; a testamentary class is the group of persons who will eventually inherit from a will.

Testator: A person who makes a will.

Treasury bill, bond, certificate, and note: Documents showing that the U.S. Treasury has borrowed money. A Treasury bill comes due in 3, 6, 9, or 12 months. It pays no interest, but is sold at a discount and the face amount including interest is paid at maturity; a Treasury certificate comes due in one year and pays interest by coupon; a Treasury note is like a certificate, but comes due in one to five years; and a Treasury bond is issued for long-term borrowing.

Trust: Any transfer or holding of money or property by one person for the benefit of another. There are many types of trusts, which may be set up during lifetime or can be set up in a will.

Trust company: A bank or similar organization that manages trusts, acts as executor of wills, and performs other similar functions.

Trust fund: Money or property set aside in a trust or set aside for a special purpose.

Trust instrument: A formal declaration of trust.

Trustee: A person who holds money or property for the benefit of another person and has a fiduciary relationship with another person.

Unitrust: A trust in which a fixed percentage of the trust property is paid out each year to individual beneficiaries based on an annual valuation of trust assets and the remainder passes to charity, meeting certain tax requirements.

Will: A document taking effect at death in which a person directs the distribution of his property after death.

Will substitutes: Life insurance, joint ownership of property, trusts, and other devices to partially eliminate the need for a will.

## CHAPTER THIRTY-NINE

Financial Planning for the Development Professional

39.1 INTRODUCTION

Too often, development officers and donors think primarily of cash and gifts of securities when it comes to making major gifts and fail to consider the donor's overall financial planning objectives and how alternative gift options may be better for the donor. Experienced planned giving officers know that a donor's philanthropic desires are affected by financial and estate planning objectives and the attendant tax consequences. Therefore, it is necessary to understand financial planning in order to assist donors in achieving their philanthropic goals. Financial planning involves the successful integration of several components of a donor's financial well-being, including:

- General investments

- Portfolio analysis and management

- Pensions and retirement

- Estate planning

- Tax considerations

- Real estate investments

- Life insurance

This chapter focuses on the basics of financial planning and is designed to heighten awareness of the various types of assets a donor may hold. Each of these assets may be used by the donor to make a gift to a nonprofit organization. Planned giving officers familiar with the language of investing and with an understanding of the underlying principles of investments can assist donors in contributing a wide array of assets. See Appendix, CD-ROM Documentation, Exhibits, for a sample Personal Information Record and Net Worth Statement, which can assist donors in inventorying their assets.

39.2 ACHIEVING FINANCIAL OBJECTIVES THROUGH CHARITABLE GIVING

Philanthropic investors can achieve some of their financial goals and objectives by incorporating charitable giving into their overall investment plans. Planned gifts can assist in producing safe and secure streams of income and can substantially increase yields over and above the rates for certificates of deposit (CDs), money market funds, and stock dividends. Charitable giving also can produce positive tax consequences by reducing income taxes, avoiding capital gains taxes, and minimizing federal estate and gift taxes. For the philanthropically disposed donor, charitable giving can satisfy a variety of financial objectives while providing support to one or more nonprofits.

The planned giving officer should keep in mind that the goal of many individuals is to achieve a measure of financial independence. A person's financial independence includes some or all of the following achievements:

- Reserving three to six months of take-home income in savings

- Setting aside a 10 to 20 percent down payment to purchase a home and pay for closing costs

- Building assets to pay for children's college tuition

- Saving assets for retirement

- Securing assets to transfer at death to children and grandchildren

- Building a nest egg

- Producing additional streams of income

- Reducing debt

- Increasing returns on current investments

- Reducing federal and state income taxes

- Avoiding capital gains taxes

- Reducing federal estate and gift taxes

- Avoiding probate

39.3 RISK-AND-REWARD THEORY

Investment opportunities are based on the risk-and-reward theory. Investments with a greater risk, such as junk bonds, potentially offer a greater reward. Low-risk investments, such as CDs and money market funds, offer lower rewards. Because high-risk investing often fails, it is not accurate to assume that there is always a reward for the accepted risk. Exhibit 39.1 illustrates the principle of risk and reward based on various investments.

Exhibit 39.1 Risk and Reward Chart

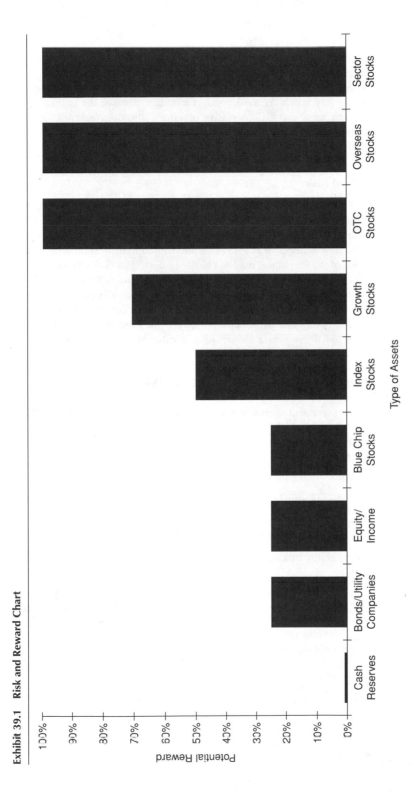

(a) Risk Tolerance

Every investor needs to reach a comfort level for risk tolerance. To be able to sleep at night, investors have to structure portfolios that complement their financial objectives and personalities. A basic theory of investment calls for every investor to accept some risk; otherwise, there will be a diminished reward. The way to achieve a risk comfort level is to regulate the amounts invested in assets that are inherently more risky. Conservative investors, uncomfortable with risk, still should consider having a percentage of their portfolio in higher-risk investments, regulating and adjusting the percentage to achieve the proper tolerance level.

(b) Time Frames and Risk

Investors also must consider the element of time as it relates to risk. Those who are otherwise aggressive in accepting a degree of risk in order to produce higher levels of return must turn to more conservative investments if the invested funds will be needed within a one- to five-year time frame. Investments such as growth stocks or growth funds are inappropriate as short-term investments, because the share price of the investment may be volatile or down at a time when these funds must be accessed. Investors with short-term windows of time should instead invest in short-term bond funds, CDs, or money market funds. For example, a donor anticipating retirement within a short time may begin to move from an aggressive position to a more conservative position. Charitable gift options, such as the charitable gift annuity, pooled income fund, and charitable remainder trust, used as a component to a donor's more conservative investments, can also supplement income.

39.4 EVALUATION OF INVESTMENT ALTERNATIVES

One way to evaluate investment alternatives is to look at the ways in which investors can obtain financial benefits, which include:

- Income—return to the investor in the form of interest or dividends

- Capital appreciation—the opportunity for an asset to increase in value over time

- Tax benefits—investments that offer tax savings, tax deferral, tax avoidance, or tax-free income

- Liquidity—the ability of an asset to be converted quickly into cash

- Pledge—the ability of an asset to be used as collateral

- Hedge—the ability of an asset to keep pace with inflation

Surprisingly, there are only five types of financial investment options from which to choose:

1. Liquid cash investments, represented by:
   a. Certificates of deposit
   b. Money market funds
   c. Treasury bills

2. Stocks, represented by:
   a. Blue-chip stocks
   b. Large-cap stocks
   c. Mid-cap stocks
   d. Small-cap stocks
   e. Micro-cap stocks
   f. Initial public offerings (IPOs)

3. Income investments represented by:
    a. Corporate bonds
    b. Government bonds
    c. Municipal bonds
    d. Zero coupon bonds
    e. Mortgage securities
    f. Utility stocks

4. Mutual funds, represented by:
    a. Growth stock funds
    b. Sector funds
    c. Index funds
    d. Bond funds
    e. Balanced funds
    f. Income funds
    g. International funds

5. Real estate, represented by:
    a. Residential properties
    b. Commercial properties
    c. Vacant land
    d. Investment properties

39.5   CASH INVESTMENTS

Cash investments offered by banks or brokerage houses earn interest on the principal invested. Currently rates are low, and many planned giving options produce streams of income that exceed the returns on fixed income investments. Elderly donors often equate financial independence with monthly income rather than the value of their portfolios. Simply put, cash flow pays the bills. Charitable gift annuities and gifts to a pooled income fund provide income streams that help produce cash flow and increase the rate of interest produced from a donor's current investment options.

(a) Certificates of Deposit

Certificates of deposit are purchased at banks and brokerage houses in amounts equal to the invested principal. The rate is fixed and locked in at the time of the investment. Certificates of deposit have maturity periods of one month, three months, six months, one year, two years, five years, and sometimes longer. The CD rate is paid periodically (monthly, annually) or when the CD matures. There is a substantial penalty for cashing a CD prior to its maturity. Donors can easily make a gift of a maturing CD to a nonprofit and obtain a charitable income tax deduction equal to the value of the CD.

(b) Money Market Funds

Money market funds are pooled funds invested in liquid assets such as Treasury bills, notes, and CDs. They are very secure and usually pay a slightly higher return than a savings account. The investment in the fund is maintained at a constant dollar value, although the rate varies daily. A money market fund can be managed through a mutual fund, a bank, or a brokerage account. The investor receives a daily rate, reflected in a monthly statement. Sometimes it is necessary to invest a minimum amount, such as $2,500. Investors can issue checks (drafts) from their market money accounts to nonprofit organizations.

(c) Treasury Bills

Treasury bills are fixed income securities backed by the full faith and credit of the U.S. government. They are issued at a discount, which means that they are sold at less than face value (the value indicated on the face of the bill). They are redeemed at face value at a specified maturity date, which may be 13, 26, or 52 weeks. The difference between the purchase price and the redemption price is the interest yield. U.S. Treasury notes and bonds also may be included in an overall investment plan, because their maturity periods are of greater length and can stabilize a portfolio. Treasury bills and U.S. government notes and bonds are exempt from state and local income taxes. Bills, notes, and bonds are readily marketable and may be contributed to nonprofit organizations.

39.6 STOCKS

A share of stock is an equity investment that represents an ownership interest in a corporation. Shareholders, owning stock, can earn a profit in two ways. First, they receive a proportionate share in the corporation's profits, measured as dividends. The dividend is declared by the board of directors of the corporation. The board may choose not to declare a dividend even if the corporation has profits if, in the judgment of the board, the profits need to be reinvested in the corporation. Second, shareholders also have an opportunity to receive capital gains or appreciation when the stock is sold if the value of the stock increases. The difference between what the stock cost (the cost basis) and its fair market value (FMV, the current value if sold today) is considered gain. The capital gains tax on most investment assets held 12 months or more is 15 percent on all gains, which means that any profit received by the shareholder is shared with the Internal Revenue Service (IRS). Donors can make gifts of stock to a nonprofit organization and obtain a charitable income tax deduction equal to the FMV of the stock, and they also avoid capital gains when making a gift of appreciated securities. Donors who want to avoid paying capital gains taxes but want to receive an income may choose to make a gift to a pooled income fund or to a charitable remainder trust, both of which avoid capital gains taxes on gifts of appreciated assets, such as securities.

(a) Types of Stocks

Blue-chip stocks are stocks issued by corporations that are large, very well known companies that have historically paid dividends in both good and bad times. Blue-chip stocks provide opportunities for both capital appreciation and periodic income from dividends, although the dividend yield is usually no more than 1 to 3 percent. These stocks, usually a safe and stable investment, form the foundation for many investors' portfolios. Blue-chip corporations are considered to be well managed and have high name recognition among the general public. Pooled income fund and gift annuity rates typically exceed the dividend rates earned on blue-chip stocks, so enterprising and philanthropic investors may look to nonprofits to achieve a higher yield while benefiting the nonprofits through planned gifts.

    Growth stocks are stocks in a variety of corporations. They usually form the aggressive portion of an investment portfolio and have opportunities for superior growth over time. These stocks may pay low dividends or no dividends. The "growth" factor is an opportunity to obtain capital appreciation, reflected in the growth of the business. Growth corporations include large caps, mid-caps, small caps and micro-caps. The "cap" refers to the market capitalization, which is the dollar value of the number of shares of issued stock multiplied by the price per share. The larger the number, the bigger the corporation. "Start-up" corporations typically have a high rate of failure, and investors should understand the inherent level of risk in owning stock in such businesses.

(b) Evaluating a Stock's Performance

There are several ways to assess a stock's performance. One of the most common is to look at a stock's price-earnings ratio. A price–earnings ratio (PE) describes the relationship between a stock's price and the earnings per share. To determine the ratio, simply divide the price of the stock by its earnings per share. For example, if a stock is selling for $20.00 per share and earnings per share is $2.00, then the PE is 10 ($20 ÷ $2 = 10). Blue-chip companies with solid earnings have lower PE ratios, and growth companies have higher PE ratios. Individual stocks' growth can be followed by reading the *Wall Street Journal*, other financial papers, or on the Internet.

A number of indexes provide points of comparison in measuring a stock's performance. The following are two of the most important:

(i) Dow Jones Industrial Average.   To find out how the stock market is doing, follow the "Average," or the "Dow." The Dow Jones Industrial Average is a measure of the movement of 30 industrial stocks' gains or losses. It includes corporations that are selected to be representative of various industries, such as manufacturing, high technology, and retail.

(ii) Standard & Poor's 500.   Known as the S&P 500, the Standard & Poor's 500 is a broad index of movement among 500 large corporations. The movement of the S&P 500 is a better measure of movement than the Dow Jones Industrial Average, because it represents a larger segment of corporate America.

39.7   INCOME INVESTMENTS

Income investments have the potential to offer greater returns than cash investments. These investments can include bonds, mortgage securities, and utility stocks. The bonds may be issued by the U.S. government, a municipality, or a corporation.

(a) Bonds

A bond is a debt instrument, considered a loan to the issuer, through which the bondholder receives income. Bonds, like stocks, also have a market value, referred to as par or face value, which is affected by interest rate changes or changes in the credit rating of the issuer. Most bonds are based on a value of $1,000. A bondholder receives an income in the form of a yield, and the $1,000 that was originally invested is returned on the bond's maturity date. A donor can make a gift of a bond to a nonprofit and obtain a charitable income tax deduction equal to the FMV of the bond. Any brokerage house can provide information on bond values as long as the name of the issuer, the maturity, the bond rate, and the face value are known.

(b) Types of Bonds

Bonds are classified according to the issuer.

Corporate bonds are essentially loans made to a corporation. An individual who purchases an IBM bond is, in fact, financing IBM. Bonds are rated with letter grades, which represent a judgment on the creditworthiness of the bond and the corporation. The lower the rate, the higher the return and the higher the risk in receiving the original investment at maturity.

Government bonds are loans made to the federal government that provide funding for operations and development. Backed by the U.S. government, these bonds are generally considered very safe and stable investments.

Municipal bonds, also known as "munies," are loans made to a municipality, state, or political subdivision to finance such activities as the maintenance of roads and bridges and the construction of a stadium or a school. Municipal bonds pay income to the bondholder free of federal income taxes and may also be free of state income taxes. Like other bonds, municipal bonds have a value and can be donated to a nonprofit organization.

Zero coupon bonds are issued by governments and private corporations. They have $1,000 to $10,000 face values and are sold at steep discounts below face value. The yield or interest is not distributed to the bondholder but is instead reflected in the value of the bond as it progresses toward its date of maturity. Although the income is not distributed, it is imputed to the bondholder and is included as income for tax purposes. This income, often called "phantom income," is costly to the donor, because the donor is taxed on income not yet received. A donor can make a gift of a zero coupon bond to a nonprofit organization and obtain a charitable income tax deduction equal to the FMV of the bond.

(c) Bonds and Interest Rates

Bonds are interest rate sensitive. This means that bond prices—prices investors would pay for the bonds—increase when interest rates fall and decrease when interest rates rise. A 6 percent bond may look good today, but if rates rise to 8 percent on new bonds, the value of the 6 percent bond falls. Conversely, if interest rates fall and new bonds are issued at 5 percent, a 6 percent bond would be attractive to an investor, who would likely agree to pay a premium above the bond's $1,000 face value.

39.8 MUTUAL FUNDS

A mutual fund is an option for investors to pool their capital to buy stocks or other securities selected by professional managers. There are hundreds of mutual fund companies that offer families of funds. Investors can move from stock funds to bond funds to income funds while staying within one mutual fund company. The investor selects a fund, and the investment is used to acquire shares in the fund. The value of the share, called the *net asset value*, varies like a stock's value, and the shares in the fund are bought and sold just like stock. Depending on the fund selected, investors have an opportunity for capital gains, as the net asset value reflects increases in the fund's underlying investments and income. If the fund is a stock fund, dividends from the underlying investments are distributed to the investor. If the fund is a bond fund, then income in the form of a yield is distributed to the investor. Donors can make gifts of shares in a mutual fund to a nonprofit. The planned giving officer should contact the mutual fund company to determine the exact value of such a gift and to facilitate the transfer of the shares from the donor's to the nonprofit's account. See Chapter 30 for a more complete discussion of gifts from mutual funds.

(a) Load versus No-Load Funds

A *load* is a fee charged to the buyer of a mutual fund and is based on a percentage of the investment. The fee may be a "front load" or an "exit load," sometimes referred to as a "redemption fee." A front load is a fee charged when the buyer buys into the mutual fund; an exit load or redemption fee is charged when the purchaser sells the investment. The load is usually between 2 and 8.5 percent, which is the maximum that a fund can charge. A no-load fund does not charge a fee when the purchaser buys into or leaves the mutual fund. Sometimes hidden operations fees are applied against earnings, which can diminish returns. These fees are often referred to as 12b-1 charges, named after the Securities and Exchange Commission rule of the same number. These charges include costs for marketing, advertising, and promotion of the mutual funds. Investors should not assume that because there is a load there will be better management or a greater opportunity for earnings. Studies have shown that there is no significant difference in the performance of load funds as compared with no-load funds.

(b) Types of Mutual Funds

Mutual funds are classified according to their investment objectives.

Growth funds invest in stock of corporations that are usually young and not well known. These corporations are in various types of product development and may be years away from profitability. Nevertheless, a growth fund represents an opportunity to achieve capital appreciation in the net asset value of the fund.

Sector funds are generally more risky than most other investments, because the investor is committing funds to a nondiversified, single-market investment. Sector funds invest in stocks of one industry group, such as retail, pharmaceuticals, or manufacturing. An investor who selects an industry that performs well enjoys a reward for the risk.

Index funds may be selected by investors who want to commit portions of their portfolio to reflect the makeup of the Dow Jones Industrial Average or of a broad index such as the S&P 500. Mutual fund companies have established index funds that invest in these corporations that make up the various indexes. Thus, it is possible to invest in all of the 30 industrial stocks that constitute the Dow Jones Industrial Average simply by investing in one index fund.

Bond funds invest in bonds of a variety of corporate and government entities. The goal of any bond fund is to produce income, measured against risk and interest rate sensitivity. Bond funds are structured by the selection of bonds with various maturity periods (1 year, 5 years, 10 years, and 30 years) so as to control risk.

Multipurpose funds, equity-income funds, growth and income funds, and *balanced funds* provide opportunities for both capital appreciation and income. The portfolio of a balanced fund consists of equities or stocks and income investments such as bonds or CDs.

Income funds are designed to produce income rather than capital appreciation. These funds invest in bonds, utility companies, mortgage securities, and CDs.

International funds are established by mutual fund companies that invest in foreign markets, which include a wide variety of geographic regions, including Japan, the Pacific Basin, Europe, the United Kingdom, Asia, and many others. These funds, which can be stock, bond, or balanced, enable investors to easily acquire ownership interests in foreign corporations without the confusion of dealing with foreign stock exchanges. Foreign currency price fluctuations can affect the investment.

39.9   REAL ESTATE

Aside from a personal residence or a vacation home, an individual may choose to make an investment in real estate. Investments in commercial property, vacant land, or residential units such as condominiums, cooperatives, duplexes, or multiplexes provide opportunities for both capital appreciation and rental income. Real estate investments are illiquid and subject to market fluctuations and economic conditions. If structured carefully, gifts of real estate can be used to make major contributions to nonprofits. See Chapter 31 for a more detailed discussion of gifts of real estate.

39.10 PORTFOLIO MANAGEMENT AND PLANNING

The portfolio, a blend of investment assets, might be compared to a restaurant menu. It contains specific investments chosen from several categories of investment opportunities. The individual percentage of each asset can be controlled to regulate an investor's risk and, therefore, the anticipated reward. The mix of each portfolio needs to be fine-tuned according to the objective and risk tolerance of the investor. Portfolio management is really a function of time: How much time is there before retirement? Before children reach the college years? The more time there is, the greater the opportunity to increase return by assuming greater risk. The shorter the time, the less opportunity to accept risk. Exhibits 39.2, 39.3, and 39.4 show how the mix of assets can change, depending on the investor's age, needs, and expectations.

An individual's financial planning goals must be revised regularly. At the very least, investment strategies and portfolio mix should be adjusted as an investor reaches a new decade and objectives and needs change. A charitable gift planner may find that as individuals reach a new decade, they may be more likely to review financial portfolios and incorporate charitable giving into their overall investment plans.

Exhibit 39.2   Sample Investment Portfolio for a 30-Year-Old

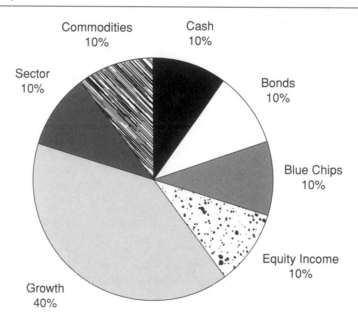

Exhibit 39.3 Sample Investment Portfolio for a 50-Year-Old

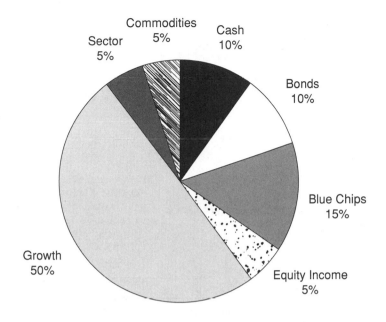

Exhibit 39.4 Sample Investment Portfolio for a 70-Year-Old

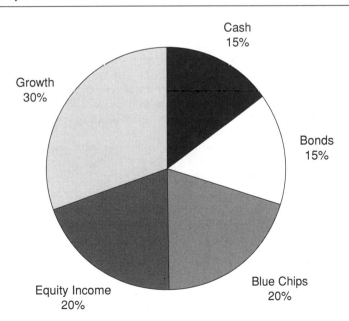

## CHAPTER FORTY

Retirement Planning and Planned Giving

40.1 INTRODUCTION

Gifts of retirement plan assets can be of significant value to a nonprofit organization, but for a variety of reasons they also can be a challenge to handle for both the donor and the charity. Tax considerations can limit the effectiveness of gifts of retirement plan assets, although new legislation might make these gifts more attractive in the future. Nonprofit organizations and donors should consult with professionals knowledgeable in the field of retirement planning before a gift is made.

40.2 GIFTS OF RETIREMENT PLAN ASSETS

Retirement vehicles such as employee benefit plans, individual retirement accounts (IRAs), Roth IRAs, corporate savings plans, 401(k) pension and profit sharing plans, and tax-sheltered 403(b) annuities provide individuals with opportunities for tax-deferred investments that also may be used to help nonprofit organizations. Individuals who shelter income through retirement plans are not taxed on either the income earned or the capital appreciation of the assets until the funds are withdrawn. When a donor participates in a 401(k) or 403(b) plan, her employer may make an additional contribution to the retirement plan, thereby increasing the retirement benefits. Moreover, the initial 403(b) and 401(k) contribution are made prior to income taxes being assessed against the employee's contributions. The Economic Growth and Tax Relief and Reconciliation Act of 2001 (EGTRRA) permits increases in annual contributions to both 401(k) and 403(b) plans: $12,000 in 2003, $13,000 in 2004, $14,000 in 2005, and $15,000 in 2006.

For IRAs, federal law limits the amount an individual can contribute each year. For example, if a donor qualifies, he can contribute a maximum of $3,000 per year in 2002 to 2004 to a traditional

IRA, provided he is not a participant in any other retirement plan and meets certain income limitations. The Roth IRA also has a $3,000 ceiling from 2002 to 2004, but a donor can establish one even if he participates in a retirement plan if certain income limitations are met. The EGTRRA allows increases in annual contributions to both Roth and traditional IRAs. The previous ceiling of $2,000 for contributions to a traditional IRA and a Roth IRA will increase gradually each year, rising eventually to $5,000 by the year 2008 ($3,000 in 2002–2004, $4,000 in 2005–2007, and to $5,000 in 2008–2010. Beginning in 2009 and onward, the amount will be adjusted to inflation.) Unlike the IRA, there is no ceiling on the amount of money that a donor can contribute to a charitable gift, although a donor's charitable income tax deduction may be limited by the annual percentage limitation applicable to charitable contributions.

In theory, retirement vehicles such as IRAs, tax-sheltered annuities, and qualified employee benefit plans may be used to make gifts to a charity, but in practice there are a variety of obstacles. Some plans permit the participant to name only the participant's spouse or certain other individuals, such as children, as plan beneficiaries. When a charity can be named, federal law also requires in most cases that the participant's spouse consent to the designation of a charity as beneficiary of a retirement plan at the employee's death. Because most retirement plans are funded with pretax income, the Internal Revenue Code requires that the assets of such plans be taxed at ordinary income rates upon any distribution of the asset during the donor's lifetime, even if the asset will be used to make a gift to charity. The donor obtains an offsetting charitable income tax deduction subject to the applicable income percentage limitations. Some attractive options still exist if the donor's retirement plan does not prohibit the transfer of plan assets to a charity or other planned gift vehicles.

Legislation has been proposed that would allow donors to make gifts of IRAs directly to a charity without first having to pay income taxes on the withdrawal and without receiving a charitable income tax deduction. If passed, this legislation will allow donors to make charitable gifts of IRA assets and, if future legislation is broad enough, perhaps other retirement plan assets, such as 401(k), 403(b)7, self-employed retirement plans (SEPs), and other related employer-sponsored plan assets without being affected by the income percentage limitations. At the time this book went to print, legislation had not been passed. Check with senators, representatives, certified public accountants, or charity's general counsel or planned giving consultant for more information on the status of this legislation.

40.3   TAX CONSEQUENCES OF CHARITABLE GIFTS OF RETIREMENT ACCOUNTS AT DEATH

As discussed, most withdrawals of or distributions from retirement account assets are fully taxable as ordinary income to the plan participant or to any noncharitable beneficiary. In addition, for estate tax purposes, the value of these assets is includible in the participant's estate. If the donor's spouse (a U.S. citizen) is designated as beneficiary, the estate tax is avoided because of the estate tax marital deduction; however, the assets are taxed in the estate of the donor's surviving spouse. If a nonprofit organization is designated as beneficiary, the estate tax also is avoided due to the estate tax charitable deduction.

Retirement accounts are characterized as income in respect of a decedent (IRD). These IRD items are taxable to the beneficiary and also are includible in the decedent's estate. The beneficiary may obtain an income tax deduction for estate taxes paid with respect to the IRD assets. Retirement accounts transferred to a charity at death avoid income tax because of the charity's tax-exempt status. Assets transferred to a charitable remainder trust will avoid income tax upon distribution because the trust itself is tax-exempt. Although ordinary income will be carved out with distributions, estate taxes also will be reduced by the charitable income tax deduction in respect of the remainder interest.

40.4 TYPES OF RETIREMENT PLANS

There are many types of retirement plans. The most common types are:

- *Individual retirement accounts (IRAs).* Individuals make contributions to IRAs up to a maximum of $3,000 per year (gradually increasing to $5,000), subject to various limitations and tax consequences upon distribution.

- *Roth IRAs.* Roth IRA provisions enable taxpayers to transfer up to $3,000 (again increasing to $5,000) posttax to an IRA account, provided their adjusted gross income is below certain limits. Any capital appreciation or income produced by the principal may be withdrawn tax-free so long as the taxpayer is 59½ years old or older and the principal has been in the account for five years or more. The new IRA provisions apply even if the taxpayer is covered under an employer's retirement program.

- *Section 401(k) plans.* Pretax voluntary contributions by an employee often are matched by the corporate employer.

- *Section 403(b) plans (sometimes referred to as tax-sheltered annuities).* Retirement plans for employees of nonprofit (501)(c)(3) organizations and public schools.

- *Qualified pension plans.* Regular contributions by an employer are used to fund retirement benefits for qualifying employees.

- *Qualified profit-sharing plans.* These are similar to pension plans, but the employer contributions are based on profits, and the amount of the contribution may vary from year to year.

- *Self-employed retirement plans (SEPs).* These include Keogh and SEP-IRA plans along with other self-directed retirement plans.

Many wealthy donors, especially those with fully funded retirement programs, were adversely affected by a 15 percent excise tax on excess distributions from qualified retirement plans, tax-sheltered annuities, and individual retirement accounts. The Taxpayer Relief Act of 1997 repealed this 15 percent excise tax, which acted as a deterrent to donors wishing to make a gift of such assets. Donors who now make a lifetime gift of retirement plan assets will pay federal and state ordinary income taxes on the distribution (as ordinary income, not capital gain) but will receive a charitable income tax deduction that may largely offset the income tax effects of the distribution.

40.5 WAYS TO TRANSFER RETIREMENT ASSETS TO A NONPROFIT

There are several ways to make gifts of retirement accounts to a charity. These options include: outright gift, designation of a beneficiary, bequest, and transfer to a charitable remainder trust.

(a) Retirement Assets Transferred through Outright Charitable Gifts

A donor can make an outright gift of a retirement account to a charity during her lifetime. Unfortunately, the donor must withdraw the assets, pay income taxes, and transfer the balance to the charity. These assets are fully taxable to the donor as ordinary income at her marginal tax rate. The donor can obtain a charitable income tax deduction, although it is limited to 50 percent of her adjusted gross income for gifts of public charities. If the donor is under age 59½, then additional penalties are imposed for early withdrawal unless the donor has retired and is at least 55 years old. Individuals must commence withdrawal of their retirement accounts by age 70½. Many donors choose to make the gift at that age because they want to offset the additional income. The inclusion in the donor's income of distributions from the retirement account and the subsequent charitable income tax deduction for the value of the donation results in a wash, at best, and the income percentage limitations may mean that the income will not be offset fully. Since the donor does not obtain favorable tax consequences and may incur relatively unfavorable tax consequences for a gift of a retirement plan, the use of this option is limited, but it is one way to make a gift.

(b) Designation of Beneficiary

If the donor's retirement plan is not depleted at death, he can designate a charity as a beneficiary to receive all or a stated percentage of his retirement account upon death. The donor receives an estate tax charitable tax deduction for the value of the assets distributed to a nonprofit organization. Like a bequest, a beneficiary designation provides the donor with an opportunity to make a considerable gift while avoiding income and estate tax on the assets remaining in the retirement account upon his death. The donor's estate obtains an estate tax charitable deduction for the value of the gift, and the charity is not taxed on the income arising from distribution. Unless the donor has created a separate account within the retirement plan and has designated the charity as the beneficiary of that separate account, designating both an individual and a charity as partial beneficiaries of a retirement plan will severely limit the individual beneficiary's withdrawal options and may have adverse income tax consequences.

(c) Bequest of Retirement Account

Donors transfer retirement accounts by designating a recipient as a beneficiary at death. In the absence of a beneficiary designation, the account generally will be payable to the donor's estate, if not the donor's spouse, and the donor may then transfer her retirement account through a bequest in her will. Technically the bequest should be a specific transfer. A specific transfer identifies the particular account to be distributed as compared to a gift through the donor's residuary clause. A transfer of a retirement account to charity, if properly made, avoids income taxation on the assets remaining in the retirement account at death. Because the transfer is made to a tax-exempt organization, the donor's estate also obtains an estate tax charitable deduction for the value of the account.

(d) Transfer to a Charitable Remainder Trust

If the retirement plan permits it, the donor may transfer the retirement account to a charitable remainder trust. The plan participant will be taxed on distributions from the retirement account as they are paid during life. At death, the assets remaining in the retirement account will be transferred to a charitable remainder trust, providing income to an individual beneficiary for life, with the remainder going to a nonprofit organization at the individual beneficiary's death. Ordinary taxable income is distributed to the income beneficiary according to the terms of the trust. The retirement account also is included in the donor's estate, but the estate receives an estate tax charitable deduction for the remainder value of the unitrust. *Caveat:* The full value of the account is included in the donor's estate, and the estate tax charitable deduction for the remainder is significantly less than the value of the account. Since a qualified charitable remainder trust is exempt from income tax, the retirement account proceeds are not taxed to the trust and the corpus is preserved. In addition, although retirement accounts are IRD items, IRD items transferred to a qualified charitable remainder trust avoid taxation because of the trust's tax-exempt status. As the income distributions are subsequently made to the life income beneficiary, they are taxed as ordinary income to the beneficiary.

(e) Charitable Remainder Unitrust for Spouse Funded with a Retirement Plan

A charitable remainder unitrust can be named as a beneficiary of a retirement plan that can provide income for life to a spouse, with the remainder going to a nonprofit. Upon the death of the first spouse, the qualified plan assets are distributed to the charitable remainder unitrust. The estate of the first spouse to die receives an estate tax charitable deduction for the remainder of the trust. However, the difference between the remainder and the initial transfer passes as a surviving spouse's income interest that qualifies for the marital deduction and therefore avoids estate taxes completely.

40.6 SUMMARY

The use of planned giving vehicles to assist in retirement planning is well accepted. The real challenge is finding ways to access the retirement plans to benefit nonprofits and satisfy a donor's financial and estate planning goals (see Exhibit 40.1).

Exhibit 40.1. Gifts of Retirement Assets

- Many plans prohibit the transfer of assets to a charity whether by outright gift or beneficiary designation.
- In cases where there is no prohibition, there may be little net tax benefit because the donor must withdraw assets that will be fully taxed. The donor receives a charitable income tax deduction equal to the withdrawal, but it may not fully offset the income.
- Retirement plan assets are characterized as IRD income. They are includible in the donor's estate for federal estate tax purposes and are subject to an income tax assessed to the beneficiary recipient. The recipient receives an income tax deduction for the estate tax paid attributable to the retirement account.
- If the plan permits, donors may transfer retirement plan assets at death by designating the charity as the beneficiary or by making a bequest of the assets to a charity or to a charitable remainder trust. Doing this may avoid or at least defer income taxation because the charity is tax exempt and income realized by the charitable remainder trust is not taxable until distributed to the income beneficiary.
- In the case of a charitable remainder trust funded at the donor's death and paying income to a survivor beneficiary, the value of the retirement account assets is included in full in the donor's estate but the donor's estate receives a charitable estate tax deduction for the value of the charitable remainder.
- However, in the case of a charitable remainder trust that provides only for the donor's spouse for life with no other income beneficiary (either concurrent or subsequent), the spouse's interest qualifies for the estate tax marital deduction and the entire value of the plan assets thus escapes federal estate taxation.
- Watch for legislation that will allow for transfers during the donor's lifetime of retirement plan assets to charity without having to pay income taxes on the withdrawal but also without receiving a separate charitable deduction.

40.7 CONCLUSION

In some circumstances, if a donor's retirement plan permits it, a donor may make distributions from retirement plan assets to a nonprofit organization. In the future, Congress may pass legislation that would allow transfer of retirement fund assets without individuals first paying taxes on the withdrawal. If so, gifts of retirement fund assets can provide valuable tools to donors who want to make charitable gifts.

## CHAPTER FORTY-ONE

Long-term Healthcare Insurance and Planned Giving[1]

41.1 INTRODUCTION

Planned giving officers should learn as much as possible about what concerns their donors. One issue of great concern to many donors and prospects is long-term healthcare insurance. Many worry whether they should purchase long-term healthcare insurance either for themselves or for a loved one. They wonder about whether they need such a policy, how policies work, the cost, their current medical conditions, and waiting periods to qualify for coverage. Their concerns may affect their desire or ability to make a major or planned gift, or force them to defer making a gift until death. It is helpful to the donor if the planned giving officer can knowledgeably discuss the ins and outs of long-term healthcare insurance and provide insight into what other donors have done about this issue. If a problem concerns one elderly donor, it is likely to concern others.

Long-term healthcare insurance is now viewed as part of a donor's overall estate plan. In addition to understanding long-term healthcare insurance, a planned giving officer should have a working knowledge of estate planning, financial planning, Social Security, and Medicare. This will help the planned giving officer understand what donors are concerned with and how these concerns

---

[1] The authors wish to acknowledge the following: *A Shopper's Guide to Long-Term Health Care Insurance* (Kansas City, MO: National Association of Insurance Commissioners), *Your Options for Financing Long-Term Care: A Massachusetts Guide* (Boston: Division of Insurance); and Benjamin Lipson, *J.K. Lasser's Choosing the Right Long-term Care Insurance* (Hoboken, NJ: Wiley, 2002). The authors also acknowledge the following disk documents: Availability and Cost of Long-term Care (*Massachusetts Guide,* pp. C-1, C-2) and Facts About Your Long-Term Care Insurance Policy (*Massachusetts Guide* p. F-1).

can affect a donor or prospect's ability to make a gift, as well as help the donor select the best type of gift vehicle to make a charitable gift.

41.2 DEFINITION

(a) What Is Long-term Healthcare Insurance?

Long-term healthcare insurance is insurance that pays for nursing home care and other long-term medical care, including, in some cases, custodial care or an assisted living residence. The care may be provided either at the patient's home or in some other facility, such as a nursing home. Long-term healthcare insurance helps protect one's personal assets against the risk of high nursing care expenses. Long-term healthcare insurance is usually paid for by an individual or an individual's family, although in some instances Medicaid (the federal and state program that provides medical costs for people with low incomes) may pay for long-term healthcare insurance. It is usually not covered by Medicare (the federal healthcare insurance for those over age 65) or private health insurance. See the glossary at the end of the chapter for additional definitions.

(b) Who Should Buy Long-term Healthcare Insurance?

One national study projects that 43 percent of people who turned age 65 in 1990 will enter a nursing home at some point during their lifetime. These could be short-term stays, a year or more stay, or over five years. The number of people receiving long-term care will greatly increase as the baby boomer generation ages. Many people between 50 and 79 years of age who are in good health and currently are able to care for themselves buy long-term healthcare insurance; about 6 million people in the United States have already purchased long-term healthcare policies. Because so many planned giving donors are age 65 or older, many face the decision of whether to purchase long-term healthcare insurance.

   For many individuals, long-term healthcare insurance is attractive. It helps to maintain independence and buys security and peace of mind. An individual should buy it only if the annual premiums will not be a financial hardship and after examining a number of factors, including age, health, income, and retirement objectives. Individuals with significant financial assets may wish to purchase long-term healthcare insurance to help protect their existing assets. Unfortunately, many people who can afford it may not need it—they can pay for long-term care costs out of pocket—while people who need it probably cannot afford it, as they may not be able to meet the cost of annual premiums. Because many planned giving donors have significant assets, yet not necessarily unlimited resources, whether to purchase long-term healthcare insurance can be a dilemma and affect their thought process about making a charitable gift.

(c) What Is the Cost?

   (i) Cost of Long-term Care.   The cost of one year in a nursing home varies tremendously from state to state and city to city. Costs may run from $40,000 per year to $75,000 per year and above. Expenses can be less if the individual receives skilled nursing care in his or her home, but on occasion, in acute cases, can be more than the daily nursing home rate. Cost is based on type of care received, the skill of the provider, and the number of times per week one is scheduled to receive care. Donors are concerned about this high cost of nursing home care and may be reluctant to commit to a major gift. Others may already be paying for nursing home care for a parent or a loved one and cannot make as large a gift as they wish or a gift at all.

   (ii) Cost of Long-term Healthcare Insurance.   Long-term healthcare insurance is expensive, depending on the amount and type of care needed and the setting in which the care is

provided, but is less expensive than what would be paid for long-term care. Potential purchasers of such insurance will want to be sure that they can cover the cost of the premiums, as well as continue to pay the premiums for other health insurance. The annual premium for long-term care insurance policies with inflation protection can run as much as $3,000 per year for a 65-year-old. The premium is higher for older individuals; cost could run to be twice as expensive, or more, for a 75-year-old. It should be noted that premiums are not guaranteed for the life of the policy.

A healthy 55-year-old can buy a long-term healthcare insurance policy that will cover home health services and up to four years in a nursing home or other facility for about $2,000 per year. In examining this over time, in 25 years at age 80, this individual will have spent about $25,000 on annual premiums. Just one year in a nursing home beginning at age 80 would cost significantly more than $25,000. He would recover the premium costs in less than one year of extended care.

(d) How Long Could Long-term Healthcare Be Needed?

One cannot predict his or her individual chances of needing long-term care. The need may evolve gradually or follow a major illness. Care may be needed for many years or perhaps for just a few months. Chances are greater that a woman will need nursing home care because statistically women live longer. Predictions are difficult to make with medical advancements and lifestyle changes that now allow people to live longer.

41.3 HOW POLICIES WORK

It is important for the planned giving officer to understand the basics of long-term healthcare insurance, including how individual policies work and generally what protection is likely to be included. Having this knowledge may help the planned giving officer work with a donor or prospect who is contemplating buying such insurance and how having or not having the insurance would affect his ability to make a gift.

(a) What Is Covered

It is difficult to understand the subtle differences among policies, differentiating between what is and is not covered. Some policies cover only in-home care. Many long-term care policies cover only care provided in licensed nursing homes; type or level of care does not matter. Other policies cover both. Many policies cover services that are provided in adult day care centers and other community facilities.

Home care coverage can vary. Some policies pay only for care performed at home by registered nurses or licensed practical nurses and occupational, speech, or physical therapists. Other policies offer a longer range of home care benefits—coverage such as care provided by home health aides and homemaker or chore workers. Most policies do not cover benefits to family members who perform home care services.

(b) What Is Not Covered

Policies generally do not cover services needed by an individual who has:

- A mental or nervous disorder other than Alzheimer's disease, although some states now require insurers to cover mental and nervous disorders
- Alcohol or drug addiction
- An injury caused by war

- Treatments already paid for by the government
- Attempted suicide or self-inflicted injuries

(c) When Individuals Are Eligible for Benefits

Long-term healthcare insurance policies' coverage varies dramatically, so each policy must be read carefully. When a policy begins to pay, benefits generally fall into the following categories (in tax-qualified policies):

- *Inability to perform activities of daily living.* This is the most common method for determining when benefits are payable. Coverage will begin when an individual cannot perform activities of daily living (ADLs) such as bathing, maintaining continence, dressing, eating, toileting, and transferring in and out of beds and chairs. Generally, benefits are payable when an individual is unable to perform a certain number of ADLs, such as two or three ADLs out of six. The ADL activity must be expected to last for at least 90 days. Recertification must occur every 12 months by a physician to confirm the disability. The more specific the policy is in describing a failure to perform one of the above functions, the easier it is to file a claim. Research has shown that bathing is usually the first ADL that an individual is unable to perform.

- *Cognitive impairment.* This provision provides benefits if an individual is unable to pass certain tests related to mental function. It is especially important for individuals with Alzheimer's disease.

- *Doctor certification.* Under some policies, an individual qualifies for care if a physician certifies that medical care is necessary.

- *Prior hospitalization.* A few states allow insurance companies to refuse to pay benefits unless the insured has had a prior hospital stay of at least three days. While this is considered quite restrictive, Medicare requires a three-day prior hospital stay for eligibility for skilled nursing facility benefits.

- *Waiting periods.* Many policies do not begin to provide coverage the day an individual enters a nursing home or begins using home care. Most policies include a waiting period, sometimes 20 to 100 days, once an individual enters a nursing home before benefits can be received. During a waiting period, the individual will be responsible for covering the cost of her own care. A policy without a waiting period will cost more.

Be clear about how a policy pays if there is a repeat stay in a nursing home. Some policies require an individual to be out of a facility for a certain period of time before benefits can be received for a second stay. Other policies consider the second stay as part of the first stay. Repeat nursing home stays, however, are not typical.

(d) When Long-term Care Costs Rise

Inflation protection adds to the cost of a policy. Years from now an individual does not want to find himself owning a policy that cannot cover the cost of needed care. The younger the individual is when purchasing the insurance, the more important it is to add inflation protection.

Two options usually exist for protecting against inflation. One option is for the cost of benefits to rise each year. A second option is for benefits to increase periodically, such as every three years. The donor should be sure to check the inflation adjustment of a policy to determine how the policy increases, which will ultimately determine the amount of coverage.

(e) Tax Deductibility

For individual itemizers, premiums paid for long-term healthcare insurance can be added as medical expense deductions. Medical expenses are deductible to the extent that they exceed 7.5 percent of adjusted gross income and are subject to maximum limits based on the policyholder's age. The extent to which one may treat long-term healthcare premiums as medical expenses increases with age. Additionally, the money paid out as a benefit is not taxable. If a corporation is paying the cost of premiums, the entire amount of the premium is deductible for a C corporation and partially deductible for an S corporation. The insurance industry is also lobbying Congress to make paid premiums fully tax deductible, as an incentive to buy insurance.

(f) Does Health Affect Ability to Be Covered?

Long-term healthcare insurance underwriting varies from company to company, but all are likely to look at one's current health and health history before issuing coverage. Depending on the company, the individual applying for coverage is likely to be asked for a medical history, to produce medical records, and to produce a health statement from her physician. Having a condition like Parkinson's disease that is likely to require a nursing home stay in the near future probably will disqualify coverage. Some group policies, often available through an employer, may provide coverage without some of these requirements.

   If one has a preexisting condition, wherein medical advice or treatment was sought or there were symptoms within a certain period of time before applying for the policy, the company may not pay benefits for this condition if the preexisting condition was not disclosed to the insurance company. Insurance companies also will vary in different policies the length of time that they look back at health status. It is important to answer all questions truthfully when completing an insurance application so that a policy cannot later be rescinded or canceled.

(g) Health Assessment

An assessment of health may be required when an individual applies for long-term healthcare insurance. This assessment is a conversation between the potential insured and a trained assessor, usually a nurse or social worker. The individual will have his blood pressure read and have height and weight measured. There will be questions to test cognitive abilities that are quite basic. Additionally, during the interview with a trained assessor, the following information is likely to be requested:

- An outline of daily activities
- Household chores
- Transportation
- Meal preparation
- Present and past health
- Current medications
- Recent physician visits

All information is confidential. No disrobing is required, and family or friends may be present. A donor or prospect who is competent to consider making a major gift is likely to pass this type of examination.

41.4 EMOTIONAL ASPECTS

It may be difficult to discuss long-term healthcare insurance. The individual who may need insurance may find it hard to discuss a future serious illness. Most people fear becoming a burden on their children. For the child, it may be hard because she does not want to place a parent in a nursing home. Planned giving officers may find discussing long-term healthcare insurance like discussing a bequest, where people do not like thinking about death or disability. It may be helpful to include children or others in the discussion; perhaps a child will be paying the cost of a parent's insurance premiums.

The planned giving officer's role may be that of a sounding board when this topic arises. Good listening skills come into play, as well as knowing that it is not the planned giving officer's job to make this decision for the donor. The planned giving officer needs to encourage the donor to discuss long-term healthcare insurance with family, friends, and a financial advisor. Keep in mind that the individual, not any third party, is the one to make the final decision as to whether or not to buy long-term healthcare insurance.

41.5 CHOOSING A PLANNED GIFT OPTION

If prospects or donors become unsure about their ability to make a gift, either worrying about the cost of long-term healthcare insurance or the cost of extended care for themselves or a parent, the planned giving officer may want to suggest a gift option to the donor that would provide a set amount of income each year that he could count on to pay the cost of long-term healthcare insurance premiums. A likely option would be a charitable gift annuity or a charitable remainder annuity trust. The donor enjoys a charitable income tax deduction while counting on a specific amount of income each year to apply toward the premiums. If the donor is very concerned about future costs of long-term care or the price of annual insurance premiums and wants to make a charitable gift, a bequest may be the best option. Because a bequest gift will come to the charity only at the donor's death, the donor will feel more secure about any cash needs during his or her lifetime.

Some final thoughts to consider when working with a donor who is considering purchasing long-term healthcare insurance include:

- A donor should not buy long-term healthcare insurance out of fear. The entire situation should be examined, and a rational decision should be made, not based on sales hype.

- A policy that was purchased before December 31, 1996, should most likely not be replaced, because some policies issued prior to that date are likely to contain benefits not available in current plans.

- Once a decision to buy or not buy long-term healthcare insurance is made, an individual should commit to the decision; otherwise, the individual will continually feel frustrated if second guessing his decision.

- The donor should not let an approaching birthday create pressure to buy long-term healthcare insurance. Some policies can be backdated.

Checklist for Buying Long-term Healthcare Insurance

- Examine this topic rationally and unemotionally, if possible.

- Look for the daily benefit, duration of benefit, and inflation coverage.

- Take into account that insurance premiums may rise.

- See what, if anything, is available under Medicare.

- List all medications and physician information if deciding to purchase coverage.

- Maintain current level of medical coverage.

- Buy just one long-term healthcare insurance policy.

- Consider paying premiums on an automatic basis from a checking account.

- Select a financially stable insurance company for insurance coverage.

41.6   CONCLUSION

Planned giving officers should strive to learn as much as possible about long-term healthcare insurance. Some donors and prospects may delay thinking about charitable giving, question their ability to make a life income gift, or choose to make a bequest or no gift at all until they can resolve whether they or a loved one need this type of insurance. Issues to consider include who should buy long-term healthcare insurance, its cost, what is covered, when one is eligible for benefits, tax deductibility, and how health affects opportunity for coverage. Planned giving officers should be knowledgeable on all of these topics because many donors, prospects, and families are concerned with this issue.

APPENDIX 41.1   GLOSSARY OF TERMS

Activities of daily living (ADLs): Activities usually performed in the course of a normal day. Although definitions differ, ADLs are usually considered to be everyday activities such as walking, getting in and out of bed, dressing, bathing, eating, and toileting.

Benefits: The money or services provided by an insurance policy. In a health plan, benefits take the form of healthcare.

Custodial care: Personal care such as bathing, cooking, shopping, etc.

Disenroll: Ending your healthcare coverage with a health plan.

Exclusion period: A period of time of up to six months when an insurance company can delay coverage of a preexisting condition.

Home healthcare: Medical care that is provided at home, such as physical therapy or skilled nursing care. It is different from at-home recovery care, which is help with bathing, eating, and other activities of daily living.

Long-term care: Custodial care provided at home or in a nursing home for people with chronic disabilities and prolonged illness. It is not covered by Medicare. Long-term healthcare insurance coverage can be purchased from a private insurance company.

Medicaid: A joint federal and state program that helps with medical costs for some people with low incomes. Programs vary from state to state, but most healthcare costs are covered if one qualifies for both Medicare and Medicaid.

Medical underwriting: The process that a company uses to determine whether to accept an application for insurance and how much to charge for that insurance.

Medicare: A health insurance program for people 65 years of age or older, certain young people with disabilities, and people with end-stage renal disease (people with permanent kidney failure who need dialysis or a transplant).

Premium: Periodic payment to Medicare, an insurance company, or a healthcare plan for healthcare coverage.

Preventive care: Care to keep one healthy or prevent illness, such as routine checkups and some tests like colorectal cancer screening, yearly mammograms, and flu shots.

Provider: A doctor, hospital, healthcare professional, or healthcare facility.

Skilled nursing facility (SNF): A facility that provides skilled nursing or rehabilitation services to help recover after a hospital stay.

Waiting period: The time between when one signs up with a Medigap insurance company or Medicare health plan and when coverage starts.

PART EIGHT

Policies and Procedures

Gift Acceptance Policies

42.1 INTRODUCTION

Nonprofit organizations that offer planned gifts need to have a written gift acceptance policy to address issues involved with accepting noncash gifts. Outright cash gifts are straightforward, offering very few challenges to a development program. However, because many deferred gift arrangements have long-term implications and obligate a charity to make payments to a donor for life, they must be monitored by the charity to protect both the donor and the charity.

The nonprofit that accepts life income gifts is obligated to pay a stream of income for life to a donor or another beneficiary. For example, if a 65-year-old donor creates a charitable gift annuity, charitable remainder trust, or pooled income fund gift, the gift has the potential of running for 25 years or more for the benefit of the first beneficiary, often the donor, and longer than 25 years if payments are made to a younger, second beneficiary. Other types of planned gifts also can obligate a charity for years. Gifts of real estate can obligate a charity to act as a landlord and real estate agent, sometimes for out-of-state property. Tangible personal property gifts may need insurance, storage, and special display cases, committing a charity to incur substantive out-of-pocket costs for years.

A gift acceptance policy is a written compilation of guidelines and suggestions for everyone involved in the gift process to understand and abide by. Development staff members need to understand the difference between a planned gift that is truly a gift to the charity, given by a donor who really wants to benefit the nonprofit, and a "gift" that is motivated by personal financial gain, which could obligate the charity to a lifelong arrangement that is not in its best interest. A written gift acceptance policy helps everyone involved to understand the difference.

In their eagerness to raise money, some inexperienced planned giving officers may move too quickly when a prospect wants to make a gift of real estate to the charity. A development officer who is inexperienced in handling gifts of real estate may see this as an opportunity to add to the gift totals for that year. Unfortunately, the development officer may spend valuable time pursuing the gift, only to discover that the property would provide no benefit and would instead be a burden on the nonprofit, requiring substantial financial outlay and management.

Development officers also may be approached by a financial advisor who suggests that the charity create a charitable remainder trust for a donor who wishes to receive a very high payout rate, such as 15 percent. The development officer may feel that this arrangement is better than no gift at all and not realize that the trust is likely to be exhausted by paying such a high annual rate of return to the donor, depleting the remainder, or gift, to the charity. Such gifts often require significant management, time, and expense on the charity's part.

A gift acceptance policy provides a way for planned giving officers to decline such arrangements graciously. They can cite a policy that does not allow certain types of real estate arrangements or payout rates greater than a certain percentage. Such a policy also provides an outline for staff members to follow for most gift arrangements.

Donors need to understand that a gift policy exists to protect the charity, because some so-called gifts provide only an incidental benefit, if any at all, to the charity. If the transaction is a way for the prospect to unload burdensome property that cannot be disposed of in any other way, or is made as a way to recoup lost principal through a charitable income tax deduction because of falling real estate prices, a gift acceptance policy can help the donor see that the gift would not benefit the charity. Citing a policy helps prevent the donor from feeling singled out and avoids alienating the prospect from the charity. This is especially helpful if the donor has a strong relationship with someone at the charity, such as a trustee or high-level administrator, dean, or physician.

A sample gift acceptance policy is included at the end of this chapter and is also found in Appendix, CD-ROM Documentation, Administrative Documents. This chapter outlines the elements of a gift acceptance policy for gifts of cash, securities, life income arrangements, bequests, tangible personal property, real estate, and life insurance. The chapter concludes by exploring administrative issues that can arise in a planned gift program that should be included in a gift acceptance policy.

(a) Who Should Draft the Policy

Several departments should be involved in drafting a gift acceptance policy. The need for the policy is likely to originate in the development office and should be reviewed first by the vice-president for development, the director of development, and the planned giving director. Legal counsel, whether inside or outside the nonprofit, should then review the draft to offer legal opinions on certain gift arrangements, especially gifts of real estate, life insurance, and gifts of tangible personal property. Outside legal counsel also can offer insight about provisions that other charitable organizations include in their gift acceptance policies.

The treasurer's office and financial administrator should be involved in the drafting process to protect the charity from entering into gift situations that are financially questionable for the charity, such as establishing charitable remainder trusts with extraordinarily high payout rates or gift annuities with rates that greatly exceed those suggested by the American Council on Gift Annuities. The treasurer's office or business office also can assist in outlining procedures for accepting gifts of real estate creating parameters for endowed funds by establishing the rate of income to be paid out on a fund and, fees and how much, if any, income should be returned to principal.

(b) Flexibility

A gift acceptance policy must be flexible because exceptions in the gift acceptance process always arise. Planned gift situations can be unique and are very different from annual fund gifts. A donor's relationship with the nonprofit can create a reason for the charity to deviate from the policy. A trustee or administrator at the charity may propose a gift option that is not terribly attractive to the charity, but the donor's connection to the organization may sway the charity to accept the gift. So, too, a charity may want or need to make an exception for a donor who has a giving record that includes substantial gifts over a long period of time to the charity. Development officers also may wish to deviate from an existing policy because of potential future gifts to the charity. Whether to deviate from the existing policy is a decision that should be made by the organization's restricted gift committee, if one exists, or informally after consultation with members of the development staff, treasurer's office, and legal counsel. See Chapter 38 for more about restricted gift committees. No policy should be written that does not allow for exceptions.

42.2 CASH

Gifts of cash (including checks) of all sizes are regularly accepted by nonprofits. All checks should be made out in the legal name of the charity; although it seems self-evident, checks should never be made payable to an individual working on behalf of the nonprofit.

Gifts of cash should be turned down by a charity if a donor tries to place restrictions on the gift that are unacceptable to the charity, contrary to public policy, or potentially illegal, such as excluding members of a race from benefiting from an endowed fund or establishing a fund to benefit an individual selected in advance by the donor. A charity may also want to turn down a cash gift when a donor asks the nonprofit to use the gift in a way that is incompatible with the charity's mission or long-range plan. For example, a nonprofit hospital might choose to turn down a gift from a donor who wishes to establish a fund to provide medical training for Polish physicians to study in the United States and then return to Poland. Such an arrangement could require work well beyond the hospital's mission of providing medical education.

42.3 SECURITIES

(a) Publicly Traded Securities

All charities accept marketable securities, including those readily traded on national or regional stock exchanges. Before the gift is made, the development professional involved with a transfer of public securities should tell a donor who wishes to make a gift of securities that the nonprofit organization's general policy is to sell gifted securities. Donors often think that the charity should keep the gifted securities because the donor is emotionally attached to the securities and feels that they are a particularly good investment. For ease of management and strategic investing, most charities do not keep small blocks of stocks representing many different companies gifted from donors; the stocks do not fit the charity's overall portfolio, which contains a diverse range of investments.

It is the charity's right, as owner of the gifted securities, to decide whether to sell them, and the planned giving officer should remind the donor of this in the beginning of the gift process to prevent misunderstandings or ill will. Having a gift acceptance policy that mandates sale of gifted securities as soon as they are received helps the charity if the donor criticizes the charity's decision to sell securities that later increase in value, and also helps prevent donors from tracking the price of the securities, staying involved with the gift long after they should.

(b) Closely Held Securities

Closely held securities, those that are not publicly traded, can be accepted by most charitable organizations. Many gifts of closely held securities represent gifts from donors that are private or family-owned businesses. Before accepting a gift of closely held securities, the charity should explore how the securities could be redeemed, such as whether they will be bought back by the company itself or by one of its shareholders. Many types of closely held stock have restrictions on transfer, as most closely held businesses do not want to see ownership move out of a small group of owners. Many companies will work with the charity to arrive at a price to buy back or redeem the securities. However, the charity has a limited number of options when deciding who will buy back the shares of stock and may have less bargaining power than it appears.

No prearrangement with respect to the sale of stock may be in place before the gift. The charity must have full discretion to decide whether and when to sell. Nevertheless, it is important to locate a potential purchaser who may buy back the shares of stock. At that point the charity can move forward with accepting the gift and completing acceptance of the gifted securities. When the charity is holding the securities, it can then negotiate with the company or individual the price per share to be paid for the closely held stock. A redemption of stock to the company can be a quick process, but at other times may take years, depending on how long the charity is willing to hold out for a specific price. A commitment for sale or redemption of closely held securities should not be entered into before the gift to the charity is completed, as this amounts to a preexisting agreement and could cause the donor to be taxed. A gift acceptance policy that addresses gifts of closely held stock should include determining who will buy back the shares of stock and the necessity of working with the charity's treasurer's, business, or legal counsel's office before accepting the gift. The charity also may want to include its restricted gift committee in its decision-making process. See Chapter 30 for a complete discussion of closely held securities.

42.4 LIFE INCOME GIFTS

Because of the charity's lifetime obligation to a donor, life income gift arrangements should not be entered into lightly. Life income gifts can cause conflict between a donor and the charitable organization that is offering the gift arrangement. The charity must have an investment strategy that allows it to meet its financial obligation to pay lifetime income to the donor, as well as administrative systems that can be maintained many years into the future. The charity must balance the desires of the donor to make a gift, and the development staff's wish to receive it, along with the nonprofit's goal to build endowment with the charity's need for current income and its willingness to spend time and money on administering a gift for many years without use of the principal.

A typical challenge presented by a life income gift is illustrated when prospects want their young children or grandchildren named as beneficiaries of a pooled income fund gift. Although legal, such an arrangement can result in a small gift received by the charity well into the future, because of the life expectancies of the young beneficiaries. The charity must decide whether the remainder value is sufficient to justify managing such an arrangement for so many years. Charities also must be alert to life income arrangements that primarily benefit the donor, leaving little or no gift for the charity. This often occurs when individuals wish to establish charitable remainder trusts with high rates of annual payout that could be difficult or impossible for the charity to meet and would, over time, result in erosion of the trust principal.

The following text examines issues that affect charitable remainder trusts, pooled income funds, and charitable gift annuities. These issues include amount of initial and subsequent gifts, payout rates, and ages of beneficiaries.

(a) Amount of Initial Gift and Subsequent Gifts

Most nonprofits require a minimum-size life income gift because, among other things, the cost of investing and administering such gifts is high. The following subsections suggest typical gift minimums, which vary depending on the size of the charity's development program and the wishes of its vice-president for development, board of trustees, treasurer's office, and outside money manager. Most charities need to balance the management and administrative costs of the gift (fees charged by the asset manager for investing the assets and the administrator for sending income payments and tax information to beneficiaries) with the possibility of discouraging donors from making a gift because of high gift minimums.

(i) Charitable Remainder Trusts. Many charities that have their programs managed by asset managers feel that charitable remainder trusts cannot be established for less than $100,000, because of the time required to manage separately invested funds. For a donor who wishes to establish a charitable remainder trust for a smaller amount, the asset manager may be willing to accept a charitable remainder trust for $75,000 if the trust's assets can be combined with the financial institution's common trust funds, reducing the time involved in managing the account.

Some nonprofits, often larger organizations such as Ivy League and older colleges, universities, and secondary schools with well-established development programs, manage their own charitable remainder trusts in-house and elect a lower gift minimum. A common figure found for charitable remainder trusts managed in-house is $100,000.

Additional gifts cannot be made to a charitable remainder annuity trust, but additional gifts can be made to a charitable remainder unitrust. Many charities prefer not to establish gift minimums for additional gifts to charitable remainder unitrusts and allow donors to make additional gifts of any amount. Other charities, especially those that have older, more established development programs, set gift minimums for additional gifts to a charitable remainder unitrust as low as $1,000. Many organizations find that the time and expense associated with processing the additional gift requires a specific minimum dollar amount.

(ii) Pooled Income Funds. Many charities choose $5,000 or $10,000 as a minimum gift amount for donors to enter the pooled income fund. This figure is lower than most gift minimums for charitable remainder trusts because the large number of beneficiaries in a pooled income fund reduces the number of investment decisions and administrative responsibilities (compared to those of a separately invested charitable remainder trust, where decisions are made for just a few beneficiaries). Selecting $10,000 as a gift minimum can set donors' giving sights higher, but hopefully is not done at the expense of losing gifts that might have been made if the minimum were $5,000.

Many charities that offer pooled income funds set $1,000 as a minimum additional gift amount, whereas other charities set no minimum for additional gifts, taking into the fund whatever amount the donor chooses to give.

(iii) Charitable and Deferred Gift Annuities. Many charities require a gift minimum of $5,000 to establish a charitable gift annuity or deferred gift annuity; others have increased that amount to $10,000. Again, the charity must balance the administrative cost of the gift with the potential loss of a gift when establishing a higher gift minimum.

Because charitable gift annuities cannot be augmented, but must be established as new gift annuities each time a donor wishes to establish one, many organizations choose to keep the establishment of a second charitable gift annuity at the same minimum amount as the first gift annuity. To encourage subsequent gifts, however, some charities allow donors to establish a second charitable gift annuity at a lower amount. When the charity allows subsequent gift annuities to be established at smaller amounts, it should determine how much benefit it receives from smaller subsequent gifts after the cost of administration is considered.

(b) Payout Rates

The charity must decide on a policy for dealing with the payout rate on life income gifts, because the charity will frequently be asked by donors and their financial advisors about the maximum payout rate allowed by the charity. The nonprofit must be sure that it is comfortable with the guidelines it establishes, because they are likely to be challenged often by donors seeking high payout rates. The desire to receive a high payout rate can encourage donors to shop around at different charities for the highest rate, creating competition among charities and undermining the spirit of philanthropy. Planned giving officers, disappointed by a prospect who made a gift to another charity that offered a higher rate, should remember that this prospect was not motivated by donative intent.

(i) Charitable Remainder Trusts. Although Congress has established 5 percent as the minimum amount for a charitable remainder trust payout rate, the minimum payout rate is rarely ever the issue with donors; the discussion more often revolves around the maximum rate allowed by charity that serves as the trustee of the trust for the donor. Many charities prefer a payout rate of 5 or 6 percent. A charity may accept a payout of 7 percent or higher if the youngest beneficiary of the trust is older, if the size of the trust is quite substantial, or the donor has a special relationship with the charity. A charity also can select rates between whole percentage points, such as 5.5 percent, to pay a donor.

Higher payout rates may be acceptable for trusts that are established for a term of years rather than a donor's lifetime. Trusts established for a small number of years, such as fewer than 10 years, may be high, such as 7 or 8 percent, especially if the donor has a specific objective that can be accomplished in a few years, such as paying college tuition for four years. The size of the gift also can be a factor when choosing a higher payout rate because, although more income will be paid to the beneficiary, the remainder amount to the charity will still be significant because of the gift's size. Donors also may select an outside institutional trustee, such as a bank or trust company, to serve as trustee, one who is not affiliated with the nonprofit. In this case, the payout rate is determined by the donor and the institutional trustee. The nonprofit organization is excluded from the process and, in many cases, may never know about the trust until the death of the donor, when the remainder is transferred to the nonprofit organization.

(ii) Pooled Income Funds. Because the payout rate from a pooled income fund is based on the income earned by the fund, and is always variable, determining a maximum payout rate is not applicable. A charity may wish to establish several different pooled income funds with different investment objectives. When the funds are first established, investment objectives must be considered so that approximate rates can be met.

(iii) Charitable Gift Annuities. The need for a written gift acceptance policy that establishes maximum payout rates allowed by the charity for donors at certain ages is important because, as mentioned earlier, some donors shop for the highest gift annuity payout rates among charities. Chapter 23 discusses the American Council on Gift Annuities (ACGA) and the reasons that nonprofits may wish to follow the Council's suggested gift annuity rates. The suggested rates are based on actuarial information that factors life expectancies, inflation, and investment returns.

The planned giving director, consulting with the organization's treasurer, should decide whether to follow the ACGA's suggested rates. Many charities choose to follow the ACGA's suggested rates but place a cap on their highest payout rate at a number lower than the ACGA's current highest rate of 14 percent. It is helpful when working with donors to refer to the ACGA's suggested rates and the importance of following them when prospects challenge the charity to provide them with a higher rate of return.

(iv) Deferred Gift Annuities. As with charitable gift annuities, the charity may want to include a policy statement that addresses the payout rates for deferred gift annuities. Because a deferred gift annuity does not begin to pay an income to the donor until a date in the future, often many years later, the charity should consider whether rates should be capped at a certain amount, and whether the nonprofit will establish deferred gift annuities for donors who are quite young, such as 25 or 30 years old. The charity may want to devise a formula that places a cap on the payout rate of both deferred and regular gift annuities.

(c) Ages of Beneficiaries

Many nonprofits establish age minimums for donors who wish to make life income gifts. Charities do not want to commit to pay income to donors who are too young, because there is a great chance of depleting the principal of the gift, leaving the charity with little or no gift. This happens most often when donors wish to include their children as successor beneficiaries, extending the obligation of the charity. Each charity needs to decide, based on the type of life income gift, the minimum age of the youngest beneficiary.

(i) Charitable Remainder Trusts.   The minimum age allowed for a beneficiary of a charitable remainder trust should be determined on a case-by-case basis, if at all. Many donors want to benefit their children in their estate planning, which may include naming the children as beneficiaries of a charitable remainder trust. The younger the beneficiary, the longer the trust will run, incurring greater administrative costs, and, because of the long time the trust must pay an income to beneficiaries, perhaps a smaller remainder gift will be left to the charity. Factors to consider include:

- Whether the trust is being established for a term of years
- Whether the charity has a special relationship with the donor
- The total number of beneficiaries of the trust
- The trust's proposed size
- The expected total return of the trust

Many charitable remainder trusts are established without involvement from the charity, so the planned giving officer who is brought into the planning process by the donor must be diplomatic in making suggestions, but remind the donor about the size of the gift that will eventually come to the charity. A donor who really wishes to benefit the charity will strike a balance in taking care of individual beneficiaries and making a gift to the nonprofit.

(ii) Pooled Income Funds.   The nonprofit should consult with the manager of its pooled income fund(s) to determine the minimum age for donors to the fund. Allowing a young, 40- to 50-year-old donor to become a beneficiary of a pooled income fund reduces the remainder gift to the charity. A wise strategy is to create several different pooled income funds, each with a different investment objective. Donors will choose which fund they wish to enter, based on how much they wish the charity to receive at their death, their need for annual income and a charitable income tax deduction, and their desire to preserve the principal of the fund. Ideally, a pooled income fund should have a balance of different-aged beneficiaries; for example, if a fund contains only older beneficiaries and most of the beneficiaries die, the pooled income fund risks extinction.

(iii) Charitable Gift Annuities.   Payout rates to donors who establish charitable gift annuities are highest for older donors, because the rates are based on actuarial tables. The older the donor, the higher the rate of return. Financially, it is generally not worthwhile to younger donors who wish to receive a high annual payout rate to establish a charitable gift annuity, because the rate they will receive is low. Donors aged 40 to 55 may receive a higher rate by joining a charity's pooled income fund.

(iv) Deferred Gift Annuities.   The charity may choose to establish a minimum age for donors who make deferred gift annuities. With deferred gift annuities, the younger the donor and the longer the payment is deferred, the higher the rate to the beneficiary. Because donors often select retirement age to receive their annual income payments, the charity may consider a 30-year-old donor too young to pay what appears to be a high rate of return for such a long time, even

though the charity invests the donor's gift for many years. The charity also needs to consider the responsibility of tracking the gift internally for that amount of time.

(d) Number of Beneficiaries

All life income gifts require that the beneficiaries be alive at the time the gift is created.

(i) Charitable Remainder Trusts. Too many beneficiaries of a charitable remainder trust may be unwieldy for administrative purposes and are likely to reduce the ultimate gift to the charity. The charity may wish to limit the number of beneficiaries of a charitable remainder trust when the charity is involved in its establishment.

(ii) Pooled Income Funds. It is smart to have many beneficiaries owning an interest in a pooled income fund. Multiple beneficiaries in a pooled income fund results in more gifts going to the charity and allows the charity to invest in larger sums at lower cost. It is unwise, however, to have one beneficiary own a disproportionate number of units in the fund, because when that donor dies the fund will shrink considerably. More donors in the pooled income fund reduce this risk. Too many beneficiaries on one gift will reduce the pooled income fund donor's charitable income tax deduction and will stretch out the gift to the charity, resulting in the proceeds coming many years in the future. The charity may want to cap the number of beneficiaries allowed on a single pooled income fund gift.

(iii) Charitable Gift Annuities. The Internal Revenue Service (IRS) allows a maximum of two beneficiaries for a charitable gift annuity. For example, a husband and wife who create a charitable gift annuity cannot also include their children as annuitants.

(iv) Deferred Gift Annuities. Like a charitable gift annuity, no more than two annuitants are allowed by the IRS.

42.5 BEQUESTS

Gifts made through a bequest can benefit a charity without any involvement from an organization's development staff. If, however, a development professional is asked to respond to an inquiry from a donor who wishes to make a bequest other than a cash gift, guidelines should exist for the planned giving officer to follow. Guidance is needed most often when a donor wants to make a gift of real estate or tangible personal property to the charity.

(a) Unwanted Property

It is helpful to both the charity and the donor if the charity is involved when a donor makes a non-cash gift by bequest to the charity. For example, a charity should discourage a donor from making a gift of a home located in another part of the country that may be difficult for the charity to sell, although this problem may be minimized if the donor's executor is authorized to sell the home and give the proceeds to the charity. The planned giving officer should explain the burdens and costs that the charity will have to bear. Although the intent may be charitable, a donor who resides in Florida and leaves the entire estate, consisting of an old car and a motor home, to a Massachusetts charity may make only a minimal gift to the organization. The charity will have to retain counsel in Florida to probate the estate and sell anything valuable. Similarly, a vacant warehouse in an unsafe part of an out-of-state town is property that a charity is unlikely to be able to sell quickly; insurance and maintenance costs make such a gift more of a burden on the charity, and such a gift should perhaps be disclaimed.

(b) Disclaimed Bequests

When a donor dies and makes a bequest of some type of property that the charity does not want to accept, the bequest should be disclaimed according to procedures established under applicable state and federal laws. A bequest recipient can refuse a gift made by bequest, but laws vary with regard to filing requirements, timing, and procedures for disclaiming unwanted property.

42.6 GIFTS OF TANGIBLE PERSONAL PROPERTY

Gifts of tangible personal property can present special challenges for a charity. For a complete discussion of gifts of tangible personal property, see Chapter 33. A gift acceptance policy should include restrictions on accepting gifts of tangible personal property and provide guidelines for analyzing such gifts. The charity should examine a potential gift of personal property for the item's financial value, its potential use by the charity, and its ability to be sold quickly and converted into cash. A comprehensive gift acceptance policy also should include the existence of a committee that will review gifts of tangible personal property (including jewelry, art, collections, computers, and equipment) before they are accepted.

(a) Gifts Used by the Charity

Each nonprofit should decide whether it should set a minimum value for accepting a piece of tangible personal property and then consider whether the charity can use the gift. Some charities may choose to accept only gifts of tangible personal property that relate to their charity's mission, such as books to a university and medical equipment to a hospital. Gifts with a less directly related use, such as a stamp collection to a hospital, may cause more expense than value after considering moving and display costs and insurance. The collection could attract few buyers if the hospital eventually decided to sell it.

(b) Liquidity of the Gift; Gifts Not Used by the Charity

The charity also should determine whether it will accept gifts of tangible personal property that will be sold by the charity. The charity must consider whether significant costs will be involved with holding and selling the asset; if the charity cannot sell the property immediately, can it afford the maintenance, insurance, taxes, and management costs for the property? How expensive will it be to hire a specialist, if necessary, to sell the property? Will the property require sale at a special auction held in London only once a year? These and other questions should be explored before accepting a piece of property that the charity hopes to sell.

(c) Acceptance of the Gift

An individual or group of people should have the authority to accept gifts of tangible personal property on behalf of the charity. If the planned giving officer is undecided as to whether a piece of tangible personal property should be accepted, an individual or governing body should be available to help make the decision. Remind the donor that the charity follows rules issued by the IRS relating to accepting gifts of tangible personal property, including filing Forms 8282 and 8283. See Chapter 33 for a full discussion of tangible personal property.

(d) Internal Revenue Service Form 8283

A gift acceptance policy that deals with gifts of tangible personal property should include a statement about whether the charity will send, as a matter of course, copies of IRS Form 8283 to a donor.

A donor attaches Form 8283 to his tax return in the year a gift of noncash property over $500 is made to a charity. The charity is not legally responsible for sending the form to donors, but for stewardship purposes the charity should routinely send it. See Chapter 33 for more on Form 8283.

42.7 GIFTS OF REAL ESTATE

Because gifts of real estate can be challenging, even for the most experienced planned giving professional, guidelines must be established to handle them. These policies will help deal with the many complex and multifaceted issues associated with gifts of real estate, including whether to accept the gift, use of an outside appraiser, and environmental concerns.

(a) Deciding to Accept the Gift

A number of factors determine whether to accept a gift of real estate. A full discussion of real estate is found in Chapter 31. Threshold guidelines should be established to determine whether the charity should even explore taking the potential gift of real estate. Issues to consider include:

- Estimated value of the real estate
- Likelihood of selling the property
- Whether the property is mortgaged
- Location of the property
- Likelihood of the nonprofit's using the property
- Relationship of the donor to the nonprofit

(b) Selecting an Appraiser

The nonprofit should establish guidelines for valuing a potential gift of property by an outside, independent appraiser. If the charity is unsure of the appraiser's figure, it should thoroughly analyze the appraisal and speak with the appraiser. If still unsatisfied, the charity may want to conduct its own appraisal to determine the real market value of the property. Appraisers also can help determine the property's potential for resale and discover environmental problems with the property.

(c) Environmental Concerns

If the charity decides to accept a gift of real estate, it should include in its gift acceptance policy the necessity of hiring a specialist to do an environmental study on the property to rule out any hazards that, if discovered, would require the charity to reject the potential gift. When an environmental hazard is discovered on a piece of property, the present owner is generally responsible for curing the problem, including any charity that was given damaged property as a gift. If the state determines that a piece of property was once the site of a toxic waste dump or was located next to a gas station and underground gas tanks have now spread gas contaminating the property, federal law could cause the charity to assume millions of dollars of liability for cleanup. This potential liability, which can turn a gift into a financial disaster, makes an environmental examination of the property absolutely necessary before accepting it.

(d) Procedures for Accepting Gifts of Real Estate

Because various departments at the charity have to be brought into the process, each charity needs to have a system in place to accept gifts of real estate. The planned giving officer should speak with someone in the charity's real estate or business office to determine if the charity wishes to accept the property. A professional with real estate experience representing the charity should make a site visit to examine the property, indicate its estimated value, and note any potential problems associated with it. This initial visit should take place before the charity hires an appraiser and makes an environmental examination of the property.

(c) Retained Life Estates

A charity should decide to accept a gift of a farm or residence with a retained life estate only after exploring all factors relevant to accepting a gift of real estate. Consideration should be given to the potential use or sale of the property at the end of the life estate.

A gift acceptance policy should state that donors will continue to be responsible for taxes, insurance, and maintenance on the property. If the donor wishes to sell the home or farm prior to death or measurable retained interest, the donor and the charity will jointly negotiate the terms of the sale. The split of sales proceeds equals the then-calculated remainder and life estate values.

42.8 LIFE INSURANCE

If a completed gift of a life insurance policy is to be made, the charity must be named as owner and irrevocable beneficiary of the life insurance policy. Gifts of life insurance that require the charity to accept a donor's premium payments as gifts and send them to the life insurance company on a regular basis should generally be discouraged, because the administrative burdens often outweigh the benefit to the charity. If the donor stops making premium payments, the charity is confronted with an awkward decision as to whether to continue the payments.

Under no circumstances should a member of the development staff give a life insurance agent a list of the nonprofit's donors for the salesperson's marketing efforts. If a donor is solicited by a life insurance company and discovers that his name was given to the life insurance agent by the charity, the donor could become angry and choose not to make additional gifts.

42.9 NAMING OPPORTUNITIES

Each charity should outline the policies in place for naming opportunities. This includes gift levels required for establishing funds, chairs, professorships, fellowships, and lectureships. Additionally, amounts required to name various facilities, such as buildings, floors, wings, and other areas, should be included.

42.10 ADMINISTRATIVE ISSUES

(a) Management Fees

Each charity should establish how it will pay various expenses, such as management fees for administration of its planned gifts, including charitable remainder trusts, pooled income funds, and charitable gift annuities. Charities need to determine whether the fees will come from a department budget set aside specifically for this purpose or from income generated from the gift.

If the nonprofit pays the administrative fees from a budget set aside for this purpose, the donor does not obtain a charitable income tax deduction for the cost of administering the gift. Under certain circumstances, a donor can take a charitable income tax deduction on her tax return if the administration fees are paid directly from the income generated by the gift. But if the charity pays the fees from income earned on the charitable remainder trust, pooled income fund, or charitable gift annuity fund, the donor's annual payment is ultimately reduced.

Some organizations follow the practice of taking administrative fees from the income earned on the trust or gift annuity fund; if the trust or fund is large, administration fees are spread to more donors, causing less of a financial impact on each donor. Smaller charities or new programs without many participants may choose to pay the administrative fees out of a separate budget so that their few donors will receive as much income as possible. They may wait to pay the administrative fees out of the income earned when their planned giving program includes more donors. Although donors rarely ask how administrative fees will be paid, the charity's gift acceptance policy should address this.

(b) Legal Fees

Charities also must decide whether they will pay any legal fees on behalf of a donor and should address this in the organization's gift acceptance policy. Some charities are willing to pay for drafting trust documents for donors who name the charity as primary remainderman of a charitable remainder trust. The charity should require that the donor have her own legal counsel review the documents to avoid having a donor later say that she was not satisfied with the way the charity's attorney drafted the document. Some charities believe that they should pay legal fees for drafting a donor's will if the charity is the sole beneficiary under the will, but the charity could be in a conflict-of-interest situation, and also runs the risk that the donor will change his mind and revoke the interest to the charity.

Charities should also insist that donors pay their own appraisal costs. Otherwise, the charity could displease the donor if the property is sold at a price the donor believed should have been higher. The donor often can deduct the cost of the appraisal as a miscellaneous deduction on his tax return, to the extent that this expense and other miscellaneous deductions exceed 2 percent of the donor's adjusted gross income. For a complete discussion of paying legal fees, see Chapter 52.

(c) Charity Acting as Trustee or Executor

It is a rare circumstance that allows a nonprofit organization to act as executor for a donor's estate or as trustee for a donor's trust. Nonprofit organizations are not equipped to make the decisions that an individual or professional trustee can make, though the charity may have the right under the donor's will or trust to appoint an individual to serve as executor or trustee. For example, a nonprofit should not act as a sole trustee making discretionary payments from a trust to an income beneficiary. So, too, a nonprofit should not accept the duties of executor, settling a donor's estate and collecting, securing, and distributing a donor's assets, unless it is the sole beneficiary of the donor's estate or the donor's family wants the nonprofit to assume that duty. A charity that acts as executor of a donor's estate also creates a conflict of interest between the rights of any individual beneficiaries and the charity. A well-drafted gift acceptance policy should include language that strongly advises a charity about assuming this fiduciary responsibility.

42.11 ETHICS

A charity should make every effort to ensure that each gift is in the best interest of both the charity and the donor. Factors to be considered include the donor's charitable interest, financial position, relationship with the charity, and the effect the gift may have on the donor's family. A gift acceptance policy should include a statement outlining the above and urge a donor to have legal representation (see Exhibit 42.1).

Exhibit 42.1   Sample Gift Acceptance Policy

PURPOSE

This policy serves as a guideline to members of the <ORGANIZATION> staff involved with accepting gifts, to outside advisors who assist in the gift planning process, and to prospective donors who wish to make gifts to <ORGANIZATION>. This policy is intended only as a guide and allows for some flexibility on a case-by-case basis.

CASH

1. All gifts by check shall be accepted by <ORGANIZATION> regardless of amount.
2. Checks shall be made payable to <ORGANIZATION> or to a particular program or project at <ORGANIZATION>. In no event shall a check be made payable to an individual who represents <ORGANIZATION>.

PLEDGES

Pledges may be payable in single or multiple installments and must have a value of at least $1,000. The pledge may not exceed <3–5> years in duration. All donors must complete a pledge form or confirm the pledge in writing.

PUBLICLY TRADED SECURITIES

1. Readily marketable securities, such as those traded on a stock exchange, can be accepted by <ORGANIZATION>.
2. Gifts of securities are likely to be sold immediately by <ORGANIZATION>.
3. For <ORGANIZATION> gift crediting and accounting purposes, the value of the securities is the average of the high and low on the date of the gift.

CLOSELY HELD SECURITIES

1. Nonpublicly traded securities may be accepted after consultation with the Treasurer's Office and/or Office of the General Counsel.
2. Prior to acceptance, <ORGANIZATION> shall explore methods of liquidation for the securities through redemption or sale. A representative of <ORGANIZATION> shall try to contact the closely held corporation to determine:
   ■ An estimate of fair market value
   ■ Any restrictions on transfer
3. No commitment for repurchase of closely held securities shall be made prior to completion of the gift of the securities.

REAL ESTATE

1. Gifts of real estate must be reviewed by the Gift Review Committee of <ORGANIZATION> before acceptance.
2. The donor is responsible for obtaining an appraisal of the property. The cost of the appraisal is borne by the donor.
3. Prior to presentation to the Gift Review Committee, a member of the staff must conduct a visual inspection of the property. If the property is located in a geographically isolated area, a local real estate broker can substitute for a member of the staff in conducting the visual inspection.
4. Due to the expenses associated with gifts of real estate, only gifts in excess of < $ > will be accepted.
5. Prior to presentation to the Gift Review Committee, the donor must provide the following documents:
   ■ Real estate deed
   ■ Real estate tax bill
   ■ Plot plan
   ■ Substantiation of zoning status

(Continued)

GIFT ACCEPTANCE POLICIES

Exhibit 42.1 *(Continued)*

6. Depending on the value and desirability of the gift, the donor's connection with <ORGANI-ZATION>, and the donor's past gift record, the donor may be asked to pay for all or a portion of the following:
   - Maintenance costs
   - Real estate taxes
   - Insurance
   - Real estate broker's commission and other costs of sale
   - Appraisal costs
7. For <ORGANIZATION>'s gift crediting and accounting purposes, the value of the gift is the appraised value of the real estate. (Note: A nonprofit can choose to exclude from the value of the gift costs for maintenance, insurance, real estate taxes, broker's commission, and other expenses of sale.)
8. A gift of a retained life estate will be accepted after exploring all factors relevant to accepting a gift of real estate. Donors continue to be responsible for taxes, insurance, and maintenance on the property.

LIFE INSURANCE

1. <ORGANIZATION> will accept life insurance policies as gifts only when <ORGANIZA-TION> is named as the owner and beneficiary of 100 percent of the policy.
2. If the policy is a paid-up policy, the value of the gift for <ORGANIZATION>'s gift crediting and accounting purposes is the policy's replacement cost.
3. If the policy is partially paid up, the value of the gift for <ORGANIZATION>'s gift crediting and accounting purposes is the policy's cash surrender value. (Note: For IRS purposes, the donor's charitable income tax deduction is equal to the interpolated terminal reserve, which is an amount slightly in excess of the cash surrender value.)

TANGIBLE PERSONAL PROPERTY

1. Gifts of tangible personal property to <ORGANIZATION> should have a use related to <OR-GANIZATION>'s exempt purpose.
2. Gifts of jewelry, artwork, collections, equipment, and software shall be accepted after approval by the Gift Review Committee.
3. Such gifts of tangible personal property defined above shall be used by or sold for the benefit of <ORGANIZATION>.
4. No property which requires special display facilities or security measures shall be accepted by <ORGANIZATION> without consultation with the Gift Review Committee.
5. Depending upon the anticipated value of the gift, <ORGANIZATION> shall have a qualified outside appraiser value the gift before accepting it.
6. <ORGANIZATION> adheres to all IRS requirements related to disposing gifts of tangible personal property and filing appropriate forms.

PLANNED GIFTS

<ORGANIZATION> offers the following planned gift options:

1. Charitable gift annuities
2. Deferred gift annuities
3. Pooled income funds
4. Charitable remainder trusts
5. Bequests
6. Retained life estates

Charitable Gift Annuities

1. Administrative fees shall be paid from the income earned on the charitable gift annuity.
2. There shall be no more than 2 beneficiaries on a charitable gift annuity.
3. The minimum gift accepted to establish a charitable gift annuity is $5,000.
4. No income beneficiary for a charitable gift annuity shall be younger than 60 years old.
5. <ORGANIZATION> follows the American Council on Gift Annuities suggested rates. Rates are capped at < % >.

Exhibit 42.1 *(Continued)*

Deferred Gift Annuities
1. Administrative fees shall be paid from the income earned on the charitable gift annuity.
2. There shall be no more than 2 beneficiaries on a deferred gift annuity.
3. The minimum gift accepted to establish a deferred gift annuity is $5,000.
4. No income beneficiary for a deferred gift annuity shall be younger than 30 years old.
5. <ORGANIZATION> follows the American Council on Gift Annuities suggested rates. Rates are capped at < % >.

Pooled Income Funds
1. Administrative fees shall be paid from the income earned on the pooled income fund.
2. No income beneficiary in the fund shall be younger than 45 years old.
3. The minimum initial contribution to the fund shall be $5,000. Additional gifts may be added for amounts beginning at $1,000.

Charitable Remainder Trusts
1. Due to the cost of drafting and administration, the minimum to establish a charitable remainder trust is $100,000.
2. Management fees for the administration of a charitable remainder trust when <ORGANIZATION> is named as trustee or co-trustee shall be paid from the income of the trust.
3. Investment of a charitable remainder trust shall be determined by the fiduciary hired to manage the trust. No representations shall be made by an <ORGANIZATION> employee or person acting on behalf of <ORGANIZATION> as to the management or investment of such charitable remainder trust.
4. The payout rate of a charitable remainder trust shall be determined in consultation with the donor and <ORGANIZATION> investment advisor. By law the payout rate cannot be lower than 5 percent. The payout rate shall be negotiated between the donor and <ORGANIZATION> and shall reflect the number of beneficiaries, their ages, and the size of the trust.

Bequests
1. Assets transferred through bequests that have immediate value to <ORGANIZATION> or can be liquidated shall be encouraged by the development staff. Gifts that appear to require more cost than benefit shall be discouraged or rejected.
2. Donors who have indicated that they have made a bequest to <ORGANIZATION> may, depending upon the individual situation, be asked to disclose, in writing or by copy of the will, the relevant clause that benefits <ORGANIZATION> as evidence of their gift. This information is used for internal financial purposes and is not binding on the donor.

ENDOWED FUNDS
1. To establish select endowed funds, the following minimum levels must be achieved:

Distinguished Chair	< $ >
Chair	< $ >
Professorship	< $ >
Lectureship	< $ >
Scholar-in-Residence	< $ >
Institute	< $ >
Center	< $ >
Fellowship	< $ >
Endowed Scholarship	< $ >
Endowed Fund	< $ >
Current Use Fund	< $ >

2. To establish an endowment:
   - For an outright gift, the fair market value of the asset used must meet the minimum endowed level.
   - For a planned gift, the fair market value of the gift must meet the minimum endowed level. (Note: A nonprofit organization may choose an alternate method of valuation such as present value.)

(Continued)

Exhibit 42.1 *(Continued)*

3. The endowed fund pays out < PERCENT > of income earned each year to the program or project designated by the donor.
4. Donors shall receive an annual report detailing the investment performance and use of the fund.

ETHICS

1. <ORGANIZATION> will make every effort to ensure that each gift is made in the best interest of <ORGANIZATION> and the donor. The donor's charitable interest, finances, relationship with <ORGANIZATION>, and family will be considered before accepting the gift.
2. Every effort will be made to ensure that the donor has legal representation.

OTHER NAMING OPPORTUNITIES

1. All significant naming opportunities will be approved by the gift acceptance committee or board of trustees
   - Chair/Professorship   < $ >
   Provides income to support a professor's salary.
   - Lectureship   < $ >
   Provides for travel and honoria for speakers and publication costs of lectures.
   - Facilities
   The following represents approximate amounts of funding needed to name a specific area.

Building	< $ >
Wing	< $ >
Floor	< $ >
Auditorium	< $ >
Rooms	< $ >

   A list of locations for naming is available from the development office.

ADMINISTRATIVE ISSUES

1. <ORGANIZATION> shall not act as an executor (personal representative) for a donor's estate.
2. <ORGANIZATION> may act as co-trustee on a charitable remainder trust when the trust names <ORGANIZATION> as a beneficiary of 50 percent or more of the trust.
3. <ORGANIZATION> will pay for the drafting of legal documents for a charitable remainder trust when <ORGANIZATION> is named as a beneficiary of 50 percent or more of the trust. The donor's own counsel must review the documents at the donor's cost.

## CHAPTER FORTY-THREE

Policies and Procedures for Naming Opportunities

43.1   INTRODUCTION

Naming opportunities are wonderfully effective ways for charities to raise significant financial support from committed donors. These gifts also create opportunities to establish permanent relationships between donors, their families, and charities. The naming opportunities are limited only by the imaginations of the donor and the charity. In exchange for a specific dollar amount, a donor may name a part of the charity's facilities or provide resources to name a department, program, center, chair, or institute, thereby permanently linking the donor's name with the charity. Naming opportunities equip the charity's facilities, provide support for faculty and staff, and provide resources to promote creative ventures. The gift may be in the form of an endowed fund; however, it also may be a current-use gift. Depending on the charity, the gift may be an outright gift, planned gift, or gift through a donor's estate or a combination of all three types of gifts.

43.2   POLICES AND PROCEDURES

To manage naming opportunities in a fair and equitable way, most charities establish polices and procedures for naming opportunities. The policies and procedures are designed to achieve these objectives:

- Fairness and equity to both the donor and the charity

- Consistency in application

- Uniformity among the charity's administrative division

- To inform donors about costs associated with a charity's operations and enterprises

- Financial integrity

- Systematic approach

- To discourage competition among the charity's departments

- To protect the charity's resources

■ To maximize fundraising potential

■ To promote institutional/organizational values

43.3 NAMING COMMITTEE

Each nonprofit organization should establish a committee to oversee the naming of all gift opportunities. The charity should strive to achieve consistency, fairness, and uniformity when establishing policies and procedures for naming opportunities. The planned giving officer and development staff may need to cite a decision of the naming committee to reinforce certain decisions. Usually the committee consists of three to five members, including the vice-president of advancement, vice president of business, and three other members designated by the charity. The committee should be autonomous so that decisions can be made efficiently. For very significant naming opportunities or potentially controversial gifts, the president and board of trustees should be consulted.

43.4 PRICING NAMING OPPORTUNITIES

Properly drafted policies and procedures protect the interests of both the charity and the donor. The minimum naming amount should be set at a level so that the amount is a stretch gift for most donors. At the same time, the amount should not be too high so that only a few donors could fund such a gift. Donors also do not want to learn that they paid too much for a naming opportunity compared to amounts that other donors paid for similar opportunities. To be fair, develop a "fee schedule" or "price list" to set minimums.

The minimum for capital projects should be based on a formula that approximates replacement cost, discounted by a percentage reflecting a donor's capacity to give based on the charity's financial traditions. Remember that the exact amount for a naming opportunity is determined through negotiation. For example, most donors cannot afford to pay for 100 percent of the replacement cost of a building. A charity could set naming levels at 30 to 50 percent of the replacement cost of a building, thereby making the cost more affordable and financially realistic. Conference rooms, classrooms, and exhibit areas can be prorated based on the square footage of the area to be named following the discounted formula. For example, if a charity determines that per-square-foot construction costs are $125, a 400-square-foot classroom would cost $50,000. If the charity discounted the cost by 50 percent, the amount to name a classroom would be $25,000. Minimums need to be set based on the financial traditions of the charity and the capacity of donors to make gifts at those levels. Keep in mind the minimum is just that—a minimum. For special new buildings in desirable locations, the minimum can be raised to a higher level. For buildings housing medical or scientific equipment or technology, the minimum amount needs to be adjusted accordingly.

Amounts for other naming opportunities should be established in relation to the cost of the opportunity. For example, at a college or university, if tuition for an individual student is $5,000 a year, a full tuition–endowed fund minimum should be set at $100,000 if the distribution rate (spending rate) is 5 percent. If graduate tuition is $7,500 per year, then a full tuition-endowed fund minimum should be set at $150,000. The endowed fund minimum for a chair should be set at a level that covers the cost of the holder's salary along with the cost of secretarial support and a research stipend. For a named professorship, the amount should cover the cost of the faculty member's salary.

Exhibit 43.1 lists many types of naming opportunities and includes a suggested approval process and minimum amount. Readers can study this policy and procedure and develop one for their charity to fit their particular needs.

43.4 PRICING NAMING OPPORTUNITIES

Exhibit 43.1   Naming Opportunities at <ORGANIZATION>

Naming Opportunity	Approval	Minimum Amount
Capital Projects		
Capital Projects/Facilities	Board of Trustees	Not less than 30 percent of new construction costs
New Buildings* or Buildings Under construction	Reviewed by Naming Committee; subject to Board of Trustees	
Existing Buildings	Board of Trustees Reviewed by Naming Committee; subject to Board of Trustees approval	Building 10 years old or less: Endowment of 30 percent or more of the original construction costs, including any subsequent renovations and/or additions. Building 10+ years old: Endowment of 30 percent or more of the calculated square footage cost.
Building Additions and Renovations	Board of Trustees Reviewed by Naming Committee; subject to Board of Trustees approval	Not less than 30 percent of project costs
Donor-Initiated Construction Projects	President/CEO and Board of Trustees; Reviewed by Naming Committee; subject to President and Regents' approval	100 percent of project cost
Science Laboratory	Reviewed by Naming Committee; subject to Board of Trustees	$100,000 to $300,000
Electronic Classroom	Reviewed by Naming Committee; subject to Board of Trustees	$200,000 minimum
Computer Laboratory	Reviewed by Naming Committee; subject to Board of Trustees	$250,000 @$10,000 /worksite
Floors	Reviewed by Naming Committee; subject to Board of Trustees	$500,000 to $1,000,000
Library	Administrative Officer	$ **
Nursing Stations	Administrative Officer	$ **
Elevator Banks	Naming Committee	$ **

*Less than three years old
**Depending on scope and cost

(Continued)

Exhibit 43.1 *(Continued)*

Naming Opportunity	Approval	Minimum Amount
Classrooms/Patient Rooms	Reviewed by Naming Committee; subject to Board of Trustees	$100,000
Conference Room	Reviewed by Naming Committee; subject to Board of Trustees	$100,000
Benches, fountains, walkways, other outdoor structures or areas	Reviewed by Naming Committee; subject to Board of Trustees	Case-by-case basis Gift must cover the entire cost of the structure or installation, and if significant ongoing costs will be incurred, an endowment sufficient to cover these costs may also be required.
Departments, Programs, and Units		
College	President and Board of Trustees	$5,000,000 addressed on a case-by-case basis
Department Programs	President and Board of Trustees	$2,000,000 addressed on a case-by-case basis
Center	President and Board of Trustees	$3,000,000
Institute	President and Board of Trustees	$1,000,000
Faculty/Staff		
Chair/Professorship	President and Board of Trustees	$500,000–$2,000,000 and up
Visiting Professorship	President and Board of Trustees	$750,000
Faculty Development Fund	All are reviewed by Naming Committee; subject to Executive Vice President	$100,000
Young Faculty Award	Dean and VP for Advancement	$250,000
Release Time	Dean	$250,000
Faculty Support	Dean	$250,000
Public Programs		
Speaker Series	Dean and VP for Advancement	$250,000
Lecture Series	Dean and VP for Advancement	$250,000
Distinguished Lectureship	Dean and VP for Advancement	$250,000

Exhibit 43.1 *(Continued)*

Naming Opportunity	Approval	Minimum Amount
Visiting Lecture Series	Dean and VP for Advancement	$100,000
Research Fund	Dean and VP for Advancement	$100,000
Screening Funds	Administrative Officer	$100,000
Service Funds	Administrative Officer	$100,000
Scholarships		
Postdoctoral Fellowships	Dean and VP for Advancement	$300,000
Full-Tuition Graduate Fellowship	Dean and VP for Advancement	$300,000
Research Fellowship	Dean and VP for Advancement	$300,000
Full-Tuition Graduate Scholarship	All are reviewed by Naming Committee; subject to Executive Vice-President	$100,000
Scholars in Residence	Dean and VP for Advancement	$100,000
Full-Tuition Undergraduate Scholarship	Dean and VP for Advancement	$100,000
Undergraduate Award	Dean and VP for Advancement	$30,000
Endowed Scholarship or Endowed Student Award	Dean and VP for Advancement	$10,000–$50,000
Equipment		
Computers	Administrative Officer	$3,000/workstation
Technology	Administrative Officer	$ **
Scientific Equipment	Administrative Officer	$ **
Projects		
Displays	Administrative Officer	$ **
Exhibitions	Administrative Officer	$ **
Presentations	Administrative Officer	$ **
Performances	Administrative Officer	$ **
Restoration	Administrative Officer	$ **
Entrepreneurial Funds		
Innovation Funds	Naming Committee	$ **
Entrepreneur Funds	Naming Committee	$ **

**Depending on scope and cost

(Continued)

Exhibit 43.1 *(Continued)*

Naming Opportunity	Approval	Minimum Amount
Resources		
Books	Administrative Officer	$ **
Periodicals	Administrative Officer	$ **
Online Publications	Administrative Officer	$ **

**Depending on scope and cost

43.5 BACKGROUND CHECK

Before a charity agrees to a major naming opportunity, it could consider conducting a background check on the donor and his family. Most charities have close relationships with law enforcement departments and private security companies, and some even have their own campus police departments. Law enforcement officials can advise charities on ways to conduct background checks on donors interested in linking their names to charities, to avoid potential embarrassment to the charity later on, in case the donor's wealth was derived from questionable sources. Each charity should check:

- How did the donor and donor's family acquire wealth?

- In what type of employment/business is the donor engaged?

- Would the family name bring disfavor to the charity?

- Has the donor or donor's family ever been charged or convicted of any criminal offenses?

43.6 CONCLUSION

Structured properly, naming policies and procedures will assist a charity in raising funds in a consistent and equitable manner. Policies and procedures help charities maximize fundraising potential and are helpful fundraising documents in their own right. Donors respond favorably to well-drafted documents that demonstrate ways donors help charities achieve their goals and fulfill their missions.

CHAPTER FORTY-FOUR

Nonprofit Investment Policies and Procedures

44.1 INTRODUCTION: INVESTMENT IN CONTEXT FOR PLANNED GIVING OFFICERS

Investment policies, procedures, and fundamentals are an integral, though often invisible, component of a planned giving officer's job. The issues of investment are presented in several contexts:

- A donor's endowed fund is managed by the nonprofit organization.

- A donor's charitable remainder trust may be invested by an independent trustee, the nonprofit organization, an outside asset manager, or an institutional trustee.

- The nonprofit's pooled income fund is invested and managed to produce a return impacted by prevailing market conditions.

- The nonprofit may manage a life income investment fund that manages charitable gift annuities and deferred gift annuities.

The nonprofit organization's donors often have questions about investment strategies and performance, and planned giving officers must understand the issues, return, and risk involved in investing these funds. Under the Philanthropy Protection Act of 1995 (PPA), nonprofit organizations must disclose to donors information about the investment of the principal of their planned gifts if the principal is commingled in a collective investment pool.

In the past, donors who established endowed funds and made planned or outright gifts often inquired about the nonprofit's investment performance and spending provisions. These inquiries were routinely referred to the nonprofit's business or financial affairs office. Now planned giving officers are involved in handling inquiries from donors that previously would have been referred to the nonprofit's financial staff. Communicating information to donors regarding investment policies and procedures is a shared responsibility. Both financial staff and planned giving staff will need to become more knowledgeable about each other's operations to provide complete and accurate information to donors.

For most nonprofit organizations, planned gifts are an important component of the nonprofit's investment operations. To understand the investment requirements for planned gifts, it is necessary to understand the strategies, policies, and procedures for the nonprofit's endowment and investment program. Planned giving officers should become more familiar with financial issues in managing the nonprofit's common endowment pool, including investment mechanics and strategies, as well as with issues in managing separate life income gift endowment funds. These endowments may be managed internally by the nonprofit or they may be managed by an outside investment manager who invests on behalf of the nonprofit.

To understand the internal investment management issues and the decision-making process, planned giving officers need to develop effective working relationships with the nonprofit's financial staff and outside managers. Concurrently, the nonprofit's financial staff often needs input from the planned giving officer regarding the unique requirements of specific planned gifts so that investment strategies can be coordinated with the type of planned gift. For example, the investment objectives for charitable remainder annuity trusts and charitable remainder unitrusts are different. The investment objectives and strategies for these vehicles should vary depending on the donor's age and the nature of the payout to the donor. Planned giving officers must understand the long- and short-term investment strategies that must be selected to produce immediate income or to plan for future growth.

The language of investment and its principles and concepts are unfamiliar to many nonprofit employees. Often the distinction between the planned giving options that is so clear in the planned giving officer's mind becomes clouded in the minds of the nonprofit's financial staff. Planned giving officers work with complex cases, sophisticated donors, the business activities of the nonprofit, and the disclosure requirements of PPA.

This chapter is divided into seven parts: investment issues common to most nonprofit organizations; an overview of the major developments affecting nonprofit investment; issues in managing the endowment; investment strategies and model portfolios; unique aspects of investing funds for planned giving purposes; the important relationship between donors and investment policy issues; and last, general guidelines, policies, and procedures.

44.2 NONPROFIT INVESTMENT ISSUES

(a) Endowments

The financial worth of a nonprofit organization consists largely of the value of its real estate, physical plant, and endowment. An endowment provides stability, serves as a foundation on which to build a nonprofit organization, and provides a vehicle for the nonprofit to store financial resources and for donors to designate bequests and other gifts. The endowment subsidizes a nonprofit organization's budget, generating income for new programs while preserving the principal for the future. In addition, a sizable endowment is important for short-term borrowing for equipment, for securing mortgages, and for long-term borrowing for new construction projects. Some public institutions, such as state universities and libraries, museums, and healthcare organizations, manage their endowments to reduce dependence on government budgets.

A nonprofit serves as a fiduciary, holding in trust funds transferred by the donor to the nonprofit to benefit the nonprofit's tax-exempt charitable purposes. In many cases the donor has designated specific restricted purposes for which the funds must be used—for example, for the medical school or department of engineering. The nonprofit must hold, manage, and invest these funds to manage risk, preserve principal, and obtain appropriate investment gains. Donors who establish endowed funds do so to provide income in perpetuity to support the nonprofit's mission, and the principal of these endowed funds is managed as part of the nonprofit's endowment. The endowed fund distributes income to provide for purposes designated by the donor, or if undesignated, for the organization's general charitable purposes including research, chairs, departments, programs, professorships, scholarships, displays, exhibits, operations, or almost any other purpose.

Many major gifts create endowed or restricted funds from which only income can be expended. Such funds are managed as part of the nonprofit's endowment, preserving the principal and distributing a portion of the earnings in perpetuity. Excess earnings, if any, are returned to principal or may be accumulated for future use. In most cases, gifts to endowment are restricted in that their income is designated to benefit a specific department or program at the nonprofit. Nonprofit departments and programs depend on endowment income to meet the operating budget and to continue programs from year to year. Unrestricted gifts of any amount usually can be placed in the endowment to benefit the entire nonprofit.

(i) Purposes of Endowment. Once the nonprofit's endowment has been established, it should be professionally managed. To protect the endowment from inflation and to protect donors' contributions from erosion, nonprofit organizations should develop investment policies and procedures for these purposes:

- To ensure proper financial integrity in the management of the assets

- To protect the donor's funds entrusted to the nonprofit

- To manage the endowment pool in a prudent manner

- To formulate an asset investment strategy designed to meet the organization's needs for income while preserving the corpus

- To establish objectives to measure the performance of investment managers against mutually agreed-on standards

- To establish multiple portfolios to accommodate the types of endowment needed by the nonprofit

- To enter into a written gift agreement with donors concerning the investment policy

- To develop a compliance system to ensure that all funds are used in accordance with the donor's wishes and that all restrictions are adhered to according to the terms of the gift

(ii) Types of Endowments. Nonprofit organizations are likely to have several endowed pools of funds to meet the long- and short-term needs. Three examples of these endowments are:

1. *Common pooled endowment.* This endowment holds funds that form the basis of the non-profit's general endowment and includes contributions from donors used to fund separate endowed funds.

   Common pooled endowments include:

   (a) *Pure endowments,* also known as *donor-restricted funds,* which distribute earnings often in accordance with a spending rule or policy and do not permit invasion of principal.

   (b) *Quasi-endowments,* which hold funds that are considered to be part of the endowment. These endowments, often called "funds functioning as endowment," hold funds for the benefit of a unit or department of the nonprofit or for the nonprofit itself that may be withdrawn at a point in the future at the discretion of the trustees of the nonprofit.

   (c) *Term endowments,* otherwise known as temporarily restricted funds, which are similar to pure endowments except that they exist for a specific length of time or cease to exist upon the occurrence of a specific event. During their existence, earnings may be distributed or may be returned to principal, and upon the end of the term, all earnings and principal are distributed. If the term is significant (e.g., at least five years), the endowment may be invested as part of the common pooled endowment since the time horizon often is compatible with long-term investment strategies characteristic of most endowments. If, however, the term is short (e.g., less than five years), the fund should be invested conservatively to reduce exposure to market fluctuations, to preserve principal, and to anticipate the distribution of principal and income upon the completion of the term.

2. *Life income gift fund.* This endowment holds funds transferred by donors who wish to provide life income streams to beneficiaries through planned gifts the remainder of which benefits the nonprofit. Life income gifts, such as charitable remainder annuity trusts and unitrusts, may be added to this pooled fund. Charitable gift annuities may be treated as part of the life income fund or may be merged with the nonprofit's endowment. There is no legal obligation to hold or identify such annuity funds separately. The nonprofit will, under all circumstances, have an obligation to make the annuity payment.

   As an alternative, life income gifts can be commingled with the nonprofit's endowment. Many nonprofits, to reduce costs and improve management, commingle or pool life income gifts with the nonprofit's endowment. To commingle these funds, many technical issues must be addressed and a partnership must be created to hold the pool of funds. A unitized system of accounting for income and expenses must be adopted.

   As the number of life income gifts increases, it may be more appropriate to manage some or all of the pool as a discrete fund to meet the income obligations to the beneficiaries. In some cases, the investment strategies for the life income fund differ from those of the nonprofit's endowment fund.

3. *Pooled income fund.* This endowment holds assets transferred by donors to establish pooled income fund gifts. This fund is a discrete fund and may be commingled with non-pooled income fund assets, but such commingling may not be wise unless the investment philosophies are similar. Pooled income funds are prohibited from holding tax-exempt assets and are subject to certain other investment limitations.

(b) The Nonprofit's Investment Players

Nonprofits may either directly or indirectly manage the day-to-day investment of the endowment depending on the nonprofit's traditions, size of the endowment, and the endowment's maturity. Nonprofits involved in direct management are more likely to design portfolios, assign asset allocations, and select specific investments for those allocations. Nonprofits that indirectly manage delegate responsibilities and decision making to external investment advisors, who oversee the process and measure the performance of the investment advisors.

Increasingly, public nonprofit organizations have established affiliated foundations to manage endowment funds. Many nonprofits are not equipped to staff and manage investments and so establish an affiliated foundation to raise, manage, and invest funds for the benefit of the nonprofit organization. These foundations are structured as separate organizations having Internal Revenue Code Section 501(c)(3) tax-exempt status. These foundations elect members of the foundation's board of directors to oversee investment management and often use outside investment advisors and several investment managers to invest pools of funds on behalf of the nonprofit organization.

(c) Investment Committee

In most nonprofits, a variety of individuals are involved in managing and investing the endowment. Many private nonprofits use an internal investment committee that consists of representatives from its board of trustees, from the treasurer's office, and from the business office or financial affairs office. Outside consultants are brought in for investment advice and for market forecasts. The nonprofit's board of directors oversees the nonprofit's investment strategy, and most of the financial decision making is done in-house. The treasurer or financial affairs office plays a key role in investment decisions and in implementing and executing policies. The planned giving officer may be consulted about specific gift options and about the obligation of the nonprofit to make payments to life income beneficiaries. To supervise the performance of the investment managers, to approve asset allocation, and to set distribution levels, the nonprofit usually establishes an investment committee. The investment committee can include these representatives:

- Vice-president of development to oversee the investment policy as it relates to the nonprofit and its development functions

- Representatives of the financial community to provide expertise to the rest of the committee

- Treasurer to actively manage the funds

- Vice-president of business affairs to make certain that the income liabilities of the nonprofit are met.

- Members of the nonprofit's board of directors or board of trustees to oversee the nonprofit's investment performance

Even if there is no formal appointment of staff and board members to an investment committee, most nonprofits have at least an informal committee to oversee investment management.

44.3 MAJOR ACTS AFFECTING NONPROFIT INVESTMENT MANAGEMENT

Nonprofit management of endowment has evolved over the years. Extensive common law and legislation exist governing trust management. The most important areas of the law dealing with endowment investment are as follows: the Prudent Man Rule, the Principal and Income Act, the Uniform Management of Institutional Funds Act, and the Uniform Prudent Investor Act. A discussion of these developments and their impact on endowment management follows.

(a) Prudent Man Rule

Historically, endowments in the United States were managed according to English trust law that limited investments made by charitable organizations to specific prescribed securities. The common law traditionally required that the trustee be held to the standard of a "prudent man," which meant that the trustee was required to perform and make investment, distribution, and other decisions in a prudent or reasonable manner. In 1830 the case of *Harvard College v. Amory* established the Prudent Man Rule, which gave institutions choices about their investments so long as they invested as a prudent person would invest. The rule gave institutions more discretion in their investing than had been previously allowed. The court held in this case that "[a]ll that can be required of a trustee to invest is that he shall conduct himself faithfully and exercise a sound discretion. He is to observe how men of prudence, discretion, and intelligence manage their own affairs, not in regard to speculation but in regard to the permanent disposition of safety of the capital invested."

The Prudent Man Rule applied to fiduciaries, such as trustees, and many nonprofit organizations apply the Prudent Man Rule to investment decisions regarding their endowments.[1]

(b) Principal and Income Act

The Principal and Income Act applies to trustees of private trusts and defines the duties of the trustee in dealing with the respective interests of the income beneficiaries and the remaindermen. The Act identifies whether receipts and expenditures should be charged to income or to principal. The Act defines "income" in the strict sense as interest, dividends, and rents. Capital gains are considered principal. Traditionally, many nonprofit organizations applied the provisions of the Principal and Income Act to their endowments and, consistent with this, Act defined earnings as income only, exclusive of capital gains.

(c) Uniform Management of Institutional Funds Act

To deal with issues of permissible investments, delegation of investment authority, and the appropriateness of investing for total return, the Uniform Management of Institutional Funds Act (UMIFA) was approved by the National Conference of Commissioners on Uniform State Laws in 1972. The Act has been adopted in at least 40 states, including California, Massachusetts, New Jersey, New York, Ohio, and Texas.

The Act provides:

- Authority to pool endowed funds for investment purposes

- A standard of prudent use of appreciation in invested funds

- Specific investing authority

- Authority to delegate investment decisions

- A standard of business care to guide governing boards in the exercise of their duties under UMIFA

- A method of releasing restrictions on the use of funds or selection of investments by mutual agreement with the donor in order to obviate the need for court action

Many attractive investment options that produced capital gain were ignored because under trust law and the Principal and Income Act, only income could be distributed. The restrictive definition of *income* caused poor investment decisions. The UMIFA broadly defined income to include a limited amount of capital appreciation, although the Act allowed donors who wished to exclude capital appreciation from the definition of income to do so. The UMIFA expressly authorized nonprofits to delegate investment management and, if desired, to purchase investment advisory or management services. It redefined the standard of care of a nonprofit's governing board member, making a member's responsibilities similar to those of a director of a corporation rather than those of a private trustee. The UMIFA acknowledged the right of a donor to place restrictions on the use of a gift and authorized the governing

[1] From William F. Massy, "Endowment Management in a Global Economy," in *Reinventing the University* (New York: John Wiley & Sons, 1995).

board of the nonprofit to resolve with the donor restrictions that were outmoded or obsolete. Unless the donor is alive and consents to elimination or modification of the terms of the restricted funds, it is necessary to seek the assistance of the probate court to remove such restrictions. The UMIFA permitted nonprofits to invest without regard to whether the return was characterized as income or capital gain.

(d) Uniform Prudent Investor Act

The Uniform Prudent Investor Act, approved by the National Conference of Commissioners on Uniform State Laws in 1994, applied to trustees of private trusts, including institutional and noninstitutional trustees of charitable remainder trusts. The Act removed limitations that were imposed under the Prudent Man Rule and protected trustees who comply with the terms of the Act. Many nonprofits work closely with trustees of charitable remainder trusts, and it is essential for nonprofit staff to have an understanding of this Act. The Act, adopted in most states, sets standards of care, portfolio strategy, and risk and return objectives. Even if it has not been adopted in the state where the nonprofit does business or is incorporated, the Act serves as an effective model to follow and provides a modern approach to investment issues.

 The Act imposes duties on trustees to exercise reasonable care and skill in investing and managing trust assets, taking into consideration the purposes, terms, distribution requirements, and circumstances of the trust. The trustee must consider a broad scope of issues, including:

- Impact of inflation and the economy
- Impact that a specific investment has on the portfolio
- Expected total return from income and capital appreciation
- Need for liquidity and the regularity of income
- Preservation or appreciation of capital

 The trustee's decisions must be evaluated in the context of the trust portfolio with risk and reward objectives reasonably suited to the trust. The Act also imposes on the trustee a duty to diversify and to manage the trust assets impartially for the benefit of the beneficiaries. In cases in which the trustee wishes to delegate investment and management functions, the Act defines the nature of the relationship between the trustee and the investment manager and outlines the duties of the trustees in selecting a manager.

 With the passage of UMIFA, which applies to nonprofits, and the Uniform Prudent Investor Act, which applies to trustees, portfolio management focuses more on performance, investment strategy, and asset allocation.

44.4 ENDOWMENT MANAGEMENT

The endowment may be invested to produce (1) growth (capital appreciation) through investments in stocks or (2) income through investment in bonds or in stocks that pay interest and dividends. Recently endowments have been invested in a blended portfolio of diversified assets, including domestic and international stocks and bonds with varying maturities, all of which increase the return while reducing the risk. The return is called *total return,* which measures the growth of the portfolio without regard as to whether the return is produced by capital appreciation or income. In this way, the endowment may be managed flexibly to produce the greatest return with the least risk.

(a) Earnings

Earnings on an investment can be produced in one of two ways, either through income or through capital appreciation. Income is produced through interest earned on certificates of deposit, money market funds, treasuries or other bonds, dividends from stocks, or bond income, or by rents and royalties. Capital appreciation is growth in the value of an asset, such as shares of stock that were bought for $10,000 and are now worth $15,000. If sold, the stock would produce a capital gain of $5,000.

Traditionally, under the law of private trusts and the Principal and Income Act, the gain on the sale of an asset held for more than a year and a day (a long-term capital gain) is considered principal and not income. In some cases, short-term gain generated on sale of assets held for less than a year and a day is also considered principal. Many nonprofits managed endowments as if they were private trusts and applied the Principal and Income Act. To produce the necessary income, assets such as bonds and mortgages were selected that would produce income only, since only income could be distributed. Investments that produce capital gains were purchased solely to achieve diversification and to provide balance and stability to the portfolio. This strategy limited investment opportunities since many assets that produced gain failed to produce income. This approach created an investment strategy, forsaking growth for income, that hampered long-term growth of the underlying pool.

Portfolio theory has changed over the last 45 years, and many nonprofit organizations have chosen to invest for total return regardless of whether the investment produces income or capital appreciation. In addition, most nonprofit endowments measure the annual distribution from the portfolio as a percentage of the market value of the endowment pool rather than as income from interest and dividends.

(b) Distributing Earnings

Donors establish restricted endowments or funds to provide income in perpetuity to benefit a nonprofit, its programs and departments. Nonprofit organizations use a variety of methods to calculate the distribution from the endowment, commonly known as the *spending rule*. There is no one correct way to measure the distribution, nor is there one correct way to invest so long as the investment portfolio is compatible with the distribution requirements. Nonprofits usually make the distribution in one of these ways:

- Distribute income only from dividends, interests, rents, and royalties.

- Distribute a percentage of the market value of the portfolio. This method is the most common approach.

- Use a combination of both.

Depending on the donor's wishes, once the earnings are distributed, all of the earnings may be expended, all or a portion of the earnings may be returned to principal, or all or a portion may be accumulated in a separate account for future use.

Many nonprofits now invest on a total return basis and measure spending based on two models: (1) the fixed percentage unitrust and (2) the net income unitrust. Some nonprofits have borrowed the unitrust concept to determine the payout. The language "fixed percentage of the market value of the portfolio" is the method used for calculating the payout for a charitable remainder unitrust. In an endowment, the payout (or distribution) is measured as a fixed percentage of the value of the unitrust assets as valued annually, and no distinction is made between income and principal.

Other nonprofits measure spending as the lesser of the net income and a fixed percentage, which is the method used to calculate the distribution to an individual beneficiary from a net income unitrust. Using this method, the endowment distributes the net income or a fixed percentage, whichever is less.

Whether the nonprofit makes a distribution based on a fixed percentage of fair market value or on net income, for many nonprofit organizations either choice is an improvement over the traditional income-only approach to investing. Because planned giving officers understand the unitrust better than do most nonprofit staff members, they can be very helpful in explaining the concept of a unitrust, as applied to endowment, to other nonprofit staff members and donors.

(c) Realized and Unrealized Gains

The endowment fund includes both realized and unrealized gains. *Realized and unrealized gains* refer to capital appreciation in the underlying principal of the endowment. Realized gains are achieved when assets are sold for more than their cost basis. Unrealized gains are increases in the unsold capital appreciation of the market value of the asset; these gains are gains only on paper and are not realized until the asset is sold. The challenge to nonprofits and their investment managers is in determining how to access the unrealized gains, as needed, to subsidize cash flow requirements. In recent years, investment returns on many portfolios, even those invested conservatively, have come largely in the form of capital gains, while interest and dividend income have generally declined as a percentage of asset value. If the portfolio has had significant gain in capital appreciation but has not produced sufficient dividends and interest income to cover the distribution requirements, a portion of the appreciated assets may need to be sold to generate sufficient cash. This approach allows portfolio managers to invest for total return and to make investments that offer the greatest potential for return regardless of whether the return is income or capital appreciation.

Some argue that the distribution should never exceed the realized gains and actual income, which might result in the principal's being invaded to meet the distribution requirements. If, however, the portfolio includes significant unrealized capital appreciation, a portion of that appreciation may be realized to supplement other realized gains, and the portfolio will nevertheless experience growth. Still others take the position that only income in the form of interest and dividends should be distributed, and gains, whether realized or unrealized, should remain as a part of the principal of the endowment. Nonprofits should establish a consistent method for measuring the payout and adopt an investment strategy consistent with the method of measuring the distribution.

For nonprofits that measure spending as a percentage of market value, excess earnings are returned to principal; over the years, this has historically increased the size of the endowment, which in turn produces a greater distribution. In some years, due to the economy, poor investment performance, or a decline in the stock market, there may not be sufficient earnings to cover the spending rate, and assets may need to be sold to generate earnings equal to the percentage. Donors must take the good with the bad. Donors enjoy seeing endowments grow but dislike decreases in the value of the endowment that occur when assets are sold to satisfy the spending rate.

One alternative is to establish a reserve fund, a separate account that holds a portion of the excess earnings. In years in which there are excess earnings, rather than returning all excess earnings to principal, a portion of the excess earnings could be segregated for use in future years when poor performance of the endowment fails to produce sufficient earnings. Once the reserve fund reaches a specified amount, such as 2 percent of the market value of the endowment, then all excess earnings could continue to be returned to principal. Rather than deducting 2 percent at the outset, the 2 percent could be built up over a three- to five-year period.

Establishing a reserve fund stabilizes the portfolio and offsets fluctuations in the principal value of the endowment that may affect the long-term growth of the portfolio. In addition, the reserve fund provides a cushion during times of poor performance and may help to resolve the uneasiness that donors feel about decreases in the market value of the endowment, especially when the decrease is partly due to a sale of assets to produce cash for the distribution.

(d) Spending and Expense Provisions

Spending provisions enable nonprofit organizations to make distributions from the endowment pool. Nonprofit investment committees adjust the specific spending provisions on an annual basis as provided in a gift agreement. Each year the committee votes to distribute earnings from the endowment based on investment performance, the economy, the nonprofit's internal needs for income, and the general wishes of donors. The distributable earnings can be expressed as an annualized percentage of the fund's market value or can be defined as actual income. Measuring distributable earnings over a longer term, such as over a three-year average, reduces fluctuations in income. In order to produce a full 12 months of distributable earnings to benefit the object of a donor's endowed fund, the principal must be invested in the nonprofit's endowment for a full 12 months. Like a mutual fund, a nonprofit usually assigns units for contributions to the endowment. For ease in assigning unitized value to the endowment, the vast majority of nonprofits require that contributions to the endowment coincide with the quarters of the year—January 1, April 1, July 1, and October 1—or at other specified times. Funds transferred to the nonprofit as contributions to endowment prior to the quarter do not become invested until the next quarter. Most nonprofits return excess earnings to principal to promote the growth of the portfolio and thereby maintain its purchasing power. Nonprofits with large endowments tend to have lower spending rates.

The spending rate is linked to a variety of factors, including:

- History of the endowment

- Investment performance

- Size of the endowment

- Investment philosophy

Expenses for professional money management, commissions, and fees range from approximately 0.25 to 1 percent and are deducted from the earnings of the fund; fixed income managers that invest cash and cash equivalents charge approximately 0.25 to .50 percent, and equity managers that manage stock portfolios charge approximately 0.75 to 1.50 percent. In addition, costs for international equities are likely to be higher than costs for mainstream domestic corporations. Some managers measure expenses by basis points rather than by percentages. One percent is equal to 100 basis points. Calculating expenses by basis points is a more precise method of calculation, and some managers are willing to "shave off" basis points to reduce expenses.

44.5 INVESTMENT STRATEGIES

There is no one all-purpose model portfolio for nonprofits to use. Many nonprofit portfolios do have some similarities; however, asset allocations may be different. Asset allocations refer to three broadly classified types of investments: (1) equities, (2) fixed income, and (3) cash and cash equivalents. Nonprofits may also maintain "other" asset allocations that can include real estate and venture capital investments.

A discussion of the asset allocations follows.

(a) Equities

A share of stock is an equity investment that represents an ownership interest in a corporation. Depending on the stock, shareholders can earn a profit in two ways.

1. Shareholders who own stock receive a proportionate share in the corporation's profits, measured as dividends. The dividend is declared by the board of directors of the corporation.

2. Shareholders also have an opportunity to receive capital gains or appreciation when the stock is sold if the value of the stock increases.

44.5 INVESTMENT STRATEGIES

Common stocks include small-cap (capitalization), mid-cap, and large-cap stocks. The term *cap* refers to the capitalization, or market value, of a corporation. Small caps are aggressive growth companies whose value does not exceed $500 million, mid-caps are moderate growth companies whose value exceeds $500 million; and large caps are conservative growth companies whose value exceeds $1 billion, such as corporations included on the Dow Jones Industrial Average and the Standard & Poor's 500.

(i) Blue-Chip Stocks. Blue-chip stocks are stocks from large-cap corporations that are very well known companies and have historically paid dividends in both good and bad times. Blue-chip stocks have opportunities for both capital appreciation and income from dividends, although the dividend yield is usually no more than 2 to 4 percent. Blue-chip stocks are a safe and stable investment and form the basis of many nonprofit organizations' portfolios.

(ii) Growth Stocks. Growth stocks are investments in high-risk or young small-cap corporations that form the aggressive portion of an investment portfolio. The "growth" factor is an opportunity to obtain capital appreciation reflected in the growth of the business. These stocks do not pay much, if any, dividends because earnings, if any, are reinvested in the corporation to allow for growth or expansion.

(iii) Utility Stocks. Utility stocks represent ownership interests in gas, oil, electric, or telephone companies. The stock's price may rise to produce a capital gain, but, primarily utility stocks produce a steady stream of dividends. Although they are classified as stocks, they have characteristics of bonds and they may also be included in the fixed income allocation of the portfolio.

(b) Fixed-Income Investments

A bond, issued for $1,000 face value, is a fixed-income investment, considered a loan to the issuer, through which the bondholder receives income. The price of a bond, called *par* or *face value*, is affected by interest rate changes or changes in the credit rating of the issuer. Bondholders who hold the bond for the duration of its term, called *maturity,* receive their initial investment upon the completion of the term. A bondholder receives an income, called *yield*

(i) Corporate Bonds. Corporate bonds distribute income to investors based on the earnings and profitability of a corporation. Bonds are rated with letter grades, which represent a judgment on the creditworthiness of the bond and the corporation. To attract investors, low-rated corporations offer higher rates that reflect the increased risk of default.

(ii) Government Bonds. Government bonds are loans made to the federal government that provide funding for government operations.

(iii) Zero Coupon Bonds. Zero coupon bonds, issued by governments and private corporations, are sold at steep discounts below the face value. The yield or interest is not distributed to the bondholder but is instead reflected in the value of the bond as it progresses toward its date of maturity. A taxable investor will be taxed on the interest as earned even though it is not paid out.

(iv) Mortgaged-backed Securities. Mortgaged-backed securities include investments in U.S. government agency mortgage programs such as the Federal National Mortgage Association and the Government National Mortgage Association. Mortgage securities can also include commercial mortgage securities.

(c) Cash and Cash Equivalents

Cash and cash equivalents earn interest on the principal invested. Currently rates are fairly low on these investments. These investments have little risk and help to stabilize a portfolio.

(i) Certificates of Deposit. Certificates of deposit (CDs) distribute a fixed rate of income that is locked in at the time of the investment. Certificates of deposit have maturity periods of one month, three months, six months, one year, two years, five years, and sometimes longer. The CD rate is paid periodically (monthly or annually) or when the CD matures.

(ii) Money Market Funds. Money market funds invest in liquid assets such as Treasury bills, notes, and CDs. The investment in the fund is maintained at a constant dollar value, although the rate varies daily. Money market funds usually pay a slightly higher return than does a savings account.

(iii) Treasury Bills. Treasury bills are securities backed by the U.S. government. They are issued at a discount, which means that they are sold at less than face value and are redeemed at a specified maturity date, which may be 13, 26, or 52 weeks. The difference between the purchase price and the redemption price is the interest yield. U.S. Treasury notes and bonds may also be included in an overall investment portfolio since their maturity periods are longer and can stabilize a portfolio.

(d) Other Investments

Nonprofits diversify their portfolios by making limited investments in real estate and venture capital.

(i) Real Estate Investments. Real estate investments include ownership interests in the real estate that houses the nonprofit or is adjacent to the nonprofit. The real estate may be in a more remote location. The real estate may be commercial or residential property. Nonprofits also make investments through real estate investment trusts that provide opportunities for income and capital appreciation.

(ii) Venture Capital. Venture capital refers to the principal used to fund business start-ups. Some nonprofits, with large endowments, invest principal with venture capital companies that raise money to fund the start-ups. The nonprofit receives an equity or ownership interest in the start-up. If the business start-ups are successful, the nonprofit is rewarded when the equity interest is sold to other investors or is redeemed. Many such businesses are not successful. The investor must be willing to accept risk and loss of the investment.

(e) Portfolio Development

Portfolios are built to match the need for income with the need for growth while limiting exposure to risk. Designing a portfolio to produce income and growth in exactly the right proportions is no simple task. Growth portfolios include equity investments in large-cap stocks, small-cap stocks, venture capital markets, and real estate investment trusts, all of which maximize growth potential. Income portfolios invest in domestic and foreign bonds, mortgage-backed securities, and utility stocks. The assets that produce income do not necessarily produce growth and vice versa, although certain assets such as blue-chip stocks pay modest dividends and have the potential for capital appreciation. Portfolios may be invested in assets that produce either income, growth, or both growth and income. Combining income and growth assets produces a growth and income portfolio that is funded with a blend of investment assets.

Prior to determining the appropriate asset mix of the investment portfolio, it is necessary to gauge the types of returns that are necessary to meet anticipated spending needs. These liabilities can be real or anticipated and can occur now or in the future. Real liabilities include, for example, the need to provide income to fund existing scholarships. Anticipated liabilities include expected budget shortfalls or funding for new programs. Selecting the portfolio type and adjusting the asset allocations within the portfolio to reflect market conditions or to limit exposure to risk affects both the performance and the return. Investment managers research and select specific companies to be purchased for the portfolio's asset allocations. Nonprofits frequently select several managers to invest a single asset allocation to further diversify the portfolio to reduce risk.

(i) Growth Portfolios. A growth portfolio is heavily weighted in equity investments, with smaller percentages in fixed income and cash (see Exhibit 44.1). The equity portion is invested in a variety of equities, such as large-cap stocks, small-cap stocks, foreign equities, utilities, real estate investment trusts, and venture capital investments. Depending on market conditions and other economic factors, the equity portion may range from 60 to 80 percent of the portfolio, leaving a balance of 20 to 40 percent to be invested in fixed income and cash investments. This portfolio has potential for capital appreciation but has a greater level of risk due to its significant equity investment. A growth stock's share price can fluctuate greatly over time.

(ii) Income Portfolios. An income portfolio is weighted heavily with fixed-income investments such as domestic corporate bonds, foreign bonds, and mortgage-backed securities. A small percentage is invested in equity investments and an even smaller portion in cash and cash equivalents (see Exhibit 44.2). This portfolio generates income from its fixed-income investment and has little opportunity for capital appreciation. Bonds are adversely affected by interest rate increases, and the value of bond portfolios can fluctuate.

(iii) Growth and Income Portfolios. A growth and income portfolio is composed of a combination of equity and fixed-income investments, along with cash and cash equivalents (see Exhibit 44.3). The balance between equity investments and fixed-income investments is adjusted periodically to reflect market conditions and the economy.

(f) The Portfolio and Total Return

Portfolio performance must not be measured solely in terms of income produced or capital appreciation, but by total return, which is the value of the capital appreciation of the principal in

Exhibit 44.1   Sample Growth Portfolio

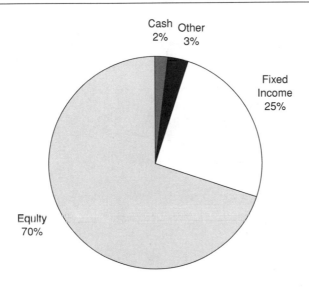

Exhibit 44.2   Sample Income Portfolio

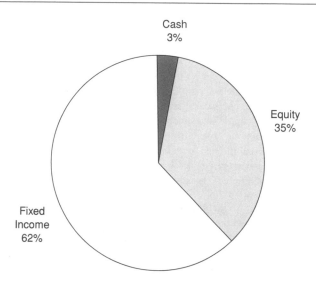

Exhibit 44.3   Sample Growth and Income Portfolio

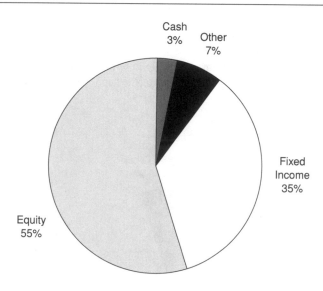

addition to all income produced. Total return enables fund managers, considering market conditions and forecasts, to allocate assets for the highest possible return without an obligation to produce income for specific purposes or for liquidity. Fixed-income investments are used as much to regulate risk as to produce income.

Nonprofit organizations, unlike individuals, are not measured in lifetimes but in decades and centuries. Some nonprofit organizations have been in existence for hundreds of years, so it is logical to think of establishing investment objectives for long-term horizons. Nonprofits can invest a portion of the endowment more aggressively to produce more growth. However, nonprofits also need to structure investment portfolios to produce income consistent with their anticipated liabilities, and the portfolio should be structured to provide for liquidity from investments such as corporate bonds, CDs, and utility stocks that also reduce risk but limit return.

A total return portfolio invests in assets that have the greatest potential for capital appreciation, dividends, interest, bond income, and other income. Investments are selected that combine characteristics of income and growth investments to reduce risk and emphasize potential for return.

At least quarterly, asset allocations to the portfolio are evaluated based on market performance, investment trends, and the potential for profitable returns.

(g) Diversification

Diversification reduces risk and provides a more stable investment portfolio. A completely diversified portfolio should consist of many types of assets from different asset classes, including fixed income, equities, and cash and cash equivalents. For example, adding investments in mortgaged-backed securities, utility stocks, and corporate bonds can help to stabilize a portfolio heavily weighted in growth stock.

A portfolio invested in a single asset class may accept a greater level of risk and may also underperform a more diversified portfolio. International investments are an increasingly important component of many nonprofits' portfolios and help to diversify the portfolio. The domestic markets represent approximately one-third of the world's economy; to tap into the world's investment opportunities, it is necessary to have some foreign investments.

(h) Risk Tolerance

Risk is a concept that is often confused with a number of other issues. Risk is measured by standard deviation. To what extent will the performance of the asset deviate from the mean or average? The greater the deviation, the greater the risk. Volatility—the rapid movement in the price of the asset—is really an issue of market timing: If the asset has to be sold, will the market be up or down?

There are several types of risk, including:

- Quality risk: Will the asset hold its value?

- Inflation (or purchasing power) risk: Will the asset return exceed inflation?

- Interest rate risk: Will the return be affected by the movement of interest rates?

Exhibit 44.4 depicts asset allocation ranges for three types of portfolios.

Exhibit 44.4   Sample Portfolio with Asset Allocation Ranges

Portfolio	Equity Range	Fixed Income	Other	Cash
Income	30–40%	55–65%	1–5%	1–4%
Growth and Income	50–60%	30–40%	3–10%	1–4%
Growth	65–75%	20–30%	1–5%	1–4%

Exhibit 44.5 depicts asset allocations for components of a portfolio.

Exhibit 44.5 Sample Diversified Portfolio Asset Allocations

	Income	Growth and Income	Growth
Equity			
Large cap	15%	15%	20%
Utilities	10%	15%	20%
Small cap	5%	20%	20%
Foreign equities	3%	5%	10%
Subtotal	33%	55%	70%
Fixed Income			
Treasuries	5%	5%	3%
Mortgage securities	25%	10%	8%
Inv. grade corp.	25%	10%	8%
High yield	5%	5%	4%
Foreign bonds	2%	5%	2%
Subtotal	62%	35%	25%
Other			
Venture cap	1%	2%	1%
Real estate	1%	6%	2%
Cash	3%	2%	2%
Total	100%	100%	100%

Nonprofit organizations must be sensitive to the level of risk associated with the endowment portfolio. A portfolio's return can be enhanced by investing in assets that have a greater level of risk, thus offering a potential for greater returns; but greater risk also means the possibility of greater loss. Frequently a loss results from risk, volatility, or market sensitivity in the portfolio over a short term, whereas over a longer term that same risk can produce positive results. As previously discussed, a nonprofit's existence is measured over long-term durations that enable nonprofits to place a portion of the endowment in investments that are inherently more risky but that have the potential for greater reward.

44.6 PORTFOLIOS FOR PLANNED GIVING OPTIONS

A planned giving officer's input is sought by nonprofit financial staff regarding the unique financial requirements of planned gifts, such as life income gifts that impose financial liabilities on nonprofit organizations. These discussions often lead to additional requests for recommendations for the handling of life income funds. Planned giving officers also are actively involved in working with donors to establish endowed funds.

Each individual donor's endowed fund is managed as part of the nonprofit's endowment, unless the donor requests that the fund be managed as a separately invested fund. If the endowed fund is to be established through a planned gift, the planned gift first must be managed for the benefit of the life income beneficiaries. It is important that the donor and the nonprofit staff members recognize that when a planned gift is used to establish an endowed fund, income to support the endowed fund is available only upon the death of the life income beneficiary. Upon the death of the life income beneficiary, the remainder of the planned gift is removed from the life income gift fund and is transferred to the nonprofit's endowment fund, where it is managed and invested as part of the endowment pool.

Two of the key challenges faced by the nonprofit are to manage planned gift assets for an extended period of time and to distribute the income to the beneficiaries for life while preserving principal for the nonprofit. Some gift options, such as the charitable gift annuity, charitable remainder annuity trust, and the straight percentage charitable remainder unitrust, require the invasion of principal if necessary to achieve the stated payout rate. To achieve a cash flow commensurate with the nonprofit's financial obligation to make income payments, the nonprofit's asset mix for a life income gift fund may need to be modified and invested separately. Greater demands for income can limit investment options and investment returns by restricting investments in growth stock that enhance portfolio performance but produce little income.

(a) Philanthropy Protection Act of 1995

The PPA codified certain exemptions from the registration requirements of federal and state securities laws for charitable organizations that establish and maintain certain collective investment vehicles, including charitable gift annuities. The PPA provides that employees, volunteers, officers, directors, and trustees who solicit funds on behalf of a charitable organization are exempt from the registration requirements of federal securities laws, providing these individuals do not receive a commission or special compensation based on the number or value of donations collected for the fund. The exemption applies to charitable income funds, which include pooled income funds, collective trust funds, collective investment funds, and other funds maintained by charitable organizations exclusively for the collective investment and reinvestment of one or more of the following:

- Assets of the general endowment fund or other funds of one or more charitable organizations
- Assets of a pooled income fund
- Assets contributed to a charitable organization in exchange for the issuance of charitable gift annuities
- Assets of a charitable remainder trust or any other trust, the remainder interests of which are irrevocably dedicated to any charitable organization
- Assets of a charitable lead trust

Revocable trusts require special treatment and, in general, should not be commingled with the gift vehicles listed above.

The PPA requires nonprofit organizations to provide written disclosure to donors of property, who retain an interest in the property, if the property will be commingled with other charitable funds. This requirement became effective as of March 7, 1996, for gifts made on or after December 8, 1995. For years, nonprofits that have offered pooled income funds have commingled gifts from donors into a collective investment pool. The provisions of the PPA should pose no real reporting obstacles. The PPA does not describe the elements necessary for a disclosure statement to comply with the Act; however, the following may be considered to be elements of such disclosure:

- The name and address of the nonprofit organization
- The name of the nonprofit organization's governing board or committee responsible for managing the fund
- A description of the investment objective of the fund, with an explanation as to the method of distributing earnings (income and capital gains) to the fund
- The names and addresses of investment advisors and other fund managers who invest assets on behalf of the nonprofit organization
- A statement describing whether the fund is a trust, corporation, or pooled fund

- A representative list of the types of securities held by the fund

- A statement that the donors' funds will be commingled with other donors' funds in a collective investment vehicle

- A statement that the fund is exempt from registration under federal securities laws

- A statement regarding the total market value of the fund

- A statement regarding restrictions or limitations for the investments of the fund

- A statement regarding the impact of risk on the market value of the investments in the pool

- A statement outlining the income, gift, and estate tax consequences of the gift

In the past pooled income funds were required to provide a prospectus to donors that details the fund's objective, fees, expenses, returns, holdings, and performance so that donors would know the consequences of their contributions to the pooled income fund. Now other life income donors whose gifts are commingled, through the PPA, have similar opportunities to be informed about these issues, and the nonprofit may need to develop a prospectus for life income gift funds. As donors become more aware of the impact of the PPA and disclosure, they may want additional information that, in the past, had been unavailable or inaccessible. Sample tax and PPA disclosure statements for charitable remainder trusts and charitable gift annuities appear in Appendix, CD-ROM Documentation, Administrative Documents.[2]

Consumer protection laws have provided consumers with rights, and the PPA may provide donors with similar rights regarding the nonprofit's investment policies and procedures. However, as donors learn more about the unique challenges of nonprofit investment, they will learn more about the importance of private support in building the endowment.

(b) Gift Annuities

Through a *charitable gift annuity,* a donor makes a gift to the nonprofit and receives an income for life. The income is based on a rate reflecting potential investment returns and a return of a portion of the donor's initial principal. The annuity payment is an immediate obligation of the nonprofit. The principal from charitable gift annuities may be placed in a life income gift fund, in a separate annuity fund, or treated as part of the nonprofit's endowment. The organization must have liquid funds sufficient to cover the income stream, and, at the same time, the funds should be invested to preserve the principal for the benefit of the nonprofit. A portfolio for charitable gift annuities may be structured at the discretion of the organization's advisors.

To estimate the income stream payable to the beneficiaries, take an average of the payout percentage of all charitable gift annuities or total the actual income payout to the beneficiaries. The annuity can be produced from the income-generating portion of the portfolio or from capital gains produced on the sale of assets. For example, if the average payout is 7 percent and the endowment pool generates 4 percent in income, then either assets will have to be sold to generate capital gain or produce proceeds to meet the obligation or the portfolio will have to be structured to produce actual income at or near the rate of 7 percent. For example, long-term bonds may meet the income obligation, but they generally do not appreciate as stocks do and therefore are unlikely to appreciate in value to preserve the purchasing power in future years.

Through a *deferred gift annuity,* a donor makes a present gift and defers the income to a predetermined point in the future. In most cases, the deferral is in excess of five years and may exceed 10 years. This deferral permits investment of principal on a total return basis, with emphasis on cap-

---

[2] Provided by Carolyn Osteen, Esquire, Ropes & Gray, Boston, Massachusetts.

ital appreciation. As with gift annuity funds, the nonprofit can commingle deferred gift annuity funds with the nonprofit's endowment or with its life income gift fund. As beneficiaries approach the predetermined age when income is to be distributed, the fund manager may wish to convert a portion to an income fund to pay out the necessary income, while the balance may continue to be invested for total return. Alternatively, the manager may also sell a portion of the portfolio to cover the income stream to the beneficiaries.

(c) Pooled Income Funds

Through a gift to the pooled income fund, a donor makes a gift to the fund and receives an income for life and a charitable income tax deduction. The payout rate is variable because it is based on the earnings produced by the underlying investments of the pooled income fund. The pooled income fund distributes income based on an allocation of income to each unit that is determined by dividing the income for the taxable year by the outstanding number of units. For example, a donor holds 1,000 of 10,000 units in the pooled income fund, and the fund earns $1 million in income; each unit receives $10 in income, so she receives $10,000 in income.

Pooled income funds define income as earnings on investments such as interest income, CD interest, bond income, and dividends from stock, net of investment expenses and management fees. The following four items are generally principal rather than income and therefore may not be distributed to income beneficiaries:

1. Long-term capital gains and losses from the sale or other disposition of investments

2. Stock dividends or stock splits

3. Capital gain distributions of regulated investment companies, such as mutual funds

4. Distributions from liquidations and all other dividends not deemed taxable under the Internal Revenue Code

Short-term capital gains from the sale of assets held by the fund for less than one year are considered principal rather than income, unless the short-term gains are earned as a substitute for interest and dividends. In addition, short-term capital gains from the sale of assets held by the donor for less than one year and contributed to the fund, and sold before the holding period equals one year, are also considered principal rather than income. Short-term gain earned by mutual funds is converted to income, as are interest and dividends, and is generally distributed to the fund's beneficiaries. The principal cannot be distributed to the beneficiaries. Instead, the actual income produced by the fund, less expenses, is distributed to the beneficiaries. A nonprofit generally offers one or more pooled income funds:

■ Income

■ Balanced

■ Growth funds

A high-income fund is invested in high-yield corporate bonds, mortgage-backed securities, and utility stocks. The bonds are "laddered" so that they mature at 5-, 10-, 15-, and 20-year intervals. Laddering stabilizes income and preserves the underlying value in the bonds. A balanced fund contains some fixed-income investments, such as assets included in the high-yield fund and growth assets such as blue-chip stocks and other dividend-paying stocks. A growth fund produces little income except for dividends from blue-chip stocks and other equity investments. A growth pooled income fund preserves and "grows" the principal from the capital appreciation of the assets that provides maximum benefit to the nonprofit; there is little income immediately, but as the fund grows, so does the income.

(d) Charitable Remainder Trusts

Charitable remainder trusts are personalized planned giving vehicles that provide income to beneficiaries for life or for a term of years. Upon the death of the income beneficiary or upon the completion of the term of years, the remainder is distributed to the nonprofit organization. These trusts are personalized in that the donor, within limits, selects the payout rate and determines whether the trust is to distribute income to beneficiaries for life or for a term of years. The trustee must select appropriate investments to meet the objectives and charitable purposes of the donor and the income needs of the beneficiaries, and, at the same time, preserve the remainder for the nonprofit. Trusts that are established for short-terms are subject to market volatility and may need to be invested with a blend of fixed-income investments, supplemented with equity investments.

(i) Charitable Remainder Annuity Trust. The charitable remainder annuity trust provides a fixed, guaranteed dollar amount that represents not less than 5 percent and usually not more than 7 percent of the value of the trust's assets at the time the trust is established. The distribution is paid regardless of the trust's investment performance, and the trustee must invade the principal of the trust, if necessary, to make the distribution to the beneficiaries. The distribution may be obtained from income from fixed-income investments or from the sale of capital assets. If the trust's investments fail to perform, the trust principal can be depleted by the trustee in making the fixed, guaranteed dollar distribution to the beneficiaries. Depletion of trust assets further strains the ability of the trust to grow, resulting in further depletion of assets to make distributions in future years while reducing the value of the remainder to the nonprofit. The IRS publishes a monthly discount rate to value remainder interests. The rate is linked to Treasury bonds; for example, the discount rate for April 2003 is 3.6 percent. Donors who select an amount that represents more than the applicable discount rate risk depleting the principal of the trust. Because the payment obligation is known at the time of the creation of the trust, the trustee, if appropriate, can take a more aggressive position in investing in growth investments.

(ii) Charitable Remainder Unitrust 1/Straight Fixed Percentage. The straight fixed percentage charitable remainder unitrust pays to the beneficiary a fixed percentage of the trust's assets as valued annually. Like the annuity trust, the trustee is obligated to make the distribution and must invade the principal of the trust, if necessary. Unlike the annuity trust, the payment is variable and is affected by the increase or decrease in the market value of the trust's assets. Depletion of principal is a concern to both the beneficiaries and the nonprofit, as a diminution of principal jeopardizes the production of income and the remainder value. Trustees have some protection because the distribution is a function of the market value, calculated by multiplying the fixed percentage by the annual market value of the fund. Depending on the needs of the lifetime beneficiaries, trustees can invest in equity and fixed-income assets to promote growth and generate income.

(iii) Charitable Remainder Net Income Unitrust. The net income unitrust requires a payment of the net income or a fixed percentage, whichever is less. Income is defined under state and local law, and most trusts define income as interest income and dividends from stocks. In most states, capital gains are considered to be principal, not income, unless the trust instrument specifically defines net income to include realized net capital gain. If no income is produced, then nothing is distributed. The trustee may not invade the principal to make the distribution since the distribution is measured as the lesser of actual net income or fixed percentage. The trustee must fully understand the wishes of the donor when this type of trust is established. For example, investments in growth stocks will produce little or no income, although if market conditions are favorable, the portfolio may grow in value. This type of trust may be appropriate for a beneficiary who is younger and who would like to receive income in the future. A couple in their 50s who wish to retire after age 65 could fund the portfolio with growth stock.

Over time, the growth stock may increase the value of the corpus. As the couple approaches retirement, the trustee can gradually convert the growth assets to income assets, enabling the beneficiaries to receive net income or the fixed percentages of an asset pool that has greatly increased in value during the investment period. See Chapter 40 for an illustration of the use of growth stock to fund a charitable remainder net income unitrust for retirement.

> *Capital Gain as Income.* The Internal Revenue Service has approved the capital gain unitrust, allowing a net income unitrust to define income to include capital gains so long as state law allows such a definition in the trust. Historically, trustees selected investments that produced income equal, or as near as possible, to the percentage amount. However, the investment climate in recent years has favored capital growth rather than dividend income. Most trustees prefer to invest for total return by selecting investments based on their potential for performance rather than on whether their return would be considered income or capital gain.[3]

(iv) Charitable Remainder Net Income Unitrust with Makeup Provision.   A net income unitrust with a makeup provision pays the lesser of the net income or fixed percentage and allows for making up a shortfall. Funding this trust with growth assets may be attractive because the makeup provision enhances the probability of income in the future to the donor since lost income is made up in a later year when income in excess of the fixed percentage is earned. The makeup provision, however, can reduce the return of earnings to principal since the earnings are distributed to the beneficiary to make up for lost earnings. In future years, the principal can be further diminished, which in turn will reduce the income to the beneficiaries.

44.7   DONOR RELATIONS

Sophisticated donors with large estates often accumulate or preserve their wealth through significant investments in the stock and bond markets. These individuals may have experienced significant market returns in the stock market. Sometimes they are disappointed to learn that returns from the nonprofit's investment portfolio are less than expected, that not all income is distributed, or that a portion of the income is used to pay a management fee. Investment policies and donor relations are inextricably woven together. The nonprofit must have an investment policy in place to govern the management and investment of donors' funds. An overly restrictive investment policy that donors perceive is weighted in favor of the nonprofit frustrates the wishes of the donors and jeopardizes their present and future philanthropic support. Interpreting and translating the policy to donors is an important part of a planned giving officer's job.

A gift agreement (fund description) defines the roles and responsibilities of the donor and the nonprofit organization and outlines the use of the funds, restrictions, and investment specifics, such as spending provisions and expenses. Chapter 27 provides a detailed description on the use of gift agreements and the issues to be addressed in preparing these agreements. The gift agreement, signed by both the donor and a representative of the nonprofit organization, is, in many ways, like a contract that defines the rights, responsibilities, duties, and obligations of all parties to the contract. In addition to the donor-related and gift-planning aspects covered in Chapter 27, a gift agreement specifically defines the distribution and earnings upon which the distribution is based and states the method for distributing earnings, the rate of distribution as set by the investment committee, and the costs and expenses for investment and professional management.

---

[3] From Carolyn Osteen, Esquire, Ropes & Gray, Boston, Massachusetts, *Memorandum to Nonprofit Clients,* December 1996.

NONPROFIT INVESTMENT POLICIES AND PROCEDURES

The following language can be included in a gift agreement to define the nonprofit's investment policies for an endowed fund:

> Contributions from the donor to establish an endowed fund will be managed as part of the principal of <ORGANIZATION's> Pooled Endowment. The distribution from the endowed fund will be determined annually by the <ORGANIZATION's> Investment Committee. Distribution is measured as <Note: Select one of the following three options. Option 1, A PERCENTAGE OF THE MARKET VALUE OF THE POOLED ENDOWMENT; Option 2, ALL INCOME PRODUCED BY THE ENDOWMENT; or Option 3, DESCRIBE OTHER METHOD OF DISTRIBUTION.> <ORGANIZATION> has the right to charge reasonable administrative expenses, including a management fee.

Organizations that use reserve funds must add a clause to the gift agreement governing the use of such funds. Because most funds operate in perpetuity, an agreement defines the terms by which the nonprofit will manage and use the funds. The gift agreement can be used for outright gifts, life income gifts, and gifts through a will or trust. It is especially important to have a pledge document in place committing to future gifts for any donor who wishes to provide future funding, for example, upon the death of a donor (a bequest), gift through a trust, or life income gift. If the gift is to be made from a charitable remainder trust or private foundation, the commitment or pledge should be made by the trustees of the trust or foundation, not the donor.

Often donor-endowed funds are established over a 3- to 5-year period. It is important that the gift agreement describe the terms of the transfer of funds from the donor to the nonprofit. For example, the following language can be helpful in dealing with funds established over a period of time:

> It is the donor's intent that this endowment may reach the endowment fund level of <$> within <#> years from the date of this agreement. If the fund fails to reach this level, then the fund shall be considered to be available for current use, and all funds shall be distributed within one year.

Sometimes donors have a change of heart regarding restrictions and provisions in selecting recipients, so the gift agreement may need to be amended after the fact to conform to the wishes of the donors. Providing information on investment policy, procedures, and expenses raises issues that donors may not have considered; therefore, the gift agreement provides a working document that prevents confusion and eliminates misinterpretation.

(a) Working with Donors' Advisors

During the normal course of doing business, planned giving officers and nonprofit staff members regularly deal with investment advisors who represent the nonprofit's prospects and donors; these investment advisors may be employed by investment or brokerage houses or by financial institutions that offer investment, financial, or trust management services to nonprofit organizations. Representatives from these institutions often inquire as to the procedure to compete or bid for all or a portion of the nonprofit's investment business. Nonprofit staff must be prepared to respond to these inquiries, otherwise advisors may feel alienated and excluded, potentially jeopardizing the donor's gift.

(b) Balancing Donor's Expectations and the Nonprofit's Needs

Endowment policies that are understandable, logical, and reasonable encourage prospects to become donors and promote additional gifts from existing donors. In establishing gift agreements, nonprofits must consider the donor's intent along with the practical needs of departments, programs, or recipient beneficiaries. Donors to endowment funds usually hold one of two philosophies regarding investment objectives: Either they want maximum income to be distributed to designated programs from an endowment or they wish to see the principal value of the endowment increase in value through favorable investment performance or through reinvestment of excess earnings to principal.

Most nonprofit's operating costs have grown faster than increases in inflation, which places additional pressure on nonprofit endowments and their money managers to perform well to equal prior distributions. To keep pace with these increases, the principal of the endowment must grow in an amount in excess of the rate of inflation to maintain its purchasing power. As operating costs increase over time, income portfolios have at times failed to produce growth in the underlying principal sufficient to preserve purchasing power. For example a $1 million portfolio of bonds with a maturity of 20 years, paying 7 percent, may produce income of $70,000 each year. That $70,000 may provide seven $10,000 full-tuition scholarships in year 1. But, by year 20, if tuition increased 7 percent per year, tuition has grown to $38,700 and that same $70,000 would produce only 1.8 full scholarships.

Nonprofits may choose not to offer donors the choice of directing contributions to one of three investment portfolios: maximum income, growth and income, or growth. Some mature nonprofits wish to offer donors the option of allocating contributions among all of the nonprofit's endowment funds, each of which has different objectives and different investment strategies. Conservative donors may wish to allocate a major portion of their endowed fund to high-grade corporate bonds that have less risk, little growth, but favorable income streams. Giving donors a choice helps to meet their needs and provides realistic expectations to the nonprofit's staff who prepare budgets in anticipation of endowment earnings. Like a mutual fund that offers growth, growth and income, and income funds, a nonprofit can allow donors to allocate their charitable gifts to the endowment compatible with their goals.

Many donors enjoy seeing their endowed fund grow to a specific dollar amount, for example, $100,000, and then distributed in accordance with their wishes as defined in the gift agreement. A growth portfolio would accommodate such a donor who could designate gifts to a portfolio that would offer opportunities for capital appreciation; once the fund reached the level of $100,000, it could be transferred to an income endowment designed to provide maximum income to satisfy the endowment's objectives. Investment portfolios may be developed to balance the often conflicting interests of the donor and the nonprofit.

In the past, for large gifts such as gifts in excess of, perhaps, $250,000, nonprofits considered the feasibility and practicality of separately investing endowed funds as an incentive to donors. In such a case, the endowed fund is invested in accordance with recommendations made by the donor, is designed to achieve a specific investment objective, and is funded with assets designed to accomplish those purposes. Separately invested funds can meet the donor's needs but can be more expensive to manage and cause administrative inconvenience due to separate reporting and accounting requirements when investing discrete funds for specific purposes. For donors who would be dissatisfied with the nonprofit's investment policy or investment returns, however, a separately invested fund may be the only answer. Nonprofits always must evaluate the specific accommodations requested by a particular donor to make certain that the benefit exceeds the cost. In any event, the nonprofit should have the right to commingle such funds with other nonprofit funds. Because most mature organizations have utilized their portfolios to allow proper allocation of income and expenses, it is possible to invest a fund to achieve specific investment objectives without requiring separate investments. Separate investment of funds is not something that a nonprofit should agree to unless the fund is quite large and alternative options have been fully explored with the donor.

(c) Inappropriate Investments

The nonprofit organization should consider whether certain assets should be excluded from the nonprofit's investment portfolios. Although members of the committee may structure their personal investment portfolios with a wide array of investment options, while acting on behalf of a nonprofit, they must make investment decisions to avoid unnecessary risk and market volatility, satisfy the public trust, and meet fiduciary responsibilities.

Depending on the policy and philosophy of the nonprofit, the following investments might not be considered financially appropriate investment options due to high volatility, risk, or their speculative nature:

- Unregistered or restricted stock

- Commodities, including gold or currency futures

- Conditional sales contracts

- Options including the purchase, sale, or writing of options

- Warrants

- Margin purchases that create unrelated business taxable income

- Short selling

- Unhedged derivatives

Furthermore, tax-exempt securities, either state or federal, are considered inappropriate investment options. Since the nonprofit is tax exempt, it does not benefit from investments in tax exempt securities such as municipal bonds.

In addition, the social, political, and cultural climates help to shape the nonprofit's investment policies. A nonprofit's constituents and donors often look to see whether the nonprofit is investing in funds that are socially responsible. Investment committees should consider their philosophy toward such investments. Regardless of its final decision, the committee must be prepared to explain its position to concerned donors.

(d) Disclosure of Management Fees and Expenses

Fees for professional investment services are a natural cost of doing business. Fees may be measured by basis points or as a percentage of the portfolio's market value, for example, 1 to 2 percent, or they can be charged on a fee-for-service basis, or can be assessed depending on the nonprofit's investment policy. Some nonprofits do not allocate fees or expenses to funds that support vital activities that are generally underfunded. For example, many organizations do not impose fees against funds restricted for scholarships since restricted funds are generally insufficient to fill the need and unrestricted funds must be utilized.

Fees can represent a significant percentage of distributable income. In addition, fees are deducted from the portfolio's market value prior to calculating the distribution. For example, on an endowment of $100,000, if the management fee is assessed at a rate of 2 percent of market value ($2,000), and the spending provision calls for a payout based on 4 percent of market value ($3,920), the management fee represents over 50 percent of the payout, which seems excessive to many donors. Some donors assume that investment expenses will be paid by the nonprofit rather than being deducted from the principal or earnings of their gift. Investment expenses may reasonably be allocated to donors' funds on a prorated basis. Donors must be reminded that there is a cost for professional management of their funds.

Planned giving donors inquire about the way their funds are invested and by whom. They also want to know about returns on their contributions and the amount of fees and expenses that are charged against their gifts for management. Sometimes donors insist that they could get a better return from a bond than from a gift annuity backed by the nonprofit's endowed fund. At times, it is true that a bond or a CD can produce more income than can the nonprofit endowment and at less cost. However, interest rates change, CD rates fall, and a bond's fixed rate fails to keep pace with the nonprofit's expenses, which are not fixed. Other donors are concerned that nonprofit management expenses are excessive compared to those of institutional trustees. These donors consider establishing private charitable trusts or private foundations to avoid placing funds with the nonprofit's endowment. Nonprofits must consider the competition when it comes to setting the policy on expenses so as not to alienate the donor.

The degree of disclosure about management fees and expenses varies from nonprofit to nonprofit. Some nonprofits provide complete disclosure about expenses by including a statement in each donor's gift agreement that explains how expenses will be handled. Others choose to maintain flexibility and may provide less than complete disclosure by providing spending and performance figures net of fees and expenses. Both methods can create problems. Because full disclosure calls attention to the issue of expenses, the organization must justify their expense policy. Those that provide only net spending figures have donors that suspect hidden expenses and challenge the validity of the available distributions.

In setting the policy, the nonprofit's investment committee must consider the historical precedents for distributions from endowment since donors and nonprofits are aware of these as well. Departures from past precedents must be carefully explained to avoid alienating donors and staff. Over the years, nationally the trend has been to reduce the distribution to 5 percent or less of market value for organizations that measure the distribution as a percentage market value and invest for total return. Management fees typically average 1 to 1.5 percent of market value.

44.8 INVESTMENT GUIDELINES

The investment policy defines the objective of the fund and establishes time frames for making transfers and withdrawals from the endowment. The policy describes appropriate and inappropriate investments and imposes restrictions and limitations regarding the acquisition of specific securities. Securities in the portfolio that fall below the restrictions or limitations must be disposed of within a reasonable period of time.

The investment policy also dictates the reporting requirements of the investment managers to the nonprofit organization. Quarterly reports are provided that define investment performance, security holdings, and market forecasts. The nonprofit through its investment committee may make decisions regarding reallocation of assets or transfer of accumulated cash to a specific portfolio. Alternatively, the cash may be distributed proportionately to all investment managers. The policy also sets targets for performance and establishes investment goals and objectives. The policy also establishes procedures to evaluate the performance of managers compared to agreed-on standards.

(a) Standards of Performance

A nonprofit's investment manager should be presented with an investment policy statement. The policy statement should provide information as to the nonprofit's investment objectives, guidelines, asset mixes, and benchmark portfolios. The performance of managers entrusted with the investment of the nonprofit assets is measured against agreed-on benchmarks composed of unmanaged and model portfolios and indexed investment funds. Portfolio risk is measured in comparison to the risk associated with the specified benchmark. For example, investments in the Far East may be measured against the Europe, the Australia, and the Far East Index. Domestic stock investments may be measured against the return of indexes such as the S&P 500, Russell 2,000, or Wilshire 5,000. The Russell and Wilshire Indexes represent broad market indexes of 2,000 and 5,000 corporations, respectively. A nonprofit ideally would prefer less risk and greater return than the agreed-on investment performance index. One measure of return is the consumer price index (CPI) plus an agreed-on percentage, such as CPI and 5 percent. The CPI is the U.S. government's measure of inflation; it reflects increases or decreases in the price of consumer goods and services. A portfolio must have returns at least equal to the CPI in order to maintain the purchasing power of the preceding year. Depending on the distribution rate set by the nonprofit and the acceptable level of risk, a nonprofit's investment portfolio performance should exceed the measure of CPI by 2 to 6 percent. The Higher Education Price Index measures institutional increases in the cost of doing business; these increases have exceeded the CPI and inflation.

(b) Investment Policy Guidelines

Investment policy guidelines control investments to limit risk by promoting diversification so that no more than a specific percentage of the portfolio should be invested in any one company and no more than a specific percentage of the portfolio should be invested in any one industry. In addition, nonprofit investment committees may set maximum percentages for these assets:

■ Domestic securities, including small- and large-cap stocks

■ Fixed-income investments, including high-grade (investment grade) bonds and high-income (junk) bonds

■ Cash and cash equivalents

■ Real estate securities

■ International securities or real estate investment trusts and emerging markets

■ Venture capital

A diversified investment strategy includes a blend of stocks, bonds, real estate, international securities, and venture capital investments that, over time, will produce a greater return with less risk.

44.9 CONCLUSION

Investment management is one of the most important yet underpublicized areas of nonprofit management. Much more is known about the nonprofit's mission, services, and needs for funding than about the use and management of those funds. Donors transfer billions of dollars to nonprofits, of which a significant percentage is contributed to the endowment fund or to the life income gift fund. Nonprofits have a responsibility to preserve the principal of the donor's gifts and to use the donor's funds to provide support to the nonprofit and its programs and departments, consistent with the donor's wishes. Nonprofit staff and planned giving officers can be instrumental in sharing with donors the details that surround the management and investment of nonprofit funds. As donors learn that nonprofits are careful, scrupulous, and diligent in the management of funds, donors are likely to provide additional funds.

Occasionally donors must be reminded that their funds contributed to endowment are vigorously managed by the nonprofit as a part of its endowment pool or life income gift fund. Their contributions are pooled with thousands of other donors' funds, providing stability to the nonprofit. An investment policy must permit donors to feel good about their charitable gifts rather than to feel that the investment policy is designed only for the benefit of the nonprofit organization. A properly drafted investment policy can be of tremendous value, demonstrating to donors the nonprofit's care and concern in managing endowment to safeguard the principal and ensure that the nonprofit's endowment and life income funds will support the donor's wishes in perpetuity.

## CHAPTER FORTY-FIVE

Administering a Nonprofit Bequest Program

45.1 INTRODUCTION

Many charities receive their largest charitable gifts from bequests, yet very few charities place enough importance on managing gifts that come from donors' wills and trusts. Often charities passively manage a very important part of their development programs.

Active management can increase distributions, speed the estate administration process, and build strong relationships with donors, their families, and professional advisors. Charities need to make administering bequests a priority. A less vigilant charity may receive less money than it would with better, active oversight. The executor, without the charity's input, can make decisions—and mistakes—that can result in a smaller gift to the charity: The executor might interpret a clause in a way that directs the gift elsewhere, pay or charge fees that are too high, or be slow in making the charitable distribution. This leaves the charity with less time to invest the proceeds, and ultimately it earns less on the gift.

With active participation on its part, the charity may collect more money from bequests and may be able to make educated estimates of bequest distributions each year. If a charity has a small development program and receives just a few bequests each year, active participation by the development staff may be likely because there are few other gifts coming in; or it may be passively managed because there are so many other jobs to do. A charity that receives any bequests should be looking carefully at the distribution and the estate settlement process. Charities that have larger development programs, receive a substantial number of bequests each year, and have a large development staff should consider having the planned giving officer include in her responsibilities active participation of the bequest administration process. It is not uncommon at the largest charities to see individuals whose entire job is bequest administration. Depending on the organization, bequest administration could be a full-time job.

This chapter begins by providing an overview of the probate process as it relates to administering gifts from bequests. It continues with reducing potential bequest losses in administering bequests and provides suggestions for managing a bequest program internally.

45.2 GUIDE TO THE PROBATE PROCESS

Chapter 38, which provides an overview of the probate process, should be read before beginning this chapter. The following explores in more detail the intricacies of the probate process as it specifically relates to administering monies received from bequests at a nonprofit organization.

State laws vary on the timing and issues involved in the probate process. Many states follow the Uniform Probate Code or have modified or adopted parts of it. Most legal terms used here apply to every state's probate process, but timetables vary. Be sure to check your state's specific probate laws.

(a) The Perfect Case

A donor has passed away and made a charitable gift to a nonprofit from his estate. The gift is significant. If perfect, the estate would be settled in approximately one year or less, and the charity would receive all of the gift before the year expires. There would be no claims or challenges against the estate by creditors or other individuals. Unfortunately, in practice it rarely works this way.

(b) Filing the Will

The executor files the donor's will shortly after the donor's death. The executor locates the donor's will and files it with the probate court for the county where the donor was domiciled, the place where the decedent had a permanent home. The will is then likely to be probated, which means that the will is allowed, or accepted as true, and the executor is formally appointed.

Once the will is probated, it becomes part of the public record and is assigned a docket number in the county probate court where the donor permanently resided. A representative from the charity can easily locate the will by looking under the deceased's name in the probate court and review the will if the planned giving officer has not already received a copy from the executor. The charity routinely receives a copy of that portion of the will that relates to the charity, making it unnecessary to obtain it from the probate court.

(c) Revocable Trusts

Donors with large estates or complex estate plans often have a revocable trust as part of their estate plans. A revocable trust is much like a will in that it provides for disposition of assets at death. The revocable trust is not available to the public nor is it subject to the jurisdiction of the probate court, which is one of the reasons why it is regularly used in sophisticated estate plans. The trustee of a revocable trust that provides for a gift to charity at the donor's death is obligated to notify the charity and to account for the charitable funds. The specific method of notification is discretionary with the trustee, unless the trust proscribes the method of notification.

The probate court will appoint the executor and issue a citation, which is a form of notice of the petition for allowance of the will. Notice from the court must be sent to all beneficiaries under the will and to all relatives of the decedent who would be eligible to receive a portion of the estate, if the decedent had died intestate (without a will). When a charity is involved, notice generally is sent from the probate court to the state's attorney general's office. A sample petition appears in Appendix, CD-ROM Documentation, Exhibits.

The notice will set forth a time period within which an objection or will contest must be filed. If there is an objection, there may be a hearing and possibly the appointment of a special administrator, an individual appointed by the court to try to resolve this dispute. The executor will not be appointed, and no assets will be collected or distributed until the matter is resolved. When there is no objection by any party, the probate court will routinely allow the will and appoint the executor.

(d) Inventory

An inventory for the donor's estate must be filed by the executor shortly after the donor's death; the time period varies from state to state. The inventory shows all of the donor's personal property and real estate held at the time of death and their total financial value. An individual's estate includes, among other things, cash, stocks, bonds, notes, partnership interests, tangible personal property, and any life insurance and pension plans payable to the estate. Jointly owned property, real estate located outside of the donor's state of domicile, life insurance not payable to the estate, and trust assets should not be included. Probate accountings (see below) are based on the inventory. A sample inventory appears in Appendix, CD-ROM Documentation, Exhibits.

Planned giving officers should review the inventory for assets that may cause complications when being transferred or sold, such as closely held stock, foreign securities, limited partnerships, and real estate. They should call the executor and ask how these assets will be handled. Eventually they should try to match all inventory items with items listed on the estate's tax return if the lawyer will share the return; the executor is not required to send it to the charity, and it is not filed in the probate court. If some personal items from the donor's estate do not appear on the estate tax return, the planned giving officer should ask the executor about the location of those items because their loss could decrease the estate's value and result in a smaller gift to the charity.

(e) Creditors' Claims

Creditors have a specified amount of time from the date of the donor's death, often nine months or one year, to file claims against the estate. To ensure that the estate has enough money to satisfy all claims, the executor usually will wait as long as possible before making any distributions from the estate. At the least, the executor will wait until all federal and state estate taxes have been paid, the timing of which varies from state to state.

Creditors' claims against an estate may take many forms. A typical example is one made by a caretaker for the deceased; the claim is that the caretaker is owed payment for care or services rendered to the decedent before death. The executor, or a lawyer hired by the executor for the estate, will want to determine the relationship of the claimant to the deceased, whether payment for services was understood and paid in the past, and the fair market value of the services. Most likely the deceased's representative and the claimant will attempt to reach a compromise. Another common creditors' claim is that the deceased owed money to a store owner for goods that were not paid for but perhaps placed on a store credit card, before the donor's death. The charity will need to wait for this holdup in the estate settlement process until it is resolved; if the charity is the sole beneficiary of the donor's estate, most likely it will be asked to okay any resolution that is offered to a claimant.

The planned giving officer should review all claims against the estate and when possible work with the executor to pay claims that are reasonable and appropriate.

(f) Charitable Bequests

As soon as the creditors' claims statute has run, the executor will want to pay any charitable bequests to avoid paying interest on the bequest to the charity. Interest on certain types of bequests begins, in some states, to accrue one year from the donor's date of death for bequests under a will and in some cases earlier if the bequest is from a trust. Other states do not select a time frame but instead require interest after a reasonable amount of time has elapsed.

(g) Probate Accountings

Probate accountings show all receipts by the estate and expenditures made from the estate by the executor. When a final accounting is made, the balance in the estate will be zero. The idea behind a probate accounting is to provide all interested parties, such as heirs, legatees, and creditors, with information to determine whether the executor's actions have been proper. A sample probate accounting appears in Exhibit 45.1.

Once the executor receives notice from the federal and state authorities that no tax liability remains, the executor will distribute any assets that had been held in reserve in the event that additional taxes were assessed against the estate. When the estate is entirely distributed, the executor will file a final accounting of the assets collected and distributed. The filing of an accounting is required for each year that the estate exists, and a final accounting must be allowed before the executor is absolved of responsibilities. The charity, as well as any other beneficiaries of the estate, may have to sign a release indicating that they agree to the accounting. The planned giving officer must be sure to review all detailed accountings to confirm whether all payments to the clients have been made, and that expenses charged were appropriate and reasonable.

(h) Receipt and Release

After all the distributions from the will or trust are made to the charity, the executor or trustee will ask the charity to sign a receipt and release form, acknowledging satisfaction of the gift and releasing the estate from any further responsibilities to the charity, preventing the charity from making any further claims against the estate. The charity may be willing to sign a release and receipt for a large partial distribution from the estate with the understanding that the small remaining balance to the charity will come shortly. A sample receipt and release form appears in Appendix, CD-ROM Documentation, Exhibits.

45.3 THE PLANNED GIVING OFFICE AND BEQUEST ADMINISTRATION

The process of receiving a distribution from a bequest may be straightforward or complex. Often a charity receives the gift due from an estate and can distribute it to the internal individual recipient or fund within the charity with very few problems. The charity needs to have a process in place to deal with bequest administration to more easily overcome problems that arise. This section deals with external and internal administrative considerations to make the process run more smoothly.

45.3 THE PLANNED GIVING OFFICE AND BEQUEST ADMINISTRATION

(a) External Considerations

(i) Notification to the Charity. A department or individual at the charity will receive notice from a family member, executor, or probate court that the charity is the beneficiary of a charitable bequest. Someone in the charity's treasurer's or general counsel's, accounting, or development office may learn first about the bequest. An individual who works at the charity, such as a dean, physician, or administrator whose department or program is the beneficiary of the gift, may receive the notice. Notice can come in many different forms: through a telephone call from the executor or a family member, or by formal notice, known as a citation, from the probate court or executor notifying the charity that it has been named as a beneficiary. A sample citation notice appears in Appendix, CD-ROM Documentation, Administrative Documents.

(ii) First Contact with Executor/Personal Representative. When notice is received by mail, telephone the executor immediately to begin a dialogue. Ask for a copy of the will or trust instrument that describes the gift to the charity, as well as copies of the inventory once it is completed and an accounting once it is filed. The will and inventory can be obtained from the probate court. Try to receive a commitment from the executor during the first conversation about when the bequest will be paid or the first distribution will arrive at the charity. If the gift due to the charity is significant, encourage a partial distribution, which would put some of the gift in the charity's hands with less delay. The executor is unlikely to make a distribution of any amount until he feels comfortable with the financial status of the estate, such as when the creditor's claims period has run, claims have been paid, and the estate's taxes are filed and accepted. If the charity does receive a partial distribution before the expiration of the creditor's claim period, it will most likely be asked to sign an agreement that says the charity will return any monies necessary to pay final expenses of the estate. This is considered an acceptable practice. The actual form of the agreement is likely to vary.

Exhibit 45.1 Sample Probate Accounting

[STATE]

[COUNTY] ss.   PROBATE COURT

To [NAME OF EXECUTOR/TRIX]
of [CITY] [COUNTY] [STATE]
Executor (trix)

You are directed to appraise, under the penalties of perjury, the estate and effects of [DECEDENT] Late of [CITY] in the County of[COUNTY] which may be in said [STATE]; and return to the Probate Court for said County of [COUNTY].

_____[SIGNATURE]_____ Register of Probate Court Pursuant to the foregoing   order to _____ said estate is appraised as follows:
Amount of Personal Estate, as per schedule exhibited, . $_____
Amount of Real Estate, as per schedule, exhibited, ... $_____

[COUNTY], SS. [DATE]
I, _____ the executor (trix) of the estate of said deceased, certify under the penalties of perjury that the foregoing is a true and perfect inventory of all the estate of the within named that has come my possession or knowledge, and sets forth the actual market values of the various items thereof ascertained by me to the best of my knowledge, information and belief.

[Signature of executor/trix]
Executor/trix

Exhibit 45.1 *(Continued)*

SCHEDULE K-1 (Form 1041)	Beneficiary's Share of Income, Deductions, Credits, etc.		OMB No. 1545-0092
Department of the Treasury Internal Revenue Service	for the calendar year 2002, or fiscal year beginning .... , 2002, ending .... , 20 .... ▶ Complete a separate Schedule K-1 for each beneficiary.		**2002**

Name of trust or decedent's estate ☐ Amended K-1 ☐ Final K-1

Beneficiary's identifying number ▶	Estate's or trust's EIN ▶
Beneficiary's name, address, and ZIP code	Fiduciary's name, address, and ZIP code

(a) Allocable share item		(b) Amount	(c) Calendar year 2002 Form 1040 filers enter the amounts in column (b) on:
1	Interest.	1	Schedule B, Part I, line 1
2	Ordinary dividends	2	Schedule B, Part II, line 5
3	Net short-term capital gain	3	Schedule D, line 5
4	Net long-term capital gain: **a** Total for year	4a	Schedule D, line 12, column (f)
b	28% rate gain	4b	Schedule D, line 12, column (g)
c	Qualified 5-year gain	4c	Line 5 of the worksheet for Schedule D, line 29
d	Unrecaptured section 1250 gain	4d	Line 11 of the worksheet for Schedule D, line 19
5a	Annuities, royalties, and other nonpassive income before directly apportioned deductions	5a	Schedule E, Part III, column (f)
b	Depreciation	5b	Include on the applicable line of the appropriate tax form
c	Depletion	5c	
d	Amortization	5d	
6a	Trade or business, rental real estate, and other rental income before directly apportioned deductions (see instructions)	6a	Schedule E, Part III
b	Depreciation	6b	Include on the applicable line of the appropriate tax form
c	Depletion	6c	
d	Amortization	6d	
7	Income for minimum tax purposes	7	
8	Income for regular tax purposes (add lines 1, 2, 3, 4a, 5a, and 6a)	8	
9	Adjustment for minimum tax purposes (subtract line 8 from line 7)	9	Form 6251, line 14
10	Estate tax deduction (including certain generation-skipping transfer taxes)	10	Schedule A, line 27
11	Foreign taxes.	11	Form 1040, line 45 or Schedule A, line 8
12	Adjustments and tax preference items (itemize):		
a	Accelerated depreciation	12a	Include on the applicable line of Form 6251
b	Depletion	12b	
c	Amortization	12c	
d	Exclusion items	12d	2003 Form 8801
13	Deductions in the final year of trust or decedent's estate:		
a	Excess deductions on termination (see instructions)	13a	Schedule A, line 22
b	Short-term capital loss carryover	13b ( )	Schedule D, line 5
c	Long-term capital loss carryover	13c ( )	Schedule D, line 12, columns (f) and (g)
d	Net operating loss (NOL) carryover for regular tax purposes	13d ( )	Form 1040, line 21
e	NOL carryover for minimum tax purposes	13e	See the instructions for Form 6251, line 27
f	....	13f	Include on the applicable line
g	....	13g	of the appropriate tax form
14	Other (itemize):		
a	Payments of estimated taxes credited to you	14a	Form 1040, line 63
b	Tax-exempt interest	14b	Form 1040, line 8b
c	....	14c	
d	....	14d	
e	....	14e	Include on the applicable line of the appropriate tax form
f	....	14f	
g	....	14g	
h		14h	

For Paperwork Reduction Act Notice, see the Instructions for Form 1041.   Cat. No. 11380D   **Schedule K-1 (Form 1041) 2002**

45.3 THE PLANNED GIVING OFFICE AND BEQUEST ADMINISTRATION

The planned giving officer will want to ask the executor about the donor's estate in order to learn about the size and timing of the distribution due to the charity. Some questions to consider include:

- What is an estimate of the overall size of the donor's estate?

- How are most of the assets held?

- Are they easily liquidated?

- Is there real estate that needs to be sold?

- Are there any claims by creditors against the estate?

Answers to these questions will help determine how soon the charity will receive its distribution. It is very important to let the executor know at this early stage that the charity is interested and involved in the settlement of the estate. It reminds the executor that the charity is waiting to receive the distribution that it is due and that it has its nonprofit mission to continue, with the help of this financial distribution. A good, solid dialogue with the executor may help dissuade an executor from thinking that the charity is "fortunate" to receive this gift and that it should simply take the distribution when it is given. It reminds the executor of the planned giving officer's obligation to pursue this gift for the charity and of the donor's wish to benefit the charity. The planned giving officer should not hesitate to speak up and ask appropriate questions. A sample follow-up letter to the executor appears in Appendix, CD-ROM Documentation, Correspondence.

(iii) The Nonlawyer Executor. Sometimes an experienced attorney is the executor for a donor's estate. Attorneys are likely to be well versed in estate settlement issues and receive support from other attorneys and legal assistants who help move the estate settlement process along more quickly. The executor may, however, not be an attorney but rather a family member or trusted friend, someone who has never settled an estate. When dealing with a nonattorney executor, the charity needs to be especially persistent in facilitating the estate settlement process. Tasks that can be done quickly by an experienced trust and estate lawyer can move very slowly for a layperson who, never having settled an estate, may feel overwhelmed.

The nonattorney executor may decide to hire an attorney to help in settling the estate, causing the planned giving officer to work with both the executor and an attorney for the estate. Remember that the attorney hired by the executor represents the estate, not the charity; the planned giving officer may find himself relying on advice from the estate's lawyer because the executor does not know answers to certain questions, but the lawyer for the estate is not working for the charity. An attorney hired to help settle the estate will cost the estate additional fees, but the settlement will likely be smoother and quicker and information can be received more easily and accurately.

(iv) Determine Form of the Bequest. The donor's bequest may take several different forms but is likely to be one of four types:

1. *Specific.* A specific bequest will be paid with cash, securities, or tangible personal property. For example, "$5,000 worth of DuPont stock to the University of Minnesota," or "My Picasso print to the Metropolitan Museum of Art in New York."

2. *Percentage.* The designated charity will receive a percentage of the donor's estate, for example, "10 percent of my gross estate to Northwestern University." If the gift is a percentage of the donor's estate, the will generally specifies whether the gift is based on the gross or the net estate. The planned giving officer should ask what the amount of the gift will be based on and for an estimate of the size of the estate. Most likely the executor can esti-

mate the amount of the bequest to the charity and disclose it. If the will is unclear, the charity should ask whether the percentage is based on the gross or net assets of the estate; the charity hopes that the percentage will be applied to gross assets of the estate, resulting in a larger gift.

3. *Rest, residue, and remainder.* The charity is the beneficiary of the entire rest, residue, and remainder of the donor's estate, all that is not given to specific, named beneficiaries (e.g., "Reed College to receive the rest, residue, and remainder of my estate"). Frequently the gift is a fraction or percentage of the residue. Learn the names of the other individuals or charities who share a gift from the residue of the donor's estate by asking the executor or looking at the will itself. Knowing the names of other charities may be helpful in future dealings. If there is a question about fees or receiving estate distributions, pressure from a group of beneficiaries may be more effective than one beneficiary handling things alone.

4. *Ongoing trust payment.* The gift is a payment from a trust that will continue once a remaining beneficiary dies. The planned giving officer should ask what specific amount the charity will receive. The planned giving officer should inquire about the tax status of the trust and whether it has or should be determined tax exempt. Knowing this information can help the charity determine a timetable for distribution from the trust and to anticipate a certain amount of income coming from the trust each year. The recipients within the charity can then make plans for using the distribution.

(v) Charity Needs an Attorney. The charity may need to hire outside counsel to assist during the probate process or turn to its general counsel for assistance. Most charities hire outside legal counsel to represent them in court. An attorney may be needed when a formal petition must be filed with the probate court; when there is a court proceeding and the charity needs to have legal representation; when a legal opinion is needed; and when ancillary administration is required. For ancillary administration, the attorney is likely to be located in the state where the donor held property outside his domicile. See Chapter 38 for more information on ancillary administration.

When working with outside attorneys who will bill the charity for their work, obtain detailed statements of the attorney's time and record in the file all discussions with the attorney. Legal fees paid to an attorney reduce distributions from the estate, so monitor billing carefully. Investing early in competent legal advice can save the charity a considerable amount of money and time.

As the planned giving officer builds professional relationships with a group of outside attorneys, contacts should be maintained after the estate is settled. If the number of bequests to the charity is large, consider honoring attorneys who handle bequests at a special event and include their names on the planned giving office's mailing list to build relationships for future potential gifts. Remember to thank the executor and attorney for the estate for their help in settling the estate.

(vi) Request for Special Notice. For large bequests, the planned giving officer should file a request for special notice with the probate court, which will inform the charity of all actions taken by the executor and all documents that the probate court will ultimately review. The charity can withdraw the request for special notice once it receives its bequest.

(b) Internal Considerations

(i) Designated Bequest Administration Department. One office at the nonprofit should be chosen to administer the bequest monies. Within the nonprofit sector, charities have not found a consistent department for bequest administration. While advice often is needed from the development, treasurer's, and legal offices, the development office is likely to have the greatest impetus to receive and handle the gift and should be responsible for its administration. Because the development office is charged with raising money, it is likely to care the most both about the timing of the

distribution and ensuring that the charity receives the appropriate total amount it is due. The planned giving officer is also the individual most eager to establish contacts with the executor handling the gift because these strong relationships may be helpful in future fund-raising efforts. Selecting one department within the charity and letting individuals know which is the designated area will reduce the confusion both internally and externally in knowing where to send bequest documents when they arrive at the charity.

(ii) Research.   Once the planned giving officer learns of the donor's bequest, work must begin internally. Check development office files to determine whether the charity was aware of the bequest and to learn about the donor's relationship with the charity.

Ask the executor for the names of family members who should be contacted to thank for the donor's bequest and extend sympathies on behalf of the charity. Maintaining or establishing contact with family members can help the planned giving officer learn more about the donor's connection to the charity and possibly produce future gifts from other family members. It is important for the charity to maintain cordial relations with the donor's family members; it can help family members who did not support, know of, or understand the relationship between the donor and the charity.

It is likely that the donor's family would appreciate receiving a letter of sympathy from a trustee, administrator, physician, or other individual who knew the donor and was originally involved with securing the bequest. The planned giving officer also should thank any other internal person who helped secure the donor's gift and encourage him to write a note to the family.

(iii) Internal Tracking System.   The planned giving officer who manages the bequest and trust distributions must be organized and know the status of every bequest gift known to the charity. A tickler system should be established to determine where each future distribution stands. A typical system, whether on paper or by computer, should include a timetable illustrating various dates and stages of the process:

- Date notice received

- Conversations with executor

- Documents requested, either from executor or probate court

- Letters of sympathy and thanks

- Distributions to be received

- Follow-up conversations and correspondence with executor

- Potential litigation that may arise

The charity also will want to try to determine the amount that it will receive from bequests in a given year, to anticipate distributions that, once they arrive, can be added to development gift totals. When estimating future distributions, always underestimate. Unforeseen delays in the estate settlement process will occur, and the charity should never rely on future bequests that may not be received in time to meet development goals. A sample internal tracking system for bequests appears in Appendix, CD-ROM Documentation, Administrative Documents.

(iv) Computer Program to Manage Bequest Administration.   The planned giving officer may find it helpful to produce a computer program to help manage the internal tracking of bequest and trust distributions and to create a timetable for future distributions. As the charity begins to receive additional bequests, and bequests begin to make up a significant share of the charity's overall development efforts, a good computer program allows the planned giving officer to record information about the estate, such as:

- Donor's name

- Donor's date of birth

- Donor's relationship with nonprofit

- Family members involved with the charity

- Estimated distribution

- Timing of distributions

- Type of bequest, such as specific, percentage, gift from residue, ongoing trust payment

- Name of individual, department, or program that benefits from the gift

- Restrictions on the gift

- Names of internal individuals who helped with the gift or knew the donor

- Outreach list

A good computer program also can produce management reports that help categorize the type of bequest the charity most often receives and that assist with the planned giving office's marketing efforts. These reports can track and monitor the status of the nonprofit's distributions. Such reports include:

- Next step reports, indicating action to be taken on specific estates. This is especially valuable to the planned giving officer in tracking the progress of each estate, determining whether the executor completed each step of the probate process. If a step has not been completed, the planned giving officer may need to move the process forward.

- New bequests received, sorted by month or year.

- Estates that hold noncash assets waiting to be sold.

- Estates in litigation.

- Expected distributions for the charity by month and year.

- Status of estate tax filing and audits.

The number of professional software programs available for the administration of bequests is currently somewhat limited. To acquire a program specifically for the administration of trusts and estates, the charity can turn to its outside development office software provider to ask whether it is possible to create a new program for this specific purpose, or the charity can contact companies that currently provide software solutions. Programs can be expensive but can be tailored specifically to the charity's needs. Planned giving officers may also consider creating their own spreadsheets to track individual estates and expand functions as the program's needs grow.

(v) Handling the Real Estate Gift.   Sometimes the charity will receive a bequest consisting of real estate. Often the charity will want to sell the property and may need to hire a Realtor to sell it. If so, hire a competent real estate firm and broker, one that preferably comes recommended by someone with firsthand knowledge of the broker's work. Agree on an appropriate fee for the broker and commit to it in writing. Consider carefully the broker's advice when establishing a selling price and revise the price if necessary. A charity does not want to own, indefinitely, a piece of property

that it cannot use. Monitor the broker's activities to ensure that the property is properly marketed for the best possible price.

Establish the appropriate team within the charity to handle the real estate gift. It is likely that there is an office better equipped to handle the sale than is the development office. For example, the charity may have a separate real estate office, or it may be the general counsel's, planning, business, or treasurer's office. Any of these offices may have greater authority within the organization to make long-term decisions about whether the charity wishes to own such a piece of property, its potential long-term use, a fair price, and so forth. The charity will want to be especially careful about potential environmental problems associated with the gifted property.

45.4 TYPICAL PROBLEMS ENCOUNTERED WITH BEQUESTS

Bequests often are very straightforward; the charity is named as a beneficiary in the donor's will or trust, and the charity receives the gift. Sometimes, however, the donor's intention is unclear. The following sample bequest provisions can cause confusion and potentially lost gifts to the charity; these examples are followed by some suggestions for preserving the bequest.

(a) Incorrect Name of Charity

Sometimes the charity is designated as the beneficiary of a gift but there is confusion because the language in the donor's will or trust is inexact or unclear, making it difficult to identify the nonprofit beneficiary. Some examples include:

- "New Hampshire College." Does the donor wish to benefit the University of New Hampshire, the state university located in New Hampshire, or Hampshire College, a small private college located in Massachusetts? Or is there a college with this exact name?

- "University of California." The donor names the California state system without indicating the specific location. Is it the university's school located in Berkeley, California? Los Angeles? Another city?

- "The American Red Cross." Does the donor wish to benefit the national Red Cross located in Washington, DC? Or to benefit a local chapter?

- "The University Hospital in Boston, Massachusetts." This is the former name of a hospital since known as the Boston University Medical Center, which includes a merger with another hospital, Boston City Hospital, whose name has changed once again. Does the donor wish to benefit the hospital formerly known as the University Hospital, eliminating Boston City Hospital? Can this be done legally? Does the donor wish to benefit any future hospitals that come under this network? Could the donor's gift benefit the medical school at Boston University?

To resolve confusion, the planned giving officer may need to convince the executor that the gift was intended to benefit the charity he or she represents. Gather as much proof as possible to demonstrate that the donor had a relationship with the charity and wished to benefit it. Look through files to find records of conversations that the donor had with individuals at the charity and letters sent to the charity from the donor, and include the donor's past giving history. Let the executor know if the donor was a patient, alumnus, or a patron of the charity. Ultimately the gift may go to another charity with a name more similar to the name used by the donor; but the planned giving officer should strive to demonstrate that a relationship existed between the charity and the decedent.

When working with donors who wish to make a bequest, the planned giving officer should provide donors or their lawyers with the correct legal name of the charity and its federal tax-exempt identification number. To help avoid confusion with other charities, the lawyer drafting the donor's will should include the charity's address, including the city and state, when naming the charity as a recipient. The planned giving officer should also encourage donors to provide their attorneys with a contact name and telephone number at the charity.

(b) Provision Subject to Interpretation

Perhaps the named charity is easy to ascertain but the provision in the will that refers to the gifted item is unclear in its wording. The donor intended to make a specific type of gift, but the wording causes confusion for the executor. For example:

- "I give $50,000 to the following three charities." Does this mean that each charity receives $50,000, or is $50,000 to be split among three charities, resulting in a much smaller gift to each charity?

- "I give my entire library to the Groton School." Will Groton receive all of the donor's books, wherever located, or only books and tangible personal property located in the donor's home library? Does this provision give Groton the donor's rare books, manuscripts, and special collections?

- "All of my cash to Stanford University and all of my securities to Johns Hopkins Medical School." Is it possible that the executor will mislist an asset on the inventory, such as money market funds, as securities rather than cash, leaving Stanford University with a smaller gift?

A planned giving officer who is following the estate distribution closely should look for such interpretations that may be construed in different ways. Recalling conversations with the donor or written correspondence can help. Family members who know what the donor intended also can help, as can the attorney who drafted the donor's will. Ultimately the executor must interpret the bequest, and if the executor is uncertain, she can ask the probate court for clarification. If the ultimate decision is unfavorable to the charity, the charity can petition the probate court to contest the executor's decision.

(c) Payment of Debts Is Unclear

The donor probably had debts at the time of death. The planned giving officer will want to avoid having the charity's interest reduced by the debt. Debt that reduces a charitable bequest has an adverse tax impact on the decedent's estate because it reduces the charitable deduction. A dialogue with the executor allows the planned giving officer to suggest to the executor how debts should be paid. For example, if the charity is receiving property subject to debt due to state law and terms of the will, request that the executor pay the debt from other estate assets. The will or trust should provide how debts are repaid; if not, state law will provide some guidance.

(d) Extraordinary Fees Charged to the Estate

Sometimes the settlement of an estate can require payment of extraordinary fees for additional or unusual work done when settling an estate. Fees that are justifiable include those that are paid to the executor, attorney for the estate, or another individual for the sale of real estate or personal property, as at auction; preparing estate, income, or other tax returns; litigation associated with any part of the estate such as payment of taxes or a will contest; and work involved with carrying on the decedent's business. The planned giving officer should look closely at the probate accountings to determine whether extra fees were justified. If there is any question, the planned giving officer should ask the executor whether the fees were reasonable and ask to see a detailed billing of the professional's work. The planned giving officer may suggest that the executor reduce the fees if they are his own, or ask that the other professional who did the work reduce her bill.

(e) Donor's Will Contested

A donor's will is sometimes challenged. The challenge may seek to invalidate the donor's entire will or a portion of the will. See Chapter 38 for more on will contests. The challenge to the will may come from a disgruntled heir—sometimes the donor's son or daughter who feels entitled to receive a gift, or a larger gift, from the donor's estate and is challenging one provision in the will or the entire will. Typical challenges include that the donor was not competent at the time she created her will and therefore the will is invalid, or that a representative from the charity or another interested party coerced the donor into making a charitable gift. A challenge also can be made because of the type of will drafted. For example, if a donor's will is a holographic will, one not written in legal form or properly witnessed, it may be challenged as invalid. State laws vary; some states permit the probate of holographic wills.

When a gift is challenged, the charity may wish to retain outside legal counsel to protect its interest. There may be long delays, and costly litigation, before the suit is resolved. The charity will have to decide how actively it wants to litigate the case and how much money it wants to spend, based on the size of the gift and the likelihood of the charity's prevailing. The charity also should consider whether there will be any unfavorable publicity surrounding the will contest and what effect it could have on its donors and development program.

Through correspondence that shows the donor's intent, such as letters and records of conversations, the planned giving officer should try to demonstrate the charity's relationship with the donor. The burden will be on the party contesting the will. When more than one charity is involved, it may be possible to reduce costs by hiring one attorney to represent all the charities and share legal fees.

(f) Disclaiming the Gift

Sometimes a charity may wish to disclaim a gift it receives under a bequest. Most often a gift is disclaimed because it is of limited use to the charity, such as tangible personal property that is difficult to maintain or sell, or gifts of real estate located out of state that contain environmental hazards. See Chapter 42 for an introduction to disclaiming gifts.

State laws vary with regard to the timing and legal requirements for disclaiming a gift to charity. For federal tax purposes, a gift by will or trust must be disclaimed no later than nine months from the time that the charity is determined to be the beneficiary of the gift. A disclaimer form that states the charity's wish in writing must be filed. It describes the property being disclaimed and is signed by a representative from the charity. The disclaimer is filed with the executor in the court where the executor is required to file accountings. If the property is real estate, the disclaimer probably should be filed in the Registry of Deeds. The disclaimer must be mailed to the individual known to have custody or possess the property. The effect of disclaiming is as if the beneficiary did not exist, and the property will pass to other beneficiaries as if the charity were not named to receive it. Check individual state laws about how to disclaim a gift.

Most charities accept gifts and dispose of them as they wish. The charity that chooses to disclaim should consider whether disclaiming will negatively affect living members of the donor's family who have a relationship with the charity. Family members will want to feel that the donor's wishes have been upheld and that the gift is appreciated.

(g) Charity Asked to Renounce Share

Occasionally a charity is asked to release its interest in a bequest by a family member who needs the money for himself or for a loved one. The family member may ask the charity to renounce its share, but the request ultimately should come formally from a lawyer representing the donor's family.

While the charity may be willing to release its interest in the bequest, the planned giving officer may not be able to make this decision on his own. A request like this may happen so infrequently that there are likely to be no policies or procedures in place that address the situation. The request may need to be presented to the charity's board of trustees for a vote, and the charity should notify the state's attorney general. The charity has an obligation to protect its assets including gifts made to it. If the charity disclaims the will, it may cause the released or disclaimed property to pass to persons other than the needy family member. The charity must consider carefully the consequences of such a release and decide what is best for all parties involved; it should consider potential public relations issues when choosing to reject such a request by a truly needy family member and work with the donor's family to reach a compromise.

(h) Gift from Trust

The gift to the charity may come from a donor's trust at the donor's death rather than through the donor's will. A trustee of a trust is not necessarily supervised by the probate court as an executor is; the trustee's powers may come from the trust document itself and are usually quite broad. If the donor's gift is from a trust that is created by the donor's will—a testamentary trust—the trustee is required to file accountings for the trust just as the executor is. If, however, the trust was not created under the donor's will—a living or inter vivos trust—such a trust is private, and the trustee is not required to file accountings, and more is left to the trustee's discretion. It is hoped that the deceased held the trustee in great regard, and the trustee is highly ethical and will work with the charity. It is possible that the trustee will be the executor, a family member, or an institution such as a bank, trust company, or law firm.

The planned giving officer should request a copy of the trust document from the trustee of the trust, who should, but is not obligated to, comply with this request if the trust is an intervivos trust. If the charity is not satisfied with the trustee's actions, it can suggest changes, such as to the trust's investment strategy. Recognize that challenging a trustee's actions may be difficult.

45.5 DISTRIBUTION WITHIN THE CHARITY

Once the charity receives the actual distribution from the will or trust, it must manage the distribution within the charity. First, the internal recipient at the charity, such as the dean, physician, or administrator who benefits from the gift, should be notified. Depending on the amount of the gift and the donor's relationship with the charity, the president or chief executive officer of the organization should also be notified. Thank-you letters should be sent to family members from all appropriate individuals at the charity. A sample notification memo to an internal charitable beneficiary appears in Appendix, CD-ROM Documentation, Correspondence.

Depending on the type and size of the gift, the organization's chief financial officer (CFO) may wish to be notified. If there is any discretion involved in deciding where the money will go within the organization, the CFO may wish to make that decision; this will vary from organization to organization. For example, if a bequest to a hospital is stated as "to benefit cancer programs," it could be directed to cancer research, patient care, or any other area involved with cancer at the hospital, and the CFO may wish to benefit one area over another.

Often bequests establish endowed funds at the charity, perhaps in the name of the donor or his family. Within the nonprofit, the fund must be created and assigned a fund number. An endowed fund description, which complies with the donor's wishes, should be drafted and confirmed by various individuals and departments. Once the recipient at the charity has use of the funds, the terms of the gift must be adhered to or its use may be subject to challenge by the state's attorney general. At many charities, compliance with the donor's wishes is left to the internal recipient; the development office does not generally become involved in policing the charity's individual endowed funds and how they, or other gifts, are used by the internal recipient. If the charity wishes to use bequest proceeds for something that is close to but not exactly representative of the donor's wishes, the charity may try to work with remaining family members and the executor of the estate to direct the proceeds at the charity. Ultimately, any significant change from the donor's wishes will need to be reviewed and approved by the state's attorney general's office.

45.6   FACILITATING BEQUEST ADMINISTRATION: WORKING WITH DONORS TODAY

Working with donors today who wish to make a gift through their estates can help the bequest process run more smoothly once the donors die. Explaining the process that will take place and the advantages and disadvantages of making a gift in a certain way will help donors understand the importance of various decisions. Listed below are seven ways to work with donors today to help alleviate problems tomorrow.

1. Encourage donors to provide the development office with copies of their wills and trusts and the names of executors and attorneys. This saves time in locating copies of documents and helps the charity prove a donor's intent if necessary. If the donor is willing, have him sign the charity's standard bequest form indicating the amount of the gift and its designation. A sample standard bequest form is included in Appendix, CD-ROM Documentation, Administrative Documents.

2. When possible, and with the donor's permission, speak directly with the donor's attorney to make sure that the attorney has a contact at the charity, that the correct name of the charity is named in the will, and that the gift is directed to the intended program or area of work the donor wishes to benefit.

3. Suggest that the donor consider an alternative use for the bequest. If the program or physician does not exist at the donor's death, the charity will still know exactly how to distribute the gift.

4. Encourage gifts of unrestricted moneys. Charities always have needs, and an unrestricted gift is most welcome because it allows the charity to use the gift wherever the need is greatest. Most charities have a large fund for unrestricted gifts, like an annual fund, and there will be no question where the monies will go.

5. When working with a donor who wishes to make a bequest to fund a specific named program or project, remind the donor that the price of funding the item, project, or program is likely to cost more at the time of the donor's death. A naming opportunity such as a chair or professorship will cost more in the future than it does today. The donor may want to consider increasing her gift to make it equally valuable at her death as it is in current dollars.

6. Make a point of meeting with donors' trust officers and attorneys both locally and when traveling on business. If one of these individuals is involved with settling a donor's estate and the charity is a beneficiary, the relationship with the charity is already established and the distribution process may run more smoothly when the donor dies.

7. Have a list of attorneys, financial institutions, and other financial advisors available for donors who ask for recommendations. Provide them with several names so that they can make their own choices and the charity does not appear to be directing donors toward one professional or firm. Referrals can be a real service to many donors who do not know where to turn for advice.

## CHAPTER FORTY-SIX

Financial Accounting Standards Board Rules Nos. 116 and 117: Application to Development Programs[1]

46.1 INTRODUCTION

In 1993 the Financial Accounting Standards Board (FASB) issued new Statements of Financial Accounting Standards (SFAS) to standardize reporting among charitable organizations. SFAS Nos. 116 and 117 mandated significant changes in the way nonprofits report charitable contributions on their balance sheets. SFAS No. 116, "Accounting for Contributions Received and Contributions Made," requires that nonprofits recognize contributions received as revenue in the period received, at fair market value. This includes unconditional promises or pledges. Organizations must now report as revenue pledges that may not be paid for a number of years, even if they are not legally binding pledges.

More important to development offices is SFAS No. 117, "Financial Statements of Not-for-Profit Organizations." This treats capital gains and losses on all investment assets as *unrestricted*

---

[1] Portions of this chapter were adapted from *Financial Reporting and Contributions: Guidance for Implementation of FASB Nos. 116 and 117* by Coopers & Lybrand L.L.P., April 1995.

net assets, unless their use is temporarily or permanently restricted by explicit donor restrictions or by law.

SFAS No. 136 amends SFAS Nos. 116 and 117 effective for financial statements issued for fiscal periods beginning after December 15, 1999. SFAS No. 136 does not directly affect the work of planned giving officers, but requires that a recipient organization that accepts cash or other financial assets from a donor and agrees to use those assets on behalf of, or transfer those assets, or both, to a specified unaffiliated beneficiary recognize the fair value of those assets as a liability to the specified beneficiary concurrent with recognition of the assets received from the donor. Additionally, the statement establishes standards requiring institutional beneficiaries to report their rights to assets held in charitable trusts.

Development officers should become familiar with these reporting standards so that communications with potential and existing donors can be structured to achieve the charity's operational and financial reporting objectives. A good dialogue needs to take place with the organization's finance office. This chapter outlines the changes in the reporting rules that most affect planned giving programs and development offices.

46.2 CONDITIONAL VERSUS UNCONDITIONAL PROMISES TO GIVE

How to record a gift depends on whether the gift is given with an attached condition, is an unconditional promise to make a gift, or comes with a restriction. The key is understanding the type of limitation placed on the gift. The differences are explored in the rest of this section.

(a) Conditional

A donor may impose a condition on the gift; the gift depends on a future, uncertain event before it becomes binding on the donor. The condition must be met before a promised gift is recognized as a contribution. A *conditional gift* means that the charity must do something before the gift is completed. For example, the donor pledges $50,000 to a special program if the charity will match the gift by raising another $50,000 from other donors. The condition is met when the organization raises the other $50,000.

A transfer of assets, such as a loan, with a conditional promise to contribute them at a later date must be accounted for as a refundable advance until the conditions have been substantially met.

(b) Restricted

A conditional gift differs from a restricted gift in that the condition affects the timing of recognition, not necessarily the purpose for which the contribution may be used. The conditional nature of the gift determines the timing of the recognition, whereas the restrictive nature of the gift determines the period or type of use (e.g., explicit instructions from the donor for use of the gift, which must be followed).

Restrictions may be permanent or temporary. A *permanent restriction* attaches to any gift where the corpus of the gift cannot be invaded, such as with an individual named endowed fund. A *temporary restriction* limits use of donated money to a particular program or use by a special individual. For example, "This gift is given for classical studies" or "This gift shall be used by the Department of Infectious Diseases." Gifts should not be made for the use of a particular named researcher or other individual, because questions arise when that individual leaves the donee institution. If possible, the donor should be encouraged to give to a department or particular area of interest rather than for the particular researcher's use.

A temporary restriction also may reference a stipulated time that must elapse before the gift can be spent. Unrestricted gifts can be used at the organization's discretion. A gift given to "Carleton College" is money that can be used in any way by that college.

(c) A Condition Met in Phases

If a gift is given with the condition that the gift will be matched by every dollar that the organization raises, the contribution should be recorded as each dollar is raised. Conditional promises to give should not be recognized until the conditions are substantially met.

46.3 PLEDGES OR ASSETS TO BE RECEIVED IN THE FUTURE

This area is of great importance to development offices. When a charity receives an unconditional promise of a gift to be made more than one year after the financial statement date, it should be measured at the net present value of the expected future cash flows. For example, a promise to give cash with payments due in future periods should be reflected at the net present value. The gift should be treated as unrestricted unless the explicit donor stipulations surrounding the promise make it clear that the donor intended it to be used to support specific activities.

If the contribution is an unconditional promise to give noncash assets more than one year after the financial statement date, the contribution should be recognized at the assets' current fair market value (FMV). Current value is, by definition, the present value of expected future value. The fact that the institution must discount such a gift for financial statement purposes does not mean that, for purposes of crediting inside the donee institution, the gift also must be discounted. Internal credit policies need not coincide with financial statement reporting.

46.4 FUNDS HELD IN TRUST BY ANOTHER INSTITUTION

When a donor establishes an irrevocable trust, such as a charitable lead trust, from which the charitable organization is to receive the income for a period of years (or sometimes in perpetuity), but the principal is held in trust by another entity, such as a bank, the principal will never be available to the charity. The perpetual stream of income should be viewed by the organization as a promise to give by the donor and should be recorded at FMV, like any other promise to give. The net present value of the income stream should be recorded as a contribution. Given the nature of the promise, it is acceptable to reflect the contribution as restricted and adjust its value annually using the same method used to initially record the promise. The income should be recorded based on the donor's stipulations.

46.5 RECORDING GIFTS-IN-KIND

Gifts-in-kind should be measured at FMV on the date of receipt. The same concepts used to determine if a promise to give cash is an unconditional contribution should be used to determine when, and if, gifts-in-kind should be recorded. Unconditional gifts in kind may be capitalized under most circumstances.

When the assets are later sold, any gain or loss should be reflected within the appropriate funds of the organization. For example, gifts used for auctions or other fundraising activities should result in the recognition of an additional contribution or a contribution adjustment within fundraising funds.

(a) Collections

For collections (defined later), capitalization will depend on the organization's policy of recognizing collections as assets. When organizations initially adopt SFAS No. 116, they may choose to capitalize their collections, capitalize only items acquired after initial adoption, or capitalize none of their collections. Capitalization of only part of an existing collection is prohibited. Contributions to the collections of organizations that capitalize their collections should be recognized as revenues or gains.

Collections are defined as works of art, historical treasures, or similar assets that are:

- Held for public exhibition, education, or research in furtherance of public service rather than financial gain

- Protected, kept unencumbered, cared for, and preserved

- Subject to an organization policy that requires the proceeds of items sold to be used to acquire other items for collections

(b) Accounting for Noncollection Assets

Many charities are recipients of works of art and collections. If the contributed collections received by the organization meet the definition of *collection,* the options available to account for collections may be used. Otherwise these works of art and similar items should be capitalized.

When the charity receives a valuable painting, a coin collection, a statue, or other works of art or collections, and capitalization is required, the items should be recognized as assets and contributions at FMV.

46.6 LIFE INCOME FUNDS

Suppose that a donor makes a gift to a charitable remainder trust requiring that, during his lifetime, all income or another fixed payment generated by the trust assets must be paid to him and that upon his death the principal of the trust investment must be paid to the charity and held as an endowment. Such a contribution should be recorded in the permanently restricted (defined later) net asset category at the net present value of the amount expected to be received upon the donor's death. The difference between the FMV of the investment at the date of the gift and the net present value of the amount expected to be received is reflected as a discount.

If the donor does not stipulate that the funds must be held as an endowment, the amounts should be classified as temporarily restricted assets at the net present value of the amount expected to be received, because there is an inherent time restriction on the gift. This is likely to represent a change for many planned giving programs that have been booking life income gifts at their full face value.

(a) Interest in a Will

Notification by a donor that the charity is a beneficiary in her will is merely notification of an intention to give; it does not meet the criteria of an unconditional promise to give. In the event of death, the charity would recognize a contribution of its valid interest in the estate when notified by the appropriate representative of the estate.

(b) Gifts of Life Insurance Policies

When an outright present gift is made of a life insurance policy by the donor, relinquishing all incidents of ownership, the donor has in effect given the cash surrender value of the policy. The premiums related to the policy, if paid by the charity, are an expense as incurred.

(c) Contributed Services

Contributed services should be recorded as a contribution only if the services create or enhance a nonmonetary asset or the services typically would have to be purchased by the organization if not provided by contribution, require specialized skills, and are provided by individuals with those skills.

46.7 CAPITAL CAMPAIGN DONATIONS

When a donor makes a promise to give in a capital campaign for a building that is not scheduled for construction until future years, the pledge should be reflected as revenue and a receivable when the promise is made. The contribution should be recorded as temporarily restricted at its net present value, because both its purpose and its time are restricted.

46.8 ENDOWMENTS

To determine whether an endowment gift is restricted or unrestricted, view the gift from the donor's perspective: The test is whether the donor allows the principal of the gift to be invaded. Examine the donor's intent. This is different from a gift given with no restrictions but then restricted by the charity's board of trustees.

To determine the origin of the restriction, a staff member may need to go through and look at the terms of funds that were established years ago, to determine whether the language in a will or trust imposes the restriction. For newly created funds, development officers may want to use a questionnaire that asks about the nature of the endowed fund, such as its specific restrictions and whether the principal can be invaded. The donor should explicitly state the conditions or restrictions on the gift and the income it generates. A sample current-use form appears in Appendix, CD-ROM Documentation, Agreements. Also included are a sample permanently restricted endowed fund description and a sample board-designated endowed fund description.

(a) The Financial Accounting Standards Board and the Uniform Management of Institutional Funds Act

The FASB rules also detail how a nonprofit organization should treat endowments on its financial statements. They take the position that the donor's explicit or implicit intent governs the organization's treatment of a gift as a permanently restricted endowment. No longer will board-created endowments be treated as permanently restricted. The rules do not define an *endowment,* as that is determined by the laws of the state where the nonprofit is organized. At least 40 states have adopted a form of the Uniform Management of Institutional Funds Act (UMIFA), which contains a definition of endowment fund. Other statutory or common law in an individual state may also affect interpretation of endowment funds.

Under UMIFA, an *endowment fund* is an organizational fund not wholly expendable on a current basis under the terms of the donor's gift agreement. An example of an explicitly created endowment is when a donor signs a gift agreement that specifically creates an endowment fund. The FASB requires that the gift be treated as permanently restricted on the financial statement of the organization. If donors respond to a fundraising appeal to create an endowment fund, they have implicitly made permanently restricted gifts, which should be treated as such on the organization's financial statement.

Pursuant to UMIFA, the net appreciation of the endowment may be appropriated "for the uses and purposes for which an endowment fund is established." Net appreciation includes both realized and unrealized gains above the value of the fund when it was created, each addition to the fund, and each accumulation made pursuant to a donor directive at the time it is added to the fund. All net appreciation is available for appropriation by the nonprofit's governing board unless the donor specifies to the contrary. However, in some states, such as Massachusetts, other statutory or common law restricts the governing board's appropriation of net appreciation pursuant to UMIFA. In the absence of governing law other than UMIFA or donor-imposed explicit or implicit restrictions, the FASB rules treat net appreciation as temporarily restricted or unrestricted on the financial statement. This does not mean that the net appreciation can be used for any purpose; it means that it may be used for the purposes of the fund in the period of the financial statement and will not be permanently restricted as is the principal of the fund.

Planned Giving
Programs on Location

Planned Giving in a Small or One-Person Organization

47.1 INTRODUCTION

In a small development office, especially a one-person office, the development director may be the primary fundraiser for the entire organization, meaning that the development director meets with the trustees, runs the annual fund, and writes grant proposals to foundations and corporations. He also crafts the solicitations, organizes the volunteers, makes the personal visits, and manages the staff. The development director may know very little about planned giving and may not have much time to master its complexities—an essential step. Perhaps the nonprofit organization is considering the idea of building a nucleus fund and planning to announce a campaign in a few years.

As a newcomer to planned giving, the development director needs to feel confident that a planned giving program can be managed without his being a financial expert, lawyer, or accountant. There are some highly technical aspects to planned giving, and the development director will learn the specifics as he goes along. A good planned giving program is built on basic development principles, in which the development director is most likely already grounded. A support network must be built so that other professionals can assist the development director as situations and questions arise. If the development director is interested in how other small organizations are marketing bequests, he may want to contact professionals who are working in similar situations to discuss the specifics of their brochures, advertisements, and bequest societies.

The development director should start by setting specific personal and program goals. A timetable and a time frame, such as one year, should be established to accomplish planned giving objectives. He or she should set aside a certain amount of time each week or month to focus solely on planned giving. The development director has to be realistic about what can be accomplished in this time, taking into consideration other work demands. It is important to begin a planned giving program, however small, because its rewards are eminently worth the investment of time and resources. This chapter builds on fundraising principles and ideas presented in other chapters.

47.2 EDUCATION

The first goal for the development director is planned giving education. A course designed as an introduction to planned giving can provide an overall picture of the planned giving basics, including the life income vehicles, marketing, and working with planned giving donors. By attending such a course, the director of development will meet colleagues with similar problems and concerns. Do not be anxious about the unfamiliar legal and financial technicalities. Planned giving can also be learned from books, monthly newsletters, and attending one-day programs and seminars. Day-to-day, hands-on experience will, however, offer the best education.

Join a professional organization that holds monthly or quarterly meetings at which speakers discuss planned giving topics. Every state is part of a district that offers a planned giving council. For example, the Planned Giving Group of New England was established to serve the states of Maine, Vermont, New Hampshire, Massachusetts, Connecticut, and Rhode Island. Some states, such as Rhode Island, offer their own planned giving groups, and others, such as New York and California, have more than one planned giving group located in different parts of the state. Call the National Committee on Planned Giving at (317) 269-6274 to learn the location of a local planned giving council.

Joining a professional planned giving organization is important for at least two reasons:

1. Planned giving requires continued learning because of changes in the tax laws, new estate-planning techniques, and new gift opportunities and ideas.

2. Regular interaction with planned giving colleagues is extremely important because they can provide referrals to lawyers and financial managers, share marketing ideas, and make available preliminary advice before consultation with a lawyer or a financial advisor. Building a network is essential to sharing information.

47.3 SUPPORT NETWORK AND ADMINISTRATION

Next, take a close look at the organization's internal administration. Chances are that there is little room in the budget for additional staff, so it is important to determine who will provide assistance, both inside and outside the organization, in developing a viable planned giving program. First and foremost, the backing of the president and board of trustees is needed to establish a program that works. The president and the board, by their actions and speech, communicate the importance of planned giving, and they support the program financially by allocating the necessary funds. The president and board of trustees also have a great deal of influence on the vice-president for development in making the planned giving program a priority. If the president and board members are not knowledgeable about planned giving, the development director has to educate them about the benefits of a planned giving program. Work with board members individually on specific planned giving assignments, and make an effort either to speak at a board meeting about the importance of planned giving or to bring in an outside speaker to address the subject.

Consider inviting volunteers to help with various components of the program. Do not establish any formal committee until it has been determined exactly what its members should do. Select individuals who are truly interested in planned giving and are committed either to raising money through planned gifts or to donating their professional skills. For example, a trusts and estates attorney might contribute to the program by answering relevant questions as they arise. An individual who wants to help raise money and has made a planned gift to another organization might speak to a group of potential donors about the benefits of planned giving. As the program grows, consider establishing an advisory board.

The internal administration should include an assistant who can learn the basics of planned giving and help with the administration of the program and the potentially voluminous paperwork.

47.4   LEGAL ISSUES

Determine who will answer the program's legal questions. Experienced in-house counsel, if available, is unlikely to have expertise in charitable giving or the time to devote to learning about it. Even a tax lawyer on staff may not be knowledgeable about the legal ramifications of charitable giving. Often questions must be answered quickly, and the development director does not have time to wait for the in-house attorney to research and provide the answer. It is essential to have access to talented legal counsel when various legal issues arise, as they will when the program grows. Negotiate the need and cost of legal counsel with the in-house attorney and, if necessary, the organization's president.

Sometimes in-house attorneys want to participate in the selection of outside counsel. It is also likely that in-house counsel is responsible for legal bills and will want to negotiate fees. If possible, include money for legal fees in the planned giving budget so that outside counsel can be called as necessary, without advance approval from the in-house attorneys.

47.5   USE OF A CONSULTANT

Many organizations require the services of an outside consultant when creating a planned giving program. A consultant can help to focus on the most important areas of the program and educate the development director about planned giving. Planned giving consultants are readily available. Many are employed by large planned giving consulting companies, and others work independently on their own. Ask colleagues to recommend planned giving consultants and interview several before making a selection.

If a consultant is hired, work together to define her role. A consultant's responsibilities may include training board members and staff, helping to identify and solicit donors, marketing the program, helping to select an outside manager for administering life income vehicles for the program, and meeting with individual donors when necessary. As the program progresses, do not rely heavily on the consultant to do the work of the development director, but work with him to learn as much as possible about planned giving. Over time, as the program grows, the consultant's role will decrease.

47.6   MANAGEMENT PLAN

The next step is to develop a management plan for the planned giving program. Determine what should be accomplished in the first 12 to 18 months of the program. For a new program, goals could include increasing the number of planned giving donors; increasing the number of bequest donors; marketing planned gifts; and establishing a particular life income program, such as a charitable gift annuity program or a pooled income fund. As the program is established, build an operational plan. Divide the plan into different areas: establishment of gift vehicles; marketing, including mailings, events, and brochures; identification and solicitation of planned giving prospects; and support areas such as management of gift vehicles, computer software, and gift crediting. To do this well an internal mini-audit may need to be done on the program, asking:

■ How many planned gifts currently exist?

■ What types of gifts currently exist?

■ What is the average gift size?

For the first year in a one-person office, marketing bequests may be sufficient, although the organization may be ready to establish a pooled income fund or to offer charitable gift annuities. In marketing these vehicles, begin by selecting one publication and run an ad or column in each issue. If a development newsletter already is being sent to donors, include marketing materials in it. Target several donors who are good prospects and solicit them for a planned gift. Be realistic about what can be accomplished in the first year in a one-person office. Do not promise more than can be delivered.

47.7 ESTABLISHMENT OF GIFT VEHICLES

Begin the planned giving program simply by learning how to handle the bequests, trusts, securities, and cash that come into the program. It takes very little effort by the organization to accept these types of gifts, and most nonprofits are skilled in dealing with them. With a charitable remainder trust, the nonprofit can accept these gifts without needing to be very involved. The development director should work with the donor or advisor to get a copy of the trust document and to build a relationship with the donor and advisor. As the program matures, consider adding charitable gift annuities and a pooled income fund to the offerings. It is important to determine whether the donor base merits the time and expense of creating a pooled income fund and a gift annuity program, because donors will not make these gifts simply because the organization now offers these vehicles. If a choice must be made between gift annuities and a pooled income fund, start with the gift annuities; they are easier to administer and less expensive to operate. Gift annuities should be promoted if there is an older donor base that may find them attractive and if they can initially be managed in-house at little cost. Consider joining a pooled income fund administered by a community foundation to keep costs down. The nonprofit should also determine whether endowed funds can be created.

47.8 MARKETING

Let donors know that the organization has a planned giving program, even if it is a modest one consisting only of bequests, trusts, and securities gifts. Even without a pooled income fund or charitable gift annuities, promote the planned giving program. Consider the following specific marketing ideas to promote a planned giving program in the first year.

(a) Advertisements

First, determine which gift vehicles to promote; then draft advertisements for those vehicles and place them in select existing publications of the organization, such as an alumni magazine, donor newsletter, or publication for subscribers. Be sure to include a response form for donors to request additional information about including the organization in their wills or to indicate that they have already made a bequest to the organization. Consider including a check-off box that allows donors to ask for more information about creating a charitable remainder trust to benefit the organization.

In response to a donor's asking for more information, create a standard letter that outlines the financial benefits a donor receives by creating a trust or bequest and the areas or programs that a donor can support in making a gift. Even if the organization does not yet have planned giving software, educate the prospect about the basic tax and financial benefits of charitable remainder trusts without discussing specific numbers. If a prospect materializes, ask a colleague or an attorney who specializes in charitable gift planning to produce financial calculations.

(b) Annual Fund Appeal

The organization may already be receiving gifts of securities to the annual fund without actively promoting them. As part of a planned giving effort, include in the annual fund appeal letter a check-off box that urges donors to request information about making a gift of securities. The return letter to a responding donor should discuss the benefits of making a gift of securities, including the charitable income tax deduction and the avoidance of capital gains taxes. Describe in the letter how a stock transfer is made and how easy it is for the donor to make this type of gift. See Chapter 30 for more information on gifts of securities, and see Appendix, CD-ROM Documentation, Marketing, for an overview of planned gift types.

(c) Targeted Mailing

Planned gifts are not well suited for direct mail appeals and are far more complex than an annual fund gift. One-on-one personal contact is the key to successful planned giving solicitations, but direct mail strategies can help to identify prospects. Use targeted mailings for identifying prospects, never for soliciting them. Consider targeting all donors to the annual fund who have made gifts for two to three years and are over a certain age, perhaps 65. Send a personal letter describing what the organization offers in the area of planned giving and include a way for them to request more information. The letter can be signed by the development director or by a trustee, the president, or a volunteer who has made a planned gift. The letter also may be targeted at donors who recently have made stock gifts to the annual fund or, depending on the size of the development program, can be mailed to all donors. Be sure to distribute the letters in a way that allows adequate time for the office to respond appropriately to inquiries. Send letters in batches so that follow-up is done in a timely manner, rather than inundating the office with inquiries.

In addition, a special letter can be mailed to trustees. The aim of this letter is twofold: First, it shows the trustees that a planned giving program is being launched. Second, a planned giving program can be "jump started" with a planned gift from one of the trustees. A lead planned gift from a trustee can be used to encourage other trustees to give, and the donor trustee can be profiled in an upcoming newsletter.

(d) Brochures

Brochures are an important part of the marketing effort. Depending on which gift option is offered, a new brochure, different from any currently in use, may be needed. Prepare one that describes the history and philosophy of the organization and how a donor can make a cash gift, a gift of securities, or a gift through a bequest or a trust. If the organization is offering a pooled income fund and charitable gift annuities, describe them. Outline the benefits to the donor of making each kind of gift, mentioning areas and programs that need private support.

A brochure does not have to be expensive or complicated. To keep expenses down, produce it in-house if possible. If expertise is needed on specific tax or financial advantages of various gifts, ask a planned giving colleague to review the brochure and suggest appropriate changes.

(e) Bequest Language

Standard bequest language should be available to donors who request information about making gifts through their estates. Donors want to learn how a gift is made and to obtain the necessary language for their attorneys. An attorney usually requires the legal name of the nonprofit, proof that the organization is a nonprofit organization, and the name of the program or department the donor wants to support. For a planned giving donors detail spreadsheet, see Appendix, CD-ROM Documentation, Administrative Documents.

(f) Events

In the first 12 to 18 months of a planned giving program, the development director may not want to invest the time necessary to hold an event for planned giving donors or prospects. Instead, consider "piggybacking" with another event the nonprofit is already hosting and invite planned giving donors and prospects. For example, a dinner may be held to honor annual fund donors who give at a certain level, such as $1,000 and up; invite planned giving donors and prospects to attend. The host of the event, a trustee, or the president can welcome these new attendees and talk briefly about the benefits of planned giving and how planned gifts help the organization. Invite planned giving donors to the event through a formal invitation or mailing. As the program matures and the number of planned giving donors increases, consider sponsoring a luncheon program that is geared strictly to planned giving donors and prospects. A planned giving event offers donors the opportunity to be recognized as a group.

47.9 IDENTIFYING AND SOLICITING PLANNED GIVING PROSPECTS

Part of an overall planned giving program includes identifying and soliciting planned giving prospects. Begin the process by sorting through files to rejuvenate relationships with any prospects who have ever requested planned giving information in the past. Discussing the planned giving program at functions and meetings also will help to attract new prospects. Look at those donors who have made regular annual fund contributions over the years, as well as trustees or volunteers who are close to the organization. Also determine how much time can be allocated to personal visits with planned giving prospects; be realistic about the number of people who can be seen, and focus on the best prospects first. Determine what types of materials to take on personal visits, such as brochures, calculations, bequest language, and marketing pieces.

47.10 STEWARDSHIP

Remember the importance of stewardship for all donors and gift types. Bequests are revocable, so relationships need to be maintained over a donor's lifetime. Report regularly to donors about their gifts, and remember to recognize them publicly when appropriate.

47.11 CREATING OR RESTRUCTURING FINANCIAL SUPPORT AREAS

In the first year of a new program, closely examine its current or potential financial support areas. Look at the current financial management of gift vehicles, existence of planned giving computer software, and any gift-crediting policies. Do not accept the status quo, especially if systems are not in place to make the program run smoothly and efficiently.

If the organization decides to establish a pooled income fund and offer gift annuities to prospects, determine who will manage the gifts. Charitable gift annuities can be managed in-house, but if these vehicles are new to the program, the development director must thoroughly educate the treasurer about them. An outside manager, such as a bank or trust company, also can be selected to manage the program and provide planned giving information and advice. If the organization chooses an outside manager, determine what is needed by the planned giving manager and communicate those needs to the individual assigned to the account at the selected outside organization. Be sure that all expectations are clear from the start. A professional planned giving manager also can provide information on real estate, financial, legal, and tax matters. The organization's size and the willingness of its treasurer will help to determine whether it is best to manage the program in-house or outside the organization. If a decision is made to engage an outside manager, help the treasurer to understand why assistance is needed from outside.

47.12   SOFTWARE

A complete planned giving program requires planned giving software. Planned giving software programs are specific to planned giving and are not linked to other development or financial planning software. If the organization offers charitable gift annuities or a pooled income fund, planned giving software can determine the specific financial and tax benefits donors receive by making different types of planned gifts. Select a software program that is easy to use and attend a training program to learn how to use it.

Planned giving software allows a development officer to compare the types of charitable gifts a donor can make and to illustrate the various benefits to the donor. For example, if a donor wants to make a gift through a charitable gift annuity, through planned giving software calculations the development director can learn the donor's rate of return from the gift, amount of annual income, charitable income tax deduction, and amount of ordinary capital gain and tax-free income the donor will receive. There are several planned giving software programs on the market, and the development director should explore all options to determine which package is best for the organization's needs.

47.13   GIFT CREDITING

Determine at the beginning of the program how the organization will credit the various planned gifts. The way gifts are credited internally may be different from the way credit is given to the donor. For example, the nonprofit may credit a donor who made a $25,000 bequest to the organization by thanking the donor for the $25,000 gift through a personal letter. The donor's name may be published in a gift roster listing those donors who have made contributions to the organization through a bequest over the amount of $25,000. The donor receives campaign credit if the organization is currently conducting a campaign. Internally, however, the organization may choose not to credit the gift at all, knowing that a bequest donor can change her mind. Decide how to credit planned gifts, and keep the crediting policy consistent from year to year.

47.14   CONCLUSION

It is difficult for a small development office to establish and administer a planned giving program while being responsible for several different programs. However, it can and should be done. Focus on putting the basics in place and build on this foundation to expand the program as it matures. Eventually staff may be added to assist in the operation of the program.

Appendix 47.1

DEDUCTION CALCULATIONS:
SUMMARY OF BENEFITS*

7.3 Percent Charitable Gift Annuity

ASSUMPTIONS:

Annuitant	75
Principal Donated	$10,000.00
Cost Basis	$3,000.00
Annuity Rate	7.3%
Payment Schedule	quarterly at end

BENEFITS:

Charitable Deduction	$3.914.30
Annuity	$730.00
Tax-free Portion	$147.16
Capital Gain Income	$323.40
Ordinary Income	$239.44

Total reportable capital gain of $4,259.99 must be reported over 12.4 years, the expected lifetime of the donor age 75.

After 12.4 years, the entire annuity becomes ordinary income.

IRS Discount Rate is 4%

*These calculations are estimates of gift benefits; your actual benefits may vary.

## CHAPTER FORTY-EIGHT

Planned Giving at Educational Institutions

48.1 INTRODUCTION

Many planned giving principles and practices were fine-tuned at educational institutions. The components of planned giving—gifts of assets other than cash, life income gifts, gifts through estates, and endowed funds—matched the resources of the donors and the financial needs of the institution.

Educational institutions recognized that planned giving provided a way to link the permanency of the institution with donors who held valuable assets such as real estate and securities. Donors with landholdings made gifts of real estate to provide a site for the educational institution, to expand the campus to offer housing for students or faculty, or for another purpose. These donors provided real estate for trade, exchange, or to be sold, allowing the educational institution to use the proceeds from the sale to support its programs and activities.

Donors with holdings other than cash or real estate made gifts of tangible personal property, stock, and gifts of intangible assets such as patents and oil and gas leases and other nontraditional assets. These gifts could be used outright, converted to cash, or held to produce streams of income that benefited the institution.

Life income gifts enabled donors to receive streams of income and at the same time make significant gifts that ultimately benefit the institution. Colleges and universities exist nearly in perpetuity and have the machinery to handle the administration of planned gifts. Consequently, life income gifts became one of the favored ways for donors to make planned gifts to educational institutions.

For other donors, planned giving offered a way to preserve current assets while making substantial gifts through their estates, by will or trust. Distributions from estates, often expressed as a percentage or fraction, are typically the largest gifts that colleges and universities receive. These gifts provide opportunities for institutions to support or expand existing programs or develop new ones.

In addition, every institution needed an endowment to provide a foundation on which to build and grow. Individual donors' endowed funds provided additional sources of support, and endowed funds provide stability and a financial footing for the institution.

Because educational institutions historically existed in perpetuity and at least over many decades if not centuries, they were able to offer planned gifts, such as life income gifts, that took longer to materialize for the benefit of the institution. Endowed funds and endowments provided financial stability to organizations, enabling them to borrow funds based on the strength of their endowments.

In addition, educational intuitions had, on staff, faculty and other individuals who were knowledgeable with a variety of financial conventions. As they were familiar with the types of assets and the underlying businesses maintained by alumni and friends, these individuals were well equipped to provide service and advice on estate planning and tax planning. The institutions were able to accept almost any gift of property, unlike other nonprofit organizations, whose staff had more limited expertise in multiple areas.

Planned giving provides a way for alumni to make gifts that ensure the viability of the educational institution. Because educational institutions graduate at least one class every year, over time, graduates themselves often become donors. In many cases, second, third, and fourth generations make gifts in support of their alma maters, making the institution more like a part of their family rather than simply a nonprofit organization. Educational institutions become part of the fabric of many families, and permanent bonds develop between the institution and the family. Because of this close connection and tradition, planned giving has become the method of choice for many donors to make gifts and has become a cherished family responsibility.

48.2 TYPES OF EDUCATIONAL INSTITUTIONS

Many types of educational institutions are involved in delivering instruction and education, including these public and private institutions:

- Colleges and universities

- Junior colleges

- Community colleges

- Technical, occupational, or trade-related schools

- Secondary schools

- Elementary schools

- Preparatory schools

- Alternative schools

- Day schools

Many of the earliest institutions were private. Because of this, they relied extensively on gifts from individuals. Public institutions originally were state or government supported and now many have become state assisted or government assisted, meaning that the state or government entity provides only a percentage of the institution's operating budget and expects the institution to charge more in tuition and fees. The state or governmental unit also expects the institution to become actively involved in raising funds to supplement the cost of doing business.

Today a full range of educational institutions rely on private support, particularly through planned gifts, to support the work of the institution. The planned giving program can be established in phases over time, first promoting gifts of securities, real estate, bequests and trusts, and endowed funds, then gradually adding life income gifts to the menu of gift opportunities.

48.3   CENTRALIZED AND DECENTRALIZED PROGRAMS

Educational institutions historically have operated centralized or decentralized development programs, and some offer hybrid programs combining elements of both centralized and decentralized programs. Centralized programs at large universities and colleges hire fundraising staff members to work in a central development office and serve the needs of the colleges, programs, and departments. Staff members report to a vice-president of development or someone holding a similar title.

Decentralized programs place staff on site at the college program or department, and the staff report to a college dean or department head. Regardless of the organizational framework, almost all institutions, except the largest, hire planned giving staff to be shared among the departments, programs, and colleges of the institution. Doing this promotes efficiency and creates opportunities to collaborate and build relationships with department heads, deans, faculty, and other administrative officers.

Hybrid programs often have dual reporting line in which a planned giving officer jointly reports to the central development office and to a dean or other university or college department head. The officer may be based in the central development office or on site in a department.

Colleges and schools with small enrollments share development and planned giving duties. Truly small organizations may operate their entire development programs under the auspices of a single position, such as director of development. Regardless of the size, planned giving can be assimilated into any development program, adding on additional components as the institution and staffing grow in size and complexity.

48.4   ALUMNI: OWNERSHIP ISSUES AT EDUCATIONAL INSTITUTIONS

The institution or the graduate may view the term *alumni* in different ways. Alumni may be viewed as graduates of the institution itself, or they may be viewed as graduates of a specific department or program where they have developed strong alliances personally and professional connections. For example, a history major may have allegiances to the Latin American history faculty, or the history department, or the college where the department is based, or to the institution that granted the degree. It is important to establish a protocol or operating policies and to consider the issue of the ownership of the institution's alumni. This is especially true for planned giving staff who operate across traditional institutional boundaries. Planned giving staff often work for both the institution and its entities: colleges, departments, and programs.

Further, additional ownership issues are likely to emerge among college graduates who may have interests in supporting nonprofit organizations other than the institution that granted their degrees, creating competition for a specific graduate's discretionary income. This can even be true at a single institution for an alumnus who received degrees from two departments.

College graduates are likely to be involved or serve as volunteers in municipal government, community organizations, and other charities. They also may hold dual degrees from one or more institutions, including a degree from a professional school. Their careers in business and the professions have led them to become involved with a variety of organizations.

48.5   THE PLANNED GIVING OFFICER: FUNDRAISER OR CONSULTANT?

At educational institutions, planned giving officers typically operate based on one of two organizational models: They are either fundraisers or consultants. In the fundraising model, planned giving staff are responsible for maintaining a pool of prospects. Their success is based largely on their fundraising capabilities, measured by the number of gifts produced and the dollar value of those gifts.

In some organizations, the planned giving staff serve as consultants or advisors to other development staff, such as the vice-president or major gift officers. In this model, planned giving officers advise fundraisers on the type of planned gift that is most appropriate and prepare financial projections, planned giving calculations, and proposals for use by other staff members. If asked, they may accompany other fundraisers on cultivation visits, and they may participate in the solicitation. In most cases, the consultant model is used at large institutions, where there are many development officers on board, each of whom is likely to be working with a diversified prospect pool representing broad demographics.

There are benefits and detriments to each model for both the fundraiser and the institution. In the fundraiser model, the institution obtains the services of an additional fundraiser who is skilled in planned giving. This may help the bottom line in the short run, while thwarting the growth of the planned giving program in the long run. When hiring, consider the personality and interest of prospective candidates to increase the chances of a successful match.

In the consultant model, many institutions prefer to have a single individual provide expertise in planned gifts while asking development staff to be conversant with general planned giving techniques and strategies. This model has the advantage of ease in administration and organizational efficiency. However, general development staff may be asked to discuss planned gifts with donors and prospects, and some may not be comfortable doing so. The result may be a loss of gift revenue during the time that the planned giving consultant trains development staff in securing planned gifts. Again, when hiring, assess both the candidates' preference for serving as a consultant or fundraiser and consider the strength and comfort level of the development staff in handling planned gifts.

48.6   PREVENTING CONFLICTS: WORKING WITH DEVELOPMENT STAFF

Regardless of the institution's organizational model, to be successful, planned giving staff and other development staff members must work together in the identification, cultivation, and solicitation of prospects and donors. Conflict makes donors and prospects question the institution's organizational skills. Multiple solicitations by two or more of the institution's staff members creates confusion, often resulting in no gift to the institution.

Much of the potential for conflict begins with a breakdown in basic business courtesies and communications. As in the case of any relationship, often the little things become significant problems. Planned giving staff should adhere to these protocols to avoid conflicts:

- Prioritize the relative importance and significance of all potential solicitations. Put simply, which ask produces the greatest impact for the institution?

- Coordinate solicitations. When competing projects are equal, present them as a package and leave the decision about which to fund to the donor or prospect.

- Understand the relationship between the prospect and all fundraisers and departments with whom the prospect is likely to engage. Remember, the best prospects are likely to do business with more than one department or program.

- Competition between fundraisers and planned giving staff members prevents gifts from occurring and hurts the image of the institution.

- To all appropriate staff members, provide courtesy copies or other forms of notation regarding all meetings, visits, telephone calls, or other forms of interaction between staff members and the prospect, and share the information as much as possible.

48.7 DEVELOPING INTERNAL RELATIONSHIPS

Because educational institutions, even smaller ones, are complex, planned giving staff should develop relationships with a variety of internal and external constituents. They should try to develop working relationships with the institution's general counsel, business officer, real estate officer, treasurer, or other officers with different titles but similar functions. Relationships should be developed with all key members of the institution's staff.

(a) Working with the President and Vice-President of Development

At most institutions, the president makes many of the largest solicitations and is likely to be involved in cultivational meetings with key donors and prospects. Because planned giving options often are involved in solicitations at the highest levels, the planned giving officer must establish rapport with the president. The president should be briefed on the basics of planned giving, and the planned giving officer can act as part of the president's team or as a consultant to the president.

(b) Working with Deans, Directors, Department Heads, and Faculty

Often deans, directors, department heads, and faculty know alumni and friends who are involved in work that is similar to the work of the department. These individuals share information and collaborate on a variety of related projects. Often they can identify prospects who might be willing to make a gift in support of the particular program with which they are involved. These individuals, if properly trained, may be instrumental during a cultivational meeting or during the solicitation. Work to build trust and share information on prospects with whom they are involved. Offer to prepare lists of alumni or donors who may have an interest in the work of their department.

Many alumni maintain close relationships with former faculty members. The faculty members served as teachers, mentors, advisors, career counselors, and business and professional advisors, and often played central roles in the business and professional lives of their students. Quite often faculty members know more about their former students' wealth, status, resources, and the propensity to make a financial commitment to the institution than does the development office.

(c) Working with Boards, Volunteers, and Committees

As in the case of most nonprofit organizations, boards, volunteers, and committees at educational institutions play an important part in the leadership of the institution and in the cultivation and solicitation of prospects and donors. At colleges and universities, members of these groups may be planned giving prospects themselves. In addition, by virtue of their positions in business, law, and/or finance, they may be well equipped to host cultivational activities, and they may know professional advisors who represent wealthy clients who may need specialized advice in planned gift techniques. Educational institutions that include professional schools, such as a school of law, may offer expertise to the development office or planned giving officer in tax, estate planning, or trusts.

Planned giving staff members need to be involved with volunteer leadership in at least two ways. Volunteer leadership such as boards of directors or trustees make allocations of resources both in terms of budget allocations and staff resources. It makes good business sense to make sure that those in charge understand the function and benefits of a planned giving office. In addition, boards and volunteers also are likely to be involved in planned giving solicitations of alumni, peers, and reunion class programs.

48.8 CONSTITUENTS

Educational institutions probably have one of the broadest pools of constituents of any type of non-profit organization. These organizations "graduate" many of their prospects and donors when their students become their alumni. The concept, unique to educational institutions, insures that there is a readily available pool of prospects who have the capacity and propensity to make gifts in support of the institution.

Regardless of its size or scope, each institution has a built-in prospect pool in place. These individuals care about the quality of the institution and often are quite motivated to help ensure its quality.

Institutions have many layers of constituents. There are alumni, faculty, staff, parents, friends, corporations, foundations, vendors, and other defined groups. Planned giving staff focus on alumni, faculty, staff, friends, and parents and leave the remaining constituents to their counterparts in the development office.

There are many types of constituents at most institutions, including:

- Alumni

- Friends

- Faculty

- Staff

- Administrators

- Parents

- Corporations

- Foundations

- Vendors

Many institutions have done wonderful jobs promoting development and planned gift opportunities by inviting senior classes and sometimes other classes to provide financial support and planting the seed that philanthropy is a part of the responsibility of graduates. Philanthropy is a mind-set that is carefully included as part of the doctrine of the institution. This is particularly true of small institutions, the Ivy League colleges and universities, but it is also true at many fine single-sex or small private institutions.

When working with students and families consider the following:

- Promote a positive mind-set in the minds of students while they are still students.

- Promote giving programs that enable students to make gifts in support of projects that are important to them.

- Inform students that the majority of scholarships and fellowships come from private support.

- Make sure students understand that the names of individuals associated with buildings, programs, institutes, and centers provided private support.

- Invite parental involvement and support.

48.9 MANAGING CONSTITUENTS

The ability of colleges and universities to segment alumni by age and class year while offering events and programs to involve these constituents, over time, is central to their fundraising success. In addition, educational institutions have the ability to segment based on demographics, including age, gender, class year, regional and geographical considerations, and degree or major. Like other organizations, assumptions can be made about property values and the nature of a prospect's real estate holdings based on zip codes and other geographical criteria.

Planned giving programs should consider the geographical dimensions of the institution. For example, some institutions have alumni in all 50 states and many foreign countries while others are regional or local in nature. Design a program that reflects the demographics of the institution. Identify the locations where concentrations of alumni are located. The demographic considerations can then be cross-referenced against types of planned gift opportunities, such as bequests, life income gifts, gifts of assets other than cash, and endowed funds.

For example, gifts of real estate can be promoted to alumni with landholdings near the campus or to those who are likely to have vacation homes near the ocean or own tracts of land in rural or agricultural areas. Deferred gift annuities can be promoted to alumni who are generally younger or to those who graduated recently. Consider which planned gift options are likely to match the demographics reflecting the makeup of the alumni base. Make assumptions about the assets that alumni are likely to hold and their interests.

48.10 PLANNED GIVING PROGRAM ACTIVITIES

Institutions offer a number of programs as part of their regular activities. Reunion programs, alumni programs, and recognition events all provide opportunities for planned giving staff to become involved. Planned giving staff members can participate in these activities to promote the program's visibility. Often planned giving staff can share administrative responsibilities and expenses with other departments and piggyback to host events and programs.

To attract planned gifts, educational institutions must offer a variety of time-tested and established methods of promoting such gifts. These activities are designed to reach and educate individuals, rather than corporations or foundations. Offering a variety of activities promotes opportunities to reach these constituents. It is not necessary to offer all at once, but rather the planned giving program can be built over time. Each of these activities supports the others and provides a balanced approach to planned giving. These activities include:

- A full range of cultivational events that enable alumni to participate with the institution in meaningful ways. Promote alumni events, regional meetings, workshops, and seminars to develop and sustain traditions among alumni.

- Planned giving workshops and presentations at reunions to returning alumni and guests.

- Planned giving training programs to department heads, staff members, and other key individuals.

- Professional advisory committees that invite alumni to participate as members.

- Planned giving committees that invite alumni to serve.

- Ask the nonprofit marketing department to review the planned giving office's marketing program.

- Cooperative and collaborative relationships with other development staff members including annual giving, alumni programs, and major gift officers.

■ Philanthropy at all levels, from senior class gift programs to reunion class gift programs.

■ Seminars, symposiums, and tax and estate planning workshops for alumni in geographical regions.

■ Breakfasts, luncheons, and dinners for graduates of specific programs, majors, or departments.

■ Recognition societies and gift clubs.

■ Planned giving orientation programs to all constituents.

48.11   GIFT OPPORTUNITIES

To attract gifts at all levels and for all institutional purposes, gift opportunities should be promoted. Because institutions are so broad in scope and purpose, constituents are likely to want to support financially a variety of opportunities. Each institution has unique parts of the campus that are revered by those who came in contact with it. Most campuses are in need of funds to rehabilitate older buildings and construct new ones. Each institution has opportunities for interested individuals to link their names with its departments, programs, centers, institutes, and colleges.

Many campuses have extensive physical plants that have naming opportunities not only for parts of the campus, but also for departments, centers, institutes, programs, colleges, and other units and entities. A list of gift opportunities that educational institutions can promote follows:

Naming Opportunities for Capital Projects

■ Capital projects/facilities

■ New buildings, existing buildings, renovated or remodeled buildings

■ Floors or wings

■ Benches, fountains, walkways, other outdoor structures or areas

Classrooms

■ Science laboratories

■ Electronic classrooms

■ Computer laboratories

■ Conference rooms

Departments, Programs, and Units

■ Colleges

■ Programs

■ Centers

■ Institutes

Opportunities to Support Faculty/Staff

■ Chairs

■ Professorships, visiting professorships

- Faculty development fund
- Young faculty awards
- Faculty release time
- Faculty awards and recognition programs

Campus Public Programs

- Speaker series
- Lecture series
- Distinguished lectureship
- Visiting lecture series

Scholarships and Fellowships

- Postdoctoral fellowships
- Research fellowships
- Full-tuition graduate scholarships
- Scholars in residence
- Full-tuition undergraduate scholarships
- Undergraduate awards
- Endowed scholarships or endowed student awards

Equipment

- Computers
- Technology
- Scientific equipment

Projects

- Displays
- Exhibitions
- Presentations
- Performances
- Restoration

Special Funds

- Innovation funds
- Entrepreneurial funds
- Creativity funds

- Resources

- Research funds

- Books

- Periodicals

- Online publications

48.12 CONCLUSION

Educational institutions are an ideal environment for a planned giving program, which is why over the years these organizations have been involved in promoting planned giving as one of their most common gift options. Educational institutions have the needs, resources, prospect pools, and longevity necessary to make planned giving a natural match for almost any school, college, or university. Few other types of nonprofit organizations have such a built-in prospect pool, professional expertise, the resources to administer and manage such gifts.

CHAPTER FORTY-NINE

Planned Giving in Healthcare Organizations

49.1   INTRODUCTION

The development or planned giving officer who works in a healthcare setting, such as a hospital, hospice, or other medical organization, has fundraising prospects and donors who are or have been sick or are dying. Such donors have special needs. An individual who is grateful to the medical organization because of success from a one-time visit, such as a surgery or consultation, may differ from an individual who has an ongoing relationship with the organization because of continuing medical problems. Long-term care should result in a stronger relationship with the organization and the physician, but also may result in diminished capacity and finances. Healthy individuals whose loved ones were treated at the medical organization are also planned giving prospects, with other special needs. This chapter helps the reader work successfully in a medical environment and produce a gift that is right for both the nonprofit organization and the donor.

49.2   THE UNIQUENESS OF HEALTHCARE FUNDRAISING

The memories of grateful patients who are donors differ from those of individuals who are loyal to their college or university or give to an arts or religious organization. Membership in the class of

1925 is a more positive memory than that of a three-week stay in a hospital. However, life-threatening illnesses can inspire deep feelings of gratitude toward the nonprofit and the work it does to help save lives or improve the quality of life for a donor or a loved one.

Conversations with such donors are unique. Their experiences are extremely personal and, in many cases, have engendered a new perspective on life. Talk is likely to revolve around the donor's illness and the heroic work done by the physician and hospital staff. Grateful patients tend to be very open about their physical conditions, and the planned giving officer must be prepared to learn more than he really needs to know about that condition. For most donors, time spent at a medical organization is truly life altering.

49.3 THE HOSPITAL ENVIRONMENT

(a) In the Patient's Room

There are many advantages to visiting a prospect or donor when she is in the hospital. One advantage is that some aspect of the environment itself is what the patient will be supporting with the gift, and the patient can see firsthand how her money could be used. This is a unique opportunity to make the case for support. The prospect's hospital visit provides the planned giving officer with an opportunity to help the donor by making physician recommendations, offering tips on the best-tasting food to order, and helping the patient take a walk in the hallway. A sick donor who is alone or without family members may be especially eager to talk with the development professional. An opportunity for developing a special relationship exists, and the planned giving officer must remember to keep the relationship friendly yet always professional. When visiting any patient, remember to bring a small gift, such as a plant, flowers, or something from the hospital's gift shop that bears the hospital's name or logo.

Realize that the conversation with a patient may be interrupted by a doctor, nurse, or medical procedure. The patient may feel self-conscious if she is dressed in a hospital gown. Leave before the patient becomes too tired, and understand that the patient may be anxious and uncomfortable. Respect the patient's privacy and call before visiting. Check with the front desk on the floor where the patient is staying to make sure that this is a good time to visit (see Exhibit 49.1).

Exhibit 49.1   Tips for Success: The Hospital Visit

- Use the hospital setting to help make the case for support.
- Offer to help the donor whenever possible.
- Respect the donor as a patient.
- Be flexible; the visit may be interrupted for medical reasons.

(b) Patient Confidentiality

A planned giving officer who works in a hospital or healthcare setting will learn to respect donor confidentiality. Any information learned about the donor's health must be kept strictly confidential. Grateful patients are the lifeblood of most hospital development programs, and the planned giving officer has the responsibility of keeping personal information private.

(i) Access to Medical Information.   In April 2003, legislation known as the Health Insurance Portability and Accountability Act (HIPAA) was enacted that directly affects fundraising in

healthcare settings. How a fundraiser or physician can discuss fundraising with a prospect has been impacted greatly. See Chapter 50 for a detailed look at HIPAA regulations.

(ii) Use of Outside Vendors.   Confidentiality concerns arise when the development staff is required to send lists of patient names to an outside vendor, such as a mailing house that sends mass fund appeals, or to a research company that determines a prospect's financial holdings. Information sent outside the hospital must be thoroughly purged to avoid disclosing information that in the wrong hands could cause irreversible damage to a patient. For example, a list of names being used for an appeal letter going to individuals who are being treated for human immunodeficiency virus (HIV) or acquired immune deficiency syndrome (AIDS) that falls into the hands of an insurance carrier could spell financial, social, and medical ruin for the patient. The development office must be sure to send just individuals' names to outside vendors. Treatment information or name or type of doctor visited is strictly eliminated.

49.4   SOLICITING PATIENTS WHO ARE DONORS

(a) Letters

Letters that ask to meet a prospect for the first time should be direct. When writing to a longtime donor, stress that the organization appreciates the donor's continued support of the hospital's annual fund. For new and existing donors, mention that Dr. X suggested that the donor be contacted. If no doctor is involved in the process, discuss the many new and exciting programs and projects developing at the hospital that can be shared with the prospect. Offer to meet with the donor at his home or following a medical appointment at the hospital. The planned giving officer should discuss whether this is a good time to approach the donor with the patient's physician.

(b) Beginning the Conversation

There is an art to speaking with prospects and donors who are patients or a patient's relative. It begins with the sensitivity that one brings to dealing with someone who is ill or has recently gone through a challenging physical and emotional experience. The planned giving officer should acknowledge the difficulty of the situation at the beginning of the conversation. Express sympathy for the patient's medical condition. Ask how she is feeling and whether she feels that she received good care. Bring the conversation around to the need for the donor's support to continue work like that being done for the patient and to help others. Expand on the patient's positive experiences, and talk about what additional funding could do. Discuss strides made in research, improvements in patient care, and all that is being done to train new physicians. Show the prospect how a gift will make a difference.

(c) The Difficulty of Discussing the Gift

When discussing a gift to a medical organization, the planned giving officer needs to stay focused on the positive aspects of the potential gift rather than on a donor's questionable or poor medical condition. Discuss the good a gift could do, now and in the future. Relay to the donor that the gift will live well into the future, helping others in need. Donors who are near death need to be encouraged to complete their estate planning as soon as possible, and the planned giving officer should have the names of several attorneys to recommend to the donor. The donor may need to be reminded to complete a healthcare proxy. If the donor has a trusted family member or outside professional involved with the potential gift, bring that person into the discussion and, depending on the relationship, use him to help move the process along and discuss the difficult topic of death. The outside professional can help to determine what type of gift is most appropriate for the donor.

Keep copies of all correspondence and closely document conversations about the gift. The healthcare organization never wants to be accused of persuading an individual to make a gift that he or she did not want to make or could not afford to make. The organization also wants to be clear about the donor's intended use for the gift before the donor passes away.

49.5 WORKING WITH THE DONOR'S PHYSICIAN

(a) Bringing the Physician into the Process

There is a greater chance of securing a significant gift if the prospect's physician is involved in the gift solicitation process. Donors feel grateful to the hospital for their care, but are especially indebted to their personal physicians. Building a strong relationship with individual physicians and the general medical staff is very important in winning credibility for a planned giving program and ultimately results in larger gifts for the organization. Informing physicians of development successes when working with one of their patients will help when it comes time to bring the physician into the process.

With a new donor, the gift process can move more quickly if the physician is involved. A letter written by a doctor to the patient, asking that the patient see the planned giving professional, is rarely ignored. The prospect often wants to make the gift in honor of the physician, erecting a plaque in the doctor's name in the hospital or naming a particular project or research fund for the doctor. Donors are particularly honored by touring a doctor's laboratory, having lunch with the physician to discuss her work, and learning about cutting-edge programs.

Success in working with a physician depends on the physician's eagerness to raise money, her faith in the organization's development office, and her comfort level in talking with patients about gift giving. Some doctors are wary of the development process because they feel that asking a patient for money will compromise the doctor-patient relationship. Others believe strongly in a cause and feel that it is appropriate to ask interested patients to help.

(b) The Process

To begin working with physicians, obtain a list of their patients from a central administrative source or from the physicians themselves. Make appointments with the doctors to talk about fundraising for their programs and projects. Determine with the physicians the case for support. Review the list with the physicians and have them identify patients they believe have the potential to make a major or planned gift. Determine each doctor's comfort level in dealing with patients as fundraising prospects. Will the physician allow the planned giving officer to say that the doctor spoke about the patient and hopes that the donor can help? Is the doctor willing to write to the donor, asking her to meet with the planned giving professional? Will the doctor host a luncheon and tour of a research laboratory for a major gift prospect? Most doctors are willing to help to some degree, and the planned giving officer must find out to what extent each doctor wishes to be involved. One role the planned giving officer plays is reassuring the doctor that the planned giving officer will make the solicitation if the physician is uncomfortable doing so personally (see Exhibit 49.2).

The planned giving officer also needs to take the time to educate physicians about planned giving and development concepts. A basic overview of the life income gift options will help physicians understand that there are many ways to make a gift and that different types of assets can be used. Emphasize that a planned gift will help to endow a doctor's work and that planned gifts often result in larger gifts than outright cash donations.

The planned giving officer should write a letter to the prospect, ideally signed by the physician, asking for permission for the planned giving officer to visit the donor. For a prospect with good giving potential, a meeting at the hospital with the physician and the planned giving officer can be a logical next step. In most cases the planned giving officer will ask the prospect for a gift at the meeting or follow up with a solicitation for a specific amount. Remember that the doctor's time is very limited and that fundraising is not her profession. Engage the physician as much as possible, but control the solicitation process so that it can be moved along. Write the draft letters, make follow-up telephone calls, and make the solicitations.

Exhibit 49.2   Tips for Success: Working with a Physician

- Become familiar with HiPAA legislation.
- Make an appointment to see the doctor to talk about fundraising.
- Ask the doctor to identify potential fundraising prospects from the patient list.
- Draft a letter for the doctor to sign. Send it out from the development office.
- Manage the entire solicitation process.
- Ascertain the physician's comfort level in making solicitations. Reassure the doctor that the development officer will make the actual request for support.
- When beginning the relationship with the doctor, let her know that you want to raise money for her special fund or project, not necessarily for the hospital at large.
- Remember that doctors can compete for gifts; be sure to bring all appropriate physicians, caregivers, or administrators into the gift process at the beginning.

49.6   FROM THE DONOR'S PERSPECTIVE

(a) Donor Motivation

Some donors to medical organizations are simply philanthropic and want to further medical research by helping to find a cure for a disease, train physicians, and improve patient care. Many donors are present or former patients who are grateful for the care they received and want to give something back. Others make a gift because they want special care by their physician, either now or in the future, and believe that by making a major gift they will receive special care if they need it. The planned giving officer needs to determine what motivates the prospect to make a gift, because the strategy for approaching various donors may be different. See Chapter 11 for more about the planned giving prospect.

(b) VIP Programs

Healthcare organizations may recognize donors with special VIP programs. These programs provide the patient with certain privileges, such as personal shoppers, special escorts, flowers, and gourmet meals. Many hospitals offer luxurious rooms to patients who are willing to pay a premium for linens, views, and service.

Many donors seem to enjoy this attention and are able to pay for it. From a development perspective, these donors are apt to be good major or planned giving prospects. Find a way to regularly receive a listing of the patients who stay in these special rooms and determine if they are good prospects.

(c) If the Donor Cannot Afford to Make a Gift

On the other side of the financial spectrum, the planned giving officer needs to be especially aware of the patient who cannot afford to make a significant gift but is eager to do so. An older donor who is ill may need the money to pay for a nursing home or other medical care sometime in the future. A younger prospect, one with a severe or terminal illness such as AIDS, may need the money to live on and thus should not make a gift, or should make a smaller gift or a bequest. The planned giving officer must determine the donor's financial situation on a case-by-case basis. When a financial advisor is involved, this is easy to determine; more likely, the planned giving officer will learn of it from conversations with the donor and a visit to the donor's home.

The planned giving officer should refuse an inappropriate gift. The individual may need the gift more than the hospital does. The hospital must avoid being in the position of being asked to return a gift to a donor who needs the money for medical care.

49.7   WORKING WITH A PATIENT'S OUTSIDE ADVISOR TO COMPLETE THE GIFT

(a) Working with an Outside Advisor

The planned giving officer often must work with a donor's lawyer, financial advisor, insurance agent, stockbroker, and trust officer. These outside professionals are not likely to be connected to the healthcare organization in the way the donor is. The advisor knows the details of the donor's financial situation and can ask the donor questions that the planned giving officer may not feel comfortable asking, such as questions relating to the donor's physical condition. Sometimes donors rely so heavily on their advisors that they cannot answer questions without the advisor present (see Exhibit 49.3).

Exhibit 49.3   Tips for Success: Working with Financial Advisors

- Strive to establish a good working relationship.
- Determine and remember your role as the planned giving officer.
- Be flexible in helping to reach the donor's financial goals.
- Politely educate advisors about planned giving; this area is not likely to be their specialty.
- Understand changing Medicaid provisions.
- Always provide excellent service.

When a donor dies, it may be the outside advisor who first notifies the healthcare organization. The advisor may be named executor or co-executor of the donor's estate, and the nonprofit could benefit from a strong continued relationship with the advisor if the advisor has any discretion about making a gift to the charity. This individual is also in an excellent position to help determine what the deceased donor wished to support, if there is any confusion about this after the donor's death.

(b) Losing the Gift Because of an Advisor

The planned giving officer may lose a potential gift because of the financial advisor. Despite years of care given to the individual or a loved one by a physician at the hospital, the financial advisor may convince a donor that a gift can be made in a better way than directly to the hospital. For example, the financial advisor may encourage the donor to make the gift through a private foundation or perpetual trust managed by the advisor. If the donor has medical problems, the advisor may convince the donor that it is better to hold on to the money in case it is needed for healthcare. If this happens, the planned giving officer should continue to work with the donor and advisor so that the charity may receive a future gift from the donor's private foundation. There is nothing to be gained by terminating the relationship with the advisor.

49.8   WORKING WITH A RELATIVE OR GUARDIAN TO MAKE A GIFT

The planned giving officer may need to establish a good working relationship with a family member or guardian who is in charge of, or assisting in, making a donor's gift. The donor may be alive but incapacitated and in need of a trusted family member's advice; or the donor may die before completing the gift, leaving the relative with the power to make the gift. This individual may be a blood relative, such as a sibling or child, or a surviving spouse or paid professional.

If the relative or guardian is unwilling to complete the donor's gift, the planned giving officer needs to remind him that the donor wants or wanted to make the gift. The planned giving officer should share conversations he had with the donor and correspondence discussing the donor's intention to make a gift. If the individual now in control is a relative, he may be grieving over the loss of a loved one and not be thinking completely clearly. Give the situation some time, while staying in touch and emphasizing the donor's intent.

49.9 PATIENTS WITH TERMINAL ILLNESSES, INCLUDING AIDS[1]

Millions of individuals are infected with HIV, the virus that causes AIDS. Millions more are affected by the disease. AIDS-related planned giving prospects fall into several categories, including AIDS patients who are grateful to the organization; parents, family members, and friends of persons with AIDS who want to memorialize a loved one; and individuals who are philanthropic and wish to help find a cure for the disease.

There is still a social stigma attached to the disease and often estrangement from and denial by family members whose loved one has died of AIDS. The catastrophic nature of the disease has had an enormous impact on residuary gifts. A person with AIDS may have depleted his estate to finance healthcare. Many people with AIDS die bankrupt or in poverty. Loved ones may not wish to acknowledge a son or daughter with AIDS and choose not to support the cause. Because of a potential loss of mental capacity, whether from medications or AIDS-related dementia, HIV-positive donors should be encouraged to complete their estate planning as soon as possible.

Exhibit 49.4 and the following sections describe the best planned giving options to pursue when working with a prospect who has a terminal illness such as AIDS.

Exhibit 49.4 Suggested Gift Options for Terminally Ill Patients

- Bequests
- Charitable Remainder Trusts
- Life Insurance
- Life Estates
- Endowed Funds

(a) Bequests

A bequest may be the most appropriate gift option for a terminally ill patient. The donor still has the use of assets that may be needed during life. A bequest to a nonprofit is also easy to include when drafting a new will to address other concerns (i.e., as selecting a guardian for children and naming other beneficiaries).

(b) Charitable Remainder Trusts

Through a charitable remainder trust, a donor has the opportunity to be recognized by the charity, secure a lifetime income for himself or another beneficiary, gain tax benefits, remove assets from the estate, and know that the gift is designated as the donor wishes.

A trust for a term of years is a smart way to make a gift for a donor who has a limited life expectancy. A regular charitable remainder unitrust also may be used, and the terminally ill donor may be able to negotiate a higher rate of return because the trust is likely to run for a shorter amount of time.

[1] Adapted from Katelyn Quynn and John Weis, "Planned Giving in the Age of AIDS," *Planned Giving Today* (March 1995).

(c) Life Insurance

When a donor names a charity as beneficiary of all or part of a life insurance policy, a substantial gift may result. Life insurance also can be used as a method of wealth replacement for assets put into trust. The issue of insurability must be addressed to determine whether the donor is still insured. In 1996, one national insurance company announced a life insurance program for HIV patients who meet specific qualifications for insurability.

(i) Viatical Settlements. Individuals with a terminal illness who have several years to live can "sell" their life insurance policy through a process called *viaticating*. Viatical settlement companies typically pay between 60 and 80 percent of the policy's value. Although this is often a godsend for the sick, viatical payments are subject to federal taxation, may adversely affect entitlements, and void any previously named beneficiaries, including a charity. Gifts that have been made with life insurance and have been viaticated should be examined by the charity to see if a gift still exists.

(d) Life Estates

A life estate allows a person with a terminal illness to remain in her home while living, but determines where the home will go at the donor's death. It may be an especially attractive gift option for a donor who has no heirs and does not know what else to do with the property. Assuming the donor is capable of continuing payments for mortgage, taxes, maintenance, and insurance, the donor can take a charitable income tax deduction now for the gift and move the home out of her estate, reducing estate taxes. The donor also can enjoy recognition by the nonprofit while living.

(e) Endowed Funds

Establishing a named endowed fund is a way to make a gift and create a lasting memorial. Donors can create the fund while living and direct how their gift will be used and who will benefit from it. Most nonprofits allow endowed funds to be established both during a donor's lifetime and at a donor's death. Many donors see an endowed fund as a gift that continues to give long after the pass away. Endowed funds are also a special way to honor a loved one.

49.10 STEWARDSHIP

Unique stewardship opportunities exist in a healthcare setting. The planned giving officer who develops a good relationship with a donor can offer services and assistance to patients. Some medical organizations have departments established to help patients work their way through the hospital maze. These departments match a patient with a prospective doctor and can make appointments for the patient. The planned giving officer can act as a liaison to this department. Good stewardship includes visits to the donor when the donor is an inpatient, visits at the hospital when the donor has a medical appointment, and regular reporting on a donor's gift by sending news of medical progress.

49.11 FUNDRAISING IN TODAY'S HEALTHCARE ENVIRONMENT

The healthcare world is changing more than ever before. Hospital mergers are commonplace. For-profit corporations are acquiring nonprofit medical centers and services. Patients continue to struggle with managed care. Hospitals compete for patients. Patient-caregiver relationships are potentially weakened as lengths of stays decrease. HIPAA legislation has been enacted that directly impacts how a development office can work with potential donors.

49.11 FUNDRAISING IN TODAY'S HEALTHCARE ENVIRONMENT

Where does this leave fundraising? In need of even more financial assistance. Money is needed to continue work in progress. Research grants are being substantially pared down as government grants diminish. Healthcare organizations are having more difficulty attracting and keeping young researchers with promise who need funding to continue their work.

Patients need to be informed of system changes and reassured that their care will not suffer, and may well improve. They need to know that a past gift will continue to benefit what it was intended to benefit. If two organizations merge and the donor does not wish his gift to benefit the combined entity or the other organization, all efforts must be made to honor the donor's wishes. In this type of environment, it is especially important to list alternate beneficiaries within the organization in case a particular program or department ceases to exist.

Some prospects can use the organization's unknown future to delay giving or to decide against making a gift. The planned giving officer should emphasize the continued need for financial support for research, education, and patient care. The planned giving officer who stays at the organization throughout its changes has an opportunity to work with donors to overcome their concerns. An organization that remains financially viable also can win a patient's trust.

Special circumstances exist when planned giving officers work with prospects and donors who give to medical organizations. The hospital environment, cooperation from a physician, and the needs of the donor add to the unique challenges of fundraising in today's healthcare environment.

## CHAPTER FIFTY

Health Insurance Portability and Accountability Act: Raising Funds in a Healthcare Setting

On April 14, 2003, fundraising in the healthcare world changed. From that time on, development offices and foundations had to comply with federal legislation entitled the Health Insurance Portability and Accountability Act (HIPAA) of 1996. Under the "Administrative Simplification" subtitle of HIPAA, the final rule of the "Standards for Privacy of Individually Identifiable Health Information" was published on August 14, 2002 (see 45 Code of Federal Regulations Parts 160 and 164). Parts of this final rule affect fundraising and regulate what individually identifiable health information may or may not be used for fundraising purposes unless a patient provides specific authorization for use of this information. The intent of the legislation is to enable patients to control the use and disclosure of their health information. Use of information applies to the activity of fundraising, not just the development office. Physicians, administrators, trustees, and volunteers who do fundraising also are covered by these regulations.

50.1   PERMISSIBLE INFORMATION

Under the final legislation, fundraising is considered to be a part of "healthcare operations." Because of this, basic demographic data about a patient, such as name, address, telephone number, other contact information such as e-mail, age, gender, insurance status, and dates of treatment, may be used for fundraising purposes. Those individuals engaged in fundraising activities are not required to receive a patient authorization to use this basic information for fundraising purposes, as referenced in Section 164.514, "Other requirements related to uses and disclosures of protected health information."

50.2   IMPERMISSIBLE INFORMATION

Information such as the patient's medical diagnosis, nature of services received, or treatment cannot be used for fundraising purposes without a signed authorization from the patient allowing this information to be specifically used for fundraising purposes. Other authorizations for use of information, such as research or marketing, require separate authorization forms. The nature of service provision poses significant difficulties for healthcare fundraising. It appears that use and disclosure of specialist physician information, such as an oncologist's patient list, implies "nature of service" about his or her patients. Therefore, covered entities such as hospitals will need to have a signed authorization form before they are allowed to contact any specialist's patients for fundraising purposes. Specific need for authorization is ferenced in Section 164.514, "Other requirements related to uses and disclosures of protected health information."

50.3   NOTICE OF PRIVACY PRACTICES

Each healthcare institution will need to provide a Notice of Privacy Practices statement that states how medical record information will be used. For fundraising purposes, the Notice of Privacy Practices should include a sentence about contacting individuals to raise funds. Such a sentence may read, "We may use certain demographic information (name, address, telephone number, dates of service, age, and gender) to contact you for fundraising purposes. Money raised will be used to improve the services and programs we provide to the community." This is referenced in Section 164.520(b)(1)(ii), "Uses and Disclosures."

The notice can be delivered through a number of methods, such as e-mail, in newsletters or other publications, or in person. The notice does not necessarily need to be separately mailed to grateful patients, but it does need to be delivered to them no later than their date of first service, as referenced in Section 164.520(c)(2), "Specific requirements for certain covered healthcare providers."

Last, the hospital or related foundation may not use any health information, including demographic information, until the notice is given. For further information pertaining to all of the elements needed for the Notice of Privacy Practices, refer to Section 164.520, "Notice of Privacy Practices for Protected Health Information, 45 CFR Parts 160 and 164, Standards for Privacy of Individually Identifiable Health Information."

50.4   OPT-OUT CLAUSE

An "opt-out clause" must be included in any fundraising materials sent to patients, thus allowing patients to decide whether they wish to receive future fundraising materials or not. The following sample language should be included in the opt-out clause: "Please write to us if you wish to have your name removed from the list to receive fundraising requests supporting X Institution in the future." The nonprofit organization must make reasonable efforts to stop sending fundraising communications to those individuals who opt out. This is referenced in Section 164.514, "Other requirements relating to uses and disclosures of protected health information."

50.5   AUTHORIZATION FORM

In addition to the charity posting its Notice of Privacy Practices and including an opt-out clause in fundraising publications, the nonprofit, as indicated in the "Impermissible" section, must obtain a written authorization form from a patient to use protected information, such as the name of a patient's physician specialist, for fundraising purposes. The authorization form is applicable only when a patient's physician is a specialist, such as an oncologist, and does not apply to primary care physicians. Fundraisers will need to work with physicians and admitting staff to obtain these authorization forms. Patients may sign authorization forms at any time, such as at the point of entry into the healthcare organization. Unfortunately, this approach asks patients to consider being grateful before they have received care. Authorization forms also could be obtained after the patient's visit by a mass mailing, during checkout from the hospital, or at one-on-one subsequent visits with physicians. All required elements needed in an authorization form are referenced in Section 164.508, "Uses and disclosures for which an authorization is required."

50.6 PENALTIES

Penalties for violation of HIPAA include both civil and criminal options. The Office of Civil Rights under the Department of Health and Human Services is responsible for the enforcement of these regulations. Penalty fines range from $100 to $250,000, with criminal penalties of up to 10 years imprisonment. Further classification is given in "I. Background: The Administrative Simplification Provisions, and Regulatory Actions."

While enforcement guidelines have yet to be released, the final rule does state that the secretary and the Office of Civil Rights first will make all efforts to bring a covered entity (healthcare institution) into compliance, before pursuing civil and criminal penalties. For more details, see Section 160.304, "Principles for Achieving Compliance," and "I. Background: Enforcement."

50.7 CONCLUSION

The way healthcare development offices work with grateful patients has changed under HIPAA. A patient's personal medical information, such as the type of specialist the patient has seen, cannot be disclosed for fundraising purposes. As hospitals and healthcare providers become more experienced with this legislation, the ultimate effect on fundraising practices will be seen.

## CHAPTER FIFTY-ONE

Planned Giving in Large, Established Arts Organizations

51.1 INTRODUCTION

Planned giving efforts in large, established arts organizations have their own unique, defined set of challenges. While borrowing much from other organizations such as educational institutions and healthcare organizations that do planned giving, planned giving and development in arts organizations is different. The arts organizations are different because of the "service" or "product" they provide and the way the individual donor feels about the organization. This uniqueness results in special challenges for the planned giving officer, as well as providing the planned giving officer with fundraising tools and personal rewards. This chapter examines planned giving at large, established arts organizations, including public television and radio, the symphony, art museums, and opera.

51.2 DONOR PROFILE

Planned giving donors to large, established arts organizations tend to fit into two general profiles. Both profiles include donors who are older, well educated, and cultured. Many have a history of community involvement and philanthropy and are wealthy, coming from a background of family money. A variation on this stereotype is the planned giving donor who lives frugally and has saved his hard-earned money and through careful saving is able to make a significant life income gift or bequest. This donor has lived through the Depression and is careful about money, and may be less sophisticated, but is motivated to give something back. Both types of donors love the arts.

(a) Give Nationally or Locally

Donors to a nationally acclaimed arts organization tend to give regardless of where they live (e.g., a donor who lives in California giving to the Metropolitan Opera in New York City). Many have the financial means and interest to travel the country and the world to pursue their arts passion. Those who travel for their passion get to know other donors who give to the organization because they meet periodically at the arts organization's sponsored events. Close friendships often develop over time, giving donors another reason to become even closer to the arts organization. Many have been long-time arts organization supporters, and the arts is their primary philanthropy. They know that there are a limited number of other individuals who have the interest and financial ability to make substantial gifts to fund the arts, and they wish to see the arts continue to thrive. Many of these donors are also interested in making smaller gifts to their local arts organizations.

(b) Understand Planned Giving

Typical arts supporters are often well educated about planned giving concepts. Since most are well educated generally, they receive appeals and educational information about planned giving from other organizations they are connected to, such as their colleges, universities, and secondary schools. Their spouses also tend to receive these promotional materials, resulting in a prospect that is well versed in the advantages of making a gift through a planned gift. Many arts organizations have not had planned giving programs for very long, and are only beginning to enjoy planned giving successes. Many benefit from the education provided by other charities.

51.3 RELATIONSHIP BUILDING

Arts organizations must develop concerted marketing efforts and attempts to bring the donor to the organization. Depending on the type of arts organization, meeting donors at the organization is either much easier than at other organizations or, in some cases, takes much more effort. Unlike other institutions (e.g., a college or university), there is no reason to come to the arts organization on an annual basis, such as at homecoming or for class reunions. People come to the arts organization because they want to, but usually not on a predictable basis.

(a) Donor Meetings

Planned giving officers who work at a museum, symphony, opera, or other arts organizations sometimes can meet with donors and prospects on a periodic, regular basis. For example, the planned giving officer at a symphony can locate the prospect in her season's subscription seat. The annual subscription holder may be seen on a weekly, monthly, or other periodic basis during the musical season. Alternatively, the director of planned giving at a museum can invite the prospect in for a special dinner or function that celebrates an opening night, special performance, or exhibit perhaps a few times per year. Donors can walk favorite galleries with an experienced tour guide or curator and can be shown special pieces from the museum's collection that are not available to the public. At the opera, donors can be invited to attend a brunch in the opera house or at a restaurant before a matinee performance or before a premiere showing. Donors may attend the opera as a guest of the director of planned giving and sit in a special opera box.

At a public television or radio station, the planned giving officer generally needs to be more creative and innovative in finding a way for the donor or prospect to come to the station. There is no reason for the donor to visit on a periodic basis or at all. A donor may be invited to come to the studio to meet with a producer or view a taping of a show. This is generally seen as a special occasion that happens infrequently. Meetings with donors and prospects bring the donor closer to the organization and may allow donors to meet others who share their passion.

(b) Servicing Donors

Another benefit that the planned giving officer at an arts organization can provide to a donor or prospect is excellent service. The development officer can work to provide patrons with advance tickets for the times, shows, and seat locations they wish. Gift giving can result in easier access to ticket privileges. In addition, there is the opportunity to have special behind-the-scenes tours, hear a famous singer or performer, or experience something that only an insider might see. This type of special service brings the donor or prospect in more regular contact with the planned giving officer and can result in a growing relationship over the years.

(c) Gifts to Promote

What is the planned giving and development officer asking donors and prospects to fund at an arts organization? Institution-specific examples are listed below.

(i) Symphony.   The types of programs and projects that a donor might fund at the symphony are quite varied. Because there is a strong teaching component involved in a symphony orchestra, donors may:

- *Endow a chair in the orchestra.* Donors can pay the salary and special expenses for the musician who holds, for example, the first seated flute or is the concertmaster.

- *Fund individual concerts.* Individual concerts may be named in a loved one's honor or memory.

- *Sponsor guest conductor artists.* Sponsor a weekly/monthly artist or guest conductor who performs for a limited engagement at the symphony.

- *Provide educational funds for school programs and community activities.* It is very expensive to bring classical music to those who do not have the opportunity to learn about or hear the symphony. Donors may support or endow programs that teach music in various settings, such as public schools.

- *Provide funds for library archives that house musical scores.* Expanded facilities always are needed to house scores and catalog them.

- *Upgrade instruments.* Permanent instruments, such as the house organ or piano, need to be upgraded and maintained constantly.

- *Name auditorium seats.* Seats in the auditorium may be named for loved ones. Seats need to be replaced often and repaired regularly. A small plaque can be placed on the back of an auditorium chair.

- *Sponsor a playbill.* The playbill may be sponsored in honor or memory of someone special. The donor's name and dedication to a loved one can be stated in the program for one or more performances.

(ii) Art Museum.   The following ideas may appeal to donors who wish to support their favorite art museum:

- *Endowment for operating support, ongoing efforts, budget relief.* These gifts often come from the museum's annual fund, but donors can make these gifts specifically for operating support. Through a planned gift, a donor can support these activities in the future, after the donor's death.

- *Name an art gallery, wing, or museum entrance.* These giving opportunities usually provide facilities support to a museum, which houses its collection. These large naming opportunities represent leadership gifts for a museum campaign.

- *Endow various professional positions, such as a full curator or associate curator.* This provides support for a donor's personal interest, such as modern paintings or Greek and Roman statues.

- *Scholarships for faculty enrichment.* This is especially helpful if the museum has its own school as part of the museum.

- *Money for new acquisitions.* Donors can make gifts that enable the museum to buy pieces of their own choosing or try to designate their gift for a particular piece they wish to see the museum acquire.

- *Money for conservation of objects and paintings and support for the general work of the curators.* Museum pieces constantly must be maintained, preserved, and protected.

- *Funds for documenting the collection and information management.* Many museums are struggling to document the pieces they already own, as well as those newly acquired. Cataloging of pieces needs to be computerized and is quite time consuming.

- *Educational programs.* Money is needed to provide educational programs to the public about special exhibits, artists, and special techniques.

- *Scholarships for inner city children, senior citizens, and students.* Funds are used to benefit people with less financial means and can help bring people to the museum who might not otherwise attend.

(iii) Public Radio and Television.   Public radio and television have different needs from those of the symphony or museums. Some funding options include:

- *Seed money for research and development.* These funds allow the station to produce new educational programs and offerings.

- *Money for production of a new show or series.* Donations always are needed when a brand-new show or series is produced and aired.

- *Endowment of a producer's chair.* This provides ongoing support for a named producer's work or the work of his successor.

(iv) Opera.   Most opera companies, regardless of their fame or stature, need charitable gifts. The pool of donors can be small, and funds may be used for:

- Endowment, to provide for the long-term future of the opera.

- Stipend assistance for young artists to live on while they continue training and can be taught language, stage movement, and fencing; view rehearsals; and have time to gain performing experience.

- New productions, to underwrite or partially underwrite the great expense of producing a new show, where virtually everything from scenery to music must start anew.

- Radio broadcasts of the opera, to bring opera into the homes of those who cannot attend in person.

- Discounted senior and student tickets, viewed as a community service.

- Touring to other locations, including national and international tours. Costs may include airfare, lodging, and transportation.

51.4 GIFTS-IN-KIND

Arts organizations are the type of nonprofit that often benefit from a donor's gift-in-kind. While other types of charitable organizations enjoy and make good use of gifts-in-kind, such as computer software, books, artwork, and collectibles, it is the arts organizations that can most enjoy and benefit from such gifts. For a museum, gifts of artwork can significantly build the museum's collection, helping it to acquire pieces it might not otherwise afford. While most organizations are offered many pieces of tangible personal property, not all are accepted; many donors believe that their gift is very valuable, while the arts organization may not consider the piece rare or terribly valuable. The planned giving officer learns to be gracious about turning down proposed gifts of artwork.

51.5 TAX DEDUCTIBILITY

For a donor to deduct the full fair market value of a gift-in-kind, the gift must be given to an organization whose tax-exempt purpose has a related use to the tangible item. If a gift-in-kind is made that is not related to the charity's tax-exempt purposes, then the donor can deduct only the cost basis of the gift for tax purposes. While donors are not generally motivated by tax benefits to give, it makes financial sense for a donor to give a gift-in-kind to a nonprofit with a related use. A gift of a painting or valuable piece collected by a museum can become a part of the museum's permanent collection, and may go on display immediately. Famous or one-of-a-kind librettos and costumes may be given to an opera, playbills and musical scores to a symphony, and books to a library. All of these gifts to these institutions should provide a donor with the ability to take the full fair market value of the gift for a tax deduction.

51.6 FORM 8283

Charities that accept gifts-in-kind should send the donor a signed Form 8283, indicating acceptance of the gift. The donor will include this form when filing taxes for the year the gift was made. See Chapter 33 for a full discussion of Form 8283 and gifts-in-kind.

51.7 USE OF PLANNED GIVING VEHICLES

The charitable gift annuity may be used at an arts organization in a way that is unique. For example, a museum may want to own outright an object that has been on permanent or semipermanent loan to the museum but is still legally owned by the donor. Perhaps it has been in a family for generations, and family members are unwilling or unable to give the object permanently to the museum. By offering the donor a charitable gift annuity based on the value of the object, the museum may be able to convince the donor to give the object outright to the museum. The museum will need to find the funds internally to make the annual income payments to the donor, but depending on the item, many museums would be willing to do this for a desired piece.

51.8 MARKETING

(a) Special Marketing Efforts Unique to the Arts

Because there is no built-in constituency at most arts organizations, ways need to be developed for prospects to identify themselves as interested in the organization. Arts organizations such as public television, radio, and symphony make use of advertising on television and radio regularly. Telethons or auctions take place that offer the opportunity for solicitations that reach an enormous audience. Donors can go on the air to tell their story of making a gift to the organization, giving testimonials of what the organization has meant to them and how they have benefited by making a gift.

(b) Targeted Advertising

Targeted advertisements may be placed in magazines that cater to a special market. For example, planned giving professionals may consider placing a charitable gift annuity ad in an antiques magazine that their constituency often reads. A prospect who responds to one of these ads may be a good prospect to make a gift to the symphony. Using these specialty magazines or publications helps the planned giving officer identify prospects with interests similar to that of their institution. Some arts organizations also offer financial-planning seminars to planned giving prospects who come and can have personalized follow-up. These seminars allow prospects who have not yet indicated an interest in the arts organization to be followed up by the planned giving officer.

(c) Captive Audience

Most organizations take advantage of the captive audience at an arts performance to begin soliciting individuals for small donations to build up the pool of people who are interested in supporting the organization. Advertisements or educational pieces are strategically placed in concert and special exhibit programs. They may tell about ways to make a gift and the benefits a donor can receive by making a gift. Sometimes the general director or other administrator will appear on the stage before or after a concert and ask for financial support. Envelopes and educational materials can be placed in the concert or opera hall offering attendees the opportunity to make a gift. Offers may be made for prospects to write or call for various free publications, such as broadcast guides. The lower-level donor base must be regularly encouraged to make larger gifts.

(d) Publications

Like many other charitable organizations, most large arts organizations provide donors and prospects with a member magazine or monthly newsletter that will provide suggested ways to make a gift and can outline the advantages of planned giving. Planned giving officers at well-known arts organizations often have the advantage of having pictures or photographs of beautiful objects available from their collections to use in their marketing pieces. Some national organizations produce the definitive publication on a certain subject, such as *Opera News,* produced by the Metropolitan Opera, which allows the planned giving officer to place an advertisement in that publication, going beyond a typical planned giving newsletter or development publication.

51.9 BOARDS AND VOLUNTEERS

Many arts organizations' boards are very large and are divided into different authoritative levels, such as advisors, directors, managing directors, and trustees. They are often very high-profile boards. It is socially prestigious for individuals to serve on high-profile arts boards, and the development staff person may have little or no access to board members and no opportunity to speak about planned giving at a board meeting.

Individual volunteers such as trustees or others can have a major impact with patrons of the arts and can solicit donors and prospects as peers. They also can entertain and bring a social component to a solicitation that a staff person cannot. A volunteer who owns a valuable private art collection may be called on to host a small dinner party for donors and prospects in his home. This type of intimate gathering appeals to many prospects and can promote giving. Board members and volunteers, once they learn about the benefits of planned gifts, can also become the arts organization's best planned giving donors.

51.10   SPECIAL CHALLENGES UNIQUE TO ARTS ORGANIZATIONS

(a) Working with Museum Curators

Planned giving officers working in an art museum or library are likely to have the unique opportunity to work with a curator. These individuals often have devoted their lives to art and have been at one institution for their entire working life. The arts organization and the financial times and pressures have made the museum a different place to work, where there is greater accountability and a greater focus on fundraising and fiscal business. Their professional success is no longer judged on scholarship alone, but also on the ability to attract money for scholarships.

For the planned giving or development officer, the relationship with the curator can be a challenge. Sometimes the curator offers a real boost to a fundraising situation or acts as an obstacle that needs to be worked around. Challenges include explaining to the curator the need for consensus and for her participation in fundraising efforts and the organization's business.

Sometimes it can be enormously helpful to a fundraising situation to include the curator in the process. The curator can speak eloquently to the donor's passions and interests. Through the curator, the donor can see how his gift really will benefit the organization. The planned giving officer also has the opportunity to learn much about art and the organization from the curator.

(b) Lack of Research on Donors

Unlike an educational institution or healthcare facility, most arts organizations do not have access to donors' personal histories. It is difficult to determine a donor's age, which makes it a challenge to target a planned giving solicitation. There is no built-in constituency; the arts organization must attract the public at large to become donors. When meeting with a planned giving professional, most donors and prospects are eager to come to the organization rather than meet at the donor's home, making it more difficult for the planned giving officer to learn about the donor's personal situation, family, and wealth. At a donor's home, the planned giving officer has a greater opportunity to see the type of home the donor lives in and his personal property, perhaps indicating wealth.

(c) Benefits of Working in the Arts

Planned giving officers who work in the arts exude a real passion for their work. Their work allows them to indulge their own love of the arts, to hear famous performers and be surrounded by beautiful objects and creative minds. On a daily basis there is the opportunity to work with donors who share a personal passion. There is also the opportunity to learn and absorb, as well as develop a new awareness and appreciation for different aspects of the arts. Planned giving officers have the opportunity to work with donors who are well known in the community and may be well known nationally and internationally. There is a strong sense of institutional pride and the feeling of privilege from working with the best.

51.11   CONCLUSION

Planned giving work at large established arts organizations can be both challenging and personally rewarding. Skills can be borrowed from work at other types of nonprofit organizations, but new skills must be acquired as the planned giving officer deals with arts organizations' special needs, donors, and services.

# PART TEN

Planned Giving in Context

Ethics and Planned Giving

52.1   INTRODUCTION

Planned giving professionals have an opportunity to become intimately familiar with a donor and the donor's entire personal, professional, and business life. Consequently, conflicts can arise between doing what is best for the organization and what is best for the donor. Nonprofit organizations and development offices owe their existence to contributions of money, but this financial support cannot be obtained to the detriment of the donor. Because of the long and close relationship that can develop between a planned giving officer and a donor, planned giving is open to more potential ethical dilemmas than other areas in the development profession. This chapter examines ethical issues that may arise in a planned giving program.

52.2   DONOR RIGHTS AND NONPROFIT RESPONSIBILITIES

Donors have rights, and planned giving officers have responsibilities in handling and managing gifts. Donors may rely extensively on a planned giving officer's advice in selecting the most appropriate planned giving option to fit their needs. They have a right to expect that the gift option will be appropriate and funded with the proper asset.

Charities are increasingly under scrutiny by federal and state agencies and departments. In recent years Congress, the Internal Revenue Service (IRS), the Securities and Exchange Commission (SEC), and states, through the regulation of charitable gift annuities by the state insurance commissioners, have sought to protect donors and to encourage nonprofits to engage in practices that are designed to meet or exceed donor expectations.

52.3 TRUTH IN PHILANTHROPY

Like truth in lending, which protects consumers by requiring disclosure of financial terms, conditions, and expenses on loans by financial institutions, a nonprofit may offer to donors "truth in philanthropy." Truth in philanthropy means a number of things. It means that a nonprofit and its staff members must:

- Engage in activities that serve to fulfill the nonprofit's mission statement.

- Spend a donor's funds consistent with the mission statement.

- Engage in practices consistent with the nonprofit's tax-exempt status.

- Disclose investment and management practices about permanently endowed funds and life income gift funds.

- Disclose to the donor the cost of fundraising and administration that must be deducted before financial support reaches its intended recipient.

- Honor the donor's restrictions on the use of funds.

- Disclose the benefits and potential negative consequences of a gift.

- Distinguish planned giving vehicles from financial investment vehicles.

- Consider a donor's financial welfare when accepting gifts.

- Comply not only with the letter of the law, but also with the spirit and intent of the IRS guidelines and regulations regarding charitable giving.

52.4 DONOR RIGHTS

(a) The Planned Gift Should Be Compatible with the Donor's Goals

Individuals can make gifts in a variety of ways, including outright gifts, gifts from the donor's estate, planned gifts, or a combination of each of these options. A donor must first have donative intent to make a gift. Donative intent can be enhanced by the attractive benefits of planned gifts. Life income streams, charitable income tax deductions, estate or gift tax deductions, and capital gains avoidance provide additional financial incentives to donors. Presenting all appropriate life income gift options is an important part of the job of a planned giving officer. For example, a donor who prefers the certainty of a fixed life income stream may choose a charitable gift annuity over a gift to the pooled income fund. Some donors prefer to receive a larger charitable income tax deduction rather than income streams. Donors who wish to provide an immediate financial benefit to a department must be advised that a life income arrangement (e.g., a charitable gift annuity) provides a delayed benefit to the department, which may frustrate their intent. Those donors should be advised to consider outright gifts as a way to accomplish their goals. In any case, donors should be presented with options and printouts that achieve their goals. Safeguarding the rights of donors avoids additional government regulation and promotes practices that ensure adequate protection of donors.

(b) Time Frame

A planned giving officer is in the business of raising funds. He must not be bashful, apologetic, pushy, or aggressive. Donors do not enjoy being pushed, although at times they need gentle prodding. Every donor should have a reasonable time frame to make a decision about a charitable gift. A planned giving officer must walk a fine line between promoting gifts on behalf of the nonprofit and protecting the donor's right to have adequate time to make an informed decision. The donor must be given time to fully understand the gift option: its benefits, detriments, and consequences to the donor, her family, and her overall estate-planning objectives.

(c) Disclosure of Fees

The nonprofit is required to disclose to the donor any financial expenses associated with gift management, including the management of endowed funds. Expenses for administration of, charitable remainder trusts, or other life income gifts managed by the nonprofit, or by the outside asset manager as a trustee, must be disclosed to the donor. In addition, policies for distributing income from endowments must be disclosed so that the donor is fully informed as to the anticipated income from the endowment that can be used by the nonprofit. The donor should be told whether the fees will be taken from the income generated by the gift or charged as a separate cost of administration.

(d) Privacy

Donors have an expectation of privacy regarding their gifts, and both the nonprofit and the planned giving officer owe the donor privacy in several respects. News of the donor's gift should not be communicated to other donors or to other departments within the nonprofit organization without the donor's consent. Donors who request anonymity or confidentiality must have their wishes protected by the nonprofit to the highest level. Many donors who make anonymous gifts do not wish to open themselves to requests for funding from other nonprofits or offend other nonprofits in the area with whom they may be affiliated. They may also not want their family members to know about the gift.

(e) How to Avoid Conflicts

A donor-related conflict can arise when a planned giving officer is trying to raise money for the organization but learns something about the donor that causes him to question whether the proposed gift should be made. For example, a planned giving officer may work with a donor who, just before (or after) delivering the check for a gift, demonstrates that she does not really understand the tax consequences or financial ramifications of the gift. When making a life income gift, the donor might ask whether she can receive the money back if she later becomes ill. Or the donor may be confused when writing out the check. These are warning signs to the planned giving officer that the donor is not fully aware of the consequences of her actions.

One way to avoid a donor-related conflict is to suggest that the donor have a financial or legal advisor review a planned giving proposal or attend the meetings between the planned giving officer and the donor. If possible, send a copy of all correspondence to the financial advisor. In addition, when corresponding with a donor, include the statement, "We advise you to consult with your attorney or financial advisor." Always try to meet personally with a donor to learn more about her and determine competency.

The planned giving officer must regularly remind the prospect that the planned giving officer represents the organization, not the donor. This is especially important when the planned giving officer has an advanced degree, such as a law degree, that may encourage the donor to rely on the planned giving officer's advice. Encourage the donor who does not have her own advisor to speak with the nonprofit's attorney or outside manager, keeping in mind that these individuals are paid by the nonprofit. The goal is to permit the donor as much input as possible. All of these precautions can help to avoid a possible conflict of interest. In the end, the decision is always the donor's.

The following is a checklist of ways to avoid potential donor conflicts:

- Have the donor consult with an outside financial advisor, lawyer, trust officer, or certified public accountant before making the gift.

- Include the outside advisor in meetings with the donor. Keep the advisor involved by sending her copies of correspondence. If possible, speak directly with the outside advisor.

- Include a statement in all correspondence indicating that the donor should seek outside representation before making a planned gift. This statement should appear in letters to the donor and accompany all gift calculations.

- Give the donor enough time to consider a gift proposal; two to five weeks or more may be appropriate.

- During conversations, remind the donor that the planned giving officer represents the nonprofit, not the donor.

- Meet personally with a donor to judge whether she really understands the tax consequences of making a gift.

(f) The Size of the Gift Should Be Appropriate

Planned giving professionals sometimes are placed in a position, by their organizations or by management, of suggesting a specific gift amount to a donor. Sometimes the donor will even ask, "How much should I give?" The planned giving officer must balance the organization's need for financial support and development success with the donor's welfare. The organization would be embarrassed, perhaps humiliated, if the donor were left in an unsound financial position after making gifts to the nonprofit. For example, it is possible that a donor who makes many gifts to a nonprofit could be unable to afford healthcare or could be denied Medicaid coverage because of recent gifts. A nonprofit would be distressed to know that it was benefiting at the expense of a donor's health or well-being. This is especially worrisome if an individual development officer is involved who may have known about the donor's health or financial position.

Because it is possible that a donor may be too generous in making gifts beyond his means, the planned giving officer should consider accepting gifts gradually, over a period of time. When asked by a donor to suggest a specific gift amount, show the donor how much several gift levels "cost," such as the amount needed to endow a fund, name a patient room, or reach a particular club level.

(g) Maintaining Independence and Objectivity

Sometimes natural friendships develop between prospects and planned giving officers. However, this should be the exception rather than the rule. The planned giving officer should maintain an appropriate professional distance from prospects, because a close friendship can confuse the business relationship. A planned giving officer should be aware of a potential conflict when a donor invites the planned giving officer to after-hours social events, brings gifts, telephones him at home, wants him to stay overnight when in the area of the donor's home, and wants to leave the planned giving officer something in his will.

It is especially important to maintain some distance from older donors and prospects, especially those who are alone. Sometimes older donors can mistake business advances as acts of friendship and will continue meeting because it provides them with company and conversation. They may feel that making gifts to the organization assures them of continued attention.

The planned giving officer should keep an appropriate distance by focusing conversations on business, beginning each meeting and telephone call by talking about the business at hand. Every meeting should relate to making gifts to the organization. Include an associate in meetings with a donor who seems more interested in building a personal relationship than in making a gift to the nonprofit. If necessary, simply remind the donor at any point that a planned giving officer's role is to raise money for the nonprofit, and although it is a pleasure to get to know the donor, the primary reason for the relationship is to raise funds.

(h) Donor's Recourse

Successful businesses know that the customer is always right. The same concept applies in planned giving. Within reason, donors, as customers of the nonprofit, are always right. Donor relations extend to every nonprofit employee and each interaction; mishandling can hinder or prevent future gifts. To deal with donor relations issues, an "ombudsperson" may be appointed. The ombudsperson acts as an intermediary who resolves conflict between donors and nonprofit departments or programs. Donors who have questions regarding the use, designation, or investment of their gifts should be provided with the name of the nonprofit's officer in charge of gift administration. In most cases, questions may be directed to the vice-president for development, a stewardship officer, or, in the case of planned gifts, the director of planned giving. If the nonprofit uses outside management for planned gifts, the donor initially should be directed to the director of planned giving, rather than the outside manager, to track and monitor gift administration problems.

52.5 NONPROFIT RESPONSIBILITIES

(a) Satisfaction of Internal Revenue Service Procedures

Many retailers offer money-back guarantees—no questions asked. That may work for retailers and, to a lesser extent, professional services, but it does not work when a planned gift is made. A planned gift is irrevocable, and it is not possible to offer a money-back guarantee. In exchange for the gift, the donor obtains a charitable income tax deduction, so once the gift is made, the donor cannot take it back, nor can the nonprofit give it back.

A gift to a nonprofit organization involves three parties: the donor, the nonprofit, and the Internal Revenue Service (IRS). Both the donor and the nonprofit must ensure that the gift is in fact a charitable gift and satisfies the applicable provisions of the Internal Revenue Code. In addition, the nonprofit must protect the donor's charitable income tax deduction by complying with IRS regulations. Donors obtain charitable income tax deductions in exchange for their gifts to nonprofit organizations, and nonprofits have an obligation to issue proper receipts and to adhere to IRS procedures to protect those charitable income tax deductions. Donors must honestly and fairly value noncash gifts, such as real estate and tangible personal property. Although the burden is on the taxpayer to value these assets, a nonprofit must not be a party to an overvaluation or a transaction that gives the donor a deduction in excess of the true value of the gift. Nonprofits should share the responsibility with the donor for valuing gifts of noncash assets.

The nonprofit's gift review committee can help protect the nonprofit from "gifts" that do little to benefit the nonprofit. Planned giving officers should explain to the donor the mutual responsibilities associated with gifts of noncash assets, such as providing the donor with Form 8283, and the charity's obligation to file Form 8282 if the property is sold within two years of the date of the gift. Proactively informing the donor about the nonprofit's obligations avoids surprises and eliminates confusion.

(b) Unfair and Deceptive Practices

As charitable organizations, nonprofits operate as a public trust and for the public good. Nonprofits owe the highest of standards in upholding their position as tax-exempt organizations. Nonprofit organizations must not engage in any practice that is unfair or deceptive. False or misleading claims that misstate charitable purposes or overstate financial benefits are inappropriate. High-pressure tactics that unfairly raise funds from the elderly, impaired, or infirm, or from those who are unfamiliar with the gift options, are also inappropriate.

Nonprofits must respect other nonprofit organizations that offer similar services or operate in the same region. One nonprofit should not try to improve its standing by disparaging other nonprofit organizations. Nonprofits share volunteers, board members, professional advisors, and donors. All nonprofits owe it to each of the constituents to engage in practices that promote professionalism, integrity, and truth in philanthropy.

(c) Promoting Ethical Behavior

The nonprofit must do its job to promote ethical behavior. It should have in place, and enforce, an ethics statement or policy. An internal audit should be done each year. All state and federal filing requirements must be adhered to. Additionally, money that comes in from donors and wills and trusts must be applied as the donor wishes. When the donor is unable to direct the gift, it should be applied where the donor would most have wanted the gift to go; it should not be applied where the development office most wants to boosts its fundraising totals.

52.6 DONOR'S REPRESENTATIVES

(a) Gift Brokers and Finder's Fees

Planned giving and development officers can find themselves in awkward situations regarding finder's fees. There has been an increasing amount of charitable gift brokering by agents acting or purporting to act on behalf of prospective donors. In some cases, there is no prospective donor and the agent is merely trying to obtain a consultant relationship with the nonprofit. In other cases, the agent is genuinely acting on behalf of a donor. In both situations, the agent, in exchange for a fee, is offering to deliver a donor who will make a gift to the organization. The fee may be a lump sum amount, but it is usually a percentage of the value of the prospective gift. Because most tax shelters have disappeared, planned giving options that shelter income, avoid capital gains taxes, and generate charitable income tax deductions have precipitated more aggressive gift brokering. Agents, and some prospective donors, shop around for the best deal a nonprofit will offer, and life income gift discussions can center on the highest yearly rate of return the donor will receive. This new type of "philanthropist" has no donative intent and is treating the charitable gift purely as a business transaction.

Any agent who requests a fee for the service of identifying a prospective donor should be told that the organization does not want to become involved with the transaction or to know the name of the potential donor. This usually brings the conversation to an end and, at the very least, puts the agent and the donor (if there is one) on notice that this form of transaction is prohibited. Sometimes when an agent knows a fee cannot be earned, she will disclose the name of the prospect to the organization or may resurface several months later and offer the name of the donor free of charge in a show of good faith.

(b) Commissioned Real Estate Agents or Brokers

Sometimes an agent representing a prospective donor is a commissioned agent or broker acting in the normal course of business, such as a real estate broker or a chartered life underwriter acting on behalf of a client. When a piece of property is sold, the broker normally receives a commission, but gifted property produces no commission. If property has just been listed on the market and is subsequently given to a nonprofit, then little or no service has been rendered to the owner of the property by the broker. Therefore, no fee should be paid to a broker who delivers property to a nonprofit from a donor making a gift.

If a piece of property has been on the market for an extended period of time and the broker delivers the owner to the nonprofit to make a gift, then the broker usually asks for a commission. The nonprofit should inform the broker that it is against the organization's policy to pay a commission for a gift of property. The organization should have a policy statement in place, approved by the board of trustees, to this effect. It may be appropriate to reimburse the broker for reasonable costs incurred in listing the property, such as advertising, multiple listing service fees, and other marketing costs. If the organization receives the property as a gift, it may choose to list the property with the broker, which will return the broker back to his original position, prior to the donor's gift. Be certain that there is no formal documentation obligating the nonprofit to list the property with a specific broker.

(c) Commissioned Stockbrokers

When a donor makes a gift of securities from a brokerage account to a nonprofit, she often wants to generate a commission for her broker. Many stockbrokers do not encourage clients to make gifts, because this reduces the donor's portfolio and, therefore, the broker's commission. As described in Chapter 30, it takes an extra step for the donor's broker to set up an account in the nonprofit's name and then sell the securities. The broker could more efficiently transfer the securities to the nonprofit and have the nonprofit sell the securities; however, in this case no commission would be generated for the donor's broker.

The planned giving officer should work with the donor and let the donor make the decision as to how to transfer the securities. The planned giving officer should tell the donor that it is unnecessary and perhaps more costly to have her broker handle the transaction, but that if the donor is concerned with providing the broker a commission, the organization is happy to oblige her wishes.

52.7 PAYMENT OF PROFESSIONAL ADVISORS AND LAWYERS' FEES

Professional advisors, such as attorneys and certified public accountants, charge their clients fees in conjunction with the clients' business transactions. Donors occasionally request that the nonprofit pay these costs when a planned gift is made to the organization. This is most often the case when documents such as wills and trusts must be drafted, and the donor thinks that because the nonprofit is a primary or sole beneficiary, the nonprofit should absorb the cost. Prospects can become quite upset if they are asked to pay the drafting fees when making a substantial gift.

The donor has the legal obligation to pay for these services and can deduct, as miscellaneous deductions, expenses and fees paid to professional advisors for tax-related advice and services. A nonprofit that steps in to pay for these services is accepting an obligation of the donor and is conferring a benefit on her. When a nonprofit confers such a benefit on a donor, the payment for these services may be treated as a gain for federal income tax purposes. Advise donors that they may jeopardize their charitable income tax deduction if the nonprofit pays the fees.

Each organization must decide whether to pay for various legal expenses. Many organizations are uncomfortable with paying for the drafting of a donor's will, perhaps because a bequest to a nonprofit is revocable. Many organizations are, however, willing to pay for outside counsel to draft a donor's charitable remainder trust, especially if the charity is the sole or primary beneficiary. If the nonprofit is willing to pay for the cost of drafting a charitable remainder trust, the planned giving officer must urge the donor to have the trust reviewed by her own attorney. Do not allow the donor to rely solely on the nonprofit for legal advice; if for any reason the donor is not satisfied with the trust arrangement, she may later blame the nonprofit.

52.8 PRIOR EXISTING AGREEMENTS

For a donor to claim a charitable income tax deduction for a gift of an asset to a nonprofit, the donor must make the gift free of any conditions or strings attached. Restrictions that create problems are found most often with gifts of real estate and closely held stock. Such restrictions include:

- A specific time frame for disposing of the gift

- A preexisting written agreement that binds the nonprofit to resell the gift to a specific third party

- A requirement that the donor will oversee the investment of the gift

- An agreement that binds the nonprofit to list property with a specific broker

A nonprofit should not accept a gift that restricts the right to do with the property whatever the organization, as rightful owner, wants to do with the property. Planned giving officers must tell donors that once a gift is made, the donor will no longer retain control over it. It is up to the organization to decide whether to sell the asset, hold on to it, or invest it. Talking openly with the donor before a gift is made can reduce the likelihood that the donor will want to exercise subsequent control over the asset.

52.9 FIDUCIARY ROLE OF THE NONPROFIT

(a) Nonprofit Serving as Trustee

An important issue for any nonprofit organization is whether the nonprofit should serve as a trustee of a charitable remainder trust that benefits the organization. There is a potential conflict of interest if the organization is to receive the remainder of the trust and there are living income beneficiaries. The potential conflict usually occurs when the trustee makes decisions about how the trust should be invested. Income beneficiaries of a charitable remainder trust are likely to prefer maximum current income streams, whereas the remainder beneficiary wants to preserve the corpus (assets) for ultimate distribution. These two goals can be mutually exclusive, and it is a challenge to keep both income and remainder beneficiaries satisfied.

To avoid this conflict, a nonprofit may choose not to serve as trustee of a charitable remainder trust. If the organization is the only remainder beneficiary and the donor and/or spouse are the only income beneficiaries, then it may be acceptable to serve as trustee as long as the income beneficiaries are told of the potential investment conflict. The charity also may choose to serve as cotrustee with a bank or trust company that is responsible for the investment decisions and can balance the needs of the income beneficiaries while protecting the remainder beneficiary.

(b) Nonprofit Serving as Executor or Personal Representative

A nonprofit sometimes is asked to serve as the executor or personal representative of an estate. The executor or personal representative is responsible, upon the testator's death, to gather all assets, discharge debts, and dispose of property in accordance with the donor's wishes. This process can be fraught with problems. A nonprofit should avoid being named or having an employee be named as personal representative or executor of a donor's estate. The wishes of the organization as a beneficiary may compete with the wishes or rights of other individual beneficiaries. In addition, most non-profits are not equipped to go through this time-consuming probate and estate settlement process.

52.10   ETHICS IN MARKETING

Charitable gift planners must be aware of ethical issues in marketing planned giving options. All marketing pieces, such as ads, should inform the potential donor that gifts to the nonprofit organization are irrevocable. Although the focus of an ad may be on the financial benefits of making a planned gift, the nonprofit must not be presented as an alternative to a bank or an investment firm. The donor who makes a planned gift to a nonprofit must, above all else, have the desire to make a gift to the organization.

52.11   PLANNED GIVING OFFICER AS SALESPERSON

Planned giving officers can be inappropriately viewed as salespeople who are selling a financial product. Planned giving officers should present themselves as professionals whose expertise is in charitable gift planning. A quota-driven development program conflicts with a quality planned giving program, which requires an appropriate amount of patience and time. Be wary of an organization that bases a planned giving officer's salary on "commission," providing him with a percentage of gifts received. This practice goes directly against the nature of philanthropy and the appropriate relationship of the planned giving officer to the donor.

52.12   ETHICAL DILEMMAS IN RELATION TO OTHER DEVELOPMENT OFFICERS

In most organizations, because several members of a development staff are likely to come in contact with a particular prospect or donor, there is the possibility of a conflict between staff members when the donor makes a gift. A system of prospect control (or management) can help to avoid such conflicts, but even then there is a potential for problems to arise. Before approaching a prospect, a development staff member should always consult with the central filing system in the office to check for the existence of correspondence with the prospect and should obtain clearance from the director of prospect management.

If the prospect is connected to a specific college, department, or program (e.g., a graduate of the College of Business or a cardiac patient), the development officer assigned to that area should be consulted regarding activity with that prospect. Planned giving officers in most organizations are central office employees who work for the entire organization, and they often can find themselves at odds with other development staff. Full disclosure about activity with a prospect is the best course of action.

52.13   MODEL STANDARDS OF PRACTICE FOR THE CHARITABLE GIFT PLANNER

The Model Standards of Practice for the Charitable Gift Planner were adopted by the National Committee on Planned Giving and the Committee on Gift Annuities (now the American Council on Gift Annuities) to encourage responsible charitable gift planning by anyone involved in the charitable gift planning process. The Model Standards of Practice, which address some of the primary ethical concerns in planned giving, should be read by everyone in the planned giving profession. Exhibit 52.1 outlines these standards.

Exhibit 52.1   Model Standards of Practice for the Charitable Gift Planner*

Preamble

The purpose of this statement is to encourage responsible gift planning by urging the adoption of the following Standards of Practice by all who work in the charitable gift planning process, gift planning officers, fundraising consultants, attorneys, accountants, financial planners, life insurance agents, and other financial services professionals (collectively referred to hereafter as "Gift Planners"), and by the institutions that these persons represent.

This statement recognizes that the solicitation, planning, and administration of a charitable gift is a complex process involving philanthropic, personal, financial, and tax considerations, and as such often involves professionals from various disciplines whose goals should include working together to structure a gift that achieves a fair and proper balance between the interests of the donor and the purposes of the charitable institution.

I. Primacy of Philanthropic Motivation

The principal basis for making a charitable gift should be a desire on the part of the donor to support the work of charitable institutions.

II. Explanation of Tax Implications

Congress has provided tax incentives for charitable giving, and the emphasis in this statement on philanthropic motivation in no way minimizes the necessity and appropriateness of a full and accurate explanation by the Gift Planner of those incentives and their implications.

III. Full Disclosure

It is essential to the gift planning process that the role and relationships of all parties involved, including how and by whom each is compensated, be fully disclosed to the donor. A Gift Planner shall not act or purport to act as a representative of any charity without the express knowledge and approval of the charity, and shall not, while employed by the charity, act or purport to act as a representative of the donor, without the express consent of both the charity and the donor.

IV. Compensation

Compensation paid to Gift Planners shall be reasonable and proportionate to the services provided. Payment of finder's fees, commissions, or other fees by a donee organization to an independent Gift Planner as a condition for the delivery of a gift are never appropriate. Such payments lead to abusive practices and may violate certain state and federal regulations. Likewise, commission-based compensation for Gift Planners who are employed by a charitable institution is never appropriate.

V. Competence and Professionalism

The Gift Planner should strive to achieve and maintain a high degree of competence in his or her chosen area, and shall advise donors only in areas in which he or she is professionally qualified. It is a hallmark of professionalism for Gift Planners that they realize when they have reached the limits of their knowledge and expertise, and as a result, should include other professionals in the process. Such relationships should be characterized by courtesy, tact, and mutual respect.

VI. Consultation with Independent Advisors

A Gift Planner acting on behalf of a charity shall in all cases strongly encourage the donor to discuss the proposed gift with competent independent legal and tax advisors of the donor's choice.

VII. Consultation with Charities

Although Gift Planners frequently and properly counsel donors concerning specific charitable gifts without the prior knowledge or approval of the donee organization, the Gift Planners, in order to insure that the gift will accomplish the donor's objectives, should encourage the donor, early in the gift planning

Exhibit 52.1 *(Continued)*

process, to discuss the proposed gift with the charity to whom the gift is to be made. In cases where the donor desires anonymity, the Gift Planner shall endeavor, on behalf of the undisclosed donor, to obtain the charity's input in the gift planning process.

VIII. Description and Representation of Gift

The Gift Planner shall make every effort to ensure that the donor receives a full description and an accurate representation of all aspects of any proposed charitable gift plan The consequences for the charity, the donor and, where applicable, the donor's family, should be apparent, and the assumptions underlying any financial illustrations should be realistic.

IX. Full Compliance

A Gift Planner shall fully comply with and shall encourage other parties in the gift planning process to fully comply with both the letter and spirit of all applicable federal and state laws and regulations.

X. Public Trust

Gift Planners shall, in all dealings with donors, institutions, and other professionals, act with fairness, honesty, integrity, and openness. Except for compensation received for services, the terms of which have been disclosed to the donor, they shall have no vested interest that could result in personal gain.

*Adopted and subscribed to by the National Committee on Planned Giving and the American Council on Gift Annuities, May 7, 1991. Revised April 1999. National Committee on Planned Giving, 233 Mc Crea Street, Suite 400, Indianapolis, Indiana 46225, (317) 269-6274, FAX: (317) 269-6276, e-mail: ncpg@iupui.edu. Copyright © 1999 by the National Committee on Planned Giving. All rights reserved..

52.14 CONCLUSION

Nonprofit organizations and individual planned giving professionals have a responsibility to work ethically with all prospects and donors. As charitable gift planners, we must constantly strive to make the most ethical choices when working with donors and other individuals who are involved in the gift planning process. Regularly, we must ask ourselves if we are doing the right thing and remind ourselves that no gift is ever worth receiving if not obtained ethically.

CHAPTER FIFTY-THREE

Planned Giving and
Capital Campaigns

53.1   INTRODUCTION

A capital campaign at a nonprofit organization raises money over a specific period of time. A campaign allows an organization to announce publicly to its constituents that it is in need of financial support and is used to encourage individuals, corporations, and foundations to give. A time frame is established to encourage donors to make the largest possible gifts in the shortest period of time. A capital campaign can focus on a number of areas, including building support commonly called "bricks and mortar" endowment, an increase in the organization's cash reserves, or specific individual programs. Many campaigns raise money for a combination of building support, endowment, and programs.

A capital campaign originally was thought to be an occasional, once-every-20-years effort, but it has now become a mainstay of most development programs. Capital campaigns have increased in size, and it is now common for nonprofits to set sights on campaign totals of millions, and even billions, of dollars. In addition, the time frame for these campaigns has been extended. In the past most organizations ran campaigns for 3 to 5 years at a maximum. Increasingly, it is not unusual to witness back-to-back campaigns and campaigns that run for as long as 10 to 12 years, which mesh perfectly with planned giving.

Because planned gifts typically take a number of years to materialize, a long capital campaign represents an excellent opportunity to incorporate the components of a successful planned giving program. Many components such as marketing, tax benefits, estate planning, financial planning, trusts, life income gifts, and gifts of real estate may be started at the beginning of a capital campaign and demonstrate success by the end of the campaign.

53.2   TYPES OF CAPITAL CAMPAIGNS

(a) Buildings and Capital Projects

Planned gifts can be used to fund, most often through a naming opportunity, a specific building or a capital project. Life income gifts such as charitable gift annuities, pooled income fund gifts, and charitable remainder trusts provide funding and stability for building projects. Because buildings take years to design and erect, planned giving is especially appropriate as an organization waits for the planned gift to mature in order to access the remainder. Planned gifts are not as helpful at the beginning of a building project when cash is needed immediately. Bequests can provide even longer-term funding for capital expansion and are especially helpful in sustaining support for building projects. Although bequests, by their revocable nature, can never be completely relied on, bequests that mature can be significant in serving to supplement financial support later in a building project and in the final phase of a campaign.

Building and capital project support are often the most difficult projects for which to raise money. Often donors like to direct their gifts to particular individuals, projects, and programs. Planned gifts, though, can provide much-needed unrestricted support. Many donors are so pleased to receive the financial benefits, like an income, from their planned gift that they do not choose to restrict their gift. Many campaigns can look to life income gifts to provide unrestricted dollars that can be applied to bricks and mortar.

(b) Endowment

Planned gifts are also particularly valuable in building endowments for capital campaigns. Endowment funds are permanent funds established to support a scholarship program or provide yearly income to a specific area or program. Typically, the principal that is contributed to a specific fund is managed as part of the organization's overall endowment, and only the income from the fund is distributed to a recipient. Planned gifts can be quite beneficial in augmenting an organization's endowment. At the end of every campaign there are unfulfilled needs, and unrestricted planned gifts can be applied to meet these needs. The remainder of life income gifts can be designated to be added to a donor's specific endowed fund, or the remainder value can be left unrestricted to augment the overall endowment. The recipient of the planned gift at the nonprofit also can leverage the future planned gift to borrow current funds for a needed project or program.

(c) Specific Programs

Campaign funds also can be used to provide continuing operating support to an organization, either generally or through specific programs. Donors tend to make larger donations to specific areas or programs because of their connection to a particular school, physician, or project. Designating a gift to a specific program allows the donor to have a greater sense of control over the use of the gift and of being part of the organization. Planned gifts can provide operating support at the gift's maturity, often at the donor's death. Development officers learn that raising money for programs is generally easier than raising money for buildings or endowment. Unfortunately, the recipients of planned gifts designated for program support are eager to use the money at once, and the professor, the physician, or the program coordinator is disappointed to learn that when a donor contributes through a life income gift, he must wait for the donor to die before the gift is realized. A savvy planned giving officer should work with the planned giving donor to encourage her to make an annual outright gift to the program in addition to the planned gift. By so doing, the donor can see specific results and be involved in the process while she is still alive, knowing that the work can continue after her death.

53.3 THE NUCLEUS FUND

A nucleus fund is a mini-campaign within a capital campaign. During the preannouncement, quiet phase of a campaign, before the campaign is made public, individuals closest to the organization are solicited to make gifts to the nucleus fund in anticipation of the campaign. For example, the board of trustees may be solicited for gifts that could represent 7 to 10 percent of the total campaign goal. In addition, select top prospects may be solicited for major gifts, any one of which may represent 10 to 15 percent of the campaign goal, with two or three other smaller leadership gifts totaling 15 percent or more of the goal. These gifts, along with any other monies raised during this time, constitute the nucleus fund. This fund collectively represents 20 to 30 percent of the total campaign at most nonprofit organizations. The nucleus fund helps to ensure the success of the campaign by testing the campaign strength and the potential for leadership support. Planned gifts become an important part of the nucleus fund when top donors choose to make their gifts through planned giving or use planned giving as a component of their gifts. The staggering dollar amounts of many campaign goals would appear overwhelming to most donors and staff in the absence of a nucleus fund, which represents money in the bank and a down payment toward success. A substantial nucleus fund fosters confidence and optimism among donors, trustees, staff, and potential donors. Exhibit 53.1 shows sources of support for a balanced campaign.

Exhibit 53.1   Capital Campaign Sources of Revenue

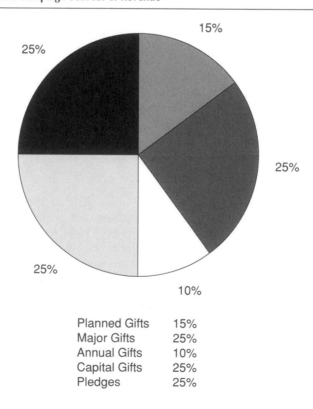

Planned Gifts	15%
Major Gifts	25%
Annual Gifts	10%
Capital Gifts	25%
Pledges	25%

53.4   TYPES OF CAMPAIGN GIFTS

(a) The Windfall

Significant, unexpected gifts, often called windfall gifts, can appear at any time, but often materialize in a campaign. Such a gift is a surprise only to the organization, because the donor has intended
to make the gift for some time. These gifts may come about as the result of a comprehensive, integrated marketing program that has delivered a cohesive, continuous message over time. Marketing
identifies and attracts windfall gifts. The combination of a solid planned giving marketing program,
coupled with a systematic annual giving program and an overall strong development effort, cultivates donors even in the absence of personal contact.

(b) The Structured Gift

One of the most important aspects of a planned giving officer's job is to assist in promoting structured gifts. A structured gift assists donors in funding a particular campaign goal. Because of their
complexity, structured gifts require initiative, specialized planned giving knowledge, and personal-
ization. Typically, most structured gifts include several components:

- An annual gift to provide regular, unrestricted support to the organization

- A major gift that is an outright gift for immediate use

- A planned gift to be used by the organization in the future

The planned giving component of a structured gift is most often a gift that provides income
to a donor during life, or it may come from the donor's estate.

(c) The Ultimate Gift

The ultimate gift, a once-in-a-lifetime gift, is typically 10 to 1,000 times larger than the donor's previously largest gift or previous cumulative gifts. The challenges of a capital campaign tend to bring out
the best in donors and increase giving substantially. For many donors, the ultimate gift is a planned
gift. The tax and financial benefits of a planned gift enhance the ability and capacity of a donor to
make his ultimate gift. The donor who makes an ultimate gift to an organization usually has a strong
bond with the organization and has been giving at lower levels for many years. Exhibit 53.2 shows a
gift pyramid for a campaign.

53.5   PLANNED GIVING TRAINING

Training in planned giving becomes more important than ever when an organization enters into a
capital campaign. Training must be conducted not only for development staff, but for external staff,
volunteers, and board members. During a campaign there is a frenzy of activity, with many individuals pursuing prospects for gifts. An effective training program prevents the dissemination of incor-
rect information to prospects and staff. The focus of training in a campaign is twofold.

1. There is a need to sensitize staff members and volunteers to planned giving concepts.
   Even staff and volunteers who have only casual contact with prospects must be made
   aware of general planned giving concepts, such as the fact that a planned gift can provide
   a donor with a lifetime income.

■   539   ■

2. Those who have extensive contact with prospects must be more conversant in all aspects of planned giving and, consequently, need more advanced training. Members of the board of trustees also should understand planned giving concepts, because they are likely to be in contact with prospects who have significant potential.

53.6 PROFESSIONAL ADVISORS

Outside professional advisors are extremely important to a capital campaign. Local attorneys, accountants, trust officers, and investment advisors must be informed of the scope and purpose of an organization's campaign, because often they are consulted by donors for advice regarding charitable giving and can suggest which charities should benefit. If the nonprofit has not yet established a professional advisory committee, there is no better time to do it than in anticipation of a campaign. If a committee has already been formed, there is no better time to invigorate the committee. See Chapter 22 for a discussion on ways to form a professional advisory committee.

53.7 PLANNED GIVING AND THE CASE STATEMENT

Case statements (discussed in Chapter 19) often describe the needs of a nonprofit, but fail to describe the ways in which donors can make gifts to assist in meeting those needs. Planned giving officers can be instrumental in marketing campaign objectives while promoting different ways to provide support. In addition, a planned giving officer can provide valuable input on the many types of assets that can be used to fund gifts in the campaign, including underutilized assets such as stocks, bonds, mutual funds, closely held stock, real estate, and tangible personal property. A bal-

Exhibit 53.2 The Campaign Gift Pyramid

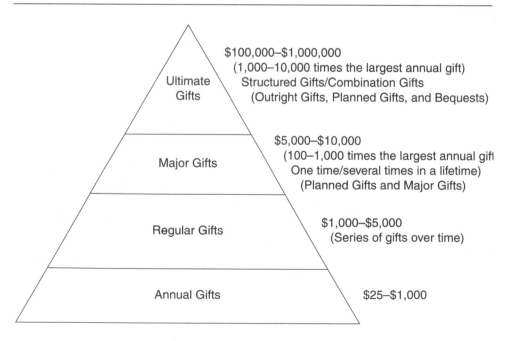

anced case statement that illustrates funding opportunities coupled with information on ways to give and the various assets that can be used is essential to campaign success.

53.8 CONCLUSION

Planned gifts provide an important giving opportunity in a capital campaign. Planned gifts can be used to provide support for buildings, endowment, and programs. Most major gifts include a planned giving component, which can be used to establish an organization's nucleus fund before a campaign is announced.

Stewardship and Planned Gifts

54.1   INTRODUCTION

What is stewardship? In a nondevelopment context, *stewardship* can be defined as the act of managing and supervising another's property while caring for the owner of that property. In the development world, stewardship represents all of that and more, and means many different things to donors, professional advisors, and development officers. Stewardship begins with thanking donors and donors' families for their gifts to our charities. If the gift is a planned gift, stewardship includes administering the gift properly at the nonprofit and providing donors with appropriate financial information about their gift. Stewardship also includes reporting information to a donor about the use of donated funds and ensuring that the donor is satisfied with the way the gift is used. A critical part of the stewardship process is continued cultivation that may include, at some point, soliciting the donor for additional gifts.

Stewardship is important because it is the lifeblood of all nonprofit organizations that hope to establish and continue long relationships with donors and their families. It is one way that the organization shows that it cares about the donor and the donor's gift, and helps demonstrate the permanence of the organization and its future. Sustained stewardship demonstrates to a donor that he is a partner with the charity in providing valuable services. Stewardship maintains a donor's positive feelings about the charity that resulted in the donor's first gift, and is a step in producing additional gifts.

Gift planners can employ conventional development stewardship methods and can enhance those methods using approaches unique to planned giving. This chapter focuses on four key functions of stewarding planned gifts: gift acknowledgment, gift-administration, donor recognition, and continued cultivation. The chapter ends with an examination of stewardship of endowed funds, which presents special challenges.

54.2 CREATE A STEWARDSHIP PLAN

To be serious about stewardship efforts, create a plan that involves various internal players at the nonprofit organization, such as trustees, volunteers, and nonprofit staff members. In the plan, outline those areas that make up the stewardship process. They may include the four functions stated earlier: gift acknowledgment, gift administration, donor recognition, and cultivation. Include timetables for completing various tasks, and begin the stewardship process at the time a donor makes her first gift. Allocate a budget for stewardship efforts; otherwise the process may not be taken seriously. The planned giving staff members should meet regularly to update the plan and report on stewardship activities.

54.3 GIFT ACKNOWLEDGMENT

A donor should be acknowledged by those at the nonprofit who were involved with the gift and by a senior administrator or manager who can express appreciation on behalf of the entire organization. Donors should be thanked appropriately, but the charity must be cautious not to thank the donor so many times that it is perceived as wasting money. The following sections discuss acknowledgment by the director of planned giving or the development professional involved with the gift; the individual for whose benefit the gift was made, such as a dean, professor, physician, or administrator; a board member or trustee; the president of the nonprofit; and the financial administrator.

(a) Director of Planned Giving

If the planned giving officer and the donor discuss the donor's potential gift and the donor is now ready to make the gift, the planned giving officer should ascertain what assets will be used to fund it and provide detailed delivery instructions for making the gift. These delivery instructions allow the securities to be transferred from the donor directly to the nonprofit or from one financial institution to another, with minimum delay.

After providing delivery instructions, the planned giving officer should notify the charity's financial administrator that a gift will arrive either by a check in the mail or by electronic transfer. If securities are being sent directly to the nonprofit or through its outside brokerage house, notify appropriate individuals that the gift securities will be delivered.

(i) Telephone Call to Donor. Good stewardship puts the donor's mind at rest that the gift was received, no matter how large or small the gift. When the gift arrives, the planned giving officer should inform the donor first by telephone that the gift has reached its destination either at the planned giving office or at the charity's financial administrator's institution. Avoid the embarrassment of being called weeks later by a donor asking if the gift arrived. Tell the donor that a written acknowledgment will follow shortly.

(ii) Thank-You Note to Donor. The planned giving officer should then write a personal thank-you letter to the donor expressing appreciation for the gift. The letter may also discuss how the nonprofit intends to use the gift and confirm any restrictions placed on it by the donor. The letter

should outline any remaining steps for completing the gift, including whether the nonprofit needs a signed instrument of transfer from the donor for a gift to the pooled income fund or that a signed gift annuity contract is in the mail to the donor. A sample acknowledgment letter appears in the Appendix, CD-ROM Documentation, Correspondence.

(b) Individual Honored by the Gift

If the donor made the gift in honor of a living individual, such as a physician at the hospital or rabbi at the temple, and the gift is not anonymous, notify the honoree immediately. Send the honoree a note informing him that a gift was made in his honor and suggest that he send a personal thank-you note to the donor. The planned giving officer should include the donor's address so that the acknowledgment note can be written quickly. Of course, the honoree may have been involved in the gift process and already be aware of the gift. However, a reminder accompanied by an address facilitates the honoree's thank you.

(c) President/Executive Director of the Nonprofit

The president, executive director, or chief executive officer of the nonprofit also should send an acknowledgment letter to the donor. Charities usually establish guidelines for when the president thanks a donor; at many organizations, donors receive an acknowledgment letter from the president only for gifts of $1,000 or more. A letter written by the development office and signed by the president is more than a symbolic gesture; it can have great meaning for the donor, who feels that the gift is important enough to be called to the president's attention. Such letters are usually generic and are drafted by the development office for the president to sign.

(d) Trustee of the Nonprofit

If a trustee participated in the donor's gift or knows the donor, the planned giving officer should ask the trustee to write a thank-you letter to the donor. If the trustee knows the donor personally, it is especially important for the trustee to acknowledge the gift. Like a letter from the president, acknowledgment from a trustee helps a donor feel that the gift is especially important to the charity.

(e) Financial Administrator/Nonprofit's Business or Treasurer's Office

When receiving a gift from a donor, the planned giving officer needs to obtain information from the donor so that the financial administrator or the nonprofit's business or treasurer's office can confirm the charitable income tax deduction and send the donor year-end tax information. Personal and financial data often are needed to properly complete the gift. Such data include the donor's Social Security number, date of birth, and, if securities were used to fund the gift, the securities' acquisition date and cost basis. It is easiest to obtain this information as soon as the donor says that a gift will be made or completes the gift, so that the planned giving officer does not have to return repeatedly to the donor for more information. Although the donor is responsible for correctly valuing her own charitable income tax deduction, in practice nonprofits and asset managers use planned giving software to calculate the remainder value of a deferred gift. Although this is helpful to a donor and her advisors, the donor must realize that the amounts used on the tax return are her responsibility and no one else's.

The planned gift should be acknowledged by the nonprofit's financial administrator or treasurer's office. A letter from the financial administrator helps to establish credibility with the donor and begins their relationship. The letter should provide financial calculations that confirm the donor's charitable income tax deduction originally estimated by the nonprofit. It should also give the donor the name and telephone number of a contact other than the planned giving officer if the donor has a question and wants to speak to the financial administrator or asset manager. The planned giving officer should, however, always be the primary contact for the donor.

The planned giving officer should discuss in advance the type of relationship the organization wishes the administrator and asset manager to have with donors. Most donors' questions can be answered by the planned giving officer, but occasionally a donor poses a question that goes beyond the planned giving officer's expertise. The financial administrator or asset manager always should telephone the planned giving officer before initiating contact with a donor and report back quickly to the nonprofit when a donor calls with a problem or question. Copies of all correspondence should be sent to the charity.

(f) Substantiation Letter from the Charity

See Section 54.3(c) for a discussion of substantiation letters to donors.

54.4 GIFT ADMINISTRATION

A second area that is important to planned giving stewardship is providing the finest possible service when administering a donor's planned gift. It is important to discuss with donors in the beginning their expectations of the gift process. Do not let surprises ruin a good donor relationship. When donors make a planned gift to a nonprofit, they should know when they will receive an acknowledgment letter from the asset manager. The donors should expect to receive distribution checks on time, with the proper amount due. Checks should be deposited directly if requested. Donors should know when tax information will arrive. Strong communication from the beginning establishes appropriate expectations for both the charity and the donor about the gift process. This section examines some important issues related to the administration of a planned gift.

(a) Date of Gift

The nonprofit, upon receiving a donor's gift, must properly determine the date of the gift, which is covered fully in Chapter 30. The date is important to the donor in the case of a securities gift because it determines the value of the gift, which in turn determines the donor's charitable income tax deduction. It also may affect the donor's club level or giving category. If the gift is made at the end of the year, the date determines the year the donor's gift was made and consequently the year in which the donor is able to claim a charitable income tax deduction. The date of the gift should be included in a letter to the donor that acknowledges the gift and confirms tax information.

(b) Planned Giving Documents

Once the date of the gift is determined and the gift is acknowledged by those involved with the gift, the donor or the nonprofit may be waiting for proper documentation to complete the gift. This section examines several documents necessary to finalize a gift.

(i) Instrument of Transfer for a Pooled Income Fund Gift. Sometimes, when a donor makes a pooled income fund gift, the donor transfers the assets before completing an instrument of transfer. The instrument of transfer is a crucial document that should be completed prior to or concurrently with making the gift. The trustee of the pooled income fund cannot assign units in the fund without this completed document. The planned giving officer should immediately send the instrument of transfer to the donor or telephone to remind the donor to return the form to the charity or the financial administrator. For a complete discussion of pooled income fund instruments of transfer, see Chapter 24. Sample instruments of transfer appear in Appendix, CD-ROM Documentation, IRS Forms.

(ii) Subsequent or Additional Gift Agreement Form for a Gift to the Pooled Income Fund. If the donor previously made a gift to the nonprofit's pooled income fund, he may use the instrument

of transfer again or may complete a subsequent gift agreement form, a shorter form that allows the donor to direct the second gift in the same way as the first gift. The donor can send the subsequent gift agreement form either to the charity or directly to the financial administrator. Like the instrument of transfer, this should be completed prior to or simultaneously with making the gift. A sample subsequent gift agreement form appears in Appendix, CD-ROM Documentation, Agreements.

(iii) Gift Annuity Contract. The gift annuity process is not complete until the donor receives a charitable gift annuity contract. Only the nonprofit is required to sign the contract, although some charities also have the donor sign it to involve the donor in the gift process. The gift annuity contract should be sent to the donor as soon as the gift is completed. The date of the donor's gift is the date the gift is received, not the date the contract is signed. A sample gift annuity contract appears in Appendix, CD-ROM Documentation, Agreements.

(iv) Bequest Intention Form. Some nonprofits ask donors to complete a bequest intention form when the donor indicates that she is leaving a gift to the charity in a will or trust. Many donors choose not to complete such a form, fearing that by completing such a form, a legally binding commitment will be made to the charity. Many donors are uncertain of the size of their estates and therefore their gifts at death. However, a bequest intention form is not legally binding unless it specifically states that the donor intends to create a binding commitment or obligation. If the nonprofit decides to ask a donor to complete a bequest intention form, it should be sent to the donor only after thanking him for the bequest intention. For a full discussion of bequests and bequest intention forms, see Chapter 29. A sample bequest intention form appears in Appendix, CD-ROM Documentation, Administrative Documents.

(v) Internal Revenue Service (IRS) Form 8283. When a donor makes a gift of tangible personal property worth $500 or more to a nonprofit, the charity may wish to provide the donor with IRS Form 8283, Noncash Charitable Contributions, when the donor makes the gift. The donor completes this form and attaches it to her tax return for the year the gift is made. Although the donor is responsible for obtaining and completing Form 8283, sending the form to the donor shows that the organization understands and complies with IRS regulations and wishes to help make the process easier. Check that the form is the latest version because it is regularly updated. For a full discussion of Form 8283, see Chapter 33.

(c) Substantiation Requirements

As covered in Chapter 37, in 1994 the IRS changed its substantiation requirements for donors who make charitable gifts of $250 or more, obligating the nonprofit to disclose if goods or services were received in exchange for the gifts, and for donors who make gifts over $75 and receive something other than a token gift in exchange for their donation. Before the law changed, a canceled check provided adequate proof for the IRS that a gift was made.

The current substantiation rules require that the charity send the donor an acknowledgment letter stating the date of the gift and the amount of the donor's gift, if it was made with cash. If the gift was made with property other than cash, such as securities or tangible personal property, a description of the property, such as "200 shares of ABC stock," is required; the actual value of the securities or tangible personal property should not be included, at least not in the required acknowledgment letter. If the donor receives no goods or services, the acknowledgment letter must nevertheless include the language "no goods or services were received in exchange for the gift." Without this language, the acknowledgment will not satisfy the requirements of the Internal Revenue Code. Anything received by the donor in exchange for the gift is commonly referred to as a "quid pro quo," and the donor must be advised that he can only take as a charitable income tax deduction the amount of the gift that exceeds the value of the quid pro quo. Any solicitation for a gift that entitles the donor to attend a dinner or event or anything of significant value must contain information about the amount that the donor may deduct.

Planned gift acknowledgment letters require additional substantiation language because of the benefit, the lifetime income, that a donor receives from making a planned gift. A planned gift acknowledgment letter—one written for a charitable gift annuity, charitable remainder trust, or gift to a pooled income fund—should include the fact that the donor reserved or received an income interest from the gift.

Many donors are aware of the requirements. Charities should provide an acknowledgment letter or receipt to the donor as soon as the donor's gift is made. Sample acknowledgment letters that satisfy 1994 IRS substantiation requirements are in Appendix, CD-ROM Documentation, Correspondence.

(d) Copies of Correspondence to Donor's Financial Advisor

Effective stewardship includes sending appropriate copies of documents to a financial advisor, certified public accountant, or attorney, if requested by the donor. At the beginning of the gift process, discuss the donor's expectations. Some donors insist that their financial advisor be copied on everything, whereas others prefer to keep the relationship between the donor and the charity.

(e) Original Documents

It is best to keep original gift documents at the charity because the organization is usually well equipped to maintain proper records. Send copies of signed documents to the donor, financial advisor, and the charity's outside financial administrator. If the donor insists on keeping the original document, the nonprofit may choose to produce two originals and give one to the donor. Whatever procedure is chosen, be consistent.

(f) Correspondence from the Financial Administrator

The charity as trustee is ultimately responsible if the financial administrator makes a mistake or is late sending information to a donor, and an unhappy donor is unlikely to make another gift. Determining what the administrator will send to the donor, and when, is critical. Discuss with the administrator the timetable for sending:

- *Initial acknowledgment letter*, indicating the donor's charitable income tax deduction and the date of the donor's gift for tax purposes. The administrator should send this letter upon receiving the gift. This letter may be more tax-oriented than the acknowledgment from the planned giving officer.

- *Distribution checks.* These should be sent according to the terms of the planned gift, which is likely to be semi-annually, quarterly, or monthly. Donors carefully watch the mail for their distribution checks, so they should arrive on a timely basis.

- *Tax information*, including the donor's K-1 and 1099-R Letters. These federal income information letters classify income for tax purposes. The K-1 letter shows income earned from a donor's pooled income fund gift and charitable remainder trust; Form 1099-R gives the same information for income earned from a donor's charitable gift annuity. These letters must be sent as early as possible for donors to complete their tax returns.

54.5 DONOR RECOGNITION

A third, important form of stewardship takes place when the planned giving office recognizes the donor's gift. This section examines several typical forms of recognition, including a planned giving society, events, plaques, names in publications, donor profiles, token gifts, press coverage, and requests for anonymity.

STEWARDSHIP AND PLANNED GIFTS

(a) Planned Giving Society

A popular way for nonprofits to recognize planned giving donors is through a planned giving society established to honor those who have made any type of planned gift to the nonprofit. Donors can be invited to attend an annual program that recognizes donors by name and announces new members of the planned giving society. Consider awarding attendees a token pin or certificate at the event. Planned giving societies provide donors with a sense of community and recognition for a gift that is often not highlighted in any other way by the charity.

(b) Small Events or Receptions

A small, private event also can be used to thank a donor for making a planned gift. If the donor made a gift in honor of a particular physician, dean, or administrator, gather those involved with the gift for a luncheon or small reception at the nonprofit. An intimate event affords the donor the opportunity to say thank you directly to the honored individual and in turn gives the honoree a chance to thank the donor. This personal meeting serves to cement the donor's ties to the charity and helps to assure the donor that the gift will be used in the manner requested.

(c) Plaques

Another form of donor recognition is a plaque used to memorialize a donor's gift. Many donors enjoy seeing their names on walls and buildings and appreciate having their pictures taken next to the plaque erected in honor of their gift. Celebrate what the donor has done, and host a photographic session and later send the donor the developed photographs. The donors can share the pictures with friends and family and potentially create new relationships for others with the charity.

(d) Donor Name in Publication

Donors also can be recognized by having their names listed in an organization's donor report. Many nonprofits produce a report each year that lists that year's donors and includes a separate listing of the organization's planned giving donors. At an arts organization, such as a symphony or opera, the donor report may be the playbill that accompanies each production.

Some donors are delighted to be profiled in an organizational magazine or newsletter. Interviewing a donor for such a publication gives the planned giving officer a chance to talk again with the donor about the gift and allows the donor to reiterate why she chose to support the charity. Most donors who allow their stories to be told feel very positive about the charity and are likely to be repeat donors.

(e) Use of Token Gifts

Many nonprofits thank donors by sending them small gifts that bear the charity's name. Examples include key chains, pens, scarves, neckties, and calendars. These token gifts can, however, be viewed in contradictory ways. Many donors, especially older ones and donors who live far away from the charity, enjoy receiving them. They act as reminders of the charity, and donors often enjoy the recognition that comes from these items when they wear them or show them to others. Other donors, however, feel that the charity is wasting money by purchasing such items. They feel that these tokens are unnecessary and that the nonprofit's financial resources would be better spent for a use the donor intended, such as improving education, furthering the arts, or conducting medical research. Some donors feel that if the charity spends money on token gifts, donors' contributions are not needed. In determining the usefulness of such tokens, the development office should examine the charity's donor base and the history of using these items and use gifts that are appropriate to the amount of the donor's gift and the image that the nonprofit organization wishes to convey.

(f) Press Coverage

Large gifts that provide a special or unique public service and that name buildings warrant press coverage. Involve the media when possible to cover a special event or to promote a major gift to the nonprofit. If the nonprofit is located in a small town or is the dominant organization in the community, the local paper usually will cover the gift. Some donors enjoy the public recognition and appreciate a photograph and press release.

(g) Request for Anonymity

Donors' permission must be obtained prior to including names in a donor list, as some donors request anonymity. Send each donor a letter asking for permission to list his name in a donor report or charity publication. Provide an opportunity for donors to list their names in the form they like. For example, "Mrs. Robert Jones" might prefer to be listed as "Esther Jones." In the letter, enclose a self-addressed stamped envelope with a card indicating permission to use the donor's name. See Appendix, CD-ROM Documentation, Correspondence, for a sample letter and form.

When contacting donors for permission to publicize their names, the planned giving officer may be surprised at the number of new business opportunities that arise. This is especially true when confirming that a donor has included a gift in her will. When a donor does not respond to a request for permission, the planned giving officer should call the donor. Despite what was thought, the planned giving officer may learn that the donor has not included the charity in the will, or that the donor is considering a bequest and the telephone call is a wonderful way to move the process along. Some donors request information about life income gifts from the planned giving officer during these calls.

54.6 CONTINUED CULTIVATION AND SOLICITATION FOR ADDITIONAL GIFT

Stewardship involves building relationships and ensuring that donors receive consistent and sustained cultivation. Cultivation includes visiting donors, sending letters and cards, periodic events, and reporting regularly on the use of funds.

(a) Donor Visits

Personally visiting a donor gives the donor a chance to talk about the gift administration process, the donor's expectations, and the level of satisfaction the donor has with the nonprofit. It also affords the planned giving officer the opportunity to update the donor on news from the nonprofit and reiterate the organization's financial needs. Visits let donors know that they, and their gifts, are important to the charity. Most significant gifts to nonprofits do not occur without one or more personal visits.

(b) Letters

Another form of cultivation includes sending donors informational letters or newsletters about new issues and programs currently being addressed or created at the nonprofit. This type of letter is especially appreciated by donors who live far from the nonprofit.

(c) Cards: Holiday, Birthday, Get Well, Sympathy

As a relationship with a donor develops, it may become appropriate to send special cards. During the holidays, a card extending season's greetings may be appreciated. Avoid religious overtones, unless the charity is a religious organization. Some donors enjoy receiving a card on their birthday; others find it too personal and are offended that the charity would send birthday greetings. If a donor becomes ill, it also may be appropriate to send get well wishes. Some charities send "thinking of you" cards at the time of a loved one's death.

At times, it may be necessary to send a sympathy card if someone close to the donor has passed away. Extend sympathies on behalf of the charity, and be sure to contact others at the charity who may need to know about the death. If a card is sent to the family of an individual who remembered the charity in her will, caution must be exercised to avoid being perceived as hovering in anticipation of a gift.

(d) Regular Events

Most charities host annual events to keep donors connected to the nonprofit. Events may be regular lectures, dinners, or seminars. These events remind donors that they are part of a larger giving community and can regularly reinforce the charity's need for support.

54.7 ENDOWED FUNDS

Stewardship at many nonprofits includes administering the organization's named endowed funds. In cooperation with the designated office, the planned giving office should assist in adhering to fund restrictions, ensuring that funds are used in accordance with the donor's wishes, and reporting to donors on the use of the endowed fund.

(a) Use of Funds

Ideally, the planned giving officer is involved in establishing the donor's endowed fund, but in many circumstances this is not the case, especially with older funds. Proper stewardship may involve assisting departments to actually use the funds, as well as use them according to the donor's wishes outlined in the will or trust. Sometimes department heads and administrators are unaware that their department has use of a particular fund, and alerting the department chair or recipient that money is available for use can help ensure that the money is used as the donor wishes. It also promotes cooperation between departments that can lead to enhanced development efforts.

At organizations with many endowed funds, it can be difficult to ensure that restrictions on funds are observed. Once a department head has use of the funds, it is possible that he will construe the terms more liberally than the donor intended. For example, a donor may designate through a bequest that funds be used for medical research at a hospital; using the funds to travel to a medical conference may be too general a use of the gift. The planned giving officer or treasurer's office must explain the restrictions on a fund to the department head and expect that they will be followed. If there is ever a question about the use of funds, the charity may wish to conduct an internal audit.

The planned giving organization may want to do an inventory of all the existing endowed funds at the organization, then determine which funds have donors who are still alive and need an annual report on the use of the fund. Putting the list together is an excellent opportunity to contact existing donors, which may result in additional gifts. Those department heads and administrators also may need to be contacted, which can strengthen ties between these individuals and those in the planned giving office.

(b) Reporting to the Donor

Reporting on an annual basis about the use of the donor's fund and its investment is another important part of stewardship. Once a donor establishes a fund, communicating to the donor that the fund is being used as the donor wishes and that it is achieving its intended purpose serves as a wonderful way to maintain relations with the donor. A report should inform the donor of the amount of principal and income available in the fund, how the fund is invested, what was spent from the fund that year, and how the money was used. If something special or unusual was done with the fund, it should be noted in the report. A proper accounting can encourage additional contributions to the fund; incomplete or no reporting can produce smaller or no additional contributions. A sample report to the donor is also included in Appendix, CD-ROM Documentation, Correspondence.

A particularly important part of reporting to the donor is having that year's fund recipient write a letter to the donor describing the importance of the funds to the recipient and how the funds were actually used. For example, a scholarship student who used an award from a scholarship fund to study French in Paris could send the donor a wonderful letter describing the study abroad. A letter from the fund recipient can have dramatically more impact on the donor than any letter from the development office staff.

CHAPTER FIFTY-FIVE

Institutionally Related Foundations

55.1 INTRODUCTION

Over the years, nonprofit organizations have recognized the importance of establishing charitable foundations to support their mission. These organizations, commonly called *institutionally related foundations*, raise funds on behalf of the nonprofit, administer planned gifts, and oversee the investment of the foundation's endowment and donors' endowed funds. The foundation manages and invests an endowment, providing a permanent source of support to the nonprofit. As part of the endowment, donors' endowed funds are managed and invested. To assist the planned giving program, the foundation may manage and invest one or more life income gift funds. The foundation's accounting office can process life income gifts and issue annuitant and life income beneficiaries' checks. This chapter provides an overview on the increasingly important role that institutionally related foundations play in fundraising and fund management.

55.2 BENEFITS OF INSTITUTIONALLY RELATED FOUNDATIONS

There are many benefits to establishing a foundation. First, institutionally related foundations are autonomous and independent and avoid the restrictive regulations and scrutiny that affect the affiliated nonprofit. This is especially true when the affiliated nonprofit is a state university, municipal hospital, or charity sponsored by a government unit, which can be subject to intense public scrutiny. Second, unlike state funds, which are lost if not spent, foundation funds may be rolled over, accrued for future use, returned to principal, or a combination of these. Finally, contributions to foundations do not affect the state's funding formula, which allocates state support to public universities, hospitals, museums, and libraries. Often nonprofits that raise money for their operations are concerned that success in fundraising can cause a reduction in future state distributions.

Many of the functions of a foundation complement a planned giving program. A foundation can assist a planned giving office in the administration and management of planned gifts. Donors, too, benefit from a foundation's financially related departments with access to investment managers. Because foundations have become so popular in recent years, planned giving officers should understand their organizational functions and operational benefits. Planned giving officers may encounter a foundation in one of several contexts:

- The planned giving officer may work for a nonprofit organization that is establishing a foundation.

- The planned giving officer may recommend the formation of the foundation to manage planned gifts and the endowment.

- A donor may direct a percentage of the remainder of a charitable remainder trust to be distributed to an entity that is an institutionally related foundation.

- A donor or an organization may be confused about the differences between an institutionally related foundation, supporting organizations, or a private foundation.

Many planned giving officers find that institutionally related foundations enhance their fundraising efforts. Foundations provide an environment and resources that foster the business of planned giving.

55.3 CONSIDERATIONS IN ESTABLISHING A FOUNDATION

The process of securing and maintaining the status of a foundation is expensive, complex, and, in most cases, takes 6 to 12 months to receive Internal Revenue Service (IRS) approval. The IRS has increasingly scrutinized entities that wish to establish themselves as Section 501(c)(3), tax-exempt organizations. Many groups who wish to establish foundations become discouraged by the formidable obstacles placed in their way. Securing the status is not the end but the beginning of the process, since running a foundation takes considerable investment of staff, time, and money.

To qualify as a foundation, organizations must meet one or more of the charitable purposes included in Section 501(c)(3) of the Internal Revenue Code (IRC):

- Religious

- Charitable, including organizations providing relief to the poor, distressed, and underprivileged; advancement of religion, education, or science or for construction and maintenance of public buildings or monuments; for lessening the burdens of government; or for the promotion of social welfare

- Scientific

- Testing for public safety

- Literary

- Educational

The organization must have a public, rather than private, focus, and no part of the net earnings may inure to the benefit of a shareholder or an individual. In addition, the organization must not expend substantial amounts in the conducting of activities or for the purpose of influencing legislation by contacting directly or encouraging the public to contact members of a legislative body for the purpose of proposing, supporting, or opposing legislation. The organization also must not engage in opposition to the election of a candidate in support of a political office.

Foundations wishing to qualify under Section 501(c)(3) must file appropriate documentation and application Form 1023 with the IRS to make the nonprofit organization exempt from federal income taxes. The application must detail specifically the intended charitable purposes of the nonprofit organization. In order to qualify as a foundation, the organization must secure a determination that is to receive contributions of a maximum deduction. It is not a private foundation in addition to Section 501(c)(3) status, it may qualify under 501(c)(1).

Once established, the foundation must file annual reports with the IRS and, in most cases, with the appropriate state agency, such as the secretary of state or attorney general's office. At this point, the foundation has a separate legal identity and is an independent and autonomous nonprofit organization. To avoid a potential conflict of interest, the foundation usually retains an attorney to serve as general counsel and an accounting firm to prepare financial statements, which are audited at least once every other year.

55.4 THE CHARITY AND THE FOUNDATION

Generally, a charity establishes foundations because the charity itself is incapable of performing the central functions of a foundation: fundraising, endowment building, fund management, and organizing volunteer leadership. Although these functions are central to their survival, many nonprofits do not have the fundraising structures and administrative machinery to perform these sophisticated functions. A foundation's sole objective is to meet these goals; therefore, nonprofit organizations are increasingly establishing institutionally related foundations.

Usually the foundation is established for the purpose of assisting the nonprofit to help it achieve its mission, and funds raised can be used for no other purpose than for the benefit of the nonprofit. The purposes can include:

- Fundraising on behalf of the related charity

- Managing and investing major and planned gifts that benefit the related charity

- Building an endowment and investing donors' endowed funds

- Enlisting volunteers and establishing boards and committees

- Organizing capital campaigns

The charity and the institutionally related foundation can share responsibilities, maximize resources, and complement efforts. Both staff and donors benefit from this arrangement. Quality services can be provided to donors, and there can be an equitable division of labor to do the job well.

To establish a relationship, an agreement between the institutionally related foundation and the nonprofit is drafted that defines the relationship between the responsibilities of each organization and the division of labor for fundraising, management, and investment of gifts.

Institutionally related foundations have a close relationship with the nonprofit organization, and, to donors, the relationship should appear seamless. The foundation has a separate legal and tax identity and its own federal tax identification number. The foundation may hold restricted and nonrestricted funds and enter into gift agreements with donors for the administration of those funds. The foundation also may hold, manage, and invest the nonprofit's segregated funds, sometimes for the benefit of the nonprofit community, with the foundation's funds. The agreement also provides for disclosure to donors and nonprofit officers about investment strategies, financial statements, membership, and committee initiatives. The nonprofit may be responsible for providing financial support for staffing the foundation and for compensating the foundation for the costs incurred in fundraising. The nonprofit also may provide office space and furnishings, insurance, utilities, and maintenance to the foundation. Prior to establishing new programs or fundraising campaigns, a mutual agreement approved by the boards of the foundation and the nonprofit is obtained to authorize such action. According to the provisions of the agreement, the terms may be amended and either party may terminate the relationship in writing.

Generally, members of the foundation's board do not receive compensation for serving on the board of directors; the foundation may never issue any capital stock. The foundations must adhere to restrictions imposed by donors on restricted gifts, as would any charitable organization, and adopt fund accounting practices to ensure that contributions are used for the purpose designated by the donor. Because institutionally related foundations hold donors' endowed funds, checks generally should be payable to the foundation rather than to the affiliated nonprofit. Unrestricted gifts may be used at the discretion of the board of the foundation.

55.5 THE FOUNDATION'S ORGANIZATIONAL FRAMEWORK

The foundation's legal framework consists of its articles of organization, bylaws, and governing board of directors (or trustees), which is organized as a committee structure. It is important to understand the organizational framework because donors often ask questions about the institutionally related foundation and its committee structure. In addition, a planned giving officer may be able to nominate financially savvy volunteers for membership.

(a) Articles of Orgnization

The articles outline the general purposes and powers of the nonprofit organization. The articles are the first document adopted by the incorporators of the nonprofit organization.

(b) Bylaws

The bylaws define the purpose of the organization, establish the fiscal year, set the number of members (if any) and directors, establish terms of office, and authorize the election of officers. Annual meetings are required in accordance with the foundation's bylaws. Apart from the formal and legal requirements, the annual meeting serves as an opportunity to conduct the foundation's business and to cultivate and solicit board members. Annual meetings also provide opportunities to invite guests who may be considered for membership. Planned giving workshops provide opportunities to involve the members and discuss appropriate gift options.

(c) Members

Many states no longer require the nonprofit corporation to have members. If the corporation has members, they perform many of the functions exercised by shareholders of a business corporation. If a corporation has no members, the powers then would be exercised by directors.

(d) Board of Directors

The board of directors is elected to serve and support the foundation. They should be recruited with the understanding that they should participate actively in the foundation's activities and meetings. Passive membership, "in name only," should be discouraged. Passive attendance and participation promotes passive foundations that do little to accomplish their intended purposes.

(i) Term Limits. Term limits vary according to the bylaws of the foundation but usually are two to six years in duration. A six-year term is a significant commitment for many busy volunteers. Some foundations instead provide for a three-year staggered term, with one third of the

board of directors terms expiring each year. To many volunteers, a three-year term is reasonable in duration, yet allows for continuity and consistency. Depending on the bylaws, members may be reappointed immediately or after a one-year absence from the board.

(ii) Size of the Board. The board's size can vary from as few as 9 to as many as 100 depending on the foundation. Small boards necessarily promote participation but limit diversity. Larger boards may signal less involvement and sometimes a lack of commitment. Extremely large boards are unwieldy and are a challenge to manage. An executive committee is vital in the case of a large board, frequently the executive committee effectively functions as the board if the board numbers more than 25.

(iii) Qualification of Board Members. Board members should be appointed to represent a variety of perspectives based on the organization's needs. Because one of the key responsibilities of all board members is fundraising, members should be selected who are willing to "give or get." The following criteria should be considered when appointing prospective board members:

- Occupation
- Regional diversity
- Cultural diversity
- Geographic representation
- Socioeconomic diversity
- Education
- Political diversity
- Gender diversity
- Racial or ethnic diversity
- Age diversity

55.6 COMMITTEES AND THEIR FUNCTIONS

The bylaws may permit or expressly prescribe the creation of several board committees of the foundation. Each of the committees has distinct functions and responsibilities. A discussion of these committees and their responsibilities follows. Donors' comfort level often is raised when they understand that several committees oversee the work of the foundation. Donors want to know that funds are managed, restrictions are honored, and administrative oversight is provided.

(a) Executive Committee

The executive committee is responsible for establishing the foundation's policies and procedures and for conducting the foundation's general business. The board, through an administrative officer, executive secretary, or executive director, is also responsible for the supervision of day-to-day operations of the foundation. The executive committee members can consist of the foundation's president, vice-president, secretary, treasurer, and other members elected by the board of directors for a one- to three-year term. As a policymaking committee, it is responsible for promulgating policies, rules, and regulations to accomplish the purposes of the foundation. The committee has the power to enter into contracts and sign legal instruments and documents on behalf of the foundation.

In many ways, the charity and its institutionally related foundation operate on parallel tracks. Like the charity, the foundation, through its committees, accepts gifts, including planned and major gifts; gifts of noncash assets such as real estate, nonmarketable securities, or tangible personal property; and restricted gifts consistent with the foundation's gift acceptance policy. See Chapter 33 for more information on the gift review committee. Managing and adhering to provisions in restricted gifts pose challenges for many nonprofits, and a foundation may provide an appropriate vehicle to screen, evaluate, accept, and manage such gifts. Through its review committee, the foundation can provide a valuable service for the benefit of the nonprofit organization in managing unique gifts and gifts that fall outside the foundation's gift acceptance policy.

(b) Nominating Committee

The nominating committee, or membership committee, typically consists of a chairperson, vice-chairperson, and other members of the board of directors, who serve two- to three-year terms. The nominating committee is an important committee because of its authority to recommend appointment of key individuals for membership on the board of directors of the foundation. In addition, the committee may nominate directors to be elected to the foundation's major committees such as the audit, investment, and executive committees. These savvy individuals can greatly assist the planned giving office. They can be as helpful in identifying prospects as in exposing the planned giving office to prospective donors. A subcommittee can also be established as a planned giving committee to assist the planned giving office in the administration of their duties or for cases that require special care.

(c) Investment Committee

The investment committee consists of a chairperson, vice-chairperson, and a select number of members from the board of directors. Typically, members of the committee serve two- or three-year terms, of which one-third expire each year. The committee has the responsibility for promulgating investment policies, selecting investment managers, and overseeing the establishment of endowed funds and the foundation's endowment pool. The committee monitors performance of the investment managers and makes recommendations for the foundation's investment portfolio. Some foundation bylaws call for at least one member of the committee to be from the financial services industry. A blend of individuals from different backgrounds and experience creates a more balanced and less technical approach to the business of investing. Novices will soon find that their knowledge base has been greatly expanded by serving on an investment committee, and their "laypersons" approach can be quite effective in educating the general foundation membership. Those skilled in investments serve an important role as advisors and can translate the language of investment and its complicated concepts to the rest of the committee. This, in turn, helps to build a knowledgeable membership who can make correct decisions for the benefit of the foundation.

(d) Audit Committee

Depending on the bylaws, the audit committee serves one- to three-year terms and is composed of a chairperson, vice-chairperson, and several additional members, who in some cases are precluded from membership on the executive and investment committees. The committee is responsible for supervising the audits of the financial business affairs of the foundation. An audit committee is authorized to retain professional independent auditors to assist them in their work. The results of any audit shall be reported to the executive committee and the board; the audit committee is accountable only to the foundation's board of directors. The committee may also review compliance with criteria imposed by restricted gifts.

(e) Major Gift/Planned Giving Committee

The creation of this committee should be one of the major reasons for establishing a foundation. A primary focus of any foundation should be on fundraising, and a major gifts committee can be an effective vehicle to secure private financial support. Members who are already major donors can provide access to other individuals, local business leaders, or large corporations that may be good prospects. Members who are appointed to this committee should know in advance that their focus is on fundraising and should be challenged by its chairperson "to give or get." The committee can play an active role in planned giving. These financially sophisticated members know other prospects likely to be interested in planned giving. Marketing materials and testimonial ads may be developed featuring members of this committee. Some members may be interested in writing a column or being interviewed for a story in a planned giving newsletter.

55.7 FUNDRAISING

Foundations involved in fundraising have dozens if not hundreds of gift prospects. These prospects are overseen by one or more of the foundation's volunteers. The prospects are targeted because of their capacity to make a leadership gift and because of the relationship of the volunteer to the prospect. The foundation volunteers augment and complement the nonprofit's staff, maximizing resources and generating enhanced gift potential. Working as teams, volunteers and staff members may make calls on prospects and donors. Often, the close personal relationship between the volunteer and the prospect can help close the gift. Volunteers can host parties or other cultivational events in their homes and attract prospects who might not otherwise attend a similar event at the nonprofit organization. Volunteers have ties to the community and social, political, and cultural networks.

(a) Volunteers and Fundraising

A foundation provides a framework to organize the nonprofit's volunteers. Individuals are selected to be members of the board of directors of the foundation because of political, social, business, and financial contacts in the community and beyond. Volunteers serve as ambassadors to the foundation, bringing news to interested prospects and opening up lines of communication between the constituents and the foundation. Foundations, through their volunteer board members and committee structures, actively raise funds on behalf of the nonprofit organization, including planned and major gifts. Fundraising provides a focal point for almost all of the foundation's activities. Members are involved in identifying, screening, and evaluating prospects' gift potential, hosting cultivational events, and, with staff support, soliciting prospects and donors. Because the members are well known with their communities, they often are involved in solicitations and are influential in promoting planned giving options.

Foundation volunteers are themselves prospects for planned and major gifts. Often the individuals are invited to become foundation board members because of their previous giving records. Many may have made planned gifts, established endowed funds, or transferred valuable assets including real estate or securities to the foundation. These volunteers represent the foundation whenever they travel and typically meet other prospects who have exceptional gift potential. A planned giving orientation for foundation board members can produce leads and new gifts. These volunteers become ambassadors and can hand-carry news about the nonprofit, funding opportunities, and gift options.

The foundation and its volunteers can offer seminars in estate planning, financial planning, taxation and charitable gift planning. As the host, the foundation can be less threatening and may elicit responses from those who would not traditionally attend a staff training program. Of course, staff is involved in presenting the information that provides a comfortable venue to meet and cultivate key prospects. Because many of the foundation board members come from the professions of law, accounting, and business, they are adept at understanding and interpreting the complexities and intricacies of planned gifts. They may be knowledgeable in retirement or preretirement planning and can translate the benefits of planned giving to a donor's overall financial objectives. Board members also have access to consultants from their respective fields, who may be retained to assist the foundation. Many are active in professional organizations or associations that offer continuing education to their members. As such, they may be able to attend workshops and can identify future speakers for foundation board meetings. In cooperation with the charity, the foundation can mount a capital campaign to benefit the charity. The infrastructure of the foundation, through its committees and volunteers, can greatly enhance the prospects for success. See Chapter 53 for more on capital campaigns.

(b) Stewardship

Stewardship and recognition programs are key functions of a foundation. Most foundations track a donor's cumulative or lifetime gifts. These gifts include a donor's annual gifts, major gifts, planned gifts, spousal gifts, and gifts from a donor's affiliated business. Depending on the foundation, some or all of these gifts may be attributed to the donor's cumulative giving record. Cumulative gift programs encourage donors to reach the next gift level. Gift levels may be established at $10,000, $25,000, $50,000, $100,000 to $1 million or more. Many donors accept the challenge and make additional gifts, including planned gifts, to climb further up the ladder. Often donors enjoy the recognition that comes from being a major donor to a foundation.

Foundations are effective in providing stewardship through gift acknowledgment, particularly for donors who make planned gifts or gifts to establish an endowed fund. A volunteer from the leadership of the foundation can personally acknowledge each gift. Often this acknowledgment may mean more to the donor than simply having the vice-president of development acknowledge the gift.

55.8   MANAGING AND INVESTING ASSETS

The foundation, through its investment committee, manages the assets of the foundation, including the principal of endowed funds and life income gift funds. As described in Section 55.6 (c), the foundation selects money managers, adopts asset allocation models, and issues performance of the foundation's portfolio. The portfolio is divided into the following components:

- Domestic stocks
- International stocks
- Corporate bonds and other fixed-income investments
- Short-term cash accounts
- Miscellaneous investments

The process that a charity employs to manage its assets is discussed in detail in Chapter 44.

Because of their flexibility and investment capabilities, foundations are effective as investment managers for planned gifts. Many nonprofit organizations' administrative restrictions and limited investment alternatives thwart their ability to manage planned gifts. A foundation may serve as an appropriate investment manager for these gifts. Because a foundation has a life span that is likely to be as long as the related nonprofit's, it is an appropriate site for the administration and management of planned gifts. Foundations typically house an accounting office and comptroller who oversee cash flow and disburse checks to annuitants or life income beneficiaries These financial functions are a valuable addition to a planned giving office that needs donor-friendly support in processing planned gifts. Alternatively, the foundation can contract with an institutional financial trustee to provide these services.

Although the nonprofit may not have the staff and flexibility to accept and manage planned gifts, the foundation does. Often it is difficult for the nonprofit organization to accept gifts of property such as real estate or nonmarketable securities like closely held stock. Accepting a gift of real estate can burden the nonprofit, but a foundation is likely to have one or more members from the real estate community who serve on the major gift committee. These members are helpful in evaluating the property and are likely to know qualified appraisers and engineering firms that can conduct environmental audits on the property. They also are likely to know something about the property, its marketability, salability, and even prospective purchasers. If they do not know the answers to these issues, they usually know someone who can provide the answers. Once the property is accepted, these individuals may be able to assist in listing and marketing the property (consistent within the foundation's conflict of interest policy) so that the foundation does not become a landlord or absentee owner.

Gifts of marketable securities also can be accepted easily. Typically, the securities are sold promptly, but, if compatible with the investment theory of the foundation, they can be added to the portfolio. If the securities are sold, the proceeds provide funding to benefit purposes consistent with the donor's wishes. Gifts of nonmarketable securities such as closely held stock can also be accepted by the foundation. The foundation is likely to have investors and business executives as members who can be of value in handling such securities. The foundation may want to hold securities for a period of years on the assumption the securities will increase in value. Many charities have policies that discourage holding closely held stock for investment, but a foundation can consider holding and/or disposing of the stock as an asset or review another appropriate option.

55.9 CONCLUSION

Institutionally related foundations can complement the efforts of the affiliated nonprofit organization. The foundation exists for the sole purpose of helping the nonprofit fulfill its mission by meeting its fundraising objectives. In addition, the foundation performs a variety of sophisticated functions that improve investment management and enhance donor relationships. Foundations provide financial expertise to planned giving staff to service the needs of donors. The foundation's volunteer structure and committee assignments help to organize leadership and augment the development efforts and the bottom line.

Outside Asset Managers: Policies and Procedures

56.1 INTRODUCTION

Working well with an outside asset manager can be a satisfying and productive experience. A collaborative partnership can help ease the planned giving officer's responsibilities, produce more gifts for the nonprofit organization, and enhance the reputation of a planned giving program with donors and prospects.

An experienced outside asset manager can accomplish things that cannot be done easily in-house. The outside asset manager deals with other nonprofit organizations and can bring a wealth of information to specific situations as well as creative solutions to planned giving obstacles. When an outside asset manager presents a solution to a board member, prospect, donor, or development officer, the idea often is viewed as having added credibility.

This chapter focuses on the relationship between the planned giving office and an outside manager, addressing when to hire an asset manager, what the manager can bring to the program, how to select an asset manager, and how to make the relationship work.

56.2 WHEN TO HIRE AN OUTSIDE ASSET MANAGER

The decision to hire an outside asset manager is made when a program can no longer effectively manage its planned giving assets on its own or chooses to remove a growing program from the nonprofit organization to ease its administration. There are times when a program grows so large that the finance, treasury, or business office can no longer manage it efficiently, effectively, or happily. The administration of the program, including sending donors' checks and direct deposits, can become overwhelming for a department that does not specialize in charitable asset management. Software programs may not be sophisticated enough to track the detail required for investment transactions and financial reporting. It may become too difficult to stay current with the ever-changing tax laws. It also may be desirable to move the planned giving assets outside the charity to give the program more options for its investments. The internal financial professionals managing the assets also are generally not focused enough on development issues and strategies to work successfully with a donor or the donor's financial advisor. A good outside asset manager that focuses exclusively on planned giving and has good donor relations skills can play an integral part in closing some planned gifts. When a program grows and becomes more successful, additional outside assistance may be warranted.

Hire an outside asset manager when

- Administration becomes too unwieldy for existing in-house structure.

- A greater range of investment options for the program is needed.

- A more donor-oriented relationship is desired when dealing with financial issues.

56.3 WHAT THE ASSET MANAGER CAN BRING TO THE PLANNED GIVING PROGRAM

Determine what is needed from an outside asset manager to satisfy the program's planned giving goals. What will the outside manager bring to the program that may not currently exist in-house?

- More professional service focused exclusively on charitable gift issues

- Sophisticated investment strategies and options

- Experience from other donor situations, charities, and planned giving officers

- Ability to work in a development-oriented fashion with donors

- A partner and sounding board with whom to articulate and clarify ideas

56.4 SELECTING THE ASSET MANAGER

At some point, a decision may be made that the planned giving assets at a charitable organization need to be moved outside to a professional asset manager focused exclusively on charitable giving. This may come when a new planned giving officer joins the development office and decides that more administration and service is needed for the planned giving program than can be obtained in-house, or the planned giving program outgrows the abilities or wishes of the treasurer's office to continue to manage the program.

Often a group decision is made to move the assets. Those making the decision may include the planned giving officer, the vice-president for development, and the treasurer. Some charitable organizations may also include their investment committee in the decision-making process, and the decision to move the assets may need to be approved by the organization's board of trustees.

It is likely that the charitable organization will choose an asset manager from a number of different providers. There currently exists only a small number of experienced asset managers for planned gifts, but the charity may not necessarily seek a highly experienced manager. Instead, the charitable organization may look for an asset manager with a connection to the organization, such as a trustee who works at a bank who could manage the assets. The charitable organization may wish to have a local organization manage the program because the organization sees the community tie as potentially attractive to donors. The asset manager may act as trustee, co-trustee, or agent for the charitable organization, and their reputation is important. A local provider can sometimes add credibility and connections to the program. Determine whether the manager selection process will be derailed if the manager chosen is located on the opposite coast. Choosing an asset manager that has offices in different parts of the country could lend credibility to the program for donors who live at a distance from the nonprofit organization.

When making the decision to move the assets outside the charitable organization, ensure that all individuals who need to be involved in the decision are included. Determine whether

- Approval is needed from one or more offices internally. The business, finance, or treasurer's office should be involved, and the organization's investment committee may need to approve not only the decision to move the assets but also the choice of manager.

- One or more trustees should be involved in the process. Identify personal connections that may help or hurt the choice of outside manager. When interviewing a prospective asset manager, ask:

  - Whether the asset manager has offices in different states around the country, for the convenience of meeting with donors or prospects who live away from the charitable organization.

  - How many years the asset manager has been in this business.

  - For a profile of other clients. Are any of the asset manager's existing clients similar to this charitable organization?

  - Whether they have a staff dedicated to planned giving.

  - What the average caseload is for a trust administrator.

  - What additional services they can offer, such as legal and real estate work.

  - Whether they conduct seminars for potential donors.

  - What their fee structure is and what additional expenses may arise. How are fees computed—monthly? Quarterly?

  - How their investment performance has fared.

56.5   FROM THE ASSET MANAGER: WHAT THE PLANNED GIVING PROGRAM WANTS AND NEEDS

When working with an asset manager, define and communicate early on the goals for the relationship. The asset manager should

- *Service donors quickly and accurately.* The planned giving program needs to stand competitively with other charitable organizations' programs and have the ability to help donors make their gifts quickly and easily and receive the documentation that they need at tax time with a minimum of confusion or demand. The information conveyed must be accurate. Donors must be responded to quickly when they call the asset manager for assistance.

- *Communicate well with donors.* When selecting the asset manager, imagine donors talking with the various members of the asset management team, and determine whether there is a comfort level with how well the team members relate to donors.

- *Provide the planned giving program and charitable organization with exceptional service.* The asset manager should act as a partner when dealing with unusual gift situations. Sometimes creativity is needed to solve and close a gift situation, and the asset manager should be able to provide solutions that will make the gift happen.

- *Facilitate growth for the program.* This will be accomplished by servicing donors and the program and providing a competitive investment return to donors and the charitable organization.

- *Provide investment expertise.* The asset manager provides an institutional strength to the program. While the organization's treasurer's office can provide the program with investment ability, it is unlikely that the treasurer's office is very experienced with charitable gift assets. Having such experience is a great value that an outside asset manager can bring to the program.

56.6 RESPONSIBILITIES OF THE OUTSIDE ASSET MANAGER

The outside investment manager is responsible for many duties that will help to lessen the workload for the planned giving officer. These duties should include administration and investment of the program.

(a) Administration of the Program

The outside manager is responsible for the administration of all of the planned gifts in the program held at the asset manager's institution, which include charitable remainder trusts, charitable lead trusts, charitable gift annuities, and the program's pooled income funds.

The reporting part of the administration of the program includes proper annual accounting of the assets to the nonprofit; federal and state compliance requirements; monthly, quarterly, or annual mailing of checks to donors; calculations and acknowledgments sent to donors once a gift is made; and, at the beginning of each new year, proper tax paperwork sent to donors. The asset manager must also do all related bookkeeping, including collecting income. In addition, the asset manager must have reports available to send to donors. Such reports include, for example, an annual report to pooled income fund income beneficiaries that provides the value of the pooled income fund, number of participants, number of units assigned, value of each unit, income earned by the fund and each unit, income yield, and description of the investment assets. A standard acknowledgment letter from an asset manager to a donor is included in Appendix, CD-ROM Documentation, Correspondence.

The asset manager is responsible for handling donor issues as they arise, including responding to donors' inquiries or inquiries by the nonprofit on behalf of donors. Discuss in advance how the asset manager should work with donors. Some charitable organizations feel strongly that the outside manager should never deal directly with a donor, while other organizations feel that dealing directly with the asset manager is more efficient.

(b) Investment of the Program

Sometimes it is helpful to physically remove the planned giving assets from the endowment assets at the nonprofit organization. The asset manager can provide asset allocation, diversifying accounts in their investment strategies. The asset manager can readily place the investments in small cap funds, international funds, and others. This should result in a balanced investment of the planned giving funds.

Similar gifts are generally invested separately from other types of gifts, all with different financial goals. For example, a charitable organization's growth pooled income fund will be invested for ultimate growth of the fund, while a charitable gift annuity is invested differently to meet a payout rate of 10 percent for a donor. The charitable remainder trusts are invested to meet the payout promised to the donor, while providing at least 50 percent remainder to the nonprofit organization at the donor's death. Outside investment management allows for the opportunity for separately managed gifts when necessary or appropriate.

Investment guidelines and policies should be put in place for all types of gifts, establishing payout rates and ideal ages for making certain types of gifts. Fees also should be addressed, such as whether fees will be charged to various accounts, taken directly from the trusts, or billed separately to the charity.

56.7 CONVERSION FROM IN-HOUSE TO OUTSIDE MANAGER

Once the decision is made to move the program from the charitable organization to an outside asset manager, the actual move must be carefully coordinated among the development office, treasurer's office, and outside asset manager. This is also the case when a program is moved from one outside asset manager to a new provider. The move is called a *conversion*.

The new asset manager will want to determine exactly what is coming under the asset manager's control. The manager will want to examine prior years' tax returns, if there are any, and see exactly what types of assets are held in individual trusts. The new provider will want to see who the various trustees of the trusts are, to see how assets are held, and to determine whether any legal work needs to be done. It is likely that the existing trustee will need to resign and the new manager be appointed, or that a new agency agreement will need to be signed.

For a conversion to run smoothly, the asset manager must do advance planning. The manager will determine who the points of communication are, such as brokers, trustees, and other administrators, and gather their telephone numbers, facsimile numbers, and e-mail addresses to have in one place for quick communication. The manager will try, if possible, to choose the slowest time of the year for the conversion, which is often the summer months. Everyone will want to anticipate and discuss situations that may arise during the conversion, such as how to handle new gifts being made and where to deposit such gifts.

One of the most important goals of this process is to keep the charitable organization's donors happy and, if possible, to make them feel that they are benefiting by this change. The planned giving officer needs to ensure that a donor does not miss a monthly or quarterly paycheck.

To help ease the transition, do some advance planning. Write a letter to donors letting them know that a change in manager is coming. Tell them why the change is being made, that better service is anticipated, and that the provider is very experienced. If moving from another provider, do not speak poorly about the previous provider, even if the program is moving because of poor service. Help the donor to understand that although no problems are anticipated, any that do occur will be straightened out quickly.

56.8 THE NONPROFIT AND OUTSIDE MANAGER RELATIONSHIP

Running a planned giving program with an asset manager requires work and cooperation on both sides. When a donor plans to make a new gift to the charitable organization, it is the planned giving officer who is likely to learn of the gift first. The planned giving officer should communicate to the asset manager that a new gift is coming. Alert the manager that a gift of stocks or cash is coming, identifying the type of stock, its value, and the name of the donor and type of gift that will be made. The asset manager can then set up an account to receive the securities. If the asset manager does not know that securities are being transferred, there is the possibility that the securities will be rejected by the receiving institution because the institution does not know where to place the incoming securities. Determine early on the best way to communicate: by facsimile, e-mail, or telephone. Once a system is established, it should run smoothly.

It is the job of the planned giving officer to gather and complete the necessary paperwork and information from the donor and to provide it to the asset manager. In the case of a pooled income fund gift, this typically means having the donor complete an instrument of transfer for a new pooled income fund gift or complete a subsequent gift agreement form that indicates the donor's wish that the current gift be made in the same manner as the donor's previous pooled income fund gift was made. Requiring this paperwork in advance allows the asset manager to invest the new gift assets quickly and at a time that is fair to all pooled income fund participants. See Appendix, CD-ROM Documentation, Agreements for an instrument of transfer and subsequent gift agreement form.

When creating a charitable remainder trust in which the asset manager is to act as trustee or co-trustee with the charitable organization, the asset manager will want to obtain a draft of the charitable remainder trust for legal review before the donor signs it. Once the trust is reviewed and signed, the asset manager will need a copy of the final trust document. This process must be completed before the assets are transferred to the manager.

A charitable gift annuity requires less advance preparation on both sides because it is a contract between the nonprofit organization and the donor, giving the asset manager less of a role to play in the establishment of the gift. Once the gift annuity contract is signed and the assets are transferred to the outside manager, the asset manager will want to have a copy of the signed gift annuity contract. See Appendix, CD-ROM Documentation, Agreements, for a sample gift annuity contract.

Information routinely needed by the asset manager for every gift includes:

■ Donor's address, including additional seasonal addresses

■ Social Security numbers

■ Dates of birth

■ Cost basis of the donor's securities

■ Direct deposit information. A canceled check from the donor's bank account will need to go to the asset manager, along with instructions for direct deposit from the donor.

For a sample Asset Manager's Gift description and donor/beneficiary information form, know your donor profile, administrative questionnaire, and sample nonprofit gift administration form, see Appendix, CD-ROM Documentation, Administrative Documents.

When possible, the planned giving officer should create standard forms together with the asset manager. Because both are looking for the same information and need to complete similar forms, they can easily anticipate each other's needs. Together, the planned giving officer and the asset manager should create standard delivery instructions to give to a donor or the donor's advisor or stockbroker. Delivery instructions for gifts made by securities is critical information that must be relayed accurately. See Appendix, CD-ROM Documentation, Administrative Documents, for a sample delivery instructions for planned gifts.

The outside manager should have established timetables for when work will be completed and should communicate this to the charitable organization. Make sure that both the charitable organization and the asset manager are comfortable with the time frames and follow them.

56.9 RECURRING ISSUES

Several issues regularly arise with donors who make gifts to charitable organizations. Establishing guidelines and confirming agreement between the asset manager and the charitable organization about how to handle these situations will help them be able to deal with problems when they arise.

(a) Date of Gift

The planned giving officer and the asset manager should agree on the best way to handle donors who think that the date of their gift is a date different from the actual, legal date of the gift. For a gift of securities, the law states that the date of the gift is the date that the assets reach the account established for the charitable organization. For gifts of cash, the date of the gift is the date that is postmarked on the envelope. Some donors, however, believe that the date of the gift is some other date, such as the date that they tell their broker to make the gift or the date on the check they write to make the gift. A strategy for handling this situation is to tell the donor in advance what the date of the gift is based on. This is especially important to do at the end of the year. Follow up in writing before the gift is made.

(b) Stockbrokers' Commissions

Another common problem encountered by the asset manager and planned giving officer is the donor's wish that her stockbroker take a commission for selling the gifted securities. It is generally easier and less expensive for the donor to make a gift of securities by sending the securities directly to the asset manager and letting the manager sell the securities. Often, however, the donor does not want to do this, wanting her own broker to receive a commission, even when the donor understands that such a practice ultimately will result in less money going to the charity.

The planned giving officer needs to evaluate each situation and respect the relationship between the donor and stockbroker. Inform the donor of the ease and convenience of transferring the securities directly to the asset manager. Tell the donor about the cost difference. If, however, the donor wishes to have the securities sold by the donor's broker, it is probably best to let the donor control this and ask the asset manager to respect the donor's decision.

(c) Gifts from Mutual Funds with Dividend Reinvestment Programs

Donors often do not understand the difficulty of making a gift from a mutual fund that has a dividend reinvestment program. Often there is a time delay in making the gift. Before accepting a gift made from a mutual fund, alert the donor to the fact that the donor's involvement in a dividend reinvestment program means the donor may have a very difficult time completing the gift quickly. The donor, his financial advisor, and the asset manager will need to work together to have the mutual fund company stop the automatic dividend reinvestment plan. There are likely to be different dates of gift for different parts of the gift because the bulk of the mutual fund gift may be transferred first, with the proceeds from the dividend reinvestment plan coming later.

Work with the asset manager to be sure that everyone understands the process and potential outcomes. The manager should have letters and procedures in place for handling gifts from mutual funds. See Appendix, CD-ROM Documentation, Correspondence, for a sample asset manager's mutual fund instruction letter.

56.10 EVALUATING THE RELATIONSHIP

Good communication is the key to a successful relationship between a planned giving officer and an outside asset manager. The planned giving officer should regularly ask himself and members of the charitable organization who work with the asset manager if the relationship is working. The charitable organization also should evaluate itself as a client to see what it can do to help things run more smoothly. A meeting between members of the charitable organization and the asset manager should be planned on a regular basis, perhaps yearly, to review the program as a whole and determine whether anything should be changed. The year's previous activities should be reviewed. The current and future investment plan for the planned giving program should be examined, as well as trends in planned giving.

Glossary

Abatement: The order of reduction or elimination. For example, if a person leaves "five hundred dollars to John and the rest to my heirs," John gets $500 and the heirs' share may abate to zero if there is only $500.

Ademption: 1. Disposing of something left in a will before death, with the effect that the person it was left to does not get it. **2.** The gift, before death, of something left in a will to a person who was left it. For example, Ed leaves a chair to Joan in his will, but gives her the chair before he dies.

Adjusted gross income (AGI): The figure that is used to measure the amount of deductions allowed for charitable income tax deductions as well as medical deductions, casualty losses, and miscellaneous deductions. The AGI is the taxpayer's total income derived from all sources, minus deductions for alimony, individual retirement account (IRA) contributions, and certain other specific expenses and items.

Administer: Settle and distribute the estate of a deceased person.

Administration: Supervision of the estate for a deceased person. This usually includes collecting the property, paying debts and taxes, and giving out what remains to the heirs.

After-born child: A legal principle that if a child is born after a will is made, the child should still inherit whatever children inherit unless the will specifically excludes late-born children.

Age of majority: Age at which a child gains full right to enter into binding contracts, make a will, vote, etc. This age varies from state to state (although it is often age 18) and from purpose to purpose.

Ancillary administration: A proceeding in a state where a decedent had property, but which is not the state where that person was domiciled or where his main estate has been administered.

Annual exclusion: The amount of money a person can give away each year to any individual without paying a federal gift tax and without using up any of the unified credit to which each person is entitled. The annual exclusion is currently $11,000.

Annual gift: A yearly gift made in response to a direct mail request or phonathon.

Assets: All money, property, and money-related rights owned by a person or an organization.

Beneficial interest: The right to profits resulting from a contract, estate, or property, rather than the legal ownership of these things.

Beneficiary: 1. A person or organization for whose benefit a trust is created. **2.** A person to whom an insurance policy is payable. **3.** A person who inherits under a will. **4.** Anyone who benefits from something or who is treated as the real owner of something for tax purposes.

Bequeath: To give personal property or money by will; to give anything by will.

Bequest: A clause in a will that enables individuals to make distributions to other individuals or charities. The bequest may be of a specific amount or a percentage. It also may transfer a specific piece of personal or real property.

Breach of trust: The failure of a trustee to do something that is required; includes doing things illegally, negligently, or forgetfully.

GLOSSARY

C corporations: A so-called "regular" corporation that includes publicly traded corporations and closely held corporations that are not S corporations. These corporations provide limited liability but allow for a dual system of taxation. The corporation pays an income tax, and income distributed to shareholders is taxed as ordinary income.

Capital gain or loss: The profit or loss from the sale of a capital asset. Long-term capital assets are assets that have been held for a year and a day. Short-term assets are assets held less than a year and a day.

Capital gains tax: A tax that is assessed on the difference between the cost basis of the asset and its fair market value. The tax is 15 percent of the gain for most types of investment property.

Charitable: A gift or organization is charitable for tax purposes if it meets several tests: A gift must be made to a government-qualified nonprofit organization to benefit humankind in general, the community in general, or some specific large group of people. In addition, the organization's and the gift's purpose must be for the relief of poverty; protection of health or safety; prevention of cruelty; for advancement of education, religion, literature, science, etc. A qualified organization must use its money and staff to advance these purposes, rather than to benefit specific individuals. If the gift and the organization meet these standards, the donor may deduct the gift from income and the organization is exempt from paying taxes.

Charitable gift annuity: A life income gift for donors age 65 and up that pays a donor and/or a second beneficiary an immediate stream of income for life. The rate is fixed and is locked in at the time the gift is made.

Charitable income tax deduction: A deduction is provided to a donor who makes a gift to qualifying charities. If the gift is to a public charity and the asset transferred is cash, the donor may claim a deduction for up to 50 percent of his adjusted gross income. If the gift is property held long term, the donor may obtain a deduction for up to 30 percent of his adjusted gross income.

Charitable lead trusts: A lead trust is the opposite of a charitable remainder trust. The lead income is paid to the charity and, after a number of years or lifetimes, the remainder is returned to the grantor (grantor lead trust) or to someone other than the grantor, such as the grantor's heirs or other beneficiaries (nongrantor lead trust).

Charitable remainder annuity trust: The form of a charitable remainder annuity trust that provides an income stream equal to a specific dollar amount based on a percentage of the trust assets at the time of creation.

Charitable remainder trust: A charitable remainder trust provides an income stream to a donor and/or second beneficiary for life or for a term of years not to exceed 20. The rate must be at least 5 percent and is usually no more than 7 percent.

Charitable remainder unitrust: A unitrust provides an income stream for life or for a term of years. There are three types of unitrusts: the straight percentage, net income, and net income with a make-up provision.

Charitable trust: A trust set up for a public purpose, such as for a school, church, charity, etc.

Codicil: A document that amends or changes clauses in a will. It is executed with the same formality as a will and avoids the need to remake a will due to minor changes.

Community property: Property owned in common (both persons owning it all) by a husband and wife. "Community property states" are those states that treat most property acquired during the marriage as the property of both partners no matter whose name it is in.

Community trust: An organization set up to administer charitable or public trust funds received from many donors in a particular community.

Competent: Having the right natural or legal qualifications. For example, a person may be competent to make a will if she understands what making a will is, knows that she is making a will, and knows generally how making the will affects persons named in the will and affects relatives.

GLOSSARY

Consanguinity: Blood relationship; kinship.

Conservator: A guardian or preserver of property appointed generally by a court for a person who cannot legally manage it.

Cost basis: The amount an individual originally paid for an asset. The cost basis may be adjusted based on the value of additional investment in the property minus allowances for depreciation and other deductions.

Current-use award: A one-time gift that is used by the charity within one year. It is the opposite of an endowed gift.

Cy pres: "As near as possible." When the provisions of a deceased person's will or trust can no longer legally or practically be carried out, a court may (but is not obligated to) order that the assets held under the terms of the will or trust are used in a way that most nearly accomplishes what the person would have wanted. If the court does not use its cy pres powers, the will or trust may be held void and no longer binding. The doctrine of cy pres is now usually applied only to charitable trusts.

Decedent: A person who has died. The term is used in the settlements of estates.

Declaration of instrument of trust: A document created by a person owning property regarding the use of property for the benefit of himself or others.

Deduction: A reduction of income for tax purposes. Itemized deductions are those expenses that may be subtracted from adjusted gross income and include certain medical payments; taxes; home mortgage interest; charitable contributions; professional expenses; etc. There are detailed tax rules for deducting each. As an alternative to itemizing deductions, a individual may choose the standard deduction, which is a specific scaled amount based on income.

Deed of trust: A legal arrangement similar to a mortgage by which a person transfers the legal ownership of land to independent trustees to be held until a debt on the land is paid off.

Deferred gift annuity: A life income gift for donors generally between the ages of 25 to 60 that pays a donor and/or a second beneficiary a stream of income for life at a point in the future.

Discount rate: The federal discount rate is set monthly and is equal to 120 percent of the federal midterm rate. The federal midterm rate is the average market yield on all options of the U.S. market that have a maturity over three years and less than nine years.

Distributee: Heir; person who inherits.

Domiciliary: Relating to a person's permanent home. For example, a domiciliary administration is the handling of a decedent's estate in the state of the person's legal residence, the primary or permanent home.

Donative: As a gift. For example, a donative trust is a trust set up as a gift for another person.

Donee: A person or organization to whom a gift is made or a power is given.

Donor: A person making a gift to another or giving another person power to do something.

Donor-advised fund: A personalized gift option through which donors transfer money to an entity and make recommendations abut the use of their gifts. These funds can be established through a charity or through the charitable services division of a for-profit corporation like a mutual fund.

DTC transfer: A depository trust company (DTC) transfer permit the electronic transfer of securities from a donor's account to a charity's account.

Durable power of attorney: A document that is part of an estate plan and allows an individual to act on behalf of another in the event of incompetence.

Earned income: 1. Money or other compensation received for work; does not include the profits gained from owning property. **2.** The earned income credit is a tax break given to certain low-income workers.

GLOSSARY

Endowed fund: A fund through which the principal of a gift is managed in perpetuity and only a portion of the earnings is distributed annually.

Estate tax: Individuals pay a federal estate tax of 35 to 49 percent on estates greater than $1 million in 2003 and increasing to $3.5 million in 2009. Under current law, the estate tax is due to be repealed in 2010. Individuals can reduce their estate by making charitable gifts through their estates. See **gift tax**.

Estate trust: A trust that holds property for a surviving spouse (which may qualify for the marital deduction) or for others.

Estimated tax: Persons with income from sources other than salaries must estimate and pay income tax four times a year.

Executor: A person named in a will to administer the estate and to distribute the property after the person making the will dies.

Fair market value: Generally, the amount that a willing buyer would pay to a willing seller assuming that all of the relevant facts are known about a piece of property and neither the buyer or seller is under an obligation to act.

Future interest: An interest in property or an income stream that begins at a point in the future. The annual exclusion applies to present interests not future interests. In addition, the creation of an income stream for the benefit of another triggers potential gift tax consequences. The gift tax is assessed only on a present interest; to avoid taxation, a donor may reserve the right to revoke the interest by will thus suspending the interest.

Generation-skipping trust: A trust that transfers payment down to grandchild or great-grandchild or unrelated person at least $37^1/_2$ years younger than the donor, for example, a trust created by a grandmother giving the trust income to her children and ultimately the trust assets to her grandchildren. Assets transferred through generation-skipping provisions may trigger tax consequences that may be diminished through the use of a special lifetime exemption.

Gift: 1. Any transfer of money or property without payment or compensation equivalent to the value of the thing transferred. **2.** Any willing transfer of money or property without payment.

Gifts to Minors Act: A uniform act, adopted by most states, that simplifies the transfer of property to a minor child and allows property to be held for a child without the need for a legal guardian. An adult acts as the child's representative and controls the property, and the child gets the interest dividends, or gains, which may be used for the child's support.

Gift tax: A tax assessed on transfers made by a donor to an individual during life. Under present tax law, in 2003 and beyond, donors may make gifts up to $1 million without being taxed. In adidtion, through the use of the annual exclusion, a donor can make gifts of $11,000 each year to as many individuals as he wishes without paying taxes. The amount of $11,000 is indexed and will gradually increase over time.

Gross estate: The total value of a decedent's property from which deductions are subtracted to determine the taxable estate on which estate taxes will be paid.

Gross income: Under the federal tax laws, gross income is all earned and unearned income minus "exclusions." It is formally defined as "all income from whatever source derived" in the Internal Revenue Code.

Heir: A person who inherits property; a person who has a right to inherit property or a person who has a right to inherit property only if another person dies without leaving a valid, complete will.

Holograph: A will, deed, or other legal document that is entirely in the handwriting of the signer. Some states require a holographic will to be signed, witnessed, and in compliance with other formalities before it is valid. Other states require less.

GLOSSARY

Incapacity: Lack of legal ability or power to do something. For example, a minor child has a legal incapacity to vote or make contracts.

Income tax: A tax on profits from business, work, or investments including capital gains tax imposed on sale of appreciated investment assets.

Incomplete transfer: An attempted gift or other transfer of property made by a person who keeps some of the control or benefits. If the person then dies, the value of that property may be included in his estate for tax purposes.

Infancy: In general, the legal status of a very young child. In some states this means the same as minority.

Individual retirement account or(IRA): A tax-deferred account or other investment arrangement.

Inheritance: Property received from a dead person, either by the effect of intestacy laws or under a will.

Insanity: In deciding whether a person has sufficient mental capacity to make a valid will, some of the signs of insanity are "inability to understand the property being given away, the purpose and manner of its distribution, and the persons who are to receive it."

Intent: The resolve or purpose to use a particular means to reach a particular result. Intent usually explains how a person wants to do something and what that person wants done.

Intestate: When a person fails to make a will or makes a will but fails to make a valid will, the state in which he is domiciled distributes his property at the person's death according to a specific formula. People can avoid dying intestate by making a valid will.

Issue: Descendants, such as children or grandchildren.

Itemizer: An individual may itemize deductions only if the total of all deductions for mortgage interest, real estate taxes, state taxes, charitable income tax deductions, and miscellaneous deductions exceeds the standard deduction levels.

Joint: Together; as a group; united; undivided.

Joint bank account: A bank account held in the names of two or more persons, each of whom has full authority to deposit or withdraw money; on the death of one joint holder, the survivor or survivors generally inherit the account assets.

Keogh plan: A tax-deferred retirement account established by a person with self-employment income; similar to an individual retirement account.

Kin: 1. Blood relationship. **2.** Any relationship.

Legacy: 1. A gift of money by will. **2.** A gift of personal property (anything but real estate) by will. **3.** A gift of anything by will.

Legacy tax: A tax on the privilege of inheriting something. This may be an inheritance tax based on the value of the property, or it may be a flat fee.

Legal heirs: 1. Persons who will inherit if a person dies without a will. **2.** Any heirs.

Legatee: A person who inherits something in a will.

Life income gift: A very popular planned gift that provides an income to a donor and/or a second beneficiary for life. There are several types, including the charitable gift annuity, deferred gift annuity, pooled income fund, and the charitable remainder trust.

Lineal: In a line. For example, lineal relationships are those of father and son, grandson and grandmother, etc.

Living trust: A trust that takes effect while the person setting it up is still alive, as opposed to one set up under a will. It is also called an inter vivos trust.

Living will: A document in which a person expresses his wish about the extent of medical treatment to be administered if unconscious because of a terminal disease or injury and that may designate a person to make decisions about treatment on his behalf.

GLOSSARY

Long-term capital asset: An asset held for at least a year and a day that if sold would not produce ordinary income or short-term gain.

Major gift: An outright gift of cash, securities, or possibly real estate. The amount may range from $10,000 to $100,000 to $1 million or more depending on the charity.

Majority: Full legal age to manage one's own affairs.

Marital deduction: A deduction that permits spouses to transfer to each other an unlimited amount of property without being taxed on the transfer.

Marriage: Legal union as husband and wife.

Mutual: Done together; reciprocal. For example, mutual wills are separate wills that were made out as part of a deal, each one made because of the other one.

Natural heir: 1. Child. **2.** Close relative. **3.** Anyone who would inherit if there were no will.

Next of kin: 1. Persons most closely related to a decedent. **2.** All persons entitled to inherit from a person who has not left a will.

Of age: No longer a minor; a person who has reached the legal age to sue, vote, make a will, etc.

Ordinary income property: Income from the sale of property that if sold would produce ordinary income or short-term gain. Gifts of ordinary income property produce a charitable income tax deduction equal to the cost basis of the property.

Outright gift: A gift that immediately transfers cash or property to a charity without the use of a life income gift option.

Patrimony: 1. All rights and property that have passed or will pass to a person from parents, grandparents, etc. **2.** All of a person's property, rights, and liabilities that can be given a dollar value.

Per capita: "By head"; by the number of individual persons, each to share equally.

Perpetuity: 1. Forever. **2.** Any attempt to control the disposition of property by transfer in trust for noncharitable purposes that is meant to last longer than the life of a person alive when the transfer is made (or at least conceived by then) plus 21 years. Most states have adopted statutes incorporating some version of the common law as the Rule Against Perpetuities.

Per stirpes: A method of dividing a dead person's estate by giving out shares equally "by representation" or by family groups.

Planned gift: Life income gifts; gifts through an estate by will or trust; gifts using assets such as securities, real estate, tangible personal property, or other assets; and endowed funds.

Pooled income fund: A life income gift that pays a donor and/or a second beneficiary a stream of income for life. The rate is variable and depends on market conditions. This option is attractive to donors age 40 to 60 and is particularly attractive to donors who fund the gift with appreciated securities.

Pour-over: A will that transfers some money or property to an existing trust is called a pour-over will, and a trust that does this is a pour-over trust.

Power of attorney: A document authorizing a person to act as attorney for the person signing the document.

Pretermitted heir: A child (or sometimes any descendant) either unintentionally left out of a will or born after a will is made. Some states have pretermission statutes that allow a child left out by mistake to take a share of the parent's property.

Private foundation: A customized gift planning option that provides control to wealthy donors. The private foundation must distribute 5 percent of the market value as earnings each year and also pays an excise tax.

Privity: A relationship between parties out of which arises some mutuality of interest.

GLOSSARY

Probate: 1. The process of proving that a will is genuine and distributing the property in a manner specified in the will. **2.** In some states the court that handles the distribution of decedents' estates handles other matters such as insanity commitments.

Real estate: Land, buildings, and things permanently attached to land and buildings. Also called realty and real property.

Related use rule: To obtain a charitable income tax deduction for a gift of tangible personal property, the donated property must be related to the exempt purposes of the charity (books to a library, artifacts to a museum, etc.). If there is a related use and if the property has been held long term, the donor receives a charitable income tax deduction equal to the appraised value. If the gift is made for auction, it does not satisfy the related use test. If there is no related use or the property has been held for less than long term, a donor receives his cost basis as a charitable income tax deduction.

Residuary: The part left over. For example, a residuary clause in a will disposes of all items not specifically given away.

Restricted gift: When a donor places a condition or limitation on a gift or imposes criteria on the use of the gift, the gift is restricted.

Retained life estate: A planned gift option that allows a donor to make a gift of a personal residence by deed to a charity but retain a life estate, allowing the donor to live in the property for life.

Retirement plan assets: Assets including an IRA, Roth IRA, tax-sheltered annuities, 403(b)(7) assets, and self-employed plan (SEP) assets.

Reversion: Any future interest kept by a person who transfers property. For example, John transfers his land in trust, providing income to charity for 10 years. His ownership rights during those years, his right to take back the property after 10 years, and his heirs' right to take back the property after 10 years if he dies, are reversionary interests.

Revocation: The voiding of a document. For example, revocation of a will takes place when, for example, a person tears it up intentionally or makes another will.

S corporation: A corporation that has no more than 75 shareholders and provides limited liability. All losses or gains are passed through directly to the shareholders.

Short-term property: Property that is held for less than a year and a day or property that if sold would produce ordinary income.

Simultaneous Death Act: A law, adopted in most states, requiring that if there is no evidence as to who died first in an accident, each decedent's property will pass as if that person survived the others. Some states have a presumption that the younger, healthier person lived longer.

Special use valuation: The option of a person handling a decedent's land to have it valued for tax purposes on the basis of its current use, not what it would be worth if used most profitably. For example, land used for agricultural purposes may under certain circumstances be so valued, rather than valued on the basis of its development potential.

Spendthrift: A person who spends money unwisely who may need a trustee to look after his property and/or principal. This protection of a person's property against himself, or creditors, is called a spendthrift trust.

Sprinkling trust: A trust that gives the trustee discretion to distribute income to many persons at different times.

Statute of wills: Various state laws, modeled after an old English law, that require a will to be in writing, signed, and properly witnessed in order to be valid.

Step up (or down) in (cost) basis: An increase (or decrease) in the tax basis of property to fair market value at the date of death of the person from whom the present owner inherited the property.

Stock: Shares of ownership in a corporation.

GLOSSARY

Stock dividend: Profits of stock ownership paid out by a corporation in more stock rather than in cash. This additional stock reflects the increased worth of the company.

Street name: Stock or other securities held in the customer's account, in the name of the brokerage or other firm acting for the customer.

Structured gift: A combination of two or more types of gifts using a pledge, annual gift, major gift, planned gift, and a gift through a donor's estate.

Succession: The transfer of property at death. Intestate succession is the transfer of property by law to heirs where that person leaves no will.

Survivorship: The right to own property after the death of another person.

Take: Acquire when a person inherits property.

Tangible: Capable of being touched; real.

Tangible personal property: Includes books, artwork, artifacts, furniture, boats, automobiles, collections, collectibles, and a variety of other forms of physical property.

Tax avoidance: Planning finances carefully to take advantage of all legal tax breaks, such as deductions and exemptions.

Tax rate: The percentage of taxable income or taxable estate paid in taxes. The federal income and estate taxes have graduated rates.

Taxable estate (or gift): The property of a decedent, or a gift, that will be taxed after subtracting for allowable expenses, deductions, and exclusions.

Testamentary: Having to do with a will. For example, testamentary capacity is the mental ability needed to make a valid will; a testamentary class is the group of persons who will eventually inherit from a will.

Testator: A person who makes a will.

Treasury bill, bond, certificate, and note: Documents showing that the U.S. Treasury has borrowed money. A Treasury bill comes due in three, six, nine, or twelve months. It pays no interest, but is sold at a discount and the face amount including interest is paid at maturity; a Treasury certificate comes due in one year and pays interest by coupon; a Treasury note is like a certificate, but comes due in one to five years; and a Treasury bond is issued for long-term borrowing.

Trust: Any transfer or holding of money or property by one person for the benefit of another. There are many types of trusts, which may be set up during lifetime or can be set up in a will.

Trust company: A bank or similar organization that manages trusts, acts as executor of wills, and performs other similar functions.

Trust fund: Money or property set aside in a trust or set aside for a special purpose.

Trust instrument: A formal declaration of trust.

Trustee: A person who holds money or property for the benefit of another person and has a fiduciary relationship with another person.

Unitrust: A trust in which a fixed percentage of the trust property is paid out each year to individual beneficiaries based on an annual valuation of trust assets and the remainder passes to charity, meeting certain tax requirements.

Unrestricted gift: A gift that can be used at the discretion of the charity for any purpose determiend by the charity.

Will: A document taking effect at death in which a person directs the distribution of his property after death.

Will substitutes: Life insurance, joint ownership of property, trusts, and other devices to partially eliminate the need for a will.

CD-ROM Documentation

A.1   INTRODUCTION

The third edition of *Planned Giving: Management, Marketing, and Law* comes with a CD-ROM containing over 250 documents that relate to the chapters within the book. The documents on the CD-ROM are all customizable, so that they can be tailored to fit the specific requirements of any organization.

A.2   ABOUT THE CD-ROM

The forms on the enclosed CD-ROM are saved in Microsoft Word for Windows version 7.0. In order to use the forms, you will need to have word processing software capable of reading Microsoft Word for Windows version 7.0 files.

A.3   SYSTEM REQUIREMENTS

- IBM PC or compatible computer

- CD-ROM drive

- Windows 95 or later

- Microsoft Word for Windows version 7.0 (including the Microsoft converter*) or later or other word processing software capable of reading Microsoft Word for Windows 7.0 files.

  *Word 7.0 needs the Microsoft converter file installed in order to view and edit all enclosed files. If you have trouble viewing the files, download the free converter from the Microsoft web site. The URL for the converter is:

  http://office.microsoft.com/downloads/2000/wrd97cnv.aspx

  Microsoft also has a viewer that can be downloaded, which allows you to view, but not edit documents. This viewer can be downloaded at:

  http://office.microsoft.com/downloads/9798/wdvw9716.aspx

APPENDIX

NOTE: Many popular word processing programs are capable of reading Microsoft Word for Windows 7.0 files. However, users should be aware that a slight amount of formatting might be lost when using a program other than Microsoft Word.

A.4   USING THE FILES

(a)   Loading Files

To use the files, launch your word processing program. Select **File, Open** from the pull-down menu. Select the appropriate drive and directory. A list of files should appear. If you do not see a list of files in the directory, you need to select **WORD DOCUMENT (*.DOC)** under **Files of Type.** Double click on the file you want to open. Edit the file according to your needs.

(b)   Printing Files

If you want to print the files, select **File, Print** from the pull-down menu.

(c)   Saving Files

When you have finished editing a file, you should save it under a new file name by selecting **File, Save As** from the pull-down menu.

A.5   USER ASSISTANCE

If you need assistance with installation or if you have a damaged disk, please contact Wiley Technical Support at:

Hotline: (201) 748-6753

Fax: (201) 748-6450 (Attention: Wiley Technical Support)

Email: *techhelp@wiley.com*

URL: *www.wiley.com/techsupport*

To place additional orders or to request information about other Wiley products, please call (800) 225-5945.

APPENDIX

A.6 SUMMARY CD-ROM CONTENTS

Section 1: Marketing Materials

a. Planned Giving Brochures   Documents 1–4

b. Advertisements for Organizational Publications Documents 5–13

c. Planned Giving Buckslips   Documents 14–22

d. Columns for Organizational Publications   Documents 23–26

e. Planned Giving Newsletters   Documents 27–29

f. Response Forms   Documents 30–32

g. Fact Sheets   Documents 33–39

Section 2: Agreements

a. Endowed Fund Descriptions   Documents 40–51

b. Current Use Awards   Documents 52–55

c. Chairs/Professorships   Documents 56–61

d. Life Income Gifts   Documents 62–68

e. Securities   Documents 69

f. Real Estate   Documents 70–73

g. Nontraditional Assets   Documents 74–78

h. Miscellaneous   Documents 78–80

Section 3: Correspondence

a. Life Income Gifts   Documents 81–88

b. Real Estate   Documents 89–96

c. Securities   Documents 97–103

d. Life Insurance   Document 104

e. Wills and Trusts   Documents 105–114

f. Gifts of Nontraditional Assets   Documents 115

g. Endowed Funds   Documents 116–123

h. Follow-up Letters   Documents 124–135

i. Miscellaneous   Documents 136–152

Section 4: Administrative Documents

a. Office Management   Documents 153–175

b. Donor Management   Documents 176–191

APPENDIX

Section 5: Exhibits

Section 6: Presentations

Section 7: IRS Forms and Tax-Related Documents

Excel Worksheet listing all documents by name, number, and category

Index

INDEX

INDEX

For information about the disk, see the CD-ROM Documentation section on pages 576–580.

DATE DUE

HV
41.9
.U5
J67
2004

Jordan, Ronald R., 1950-

Planned giving